90 AL 1490

6989796

Andrews University Monographs
Studies in Religion
Volume V

THE REMNANT

The History and Theology of the Remnant Idea
from Genesis to Isaiah

by

GERHARD F. HASEL

14192/Eisenbrauns/

BS
1199
.R37
H37
1980

Andrews University Press
Berrien Springs, Michigan

© Andrews University Press 1974

All Rights Reserved

First Edition, 1972
Second Edition, 1974
Third Edition, 1980

Dedicated
to
my wife,
Hilde

45962

INTERNATIONAL SCHOOL
OF THEOLOGY LIBRARY

CONTENTS

PART IV

THE REMNANT MOTIF OF ISAIAH OF JERUSALEM

PART V

PREFACE

Modern man lives in a situation of constant threats with the real possibility of total global destruction. Recognizing his existence to be threatened, man's existential concern leads him inevitably to raise the question of survival, the securing of his life and existence, which is the question whether there will be a remnant and who will belong to it. Man is thus driven to ask questions of ultimate concern and future existence. The intensely theological idea of the remnant as found in the Biblical testimony aids man in the securing of his existence, for the hope of modern man's survival and future existence hinges upon his response to the urgent call to return to God.

The purpose of this study is to investigate the origin, development, and theology of the remnant idea in the Old Testament where it is one of the major theological motifs. Due to the fact that the remnant motif is not limited to the Biblical writings and that it has been claimed to have its roots in either the political-social sphere of Assyria or the cultic one of Babylonia, it became imperative to examine the remnant idea in the various genres of Sumerian, Akkadian, Hittite, Ugaritic, and Egyptian literary texts. This comparative approach is not only extremely important for determining the origin of the remnant idea but also for delineating the uniqueness and richness of the Old Testament remnant motif, and its significant place in Old Testament thought and theology over against its appearance in the ancient Near Eastern texts.

The investigation of the remnant motif in the Bible begins with its earliest explicit appearance in the old materials of Genesis and proceeds to Isaiah, the greatest eighth century prophet, ministering to Israel at some of the most crucial turning points in her history. The writings of this prophet had to be chosen as a cutoff point for our study not merely because the remnant idea comes to a high point as a key element of his theology but primarily because limitations needed to be imposed on the basis of the length of this study. The latter reason also determined the omission of a detailed examination of the Hebrew remnant terminology under due consideration of linguistic semantics and comparative Semitic philology. This examination has shown among other things that the 580 usages of derivatives of five separate Hebrew roots exhibit a basic bi-polarity of negative and positive aspects of the remnant idea in their individual contexts, word- and sentence-combinations. A discussion of the most prominent remnant terms and their usage and meaning in the OT is now discussed in my articles entitled, "Semantic Values of Derivatives of the Hebrew Root Š'R," AUSS, 11 (1973), 152-169; "Remnant," IDBSup., pp. 735f.; "'Remnant" as a Meaning of 'aḥarîṯ" in The Archaeology of Jordan and Other Studies. Presented to S. H. Horn, ed. L. T. Geraty (Berrien Springs, Mi.: Andrews University Press, 1980).

The Old Testament remnant idea appears to undergo considerable development from its earliest usage in Genesis, where it is from the start intensely theological which shows itself from its immediate incorporation into salvation history up to its usage as a vehicle to express the election of God's people. In the Elijah narratives new aspects will become transparent. A religio-cultural threat leaves a remnant after a past catastrophy and climaxes in the survival of a remnant in the future judgment that has characteristics qualifying it to become the nucleus of a new Israel faithful to Yahweh. Amos will be seen to refute popular remnant hopes while at the same time expressing his hope that a remnant from Israel may emerge from an eschatological judgment. It will become apparent that the remnant idea is a central element in the theology of Isaiah. The notion of a purified and holy remnant will present itself as a main aspect of Isaiah's eschatology. At the same time Isaiah knows a non-eschatological-historical remnant of Israel and the nations and employs this aspect to call the people back to God in order to create conditions for an eschatological remnant to emerge from future judgment. It is hoped by the present writer that he can in the near future continue his investigation of the remnant motif in the remaining Biblical writings.

This study is a considerably shortened but slightly revised and updated version of the writer's dissertation which was accepted in the spring of 1970 at the Department of Religion of the Graduate School of Vanderbilt University, Nashville, Tennessee, under the title "The Origin and Early History of the Remnant Motif in Ancient Israel." Warm thanks and deep appreciation are expressed to Prof. Dr. Walter Harrelson, Dean of the Divinity School of Vanderbilt University, for his encouragement and helpful guidance, and to the late Prof. Dr. J. Philip Hyatt, Harvie Branscomb Distinguished Professor of Old Testament, for his valuable suggestions during the final phases of the preparation of the writer's Ph.D. dissertation. My deepest appreciation goes to all those known and unknown who made it possible to have this contribution appear in the series of "Andrews University Monographs."

The very favorable reception of this monograph made it necessary to let it appear again only two years after the first edition came off the press. The body of this edition is virtually identical to that of the first edition of 1972. It was felt desirable to add one appendix. The Appendix (pp. 461-474) discusses the pertinent literature dealing with the various aspects of the remnant idea which appeared since the completion of the manuscript of the first edition thus updating the entire monograph.

Several years have passed since the second edition appeared. Continuing demand has made it necessary to have this third edition appear. The content of this investigation remains largely the same except that in the text all quotations of sources in foreign languages are translated into English and that all Hebrew and Greek terms and phrases are now transliterated. These changes hopefully make this study more readable for a larger group of readership.

My innermost desires were fulfilled if this study would provide at least for some of its readers in an age threatened by global annihilation the kind of theological stimuli on the basis of which they were able to expect the near and distant future with hopeful anticipation and deep inner joy.

Berrien Springs, Michigan
June 1980

GERHARD F. HASEL

PART ONE

THE REMNANT MOTIF IN RECENT RESEARCH

This chapter serves as a general introduction to our investigation. We attempt to present a concise history of research of the Hebrew remnant motif from its beginnings in modern Biblical scholarship to the present. Special attention will be placed upon the leading trends in the major studies on the origin, meaning, and history of the remnant motif in the Hebrew Bible from its earliest appearance to Isaiah of Jerusalem. This procedure will enable us to focus on methodological, historical, and theological problems, to build upon the present state of inquiry, and to carry forward the discussion at crucial points.

A. SURVEY OF RESEARCH

The credit for the pioneering study of the remnant motif since the rise of modern Biblical scholarship belongs to Johannes Meinhold. In the year 1903 he published the first part of his Studien zur israelitischen Religionsgeschichte which is devoted to the sole task of investigating on a large scale, the "origin, meaning and history of the term š'r"[1] in the Old Testament. Meinhold's noble endeavor was never finished. His study remained a torso, for he was not able to go beyond the

---

[1]Johannes Meinhold, Studien zur israelitischen Religionsgeschichte. Band I: Der heilige Rest. Teil I: Elias Amos Hosea Jesaja (Bonn, 1903), p. 1.

prophetic traditions of Elijah, Amos, Hosea, and Isaiah.[2]

It must be clearly stated right at the outset that Meinhold operates with his own definition of the remnant motif. The term "remnant" is always understood and used in a very limited and narrowly defined sense, namely as a "holy remnant"[3] or "pious remnant."[4] The adjectives "holy" (heilig) and "pious" (fromm) are used synonymously in connection with the remnant motif. The "holy remnant" is a "Remnant of pious Israelites, who escape from the destructive judgment only because of their piousness of heart and their way which is acceptable to Yahweh, . . ."[5] It is Israel kata pneũma in contrast to Israel kata sárka. The latter constitutes merely a unified national entity.

On the basis of this definition Meinhold maintains that the remnant of 7,000 in the Elijah cycle constitutes actual Israelites, because the others excluded themselves from the national community by their abandoning the national God.[7] "But the seven thousand are the Israel oú kata pneũma ålla kata sárka ,..."[8] With regard to the book of Amos Meinhold's conclusions are not much different. "It is clear that in Amos there remains actually a remnant, namely Judah ."[9] But this

---

[2]Meinhold had hoped to continue his investigation of the remnant motif in the remaining Hebrew prophets. In his opening statements he declares that he does not know when his investigation of the "holy remnant" will be finished. Ibid., p. V.

[3]Ibid., pp. 3, 22, 32, 88.

[4]Ibid., pp. 33, 63, 86.

[5]Ibid., p. 33.

[6]Ibid., p. 32.

[7]Ibid., p. 31.

[8]Ibid., p. 32.

[9]Ibid., p. 63.

remnant, i.e., Judah, does not correspond to the "holy remnant" and is therefore of no importance for Meinhold's delineation of the remnant motif.[10] Hosea does not exhibit any remnant terminology. In the prophet Hosea the notion of a "holy remnant" has no place, because there is no division between the pious and impious.[11]

It was Isaiah's achievement, according to Meinhold, to develop after "hard inner struggles"[12] the notion of a "holy remnant," i.e., a remnant which remains on the basis of faith and constitutes only a part of the people. It is maintained that at the beginning of Isaiah's ministry, namely before the birth of his first son, the prophet did not entertain any remnant idea. At this time the people still constituted a unity as in Amos and Hosea.[13] A dramatic change took place at ca. 738 B.C., when he named his son Shear-jashub.[14] The remnant to which this name testifies is at first a part of Israel, namely the political entity Judah.[15] Out of the encounter with Ahaz the recognition ripens that faith cannot be forced upon the masses but grows out of divine promptings and consequently only a part of Judah will escape judgment. During his third period of prophetic ministry the conviction grows that the

---

[10]The passage of Amos 5:15 is interpreted to refer to the whole of Judah as compared to Ephraim (=Israel). Meinhold, ibid., pp. 47, 62 n. 1, denies any notion of distinction between the faithful and unfaithful in 5:4, 5, 15. These passages reflect only the cultic acts of the Israelites.

[11]Ibid., p. 88.

[12]Ibid., p. 110.

[13]Ibid., p. 106.

[14]Ibid., p. 108.

[15]Ibid., p. 110.

remnant will be a remnant from Judah, i.e., it will not be made up of the whole of Judah.[16] This remnant will consist of those who oppose Ahaz and the masses by faith and trust in Yahweh.[17] As a result Isaiah forms "a small group, . . . at whose center he is himself. . . ."[18] The members of this community are his family and the "poor,"[19] who are Israelites that are united in showing their trust towards Yahweh and his prophet.[20]

In short, the originator of the remnant motif, namely the idea of the "holy remnant" as understood by Meinhold, is Isaiah of Jerusalem. The remnant motif is not encountered in the Elijah cycle nor in Amos and Hosea. These conclusions are dependent upon a number of presuppositions which may be briefly stated. Meinhold works with a preconceived notion of the remnant motif. He links the origin of the remnant motif with that of ethical monotheism.[21] Insofar as ethical monotheism did not arise prior to the 8-7th century B.C. the remnant motif cannot be older. The connection of the remnant motif with ethical monotheism is to a large degree due to Meinhold's definition of the meaning of the remnant motif. He sees the remnant motif only in terms of a positive notion: the "holy remnant" are those who survive a catastrophe on the basis of their "holiness" or "piousness." This onesided limitation of the remnant motif determines most of the results of Meinhold's study. It will be seen that Meinhold's concept of the "holy remnant" is inadequate, for it does not allow a full appreciation of the Hebrew remnant motif. Des-

---

[16] Ibid., pp. 112, 114.

[17] Ibid.

[18] Ibid., p. 123.

[19] Ibid., pp. 130-1.

[20] Ibid., p. 135.

[21] Ibid., p. 3.

pite these problems and methodological flaws Meinhold's investigation is important. He focused scholarly attention upon the problem of the Hebrew remnant motif. It is unfortunate that he was not able to carry his study through the remaining Hebrew prophets.

Two years later (1905) appeared Hugo Gressmann's Ursprung der israelitisch-jüdischen Eschatologie, a study that touched on the remnant motif within a discussion of the origin of eschatology in ancient Israel.[22] As is well known Gressmann argued that the popular Israelite eschatology derived from Babylonia,[23] and that it was primarily an eschatology of salvation.[24] He pointed to the unadjusted juxtaposition of the eschatology of doom and of salvation in the proclamation of the prophets.[25] The only explanation of this phenomenon, according to Gressmann, is that the prophets adopted both types of eschatology leaving them in their original fragmentary state which they had from the start without integrating them into one system.[26] This hypothesis came as a reaction against the extremes of Wellhausenism, which considered the

---

[22]Hugo Gressmann, Ursprung der israelitisch-jüdischen Eschatologie (FRLANT, 6; Göttingen, 1905), pp. 229-38.

[23]Ibid., pp. 237, 244-7. Gressmann believes that the eschatology of doom and the eschatology of salvation are originally mythical in nature and derive from the Babylonian myths of the procession of the equinoxes. These views he shared with Hermann Gunkel, Genesis (HK; 2nd ed.; Göttingen, 1902), p. 234, and Hugo Winckler.

[24]Gressmann, op. cit., p. 236.

[25]Ibid., p. 232: "We are concerned here with the eschatology of doom and the following eschatology of salvation, as if there were before us two fragmentary fields. Both are separated and yet they are close together."

[26]Ibid., pp. 232-3.

prophetic passages containing an eschatology of salvation as late interpolations frequently opposing the prophet's original message of doom,[27] and against Meinhold's psychological reconstruction of positive eschatology.[28]

The remnant motif is a part of the popular eschatology of doom.[29] As such it is utterly negative stressing complete destruction and full annihilation. Gressmann argues that whenever the remnant idea appears within the eschatology of salvation it is a "dogmatico-technical term."[30] In the course of time the remnant motif was adopted to bridge the abyss between the eschatology of doom and the eschatology of salvation. This usage of the remnant motif was relatively late in popular Israelite eschatology but still earlier than Amos.[31] It is to be linked with the prophetic movement in Israel.[32] The writing prophets, claims Gressmann, adopt the remnant motif in its original negative sense as a chief element of their proclamation of doom and disaster. This is the reason why the eschatology of doom and the eschatology of salvation remain in an unadjusted juxtaposition in the prophetic writings.[33] Nevertheless, in the writing prophets the remnant motif broke through the rigid eschatology of doom and linked it up with the eschatology of salvation in an

---

[27]Hugo Gressmann, Der Messias, ed. by Hans Schmidt (Göttingen, 1929), p. 70: "It is believed that the prophet is unable to threaten and to promise in the same breath. He does not actually do that, but as a rule a threat is at one place and a promise at another. Why should the prophet not threaten and then promise?"

[28]Gressmann, Ursprung der . . . Eschatologie, p. 244.

[29]Ibid., p. 233.

[30]Ibid.

[31]Ibid., p. 237.

[32]Ibid., p. 235.

[33]Ibid., pp. 236, 242-3.

unwilling accommodation of popular eschatology.[34] The writing prophets then either affirm or reject the popular Israelite eschatology according to time and mood.[35]

Gressmann maintains over against Meinhold that the remnant motif originated long before Isaiah of Jerusalem. As a matter of fact it is even older than Amos. Both Isaiah and Amos use it already in a rather technical sense. Gressmann's rejection of the origin of the remnant motif from ethical monotheism and his joining it with eschatology has been of lasting influence among many scholars. But it remains to be seen whether his contention that the origin of the remnant motif is to be sought in the mythical origin of eschatology is a likely position.

Gressmann's attempt to solve the problem of the interrelation of the two apparently opposing types of eschatology was aimed to counter the critical solution of the Wellhausen School, which denied that there is an eschatology of salvation in pre-exilic prophecy. It was also aimed to counter the psychological solution, which explained the duality of doom and salvation as due to the varying moods of the prophets caused by

---

[34] Ibid., p. 243.

[35] Gressmann claims in an essay entitled, "Foreign Influences in Hebrew Prophecy," JTS, 27 (1926), 241ff., that doom and salvation are often united in Egyptian "prophecy." See also C. C. McCown, "Hebrew and Egyptian Apocalyptic Literature," Harvard Theological Review, 18 (1925), 357-411; James H. Breasted, The Dawn of Conscience (Chicago, 1933), pp. 363ff.; T. J. Meek, Hebrew Origins (3rd ed.; New York, 1960), pp. 181-2. Much more cautious conclusions have been reached with regard to the supposed influence of Egyptian "prophecy" on Israelite prophecy by N. Schmidt, "The Origin of Jewish Eschatology," JBL, 41 (1922), 102-14; T. H. Robinson, "Die prophetischen Bücher im Lichte neuer Entdeckungen," ZAW, 45 (1927), 3-9. It should be noted that the Gattung "prophecy" which is itself much debated has nothing to do with prophecy in ancient Israel.

different historical or external circumstances.[36] Yet Gressmann himself offered a psychological solution to the problem of the interrelation of the two types of eschatology.[37] He too did not recognize that the essential weakness of the psychological solution lies in the fact that it does not take account of the prophets as recipients of divine revelation.[38] Furthermore, Gressmann is not convincing in his arguments with which he attempts to show that the remnant motif bridges only inadequately the tension between the eschatology of doom and the eschatology of salvation. E. Sellin has provided a critique of Gressmann in his study about Old Testament eschatology in which he shows that the remnant motif does not mediate artificially between the proclamation of doom and the proclamation of salvation but is an integral part of both.[39] Gressmann is not objective in his evaluation of the prophetic message of salvation because he considers the prophetic proclamation of salvation as a "sub-prophetic" (unterprophetische)[40] adoption of popular belief. He is thus still following the Wellhausen School to which he tries to provide an

---

[36]For example, Meinhold, *op. cit*., p. 108, speaks of such psychological changes in Hosea, Jeremia, and Isaiah.

[37]See especially Volkmar Herntrich, "λεῖμμα κτλ.," *TDNT*, IV, 199. For criticisms of deriving Hebrew eschatology from Babylonia and the problem of nature myths, see Ernst Sellin, "Alter, Wesen und Ursprung der alttestamentlichen Eschatologie," in *Der alttestamentliche Prophetismus* (Leipzig, 1912), pp. 124ff., and A. von Gall, *Βασιλεία τοῦ θεοῦ. Eine religionsgeschichtliche Studie zur vorkirchlichen Eschatologie* (Heidelberg, 1926), pp. 28ff.

[38]On this aspect, see Johannes Lindblom, *Prophecy in Ancient Israel* (Philadelphia, 1962), pp. 105-22, 423-4.

[39]Sellin, *op. cit*., pp. 119, 133, 154-6.

[40]Gressmann, *Ursprung der . . . Eschatologie*, p. 237.

alternative. Gressmann's attempt is hardly a success.

In the year in which World War I broke out Herbert Dittmann devoted an article to the topic of "Der heilige Rest im Alten Testament."[41] He rejects Meinhold's psychologizing and builds on Gressmann's emphasis upon the antiquity of Israelite eschatology. Dittmann takes up Sellin's notion that the proclamation of doom and salvation are "only two different aspects of one and the same expectation."[42] Taking this as his starting point he shows that the remnant motif "is an actually powerful bridge between both thoughts."[43] With regard to Amos Dittmann states that he is the first prophet who speaks of a "holy remnant" consisting of converted Israelites.[44] Then Dittmann argues that Meinhold's outline of the development of Isaiah's remnant motif is completely untenable. The supposition that Isaiah did not use the remnant motif at the beginning of his ministry cannot be supported.[45] Isaiah used the remnant motif right from the beginning of his prophetic activity and at that always in the sense of a remnant <u>from</u> Judah. The remnant motif is not only a part but actually a "foundation pillar of the whole of Israelite eschatology."[46] It is an original constituent of eschatology and was not created by the prophets as a deficient connection between the eschatology of doom and the eschatology of salvation. The contribution of the

---

[41]This article appeared in <u>Theologische Studien und Kritiken</u>, 87 (1914), 603-18.

[42]<u>Ibid</u>., p. 607.

[43]<u>Ibid</u>.

[44]<u>Ibid</u>., p. 610.

[45]<u>Ibid</u>., pp. 610-11.

[46]<u>Ibid</u>., p. 617.

prophets to the remnant motif, which was adopted by them as part of their eschatology, was an ethical deepening and undergirding.[47]

Dittmann appears to be an extreme supporter of those who connect the remnant motif with eschatology. Dittmann and his predecessors fail to account for the Hebrew remnant motif prior to its appearance in the writing prophets and thus possibly prior to the rise of eschatology.

Another great representative of the line of scholars that connect the remnant motif with eschatology is Sigmund Mowinckel. In 1922 he published his Psalmenstudien II. Das Thronbesteigungsfest Jahwäs und der Ursprung der Eschatologie.[48] In this work he treated the remnant motif as a part of his discussion of Israel's eschatology.[49] Mowinckel maintains against Gressmann that the remnant motif does not originate in the Babylonian nature myth but it is part of the Babylonian enthronement myth out of which Israelite eschatology developed.[50] He distinguished between

---

[47]Ibid., pp. 612, 617.

[48]The present writer cites from the 2nd ed. published in Amsterdam by P. Schippers, 1961.

[49]Sigmund Mowinckel, Psalmenstudien II, pp. 276-82.

[50]Mowinckel, ibid., p. 262, states, "if eschatology derives from the enthronement festival, then it is most likely to think about the Tiamat myth." It is curious that he denies the earlier claim in the preface to the second edition that he never wrote that eschatology originated from the enthronement festival: "I have certainly never written that the eschatology 'originated' out of the cult festival. The Jewish future hope and eschatology 'originated' as such in a definite historical situation--the collapse of the national existence of the covenant people--out of the primeval depths of Yahwistic religion." Despite this disclaimer Mowinckel had written on p. 314: "From all these assumptions we can draw the final conclusion: eschatology originated from the enthronement festival."

a "pre-Amos eschatology,"[51] which is the old popular eschatology of salvation,[52] and a "post-Amos eschatology,"[53] also called later eschatology,[54] which began with Amos and is attested in Hosea, Isaiah, etc.[55] The "pre-Amos eschatology" contains oracles of doom and of salvation, because the "the day of Yahweh's accession to the throne brings doom to Israel's enemies and salvation for Israel, these have been always both aspects of its ex-

---

[51] *Ibid.*, pp. 263, 338.

[52] Mowinckel employs a number of terms for this such as "ältere Eschatologie" (*ibid.*, pp. 266, 269), "ältere Heilseschatologie" (*ibid.*, pp. 267, 274), "alte Heilseschatologie" (*ibid.*, p. 277), and "alte volkstümliche Eschatologie" (*ibid.*, p. 271).

[53] *Ibid.*, p. 267.

[54] *Ibid.*, p. 270.

[55] In more recent publications Mowinckel retracted his earlier view of a pre-prophetic or pre-Amos eschatology. In *He That Cometh*, transl. by G. W. Anderson (Nashville, 1956), p. 130, he writes, ". . . it is established as a result of the historical and critical study of the Old Testament tradition and literature during the past generation that there is no eschatology in the strict sense in the early pre-prophet age." Cf. S. Mowinckel, *Prophecy and Tradition* (Oslo, 1946), p. 14. In *He That Cometh*, p. 132, Mowinckel denies also any aspects of a pre-exilic prophetic eschatology. This reversal on the part of Mowinckel is to a large degree due to a new definition of eschatology. In his *Psalmenstudien II* eschatology is viewed in a broad sense referring to the future of Yahweh's people in which the circumstances of history are changed without, in so doing, necessarily leaving the plane of actual history. Now he states that "the belief that there always will be a 'future' for Yahweh's elected people is no eschatology" (*The Psalms in Israel's Worship* [Nashville, 1962], II, 225 n. VIII). In *He That Cometh*, p. 125, a succinct definition is given: "Eschatology is a doctrine or complex of ideas about 'the last things', which is more or less organically coherent and developed." This change has not brought about a new interpretation of the remnant motif except that it is denied its eschatological nature and assigned to the "future hope" (*He That Cometh*, pp. 132, 134-6).

pectation."[56] Amos, the first writing prophet, reversed this original eschatological scheme by making the "day of Yahweh" a day of doom.[57] Amos is a consistent prophet of doom; he knows no remnant that will escape the future disaster.[58] The "remnant of Joseph" in Amos 5:15 is a reference to the present entity of Israelites, i.e., those that are addressed by the prophet.[59] This questionable exegesis of Amos 5:15 is due to Mowinckel's notion that the remnant motif is a part of the eschatology of salvation for which there is no room in a consistent prophet of doom.

With regard to Isaiah Mowinckel follows Wellhausen and his school by accepting only Isa. 7:3 and 37:32 as genuine remnant passages.[60] He revives the theory of Meinhold without mentioning him by name that the Hebrew remnant idea first appears in Isaiah of Jerusalem, who was at first a prophet of doom and only later became a prophet of salvation.[61] The reason for Mowinckel's notion that the remnant motif is not at least as

---

[56]Mowinckel, Psalmenstudien II, p. 263.

[57]Ibid., pp. 264-6, against Sellin, op. cit., pp. 119ff., who argued that the negative aspect was already present in the tradition of the "day of Yahweh" prior to Amos.

[58]Mowinckel, Psalmenstudien II, p. 266.

[59]Ibid., p. 265.

[60]Ibid., p. 278. Mowinckel gives no reason for rejecting the large number of remnant passages in the book of Isaiah except that he points out that he has no desire to follow Gunkel's and Gressmann's search for the old prophetic eschatology of salvation nor for Sellin's attempted defense against critical extremes.

[61]Ibid., p. 279.

as old as Amos lies with two aspects which he assigns to the term remnant. The negative aspect is employed in connection with prophecy of doom[62] and in such cases it is not an independent motif but merely a part of the picture of doom.[63] He believes that in passages in which no survivors are left one cannot speak of the remnant motif. This explains, he believes, why the remnant motif could not have arisen from an eschatology of doom, as Gressmann argues, and serve as a bridge between it and the eschatology of salvation. Thus Mowinckel takes the other extreme and connects the remnant motif solely with the Israelite eschatology of salvation.[64]

Isaiah of Jerusalem is the first to make use of the "positive" aspect of the remnant.[65] He linked it with faith and repentance and introduced the idea that the remnant refers to a part of the whole. This is a decisive departure from the idea of an escaped remnant of the "pre-Amos eschatology" in which the remnant motif was always used of the whole of Israel which Yahweh delivered from the catastrophe.[66] Mowinckel bases this view of the remnant motif upon arguments of terminology. He argues that since there are only phrases such as <u>šeʾār</u> <u>yiśrāʾēl</u> and never

---

[62]Amos 3:12; 5:2-3; Isa. 6; 7:3; 24:13.

[63]*Ibid.*, p. 278.

[64]Lindblom, *op. cit.*, pp. 362ff., follows much the same line of argumentation. He links it with what he calls "positive eschatology" which is virtually the same as Mowinckel's eschatology of salvation.

[65]Mowinckel, *Psalmenstudien II*, pp. 279-80.

[66]*Ibid.*, pp. 281-2.

šeʾār miyyiśrāʾēl the remnant motif must invariably have referred to the whole and not part of the people. Isaiah adopted the term in this sense, but it is his contribution to the religion of the history of Israel to make the remnant motif to mean a part of the whole.[67]

The linguistic considerations do not justify the conclūsions which Mowinckel draws from them. This is shown by such expressions as *šeʾērîṯ-haggôyim* and *pelêṭaṯ-haggôyim* from which one would then be forced to conclude that the whole and not part of the nations would constitute the remnant.[68] This is exactly what Mowinckel does not want to say. The idea of separation and sifting is inherent in that of the remnant. Furthermore, Mowinckel's notion of a "positive" and "negative" remnant motif where the former is a separate idea but the latter is a supposedly inseparable part of the eschatology of doom is seemingly an arbitrary and artificial distinction which can hardly be supported by detailed exegetical study.

Father Roland de Vaux published in the year 1933 his essay on the "remnant of Israel" in the Old Testament prophets.[69] Father de Vaux has the credit to be the first scholar to take as his point of departure etymological considerations of some major roots employed in the Hebrew Bible in connection with the remnant motif. His terminological considerations, however, are very limited. While he asserts an Israelite

---

[67]*Ibid.*

[68]Cf. Herntrich, *TDNT*, IV, 200.

[69]R. de Vaux, "Le 'reste d'Israël' d'après les prophètes," *RB*, 42 (1933), 526-39, now reprinted in *Bible et Orient* (Paris, 1967), pp. 25-39. All citations are from the original publication. See Appendix II, p. 461.

The King's Library

origin of the remnant motif no attempt is made to investigate its origins in the Hebrew Bible or in the prophetic materials. De Vaux sees the remnant motif as a bridge binding the threat of punishment to the hope of restoration.[70] He points to the dual aspects of doom and hope as expressed through the prophetic use of the remnant motif. Three stages emerge, according to de Vaux, in the prophets' use of the expression "remnant": (1) In the pre-exilic period it is a designation for the few remaining Israelites on Palestinian soil; (2) in exilic times it serves to designate the deportees; and (3) in the post-exilic era it is used to mark the congregation of Ezra. With regard to the relationship between the remnant motif and the future hope of the prophets de Vaux presents the following conclusion:

> In every age the remnant is first of all that which will escape the danger of the present. But back of this first plane on which contemporary events are more sharply drawn in the mind of the prophet, a second may be discerned, dominated by the person of the Messiah: the remnant is there identified by the New Israel; established in the promised land where it forms a holy community which lives in the love and fear of Yahweh and receives his blessings. Yet this is not all, for a yet more distant and vaster plane is to be seen: it spreads to the horizon of time, when the remnant, not only the new Israel, but spiritual Israel, having gathered at once all the dispersed of the people and all the converted of the nations, will alone remain before Yahweh in the final annihilation of the wicked.[71]

In 1938 the fascicle of the TWNT came off the press which con-

---

[70] *Ibid.*, p. 538.

[71] *Ibid.*, p. 539.

tained Volkmar Herntrich's article on λεῖμμα κτλ.[72] Herntrich rejects the derivation of the remnant motif from mythology as argued by Gressmann and Mowinckel.[73] He does agree, however, with these two scholars that the rise of the fixed theological remnant motif is closely connected with the origin of Israelite eschatology.[74] Herntrich follows F. Baumgärtel[75] in his argument that eschatology has its basis in the coming of God himself, who is continually present and active in the actual event of revelation.[76] The remnant motif, in the view of Herntrich, "has its origin at the same point as eschatology generally, namely, in the coming of God into this world-time in which he reveals Himself to men as the Holy One."[77] This means that the inbreaking of God into the here and now by means of his revelation is eschatology. Along this line of reasoning it is argued that the origin of the remnant motif is grounded in the "Setzung Gottes,"[78] i.e., the action of God. "God creates the remnant."[79] Through divine action doom and salvation are united in the

---

[72]V. Herntrich, "λεῖμμα κτλ.," TWNT (Stuttgart, 1942), IV, 200-15, English translation, TDNT (Grand Rapids, Mich., 1967), IV, 196-209. The present writer follows the English translation unless otherwise noted. References are given both to the German and English publications.

[73]TWNT, IV, 203-5; TDNT, IV, 198-200.

[74]TWNT, IV, 203; TDNT, IV, 198.

[75]Friedrich Baumgärtel, Die Eigenart der alttestamentlichen Frömmigkeit (Schwerin, 1932), pp. 66ff.

[76]TWNT, IV, 206 n. 25; TDNT, IV, 201 n. 25.

[77]TWNT, IV, 205; TDNT, IV, 201.

[78]TWNT, IV, 205.

[79]TWNT, IV, 208 (translation is mine).

remnant motif in such a way that the continuity of history is grounded solely in the work of God.[80] Since it is none other than God who established and creates the remnant by his own action, the question of the "temporal origin"[81] of the remnant motif is no more the question of the origin and development of a motif. The latter question has become inappropriate; the question of the "temporal origin" is identical with "the question of the witness to the reality of God, who established a remnant by His own action."[82]

Herntrich's study lacks not only an appreciation for the importance of the historical question of the origin and development of the remnant motif in the Hebrew Bible, but he also presents an excessive overemphasis on the action of God for the constitution of the remnant.[83] Due to this one-sided stress man's action or disposition can have no influence on whether or not he may become a member of the remnant. "Faith is not the condition for belonging to the remnant."[84] The remnant does not have "its existence in the holiness of its members."[85] While these notions remain highly debatable, Herntrich must be credited to be the first to recognize the important connection between the remnant motif

---

[80] TWNT, IV, 204; TDNT, IV, 200.

[81] TWNT, IV, 206; TDNT, IV, 202.

[82] TWNT, IV, 205; TDNT, IV, 200.

[83] F. Rienecker, "Rest," Lexikon zur Bibel (5th ed.; Wuppertal, 1964); cols. 1138-40, follows Herntrich on this particular point.

[84] TWNT, IV, 212; TDNT, IV, 207.

[85] TWNT, IV, 213; TDNT, IV, 207.

and the election tradition.[86] But he fails to delineate this connection in detail.

Herntrich's investigation of the remnant terminology is valuable in a number of areas but inadequate in a number of other areas. The distinction between a "secular" and a "theological" remnant concept is artificial. It is claimed that the remnant motif is "theological" since the time of Isaiah, because from then on it "belongs to the context of expectation of salvation and judgment."[87] Herntrich was apparently unacquainted with de Vaux's study of some remnant terminology.

Werner E. Müller's inaugural dissertation of the year 1939 entitled Die Vorstellung vom Rest im Alten Testament[88] is a highly original study. Müller followed the lead of Herntrich in distinguishing the secular from the religious use of the remnant motif in the Old Testament. His very consistent application of this distinction has led to conclusions which have been of great influence on later scholarship.

Müller's study opens with an investigation of the "political meaning of the remnant for a people"[89] in ancient Near Eastern materials, namely the war annals of the Hittites, Egyptians, and Assyrians. As a result of this investigation of the ancient Near Eastern annalistic background Müller concludes that the remnant motif originated out of the practice of complete annihilation in the Assyrian method of total war-

---

[86] TWNT, IV, 206; TDNT, IV, 201.

[87] TWNT, IV, 201-2; TDNT, IV, 197.

[88] Werner E. Müller, Die Vorstellung vom Rest im Alten Testament (Inaugural-Dissertation; Borsdorf-Leipzig, 1939).

[89] Ibid., p. 4.

fare.[90] To be precise, "The origin of the remnant [motif] lies in the breakdown of this principle [of total warfare] as in Assyrian practice."[91] The Old Testament reflects the same situation as in the ancient Near Eastern surroundings. In other words, the remnant motif derives from the sphere of politics and not from mythology or mythology and cult as Gressmann and Mowinckel had maintained respectively.

Next Müller turns to a delineation of the content of the remnant motif. He points out that while the fate of the surviving remnant was on the whole a wretched one--it could be destined for complete annihilation or it could be totally insignificant--this remnant could very well be the nucleus of the rebirth of a people.[92] The remnant is then "the carrier and preserver of life for the community."[93] Thus Müller is the first to point to the significant connection between the idea of life and existence and the remnant motif. He is, however, not able to recognize the importance of this connection for a possible origin of the remnant motif because of his one-sided emphasis on the secular-political notion of the remnant motif.

A date for the first appearance of the remnant motif can hardly be expected, argues Müller.[94] Yet he pushes the date much farther back than his predecessors. Meinhold had supposed that the remnant motif originated at about the middle of the eighth century B.C.[95] Gressmann viewed the remnant motif as peculiar to the preaching of the prophets and connected

---

[90]*Ibid.*, p. 18.

[91]*Ibid.*, p. 27.

[92]*Ibid.*, pp. 28-33.

[93]*Ibid.*, p. 38.

[94]*Ibid.*

[95]Meinhold, *op. cit.*, p. 19.

its origin with the pre-canonical schools of the prophets.[96] Müller, on the other hand, believes that it was transferred to the language and ideology of religion even before the time of Elijah. The remnant motif is obviously used by the Yahwist.[97]

Beginning with the primeval and patriarchal traditions in Genesis Müller traces the remnant motif through the Elijah cycle to Amos and Isaiah among the pre-exilic prophets. With regard to Isaiah he argues much like Meinhold that there are several stages in his usage of the remnant motif. At the beginning of Isaiah's ministry there is supposedly no evidence for the hope of a remnant.[98] It arose during the Syro-Ephraimitic crisis,[99] and receded into the background under the stress of the judgment message. Yet it never disappeared completely.[100] Müller argues forcefully that the Isaianic use of the remnant motif follows the tradition recognizable in Elijah and Amos, namely that the possibility of the survival of a remnant is uniquely dependent upon the will of God. But over against the excessive emphasis on God's action by Herntrich, Müller maintains that the condition for the possibility of a remnant is the human reaction to the ethical demand of repentance and faith. Müller studies also the remnant motif of Zephaniah, Jeremiah, and Ezekiel[101] before he touches briefly on the remnant motif in post-exilic Judaism.[102]

---

[96]Gressmann, Ursprung der . . . Eschatologie, pp. 229ff.

[97]Müller, op. cit., pp. 42-6; cf. Gerhard von Rad, OTT, II, 22-3.

[98]Ibid., p. 54.

[99]Ibid., p. 57.

[100]Ibid., p. 61.

[101]Ibid., pp. 62-77.

[102]Ibid., pp. 78-84.

Müller's contributions to the understanding of the remnant motif are significant. He is the first to make use of ancient Near Eastern materials. But inasmuch as he restricted his investigation to annalistic records of the Hittites, Egyptians, and Assyrians his conclusions were dependent upon findings in these materials. Thus there is here a serious methodological problem. What about the remnant motif in non-annalistic records of the ancient Near East? A more inclusive and broader investigation of ancient Near Eastern literary materials is therefore mandatory. It must extend also to Sumerian, Akkadian, and Ugaritic materials. As such an investigation is carried out it will become apparent whether or not Müller's conclusions with regard to the political origin of the remnant motif can be substantiated or need to be abandoned. Secondly, the arbitrary distinction between the secular-political and religious uses of the remnant motif poses a problem of procedure and methodology for Müller which is of great consequence for the outcome of his study. He develops the "origin" and "content" of the remnant motif on the basis of the secular-political sphere, while the "development" and "history" of the remnant motif is treated under its religious sphere. As a result the remnant motif is changed, modified, and impregnated with additional aspects in its religious use, which means that the original secular-political "content" becomes thus transformed by secondary religious influences. These problematical notions raise a number of questions. If there were an original "secular-political" remnant motif, would this not also exhibit a "development" and "history" aside from having an "origin" and "content"? Would its "development" and "history" not run side by side with that of the "religious" remnant motif instead of being strictly sequential? These questions actually ask whether or not an a priori distinction between a "secular-political" and a "religious" sphere is necessary or even helpful in the study of the remnant motif.[103] It appears that these distinctions blur rather than aid our understanding of the origin, meaning, and history of the extra-Biblical and Biblical remnant motif.[104] Finally, the very fact that the earliest appearance of the remnant motif in the oldest stratum of Genesis is present in materials in which the political practice of total warfare is absent calls for a thorough reinvestigation of the origin and early development of the remnant motif.[105] Thus while Müller's contributions to the discussion of the remnant motif are important they cannot be considered to be conclusive.

---

[103]At times one even wonders whether the modern concept of the separation of politics and religion has not been subconsciously applied to the ancient remnant motif which arose in a world which knew nothing of such a separation.

[104]Müller, op. cit., p. 4, refers to Herntrich for introducing the distinction between the "secular" and "theological" use of the remnant motif. Herntrich, however, means something quite different by this distinction from what Müller makes it to be. Herntrich's "secular" use refers to a series of years, trees, food, strength, breadth, etc. and does not have any "political" aspect to it, which is primary for Müller. In the same way Herntrich's "theological" use refers to contexts in which the remnant motif is employed in connection with the eschatological expectations of judgment and salvation. This is completely different from Müller's "religious" use. In contrast to Müller Herntrich is painfully aware of the problems connected with such a distinction: "It is obvious that the boundary between the secular and the theological use of the concept is a fluid one" (TWNT, IV, 202; TDNT, IV, 197).

[105]Müller's notion that the remnant motif originated from politics, i.e., from the breakdown of the military practice of total warfare with complete annihilation, has been widely accepted. Cf. von Rad, OTT, II, 21ff.; idem, Die Botschaft der Propheten (München, 1967), p. 132; Lothar Ruppert, Die Josephserzählung der Genesis (SANT, XI; München, 1965), p. 122; Hans Walter Wolff, Frieden ohne Ende. Eine Auslegung von Jes. 7, 1-7 und 9, 1-6 (BS, 35; Neukirchen-Vluyn, 1962), p. 17; Hans Wildberger, Jesaja (BKAT, X/2; Neukirchen-Vluyn, 1966), pp. 155-6; Odil H.

In the year 1942 two Catholic doctoral dissertations were finished, both of which treated the remnant motif in the prophetic materials of the Hebrew Bible. Salvatore Garofalo entitled his monograph La nozione profetica del 'Resto d'Israele'. Contributo alla teologia del Vecchio Testamento. A brief summary appeared a year earlier.[106] Garofalo divided his monograph into two main parts. The first part[107] treats the remnant motif in the Northern Kingdom, i.e., Elijah, Amos, and Hosea, and in the Southern Kingdom, i.e. Isaiah and Micah, as well as Zephaniah, Jeremiah, Ezekiel, Daniel, Haggai, Zechariah, Obadiah, and Jonah. The second part deals with the theology of the "remnant of Israel" opening with a five-page outline of the remnant terminology and then turning to the identification and character of the remnant in a kind of systematic-theological fashion. Against Meinhold the author argues for a pre-Isaianic remnant motif; against both Gressmann and Mowinckel he supposes an Israelite origin of the remnant motif rising out of the

---

Steck, Überlieferung und Zeitgeschichte in den Eliaerzählungen (WMANT, 26; Neukirchen-Vluyn, 1968), p. 96 n. 2; Ursula Stegemann, "Der Restgedanke bei Isaias," BZ, 13 (1969), 163. On the other hand, Mowinckel, He That Cometh, p. 138, maintains against Müller that the remnant motif "had also a religious aspect from the very beginning." V. Hamp, "Rest, heiliger R. I. Altes Testament," Lexikon für Theologie und Kirche, ed. by J. Höfer und K. Rahner (Freiburg, 1963), VIII, 1252-3, outrightly states that the origin of the theological remnant motif is insufficiently explained by a connection with the military sphere in which a part of the population remains.

[106] S. Garofalo, "Residuum Israelis," Verbum Domini, 21 (1941), 239-43.

[107] S. Garofalo, La nozione profetica del 'Resto d'Israele'. Contributo alla teologia del Vecchio Testamento (Lateranum, N.S. An. VIII N. 1-4; Romae, 1942), pp. 25-193.

notion of the people of God and thus the election tradition. The remnant motif appears first in the prophetic circles of Elijah. With regard to the Isaianic use of the remnant motif Garofalo summarizes:

> Isaiah is always the great prophet of the remnant. The certainty of deliverance for the chosen people prevails over the painful uncertainty of the events; and it is above all in his preaching that the idea shines forth supremely in the light of the Messiah. He thus throws into magnificent relief the true historical and providential function of the chosen people.[108]

Garofalo apparently does not know Herntrich's study nor that of Müller. He does not bring much that is new.

The dissertation of Othmar Schilling, "'Rest' in der Prophetie des Alten Testaments" is divided into linguistic, historico-analytical, and theologico-systematic parts. The linguistic section[109] treats the Old Testament remnant terminology. On the basis of this terminological investigation he concludes that the Old Testament remnant motif is much more diffused than Müller had allowed by deriving it from Assyrian military practice. While this observation of Schilling seems to be correct, it still needs objective historical verification which he has not provided. It is at this point where our investigation attempts to contribute to the discussion. It is not enough to take seriously the terminological diffusion of the remnant motif in the Old Testament, as important as this is by itself; a failure to study seriously the appearance of the remnant motif in the available ancient Near Eastern literary materials inadvertently leaves the power of argument on the side of Müller. It is at this crucial juncture where the studies of Garofalo, Schilling, and all

---

[108]*Ibid.*, p. 191.

[109]Othmar Schilling, "'Rest' in der Prophetie des Alten Testaments" (unpublished Inaugural-dissertation, University of Münster, 1942), pp. 8-21.

later investigations are painfully inadequate.

Schilling places great emphasis on the election tradition for the origin and development of the Old Testament remnant motif. He shows that the action of God for the creation of the remnant has a corresponding human side; both the divine and human aspects belong together in the prophetic remnant motif. This emphasis is consistently recognizable in the second part of Schilling's monograph.[110] Amos adopted the remnant motif from tradition and used it to express the survival of the remnant of the nation when judgment will fall upon it. This remnant will not be the nation itself but will consist of a community of believers. Isaiah of Jerusalem is dependent upon Amos. He emphasizes Yahweh's special action in history in which salvation is the result of ethical behavior. The Isaianic remnant motif is, therefore, radically separated from politics. The remnant community is a religious entity. In Isaiah there is no development of the remnant motif; it is present from the beginning and does not show a development during the various stages of the prophet's work.[111] Schilling then continues to investigate the remnant motif in the remaining major and minor prophets. He concludes that "one cannot speak of a development of the remnant idea"[112] in the prophets; there are merely "variations."[113]

Schilling believes that there is no real connection between the prophetic remnant motif and that of the patriarchal narratives of Genesis. The relationship between the two does not go beyond that of analogy.

---

[110]Ibid., pp. 22-136.

[111]Ibid., p. 81.

[112]Ibid., p. 148.

[113]Ibid.

He does, therefore, distinguish between the origin of both. The remnant motif of the prophets is closely connected with the idea of divine retribution. The origin of the prophetic remnant motif is grounded in the sanctions of the law, especially in Lev. 26 and its Deuteronomic parallels. Israel adopted the positive sanctions for herself and developed the notion of the positive remnant motif which expressed the belief that Israel as a whole would emerge as a remnant from any catastrophe. The prophets, on the other hand, took up the negative sanctions of the law and developed the negative notion of the remnant motif.[114] "The sanction of the law and of covenant-making . . . [are] the internal reason and the external origin of the idea of the remnant."[115]

This exposition of the origin of the remnant motif seems to be hampered by insurmountable difficulties. First, it assumes an extensive popular notion of a positive remnant motif among the Israelites for which there is no support in the extant materials. More serious even is the failure to account for the origin of the remnant motif in the early stratum of Genesis which antedates the prophetic use of the remnant motif. Third, Schilling is forced to juxtapose the remnant motif of the primeval and patriarchal narratives to that of the prophets without being able to delineate an indirect or direct relationship between the two. As a matter of fact Schilling is not objective, for he depreciates the former by limiting his discussion to the remnant motif in the flood story

---

[114] *Ibid.*, pp. 141-6.

[115] *Ibid.*, p. 141.

and one incident in the Lot tradition.[116] And finally, Schilling fails to recognize the problems of dating all or parts of Lev. 26.[117] He assumes an early date and connects it with the Sinai tradition. These hypotheses need thorough study.[118] In any case Schilling's position with regard to the origin of the remnant motif is too problematical to be convincing. He is, however, on the right track in maintaining against Herntrich that the remnant motif is not solely grounded in the action of Yahweh to the complete exclusion of any human response.

G. A. Danell[119] deals with the remnant motif as a part of his study of the meaning of the name "Israel" in the Old Testament. He attempts to define the remnant motif in phrases in which a designation for Israel appears and is therefore not interested in a detailed study of the Hebrew remnant motif. H. H. Rowley[120] views the remnant motif as

---

[116]Ibid., pp. 146-8.

[117]For the various dates proposed for this part of the Holiness Code, see Eissfeldt, OTI, pp. 236-9; Georg Fohrer, Introduction to the Old Testament, transl. by D. E. Green (Nashville, 1968), pp. 137-42; Otto Kaiser, Einleitung in das Alte Testament (Gütersloh, 1969), pp. 98-100.

[118]H. Graf Reventlow, Das Heiligkeitsgesetz formgeschichtlich untersucht (WMANT, 6; Neukirchen-Vluyn, 1961) maintains that the Holiness Code is rooted in the covenant renewal festival and experienced a long development. The process of origin and development is to be assigned to the long span of time between the Sinai events and shortly after 725 B.C. Kurt Elliger, Leviticus (HAT I/4; Göttingen, 1966), on the other hand, denies that the Holiness Code ever constituted a separate corpus and maintains a post-Deuteronomic origin. Parts of the Holiness Code are, of course, very old. These scholars represent the two extremes of current positions. Kaiser, op. cit., p. 100, states, "One recognizes that in most recent research practically the full range of possibilities are present"

[119]G. A. Danell, Studies in the Name Israel in the Old Testament (Uppsala, 1946), pp. 120ff.

[120]H. H. Rowley, The Biblical Doctrine of Election (London, 1950), pp. 80ff., 86, 70ff.

an integral part of Israel's election tradition. He rejects the view of a common origin with eschatology[121] and proposes that the origin of the remnant motif is closely associated with the election tradition as seen in the election of Isaac's son Jacob over Esau.[122] It remains to be seen whether this suggestion can be supported by the evidence in Genesis.

Eric W. Heaton devoted an article to "The Root שאר and the Doctrine of the Remnant,"[123] which was published in 1952. Heaton protests against the designation "doctrine of the remnant"[124] on grounds that there is no intrinsic unity in the prophet's use of the root š'r in the genuine prophetic oracles. Heaton's study of the prophetic remnant motif is dependent upon the claim that the usage of the root š'r is the only criterion upon which one can arrive at a proper understanding of the prophetic remnant motif. It is obvious that this is a rather questionable claim. As a matter of fact the prophets did not limit themselves to the use of š'r when referring to the remnant motif.

Heaton concludes that the root š'r "primarily directs attention, not forward to the residue, but backwards to the whole of which it had been a part and to the devastation and loss by which it had been brought

---

[121]Ibid., p. 80.

[122]Ibid., p. 71.

[123]JTS, N. S. III (1952), 27-39.

[124]This designation is used frequently by scholars dealing with the remnant motif. One may refer for instance to J. Skinner, The Book of the Prophet Isaiah, Chapters I-XXXIX (Cambridge Bible for Schools and Colleges; 2nd ed.; Cambridge, 1915), pp. lxiiff. Recently J. Paterson, "Remnant," Hasting's Dictionary of the Bible, ed. by F. C. Grant and H. H. Rowley (New York, 1963), p. 841, argues that the remnant motif in the prophets is "a definite coherent doctrine."

into being."[125] Insofar as Heaton claims that "the basic meaning of the root _š᾽r_ is to remain or be left over from a larger number or quantity which has in some way been disposed of"[126] and that "in the overwhelming majority of instances the root is used in contexts which imply that the residual part is less important than the part from which it has been distinguished"[127] one wonders whether this is really so, for the investigations of Schilling and de Vaux give a different impression. When Heaton states that "other semitic languages appear to confirm this"[128] he gives the impression that his conclusions are on more solid ground than those of his predecessors.[129] In view of such conflicting conclusions and claims a re-examination and re-evaluation of the Hebrew remnant terminology is called for, including an investigation of the corresponding terms in cognate Semitic languages.

In the year 1955 two studies appeared dealing with the remnant motif in Isaiah. F. Dreyfus [130] dedicated a 25-page article to the doctrine of the "remnant of Israel" in the prophet Isaiah. Dreyfus' work

---

[125] Eric W. Heaton, "The Root שְׁאר and the Doctrine of the Remnant," _JTS_, N. S. III (1952), 29.

[126] _Ibid._, p. 28.

[127] _Ibid._

[128] _Ibid._

[129] Heaton apparently does not know Schilling's study of the remnant terminology.

[130] F. Dreyfus, "La doctrine du Reste d᾽Israël chez le prophète Isaïe," _Revue de Sciences Philosophiques et Theologiques_, 39 (1955), 361-86.

follows a systematic-theological structure with four main parts: (1) The vocation of the prophet; (2) remnant and faith; (3) the composition of the remnant; and (4) the remnant and the Messiah. This procedure prevents Dreyfus from adequately dealing with the Isaianic remnant motif in chronological order. Thus he is unable to penetrate into the variegated aspects of the Isaianic remnant motif as reflected in the various periods of Isaiah's prophetic ministry. He believes that Isaiah's message contained the remnant motif right from his inaugural vision on.[131] Isaiah does not proclaim judgment or salvation for the whole nation; rather, a dividing line separates the believing remnant from the disbelieving <u>massa perditionis</u>.[132] The remnant is clearly identified with the poor and the disciples of Isaiah.[133] "The Messiah appears in Isaiah as the personification of the remnant in the sense in which he represents the religious ideal to whom the one who desires to have a part in the new people must conform."[134] In this sense the remnant and the Messiah are "identical symbols."[135] These ideas indicate the novel nature of the presentation of Dreyfus and his independence from previous studies. Yet his contribution cannot be viewed as definitive for a proper understanding of the Isaianic remnant motif.

Reiji Hoshizaki has devoted a Master of Theology thesis to

---

[131] <u>Ibid</u>., p. 362.

[132] <u>Ibid</u>., p. 364.

[133] <u>Ibid</u>., pp. 382-3.

[134] <u>Ibid</u>., p. 383.

[135] <u>Ibid</u>., p. 384.

"Isaiah's Concept of the Remnant."[136] Hoshizaki's thesis is divided into two main parts: (1) The first two chapters--almost one half of the total length of the study--treat general introductory problems, such as authorship, unity, etc.,[137] and (2) the last two chapters deal respectively with the "importance and place" and the "content and meaning" of the Isaianic remnant "concept."[138] Hoshizaki follows the path of Dittmann and Rowley. The remnant concept "is found throughout his [Isaiah's] career from his earliest utterance to the very last."[139] Yet there is a definite development. Up to 735 B.C. Isaiah had some hope that the whole nation would return to Yahweh and be the remnant, but after the Syro-Ephraimitic crisis this hope was dashed and the remnant are the survivors left in Jerusalem. In a third stage Isaiah gave up all nationalistic hopes and "something of a universalistic element is beginning to emerge."[141] The remnant becomes an entity separate from the nation; it is connected with the concept of a "spiritual kernel" within Israel which becomes a most fruitful category for the future of Israel's faith.[142]

Despite Hoshizaki's attempt to come to grips with the Isaianic remnant motif his study is very disappointing. He is unaware of the rich

---

[136]Reiji Hoshizaki, "Isaiah's Concept of the Remnant" (unpublished M. Th. thesis, Southern Baptist Theological Seminary, Louisville, Kentucky, 1955).

[137]*Ibid.*, pp. 8-37.

[138]*Ibid.*, pp. 38-88.

[139]*Ibid.*, p. 40.

[140]*Ibid.*, p. 44.

[141]*Ibid.*, p. 86.

[142]*Ibid.*, pp. 86-8.

literature on the remnant motif,[143] and is therefore unable to carry the discussion forward at crucial points. He does not address himself to the origin of the Isaianic remnant motif. His methodology limits the results of his study in very much the same way as was noted in the case of the article of Dreyfus. Because of his methodological procedure he is unable to penetrate into the relationship between the external historical circumstances and the message of Isaiah and into the relation between the remnant motif and the prophet's proclamation of doom and salvation. Yet the studies of both Dreyfus and Hoshizaki are of value precisely because they teach us to avoid subtle pitfalls.

Donald M. Warne devoted in 1958 a dissertation to the subject of "The Origin, Development and Significance of the Concept of the Remnant in the Old Testament."[144] Warne's purpose is to investigate the place of the "remnant concept" in the development of the Hebrew religion. His monograph opens with a chapter dealing with the Hebrew remnant terminology.[145] Over against Heaton he maintains that the root <u>š'r</u> is not merely backwards-looking, but contains a bi-polarity of outlook which refers backward to the devastation and forward to the renewal. The terminol-

---

[143]Hoshizaki does not refer to such names as Meinhold, Gressmann, Mowinckel, de Vaux, Müller, Garofalo, Schilling, Heaton. His use of scholarly literature is painfully limited in virtually all areas of his endeavor.

[144]Donald M. Warne, "The Origin, Development and Significance of the Concept of the Remnant in the Old Testament" (unpublished Ph. D. dissertation, Faculty of Divinity, University of Edinburgh, 1958). The present writer is indebted to Dr. Warne for his kindness in lending him his personal copy since this dissertation was not available through regular channels.

[145]<u>Ibid</u>., pp. 1-14.

ogical part of Warne's study is on a limited scale. Therefore a more detailed investigation is still called for. The second chapter attempts to probe into the origin of the remnant motif by placing the Israelite concept of the remnant over against that of the surrounding nations.[146] We had noted earlier that this is exactly what is as yet needed on a large scale. But Warne's research hardly goes beyond that of Müller. With the exception of the inclusion of some Ugaritic materials Warne is satisfied to summarize on the whole Müller's findings with regard to the annalistic records of the Hittites, Egyptians, and Assyrians. He concludes that "nothing in the records of the ancient Near East serves to show us exactly how the concept arose in the Old Testament."[147] It must be recognized that this conclusion is based only upon a very superficial use of annalistic records of three ancient nations. A more comprehensive and careful study of all literary records of the ancient Near East and Egypt may well lead to a completely different conclusion. Such an investigation is called for even more now since Müller and Warne have arrived at opposing conclusions from virtually the same ancient Near Eastern materials.

Warne rejects the theories of Gressmann and Mowinckel, who respectively derive the Hebrew remnant motif from Babylonian mythology and cult. He follows the lead of E. Sellin[148] and L. Dürr[149] in deriving

---

[146]<u>Ibid</u>., pp. 15-44.

[147]<u>Ibid</u>., p. 24.

[148]Sellin, <u>op. cit</u>., pp. 124ff.

[149]L. Dürr, <u>Ursprung und Ausbau der israelitisch-jüdischen Heilandserwartung</u> (Berlin, 1925).

the remnant motif from the early religious experience of the people of Israel, i.e., the origin of the Hebrew remnant motif is closely bound up with the election of Israel, the origin of eschatology, and the idea of an ethical judgment.[150] On the whole "the origin of the remnant idea is closely connected with the origin of eschatology, . . ."[151]

The next four chapters trace the "development" of the remnant motif from the flood story in Genesis through the era of post-exilic Judaism.[152] Warne's delineation of the remnant motif in Isaiah of Jerusalem[153] is of special interest. The inaugural vision indicates that "his /Isaiah's/ own experience showed him that out of judgment there would come reconciliation and new life."[154] The name Shear-jashub contains the notion of threat and hope. The Immanuel sign is a threat to king and nation but a promise to the remnant. The remnant actually took shape in the band of disciples. Zion in Isa. 8:18 and Isa. 6 is not to be understood as referring to the temple on the hill, but as a designation for the remnant community of faith. While Warne has a number of valuable insights, it is strange that he fails to deal with a great number of remnant passages in First Isaiah[155] without giving a reason for this omission. Since he does not seem to follow any clear-cut procedure in dealing with Isaiah's remnant motif—he does not treat the passages with which he deals in chronological or any other order—Warne is not able to

---

[150]Warne, op. cit., pp. 34-43. [151]Ibid., p. 44.

[152]Ibid., pp. 45-142. [153]Ibid., pp. 77-101.

[154]Ibid., p. 83.

[155]Cf. Isa. 1:8-9, 21-26; 14:22, 30; 15:9; 16:13, 14; 17:3, 5-6; 21:14-17; 30:17; 37:4; 37:30-32.

discern whether or not there is any development in Isaiah's employment of the remnant motif.[156] Warne refrains from tracing the possible influences of Amos upon Isaiah or Elijah upon Amos or the patriarchal narratives on the pre-exilic prophets. Thus the term "development" must be understood in a sense different from the customary.

The final chapter of Warne's dissertation pays attention to the "significance" of the Old Testament remnant concept.[157] This chapter actually addresses itself very briefly—and in the present writer's opinion very superficially—to the remnant concept and the uniqueness of Israel's faith, judgment and salvation, Israelite nationalism,[158] holiness, and eschatology.

We have registered our strictures with regard to scope, methodology, and original research at the appropriate junctures of our review of Warne's study and do not need to repeat them again. Warne's work is of special value in its limited part on terminology and in pointing toward the idea of preserving life as a constituent element of the remnant motif.

The Isaianic remnant motif has been briefly touched in the monograph of Siegfried Herrmann[159] within his discussion of the concrete

---

[156]Thus we do not learn whether Isaiah made use of the remnant motif right from the start of his ministry or whether it is introduced at a later time.

[157]*Ibid*., pp. 143-7.

[158]In regard to this aspect, see in much more detail J. C. Campbell, "God's People and the Remnant," *Scottish Journal of Theology*, 3 (1950), 78-85; Ben. F. Meyer, "Jesus and the Remnant," *JBL*, 84 (1965) 123-30; and Julian Morgenstern, "The Rest of the Nations," *JSS*, 2 (1957), 225-31.

[159]Siegfried Herrmann, *Die prophetischen Heilserwartungen im Alten Testament* (BWANT, 85; Stuttgart, 1965).

hopes of salvation among the eighth century prophets. Herrmann points out that Isaiah's expectations of salvation are limited to three conceptions: the remnant, the house of David, and Zion.[160] "These three themes are treated by Isaiah independently from each other without any correlation or unity of its supporting elements."[161] His discussion is limited to Isa. 1:21-26; 7:3; and 30:15-17. He accepts Müller's notion that Isaiah lacked the remnant motif in his first period of ministry and began to use it only in his middle period.[162] As to the general importance of the remnant motif for Isaiah Herrmann concludes, "The remnant is found on the fringes of Isaiah's message."[163]

H. D. Preuss treats the remnant motif in a chapter that discusses the Old Testament tension of judgment and salvation.[164] The main concern of Preuss' study is a phenomenological and synthetic investigation[165] of the traditions, development, and origin of Old Testament eschatology. The thesis which he develops is that

> . . . the Yahwistic faith is itself the root of eschatology, since it has always been directed towards the future and has remained so on account of the nature of its God and its continuing fulfillment. Therefore, one cannot only speak of 'Yahwistic faith _and_ future expectation,' but one has to speak of 'Yahweh faith _as_ future expectation'.[166]

---

[160] _Ibid_., p. 127.

[161] _Ibid_. This conclusion is opposed to the impression given by von Rad, _OTT_, II, 165ff., namely that the remnant motif and the Zion tradition are closely related.

[162] Herrmann, _op. cit_., p. 128.

[163] _Ibid_., p. 130.

[164] Horst Dietrich Preuss, _Jahweglaube und Zukunftserwartung_ (BWANT, 87; Stuttgart, 1968), pp. 154-204.

[165] _Ibid_., p. 6.

[166] _Ibid_., pp. 208-9.

The remnant motif[167] bridges the abyss of doom and weal; it is an equalizing factor in the tension between judgment and salvation.[168] Amos takes up the remnant motif from popular belief and transforms it to refer to a community of faithful.[169] Thus it is not a designation for the whole people. "The remnant is thereby an entity of future expectation, . . ."[170] In Isaiah the content of the remnant motif changes with the various stages in the prophet's proclamation. "The remnant is the sprouting of new life in judgment (6:13)."[171] The "remnant" is for Isaiah a "salvatio-historical and religious entity"[172] whose goal is life. In the Syro-Ephraimitic crisis Isaiah and his son Shear-jashub represent symbolically the remnant. For a time Isaiah himself attempts to "create" the remnant in his disciples.[173] The ideas of faith, repentance, grace, and life are all closely related to the Isaianic remnant motif.

As regards the origin of the remnant motif Preuss explicates that the remnant idea was originally not an eschatological concept, but was later employed within the future expectations of Israel, namely by Amos and Isaiah.[174] The origin, usage, and content of the remnant motif are thus closely related to the analogous problems of Old Testament eschatology.

Preuss' contribution to the understanding of the Hebrew remnant motif rests largely in his cautious evaluation of most of the secondary

---

167 Ibid., pp. 179-88.

168 Ibid., p. 181.

169 Ibid., pp. 181-2.

170 Ibid., p. 181.

171 Ibid., p. 182.

172 Ibid.

173 Ibid., p. 183.

174 Ibid., p. 188.

literature and in his delineation of the relation of the prophetic use of the remnant motif to eschatology. His summary presentation of the remnant motif in the writing prophets can, of course, not be taken to represent a major contribution to the understanding and appreciation of the origin, usage, and meaning of the Hebrew remnant motif. It would be unfair to criticize Preuss for something he did not aim to do.

The article by Ursula Stegemann entitled "Der Restgedanke bei Isaias"[175] is the most recent treatment of the remnant motif in First Isaiah. While Stegemann claims that the book of Isaiah contains in its present form "A developed remnant theology,"[176] it is her aim to investigate whether or not the "term 'remnant' . . . is already used by the prophet Isaiah with a theological meaning, in how far one can attribute to him a 'theology of the remnant'."[177]

The discussion of the remnant motif in Isaiah of Jerusalem is divided into two sharply separated parts: (1) the "secular-profane" remnant motif;[178] and (2) the "theological" remnant motif.[179] She follows Müller in claiming that the "secular-profane" remnant "is that which from a larger part (a forest Is 10:19; a city; an army 21:27; a people 14:30; 17:3ff.; 30:17; a country 1:8f.; etc.) has been left after a catastrophe."[180] The "secular-profane" remnant passages in First Isaiah express (1) that the remnant will be destroyed (14:30b); (2) that there remains an insignificant and small remnant

---

[175] BZ, 13 (1969), 161-86.

[176] Ibid., p. 161.

[177] Ibid., pp. 162-3.

[178] Ibid., pp. 163-5.

[179] Ibid., pp. 165-76.

[180] Ibid., pp. 163-4.

(7:22b; 10:18-19; 17:3-6; 30:14, 17; etc.); and (3) that a real remnant is left which causes hope for the future. "These hopes are however purely this-worldly-profane"[181] and therefore theologically not relevant. The "theological" remnant passages and the "theological" expression "remnant" is "first of all a concept of promise and refers to those . . . whom Yahweh would save on account of their faith."[182] Stegemann believes that only those passages should be dealt with in a study of the "theological" remnant motif whose authenticity is largely certain. Such passages are the following: Isa. 6:9-13b; 28:16-17a; 8:16-18; 7:3. Under this presupposition Stegemann concludes that these passages do not allow one to speak of a theology of the remnant in Isaiah.[183]

Stegemann's procedure and presuppositions determine her depreciation of the remnant motif in Isaiah of Jerusalem. Her study may be considered to represent the extreme outcome of Müller's artificial distinction between a "secular-political" and a "religious" remnant motif. Stegemann transformed these designations to apply to a supposed "secular-profane" remnant motif and to a supposed "theological" remnant motif. The problem with such a distinction is the spurious division of the prophet's message along secular-profane and theological lines whereby the former is theologically irrelevant. Such a distinction is inappropriate and does justice neither to the Isaianic remnant motif nor to the proclamation of Isaiah of Jerusalem. This is inadvertently admitted by Stegemann. While she reaches her conclusion with regard to Isaiah's

---

[181]<u>Ibid</u>., p. 165.

[182]<u>Ibid</u>.

[183]<u>Ibid</u>., p. 176.

use of the remnant motif on the basis of "theological" remnant passages, the catastrophe which leaves a "secular-profane" remnant is brought about also by Yahweh, and as such it is "religiously motivated . . . so that also the survivors can be reckoned as a remnant to have been left by him . . . ."[184] If the "secular-profane" remnant is the result of the action of Yahweh in history, then it too is theologically relevant. Thus the distinction between the "secular-profane" and the "theological" remnant motif breaks down. As a result the conclusions reached by Stegemann's investigation of the supposed "theological" remnant motif in Isaiah are themselves inconclusive.[185] It has become apparent from the history of research that it is completely inadequate to account for the different levels of the Isaianic and even the Hebrew remnant motif along the lines of such distinctions as "secular" and "religious" (Herntrich), or "political" and "religious" (Müller) or "secular-profane" and "theological" (Stegemann).[185a]

This review of almost seven decades of research on the origin, history, and meaning of the Hebrew remnant motif has shown that there is no communis opinio with regard to either the origin or the history or the meaning of the remnant motif in the Hebrew Bible. With regard to the origin of the Hebrew remnant motif three major trends seem to have emerged and are supported by scholars to the present day. There are those who

---

[184] Ibid., pp. 164-5.

[185] Herbert Donner, Israel unter den Völkern (SVT, XI; Leiden, 1964), pp. 170-1, shows in his investigation of Isaiah's political judgments "dass politische und theologische Motive (in Jesaja) eine unauflösliche Einheit bildeten. . . ."

[185a] See Appendix, pp. 461-62.

argue that the remnant motif has its origin in conjunction with eschatology. Others believe that it is grounded solely in God's action in history within Israelite faith. Still others maintain that it evolved from the secular-political sphere of ancient Near Eastern practice of warfare. There is likewise no agreement on the development of the Hebrew remnant motif. The general trend is to view the appearance and usage of the remnant motif in the various parts and layers of tradition of the Hebrew Bible as in some way related to each other. It is supposed that each Biblical writer uses this motif according to his own emphasis and historical circumstances.

The nature of the remnant motif in Isaiah of Jerusalem is a matter of heated scholarly debate. Our survey of the leading studies of the remnant motif has pointed to extremely disparate scholarly positions. Many scholars consider the remnant motif to be a basic element in the theology of Isaiah;[186] others maintain that Isaiah of Jerusalem does not

---

[186]Meinhold, op. cit., p. 159: "It is in Isaiah in which we find for the first time the idea of the 'holy remnant'." C. H. Cornill, Der israelitische Profetismus (20th ed.; Strassburg, 1920), p. 59: "At the head of the theology of Isaiah is the [remnant] idea." O. Procksch, Jesaja I (KAT, IX; Leipzig, 1930), p. 84: "a theological idea of utmost importance." Herntrich, TWNT, IV, 202; TDNT, IV, 200: "Even in Is., where it [the remnant idea] has a central place. . . ." Garofalo, op. cit., pp. 70ff.; Schilling, op. cit., p. 81; M. Burrows, An Outline of Biblical Theology (Philadelphia, 1946), p. 147: The remnant idea is "one of his [Isaiah's] most characteristic teachings." Rowley, op. cit., p. 73; Dreyfus, op. cit., p. 361; Hoshizaki, op. cit., p. 89: "The remnant concept . . . [is] one of Isaiah's most characteristic thoughts. . . ." H. S. Gehman, "The Ruler of the Universe. The Theology of First Isaiah," Interpretation, XI (1957), 277: The remnant motif is Isaiah's "favorite theme." Warne, op. cit., p. 101: The remnant concept is "theologically significant." T. W. Manson, The Teachings of Jesus (2nd ed.; Cambridge, 1959), p. 176: "This doctrine of the Remnant is one of the dominant thoughts of Isaiah." E. Jenni, "Remnant," IDB, IV, 32: The "idea of a remnant. . . plays a significant role in the case of

know a religious or theological usage of the remnant motif;[187] still others attribute a subordinate role to the remnant motif in the proclamation of Isaiah.[188] There are a host of other questions which have received divergent answers. Did Isaiah of Jerusalem at the beginning of his ministry refrain from using the remnant motif[189] or was it a part of

---

Isaiah. . . ." C. R. North, "Isaiah," IDB, II, 734: The remnant is a constituent part of Isaiah's theology. J. Jeremias, Abba (Göttingen, 1966), p. 121: "The prophet Isaiah is the first great theologian of the idea of the remnant." H. Gottlieb, "Amos und Jerusalem," VT, XVII (1967), 437: " . . . in Isaiah the remnant idea has been expressed most notably." E. H. Maly, Prophets of Salvation (New York, 1967), p. 92: The remnant is "an important theological concept. . . to which Isaiah made his contribution." A. Gelin, "The Latter Prophets," Introduction to the Old Testament, ed. by A. Robert and A. Feuillet, transl. by P. W. Skehan et al. (New York, 1968), pp. 290ff.; Martin Rehm, Der königliche Messias im Licht der Immanuel-Weissagung des Buches Jesaja (Eichstätter Studien, 1; Kevelaer, 1968), p. 143; James M. Ward, Amos & Isaiah (Nashville, 1969), p. 270: "The prophecy of the remnant is. . . an essential ingredient of Isaiah's message from the outset."

[187]Heaton, op. cit., pp. 37f.; S. H. Blank, "Traces of Prophetic Agony in Isaiah," HUCA, 27 (1956), 85-90; Fohrer, op. cit., p. 373 n. 35: Isaiah has neither a proclamation of salvation nor a theological remnant motif; idem, "Die Struktur der alttestamentlichen Eschatologie," ThLZ, 85 (1960), 413 n. 69: "The investigation of all usages shows clearly that the theological or eschatological remnant idea does not derive from Isaiah." Idem, "Zehn Jahre Literatur zur alttestamentlichen Prophetie (1951-1960)," ThR, 28 (1962), 64; Stegemann, op. cit., p. 186: Isaiah is to be designated "as precursor of the doctrine of the remnant."

[188]Hamp, op. cit., VIII, col. 1253: ". . . in Isaiah the remnant idea [is] a solid even though no central part of his proclamation . . ." Herrmann, op. cit., p. 130: "The remnant appears at the fringes of the message of Isaiah." Von Rad, OTT, II, 165; idem, Die Botschaft der Propheten, p. 132: "Thus one cannot claim that Isaiah made the remnant a significant key word of his proclamation of salvation." R. Kilian, Die Verheissung Immanuels, Jes. 7, 14 (SBS, 35; Stuttgart, 1968), p. 49: ". . . the much belabored remnant idea does not at all play a decisive role in the proclamation of Isaiah."

[189]So Meinhold, op. cit., pp. 106-8; Müller, op. cit., p. 54; Herrmann, op. cit., p. 128.

his message right from the outset of his prophetic activity?[190] Did he use it at first as a sign of judgment and only later as a sign of hope[191] or did it always contain the dual aspect of doom and salvation?[192] Is it a part of Isaiah's future hope and eschatology[193] or is it singularly a part of his call for repentance?[194] Does Isaiah of Jerusalem speak of a "holy" remnant[195] or is this a development of the later Isaianic tradition?[196] Has Isaiah adopted the remnant motif from tradition[197] or is he the first to use it?[198] These and other contrasting positions in

---

[190] So for instance Dittmann, op. cit., pp. 610-1; Herntrich, TWNT, IV, 208; TDNT, IV, 203; Schilling, op. cit., p. 81; Dreyfus, op. cit., p. 362; Hoshizaki, op. cit., p. 40; Preuss; op. cit., p. 182; Ward, op. cit., p. 270; Lindblom, op. cit., 367; Eissfeldt, OTI, p. 310; I. Engnell, The Call of Isaiah (Uppsala, 1949), p. 53.

[191] So for instance G. E. Wright, Isaiah (Layman's Bible Commentary; London, 1965), pp. 36-7.

[192] So for example Herntrich, TWNT, IV, 202; TDNT, IV, 200; Schilling, op. cit., p. 81; Dreyfus, op. cit., p. 364; Preuss, op. cit., p. 181.

[193] So for instance Sellin, op. cit., pp. 124ff.; Dittmann, op. cit., pp. 612, 617; Mowinckel, He That Cometh, p. 132; Edmond Jacob, Theology of the Old Testament (London, 1958), p. 323; E. Jenni, "Eschatology," IDB, II, 129; Lindblom, op. cit., p. 367; Preuss, op. cit., p. 188; Rehm, op. cit., 143; R. B. Y. Scott, The Relevance of the Prophets (2nd ed.; New York, 1968), p. 133.

[194] Georg Fohrer, Das Buch Jesaja (Zürcher Bibelkommentar; 2nd ed.; Zürich, 1966), I, 45.

[195] So Meinhold, op. cit., p. 159; Dittmann, op. cit., p. 614; Schilling, op. cit., pp. 59, 62-3; Lindblom, op. cit., p. 367; Eissfeldt, OTI, p. 310; von Rad, OTT, II, 165; Preuss, op. cit., pp. 182-3; etc.

[196] Fohrer, Das Buch Jesaja, I, 72, 103 n. 43; Stegemann, op. cit., 169.

[197] This is the position of most scholars.

[198] So for instance Meinhold, op. cit., pp. 53, 88, 159; Mowinckel, Psalmenstudien II, pp. 265ff.; idem, He That Cometh, p. 132; Lindblom, op. cit., pp. 188, 367.

recent research with regard to the origin and early history of the Hebrew remnant motif gave the impetus to investigate the remnant motif of ancient Israel from its earliest appearance to Isaiah ben Amoz.

B. Task and Object

The present investigation attempts to provide answers in four interrelated areas. The first part of the present chapter aimed to present the problems of the origin, development, and meaning of the Hebrew remnant motif in modern Biblical scholarship. It is to provide the basis and set the stage from which our research can proceed. The second chapter attempts to investigate the remnant motif in ancient Near Eastern and Egyptian literary texts in order to examine the opposing theories of the origin of the remnant motif as propounded by Gressmann, Mowinckel, and Müller. This investigation aims to be rather comprehensive in that it will not be limited only to annalistic records of few nations but will include a study of such genres as myth, legend, epic, prophecy, prayer, hymn, letter, and annal in Sumerian, Akkadian, Hittite, Ugaritic, and Egyptian texts. It will hopefully provide information upon which more definite conclusions can be based concerning the origin and meaning of the remnant motif in extra-Biblical literature. It will also provide body of materials to which the Hebrew remnant motif can be properly compared, so that possible borrowings, influences, and similarities as well as differences will become apparent.

Another part of the study of the remnant idea should be devoted to an investigation of the remnant terminology in the Hebrew Bible, i.e., one should examine the verbal and nominal forms of such Hebrew roots through which the remnant idea has come to expression. Special attention ought to be given to the semantic values of the respective forms and terms under due consideration of the principles of linguistic semantics. Each investigation of the forms of a particular Hebrew root is to contain a concise description of usages of forms of cognate roots in other Semitic languages. This part of our investigation was undertaken by the present writer but had to be omitted from the publication of this study in the present form due to limitations of space.

The third chapter provides an exegetical study of the remnant motif from its first appearance in the Hebrew Bible up to the prophet Isaiah of Jerusalem. This is a significant part due to traditio-historical reasons. It will concentrate on the delineation of the appearance of the remnant motif in the various early materials of Genesis, in the Elijah cycle, and in the book of Amos. This investigation will give special attention to the appearance and history of the remnant idea in the variegated life situations and historical circumstances and will trace the lines of connection between the various materials in which it appears. It will provide tangible information from which conclusions can be drawn concerning the origin, history, and meaning of the remnant concept prior to the great prophet Isaiah.

In the fourth chapter the present writer will then be able to turn his attention to a main concern of his investigation, namely to trace the usage and development of the remnant motif in the various phases of the prophetic activity of Isaiah of Jerusalem and thereby to ascertain to what extent the remnant motif played a role in Isaiah's proclamation and theology. We have noted above the keen disagreements among scholars on virtually all aspects of the remnant motif in the book of Isaiah. Our investigation of the remnant idea of Isaiah of Jerusalem will therefore have to be conducted with the use of all available tools of research. It will not suffice to accept uncritically any particular passage as Isaianic nor will it serve the cause of scholarly research to reject outright the critical work of past generations. Since there is hardly a remnant passage in Isa. 1-39 which has not at one time or another been considered as inauthentic, it is essential to turn to the question of authenticity. A responsible decision on the genuineness of the individual remnant passages will have to be made in most cases. The great variety of positions does not permit the careful scholar to accept some passages and reject others on a priori grounds or on a supposed consensus of scholarly opinion. Furthermore, the remnant motif of Isaiah the prophet cannot be adequately understood nor fully appreciated without its prior history in Hebrew thought. Thus the study of the previous chapters provides the necessary background for the examination of the remnant motif in the eighth century prophet Isaiah of Jerusalem.

Having stated our task and object, it remains to clarify some matters of definition. The designation "remnant" is used by the present writer in an unrestricted and not in a narrow sense. This means that the designation "remnant" is employed for both the negative and positive aspects of the remnant idea as well as for its non-eschatological or eschatological use. The term "remnant" can express the negative idea that there was total annihilation of human life without any survivors. It is used in connection with the negligible nature of a few survivors who are a meaningless remnant for the future of a family, clan, tribe, people, or nation. Conversely, it is employed when a remnant remains, either large or small, that carries within itself the potentialities of renewal, life, and continual existence. It is used for historical and eschatological entities. This unrestricted use of the term "remnant" has the quality of including in one designation the large variety of aspects and emphases which are expressed by the Hebrew and Semitic notion of the remnant. This usage of the term "remnant" has actually grown out of the present study and avoids the one-sided and misleading emphases that are inherent in designations such as "doctrine of the Remnant," "concept of holy remnant," "idea of pious remnant," etc.

A proper definition of "eschatology" is still anything but settled in current Biblical research. Gressmann[199] was responsible for the rediscovery of the eschatological element in the Old Testament and for its establishment as a subject of research. He defined "eschatology" as a consistent body of ideas which has to do with the end of the world and with its renewal.[200] Vod Rad has criticized such a narrow definition of "eschatology" and proposed to apply the term "eschatology" to the pro-

---

[199] Gressmann, Ursprung der israelitisch-jüdischen Eschatologie, p. 1.

[200] Ibid.; G. Hölscher, Die Ursprünge der jüdischen Eschatologie (Giessen, 1925), p. 5, wished to limit the term "eschatology" to the idea of an end of the world. Mowinckel, He That Cometh, p. 131, also used this term in the narrow sense as referring to the "end of the world or last things." G. Fohrer, "Die Struktur der alttestamentlichen Eschatologie," ThLZ, 85 (1960), 401ff., also wants to restrict eschatology to events which lie beyond the scope of world history. Virtually the same definition is advanced by Herrmann, op. cit., pp. 303-4.

phetic proclamation, if (1) there is the possibility "to say that the event which they foretell is a final one even if we . . . would describe it as still 'within history',"[201] and, in addition, if (2) "there is also the contribution made by what has been called . . . the two 'aeons,' including the break which is preceded by Jahweh's great act of demolition, and followed by the new state of things which he brings about."[202] Von Rad finds such an eschatology especially in the pre-exilic prophets. The broader definition of "eschatology" has found wide acceptance. E. Rohland,[203] H. D. Preuss,[204] H. P. Müller,[205] and W. Harrelson[206] among constantly increasing numbers of scholars prefer

---

[201]Von Rad, OTT, II, 115.

[202]Ibid.

[203]Edzard Rohland, Die Bedeutung der Erwählungstraditionen Israels für die Eschatologie der alttestamentlichen Propheten (Inaugural-Dissertation; Heidelberg, 1956), pp. 1-18, 273ff.

[204]Preuss, op. cit., pp. 205-14. Preuss argues that the religion of Yahweh is itself the root of eschatology. "Since Yahweh and history belong together, both Yahweh faith and history and thus history and eschatology are related to each other" (p. 209). "The eschatology of the Old Testament is 'function of the experience of history'" (p. 210).

[205]Hans-Peter Müller, Ursprünge und Strukturen alttestamentlicher Eschatologie (BZAW, 109; Berlin, 1969), pp. 1-9, brings the discussion of the definition of "eschatology" begun by Rohland up to date and adds valuable critiques of the definition of the Wellhausen School.

[206]Walter Harrelson, From Fertility Cult to Worship (Garden City, N. Y., 1969), p. 138: "It is wrong, in my judgment, to make of biblical eschatology a hope in a future time that lies beyond this historical time, or to make it only a present meaning-filled moment in the here and now. The Bible speaks of an End which moves into the present, of a present that stretches forth toward the consummation. It is neither this-worldly nor other-worldly; it is the consummation, the summing up, the crowning of the entire historical process." Harrelson, then, points

such a wider definition of "eschatology." The broader definition of "eschatology" does justice to the message of the prophets which must be termed "eschatological" wherever it regards the old historical bases of salvation as null and void and shifts the basis of salvation to a future action of God within the historical process that stretches forth toward the future time. The prophets expected the new saving action of Yahweh to take virtually the form of the old one, and, therefore, in expounding the new, the prophets had recourse to Yahweh's saving action of the past. The term "eschatology" is used in the present study in that wider sense.

---

to the predominance of four eschatological motifs in Israel's worship: (1) the coming king, (2) the holy city Zion, (3) the new exodus, and (4) the new heaven and new earth.

INTERNATIONAL SCHOOL
OF THEOLOGY LIBRARY

PART TWO

THE REMNANT MOTIF IN ANCIENT NEAR EASTERN LITERATURE

In this chapter we attempt to examine the remnant motif in ancient Near Eastern literary texts. Although the present writer will build upon previous studies, there will be no one-sided limitation to merely annalistic records. It is hoped that a comprehensive investigation of mythological, epical, religious, didactic, and historical texts of the ancient Near East and Egypt will provide new clues with regard to the origin and meaning of the remnant motif in extra-Biblical literature. Inasmuch as the remnant motif can be expected whenever and wherever there is any reference to the destruction or threat of destruction of human life it will be our task to examine such reports without regard to whether or not the remnant motif is referred to implicitly by circumstances or explicitly be verbal expressions. We have chosen to follow the methodology that avoids "punctual comparison"[1] by treating such phenomenon in its contextual totality before any comparison with a similar phenomenon is undertaken.

A. The Remnant Motif in Sumerian Texts

Since the Sumerians established the first great civilization in

[1]Claus Westermann, "Sinn und Grenze religionsgeschichtlicher Parallelen," ThLZ, XC (1965), cols. 489-96.

INTERNATIONAL SCHOOL OF THEOLOGY LIBRARY

Mesopotamia and left their imprint in varying degrees on all things Mesopotamian,[2] it seems logical to begin with them. The remnant motif appears in the fragmentary Sumerian flood story,[3] which dates in its present form to ca. 1600 B.C.[4] M. Civil concludes, however, that the theme of the flood which destroys mankind with the exception of a handful of the human race "became popular during the Isin dynasty,"[5] which is dated from 2017-1794 B.C.[6] Some designate the Sumerian flood story as a

---

[2]Samuel Noah Kramer, History Begins at Sumer (Garden City, N. Y. 1959), pp. xviiiff.; W. G. Lambert, Babylonian Wisdom Literature (Oxford, 1960), p. 2; A. Leo Oppenheim, Ancient Mesopotamia. Portrait of a Dead Civilization (2nd ed.; Chicago, 1968), pp. 4f.

[3]It was published by Arno Poebel, Historical and Grammatical Texts (PBS, V; Philadelphia, 1914), No. 1; A. Poebel also published a transliteration and translation with detailed commentary in Historical Texts (PBS, IV, Pt 1; Philadelphia, 1914), pp. 9-70. Other translations are by L. W. King, Legends of Babylon and Egypt in Relation to Hebrew Tradition (London, 1918), pp. 41ff.; A. T. Clay, A Hebrew Deluge Story in Cuneiform and Other Epic Fragments in the Pierpont Morgan Library (Yale Oriental Series, V/3; New Haven, Conn.; 1922), pp. 69ff.; Th. Jacobsen, The Sumerian King List (Assyriological Studies, 11; Chicago, 1939), pp. 58-59; Alexander Heidel, The Gilgamesh Epic and Old Testament Parallels (2nd ed.; Chicago, 1949), pp. 102-05; Samuel Noah Kramer, From the Tablets of Sumer (Indian Hills, Colo., 1956), pp. 176-81; idem ANET[3], pp. 42-44. The most serious attempt to bring Poebel's work up to date can be found in M. Civil's, "The Sumerian Flood Story," in W. G. Lambert and A. R. Millard, Atra-ḫasīs. The Babylonian Story of the Flood (Oxford, 1969), pp. 138-45, 167-72, who presents a new transliteration and translation with philological notes of the only known tablet of the Sumerian flood story.

[4]Lambert and Millard, op. cit., p. 14.

[5]Ibid., p. 139.

[6]Since there are not yet any absolute dates for the chronologies of the ancient Near East, we quote throughout this chapter the dates of J. A. Brinkman, "Mesopotamian Chronology of the Historical Period," in Oppenheim, Ancient Mesopotamia, pp. 335-52.

"myth,"[7] others prefer "legend"[8] or "epic."[9] In view of the fact that mortals play significant role only in one of the nineteen extant Sumerian myths,[10] and that the content of the Sumerian flood narrative is roughly the same as the Old Babylonian Atraḫasis Epic, it would seem best simply to refer to is as the Sumerian flood account[11] until new evidence makes an indisputable classification possible.

Only the lower third of the single tablet which contains the Sumerian flood story is presently preserved. This makes it impossible

---

[7]S. N. Kramer consistently speaks of the Sumerian flood account as a "Sumerian myth," ANET³, p. 42; idem, From the Tablets of Sumer, p. 176; idem, Sumerian Mythology (rev. ed.; New York, 1961), p. 97; idem, The Sumerians (Chicago, 1963), p. 144; idem, "Cuneiform Studies and the History of Literature: The Sumerian Sacred Marriage Texts," Proceedings of the American Philosophical Society, 107 (1963), 486; idem, History Begins at Sumer, p. 150; cf. S. H. Hooke, Middle Eastern Mythologies (Baltimore, 1963), p. 30. Because there is a considerable amount of ambiguity in the use and meaning of the term "myth," this term will be used in this study as a designation for narratives which are concerned largely with the world of the gods or in which gods are at least to a considerable extent involved. Cf. H. Bonnet, "Mythus," Reallexikon der ägyptischen Religionsgeschichte (Berlin, 1952), pp. 496-97; S. N. Kramer, "Introduction," Mythologies of the Ancient World (Garden City, N. Y., 1961), p. 7; Hooke, op. cit., pp. 11-16; G. Fohrer, Introduction to the Old Testament, pp. 86-87.

[8]E. Sollberger, The Babylonian Legend of the Flood (London, 1962), p. 23.

[9]C. Leonard Woolley, The Sumerians (New York, 1965), p. 31; W. E. Staples, "Epic Motifs in Amos," JNES, XXV (1966), 107; Lambert and Millard, op. cit., p. 14.

[10]Kramer, The Sumerians, pp. 160-63.

[11]M. Civil, op. cit., pp. 138-9, refrains from using any designation other than "Sumerian flood story."

to know what the initial lacuna of thirty-seven lines contained. Presumably a deity is addressing other deities stating that he will save mankind from destruction,[12] because the first two lines read:

38 'I want to [. . .] the destruction of the human race,
39 For Nintu, I want to stop the annih[ilation of] my creatures.'[13]

The cause of this destruction of mankind is of an unknown nature; it is most likely not caused by a flood. The remainder of the first column says that man has been created in order to serve the gods.[14] The second column deals with the early history of man, the third and fourth cover the decision of the gods to bring a flood and Enki's divulging this secret to his client Ziusudra, the last antediluvian king of Suruppak.[15] Ziusudra is the counterpart of Atraḫasis of the Atraḫasis Epic, Utnapishtim of the Gilgamesh Epic, and Noah of the Biblical flood account. He appears to station himself beside a wall, where Enki informs him of the fateful decision of the divine assembly to send a flood. The purpose and scope of the flood are clearly stated:

157 The destruction of the descent of mankind [. . .].[16]

This may well preserve the earliest tradition of the motif of the des-

---

[12]Kramer, ANET[3], p. 42.

[13]Civil, *op. cit.*, p. 141.

[14]This motif appears also in the story of "Enki and Ninmaḫ," see L. Matouš, "Zur neueren epischen Literatur im alten Mesopotamien," *ArOr*, 35 (1967), 4; and in the didactic poem of "The Creation of the Pickax," see Kramer, *Sumerian Mythology*, p. 53.

[15]J. J. Finkelstein, "The Antediluvian Kings: A University of California Tablet," *JCS*, XVII (1963), 41ff.; Matouš, *op. cit.*, p. 4.

[16]Civil, *op. cit.*, p. 143; Kramer translates: "To destroy the seed of mankind . . ." ANET[3], p. 44; Heidel's translation is the same as Kramer's (*op. cit.*, p. 103).

truction of mankind. The implication seems rather clear: mankind's complete annihilation has been decreed by the gods; no human survivor is expected to be left over. After a gap the fifth column tells that the flood swept over the land:

203-204 After the storm had swept the country for seven days and seven nights
205 And the destructive wind had rocked the huge boat in the high water,
206 The Sun came out, illuminating the earth and the sky.
207 Ziusudra made an opening in the huge boat,
208 And the Sun with its rays entered the huge boat.
209 The king Ziusudra
210 Prostrated himself before the Sun-god,
211 The king slaughtered a large number of bulls and sheep.

After another break of forty lines the sixth column of the tablet describes how Ziusudra prostrates himself before An and Enlil

256 (Who) gave him life, like a god,
257 Elevated him to eternal life, like a god.
258 At that time, the king Ziusudra
259 Who protected the seed of mankind at the time (?) of destruction,
260 They settled in an overseas country, in the orient, in Dilmun.[17]

(end broken)

Lines 256 and 257 may possibly be understood to refer to physical life in general and to future life in particular, but they more likely refer to eternal life because of the phrase "like a god." It is fairly clear, however, that there is in this oldest preserved flood story a preoccupation with life.[18] The eternal life of the survivor Ziusudra does not

---

[17] Civil, *op. cit.*, pp. 143-45.

[18] The name Ziusudra=Zi-u-sudra, which is interpreted to mean "Life of long days" by Sollberger, *op. cit.*, p. 19, or "he saw life" by N. K. Sandars, *The Epic of Gilgamesh* (2nd id.; Baltimore, 1964), p. 18, puts additional emphasis on the motif of preservation of life.

seem to become a part of the descendants of the human race which king Ziusudra preserved. Line 259 contains textual problems. A. Poebel and A. Heidel translate, "The name of the . . . . . .'Preserver of the Seed of Mankind'."[19] S. N. Kramer renders it, "The preserver of the name of vegetation (and) of the seed of mankind."[20] It seems to be fairly clear that through the surviving remnant, Ziusudra, the future existence of the "seed of mankind" has been preserved when a flood threatened the human race with complete extinction. The motif of the preservation of the "seed of mankind" is the opposite result of the threatening intention of the gods who had decreed that this very "seed of mankind" must be destroyed by a flood.[21]

The extant Sumerian tablet does not provide information of a basic element in the common pattern of deluge stories,[22] namely the reason that caused the flood. One of the two central motifs is that the gods decide

---

[19]Poebel, *Historical Texts*, p. 20; Heidel, *op. cit.*, p. 105. The difference lies with the ambiguous nature of the text which Poebel, *op. cit.*, p. 61, transliterates "numun-nam-lù-qal-ùru' (-(š̆)â)," while Civil, *op. cit.*, p. 144, gives "numun-nam-lú-u$_x$ uri$_3$-ak."

[20]*ANET*^{3}, p. 44.

[21]Both lines 157 and 259 the Sumerian phrase is the same: numun-nam-lú-u$_x$.

[22]Sollberger, *op. cit.*, p. 11, has studied the flood stories of the ancient Near East, of Asia, Australia, the Americas, and Europe, concluding that as much as they may differ in detail, they follow a common pattern, the three basic elements of which are (1) mankind gravely offending the gods; (2) its punishment in the form of a universal flood meant to wipe out mankind; and (3) one just man and his family being spared as a remnant. Staples, *op. cit.*, pp. 106-12, comes basically to the same conclusions in his analysis of what he calls the "epic of destruction," i.e., the ancient Near Eastern flood accounts.

to destroy mankind,[23] and the other is that in the remaining survivor Ziusudra the future existence of mankind is preserved. S. N. Kramer has suggested that Ziusudra was saved because "he had humbly and piously performed the daily rites for the gods."[24] If this suggestion is correct we have here an example in which religious devotion is closely associated with the reason for leaving a remnant. Correspondingly, one could suppose that rebellion against gods brought about the flood. But this guess has no foundation in the presently available Sumerian material, while it is supported by the new finds of the Atraḫasis Epic. In short, through the surviving remnant, Ziusudra, the entire future hope for the continuity of the existence and life of mankind comes to expression and finds its realization in the preservation of the "seed of mankind."

The theme of the flood which destroys mankind but leaves a remnant appears again in a historical text, i.e., the Sumerian King List[25] which contains an account of the early history of mankind. The original, short form of the Sumerian King List may or may not have contained an opening reference to the flood, because unfortunately no single copy of the short form has the opening lines preserved. A pointer in favor of the conclu-

---

[23]See Hooke, _op. cit._, p. 30.

[24]Kramer, _The Sumerians_, p. 135. This conclusion is well supported by lines 147-48, 254-55.

[25]The standard edition is that of Th. Jacobsen, _The Sumerian King List_ (Assyriological Studies, 11; Chicago, 1939). New material and appropriate discussions have been offered by A. Leo Oppenheim, _ANET3_, pp. 265-66; M. Civil, "Texts and Fragments (36)," _JCS_, XV (1961), 79-80; Finkelstein, _op. cit._, pp. 39-51; W. W. Hallo, "Beginning and End of the Sumerian King List in the Nippur Recension," _JCS_, XVII (1963), 52-57; Lambert and Millard, _op. cit._, pp. 14-19, 25-27, 139.

sion that the opening words were "After the flood had swept over the land and kingship had come down from heaven . . ." is contained in a rival king list from Lagaš,[26] which begins with the words: "After the flood had swept [egir a-ma-ru ba-ùr-ra-ta]. . . ."[27] The oldest datable occurrences of this standard phrase, which appears in line 40 of the longer Sumerian King List,[28] come from ca. 2100 B.C. for the longer recension,[29] from a hymn[30] of Išme-Dagan, king of Isin (1923-1935 B.C.), and from a variant in a text which mentions Ur-Ninurta of Isin (1923-1896 B.C.).[31] Various copies of the longer Sumerian King List mention from eight to ten antediluvian kings in several cities ruling for vast periods of time. One tablet lists seven or eight kings who reign up to 186,000 years,[32] while the best preserved copy gives eight kings a rule of 241,200 years.[33] Another tablet mentions ten kings who rule a total of 456,000 years in antediluvian times before the flood swept over the land.[34] It seems fairly certain, despite all differences, that the theme of the flood which

---

[26] W. G. Lambert, "Enmeduranki and Related Matters," JCS, XXI (1967), i 8.

[27] Lambert and Millard, op. cit., p. 16.

[28] ANET[3], p. 265.

[29] Jacobsen, followed by Lambert and Millard, op. cit., p. 25.

[30] Transliteration is given in Lambert and Millard, op. cit., p. 26.

[31] Translation in Lambert and Millard, op. cit., p. 16.

[32] Finkelstein, op. cit., pp. 39ff.

[33] ANET[3], p. 265; Kramer, The Sumerians, p. 328.

[34] Lambert and Millard, op. cit., p. 17.

wiped out mankind is an integral part of the historical tradition of the Sumerian King Lists and that in the longer Sumerian King List a succession of eight to ten long-lived worthies is brought to an end by a divinely sent flood, which destroys the whole human race apart from one remaining survivor to whom kingship is again entrusted. Through this surviving remnant also "seed [was] preserved from before the flood"[35] as is stated in a related bilingual text from the Second Isin Dynasty. Thus the Sumerian King List preserves the motif of the destruction of mankind and the remnant motif. The latter contains two emphases: firstly, in the remaining survivor man's continuity of existence was preserved, which had been threatened with extinction by a flood; and secondly, civilized life in the form of kingship[36] was preserved. Despite the destruction of mankind and civilized life by the flood, the seeds of human existence and thus of civilization were preserved in the remaining survivor with all the future potentialities.[36a]

The remnant motif appears in the longest Sumerian lamentation, i.e., the "Lamentation over the Destruction of Ur."[37] This lamentation

---

[35]Lambert, JCS, XXI (1967), i 8.

[36]C. J. Gadd, "The Cities of Babylonia," Cambridge Ancient History (rev. ed., Cambridge, 1964), p. 19, points out that in Sumerian ideas kingship was requisite to the possibility of the continuity of civilized life.

[36a]See Appendix II, pp. 466-467.

[37]This lamentation has been published by Samuel N. Kramer, The Lamentation over the Destruction of Ur (Assyriological Studies, 12; Chicago, 1940) with transliteration, translation and notes. The same author presents a more up to date translation in ANET[3], pp. 455-63. Other translations are by M. Witzel, "Die Klage über Ur," Orientalia, N.S. XIV (1945), 185-234, XV (1946), 46-63, and Adam Falkenstein and Wolfram von Soden, Sumerische und addakische Hymnen und Gebete (Zürich, 1953), pp. 192-213.

belongs to the type that bewails the destruction of Sumerian cities or city-states.[38] Th. Jacobsen dates this lamentation to about seventy or eighty years after the destruction of Ur III at ca. 1945 B.C., plus or minus fifty years,[39] while D. O. Edzard says: "Die Entstehung der Ur-Klage ist kaum später als eine Generation nach dem Ereignis anzusetzen."[40] The essential historicity of this lamentation is commonly recognized.[41]

In the fifth "song" a detailed description is presented of a "land-annihilating storm,"[42] an "afflicting storm,"[43] or "destructive storm."[44] S. N. Kramer suggests that the term "storm" is used figuratively referring to the destruction of Ur by the Subarians and Elamites,[45] who are mentioned in line 244 as "the destroyers." This inter-

---

[38]S. N. Kramer, "Sumerian Literature: A General Survey," The Bible and the Ancient Near East, ed. by G. E. Wright (Garden City, N. Y., 1965), p. 388; idem, The Sumerians, p. 208; idem, Sumerian Mythology, p. 14.

[39]Th. Jacobsen, "Review of Lamentation over the Destruction of Ur by S. N. Kramer," AJSL, LXIII (1941), 219-21; cf. Kramer, The Sumerians, p. 32.

[40]D. O. Edzard, Die 'zweite Zwischenzeit' Babylonians (Wiesbaden, 1957), p. 57.

[41]See especially Edzard's, op. cit., pp. 50-57, convincing argumentations.

[42]ANET[3], p. 458 l. 184.

[43]Ibid., p. 459 l. 197.

[44]Ibid., l. 198.

[45]ANET[3], p. 455, following Jacobsen op. cit., p. 220 n. 4. This suggestion is based upon the evidence from a line of an inscription of Šu-ilišu, king of Isin, (1984-1975 B.C.), which reads: ". . . when he had returned Nanna from Anšan to Ur." This line refers to the return of a statue of Nanna which was taken away by the Elamites; cf. Edzard, op. cit., p. 57; Falkenstein and von Soden, op. cit., p. 377.

pretation best explains the devastation that befell Ur as a result of defeat in battle:

> Its walls were breached; the people groan.
> In its lofty gates, where they were wont to promenade, dead bodies were lying about;
> In its boulevards, where the feasts were celebrated, scattered they lay.[46]
>
> Who kept standing near the weapons, by the weapons was killed; the people groan.
> Who escaped them, by the storm was prostrated; the people groan.[47]

The record describes the fate of the remaining population which had "escaped" the destruction of the battle:

> Ur-its weak and (its) strong perished through hunger;
> Mothers and fathers who did not leave their houses were overcome by fire.[48]

The fifth "song" closes by stating that "Ur has been destroyed, its people have been dispersed."[49] This statement gives an indication that despite the great loss of life through battle, famine, and fire, there were remaining survivors who had been dispersed. A clue to the nature of the dispersion comes from the lips of the embittered goddess Ningal, who wails in the sixth "song": "My daughters and sons verily . . . have been carried off--."[50]

In short, the calamity which befell the inhabitants of Ur was war with its destruction of human life by battle, famine, and fire. A remnant of the population, however, escaped destruction and was carried off into captivity. With the fall of the Dynasty of Ur III, the Sumerians

---

[46] ANET[3], p. 459 ll. 212-14. [47] Ibid., ll. 225-26.

[48] Ibid., ll. 227-28. [49] Ibid., p. 460 l. 250.

[50] Ibid., l. 283.

disappeared as an independent nation from history.[51]

An allusion to the remnant motif is contained in a Sumerian votive inscription,[52] which commemorates a smashing victory of Entemena, son of Eannatum of Lagaš over Ur-Lumma of Umma. The battle was fought at ca. 2400 B.C.[53] It is stated that Entemena defeated the Ummaite forces including the elite troops of Ur-Lammu, who himself "fled." It is not clear whether Ur-Lammu was the only survivor of his forces or whether the phrase "he (Entemena) slew (the Ummaite forces) up into Umma (itself)"[54] should be understood to indicate that also some of the troops were able to reach the city and save themselves from destruction. Although the latter is certainly a possibility, it is clear that Ur-Lammu was able to flee to save his life.

The Sumerian "Hymn to Enlil,"[55] which is important for its poetic summary of civilization's debt to his beneficence,[56] describes in the third person the achievement of Enlil "as the lord of the world, who has

---

[51]See the summary of Sumerian history by Hartmut Schmökel, Das Land Sumer (3rd ed.; Stuttgart, 1962), pp. 76-80; Woolley, op. cit., p. 170: "The poet of Nippur was right when in his lamentation . . . he spoke not only of Ur alone but of Sumer, for the fate of the city involved that of the whole land and people. From the destruction . . . the Sumerians never recovered and their history as an independent nation stops at this point."

[52]Published by Kramer, The Sumerians, pp. 314f.

[53]Schmökel, op. cit., p. 63.

[54]Kramer, The Sumerians, p. 314.

[55]Published in Falkenstein and von Soden, op. cit., No. 12.

[56]Kramer, The Sumerians, p. 205.

conquered in battle the 'enemy land' for his father."[57] The complete victory of Enlil leaves no remnant:

> No enemy escapes from your right hand,
> no evil man flees from your left hand.
> [. . . .] you,
> the land of the enemy, to which the saying is directed, no more shall arise
> in the evil land, which you have cursed, no one is left [over].[58]

Inasmuch as this hymn was composed to glorify the god Enlil and his achievements, it remains open to doubt whether this description is based upon an actual historical event. One would not be far wrong to say, however, that Enlil is credited with the power of total victory over enemies and their land. This may well be a poetic hyperbole extolling Enlil's superior strength.

With this example the evidence for the remnant motif in Sumerian literary texts has been exhausted. It has become apparent that the remnant motif appears in a variety of Sumerian literary productions, namely in an epic, a lamentation, a hymn[59] and in historical texts. The calam-

---

[57]Falkenstein and von Soden, op. cit., p. 365.

[58]Ibid., p. 78.

[59]There is hardly any question that hymns and lamentations were composed and redacted for use in the temple cult, although in Nippur they were found not in temples but in the scribal quarters which may indicate that they must have been composed in the edubba by members of its staff rather than by priests, see Kramer, The Sumerians, p. 170; Th. Jacobsen, "Formative Tendencies in Sumerian Religion," The Bible and the Ancient Near East, ed. by G. E. Wright (Garden City, N. Y., 1965), p. 367. With regard to the Sumerian flood story, which Kramer counts among the Sumerian myths, the situation is different: ". . . it is important to note first of all that Sumerian myths have little if any connection with rite and ritual in spite of the fact that the latter played so important a role in Sumerian religious practice. Practically all the extant Sumerian myths are literary and etiological in character; they are neither 'spoken rite,' as myths have often been erroneously categorized, nor

itous catastrophes which befall mankind either leaving or not leaving a remnant are flood and war with battle, famine and fire. The Sumerian flood account is of great important for an understanding of the origin and nature of the remnant motif in the ancient Near East, because as the earliest flood story it is most likely a prototype of later flood stories which are directly or indirectly related to it and contain likewise the remnant motif. It is the only Sumerian account which contains the remnant motif and states explicitly that in the remaining survivor the existence of the "seed of mankind" was preserved for the future. No matter how total the destruction of mankind was and how small the remnant was that escaped from it, the latter contained the full potentialities of man's future existence linking in an unbroken chain past life with future life. There may here be a clue to indicate that the remnant motif originated out of man's concern to preserve life when human existence and life were threatened with extinction. It is well known that certain fears of ancient man which were brought about by threats to the very roots of existence produced various responses.[60] It appears that calamitous threats, which endangered the very roots of man's life and existence, raised the question whether or not there will be survivors who live through various catastrophes which threaten to annihilate human life as

---

verbalized appendages to ritual acts." Kramer, <u>The Sumerians</u>, p. 144.

[60]There are many different types of threats which man fears. That certain fears of ancient man were at the very roots of existence and gave various responses is generally recognized. Th. Jacobsen, "Ancient Mesopotamian Religion: The Central Concerns," <u>Proceedings of the American Philosophical Society</u>, 107 (1963), 473-84, has pointed out that fears such as of starvation and war took their place at the center of existence and produced certain religious responses.

such or the life of various social groups. The response may have grown out of empirical knowledge, which indicated that in the remnant, life continued with all possibilities for renewal, securing the continuity of the existence of man. Thus it appears that already in these Sumerian materials the remnant motif is the vehicle of thought to express the idea that continuity of existence and security of life for the future are preserved in the remnant.

B. The Remnant Motif in Akkadian Texts

It has been pointed out by A. Haldar[61] that the remnant motif is present in the best-known piece of Akkadian "epic literature," i.e., the Epic of Creation[62] or "Enūma eliš" as the Akkadians called it after its incipit. It was written relatively late. But in its earliest form it probably goes back to the Old Babylonian period.[63] It appears to represent a transformation of earlier practices to a literary level for the Marduk cult of Babylon. The story offers Marduk as creator and proceeds to present a theological interpretation of this world. However, "it was

---

[61]Alfred Haldar, Studies in the Book of Nahum (Uppsala, 1947), p. 107.

[62]It was first published by W. L. King in CT, XIII (London, 1901). For publications of additional texts and materials, see Rykle Borger, Handbuch der Keilschriftliteratur. Repertorum der sumerischen und akkadischen Texte (Berlin, 1967), I, 225-26. To this bibliography must be added W. G. Lambert and S. B. Parker, ENUMA ELIŠ. The Babylonian Epic of Creation: The Cuneiform Text (Oxford, 1966). For a bibliography of various studies and translations, see ANET[3], p. 60 and A. Heidel, The Babylonian Genesis (2nd ed.; Chicago, 1963), pp. 2-3.

[63]The extant texts do not antedate the first millennium B.C., cf. ANET[3], p. 60; Heidel, op. cit., pp. 13-14.

not read to the believers as a testimonial of the deity's achievements but was read to the god himself. It is a hymn in praise of Marduk by which the priest extols his god."[64]

In Tablet I the god Apsu, the begetter of the great gods, speaks to Tiamat about the gods:

I: 37 'Their ways are very loathsome unto me.
38 By day I find no relief, nor repose by night.
39 I will destroy, I will wreck their ways,
40 That quiet may be restored. Let us have rest!'[65]

Ea, endowed with wisdom and cunning, intervened in behalf of the gods by slaying Apsu and locking up Apsu's vizier Mummu.[66] The gods finally address Tiamat, the spouse of Apsu, who refrained from intervening when her husband was slain:

I: 116 'Let Apsu, thy consort, be in thy mind.
117 And Mummu, who has been vanquished! Thou are left alone!'[67]

The outcome of this initial struggle among the gods is that Tiamat alone remains, while Apsu has been killed and Mummu made ineffective. In the

---

[64]Oppenheim, op. cit., p. 233; cf. F. Thureau-Dangin, Rituels accadiens (Paris, 1921), pp. 136, 279-84; S. A. Pallis, The Babylonian Akîtu Festival (Copenhagen, 1926), pp. 212, 298. It is well known that the Babylonian New Year festival took place under the Late Babylonian kings, i.e., from 625 to 539 B.C. Evidence from Late Assyrian sources, both literary and other, enable us to conclude that the akîtu festival was essentially the same from about 750 B.C. How much farther back it went is a question on which almost no evidence exists. W. G. Lambert, "Myth and Ritual as Conceived by the Babylonians," JSS, XIII (1968), 106-108, following W. von Soden and A. Falkenstein, points out that there is no single piece of evidence for the death and resurrection of Marduk nor for Marduk being involved in a sacred marriage in the course of the New Year festival.

[65]E. A. Speiser, in ANET^3, p. 61b.

[66]Ibid., p. 61b, ll. 69-70.

[67]Ibid., p. 62b.

meantime, Marduk, the most able and wisest of the gods, was born to Ea and Damkina and Tiamat becomes disturbed, doubtless because of the reflection on her husband's violent death.[68] Her restlessness mounted as some of the gods, under the leadership of Kingu,[69] in their wickedness prevailed upon her to avenge the slaughter of her spouse. Tiamat, on her part, gave birth to eleven kinds of monster serpents and dragons and made Kingu her husband. He was entrusted with the high command for the planned battle. When Tiamat was almost ready for the assault with her formidable demonic host, someone informed Ea of the imminent peril. He was unable to overcome Tiamat. Thus valiant Marduk was summoned to save the gods. He engaged Tiamat with Kingu and their host:

> I:105 After he had slain Tiamat, the leader,
> 106 Her band was scattered, her troup broken up;
> 107 And her gods, her helpers, who had marched at her side,
> 108 Trembling with terror, turned their backs about,
> 109 In order to save and preserve their lives.
> 110 Tightly encircled they could not escape.[70]

Finally also Kingu, who contrived the uprising, was slain,[71] while the other apostate gods became incorporated into the group friendly to Marduk.

Thus when Marduk overcame his enemies, he killed only the two instigators and leaders, Tiamat and Kingu, while the remainder of the rebellious gods "saved and preserved their lives" (Tablet IV:109) through a change of allegiance. Thus punishment is sent, but not unto complete

---

[68]Heidel, op. cit., p. 5.

[69]ANET[3], p. 66a Tablet IV:23-30.

[70]Ibid., p. 67a ll. 105-110.

[71]Ibid., p. 68b Tablet VI:30-35.

destruction; a remnant is left that turns back to the god Marduk. The unusual thing here is that the remnant motif appears in the mythological realm of the gods. The suggestion of A. Haldar that "this development of events applied to historical conditions: to the apostate gods corresponds an apostate nation, who turns to other gods . . ."[72] may be at least partially correct. In view of conditions as reflected in the historical texts of the Assyrians, one can say that to the apostate gods corresponds an apostate or rebellious nation or vassal whose remnant is again brought into subjection.

The remnant motif is a prominent element in the Atraḫasis Epic,[73] known to the Akkadians by "Inūma ilū awīlum."[74] This epic is preserved

---

[72]Haldar, op. cit., pp. 107-08.

[73]The first fragment of the Atraḫasis Epic was published in the year 1885 by F. Delitzsch, Assyrische Lesestücke (3rd ed.; Leipzig, 1885), p. 101. From that time begins an extraordinary story of recovery of the epic under discussion. The following scholars played a major role in the recovery of texts and in recognizing in part their proper place: G. Smith, P. Jensen, V. Scheil, A. T. Clay, H. Zimmern, and A. Boissier. But it was not until 1956 that the correct sequence of the available material was demonstrated by the Danish scholar J. Laessøe, "The Atraḫasis Epic: A Babylonian History of Mankind." BiOr, XIII (1956), 89-105. Thus we find that E. A. Speiser's translation of a part of the Atraḫasis Epic in ANET[3], pp. 99-100, is separated from the former under the heading, "Creation of Man by the Mother Goddess." The most recent up to date critical edition of the epic with the publication of new tablets not yet included in W. G. Lambert and A. R. Millard, Babylonian Literary Texts (CT, 46; London, 1965), Nos. 1-15, is a volume by the same authors, Atra-ḫasīs: The Babylonian Story of the Flood (Oxford, 1969).

[74]The main and most complete Old Babylonian Recension begins with these words whose translation is rather difficult. A. T. Clay, A Hebrew Deluge Story in Cuneiform (Yale Oriental Series, V/3; New Haven, Conn., 1922), p. 14, translates these opening words, "When God, man"; Laessøe, op. cit., 98, who reads enūma ilū awīlam renders this clause "When the gods . . . man." Oppenheim, Ancient Mesopotamia, p. 266, interprets this line with "When the gods [and?] man," while Lambert translates in Lambert

in two main recensions, the Babylonian Recension and the Assyrian Recension. The former is the more complete. It was an edition in three tablets most likely from Sippar copied out in the reign of Ammiṣaduka, great-great-grandson of the famous Hammurabi, by the junior scribe Ku-Aya, also transliterated with Ellat-Aya. Tablets I and II are dated to the 12th and 11th year of Ammiṣaduka's reign respectively, i.e., ca. 1635 B.C. and 1636 B.C.[75] Tablet III is considered to derive from the same year as Tablet I. The Assyrian Recension was preserved mainly in the library of Ashurbanipal; it seems not to have exceeded two tablets[76] and consists in the main of Late Assyrian copies from about 700-650 B.C.[77] There are a good number of fragments which belong to editions other than the two presently extant.[78] Although we have no exact knowledge of the origin of the Atraḫasis Epic, W. G. Lambert, who has published recently the newly recovered Tablet I and other important fragments of texts as

---

and Millard, Atra-ḫasīs, p. 43, "When the gods like men." He believes that awīlum has the locative -um with the meaning of the comparative -iš. The translation which was produced in the last Seminar of Prof. A. Falkenstein renders the opening line "Als die Götter noch Menschen waren," quoted by C. Westermann, Genesis (BKAT, I/2; Neukirchen-Vluyn, 1967), p. 97. See Appendix II, p. 467.

[75]Lambert and Millard, Atra-ḫasīs, pp. 31-33; Brinkman, op. cit., p. 337; M. E. L. Mallowan, "Noah's Flood Reconsidered," Iraq, XXVI (1964), 66, who also points out that this is the period when Sumerian literature was being collected and systematically translated into Akkadian by scribal schools.

[76]L. Matouš, "Zur neueren epischen Literatur im alten Mesopotamian," ArOr, 35 (1967), 5.

[77]Lambert and Millard, Atra-ḫasīs, p. 5.

[78]Some belong to Middle and Late Babylonian times and others to the Late Assyrian period, see ibid., pp. 5-6.

well as a critical edition of all available materials, suggests a date of ca. 1800 B.C.[79] It seems that it is based upon a Sumerian Vorlage[80] and represents a stage in the long tradition of the great flood between the former and Tablet XI of the Gilgamesh Epic.[81]

The central theme of the Atrahasis Epic "is the flood and what it

---

[79]W. G. Lambert, "A New Look at the Babylonian Background of Genesis," JTS, N. S. 16 (1965), 292; Lambert and Millard, Atra-ḫasīs, pp. 23-24: ". . . the text can hardly have been written down more than one, or at most two centuries earlier [than the sixteenth century B.C.]."

[80]Th. Jacobsen, The Sumerian King List (Assyriological Studies, 11; Chicago, 1939), pp. 59f.; Laessøe, op. cit., pp. 91, 96, 100; Matouš, op. cit., p. 3; Lambert and Millard, Atra-ḫasīs, p. 14: "It is possible that the Akkadian author knew the Sumerian text, but this cannot be proved, and the various elements of the story are sufficiently well known outside these two texts that one must say that the Akkadian author did not need to know the Sumerian texts to write as he did." This cautious appraisal of literary relationships by Lambert may be correct. It seems, however, that the conclusions reached by the previously mentioned scholars are sound in that they are based upon a small partly bilingual fragment from Nippur, published in CT 46, No. 5, which is generally taken to be a late edition of a missing portion between columns ii and iii of Tablet III.

[81]This is the generally accepted view first proposed by George Smith; Laessøe, op. cit., p. 96: "A comparison between the flood stories of the Gilgamesh Epic and the Atraḫasis Epic will show strong evidence to suggest that the narrative contained in the latter composition is a primary source on which an editor of Gilg. 11 depends." Matouš, op.cit., p. 3: "Zwischen der sumerischen Vorlage und der Übernahme der Sintfluterzählung in GE XI liegt eine lange Entwicklung, die wir-dank der aB Fassung des Atraḫasis-Epos und der nA Rezension aus Ninive-von einer Periode zur andern verfolgen können." It has been pointed out, however, by F. M. Th. de Liagre Böhl, "Gilgameš," Reallexikon der Assyriologie und vorderasiatischen Archäologie, ed. by Wolfram von Soden (Berlin, 1968), III, 367, that, despite the close relationship between the Atraḫasis Epic and its Sumerian original and between the former and the Gilgamesh Epic, these recensions "im Wortlaut aber freier und voneinander unabhängiger [sind] als bisher angenommen wurde." See Gerhard F. Hasel, Review of Atra-ḫasīs: The Babylonian Story of the Flood by W. G. Lambert and A. R. Millard in AUSS, VIII (1970), 182-8.

caused and the escape of the Noah figure, Atraḫasis."[82] A concise summary of the contents of the most complete recension may be helpful toward a better understanding of the remnant motif. Man was created after an uprising of the junior gods to relieve the latter of the hard labor they performed for the senior gods Anu, Enlil, and Enki (Tablet I:1-139). As the human race multiplied and their noise became such that Enlil was disturbed, he resolved to reduce their number by plague. King Atraḫasis petitioned his personal god Enki to prevent the plague and was informed on how to avert this means of destruction (Tablet I:352-416). Mankind multiplied again, Enlil now tried to reduce the human population by famine caused by a drought. This attempt failed again, because Enki gave instructions to Atraḫasis on how to avert this menace (Tablet II, i-ii). Enlil renewed the drought and mankind was "on the verge of death" (Tablet II:iv:14) when Enki intervened once more (Tablet II, iii-v). Thus Enlil decided that the whole human race must be wiped out by means of a flood and Enki was bound by an oath, against his wishes, to cooperate (Tablet II:vi-viii). Tablet II closes with the following fateful words:

> II:viii:34 The gods commanded total destruction,
> 35 Enlil did an evil deed on the peoples.[83]

Tablet III contains the account of the flood and the preservation of a remnant of mankind. Despite his oath Enki instructs Atraḫasis:

---

[82]Oppenheim, Ancient Mesopotamia, p. 266; cf. G. Pettinato, "Die Bestrafung des Menschengeschlechts durch die Sintflut," Orientalia, N.S. 37 (1968), 175-76. See Appendix II, p. 467.

[83]Lambert and Millard, Atra-ḫasīs, p. 87 Tablet II:viii:34-35.

III:i:22 Destroy your house, build a boat,
23 Spurn property and save life.[84]

Atraḫasis relates this to the elders and receives aid for the construction of the boat. Animals and birds are put on board, then Atraḫasis goes aboard with his family.

III:iii:11 [. . . .] the flood [set out],
12 Its might came upon the peoples [like a battle array].
13 One person did [not] see another,
14 They were [not] recognizable in the destruction.[85]

Enki is beside himself, seeing that his "sons,"[86] his "offspring,"[87] are thrown down before him. The flood rages "for seven days and seven nights"[88] in order to bring "total destruction."[89] Then Enlil becomes aware of the boat, which contains the remnant of mankind, and questions:

III:vi:9 Where did life escape?
10 How did man survive in the destruction?[90]

Enki finally admits that he is responsible "for saving life."[91] The

---

[84]*Ibid.*, p. 89 Tablet III:i:22-24; line 24:na-pí-iš-ta bu-ul-li-iṭ.

[85]*Ibid.*, p. 95 Tablet III:iii:11-14.

[86]*Ibid.*, p. 95 Tablet III:iii:26:ma-ru-su.

[87]*Ibid.*, p. 95 Tablet III:iii:44.

[88]*Ibid.*, p. 97 Tablet III:iv:24.

[89]The term translated "total destruction" is *gamertu*. It is used in the Atraḫasis Epic only in connection with the total extermination of mankind by means of a flood decreed by Enlil, Tablet II:viii:34; III:iii:38; III:v:44.

[90]Lambert and Millard, *Atra-ḫasīs*, p. 101 Tablet III:vi:9-10:
9 a-ia-anu ú-ṣi na!-pi!-iš-tum
10 ki-i ib-lu-uṭ ⸢a-wi⸣-lum i-na ⸢ka⸣- [r] a-ši

[91]*Ibid.*, p. 101 Tablet III:vi:19:
19 [ú-uš-t]a-ṣi-ra na-pí-i[š-tam][(. .)]x x x[x x]

Atrahasis Epic ends with the salvation of mankind through a remnant:

III:viii:9 That we brought about [the flood],
10 But man survived [the destruction].[92]

For a proper evaluation of the remnant motif in the Atrahasis Epic one must be aware of the differences in the various attempts to destroy mankind. Plague and famine with drought were employed as a means "to diminish"[93] the human race without any intention of complete extermination. The flood, on the other hand, is sent for the purpose of "total destruction"[94] of mankind. Thus the remnant motif becomes most explicit in this instance in connection with the motif of the total destruction of mankind, i.e., when human life and existence as such was threatened with extinction.

The Atrahasis Epic provides welcome information concerning the cause of the destruction by a flood. With the exception of one dissenter the communis opinio of Assyriologists is that the "noise" (rigmum, hubūrum[95]) is a "joyous noise" of men which disturbs the rest and sleep of the senior gods and that this "joyous noise" leads to the capricious action to destroy mankind by a flood. G. Pettinato argues against this assumption by marshalling evidence in support of his con-

---

[92]Ibid., p. 105 Tablet III:viii:9-10:
9 ki-ma ni-iš-ku-[nu a-bu-b]a
10 a-wi-lum ib-lu-ṭ[ú i-na ka-ra-ši]

[93]This is made explicit in the Assyrian Recension by the use of the verb maṭû "to become less, to diminish," ibid., p. 107 S:iv:39.

[94]Supra, n. 89.

[95]For the appearance of these terms in the Epic, see Lambert and Millard, Atra-hasīs, pp. 193-94: rigmu; p. 184: hubūru. See Appendix II, p. 467.

tention that this "noise" is "the rebellious and complaining noise of man,"[96] which implies evil conduct and rebellion on the part of mankind with the aim to overthrow the established order.[97] The divine answer with a flood would then have been a justified action.

The Atraḫasis Epic provides the first explicit usage of remnant terminology in Akkadian "epic literature" in connection with human entities. Verbal forms of balaṭu (Heb. plṭ) in the D-stem are employed with the semantic values of "save" and "survive" (Tablet III:i:23; III:vi:10; III:viii:10), while verbal forms of waṣû[98] are used with the meanings of "escape" (Tablet III:vi:9) and "save" (Tablet III:vi:19). These verbs are used in clauses in which the subject or object is either "man" or "life." This points to a remarkable relationship between the survival of mankind and the preservation of life and existence when the existence of mankind is threatened with "total destruction" (gamertu). The corollary of the motif of "complete destruction" is the motif of the salvation of a remnant in which life is preserved. In this connection it is appropriate to refer to a Middle Babylonian[99] fragment from

---

[96]Pettinato, op. cit., p. 198.

[97]Ibid., p. 193: "Die Menschen wurden deshalb bestraft, weil sie sich der von den Göttern bestimmten Ordnung nicht fügten. Das Wehgeschrei der Menschen über das schwere Schicksal entsprach der offenen Rebellion der Igigu." See Appendix II, p. 467.

[98]The common meaning is "to go out," see the Glossary in Lambert and Millard, Atra-ḫasīs, p. 180; A. Ungnad and L. Matouš, Grammatik des Akkadischen (4th ed.; München, 1964), pp. 92, 100.

[99]A number of scholars, among them A. Heidel, The Gilgamesh Epic and Old Testament Parallels (2nd ed.; Chicago, 1963), p. 105, E. A. Speiser in ANET[3], p. 104a, argue for an Old Babylonian date; G. A. Barton and E. I. Gordon suggest a Middle Babylonian date, which has been adopted by Lambert in Lambert and Millard, Atra-hasīs, p. 126.

Nippur[100] referring to the name of the boat which will save the flood hero, "Preserver of Life" (na-ṣi-rat na-piš-tim).[101] This name places additional emphasis upon the idea of saving and preserving life which is so inextricably connected with the entire notion of the remnant motif in the Atraḫasis Epic. With the escaped remnant--the survival of Atraḫasis and his family--human life and physical existence as such were saved and preserved, making a future existence for the human race possible when this very existence was threatened with total destruction by a natural cataclysm in the form of a flood. In this instance the remnant motif appears when human life and historical existence[102] are threatened with

---

[100]Text published and translated by H. V. Hilprecht, The Babylonian Expedition of the University of Pennsylvania (Series D, Vol. V, Fasc. 1; Philadelphia, 1910), pp. 33f. Later translations by M. Jastrow, Hebrew and Babylonian Traditions (London, 1914), pp. 343f.; Clay, op. cit., pp. 81-82; E. Ebeling in ATAT[2], p. 199; Heidel, op. cit., pp. 105-06; Speiser in ANET[3], p. 105a; and transliteration and translation in Lambert and Millard, Atra-ḫasīs, pp. 126-27; cf. A. Deimel, "Diluvium in traditione babylonica," VD, VII (1927), 186-91.

[101]The Babylonian na-ṣi-rat na-piš-tim has also been translated with "Which saved life," by A. Poebel, Historical Texts (Philadelphia, 1914), p. 61 n. 3; "Welches, das Leben schützt," by Matouš, ArOr, 35 (1967) p. 9; "The Life Saver," by Lambert in Lambert and Millard, Atra-ḫasīs, p. 127. The translation "Preserver of Life" has the following supporters, E. Ebeling in ATAT[2], p. 199; Heidel, op. cit., p. 106; A. Salonen, Die Wasserfahrzeuge in Babylonien (Helsinki, 1939), p. 51 under eluppu qurqurru; Speiser in ANET[3], p. 105a; D. Hämmerly-Dupuy, "Some Observations on the Assyro-Babylonian and Sumerian Flood Stories," AUSS, VI (1968), 6.

[102]The Myth and Ritual school answers the question of the occasion of the "singing" of an epic by arguing that many myths sprang out of a cultic environment and served in the cult. The Atraḫasis Epic gives the impression of having been intended for public reading as the conclusion indicates, "I have sung of the flood to all the peoples. Hear it!" Lambert and Millard, Atra-ḫasīs, pp. 105, 7-8. At times the Epic turns suddenly to offer advice on midwifery "though this text (contrary to what has been said repeatedly) was never used as an incantation in childbirth." W. G. Lambert, "Myth and Ritual as Conceived by the Babylonians," JSS,

complete annihilation. For the moment the remnant was but a meager and woefully small lot when all existence had been blotted out; but it preserved life itself and thus possessed within itself the immense potentiality of renewal and all future life. In the remnant mankind's past existence is linked in an unbroken chain to mankind's future existence. This may be another indication that the remnant motif originates when man's life and existence are threatened with annihilation.[102a]

Tablet XI of the Gilgamesh Epic[103] contains an account of the great flood, "clearly an extraneous story,"[104] which has been fused into the main story. It is a fairly well established conclusion that the

---

XIII (1968), 104. There is no evidence that a religious aura surrounded the recitation which is not limited to scribes alone. For an evaluation of myths and mythologically embellished literary works as a source of Mesopotamian religion and cult, see Oppenheim, Ancient Mesopotamia, pp. 177-78.

[102a]See Appendix, pp. 463-64.

[103]The publication of the Gilgamesh material is a rather long story that need not be related in detail at this time. The most recent edition of the cuneiform text of the Assyrian recension with a complete transliteration of all the Semitic Gilgamesh material known at the time is found in R. Campbell Thompson, The Epic of Gilgamish (Oxford, 1930). The translation of Heidel, op. cit., is based on Thompson's edition. The latest serious attempt to bring all the new material to bear on an English translation is found by E. A. Speiser in ANET[3], pp. 72b-99a. Recent German translations of importance are by A. Schott and W. von Soden, Das Gilgamesch-Epos (Stuttgart, 1958); H. Schmökel, Das Gilgamesch Epos (Stuttgart, 1966).

[104]Oppenheim, Ancient Mesopotamia, p. 258; Laessøe, op. cit., p. 96: "As it stands, the story of the deluge has every appearance of being a separate tale which has been joined artificially, although undeniably with great dramatic effect, to the cycle which concerns Gilgamesh and Enkidu." N. K. Sandars, The Epic of Gilgamesh (2nd ed.; Baltimore, 1964), p. 42: "The flood narrative is still an independent poem inserted into the framework of the Gilgamesh Epic." Schmökel, op. cit., p. 105 n. 2: ". . . die Sintflutmythe . . . [wurde] vom Dichter geschickt, jedoch erkennbar, . . . in die Gilgamesch-Dichtung eingefügt." These quotations reflect the general opinion of scholars.

flood episode of GE XI has been taken over from the Atrahasis Epic[105] apparently in the Kassite period.[106] The Gilgamesh Epic gives no reason for the flood, very likely because it is immaterial for the plot as a whole.

The remnant motif is an integral part of the deluge story which Utnapishtim relates to Gilgamesh, who is in search of immortality.[107] Ea (Enki) addresses Utnapishtim through the wall of the reed-hut in the following words:

XI:24 'Tear down (this) house, build a ship!
25 Give up possessions, seek thou life.
26 Forswear (worldly) goods and keep the soul alive!
27 Aboard the ship take thou the seed of all living things.'[108, 108a]

---

[105]There is no need to repeat what has been said in n. 81 above, see also Benno Landsberger, "Einleitung in das Gilgameš Epos," in *Gilgameš et sa légende*, ed. by P. Garelli (Paris, 1960), p. 34; Schmökel, *op. cit.*, p. 105 n. 2.

[106]Matouš, *ArOr*, XXI (1967), p. 12; differently de Liagre Böhl, *op. cit.*, III, 367, believes that the Ugaritic flood story is dependent upon GE XI. This is an unproved assumption.

[107]Oppenheim, *Ancient Mesopotamia*, p. 257: "Gilgamesh's . . . unsuccessful quest for immortality is told on eleven of the twelve tablets." Cf. Heidel, *op. cit.*, pp. 5-13; *ANET*[3], p. 72.

[108]*ANET*[3], p. 93a Tablet XI:24-27. Transliteration in Thompson, *op. cit.*, p. 60:
24 u-ḳur bîti bi-ni iṣu elippa
25 muš-šir mešrê(e) še-ʾ-i napšâtipl
26 [m]a-ak-ku-ra zi-ir-ma na-piš-t[a] bul-liṭ
27 [š]u-li-ma zir nap-ša-a-ti ka-la-ma a-na lib-bi iṣu elippi
The second parts of ll. 25 and 26 are variously translated, Schott, *op. cit.* p. 87: "dem Leben jag nach! . . . der Seele erhalte das Leben!" Schmökel, *op. cit.*, p. 97: "das Dasein rette! . . . sichere das Leben." Ebeling in *ATAT*[2], p. 176: "suche Leben! . . . das Leben rette!"

[108a]See Appendix, p. 464.

The hero of the flood built his ark, loaded it with silver and gold.

> XI:83 Whatever I had of all the living beings I [laded] upon her.
> 84 All my family and kin I made go aboard the ship.
> 85 The beasts of the field, the wild creatures of the field, All the craftsmen I made go aboard.[109]

After the door is shut and the rudder of the vessel is handed over to Puzur-Amurri, the boatman, the gods send the flood, which all but sweeps away the last vestige of life on earth. For six days and six nights the future of life and civilization hinges on the fate of the precarious craft. After "all of mankind had returned to clay" (Tablet XI:133), the boat containing the remnant of the human race came to rest on Mount Nisir. Those who were saved disembarked when it was safe and Utnapishtim prepared a sacrifice to which the gods assembled. The closing words of a brief address by Ishtar reveal that Enlil was responsible for the destruction of mankind:

> XI:167 '(But) let not Enlil come to the offering,
> 168 For he, unreasoning, brought on the deluge
> 169 And my people consigned to destruction.'[110]

Yet Enlil arrived and having noticed the boat exclaimed in anger:

> XI:173 'Has some living soul escaped?
> No man was to survive the destruction!'[111]

---

[109] ANET^3, p. 94a Tablet XI:83-85.

[110] ANET^3, p. 95 a Tablet XI:167-69. Transliteration in Thompson, op. cit., p. 63:
167 ^{ilu}En.LIL a-a il-li-ka a-na šur-ḳi-ni
168 aš-šu la im-tal-ku-ma iš-ku-nu a-bu-bu
169 u nišê^{pl}-ia im-nu-u a-na ka-ra-ši

[111] ANET^3, p. 95a Tablet XI:173. Transliteration in Thompson, op. cit., p. 64:
173 a-a-um-ma u-ṣi na-piš-ti a-a ib-luṭ amēlu ina ka-ra-ši.
CAD, II, 57 translates: "has anyone escaped? let no one live through the destruction."

In a moving speech Ea (Enki) asked leniency of Enlil and was able to appease him. As a result Enlil boarded the ship and bestowed eternal life to Utnapishtim and his spouse:

XI:193 'Hitherto Utnapishtim has been human.
194 Henceforth Utnapishtim and his wife shall be like unto us gods.
195 Utnapishtim shall reside far away, at the mouth of the rivers!'[112]

The remnant motif in the Gilgamesh Epic contains many aspects of its prototypes, the Sumerian flood story and the Atrahasis Epic. Although no reason is advanced for the flood, the second element of the common pattern of flood stories is present, i.e., the cataclysm was meant to wipe out the whole human race. The third element is again the remnant of mankind, i.e., a family--here with the addition of all craftsmen--is "saved," because it "survived" the flood. "The seed of all living things" (Tablet XI:27) is similar to "the seed of mankind" in the Sumerian flood account. The remnant terminology of the Gilgamesh Epic is identical with that of the Atrahasis Epic. Verbal forms of balatu are used with meanings of "survive" and "save;"[113] a form of wasu is employed with the sense of "escape."[114] Again the subject or object of the clauses in which these forms appear is either "man" or "life." Thus we find again an inextricable connection between the survival of mankind and the preservation of life and existence when threatened with "destruction" (Tablet XI:169=Atrahasis Epic, III:iii:54;III:v:43). The interest in

---

[112] ANET^3, p. 95b Tablet XI:193-95.

[113] GE, XI:26, 173; Atrahasis Epic, III:i:23; III:vi:10; III:viii:10.

[114] GE, XI:173; Atrahasis Epic, III:vi:9.

life seems to be expressed also in the name of the pious flood hero Utnapishtim, the second element of whose name contains the word "life."[115] The surviving remnant that escaped the destruction of the flood links in an unbroken chain the existence and life of the human race of the antediluvian era with that existence in the postdiluvian period.[116] Thus the surviving remnant represents the carrier of life itself linking the past and future existence of mankind.

The Akkadian Erra Epic[117] contains the remnant motif, shedding additional light on its usage. From all available evidence this epic appears to have been composed in the second half of the Middle Babylonian period.[118] The number of preserved copies yields about two-thirds of

---

[115]Though there is no agreement on the translation of Utnapishtim, there is a consensus of opinion that the second element means "life", see ANET[3], p. 90 n. 164; Sollberger, op. cit., p. 19; Schmökel, op. cit., p. 80 n. 1; Hämmerly-Dupuy, op. cit., p. 2.

[116]E. A. Speiser, "Ancient Mesopotamia," in The Idea of History in the Ancient World, ed. by R. C. Dentan (New Haven, 1955), p. 50.

[117]The publication of the texts of the Erra Epic does not need to be recounted here. A presentation of all materials published up to 1924 is found in E. Ebeling, Der akkadische Mythos vom Pestgotte Era (Berliner Beitrage zur Keilschriftforschung, II/1; Berlin, 1925). A German translation by E. Ebeling is in ATAT[2], pp. 212-30. The most recent transliteration and translation of all available materials is by Felix Gössmann, Das Era-Epos (Würzburg, 1956). S. N. Kramer presents a discussion and translation of parts of the Erra Epic in his essay, "Mythology of Sumer and Akkad," Mythologies of the Ancient World, ed. by S. N. Kramer (Garden City, N. Y., 1961), pp. 127-35. For recent bibliographies on new finds and publications, see B. Kienast, "Review of Das Era-Epos by F. Gössmann," ZA, 54 (1961), 244-49, and Borger, op. cit., I, 157-58. See Appendix II, p. 468.

[118]Gössmann, op. cit., pp. 87-90, concluded that according to the texts and language a date between 1000 B.C. as the terminus post quem and 626 B.C. as the terminus ante quem is likely. But the historical events point to the year 700 B.C. as the most likely date because the Babylonians rebelled against Assyrian overlordship under Bel-ibni (702-700 B.C.) and Sennacherib quelled this rebellion causing much bloodshed and destruction. W. G. Lambert, "Review of F. Gössmann, Das Era-Epos,"

the original text of five tablets. A. L. Oppenheim[119] points out that the Erra Epic[120] enjoyed much wider currency than the Gilgamesh Epic.

Although the mythological plays a prominent role,[121] there is a common recognition that the Erra Epic reflects actual historical events.[122]

AfO, XVIII (1958), 395-401, argues forcefully on grounds of new cuneiform materials under linguistic, historical, geographic, and ethnic considerations for a date in the ninth century B.C. during the reign of Nabu-apla-iddina, who probably gave orders to compose this epic in order "to chronicle the fall and rise of Akkad." Cf. idem, "A Catalogue of Texts and Authors," JCS, XVI (1962), 76. W. W. Hallo, "On the Antiquity of Sumerian Literature," JAOS, 83 (1963), 175, assigns the Erra Epic to the Middle Babylonian period. More recently Oppenheim, Ancient Mesopotamia, p. 268 states: "It is possible that the sack of Babylon by the Elamite king Šutruk-Nahhunte [11th cent. B.C.] inspired the poet [to write the Erra Epic] and that the opus was composed, in a dark period, to promise the city a brighter future." It would seem that a date in the second half of the Middle Babylonian period is quite likely. See Appendix II, p. 468.

[119]Oppenheim, Ancient Mesopotamia, p. 256.

[120]The spelling of the god of pestilence is either Erra, Era, Irra, or Ira (but not Ura or Dibbara), Gössmann, op. cit., p. 68. His purpose of existence is to make war (Tablet I:6), to destroy lands (Tablet I:13), to destroy men (Tablet I:43). This is his "desire of the heart" (Tablet I:6).

[121]At the time of "pan-Babylonianism" it was believed that the Erra Epic contained an "Astralmythus," see for example Otto Weber, Die Literatur der Babylonier und Assyrer, ein Überblick (Der Alte Orient, Ergänzungsband 2; Leipzig, 1907), p. 108. However, internal signs of cultic influence are generally absent. There is also no mention of the Akîtu rites, and the only allusion occurs in the section containing the fifty names of Marduk. But W. G. Lambert, "Myth and Ritual as Conceived by the Babylonians," JSS, XIII (1968), 108, points out that this section is known to have been originally a separate document whose allusions often contradict the epic's own story. Other scholars looked for Messianic concepts in the Erra Epic; see M. Jastrow, Aspects of Religious Belief and Practice in Babylonia and Assyria (New York, 1911), p. 533; E. Schrader, Die Keilinschriften und das Alte Testament, rev. by H. Zimmern and H. Winckler (3rd ed.; Berlin, 1903), pp. 393-94, 412-14; Alfred Jeremias, Babylonisches im Neuen Testament (Leipzig, 1905), p. 98.

[122]The historical interpretation was first propounded by E. T. Harper, "Die babylonischen Legenden von Etana, Zu, Adapa und Dibarra," Beiträge zur Assyriologie und semitischen Sprachwissenschaft, II (1894), 437, and accepted by E. Ebeling, Bruchstücke eines politischen Propa-

This can be readily observed in the reference to devastation brought about by war and pestilence in such Akkadian cities as Babylon, Sippar, Uruk, and Der (Tablet IV:18, 66) and the mention of such peoples as the Subareans, Assyrians, Elamites, Kassites, Sutaeans, Gutaeans, and Lullamaeans (Tablet IV:131-135).[123]

The Erra Epic is actually a dialogue between gods whose protracted speeches link descriptions of pestilence and war with peace and prosperity into a logical sequence. Erra, the destructive god, resolves to let loose devastation on earth. He has to persuade Marduk to accept this, which involves Marduk's leaving his shrine to descent into the lower world of Ea. His departure releases the rage of Erra against Babylon and all of Akkad. Having his anger appeased by the good vizier Ishum, Erra pre-

---

gandagedichtes aus einer assyrischen Kanzlei (MAOG, 12/II; Leipzig, 1938), 2 note. More recently Gössmann, op. cit., pp. 84-86; Lambert, AfO, XVIII (1958), 395-401; and Oppenheim, Ancient Mesopotamia, pp. 152, 268, among others, support the historical interpretation.

[123]This is not to deny that the Erra Epic was used as a plague amulet that was kept in the house or hung on the wall of the house to safeguard the inhabitants against the raging of Erra, the plague, as the epiolgue makes clear:

"To the house where this tablet is stored,
Should Erra be irate and Sibbi rage,
The sword of slaughter will come not near,
Peace and well-being will be its lot."

Quoted by Kramer, The Sumerians, p. 135. Erica Reiner, "Plague Amulets and House Blessings," JNES, XIX (1960), 148-50, points out that the usage of the Erra Epic as a plague amulet has nothing to do with the philosophy of the poet as Gössmann, op. cit., pp. 61ff. thought, but that the epic qualified for such usage because the gods around whom the story is woven were those who could best extend their tutelage over a menaced house: Marduk as patron god of magic; Erra as the one who decides which house shall be afflicted with plague; the Seven Gods are charged with administering the scourge; and Ishum as envoy of the gods will upon seeing the amulet mark the house as one on which the plague should pass by.

dicts Akkad's rise with Babylon's pre-eminence and happiness. Despite the destruction of human life a small "remnant" will again become a great nation.

Tablet I of the Erra Epic refers to _a_ or likely _the_ flood[124] in a dialogue between Erra and Marduk. The purpose of this conversation is stated as follows:

> I:118 'I [Erra] will arouse Marduk, the princely,
> Will summon him from his dwelling place,
> Will destroy man.'[125]

Marduk rejects Erra's proposal that he leave his throne by pointing out that when he arose once before, a destructive flood ensued which diminished greatly the human race:

> I:135 When I looked again, I became utterly ill,
> 136 The number of living beings had become small,
> I did not return them to their place.[126]

---

[124] There is no unanimity among scholars whether this is the very flood referred to in Tablet XI of the Gilgamesh Epic. Lambert and Millard, _Atra-ḫasīs_, p. 27, believe that this is a flood other than the one in the story of the great flood, because every detail is either lacking from, or cannot be reconciled with, the various versions of the story of the great flood. Gössmann, _op. cit_., pp. 44, 65, however, has provided arguments that make the supposition of another flood hardly likely. In the Erra Epic (Tablet I:127-145) Marduk appears as originator of the flood and not Enlil as in GE XI. Gössmann following M. Jastrow, _Die Religion Babyloniens und Assyriens_ (Giessen, 1905), I, 112, 137-40, believes that Marduk as the successor of Enlil had to take over from the latter the heritage of responsibility and therefore appears as originator of the flood. In GE, XI:185, it is said that it would have been better if Erra had devastated the land. The author of the Erra Epic supposes that this actually happened. See Appendix II, p. 468.

[125] Kramer, _op. cit_., p. 129; cf. Gössmann, _op. cit_., p. 12; _ATAT_^{2}, p. 217.

[126] Gössmann, _op. cit_., p. 13 Tablet I:136: šiknat napištim^{tim} nab-nit-si-na iṣ-ḫi-ir-ma ul ú-tir a[š-ru-uš]-šun

Marduk takes this small number of living beings and like a sower sows "their seed" (Tablet I:137) saving thereby the remaining survivors. The future of these survivors is threatened by Erra:

> I:145 The men who remained over from the flood
> and saw the execution of the work,
> 146 Your weapons you [Erra] have raised
> and you destroyed the remnant.[127]

The identification of the "remnant" is not quite clear. The "remnant" could refer only to those who observed the execution of the work of Marduk or it could refer all-inclusively to the "remnant" that was saved at the time of the flood. If the latter were the case, it would mean that no one was left and the remainder of the Erra Epic, which constantly refers to the Akkadians and other peoples, would be rather ambiguous. If, however, the former were the case, namely that the flood decimated the human race leaving only a small number, and a part of this remnant was destroyed by Erra, then the assumed continuity of mankind in this story was preserved. While this seems to be the more likely interpretation, one cannot be absolutely certain that it is correct, because of the fragmentary nature of the text.

For the first time the substantive <u>riḫtu</u>[128] "remnant" (Tablet I:

---

[127]Following the more complete text published by O. R. Gurney and J. J. Finkelstein, <u>The Sultantepe Tablets I</u> (London, 1957), Nos. 16-17= S.U. 51/122+150:

145 nišē^{meš} ša ina a-bu-bi i-se-ta-ma e-mu-ra e-peš šip-ri
146 ^{iṣ}kakkē^{meš}-ka tu-šat-bi-ma tu-ḫal-liq re-e-ḫa
Gössmann, <u>op. cit</u>., p. 12, translates KAR 168 Rs
145 "Die Leute, die aus der Flut entkommen waren und zusahen
146 Deine Waffen hast du (gegen sie) erhoben und ihren Rest vernichtet."

See Appendix II, pp. 468-69.

[128]The present writer wants to express his gratitude to Prof. Dr. A. Leo Oppenheim who graciously granted access to the files of the project of the Chicago Assyrian Dictionary in finding the respective entries. See Appendix II, p. 469.

146) appears in Akkadian "epic literature" as well as the verb sâtu[129] "to remain over" (Tablet I:145). It is significant that the "remnant" is compared to "seed" (Tablet I:137), which has the capacity of sprouting and replenishing that which was lost.

Tablet IV recounts the main event of the entire epic: the destruction of Babylon, the city of Marduk. Erra finally aroused Marduk from his throne reassuring him that he would take full charge, seeing to it that the inhabitants of Babylon remained unharmed. But as soon as Marduk left Babylon, Erra lets loose his scourges. He "overcame, took captive, destroyed them" (Tablet IV:19). The destruction comes about through man:

IV:26 Into the city to which I send you, O man,
27 You shall not fear any god nor be afraid of any man
28 Small and great kill together!
29 The infant, the child: let no one escape![130]

First Babylon and its inhabitants together with the outskirts were destroyed. Babylon became a ruin, destruction came also on Sippar, Uruk, and Der. Ishum, the vizier of Erra, deeply disturbed by the indiscriminate slaughter and destruction, pleads with Erra, hoping to pacify him. Thus Erra proffers a note of hope, at least for the Akkadians. When the Sealander, Subarean, Assyrian, Elamite, Kassite, Sutaean, Gutaean, and

---

[129]W. G. Lambert, Babylonian Wisdom Literature (Oxford, 1960), p. 315, gives the meaning of "to remain over" for our text. For its usage in a Late Babylonian letter, see Ebeling. op. cit., p. 205, and in a ritual text, see F. Thureau-Dangin, Rituels accadiens (Paris, 1921), p. 72. See Appendix II, p. 469.

[130]Gössmann, op. cit., p. 29 Tablet IV:29 e-niq ši-iz-bi šer-ra la te-ez-zi-be a-a-am-ma.

Lullamaean will arise,

IV:135 They will kill one another
136 Then shall the Akkadian arise,
and fell all of them,
and rule them.[131]

In Tablet V Erra, who had at first planned the total destruction and complete annihilation[132] of the Babylonians and all Akkadians, instructs Ishum concerning "the scattered people of Akkad":

V:25 'Let the sparse people of the land multiply again,
26 Let short and tall alike tread (Akkad's) road,
27 Let crippled Akkad throw down the mighty Sutu.'[133]

The restoration of Babylon is finally described in the epilogue:

V:39 That for the glory of Erra this might be sung years without count:
40 How Erra was angry and set his face to devastate the lands and to destroy their peoples,
41 But Ishum, his counselor, appeased him and they left a remnant.[134]

---

[131] My translation differs slightly from Kramer, The Sumerians, p. 132; cf. ATAT^{2}, p. 228; Gössmann, op. cit., p. 32.

[132] Erra addressing the gods in a divine assembly states:
V:6 No doubt I plotted mischief at the time of the former sin;
7 In the fury of my mind I wished to overwhelm the people.
The translation is from W. G. Lambert, "The Fifth Tablet of the Erra Epic," Iraq, XXIV (1962), 121.

[133] Ibid., p. 122; cf. Kramer, op. cit., p. 133; ATAT^{2}, p. 229; A. Halder, Associations of Cult Prophets Among the Ancient Semites (Uppsala, 1945), p. 172.

[134] My translation of the passage differs slightly from that of Gössmann, op. cit., p. 36; Lambert, Iraq, XXIV (1962), p. 123. The transliteration of K 1282 Rs as given by Gössmann, op. cit., p. 37 is as follows:
39 šanāt^{meš} la ni-bi ta-nit-ti bēli rabî^{i} il Nergal qu-[ra-di liq-bu-u]
40 ša ^{il}Era^{ra} i-gug-gu-ma ana sa-pan mātāti^{meš} ú ḫul-lu-uq ni-ši-šun iš-ku-nu pa-ni-š[u]
41 ^{il}I-šum ma-lik-šú ú-ni-iḫ-šu-ma iz-zi-bu ri-ḫa-[ti]
The key term riḫtu appears in a new text as ri-ḫa-ni-iš, see Lambert, Iraq, XXIV (1962), p. 123. See Appendix, p.465.

H. Gressmann first recognized the importance of this epic for the understanding of the remnant motif. We may quote his summary:

> Babylon . . . falls into great distress and is devastated . . . in connection with a war of all against all; thus the beloved city of the gods is punished for her sins. But when it is greatly reduced, the remnant shall be saved. The city shall be restored and the Babylonians shall receive world-dominion.[135]

Though Gressmann states that the punishment came as a result of Babylon's "sins," this is not supported by the text itself, which as a matter of fact gives no reason for the destruction. What is new in the Erra Epic is not so much that there remains a remnant, but that the poet speaks of a remnant of his own people. The Akkadians were threatened with total annihilation had not the gods intervened and "left a remnant" (Tablet V: 41). Through this "remnant" (riḫtu) the "few people of the land" (Tablet V:25) will "multiply" (Tablet V:25) again and "arise" (Tablet IV:136) to be a great nation ruling other nations. The future existence of the inhabitants of Babylon was assured with the survival of a "remnant" which had been "left" (ēzib[136]). Thus the remnant motif appears here in the context of the destruction of a capital city with its surrounding cities and their inhabitants of whom only a remnant survived. But the survival of the remnant was a gracious act on the part of the gods, because in this remnant the future existence of the Akkadians was preserved, linking past and future existence in a straight, uninterrupted line. It is made explicit in the Erra Epic that the remnant possesses

---

[135]H. Gressmann, The Tower of Babel, ed. by J. Obermann (New York, 1928), pp. 52-53.

[136]Erra Epic, Tablet IV:29; V:41, cf. Ungnad-Matouš, op. cit., pp. 87-88, 104. See Appendix, p. 465.

all potentials to again become a powerful nation that will be victorious over her enemies and rule them. It seems that with the Erra Epic the occurrence of the remnant motif in Akkadian "epic literature" has been exhausted.

The Gattung of Akkadian literature designated as "prophecy"[137] contains in one instance the remnant motif. At the outset it should be stressed that the "prophecy" texts are in no way related to Old Testament prophecy. They are descriptions of the reigns of unnamed kings or princes cast in the form of predictions. The reign of each is described either in terms of a "good" time or "bad" time. These "prophecies" are post eventum and "in fact reflect the specific historical period and real historical events."[138]

Text VAT 10179 was found in Assur and first published by E. Ebeling.[139] It has been dated to the reign of the four last kings of the Kassite Dynasty (1188-1157 B.C.) and the Elamite invasion of that per-

---

[137]See especially the two important recent essays by A. K. Grayson and W. G. Lambert, "Akkadian Prophecies," JCS, XVIII (1964), 7-30, and Robert D. Biggs, "More Babylonian 'Prophecies'," Iraq, XXIX (1967), 117-32. Biggs believes that these "prophecies" must be considered simply a peculiar part of the vast Mesopotamian omen tradition connected specifically with astrology. An up to date discussion of the omen tradition is given by Oppenheim, Ancient Mesopotamia, pp. 206-27.

[138]Biggs, op. cit., p. 117.

[139]Erich Ebeling, Keilschrifttexte aud Assur religiösen Inhalts (Wissenschaftliche Veröffentlichung der Deutschen Orientgesellschaft, 34; Leipzig, 1923), II, No. 421. Translations are in ATAT², pp. 283-84; ANET³, pp. 451-52; and a transliteration with translation is given in Grayson and Lambert, op. cit., pp. 13-14.

iod[140] as well as to the Sargonid Period.[141]

ii:2 A prince will arise and [rule] for three years.
3 The remainder of the people into [. . . . . .]
4 Cities will be devastated, dwellings [will be desolate]
5 There will be rebellions and [destruction will occur]
6 Hostilities against Akkad [. . . . . .]
7 The rite of Ekur and Nippur . . .[. . . . . .]
8 . . . . . . Nippur [. . . . . .]
9 The Amorites [will put] that prince to the sword.[142]

It is obvious that this is a description of a "bad" time encountered by Babylonia under an unnamed prince (*rubû*). The "remainder of the people" (*rīḫat*^{at} *nišē*^{meš}) of Akkad either seems to experience something bad or seems to have done something bad. Since the text is destroyed there is no proof that this "remnant" will meet death as suggested by some scholars.[143] One could suppose that this "remnant" rebelled or was taken into captivity. But it seems best not to speculate in view of complete lack of evidence. It is, however, of interest that this "remnant of the people" apparently refers to Akkadians, i.e., the author of this "prophecy" speaks of his own people.

---

[140]E. F. Weidner, "Texte-Wörter-Sachen," *AfO*, 13 (1939/40), 236.

[141]F. M. Th. de Liagre Böhl, "Religieuze Teksten uit Assur (VI-IX)," *JEOL*, 7 (1940), 416-17.

[142]The present writer followed generally the translation of Grayson and Lambert, *op. cit.*, p. 14, filling in the lacunae as far as possible from E. Ebeling, *ATAT*^{2}, p. 284, and R. H. Pfeiffer, *ANET*^{3}, p. 452.

[143]Ebeling translates ii:3 rīḫat (ÍB.KÍD)^{at} nišē^{meš} ana [. . . . . .] as follows: "Der Rest der Menschen [wird] in die Erde [hinabsteigen (?)]," *ATAT*^{2}, p. 284. This is taken over by Pfeiffer in *ANET*^{3}, p. 452: "The rest of mankind [will descend] into the earth." It must be noted, however, that the text merely contains the preposition *ana*, but lacks "the earth." Thus there is no basis for the suggestion to "descend into the earth."

We may use a letter of historical relevance used in ancient international diplomatic correspondence[144] as an introduction to the various Assyrian historical texts which contain the remnant motif. This letter was uncovered among the 25,000 cuneiform tablets of the archives of Mari[145] and belongs to the reign of Išme-Dagan I, king of Assyria, (1780-1741 B.C.) who wrote to his brother Yasmaḫ-Addu, king of Mari. The latter is informed of the utter destruction of an enemy tribe:

> The men of the Awlānum tribe assembled here, their entire contingent, under Mār-Addu, in order to give battle. We fought at Tu-[.]wi and I inflicted a severe defeat on them. Mār-Addu and all the tribesmen of the Awlāmum are dead; also their slaves and their clients are killed. Not even one of the enemy escaped with his life. Rejoice![146]

This theme of total annihilation of the enemy without leaving a remnant appears again and again in later Assyrian annalistic literature. It will not be necessary to go into great details, yet one must refer to the pertinent passages in historical sequence. Inasmuch as Werner E. Müller began his study of "the remnant among the Assyrians"[147] with information obtained from annalistic records of Assurnasirpal II (883-859 B.C.), Shalmaneser III (858-824 B.C.), and Tiglath-Pileser III (744-727 B.C.),

---

[144]Published by G. Dossin, ed., Lettres (Archives royales de Mari, 4; Paris, 1951), No. 33.

[145]See A. Parrot, "Mari," Archaeology and Old Testament Study, ed. by D. W. Thomas (London, 1967), pp. 140ff.

[146]A. Leo Oppenheim, Letters from Mesopotamia (Chicago, 1967), p. 106.

[147]Werner E. Müller, Die Vorstellung vom Rest im Alten Testament (Inaugural-Dissertation, Theologische Fakultät, Universität Leipzig, 1939), pp. 9-12.

the present writer begins with the earliest available records in order to avoid arbitrariness.

The first detailed account of Assyrian military operations comes from inscriptions of Shalmaneser I (1274-1245 B.C.).[148] It is reported that the Hittite army and their Aramean ally were "slaughtered like sheep."[149] This is followed by the report of the capture of cities of a large region. The record concludes: "Their lands I brought under my sway, and the rest of their cities I burned with fire."[150] Tukulti-Ninurta I (1244-1208 B.C.), son of Shalmaneser I, gives the report[151] that he destroyed the lands of unsubmissive peoples, overthrowing "the forces of the land of Shubari in [its] totality . . . ."[152] The famous Prism Inscription of Tiglath-Pileser I (1115-1077 B.C.) informs us of his campaign against the Mushki carried out in his accession year[153]:

> With their twenty thousand warriors and their five kings I fought in the land of Kutmuhi and I defeated them. The corpses of their warriors I hurled down in the destructive battle . . . Their blood I caused to flow in the valleys and on the high places of the mountains. I cut off their heads and outside their cities, like heaps of grain, I piled them up . . . . I carried off six thousand

---

148 *ARAB*, I, 38.

149 *ARAB*, I, 40.

150 *Ibid*.

151 R. Borger, *Einleitung in die assyrischen Königsinschriften* (Handbuch der Orientalistik; Ergänzungsband, V; Leiden, 1961), p. 79, affirms that the military reports of Tukulti-Ninurta I have equal historical rank with the building record and must not be considered as relatively lengthy parentheses for self-glorification.

152 *ARAB*, I, 53.

153 *ARAB*, I, 74.

> (men), the remainder of their troops, who had fled from before my weapons and had embraced my feet, and I counted them as inhabitants of my land.[154]

D. D. Luckenbill states: "Here we have the beginning of the deportation of inhabitants of conquered territory [by the Assyrians]."[155] Tiglath-Pileser I was again forced to march against the land of Kutmuhi, because it had revolted and withheld tribute.

> I burned their cities with fire, I devastated, I destroyed (them). The rest of the people of the land of Kutmuhi who had fled from before my weapons, crossed over to the city of Shershe . . . . I crossed the Tigris and conquered the city of Shershe, their stronghold. I scattered their warriors in the midst of the hills like—, and made their blood to flow in the Tigris and on the high places of the mountains.[156]

This destruction, however, was not complete, because in the following year he marched once more against them.

> I burned their cities with fire, I devastated, I destroyed (them). The rest of their troops who took fright at my terrible weapons . . . sought the strong heights of the mountains, a difficult region, in order to save their lives . . . . I defeated them.[157]

The fate of the "rest of their troops" did not need to be defeat and death. It was not the purpose of Tiglath-Pileser I to totally destroy his enemy, if he only submitted to his yoke. In a campaign against the land of Sugi, which is the land of Kirhi, he "had mercy" on the "rest of their host," because, as the record says, they "embraced my feet."[158]

---

[154] ARAB, I, 74; Borger, op. cit., p. 115, gives a shorter account from Weidner Text III which reads in its concluding lines 19-20: "[Den Rest] ihrer [Trupp]en deportierte ich und liess ich nach meinem Lande herunterkommen. [Das Land der Mosker nahm ich in seinem ganzen Umfang] in Besitz und fügte es zum Gebiet meines Landes."

[155] D. D. Luckenbill, The Annals of Sennacherib (Chicago, 1924), p.6.

[156] ARAB, I, 74-75.

[157] ARAB, I, 77-78. See Appendix, p. 465.

[158] ARAB, I, 80.

This phrase indicates that the aim of political dependence of the enemy had been achieved. They became a vassal of Assyria which included the payment of tribute to the suzerain. Similarly, Shadi-Teshub, king of Urratinash, "embraced the feet" of Tiglath-Pileser I, when he approached the former's country:

> His sons, the offspring of his loins, and his household, I took as hostages. Sixty vessels of bronze, bowls of copper, great caldrons of copper, together with 120 slaves and herds and flocks, he brought as tribute and toll; I received them from him; I pardoned him, and spared his life.[159]

Tiglath-Pileser I reports also that the "rest of the forces" of Aramean tribes in the area of Carchemish fled to save their lives,[160] and since the outcome of his pursuit is not stated, it can be assumed that their attempt was successful. This has been a representative selection of the fairly stereotyped reports of Tiglath-Pileser I. Later Assyrian kings employed the same practices as their predecessors and recount them in very similar fashion. The main object of such military operations on the part of the Assyrians was to destroy the political independence of the enemy. The rigorous nature of this endeavor is manifested in various ways, but most tellingly by the frequent appearance of phrases such as "to save his (her, their) life (lives), he (she, they) fled"[161] and the

---

[159] ARAB, I, 76; cf. I, 82. See also the following: "The king of Kumani became frightened at the advance of my battle array, and embraced my feet. I spared his life." ARAB, I, 85.

[160] ARAB, I, 83.

[161] Shalmaneser I (1274-1245 B.C.): ARAB, I, 41; Tukulti-Ninurta I (1244-1208 B.C.): ARAB, I, 53; Tiglat-Pileser I (1115-1077 B.C.): ARAB, I, 76, 78; Tukulti-Ninurta II (890-844 B.C.): ARAB, I, 127, 128; Assurnaṣirpal (883-859 B.C.): ARAB, I, 149, 152, 160, 162; Shalmaneser III (858-824 B.C.): ARAB, I, 243, 245-46, 218, 222, 235, 238-39; ANET^3,

success is indicated by the phrase "not one escaped."[162] To reach their goal the Assyrians followed the old practice--known already from the Hittites[163]--of destroying every support of life. The orchards, groves, plantations, and gardens were cut down[164] and the grain was carried off.[165] Both the total annihilation of the life of the insubmissive enemy and the complete destruction of the support of life was to serve the aim of breaking his political independence.[166] This goal was reached when

---

p. 280; Tiglath-Pileser III (744-727 B.C.): ARAB, I, 273, 275, 279, 281, 293; Sargon II (721-705 B.C.): ARAB, II, 8, 17, 22-23, 82, 86; Sennacherib (704-681 B.C.): AS, pp. 24, 47, 56, 82; ARAB, II, 128; Assurbanipal (668-627 B.C.): ARAB, II, 293, 295-96, 367.

[162]Assurnasirpal II (883-859 B.C.): ARAB, I, 146: "I did not leave a single one among them alive to serve as hostage." Shalmaneser III (858-824 B.C.): ARAB, I, 230; Tiglath-Pileser III (744-727 B.C.): ARAB, I, 279, 285; Sennacherib (704-681 B.C.): AS, p. 26=ARAB, II, 116; AS, p. 38=ARAB, II, 123; AS, pp. 55, 57, 77; Assurbanipal (668-627 B.C.): Hugo Winckler, Keilinschriftliches Textbuch zum Alten Testament (3rd. ed.; Leipzig, 1909), pp. 22, 23, 24, 25, 31; M. Streck, Assurbanipal und die letzten assyrischen Könige bis zum Untergang Niniveh's (Vorderasiatische Bibliothek, VIII; Leipzig, 1916), II, 11, 15, 17, 67, 69, 75; ARAB, II, 317-18, 294; ANET[3], p. 299.

[163]Albrecht Goetze, Die Annalen des Muršiliš (Mitteilungen der Vorderasiatischen-Aegyptischen Gesellschaft, 38; Leipzig, 1933), pp. 34, 42, 110, 112, 120, 150, 184; idem, Kulturgeschichte des Alten Orients. Kleinasien (Handbuch der Altertumswissenschaft, III; 2nd ed.; München, 1957), p. 127; Ph. H. J. Houwink Ten Cate, "Mursilis' Northwestern Campaigns-Additional Fragments of His Comprehensive Annals," JNES, XXV (1966), 177.

[164]Shalmaneser III (858-824 B.C.): ARAB, I, 230, 243; Tiglath-Pileser III (744-727 B.C.): ARAB, I, 279, 285; Sargon II (721-705 B.C.): ARAB, II, 16.

[165]ARAB, I, 230.

[166]This is completely different from Müller's contention that the aim was always to exterminate the enemy, op. cit., p. 10.

the enemy gave up his struggle submitting to heavy tribute imposed by Assyria,[167] such tribute at times being established by formal treaties.[168] Then it is often recorded that the Assyrian kings had mercy[169] on that part of their enemies and saved their lives.[170] These are frequently designated as the "remnant" (sittu).[171] On many other occasions the Assyrian kings applied the age-old method of large-scale deportations of those who remained of their vanquished enemy.[172] This policy was already

---

[167] Tiglath-Pileser I (1115-1077 B.C.): ARAB, I, 80; Adad-Nirari II (911-891 B.C.): ARAB, I, 114, 125; Tukulti-Ninurta II (890-884 B.C.): ARAB, I, 127; Assurnasirpal II (883-859 B.C.): ARAB, I, 143, 147, 155-56; Tiglath-Pileser III (744-727 B.C.): ARAB, I, 293; Sargon II (721-705 B.C.): ARAB, II, 50-51; Sennacherib (704-681 B.C.): AS, p. 32= ARAB, II, 119-20; AS, p. 70; Esarhaddon (680-669 B.C.): ARAB, II, 207.

[168] A. R. Millard, "Fragments of Historical Texts from Nineveh: Ashurbanipal," Iraq, XXX (1968), 101: "[A treaty] sworn by the gods, more binding than before, I established with him." See also E. F. Weidner, "Der Staatsvertrag Aššurnirâris VI. von Assyrien mit Matiʾilu von Bît-Agusi," AfO, 8 (1932), 17ff.; R. Borger, "Zu den Asarhaddon-Verträgen aus Nimrud. Nachtrag," ZA, N.F. 22 (1964), 261.

[169] ARAB, I, 80, 127, 155-56; ANET³, pp. 295, 298.

[170] ARAB, I, 76, 82, 85, 127, 144, 155-56, 293; II, 295; ANET³, pp. 295, 298.

[171] ARAB, I, 114, 117, 125, 147-48; AS, pp. 32, 70; ARAB, II, 207.

[172] Tiglath-Pileser I (1115-1077 B.C.): ARAB, I, 74, 75; Adad-Nirari II (911-891 B.C.): ARAB, I, 117; Tukulti-Ninurta II (890-884 B.C.): ARAB, I, 127; Assurnasirpal (883-859 B.C.): ARAB, I, 144, 148, 149, 151, 169; D. J. Wiseman, "A New Stela of Aššur-naṣir-pal II," Iraq, XIV (1952), 25-27. Shalmaneser III (858-824 B.C.): ARAB, I, 210, 221-22, 229; Tiglath-Pileser III (744-727 B.C.): ARAB, I, 277-78; Sargon II (721-705 B.C.): ARAB, II, 7; Sennacherib (704-681 B.C.): AS, pp. 32, 35, 51, 70; Esarhaddon (680-669 B.C.): ANET³, pp. 294, 296; Assurbanipal (668-627 B.C.): ARAB, II, 300, 305, 311-12, 319.

applied by Sumerian kings of the Third Dynasty of Ur[173] and also by Hittite kings.[174]

The designation "remnant" (<u>sittu</u>) also appears frequently in connection with those who fled from the Assyrian military force in order to save their lives. Tiglath-Pileser I admits that "the rest of their forces [of Aramean tribes], which had fled"[175] were beyond his reach. In a report of Tukulti-Ninurta II (890–884 B.C.) it is stated that after a part of the enemy had been deported "the rest of them escaped and occupied a steep mountain. . . . I climbed up after them. I captured countless numbers of them. The rest of them crossed the Lower Zab, to save their lives."[176] Assurnasirpal II (883–859 B.C.) tells that Kudurru, the governor of the land of Suhi "together with seventy of his men, to save his life, cast himself into the Euphrates"[177] and escaped. Shalmaneser III (858–824 B.C.) reports rather often about the successful flight of his enemies, who saved their lives in so doing. We must limit ourselves to one example:

> I defeated Hadadezer of Damascus (Imer[i]) together with twelve princes, his allies (lit.: helpers). I stretched upon the ground

---

[173]This is shown by inscriptions of Šu-sin (2037–2029 B.C.); see Oppenheim, <u>Ancient Mesopotamia</u>, p. 363 n. 33.

[174]An example of the deportation of a total urban population is reported in the fourteenth-century treaty of Šuppiluliuma, the Hittite suzerain, and Mattiwaza, the Mittanian vassal; see E. F. Weidner, <u>Politische Dokumente aus Kleinasien</u> (Boghazköi-Studien, 8–9; Leipzig, 1923), pp. 6–15.

[175]<u>ARAB</u>, I, 84.

[176]<u>Ibid</u>., I, 128. See Appendix, p. 465.

[177]<u>Ibid</u>., I, 160; cf. I, 149, 152, 162.

> 20,900 of his strong warriors like *šu-bi*, the remnants of his troops I pushed into the Orontes (*Arantu*) river and they dispersed to save their lives.[178]

Similar reports are given by Tiglath-Pileser III (744-727 B.C.),[179] Sargon II (721-705 B.C.),[180] Sennacherib (704-681 B.C.),[181] and Assurbanipal (668-627 B.C.).[182] In a few instances the Assyrian kings do not miss the opportunity to report that this "remnant" was caught and destroyed by the sword,[183] or pardoned,[184] or deported.[185] In some cases when their escape was successful it is reported that this remnant was consumed with thirst in the desert,[186] or that famine broke out among them.[187] Yet in the great majority of cases this "remnant" seems to have been indeed able to save their lives. This constitutes an involuntary admission that the aim of breaking the political independence of the enemy or part thereof was not always reached.

It has been correctly observed that in the Assyrian annalistic

---

[178] *ANET*[3], p. 280b; cf. *ARAB*, I, 218, 222, 235, 238, 239, 243.

[179] *ARAB*, I, 273, 275, 279, 281, 293.

[180] *ARAB*, II, 8, 17, 22-23, 86.

[181] *AS*, pp. 24, 56, 82, 47=*ARAB*, II, 128.

[182] *ARAB*, II, 293, 295, 296, 302, 303, 304, 317, 318, 367.

[183] *Ibid*., I, 75, 78, 239-40.

[184] *Ibid*., I, 80.

[185] *Ibid*., I, 74.

[186] *Ibid*., I, 162; cf., II, 317-18.

[187] *Ibid*., II, 367.

literature the remnant motif is much more frequently encountered than in the reports of the Hittites and the Egyptians.[188] W. E. Müller advances the following argument: "The reason for this must lie in the different type of warfare. . . ."[189] He claims that the Assyrians employed the strategy of total warfare which meant the complete physical annihilation of the enemy.[190] This practice precludes the leaving of a remnant. Therefore, when a remnant remains, it seems a breakdown of the principle of total physical destruction. This contention leads Müller to conclude that the remnant motif originates from the breakdown of this principle:

> Another result can be derived from this for our investigation, namely that the linguistic usage of the remnant of an army or a people is rooted in the strategy of destruction of total warfare. The presence of a remnant means the breakdown of this principle.[191]

This conclusion hinges on whether or not the Assyrians acted according to a supposed principle of "complete physical destruction." As far as the present writer was able to ascertain the Assyrian texts never explicitly state such a principle nor imply it. From all extant evidence it appears that this principle is the result of a misinterpretation of the evidence.

---

[188]Müller, op. cit., p. 12. But one must not put too much emphasis upon the quantitative occurrence, because a much larger amount of annalistic literature has been preserved from the Assyrians as compared to other ancient Near Eastern peoples.

[189]Ibid.

[190]Ibid., p. 17.

[191]Ibid., p. 18.

The available evidence appears to indicate that the Assyrian strategy of warfare was designed to break the political independence of the enemy, which in the most extreme cases could lead to total destruction. The Assyrian strategy of total warfare did not aim toward "complete physical annihilation" but complete subordination. There is an obviously decisive difference between the two, because the former supposed aim would destroy life indiscriminately, while the principle of complete subordination makes the life of the enemy useful for Assyrian overlordship. The view that the Assyrian strategy of warfare aimed at complete subordination--breaking the political independence of the enemy--is supported by the preceding presentation of the evidence which may be briefly summarized. The many instances in which the enemy "embraced the feet" of the Assyrian ruler and was pardoned and made into a tribute-paying vassal of the Assyrian suzerain[192] show clearly that the Assyrian king had reached his goal,[193] which could not have been "total physical destruction," but destruction of national-political independence. Secondly, the age-old practice of deportation as employed by Assyria--and other ancient Near Eastern peoples--contradicts the supposed principle of "total physical destruction."[194] Instead it served to uproot the political sovereignty

---

[192] Supra, nn. 167, 169, 170.

[193] ARAB, I, 80, 82.

[194] That this difficulty exists in Müller's argument is admitted by him, op. cit., p. 16 n. 8. Wolfram von Soden, Der Aufstieg des Assyrerreiches als geschichtliches Problem (Der Alte Orient, 37/I-II; Leipzig, 1938), p. 35, points out that the aim of the deportations and "ihr Erfolg war die restlose Austilgung nationalen Selbstbehauptungswillens."

of the enemy. Thirdly, the presence of Assyrian treaties[195] indicates the aim of unconditional subjugation and not "total physical destruction." Finally, we may add that the cruelty--the wholesale slaughter of captive soldiers and conquered male and female youths, flaying, impaling, mutiliation, etc.--with which the Assyrians pursued their goal and which made life so cheap--is not the result of a supposed principle of "total physical destruction." Rather it served the propaganda purposes of psychological warfare:

> The inscriptions [of the Assyrian kings] as well as the later huge pictorial representations on the palace walls since the time of Assurnasirpal II served as works of propaganda the purpose to place in a dramatic way before the eyes of the enemy the danger and senselessness of any resistance. . . .[196]

Sargon states explicitly that his victories had a propaganda aspect to them. After the victory of the combined forces of Urartu and Zikirtu, he says:

> . . . the rest of the people, who had fled to save their lives, I let go free to glorify the victory of Assur my lord! . . . Their leaders, men who understand battle and who had fled before my weapons, drew nigh to them covered with the venom of death, and recounted to them the glory of Assur, . . . so that they became like dead men.[197]

---

[195] Supra, n. 168.

[196] Wolfram von Soden, "Der Assyrer und der Krieg," Iraq, XXV (1963), 132. Von Soden warns also that, therefore, these reports must be accepted as critically as the Assyrian reports of victories.

[197] Quoted by H. W. F. Saggs, "Assyrian Warfare in the Sargonid Period," Iraq, XXV (1963), 149.

These considerations militate against a supposed principle of "total physical destruction." Rather they support the view that the Assyrian strategy of warfare aimed at breaking the will of the political independence of the enemy and at his subjugation.

The frequent appearance of the remnant motif in these annalistic records of Assyria is due to the constant threat to the independent existence of the enemies of Assyria. The remarkably frequent appearance of the remnant motif in connection with phrases that express the concern to preserve life indicates again the interrelationship between these ideas. No remnant means no life and existence; a remnant means life and existence for the individual, community, tribe, city, or people. Thus we note again that the remnant motif appears whenever and wherever life and existence are threatened with destruction. Another result of our investigation of Assyrian annalistic literature is that the remnant motif is grounded in circumstances in which the life and existence of man in various independent social structures are threatened with annihilation and in which the remnant is the means by which continuity of life and existence is preserved for the future.

C. The Remnant Motif in Hittite Texts

The remnant motif is present in two different Gattungen of Hittite religious literature,[198] i.e., a mythological text and a prayer. The

---

[198]For a discussion of the various genres of Hittite texts, see the outstanding article by Annelies Kammenhuber, "Die hethitische Geschichtsschreibung," Saeculum, 9 (1958), 136-55. A survey of original publications of cuneiform texts, translations, and discussions up to 1958 is found in E. Laroche, "Catalogue des textes hittites," Revue hittites et asianique, XIV (1956), 33-38, 69-116; XV (1957), 30-89; XVI (1958), 18-64.

former belongs to the Kumarbi cycle and is commonly called "the Song of Ullikummi."[199] It is the second epic of the Kumarbi cycle whose contents is largely mythological[200] connected with the theme of celestial kingship: Kumarbi, "the father of the gods," attempts to take back from his son Teshub, the Storm-god, the kingship of the gods. The means for achieving this aim is Ullikummi. Underlying this myth is the familiar motif of rivalry between older and younger gods.[201]

Ea gives a report to the god Tashmishu about the fate of the human race on earth:

> 'My soul is sad. I have seen with my own eyes the dead [people] on the [dark] earth; they (are) str[ewn about as] dust while [. . .] stand around.'[202]

Then Ea asks the gods why they are allowing mankind's destruction by the monstrous creature Ullikummi. An almost Homeric dialogue between Teshub and Ullikummi follows, in which the latter boasts of the role which his father Kumarbi has assigned him. At this crucial juncture the tablet

---

199 A full reconstruction of the preserved parts of this most remarkable literary composition is offered by Hans G. Güterbock, "The Song of Ullikummi. Revised Text of the Hittite Version of a Hurrian Myth," JCS, V (1951), 135-61; VI (1952), 8-42. These articles are reprinted in book-form, idem, The Song of Ullikummi (New Haven, Conn., 1952). A more recent English translation is given by A. Goetze in ANET³, pp. 121-25. A German translation is provided by Heinrich Otten, Mythen vom Gotte Kumarbi (Berlin, 1952), pp. 13-25.

200 For a discussion of Hittite mythology including the present work, see H. G. Güterbock, "Hittite Mythology," Mythologies of the Ancient World, ed. by S. N. Kramer (Garden City, N. Y., 1961), pp. 139-79.

201 S. H. Hooke, Middle Eastern Mythology (Baltimore, 1963), p. 97.

202 ANET³, p. 125a.

is broken off and the end is missing. H. G. Güterbock states that "we can safely assume that the outcome of this . . . battle was the final victory of Teshub."[203] If this assumption is correct, it follows that the remainder of the human race on earth was saved from total annihilation. S. H. Hooke considers this myth as "another version of the myth of the destruction of mankind and its frustrations by the interposition of Ea."[204] The fragmentary nature of this Hittite epic leaves much to be desired with regard to a clear understanding of its remnant motif. No explicit reason is advanced in the present text for the cause that brought about the destruction of mankind. Thus "The Song of Ullikummi" makes reference to the destruction of mankind as a result of a struggle among the gods and due to the interposition of Ea a remnant of the human race is saved through the assumed victory of Teshub over his divine challengers.

The second genre of Hittite religious literature in which the remnant motif is present are the famous "Plague Prayers of Mursili II."[205]

---

[203]Güterbock, "Hittite Mythology," p. 171; cf. Goetze in ANET[3], p. 125b, says that the closing lines "must have told how Ullikummi . . . was defeated by the Storm-god." O. R. Gurney, The Hittites (2nd ed.; Baltimore, 1966), p. 194: "The end of the story is lost, but we may be sure it closed with the restoration of Teshub and the defeat of Kumarbi and his monstrous son."

[204]Hooke, op. cit., p. 98. It is still an open question whether this existing Hittite epic is a translation of a Hurrian original as suggested in the past and still supported by Gurney, op. cit., p. 190, or whether it is originally Hittite creation merely drawing its subject matter from Hurrian tradition as now held by Güterbock, "Hittite Mythology," p. 172.

[205]Translations are offered by Albrecht Goetze, "Die Pestgebete des Muršiliš," in Kleinasiatische Forschungen, ed. by F. Sommer and H. Ehelolf (Weimar, 1930), I, 161-251; O. R. Gurney, "Hittite Prayers of Mursili II," Annals of Archaelogy and Anthropology, 27 (1940), 1-163; and A. Goetze in ANET[3], pp. 394-96.

Mursili II (1345-1315 B.C.) prays to his Hattian gods asking for the removal of the plague, because he makes atonement for the sins of his father. These prayers have actual historical value, because the plague actually raged in Hittite lands as is verified from historical texts.[206]

A number of sentences from these prayers provide us with information regarding the severity of the situation faced by the Hittites: "The Hatti land, all of it, is dying."[207] "The few people who were left to give sacrificial loaves were dying too."[208] "Take pity on me and drive the plague out of the Hatti land! Suffer not to die the few who are still left to offer sacrificial loaves and libations!"[209] That this great decimation of the Hittite population must have been real is further attested by the dangerous threat from without that accompanied the threat of plague from within:

> O gods, take ye pity again on the Hatti land! On the one hand it is afflicted with a plague, on the other hand it is afflicted with hostility . . . each one has rebelled; they [the rebellious countries] do not acknowledge the gods and have broken the oaths of the gods.[210]

Again and again the cry is uttered: "Hattian Storm-god . . . save my life!"[211]

---

[206]Newly found fragments of the annals of Mursili II mention a "plague in the Hatti-land," which began to destroy the towns of the Hittite territory in great numbers. This calamitous situation was seized upon by the Gasgaean enemy to make war against the weakened Hittites. P. H. J. Houwink Ten Cate, "Mursilis' Northwestern Campaigns-Additional Fragments of His Comprehensive Annals," JNES, XXV (1966), 178-79. The war with the Gasgaeans is mentioned in a plague prayer of Mursili II, ANET^3, p. 396b; cf. Kammenhuber, op. cit., p. 147.

[207]ANET^3, p. 396a.

[208]Ibid., p. 395a.

[209]Ibid., p. 395b.

[210]Ibid., p. 396a.

[211]Ibid., pp. 395b, 396a.

The existence of the Hittite nation was threatened by plague from within and rebellious vassals from without. Only "few people" are still "left" to bring sacrifices to the gods. But this remnant too "was dying." It must be assumed that the plague finally abated, because the annals of Mursili II report his campaigns and victories. Thus whatever part remained of the Hittite population must have been able to overcome relatively quickly the decimation caused by the plague.

The earliest preserved annalistic literature comes from the Hittites. These historical texts date from the Old Kingdom (ca. 1600-1450 B.C.)[212] and the New Kingdom or Hittite Empire (ca. 1380-1200 B.C.).[213] In these records[214] the remnant motif is also present but less frequent

---

[212]From the period of the Old Kingdom come two bilingual texts: (1) the Annals of Hattusili I (1650-1620 B.C.), translated by Heinrich Otten, "Keilschrifttexte," Mitteilungen der Deutschen Orient-Gesellschaft, 91 (1958), 73-84; (2) Instruction of Mursili I (1620-1590 B.C.), translated by F. Sommer-A. Falkenstein, Die hethitisch-akkadische Bilingue des Ḫattusili I. (Labarna II.) (Abhandlungen der Bayerischen Akademie der Wissenschaften, N. F., 16; München, 1938).

[213]From the period of the Hittite Empire or New Kingdom come the (1) Annals of Suppiluliuma (1380-1346 B.C.) composed by his son Mursili II after 1350 B.C., transliterated and translated by Hans G. Güterbock, "The Deeds of Suppiluliuma as Told by His Son, Mursili II" JCS, X (1956), 41-69, 75-98, 107-130; (2) Annals of Mursili II (1345-1315 B.C.) transliterated and translated by H. Goetze, Die Annalen des Muršiliš (MVAG, 38; Leipzig, 1933); and (3) Annals of Tuthaliyas IV (1265-1235 B.C.), see V. Korošec, "The Warfare of the Hittites--From the Legal Point of View," Iraq, XXV (1963), 159-66.

[214]Müller, op. cit., pp. 5-6, discusses the "remnant motif among the Hittites" by merely referring to the Annals of Mursili II! He is followed by Donald M. Warne, "The Origin, Development and Significance of the Concept of the Remnant in the Old Testament" (unpublished Ph.D. dissertation, Faculty of Divinity, University of Edinburgh, 1958), pp. 22-23.

than in the Assyrian annals. This may partly be due to the fragmentary nature of the Hittite annals as well as to the different purpose of the Hittite records.

The Annals of Hattusili I (1650-1620 B.C.) report a campaign against the kingdom of Arzawa:

> In the following year I went against the country of Arzawa; cattle and sheep I took from [them]. But the enemy of the country of Ḫanikalbat in my back and my country and the other countries altogether fell away from me. Only the city of Ḫattusha was left over by itself.[215]

This report is unique in that the Hittite king admits the total loss of all his own land as well as his vassals, except that his own capital Ḫattuša remained. In a sense, then, his capital represents a remnant.

The recently discovered Annals of Suppiluliuma (1380-1346 B.C.) as recorded by the great annalist Mursili II, his son, contain only indirectly the remnant motif in that they refer to the deportation of the population *in toto* or in part of vanquished lands.

> [And] he burned down [the land of Ḫa]palla. And he removed it together with the population, [the cattle and sheep] and he brought them to Ḫattušaš.[216]

A similar action is reported about the country of Kašula.

> And the gods of my father helped them, (so that) they conquered all of the country of Kašula and brought its population, cattle and sheep before my father. The deportees whom they brought were one thousand.[217]

Suppiluliuma destroyed these conquered territories after he had plundered

---

[215] Otten, "Keilschrifttexte," p. 78.

[216] P. H. J. Houwink Ten Cate, "A New Fragment of the 'Deeds of Suppiluliuma as Told by His Son, Mursili II'," *JNES*, XXV (1966), 29.

[217] Güterbock, *JCS*, X (1956), p. 91.

them. The deportees must be considered a remnant, despite the fact that the report does not mention how many were slain.

The Annals of Mursili II quote a letter which young Mursili II (1345-1315 B.C.) received from a rebellious vassal:

> You are a child and you do not understand; you do not receive (any respect from me). Secondly your country is demolished, and your troops and your charioteers have become few . . . .[218]

There is no reason to doubt the essential historicity of this letter nor that it reflects actual conditions. Mursili II came to the throne after his brother Arnuwanda II and his father Suppiluliuma had suffered death by the plague. The decimation of the population, which included obviously "troops" and "charioteers," was great, so that the latter groups "had become small." The decimated Hittite forces, which were of course of great interest to a vassal, are in a sense a remnant. In the first year of his reign the Gasgaeans in the northern hills challenged Mursili II. The latter burned down two of their cities and adds: "And I took them in with inhabitants, cattle and sheep and took them to Ḫattuša."[219] But it appears that a remnant of the population must have been left behind, because one of these two cities furnished regulars for the army of Mursili II in the same year. Mursili II also reports that some of his rebellious vassals were able to save themselves from his hands by escaping.[220] Others in turn "embraced his feet" in submission pleading

---

[218] Goetze, Die Annalen des Muršiliš, p. 19 ll. 16-18.

[219] Ibid., p. 23 ll. 34-35.

[220] Ibid., pp. 31, 51, 53, 63, 65, 159, 189; H. Otten, "Neue Fragmente zu den Annalen des Muršili," Mitteilungen des Instituts für Orientforschung, 3 (1955), 174.

for vassalage.[221] About the latter Mursili II reports: "The sun [Mursili] did not destroy them."[222] The enemy or rebellious vassal seems to have had the choice between destruction of cities and lands[223] with deportation of the remaining population or vassalage or flight. Flight had been the action taken by the Timmuḫaleans in a battle with Mursili II:

> And the Timmuhalean enemy could not flee. And as soon as I came to Timmuhala--because at first Timmuhala had fled with his troops, cattle (and) sheep--I grabbed him there with his troops, cattle (and) sheep; only few people got away.[224]

These "few people" are a remnant. It may be supposed that the part of the forces of the Timmuḫaleans, which did not escape, shared in the fate which is reported in connection with other battles. "There (were) many deaths in great numbers as well as prisoners in gr[eat numbers]."[225]

This investigation of the remnant motif in Hittite literary texts has shown that it is implicitly present in religious and historical records. In "The Song of Ullikummi" of the mythological Kumarbi cycle a remnant of mankind can be spoken of only upon accepting the likely assumption of a victory of Teshub over his enemies. The remnant motif

---

[221]Goetze, Die Annalen des Muršiliš, pp. 57, 129, 135-37, 139, 153.

[222]Ibid., p. 137.

[223]There are frequent reports that cities were burned down, that the country was burned down, that all support of life was destroyed, Goetze, Die Annalen des Muršiliš, pp. 34, 42, 43, 110, 111, 112, 120, 121, 150, 184; cf. idem, Kulturgeschichte des Alten Orients. Kleinasien (Handbuch der Altertumswissenschaft, III; 2nd ed.; München, 1957), p. 127-28; idem, "Warfare in Asia Minor," Iraq, XXV (1963), 126-29; G. Walser, Neuere Hethiterforschung (Wiesbaden, 1964), pp. 9-11.

[224]Goetze, Die Annalen des Muršiliš, p. 175 ll. 20-25.

[225]Ibid., p. 123 ll. 74-75.

appears more directly in "The Plague Prayers of Mursili II" and in the annals of the various Hittite kings. In the former the remnant is spoken of in connection with the decimation of the Hittite population by a plague. The whole land was threatened with death but a "few" survived with their third king and the Hittites arose once more to be a powerful nation. In the Hittite annals the remnant of conquered enemies or rebellious vassals consists of deportees or escaped vassals and people.

D. The Remnant Motif in Ugaritic Texts

The recent find at Ugarit of a fragment of a four column tablet[226] which contains a version of the Old Babylonian flood story[227] is of great importance inasmuch as it represents the only version of the Babylonian flood story outside Mesopotamia so far. Since the remnant motif has had a prominent place in Mesopotamian flood stories the publication of this Ugaritic fragment was eagerly awaited. However, only the beginning and the end survive of this tablet which dates from the fourteenth century B.C.[228] The content of the tablet is indicated by its opening:

Obv. 1 When the gods took counsel
2 in the lands and brought about a flood
3 in the regions of the world . . .[229]

---

[226]The find of this small fragment was first announced by Jean Nougayrol, "Nouveaux texts accadiens de Ras Shamra," Comptes rendus . . . de l'Académie des Inscriptions et Bell-Lettres (Paris, 1960), pp. 170-71 and it is published by him in Ugaritica (Paris, 1968), V, No. 167=R.S. 22. 421. A transliteration and translation has been published by Lambert and Millard, Atra-ḫasīs, pp. 132-33.

[227]Böhl, "Gilgameš," p. 367.

[228]Lambert and Millard, Atra-ḫasīs, p. 131.

[229]Ibid., p. 133.

Atraḫasis begins to speak in obverse 6:

Obv. 6 'I am Atra-ḫasīs
7 I lived in the temple of Ea, my lord,
8 . . . . . [.]
9 I knew the counsel of the great gods,
10 I knew of their oath, though they did not reveal it to me.'[230]

The subterfuge of the god Ea in informing his client of the impending flood appears in the following words:

Obv. 12 He repeated their words to the reed-wall,
14 'Wall, hear [. . .[231]

At this crucial point, where it sounds as if Atraḫasis is going to tell the story of the flood with the salvation of a remnant, the tablet is broken off. The end of the story which is preserved is as follows:

Rev. 1 [. . . .]. the gods life [. . .
2 [. . .]. . your wife .[. . .
3 [. .]. help and . [. . .
4 Life like the gods [you will] indeed [possess].[232]

From this fragmentary information it would seem reasonable to assume that Atraḫasis and his "wife" were saved from the flood and represent the remnant as in the Old Babylonian Atraḫasis Epic and the later Gilgamesh Epic. To say more than that would be fruitless speculation.

The Ugaritic "Legend of King Krt"[233] contains the remnant motif in

---

[230] Ibid.

[231] The present writer's translation follows on the whole Lambert and Millard, Atra-ḫasīs, p. 133, with the exception that "wall" is replaced with the better "reed-wall."

[232] Ibid.

[233] The most recent transliteration is in UT, pp. 250-52. Important discussions and translations with bibliographies are in H. L. Ginsberg, The Legend of King Keret (BASOR, Supplementary Studies, 2-3; New Haven, Conn., 1946); C. H. Gordon, Ugaritic Literature (Roma, 1949) pp. 66-83; H. L. Ginsberg in ANET3, pp. 142-49; John Gray, The Krt Text in the Literature of Ras Shamra (2nd ed.; Leiden, 1964).

the opening part of the preserved text of Tablet I. J. Gray dates the Krt legend to ca. 1800 B.C.,[234] while W. F. Albright suggests a date in the sixteenth century B.C.[235] The essential motif of the extant Krt text is the death and life problem,[236] which presents the rehabilitation of the royal house of Krt after the extermination of his entire family--brethren, wife, and progeny--leaving Krt as the sole survivor, and the recovery of the king's lineage in old age.[237] The following lines describe the annihilation of Krt's family:

Krt:12 His lawful wife he did find,
13 His legitimate spouse
14 He married the woman, and she 'departed.'
15 *Flesh of kinship* had he:
16 One-third died *in* health,
17 One-fourth *of* sickness;
18 One-fifth pestilence gathered unto itself,
19 One-sixth *calamity*;
20 One-seventh thereof fell by the sword.--
21 He sees his offspring, doth Keret;
22 He sees his offspring ruined
23 Wholly *undermined* his seat
24 And in its entirety a posterity perishing,
25 And in its totality a succession.[238]

---

[234]J. Gray, "Texts from Ras Shamra," in *DOTT*, p. 123 n. 21, suggests this date on the basis of the mention of a "chariot" of king Krt which was still apparently a rarity when this text was composed. It was at about 1800 B.C. when the horse and light war-chariot were introduced into Western Asia.

[235]W. F. Albright, *Yahweh and the Gods of Canaan* (Garden City, N. Y., 1968), pp. 5 n. 9, 118, arrives at his conclusion through his identification of Krt with Kirta, the putative founder of the reigning dynasty of the Mitanni kingdom in the sixteenth century B.C.

[236]Ivan Engnell, *Studies in Divine Kingship in the Ancient Near East* (2nd ed.; Oxford, 1967), p. 144.

[237]Gray, *Krt Text*, p. 1; Gordon, *Ugaritic Literature*, p. 66.

[238]*ANET*^{3}, p. 143a. "Deported" in line 14 is a euphemism for "died"; Gray, *Krt Text*, p. 32. A number of scholars consider with Ginsberg the numerical forms as fractions; see Gordon, *Ugaritic Literature*,

The meaning of this passage is relatively clear. The entire "offspring" of Krt has perished. The king is the sole survivor. The disaster came about through "sickness," "pestilence," "calamity," and "sword." It has been suggested that "sword" may refer to a "local rebellion."[239] With the death of Krt's wife and progeny Krt is left as a surviving remnant without heirs to assure the succession of the throne.[240] But in Krt himself resides the potentiality to assure the continuity of the royal lineage:

Krt:296 For in my dream El granted,
297 In my vision the Father of Men,
298 Offspring should be born to Krt
299 Even a lad to the Servant of El.[241]

Thus the future life of the dynastic succession is assured through the surviving remnant Krt who is once more able to produce offspring. Krt

---

p. 67; G. R. Driver, Canaanite Myths and Legends (Edinburgh, 1956), p. 29; J. Aistleitner, Die mythologischen und kultischen Texts aus Ras Schamra (2nd ed.; Budapest, 1964), p. 89. Gray, Krt Text, p. 32, on the other hand, believes that this interpretation must be a gross exaggeration of Krt's offspring and suggests that these forms are numerals referring to successive years of ages of Krt's children which are used to emphasize the prosperity of Krt in his offspring in order that the disaster is made the more poignant. Accordingly, only line 20 speaks of the destruction of Krt's offspring: "At seven, lo! they fell one after the other by the sword." Ibid., p. 11.

[239]Gray, Krt Text, p. 33.

[240]Few consider the Krt text as a cultic myth, namely S. Mowinckel, I. Engnell, and B. Reicke. The "historical interpretation" of the text is the common view supported by C. Virolleaud, R. Dussaud, C. F. A. Schaeffer, A. Lods, W. F. Albright, W. Baumgartner, R. de Vaux, O. Eissfeldt, J. Pedersen, H. L. Ginsberg, J. Aistleitner, G. R. Driver and others. Gray, Krt Text, p. 3, states that "the main impression given by the first Krt tablet is that here we are more in touch with sober history" than in some other parts of the Krt text.

[241]Gray, Krt Text, p. 18.

is the carrier of the future of his name and dynasty.[242] In short, the remnant motif appears in the Krt text in connection with the death and life problem. The remnant Krt is the carrier of life for his own offspring through which at the same time the dynastic succession is assured.

The mythological texts of the Baal and Anath Cycle contain passages which contain the remnant motif. For the sake of convenience the story of the first thirty-seven lines of Tablet VI may be briefly summarized: The goddess Anath is filled with yearning for the god Baal, as a mother beast for her young. She seizes Mot, Baal's son born by a heifer, by his clothes and demands that Mot restore Baal to her. After observing what a difficult thing Anath is asking of him, Mot explains that he has searched every hill and mountain in quest of Baal, but that life has become extinct and when finally he met Baal at the Elysian fields he swallowed him as a wild beast swallows a kid. Anath, in turn, searches for Baal, her brother, day after day, month after month as the sun scorches the earth and rain is withheld. Anath bides her time. Then, encountering Mot again, she attacks him savagely and slays him.

49:II:31-37 She seizes the Godly Mot--
    With sword she doth cleave him.
With fan she doth winnow him--
    With fire she doth burn him.
With hand-mill she grinds him--
    In the field she doth sow him.
Birds eat his _remnants_
    Consuming his _portions_
Flitting from remnant to remnant.[243]

---

[242]J. Pedersen, "Die KRT Legende," _Berytus_, 6 (1941), 64: "Der Hauptinhalt der Legende ist die Sicherung der Dynastie durch Nachkommenschaft." Gray, _Krt Text_, pp. 2-3, points out that the permanence of the dynasty of Krt is no less vital than that of his own offspring.

[243]Ginsberg, in _ANET_^{3}, p. 140b.

It is advisable to give the transliteration of lines 35-37, which contain the crucial term šir three times, because the translations of these lines vary at two significant points among scholars:

49:II:35 tdrʿnn širh . ltikl
36 ʿṣrm mnth . ltkly
37 npr [š]ir . lšir . yṣḥ

C. H. Gordon translated these lines in 1949 as follows:

49:II:35 In the fields she plants him
So that the birds do not eat his flesh
Nor anyone destroys his portion
Flesh calls to flesh.[244]

However, there seems to be a growing consensus to translate the noun šir in this passage as "remnant."[245] Furthermore, the "l" in lines 35 and 36 should be taken in the negative sense of la[246] as in Gordon's rendering, because it seems to be required by the context. Mot somehow comes to life again.[247] If these suggestions are correct--and one cannot be absolutely sure about them--then it would seem that the remaining parts of the mutilated corpse of Mot were sown into the field, were not destroy-

---

[244]Gordon, Ugaritic Literature, p. 45.

[245]See Driver, op. cit., p. 111 n. 13; Aistleitner, op. cit., p. 20; idem, Wörterbuch der ugaritischen Sprache (Berlin, 1963), p. 299 No. 2569; A. Jirku, Kanaanäische Mythen und Epen aus Ras Schamra-Ugarit (Gütersloh, 1962), pp. 69-70; T. H. Gaster, Thespis (3rd ed.; New York, 1966), p. 221. This is reflected also in Gordon, UT, p. 425 No. 1338, who now leaves the question undecided whether to translate "remains/flesh."

[246]Both Gordon and Aistleitner make these lines negative; cf. UT, p. 425 No. 1338.

[247]Those who take the "l" as lu meaning "verily" have an almost insurmountable difficulty in accounting for the continuation of the plot in which Mot, who somehow came to life again, is still a major force. This is admitted by Ginsberg, ANET³, p. 140 n. 3.

ed or devoured, and presumably were the seed from which Mot comes to life again. The remnant motif in this instance would then also be connected with the death and life problem and the remnant represents that part from which new life springs forth.

The second passage in the Baal and Anath Cycle which has a bearing on the remnant motif at Ugarit comes from Text 76:I. G. R. Driver[248] summarizes the fragmentary lines 1-18 in the following way: Anath is ordered to fly over the hills and asked to announce to the host of heaven that rain will come again, for Baal, the Rider of the Clouds, will return to earth. He will give beautiful showers, so that "men" and "plants" will come to life and be saved. Anath follows her orders by making the announcement that Baal with life-giving rains will come to "the peoples" of the "earth" (ll. 15-16), i.e., to the remnant.

76:I:14 [And the virgin] Anath [answered],
15 [the sister-in-law] of rulers [cried]:
16 '[El Hadad will come among (?)] the peoples
17 '[and Baal] will return to the earth.
18 '. . . . . to the remnant.[249]

It is very unfortunate that this text is too fragmentary as to allow us to be completely sure on the translation of line 18 which contains the term <u>šir</u>. J. Aistleitner translates "<u>Fleisch</u>," but indicates that this

---

[248]Driver, <u>op. cit</u>., p. 19.

[249]<u>Ibid</u>., p. 117. The transliteration of Text 76:I:14-18 according to Gordon in <u>UT</u>, p. 182, is as follows:

76:I:14 [btlt] ʿnt
15 [ybmt] limm
16 [ ] llimm
17 [ ] larṣ
18 [ ] lšir

suggestion is doubtful by italicizing it.[250] C. H. Gordon is undecided rendering it with "flesh/remainder."[251] Driver, on the other hand, follows Brockelmann giving the meaning "remnant/residue" to *š*ir for Text 76:I:18 in his glossary.[252] The present writer is inclined to accept the suggestion that *š*ir in this instance means "remnant," because in ll. 10 and 19 the indication is given that "men die"[253] of the drought. Therefore, Baal, the Rider of the Clouds, is urged to return to earth with life-giving rain in order that the "remnant," i.e., the remainder of the peoples of the earth will not perish but come to life and be saved. If this interpretation is correct, then we find a calamitous drought as the cause of men's death. A "remnant" of the "peoples" on earth will be saved and continue to live by the removal of the threat to the life and existence of man. Thus we can observe again the inextricable interrelationship between the threat to the life and existence of man and the concern to preserve that life and existence of man. In the survival of a remnant this is achieved.

Let us summarize: The newly discovered flood story at Ras Shamra is too fragmentary to allow definite conclusions. It seems, however, fairly safe to assume that Atraḫasis with his wife represent the remnant that

---

[250]Aistleitner, Die mythologischen und kultischen Texte aus Ras Schamra, p. 53.

[251]Gordon, Ugaritic Literature,p. 49. In his Ugaritic Handbook (AnOr, 25; Rome, 1947), p. 271 No. 1903, he gives "flesh/remnant" for Texts 49:II:35, 37, and 76:I:18. However, see the indefinite remarks in UT, p. 487 No. 2372.

[252]Driver, op. cit., p. 147.

[253]Gordon, Ugaritic Literature, p. 49; Driver, op. cit., p. 117.

survives the great flood and that Atrahasis is bestowed with "life like the gods." The remnant motif appears in the "Legend of King Krt" in connection with the extermination of the royal house of Krt, leaving him as the sole survivor. The disastrous death of Krt's family was brought about through "sickness," "pestilence," "calamity" and "sword." The death and life problem is at the core of the Krt text. Krt, on the one hand, is the woeful survivor of the royal family without heir or progeny; he is, on the other hand, the remnant through whom the life and existence of the dynasty are assured, because of the ability to produce new offspring. Thus he, the remnant, secures the future of his dynasty. The remnant motif is here at the center of the death and life problem, the motif of progeny, and royal ideology. The mythological Baal and Anath Cycle again uses the remnant motif in connection with the death and life problem. "Men" on earth die, because of lack of rain. The calamitous drought comes to an end when Baal returns with life-giving rain, which saves the "remnant" of men and preserves human life and existence on earth. Thus the remnant motif appears when life and existence are threatened with destruction. The future of human life and existence is guaranteed through the survival of a remnant.

E. The Remnant Motif in Egyptian Texts

The remnant motif is a striking theme in the Egyptian myth of "The Book of the Divine Cow."[254] This work is of importance also for

---

[254]This work is one of three independent mythological monuments from Egypt known to date, see Siegfried Schott, "Die älteren Göttermythen," Ägyptologie: Literatur, ed. by B. Spuler (Handbuch der Orientalistik; Leiden, 1952), I, 69. The most recent comprehensive study is

Egyptian religion,[255] because in some sense it is the equivalent of the Mesopotamian flood story.[256] In this myth appears for the first and only time in Egyptian records the motif of the destruction of the human race and its salvation.[257] The oldest extant version of the Book of the Divine Cow appears on Shrine I of Tut-Ankh-Amon, but the longer versions are known from the tombs of Seti I, Ramses II, Ramses III and Ramses IV. Thus its date would go back to the fifteenth century B.C. John A. Wilson, however, believes on internal grounds that this myth "followed an older original."[258] The likely suggestion has been advanced that this work transposes actual historical events of revolutionary changes from the end of the Fifth and Sixth Dynasties (ca. 2200 B.C.) into the world of the gods, transforming the incidents into a rebellion of mankind against the sun god Re.[259]

---

by Alexandre Piankoff, The Shrines of Tut-Ankh-Amon, ed. by N. Rambova (New York, 1955), pp. 26-34; full translations or translations of parts are given by G. Roeder, Urkunden zur Religion des alten Ägypten (Jena, 1915), pp. 142-56; H. Ranke in ATAT², pp. 3-5; A. Erman, The Ancient Egyptians. A Sourcebook of their Writings, transl. by A. M. Blackman (New York, 1966), pp. 47-49; J. A. Wilson, ANET³, pp. 10b-11b; E. Brunner-Traut, Altägyptische Märchen (Düsseldorf-Köln, 1963), pp. 69-72.

[255]Schott, op. cit., I, 67; W. K. Simpson, "The Study of Egyptian Literature, 1925-1965," in AE, p. xxv.

[256]The Divine Cow's name appears in three spells in the Coffin Texts as the "Great Flood," see A. de Buck, The Egyptian Coffin Texts (Oriental Institute Publications, 49; Chicago, 1938), II, 25, 34; Brunner-Traut, op. cit., p. 266. For more information on the motif of the cow in Egyptian religion, see H. Bonnet, "Kuh, Reallexikon der ägyptischen Religionsgeschichte (Berlin, 1952), pp. 402-405.

[257]Eberhard Otto, "Die Religion der Ägypter," Religionsgeschichte des Alten Orients, ed. by B. Spuler (Handbuch der Orientalistik; Leiden, 1964), VIII, 41, says that this is "ein beinahe unägyptischer Gedanke."

[258]ANET³, p. 10b.

[259]Joachim Spiegel, "Göttergeschichten, Erzählungen, Märchen,

The Book of the Divine Cow describes the end of the reign of Re upon earth, the rebellion of mankind, the punishment of humanity, and the creation of heaven with the appointment of Thot, the moon god, to act as his deputy in the sky.

The story begins with the rebellion of mankind on earth:

> Then it came to pass that the majesty of Re, he who created himself . . . having been king of men as well as of gods. Then men began to devise evil plans against him.[260]

When Re had heard about these "evil plans" of conspiracy on the part of men, he convened the divine assembly asking the gods of their opinion with regard to the action that should be taken against the human race. Nun, the Watery Abyss, suggested that the Eye,[261] i.e., the sun eye of Re, should be sent in the form of Hathor against those who scheme against Re. Man in the meantime learned of the intended action and escaped to the desert land. But there they were caught by the goddess Hathor.

> Then this goddess came back after having killed men in the desert land.
> Then the majesty of this god [Re] said:
> Welcome in peace, O Hathor, thou hast accomplished (that) for which I came.
> Then this goddess said:
> As true as thou livest, I overpowered men, it was sweet for my heart.

Fabeln," Ägyptologie: Literatur, ed. by B. Spuler (Handbuch der Orientalistik; Leiden, 1952), I, 124; Brunner-Traut, op. cit., p. 266. This is the general period when other references to man's rebelliousness and the god's punishment of man appear, see ANET[3], pp. 417; 9; R. Anthes, "Mythology in Ancient Egypt," Mythologies of the Ancient World, ed. by S. N. Kramer (Garden City, N. Y., 1961), p. 18.

[260] Piankoff, op. cit., p. 27.

[261] Ibid.; cf. H. Bonnet, "Sonnenauge," Reallexikon der ägyptischen Religionsgeschichte (Berlin, 1952), pp. 733-34.

Then the majesty of this god said:
I shall have power over them as king by diminishing their number.[262]

This translation assumes that Re can rule mankind provided their number is reduced. Thus mankind was partially destroyed. This reflects a change of mind on the part of Re who had at first planned to destroy mankind completely. No reason is advanced for this sudden change. Now he attempts to stop Hathor from totally annihilating mankind. He orders that a beer-mash should be brewed to resemble "the blood of men."

Then the majesty of Re, king of Upper and Lower Egypt, went out with these gods to see this beer.
And when the earth was light for the killing of men by this goddess, in the dawn when they went South, the majesty of Re said:
It is good indeed, I shall protect men from her!
Re said:
Carry it to the place where she intends to kill men.[263]

The order is given to pour the beer on the fields.

When the goddess came in the morning, she found (the land) inundated and her face looked beautiful in (the beer).
Then she drank, and it was pleasant for her heart.
She became drunk and failed to recognize men.[264]

Hathor returned and Re addressed her thus:

Is there a burning pain of sickness?
And the period of sickness came into being.
Then the majesty of Re said:
As true as I live, my heart is weary to remain with them. I keep on killing them to the last one—the small remainder is not my gift!
The gods who were in his following said:
Be not disappointed, be not weary. Thou hast power over all thou wishest.[265]

---

[262] Piankoff, op. cit., p. 28.

[263] Ibid.

[264] Ibid.

[265] Ibid., p. 29.

Re had decided totally to destroy the human race. When a partial destruction had taken place, Re changed his mind and prevented Hathor from further destructive action. He believed that a diminished human race would be easier to rule, but a "small remainder" of mankind is not his gift. Re had grown so weary in his good old age that he would have kept on killing even the diminished human race. But his gift is a complete, replenished human race and not "the small remainder." Therefore, he creates the heavenly abodes and withdraws from ruling mankind.[266] The men on earth, in turn, repent of their rebellion and promise to defend the cause of Re.

A few additional remarks are in order. The destruction of mankind was not due to the caprice of the gods, but was caused by men's rebellion against their creator. The exact means of destruction is not made known in the texts. Speculation at this point is futile, but it must have been a slaughter in which blood flowed, otherwise the blood-resembling beer-mash would have been meaningless. The human race is saved from complete annihilation because of the intervention of the god of Upper and Lower Egypt, Re. The "small remainder" of mankind contained all potentialities for renewal and growth and preserved the future life and existence of the human race.

Next we turn to the so-called "prophetic literature,"[267] which has

---

[266] Brunner-Traut, op. cit., p. 71.

[267] This is actually a misnomer. Contemporary Egyptologists regard "prophecy" in Egypt with great scepticism. The supposed schematic sequence of doom and salvation in Egyptian "prophecy," said to have been taken over by Israel, was first propounded by Eduard Meyer, Die Israeliten und ihre Nachbarstämme (Halle, 1906), pp. 451-55 and accepted by Hugo Gressmann, Der Messias, ed. by Hans Schmidt (Göttingen, 1926), pp. 417ff.;

been designated more properly as "Auseinandersetzungsliteratur."[268] In

two different texts the remnant motif occurs with reference to a remnant ✓

of Egypt. The "Prophecy of Neferti,"[269] formerly designated as the

"Prophecy of Nefer-rohu,"[270] dates from the first king of the Twelfth

Dynasty, Amen-em-het I (ca. 1991-1962 B.C.).[271] That this "prophecy" is

not a prophecy in the regular sense of the term, but a vaticinium post

idem, "Foreign Influences in Hebrew Prophecy," JThS, XXVII (1926), 241ff.;
J. H. Breasted, The Dawn of Conscience (Chicago, 1933), pp. 363ff.; A.
Bentzen, Introduction to the Old Testament (Copenhagen, 1948), I, 258-59;
Th. J. Meek, Hebrew Origins (2nd ed.; New York, 1960), p. 181. However,
S. Herrmann "Prophetie in Israel und Ägypten," SVT, IX (1963), 48, has
shown that this view is based on a limited sample of Egyptian texts.
H. Bonnet, "Prophezeiung," Reallexikon der ägyptischen Religionsgeschichte
(Berlin, 1952), pp. 608-609, rejects such a Gattung. See Appendix, p. 465.

[268]This term was coined by Eberhard Otto in W. Helck and E. Otto,
Kleines Wörterbuch der Ägyptologie (Berlin, 1956), p. 206, and has been
accepted by Herrmann, op. cit., p. 62. Despite the translation of materials entitled "Egyptian Oracles and Prophecies" in ANET[3], pp. 441-49, the
volume on Egyptian literature in the series of the Handbuch der Orientalistik contains no treatment of "Prophetische Literatur," but what is
so designated by some is dealt with in an essay by Eberhard Otto entitled
"Weltanschauliche und politische Tendenzschriften," Ägyptologie: Literatur, ed. by B. Spuler (Handbuch der Orientalistik; Leiden, 1952), I,
111-19.

[269]The text was published by W. Golénischeff in 1913. A. H. Gardiner, "New Literary Works from Ancient Egypt," JEA, I (1914), 101-106,
studied and translated the text. Other translations and discussion are
found in Erman, op. cit., pp. 110-15; H. Ranke in ATAT[2], pp. 46-48; J. A.
Wilson in ANET[3], pp. 444-46; G. Posener, Littérature et politique dans
l'Égypte de la XIIe dynastie (Paris, 1956), pp. 27-60; S. Herrmann,
Untersuchungen zur Überlieferungsgestalt mittelägyptischer Literaturwerke
(Berlin, 1957), pp. 37-48. See Appendix, p. 465.

[270]G. Posener has convincingly shown that the name of the author is
not Nefer-rohu but Neferti as one of the seventeen new ostraca, ostracon
Turin 9596, indicates Revue d'Egyptologie, VIII (1951), 171-74. This new
reading of the name has been adopted by Herrmann, SVT, IX (1963), p. 48
n. 5; Simpson, op. cit., p. xxx; Helmer Ringgren, Israelite Religion
(Philadelphia, 1966), p. 257, and others.

[271]Inasmuch as the ending of this composition predicts the rise
of Amen-em-het I (1991-1962 B.C.) and the reestablishment of happy de-

eventum description must be kept in mind.[272] G. Posener emphasizes that its character is that of a work of political propaganda on behalf of the founder of the Twelfth Dynasty.[273] The uniqueness of this work for the remnant motif lies in the fact that it refers to a remnant of Egypt. Lines 23-26 read as follows:

> The land is completely perished, (so that) no remainder exists, (so that) not even the black of the nail survives from what was fated. This land is (so) damaged (that) there is no one who is concerned with it, no one who speaks, no eye that weeps. How is this land? The sun disc [Aton] is covered over. It will not shine (so that) people may see. No one can live when clouds cover over (the sun).[274]

---

liverance at a time of order, it must have been composed during the reign of this king, despite the story in the text which purports to relate how king Snefru of the Fourth Dynasty was told the downfall of the Old Kingdom and the reestablishment of a period of well-being under Amen-em-het I, see Herrmann, SVT, IX (1963), p. 53; Erman, op. cit., p. 111.

[272]The majority of scholars agree that this is not a real prophecy. Already Gardiner, op. cit., p. 100, distinguished between prediction and prophecy, the former describes foretelling of the future and the latter described in elevated and political style certain social and political evils. A. von Gall, Βασιλεία τοῦ θεοῦ. Eine religionsgeschichtliche Studie zur vorkirchlichen Eschatologie (Heidelberg, 1926), p. 54, was probably the first to designate the "Prophecy of Neferti" as a vaticinium post eventum. Posener, Littérature et politique . . ., pp. 28-29, says that this work is not a "prediction authentique," but a "prophetie post eventum." Herrmann, SVT, IX (1963), pp. 52, 60, makes the point that the Egyptian expectations of salvation are largely vaticinia ex eventu, including the "Prophecy of Neferti." Cf. Ringgren, op. cit., p. 257; Warne, op. cit., p. 21.

[273]Posener, op. cit., p. 60. S. Herrmann, Die prophetischen Heilserwartungen im Alten Testament (BWANT, 5. Folge Heft 5; Stuttgart, 1965), p. 35 n. 97, evaluates this composition as "eine eigene Form der Huldigung des regierenden Herrschers durch Kreise von Gelehrten und Schreibern . . ., die aus eigener Initiative und nicht auf Befehl handelten."

[274]$ANET^3$, p. 445a; cf. Müller, op. cit., pp. 7-8; Warne, op. cit., p. 21.

S. Herrmann[275] has pointed out that the second paragraph is composed in the form of a litany which speaks in the first part of disturbances in the microcosm of human feelings and expressions and in the second part of disturbances of the macrocosm of natural forces which threaten to put an end to life. The first paragraph, however, in which the reference to the "remnant" (d3.t.) occurs belongs to the "Gattung des Vorwurfs,"[276] which is directed against the creator god Re. This would mean that a removal of the present catastrophic state of affairs in the political sphere is related to the ordering of the cosmic sphere. A change for the better of the present political condition will be brought about when Re reestablishes the order of his creation. That "no remainder exists" is obviously an overstatement to indicate the severity of the situation. Though no explicit statement is given with regard to the means of destruction, there are indications in this "prophecy" that point to internal strife, perhaps of civil war,[277] and external threats from the Asiatics and Libyans.[278] In addition there have been natural disorders.[279] Despite all of this a "happy end" is assured. Thus a "remnant" survived through whom the future of Egypt was guaranteed.

The only other reference to a remnant of Egypt is in the 'Potter's

---

[275]Herrmann, Untersuchungen . . ., p. 40.

[276]Ibid., pp. 22-23: "genre of accusation."

[277]ANET³, p. 445b ll. 44-45.

[278]Ibid., p. 446a ll. 63-64.

[279]Ibid., p. 445a ll. 27-30.

Oracle."[280] This too must be considered as a vaticinium post eventum.[281] The presently extant Greek papyrus fragments date from the second and third century A.D.[282] But there is reason to believe that they are based on an underlying Egyptian text whose kernel goes back to one of the Amenhotep's[283] of the Eighteenth Dynasty, i.e., the sixteenth-fifteenth centuries B.C.[284] The pertinent lines read as follows:

I:16 But the hat[ed k]in[g] from Syria will occupy [. . .
17 [. . . . .] being present from [. . . . .
18 [. . . . .] he himself from the wicked ones to Egypt and [. . .
19 [. . . . .] will later be depopulated
20 [. . . . .] . . . . .
21 [. . . . .] . . . . .
22 [. . . fe]w of the inhabitants of Egypt will remain over . . .[285]

---

[280]For original publication, see ATAT², p. 49. The Greek text is again published by U. Wilcken, "Zur ägyptischen Prophetie," Hermes, 40 (1905), 546ff.; and von Gall, op. cit., pp. 70ff. The so-called "Potter's Oracle" was first identified by U. Wilcken, "Zur ägyptisch-hellenistischen Litteratur," Aegyptica. Festschrift für Georg Ebers zum 1. März 1897 (Leipzig, 1897), pp. 142-52, W. Struwe, "Zum Töpferorakel," Aegyptus: Roccolta di scritti in onore di Giacomo Lumbrosa (Milano, 1925), pp. 127-35, makes it likely that Ptolomy III Euergetes (246-221 B.C.) is the promised king.

[281]Von Gall, op. cit., p. 74; Warne, op. cit., p. 21; Herrmann, SVT, IX (1963), pp. 50, 62.

[282]ATAT², p. 49; Siegfried Morenz, "Die ägyptische Literatur und die Umwelt," Ägyptologie: Literatur, ed. by B. Spuler (Handbuch der Orientalistik; Leiden, 1952), I, 205 n. 4.

[283]The Greek form of this name is Amenopis, which appears twice in this text in l. 17 and the subscription, ATAT², p. 50.

[284]Von Gall, op. cit., p. 74, suggested Amenhotep III (ca. 1417-1379 B.C.), but it remains questionable whether one can be that exact. Cf. H. Ranke in ATAT², p. 49; Herrmann, Die prophetischen Heilserwartungen . . ., p. 40 n. 114.

[285]The present writer based his translation on the Greek text as collated by von Gall, op. cit., p. 70. For a German translation, see ATAT², p. 50, cited by Müller, op. cit., p. 8, and Warne, op. cit., p. 21.

Despite the fragmentary nature of the text it is clear that the depopulation of Egypt which will lead to a mere remnant of a few Egyptian inhabitants is caused by a political catastrophe. But in this text too there is a close relationship between political and natural events. Almost simultaneously with the political restoration the empty Nile will again be filled, winter will again run its normal course, and the winds will blow again.[286] The fact that a time of bliss follows the period of doom indicates that even through the small remnant the future existence and life of the nation are secured and that it possesses all potentialities for renewal.

A religious text in the form of a memorial prayer directed by a father and a son to the god Amon-Re contains the remnant motif. Nakht-Amon, the son of an artisan of the Nineteenth Dynasty, had acted impiously with respect to a cow and was taken with a serious illness which threatened his life. But happily he recovered from the malady.

> The Lord of Thebes does not spend an entire day angry. As for his anger--in the completion of a moment there is no remnant, and the wind is turned about in mercy for us, and Amon has turned around with his breezes.[287]

The remnant motif appears here in connection with the physical sickness of an individual. The "remnant" which had not remained except for the mercy of the deity refers to the individual Nakht-Amon.

The final category of Egyptian literary records in which the rem-

---

[286] ATAT[2], p. 50 col. II:8:14; cf. U. Wilcken, "Zur ägyptischen Prophetie," Hermes, 40 (1905), 554f.

[287] J. A. Wilson in ANET[3], p. 380b; cf. Erman in AE, p. 311; B. Gunn, "The Religion of the Poor in Ancient Egypt," JEA, III (1916), 85.

nant motif is present are historical texts. No annals have yet been uncovered from the sands of Egypt, except the so-called "war annals"[288] of Thutmose III (ca. 1490-1436 B.C.). Egyptologists assume that at least since the First Dynasty annals were prepared at the royal court, in which such events as military campaigns, construction of structures and temples, etc., were recorded, because there are "more or less complete excerpts"[289] preserved from these annals on a number of monuments. Werner E. Müller[290] claims that the remnant motif appears "only very seldom" in Egyptian historical texts. He cites only two examples, giving the impression that thereby all occurrences are exhausted. Then he draws the conclusion that the Egyptians were not interested in the remnant motif. The following discussion will show that Müller's investigation is inadequate and that his conclusions are erroneous.

During a punitive southern Palestinian campaign, Uni, commander of the armies of Pepi I (ca. 2375 or 2350 B.C.), inflicted a total defeat on a rebellious vassal.

> While a full half of this [Egyptian] army was (still) on the road, I arrived, I caught them all, and every backslider among them was slain.[291]

---

[288]H. Grapow, Studien zu den Annalen Thutmosis des Dritten und zu ihnen verwandten historischen Berichten des neuen Reiches (Berlin, 1949). But Grapow points out on p. 7 that the designation "annals" is ill-chosen and that a proper designation would be "Siegestaten."

[289]E. Otto, "Annalistik und Königsnovelle," Ägyptologie: Literatur, ed. by B. Spuler (Handbuch der Orientalistik; Leiden, 1952), I, 141.

[290]Müller, op. cit., pp. 6, 14. He cites one example from Seti I and one from Merneptah.

[291]ANET³, p. 228b; cf. ARE, I, 144.

A victory hymn of Pepi I, which describes the safe return of the Egyptian army from various Asiatic campaigns, makes reference to the fact that the troops of the Sand-Dwellers were killed by tens of thousands while at the same time a multitude of living captives was taken. Then it is added that even all support of life was destroyed:

> This army returned in safety,
> After it had cut down its [the land's] fig trees
> and its vines.[292]

Thus the Egyptians employed the same practice that is known also from Sumerian, Hittite, and Assyrian records.

The Carnarvon Tablet I from Thebes, which dates from the time contemporary to the events,[293] contains a record of the war against the Hyksos under Kamose just before 1570 B.C.[294] The report describes the following with regard to the defeat of Teti, son of Pepi, a sympathizer of the Hyksos:

> When the day broke, I [Kamose] was on him as if it were a falcon. When the time of the breakfast had come, I attacked him. I broke down his hills, I killed his people, and I made his wife come down to the riverbank. My soldiers were as lions are, with their spoil, having serfs, cattle, milk, fat and honey, dividing up their property, their hearts gay.[295]

The indication is that the people of Teti were destroyed, but Teti's spouse was spared to be a captive. Besides her, there was a remnant of the people carried off as slaves.

---

[292] ANET[3], p. 228a.

[293] A. H. Gardiner, "The Defeat of the Hyksos by Kamose," JEA, III (1916), 97; Erman in AE, p. 52; Wilson, ANET[3], p. 232a.

[294] The present writer cites the dates of Simpson in AE.

[295] ANET[3], p. 233a; cf. Gardiner, op. cit., p. 108; AE, pp. 53-54.

After Ahmose I (ca. 1570-1546 B.C.) had driven the Hyksos out of Egypt, he invaded Nubia, but was recalled to quell successive rebellions.[296] At times the revolters were carried off[297] and on one occasion they were totally annihilated.

> Then came that fallen one, whose name was Teti-en; he had gathered to himself rebels. His majesty slew him and his servants, annihilating them.[298]

No remnant was left of these revolters.

Thutmose I (ca. 1525-1512 B.C.) defeated in his second year the Nubians, conquering their land as far as the Third Cataract.

> He hath overthrown the chief of the Nubians; the Negro is helpless defenseless in his grasp . . ., there is not a remnant among the Curly-Haired, who come to attack him; there is not a single survivor among them.[299]

Remnant terminology has been explicitly employed to express the utter destruction of the Nubians.

The so-called "Annals" of Thutmose III (ca. 1504-1450 B.C.), which are actually not real annals but an account of victories[300] granted to Thutmose III by Amon-Re, contain many lists of plunder and booty carried off by the Egyptians from their vanquished enemies. When Megiddo was captured and destroyed at ca. 1468 B.C. 2,503 people consisting of officers, prisoners of war, male and female slaves, and children were

---

[296] ARE, II, 8.

[297] ARE, II, 5.

[298] ARE, II, 9.

[299] ARE, II, 30.

[300] Grapow, *op. cit.*, p. 7.

carried off.[301] This must be considered a remnant, because after this disaster Megiddo probably lay in ruins for decades. Lists of booty that mention captives are included in references to a number of other cities which were destroyed.[302] The report of the campaign against the land of Naharin ends with the following words:

> I captured all their people, carried off as living prisoners, . . . I took the very sources of life, (for) I cut down their grain and felled all their groves and all their pleasant trees. . . . I destroyed it. . . .[303]

Some cities were destroyed by fire.[304] The destruction of the sources of life, i.e., grain, groves, orchards, and trees,[305] seems to have been a standard measure to prevent the possibility of quick repopulation. The "living prisoners" must in all liklihood be understood as a remnant. However, they do not seem to have been designated as a remnant in Egyptian historical texts. It appears that the term "remnant" was used only when the remainder of the enemy force was destroyed. A victory hymn of Thutmose III states:

> Cut down are the heads of the Asiatics, there is not a remnant of them [lit. their remnant is not]. Fallen are the children of their mighty ones.[306]

---

301 ANET[3], p. 237b; cf. G. E. Wright, "Discoveries at Megiddo, 1935-1939," The Biblical Archaeologist Reader, 2, ed. by D. N. Freedman and E. F. Campbell (Garden City, 1964), p. 230.

302 ANET[3], p. 238b.

303 ANET[3], p. 240a; cf. ARE, II, 258; Grapow, op. cit., pp. 59-60.

304 ANET[3], pp. 239a, 241b.

305 ANET[3], pp. 239a, 240a, 241b; ARE, II, 165, 215.

306 ARE, II, 264.

The same usage appears in the inscription to a victory relief by Seti I (ca. 1303-1290 B.C.) depicting a battle against bedouins of northern Palestine:

> He cuts off the head of the perverse in heart. . . . His majesty kills them all at one time, and leaves no heirs among them. He who is spared by his hand is a living prisoner, carried off to Egypt.[307]

This text states explicitly that "the perverse in heart," i.e., the rebels, were destroyed with kith and kin and not even heirs were "left." But still the "living prisoners" constitute a remnant.

The famous report of the "Battle of Kadesh" by Ramses II (ca. 1290-1223 B.C.) against the combined Hittite forces gives an interesting note about the Hittite spoilers who had entered the Egyptian camp:

> Then the [Egyptian] recruits cut off the foe belonging to the vanquished chief of Kheta, while they (the foe) were entering into the camp, and Pharaoh's officers slew them; they left not a single survivor among them.[308]

Here too the remnant terminology appears to express the total defeat of the enemy.

The well-known "Israel Stela" of Merneptah (ca. 1230 B.C.) gives in the last poem a summary report of the triumph of the Egyptians over the surrounding peoples. The pertinent lines read:

> Yanoam is made as that which does not exist;
> Israel is laid waste, his seed is not.[309]

The enigmatic phrase "his seed is not" does not refer, as earlier interpreters thought, to the slaying of the male children of Israel by the

---

[307]ANET[3], p. 254a; ARE, III, 52; ATAT[2], p. 94.

[308]ARE, III, 155.

[309]ANET[3], p. 378a; cf. R. J. Williams in DOTT, p. 139; ATAT[2], p. 25.

Egyptians. J. H. Breasted cites five other examples in which this phrase is used in connection with any plundered and defeated people.[310] A. Erman states that this is a "metaphor for countries that have been laid waste."[311] It is obviously a "hyperbole for propaganda purposes,"[312] because subsequent events proved that Israel was far from desolate and without offspring.

Ramses III (ca. 1195-1085 B.C.) campaigned on a number of occasions against Libyan tribes. With regard to the Meshwesh the following is stated:

> The Meshwesh are hung up in their land, their plant is uprooted, there is not for them a survivor. . . . They say: 'Behold, we are subject to Egypt, its lord has destroyed our soul, forever and ever. . . .'[313]

The phrase "there is not for them a survivor" refers to the rebels whose "soul" has been destroyed. Their will for political independence had been broken along with the annihilation of those who sought political independence from Egypt. But there was a surviving remnant of the people. Other reports of Ramses III mention captives not infrequently.[314]

The pink granite stela of the Kushite Piankhi (ca. 740-708 B.C.)

---

[310]<u>ARE</u>, III, 258.

[311]<u>AE</u>, p. 278 n. 4; cf. H. Ranke in <u>ATAT</u>², p. 25 n. c. J. A. Wilson in <u>ANET</u>³, p. 378 n. 18, states: "The statement that the 'seed', i.e., offspring, of Israel had been wiped out is a conventional boast of power at this period." Cf. Jack Finegan, <u>Light from the Ancient Past</u> (2nd ed.; Princeton, 1959), p. 116.

[312]G. Ernest Wright, <u>Biblical Archaeology</u> (2nd ed.; Philadelphia, 1962), p. 71.

[313]<u>ARE</u>, IV, 23.

[314]<u>ARE</u>, IV, 29, 31, 56, 66, 202.

found at Napata describes among other things the battle against the Northerners:

> They /Kushite forces/ went forth against them; then they made a great slaughter among them, greater than anything. Their ships were captured upon the river. The remnant crossed over and landed on the west side before Peg-Peg. When the land brightened early in the morning, the army of his majesty crossed over against them. Army mingled with army; they slew a multitude of people among them; . . . a rout ensued among the remnant. They fled to the Northland, . . .[315]

The "remnant" designates in this stela the successively smaller parts of the beaten enemy force from the Northland. A final remnant was able to flee. This greatly disturbed Piankhi.

> Then his majesty was enraged thereat like a panther (saying): 'Have they allowed a remnant of the army of the Northland to remain? allowing him that went forth of them to go forth, to tell of his campaign? not causing their death, in order to destroy the last of them? I swear as Re loves me! . . . I will myself go northward, that I may destroy that which he has done, that I may make him turn back from fighting, forever'.[316]

This study of the Egyptian historical texts has shown that the remnant motif is much more common in them than has previously been recognized. The Egyptians pursued the goal of totally annihilating the rebels and enemy forces in order to achieve complete domination. The remnant terminology appears most frequently to express the notion that "no survivors" and "no remnant" remained. The practice of destroying all sources of life--grain, orchards, vineyards, groves--was employed as among the Sumerians, Hittites, and Assyrians. Yet a surviving remnant remained often in the form of deportees and vassals.

We may summarize our investigation of the remnant motif in Egyptian

---

[315] ARE, IV, 424-25.

[316] ARE, IV, 425-26.

literary texts in the following way. The remnant motif is present in mythological, "prophetic," and religious as well as historical texts. The remnant terminology is employed with reference to an individual, a group among a people, peoples, a nation, and mankind. The means of destruction when mentioned include physical illness, civil disorder, and war. In some cases it seems to be a combination of political and natural disorders. In texts other than historical ones a remnant is always saved. In historical texts, however, the explicit usage of the terms "remnant" or "survivor" designates as a rule the destroyed enemy or one that will be annihilated. The remnant terminology seems never to be employed with reference to the Egyptian forces. This seems to be due to the fact that the Egyptian records relate only victories. On the other hand, a remnant of the enemy survived in the "living prisoners" and the subjugated vassals. The myth of the Book of the Divine Cow speaks of a "small remnant" of the human race. Twice, explicit references are made to the "remnant" of Egypt. One of the "prophetic" texts contains the earliest Egyptian reference to a "remnant," dating to the twentieth century B.C. The remnant motif in Egyptian literary texts has both a negative and a positive aspect. Negatively, it expresses that no remnant or survivor remains, that all human life and existence has been annihilated; and, positively, it expresses the idea that in the surviving remnant the future life and existence of the human race, the Egyptian people, or a family are preserved and that this surviving entity contains all potentialities for renewal.

The Egyptians, Hittites, and Babylonians at times speak of a remnant of their own people. This idea is also present among the Hebrews to whom we must turn our attention next. Thus it is our task to examine in the remainder of this study the remnant motif in the relevant passages of the Israelite literature in the Hebrew Bible.

PART THREE

THE REMNANT MOTIF IN THE HEBREW BIBLE PRIOR TO ISAIAH OF JERUSALEM

This chapter attempts to investigate the appearance, development, and meaning of the remnant motif in the Hebrew Bible in passages which are considered earlier than Isaiah of Jerusalem. It is absolutely essential to gain an adequate understanding of the remnant motif in the earlier materials of the Hebrew Bible in order to be able to recognize its first explicit appearance, to trace its development during its long history, and to delineate the manifold connections of this motif in Israelite thought.

A. The Remnant Motif in Genesis

1. The Flood Story.--A characteristic motif of the ancient Near Eastern flood stories is that a man alone, or with his family, or with some companions, survives the flood[1] and that the future existence of mankind is preserved in this remnant.[2] It is striking that the Biblical

[1]This motif is, of course, not limited to the ancient Near Eastern deluge accounts, but appears to be a constituent part of the available flood stories around the globe. See the collection of flood stories from all continents in Theodor H. Gaster, Myth, Legend, and Custom in the Old Testament (New York, 1969), pp. 82-130; cf. E. Sollberger, The Babylonian Legend of the Flood (London, 1962), p. 11; W. E. Staples, "Epic Motifs in Amos," JNES, XXV (1966), 106-12.

[2]Supra, pp. 55-6, 71-2, 75ff.

flood story, which is ultimately connected with the Mesopotamian flood tradition,[3] explicitly refers to the remnant motif. Noah, the Biblical flood hero, is considered a remnant in the ancient Hebrew flood account according to Gen. 7:23b: "Only Noah was left [yiššā'ēr][4] and those

---

[3]The similarities of the extant ancient Near Eastern flood stories with the flood story in Genesis lead to the inevitable conclusion that a relationship exists between them. The earlier assumption of many scholars that the Biblical flood account is dependent upon Tablet XI of the Gilgamesh Epic (for instance Hermann Gunkel, Genesis [HAT, I/1; 7th ed.; Göttingen, 1967], p. LVIII: "We can prove that the flood saga is of Babylonian origin, for we possess Babylonian recensions.") is today no longer supported by an ever increasing number of scholars. The situation from the time of the "Babel-Bible controversy" in the first decades of this century has changed, because now are available a number of forms of Mesopotamian flood traditions, which make such a simple answer of dependence impossible. Among modern scholars, who reject a direct literary dependence of the Biblical flood account on the extant Sumerian or Akkadian versions, the following may be mentioned: Heidel, The Gilgamesh Epic and Old Testament Parallels, pp. 260-69; Schott und von Soden, Das Gilgamesch-Epos, p. 12 n. 17; von Rad, Genesis, pp. 119-20; Speiser, Genesis, pp. 54-55; Claus Westermann, Genesis (BKAT, I/1; Neukirchen-Vluyn, 1966), p. 67; D. Kidner, Genesis (Tyndale Old Testament Commentary; Chicago, 1967), pp. 95-97; M. H. Segal, The Pentateuch (Jerusalem, 1967), p. 30; Albright, Yahweh and the Gods of Canaan (New York, 1968), p. 98; Nahum M. Sarna, Understanding Genesis (New York, 1966), pp. 43-48. Cf. Hasel, AUSS, VIII (1970), 182-8. See Appendix, p. 466.

[4]Verbal forms of the remnant terminology occur not infrequently with individuals as well as with larger groups as is expected. The tradition of Noah as the "remnant" is reflected in Sirach 44:17:

> Noah was found perfect and righteous;
> in the time of wrath he was taken in exchange;
> therefore a remnant was left to the earth
> when the flood came.

Bruce M. Metzger, ed., The Apocrypha of the Old Testament. The Oxford Annotated Apocrypha. (New York, 1965), p. 187; Jack P. Lewis, A Study of the Interpretation of Noah and the Flood in Jewish and Christian Literature (Leiden, 1968), p. 21; F. Dreyfus, "Reste," Vocabulaire de théologie biblique, ed. by X. Léon-Dufour (Paris, 1962), col. 908.

that were with him in the ark."[5] In view of our earlier investigation in Chapter II, we are unable to follow Donald M. Warne's conclusion that "the Yahwist [in contrast to other ancient Near Eastern authors] has made the concept of the remnant an integral part of primitive history."[6] The remnant motif is also part of the "primitive history" of the Old Babylonian Atrahasis Epic. Since this is the case there is the likelihood that the histroical framework, i.e., the overall scheme of events--creation, rebellion, man's achievements, the flood--goes back to a Mesopotamian tradition[7] which closed with the story of the great flood of which the remnant motif is the key part. If this is correct, it would appear likely that the narrator in Genesis adopted this ancient tradition. In this

---

[5]There is a general consensus among scholars who subscribe to the Documentary Hypothesis or at least in some fashion to it, that this part of the text must be assigned to the Yahwist. Though J is dated most often in the era of David and Solomon, see Otto Kaiser, Einleitung in das Alte Testament (Gütersloh, 1969), pp. 75-76, or at times even down to around 800 B.C., see Fohrer, Introduction to the Old Testament, pp. 151-52, the tradition contained in the Genesis flood story is older as is indicated by the extant Sumerian and Akkadian flood accounts which date in their present form to ca. 1700-1600 B.C.

[6]Warne, "The Origin, Development and Significance of the Concept of the Remnant in the Old Testament," p. 45.

[7]It is an indisputable fact that the overall scheme of events as related in the Atrahasis Epic corresponds closely to the sequence of events in Gen. 1-11. This correspondence of sequences, however, can hardly be construed to indicate that in the latter we have a case of literary borrowing from the former, because the detail is so divergent as to discourage belief in direct literary dependence of one on the other. See A. R. Millard, "A New Babylonian 'Genesis' Story," Tyndale Bulletin, 18 (1967), 14-18; K. A. Kitchen, Ancient Orient and Old Testament (Chicago, 1968), p. 41. Yet the parallel in the overall sequence of events appears to point strongly into the direction that both accounts go back to a tradition which the Babylonians and Hebrews appropriated each in their own particular ways.

connection it is of no little importance for the understanding of the remnant motif that the tradition of the great flood treated world history from the same point of view, namely the deluge marks the end of one age of mankind and the beginning of another.[8] The remnant of mankind constitutes in the extant Sumerian, Babylonian, and Hebrew flood stories the crucial link which bridges man's past existence prior to the flood with his existence since the flood. The amazing fact is that the woeful remnant of the human race secured the future existence of that race. Thus we find that the ancient flood tradition exhibits a union of judgment and salvation. This basic unity of "salvation and doom" which Hugo Gressmann thought had disappeared long ago,[9] is to be seen still in the Israelite flood account as much as it is present in the older Atraḫasis Epic.

The concept of the history of man from creation to flood attested to both in the Babylonian Atraḫasis Epic and the Hebrew account of Gen. 1-9 has a bearing on the origin of the remnant motif in general and in Israelite thought in particular. Due to the agreement of the general sequence of events in both of these "primeval histories," it is no longer necessary or even possible to treat creation and flood separately.[10]

---

[8]S. H. Hooke, In The Beginning (The Clarendon Bible, VI; Oxford, 1947), p. 54.

[9]Gressmann, Der Ursprung der israelitisch-jüdischen Eschatologie, p. 232.

[10]Long before the parallel of the Hebrew primeval history in Gen. 1-11 appeared in the Babylonian Atraḫasis Epic, W. Wundt, Völkerpsychologie (Mythus und Religion, III; 3. Auflage; Stuttgart, 1923), VI, 290, had stated in his section about the "myths of the destruction of the world": "Die Weltuntergangssage bildet das mythologische Komplement zur Weltschöpfungssage." That this observation is correct is supported not

Claus Westermann has strongly and correctly emphasized that the narratives of the creation of the world and of man do not originally answer the intellectual question of how world and man originated, rather they answer the prior existential question which is concerned with the preservation of world and man.[11] If it is correct that creation and flood must be viewed together,[12] then the basic motif of the flood tradition, i.e., the decree to destroy man, derives from the consideration that the creating God or gods have the sovereign right to decree such an act as much as he or they had the right to create man. In other words, the creation of man leaves open the possibility of his destruction. In this sense the flood is the complement to creation in the history of primeval events. Westermann makes a further observation with regard to this complementary relationship:

> The correspondence [of creation and flood] and also the fairly same distribution of creation and flood stories means that man's knowledge concerning his creation and the creation of the world belongs together with his knowledge concerning the possibility of an end or a destruction which transcends the death of a single man as well as the temporal or spacial catastrophe. The catastrophe of the flood is concerned with the whole as the creation is concerned with the whole. It is part of being man . . . , that he is able to conceive such a possibility of total destruction. With it a completely new possibility enters into man's existence: <u>the continuation of existence on the basis of a salvation</u> (italics mine).[13]

---

only by the Genesis accounts of primeval history and explicitly by the newly recovered Babylonian Epic of Atraḫasis but also by the various other flood accounts. See Gaster, <u>Myth, Legend, and Custom</u>, pp. 84-130; Westermann, <u>Genesis</u>, pp. 69-70.

[11]Claus Westermann, "Der 'Mensch' im Urgeschehen," <u>Kerygma und Dogma</u>, 13 (1967), 231.

[12]See especially Sarna, <u>op. cit</u>., p. 55.

[13]Westermann, <u>Genesis</u>, pp. 72-73.

The unique event of the total annihilation of the existence of man in the flood actualized the possibility of a continuation of human existence through the salvation of a remnant. Thus the flood provided the complementary answer to the existential concern of man. The question of existence[14] refers to the past, to primeval times in order to secure and preserve that which exists. Thus creation gives an assurance for the continuation of human existence and life, but it leaves open the possibility of annihilation. In the story of the great flood the annihilation of man was actualized, but it provided at the same time an additional answer to the problem of existence: a remnant survived the flood. Man's continual existence is secured; human life is preserved for the future. It is obvious that the motif of the salvation of a remnant from the destruction of the flood contains the dual aspects of doom and hope. The aspect of doom comes to expression in the idea that for the moment it is but a meager and woeful remnant of the human race. All mankind has been destroyed, only a remnant remains. The corresponding aspect of hope comes to expression in the idea that the survived remnant contains all the necessary seeds of life for the continual existence of mankind and preserves human life and existence for the future. Thus the remnant motif links human existence in the past in an unbroken chain with human existence in the present and the future. The remnant motif of primeval history is firmly grounded in unique events of the past, such as creation and flood, but directing its full attention to the future. Stress is

---

[14]The placing of the existential question before the intellectual question does not in any way diminish the importance of the latter; rather this is a matter of priorities. The intellectual question seems to be subordinated to the existential question.

placed upon the fact that a remnant was actually preserved, that it survived the destructive cataclysm, and made possible the future existence of mankind. In this sense it must be stressed that the first appearance of the remnant motif in the ancient Mesopotamian flood tradition contains as a basic and fundamental constituent an innate relation to the future. One can say that it contains in a real sense an inherent future expectation, which in the later development of this motif in Israelite religion becomes enriched and further developed to a considerable degree.

It appears that certain conclusions present themselves with regard to the origin of the remnant motif. It is fairly certain that the remnant motif is neither of Israelite nor of Babylonian origin, but that both are already dependent on earlier traditions. The new evidence of the Mesopotamian sources indicates that the possibility of a remnant grew out of the death and life tension, namely the problem of existence. The remnant motif, therefore, originated in the remote past of man's existence in connection with the recognition of the possibility of continual existence on the basis of the salvation of some survivors in a unique catastrophe. The first explicit appearance of the remnant motif according to the presently available evidence is in connection with the Mesopotamian tradition of the great flood, which is reflected in the various ancient Near Eastern versions of the flood. The remnant motif of the Hebrew flood story, the earliest explicit reference to this motif in the Old Testament, ultimately goes back to this Mesopotamian source and may likely have been already a part of the tradition of the Hebrews before it found expression in written form.

The writer of the oldest Hebrew flood account has incorporated this event into his scheme of narratives as a unique "guilt-punishment-narrative"[15] bracketing it by his own theological insights.[16] The prologue of the flood story (Gen. 6:5-8) contains the motivation for the flood. Man's sinfulness and his punishment are related to each other as cause and effect. Gerhard von Rad had claimed that the motivation of the Hebrew flood account is a unique one "without dependence on older material."[17] This assumption must be called into question. The Sumerian flood story is too fragmentary[18] to allow definite conclusions with regard to the reason for the deluge,[19] but the Old Babylonian Atraḫasis Epic seems to offer an explanation. The "uproar" (rigmu) of mankind, which disturbs the sleep of the gods, has been interpreted as a metaphor of human wickedness.[20] If this interpretation is correct, then it would appear that the motivation of the Hebrew flood story has a pre-history[20a]

---

[15]Claus Westermann, "Arten der Erzählung in der Genesis," Forschung am Alten Testament, (TB, 24; München, 1964), pp. 53, 57. More recently Westermann, Genesis, p. 66, has correctly qualified his placing of the flood story to the Schuld-Strafe-Erzählungen by stressing that guilt and punishment are merely the background for its main theme, namely the salvation of one man from the destruction of all men. Thus Gen. 6-9 is actually a story of salvation.

[16]Von Rad, Genesis, pp. 112-14, 118-19.

[17]Ibid., p. 113.

[18]Supra, p. 52-3.

[19]Sarna, op. cit., p. 49; Ferdinand Dexinger, Sturz der Göttersöhne oder Engel vor der Sintflut? (Wiener Beiträge zur Theologie, XIII; Wien, 1966), p. 29.

[20]J. J. Finkelstein, "Bible and Babel," Commentary, 26 (1958), 436-37, Sarna, op. cit., p. 50; Pettinato, Orientalia, N. S. 37 (1968), 165-200.

[20a]See Appendix, p. 466.

too. Nevertheless, the Hebrew flood account contains the most explicit moral motivation. If the Hebrew narrator is dependent on the Mesopotamian tradition on this point, then he has transformed this motif to a considerable degree to make it fit his own purposes. It seems, however, to be correct that the words of the earliest author of the Hebrew flood story are preserved in the significant conclusion of the prologue in which it is stated that Noah found "favor" (ḥēn) with Yahweh (Gen. 6: 8).[21] Noah was chosen to survive the deluge because he was ṣāddîq (Gen. 7:1). This term which is normally translated with "righteous" expresses primarily "a relational concept."[22] This expression is much more comprehensive than a narrow forensic[23] or ethical[24] notion which is usually

---

[21]In none of the Babylonian versions, nor in the Sumerian recension, is any reason given for the divine favor to one individual. The Sumerian Ziusudra is the only flood hero who seems to have been thought of as pious as his acts of worship appear to indicate, see M. Civil, "The Sumerian Flood Story," in Lambert and Millard, Atra-ḫasīs, pp. 142-45, lines 147-48, 254-55; ANET[3], pp. 43-44; cf. Kramer, The Sumerians, p. 135. But regarding Ziusudra's piousness, Sarna, op. cit., p. 51, states: "Yet nowhere is it explicit or implied that his righteousness was the one and only cause of his favored treatment. On the contrary, one has constantly the impression that the moral reason played little part in the decision [of the gods to destroy mankind]."

[22]Walther Eichrodt, Theology of the Old Testament, transl. by J. A. Baker (Philadelphia, 1967), II, 394; cf. Ludwig Köhler, Old Testament Theology, transl. by A. S. Todd (Philadelphia, 1957), pp. 166-68; for further literature, see the bibliographies in E. R. Achtemeier, "Righteousness in the OT," IDB, IV, 85, and von Rad, OTT, I, 370 n. 1.

[23]Von Rad, Genesis, p. 116.

[24]Norman H. Snaith, The Distinctive Ideas of the Old Testament, Schocken Paperback (New York, 1964), pp. 59-78, 161-69.

associated with it would indicate. In the Hebrew Bible the <u>ṣāddîq</u> does justice to a relationship in which he stands. Every relationship brings with it certain claims, and the satisfaction of these claims, which issue from the relationship and in which alone the relationship can persist, is described by the term <u>ṣdq</u>. Thus Noah had no claim upon God on the basis of some intrinsic merit on his own, but he is <u>ṣāddîq</u> because he stands in right relation to God. By believing and trusting in God, Noah stands in the right relationship and thus finds favor in God's eyes.

The epilogue of the old Hebrew flood story (Gen. 8:20-22) relates how Noah built an altar and offered pleasing and acceptable sacrifices to Yahweh. The daring note struck in this epilogue is the gracious self-limitation of Yahweh's primitive holiness, his good will toward men, even though "the devisings of man's heart"[25] are still evil. This evidence of the overflow of divine grace prevents us from making the cultic act of sacrifice[26] regulate the new relationship of Yahweh to the remnant.[27] Noah's burnt offering is to be regarded as the occasion for

---

[25]Speiser, <u>Genesis</u>, p. 50.

[26]Umberto Cassuto, <u>A Commentary on the Book of Genesis</u>, transl. by I. Abrahams (Jerusalem, 1964), pp. 117-18, points out that the sacrifices offered by Noah were not sacrifices of atonement, nor to beseech protection and blessing, but are sacrifices of thanksgiving to the one who saved Noah from a terrible catastrophe; cf. Franz Delitzsch, <u>A New Commentary on Genesis</u>, transl. by S. Taylor (New York, 1899), p. 281.

[27]Concerning the grace of God von Rad, <u>Genesis</u>, p. 119, writes, "This grace is known in the incomprehensible duration of the natural orders in spite of continuing human sin. It is not yet, therefore, that grace which forgives sin . . ., but a gracious will that is above all mankind and is effective and recognizable in the changeless duration of nature's order."

God's gracious resolve[28] rather than a cultic act performed to restore a regular relationship between man and God.[29] The latter interpretation leads Werner E. Müller to a mistaken concept of Noah's "righteousness."

> It seems to follow that the ṣāddîq ["righteous one"] can derive a right to life from the knowledge of his ṣ^e^dāqāh ["righteousness"] and can demand his preservation from the coming catastrophe.[30]

Warne is correct in pointing out that the "righteousness" of Noah is not the basis for the claim of God's favor and grace.[31] It is God's grace and mercy which brings Noah safely through the judgment of the flood. Th. C. Vriezen states, "Here a prophetical element emerges again: in His mercy Yahweh saves a remnant."[32] In the final analysis God's will is seen to be "salvation and not doom."

Let us briefly recapitulate our discussion of the earliest explicit appearances of the remnant motif in the Hebrew Bible. The remnant

---

[28]So already A. Dillmann, Genesis, transl. by W. B. Stevenson (Edinburgh, 1897), I, 290.

[29]It is of significance that the purpose of the whole burnt offering, which is the type of sacrifice offered by Noah, was probably originally to express homage to God, see R. de Vaux, Studies in Old Testament Sacrifice (Cardiff, 1964), pp. 27ff.; H. H. Rowley, Worship in Ancient Israel (London, 1967), p. 120; Hans Joachim Kraus, Worship in Israel, transl. by G. Buswell (Richmond, Va., 1960), p. 115.

[30]W. E. Müller, Die Vorstellung vom Rest im Alten Testament, p. 43.

[31]Warne, op. cit., p. 49. It is also misleading to say as does Othmar Schilling, "'Rest' in der Prophetie des Alten Testaments," p. 146, that the salvation of the remnant takes place "auf Grund der Gerechtigkeit Noes." See Appendix, p. 466.

[32]Th. C. Vriezen, An Outline of Old Testament Theology (Newton, Mass., 1958), p. 44; cf. von Rad, Genesis, p. 119: ". . . the epilogue [to the flood] reveals God's grace and providence." G. E. Wright, "The Faith of Israel," The Interpreter's Bible, ed. by G. A. Buttrick (Nashville, 1953), I, 369.

motif has its origin in the remote past of man's existence in connection with the recognition of the possibility of the survival of man in a unique catastrophe which threatened the whole of mankind with destruction.[33] In the very early stages of ancient Israel, the main outline of the remnant motif has taken shape.[34] The Hebrew narrator surrounds the flood story with his own theological insights, so that the earliest explicit reference to the remnant motif in the Hebrew Bible appears in the context, language, and ideology of religion.[35] The remnant motif is from the start securely anchored in salvation history. Though the devisings of the heart of men are still evil, Yahweh's grace alone made possible the continuation of the existence of the human race by means of the righteous Noah and his family who constitute the remnant. Judgment and salvation, doom and hope, are intrinsically connected in this earliest

---

[33]O. Kaiser, "Rest," Biblisch-historisches Handwörterbuch, ed. by Bo Reicke and Leonhard Rost (Göttingen, 1966), III, col. 1592, states: "The problem of the possibility of a remnant grew out of the tension between faith in election and judgment." Our investigation has shown that the possibility of a remnant grew out of the death-and-life tension in connection with the existential concern of man's survival. Election plays a role in the earliest Biblical reference to a remnant only insofar as a man and his immediate family were chosen by God's grace to survive the great destruction. This election of Noah and his family does not, however, play any significant role in the later election tradition of Israel.

[34]Cf. G. H. Davies, "Remnant," A Theological Word Book of the Bible, ed. by Alan Richardson (2nd ed.; New York, 1962), 189; J. Nelis, "Rest Israels," Bibel-Lexikon, ed. by Herbert Haag (2nd ed.; Einsiedeln, 1968), col. 1474; E. Jenni, "Remnant," IDB, IV, 32; Preuss, Jahweglaube, p. 187.

[35]This is admitted by W. E. Müller, op. cit., pp. 43-44, and von Rad, OTT, II, 22. However, it is at the same time of great importance that the remnant motif in the Mesopotamian flood tradition does not appear in a political-civil sense. S. H. Hooke, Middle Eastern Mythology (Baltimore, 1963), p. 131.

explicit appearance of the remnant motif, but in the final analysis God's will is salvation and not judgment. As such the remnant motif is innately related to the future while at the same time human existence from the past aeon is linked with its existence in the present aeon.

2. The Abraham-Lot Tradition.--Attention has been drawn by a number of scholars to the remnant motif lying behind Abraham's intercession on behalf of Sodom (Gen. 18:22b-33).[36] The larger section (Gen. 18:17-33) to which this *intercessio* belongs represents an "enlarged announcement of judgment"[37] directed against the cities of the Plain, mainly Sodom, and not against Israel. The motif of the revelation of the judgment to the *one* who is not to meet its destruction himself, namely Abraham, appears also in the flood story of Gen. 6-9, where Noah escapes the judgment himself. The Sodom story was in its original form probably an old local tradition[38] which was adapted into the nucleus of traditions upon which Gen. 18 in its present form is dependent.[39] The antiquity of

---

[36] W. E. Müller, *op. cit.*, pp. 43-45; Schilling, *op. cit.*, pp. 147-48; Davies, *op. cit.*, p. 189; Jenni, *IDB*, IV, 32; Warne, *op. cit.*, pp. 53-59.

[37] Westermann, *Forschung am Alten Testament*, p. 72.

[38] Noth, *The History of Israel*, p. 121 n. 1; Hooke, *In the Beginning*, p. 82; Sarna, *op. cit.*, p. 143.

[39] Gunkel, *Genesis*, pp. 203-204, followed J. Wellhausen in denying Gen. 18:22b-33 to J and assigning it to the time of the prophets of the eighth and seventh centuries B.C. This position was challenged just as soon as it was propounded by Dillmann, *op. cit.*, II, 91-92; J. Köberle, *Sünde und Gnade* (München, 1905), p. 53; Otto Procksch, *Die Genesis* (KAT, I; Leipzig, 1913), pp. 123-25, who assign it to J. Martin Noth, *Überlieferungsgeschichte des Pentateuch* (Stuttgart, 1948), pp. 258ff., von Rad, *Genesis*, p. 209 and Kaiser, *Einleitung*, p. 81 also believe that it stems from the pen of the Yahwist. However, Eissfeldt, *OTI*, p. 211, states that this section "appears more like a secondary extension of the L narrative than as an original component of it." Fohrer, *Introduction*, pp.

Abraham's intercession is rather certain.[40]

An adequate interpretation of the remnant motif in Abraham's dialogue with Yahweh depends on the interpreter's understanding of the main issue of this colloquy. Werner E. Müller believes that the main point of this dialogue is the idea of the sifting of the righteous from the wicked.[41] O. Schilling follows this interpretation by adding that the sifting takes place by means of an interaction of ethico-religious values, which in turn demonstrate the inner connection between the remnant motif and ethics.[42] This line of reasoning falls short in that it does not recognize that the intercession itself is a unit to which Gen. 19:1-29 does not provide an answer.[43] The present writer believes that a proper interpretation of Abraham's intercession must begin by considering this section as an independent unit. When thus considered it becomes apparent that Abraham is not especially concerned to save Lot, nor even to save Sodom. Instead the entire colloquy unfolds a serious theological problem

---

131, 151, assigns it to the source stratum J, but notes that ultimately it derives from the oral tradition of G[1].

[40]The obvious but widely neglected parallel between Abraham's intercessory activity and that of similar material in extra-Biblical Mesopotamian sources indicates that intercessory prayers offered by a holy man on behalf of others was recognized in early Mesopotamian religion, so that the Hebrews could draw on this well developed heritage. The earlist forms of intercessory prayer date to Old Babylonian times. See John M. Holt, The Patriarchs of Israel (Nashville, 1964), pp. 163-67.

[41]W. E. Müller, op. cit., pp. 44-45.

[42]Schilling, op. cit., p. 147.

[43]With von Rad, Genesis, p. 209, against Speiser, Genesis, p. 135; cf. Warne, op. cit., pp. 53-54.

to which G. von Rad has drawn attention.[44] He protests against the interpretation of the intercession for Sodom which makes Abraham a "prophetic" intercessor,[45] just as he denies that it represents some sort of argument from collectivism to individualism, or that it reflects a concern to release the guiltless or preserve them; he takes this conversation as a "new interpretation of the concept of 'the righteousness of God'."[46] Should Yahweh destroy a community because the majority is "evil," or should not the few "righteous" avail for the salvation of the whole? This must not be construed as a problem of individualism, but one that dares to replace old collective thinking with a new one.[47] In the course of the conversation the capacity of God's gracious righteousness is more and more stretched until the astonishing answer is reached that even the very small remnant of ten "righteous" is more important in God's sight than a majority of wicked and is sufficient to stem the judgment. The answer that for the remnant of only ten righteous the city would be saved is sufficient for Abraham. To go beyond this questioning did not occur to him.[48] He was satisfied that God's ultimate purpose is not judgment and

---

[44]Von Rad, Genesis, pp. 207-208.

[45]So Procksch, Genesis, p. 116.

[46]Von Rad, Genesis, p. 208.

[47]Eichrodt, Old Testament Theology, II, 430 n. 1, points out that Gen. 18:24-32 turns the ancient view of collective liability upside down, "that instead of the sin of the few making the whole group culpable the righteousness of the few avails for the salvation of the whole." This needs to be qualified in the sense that the righteousness of Yahweh actually makes possible the salvation of the whole for the sake of the righteousness of the few.

[48]Warne, op. cit., p. 56; von Rad, Genesis, p. 209.

doom, but grace and salvation.[49]

There is in Abraham's intercession no basis for Müller's and Schilling's assertion of a sifting process in which the righteous are separated from the wicked. What we have, however, is Sodom as a pattern of a human community--not here expressly considered as outside the covenant people--for which God would use the same standard of judgment and salvation as he would for Israel. In an extremely revolutionary manner the old collective thinking, which brought the guiltless member of the guilty association under punishment, has been transposed into something new: the presence of a remnant of righteous people could have a preserving function for the whole. The conversation between Abraham and Yahweh is the product of independent reflection upon Yahweh's righteousness, which is demonstrated by the preserving function of the righteous.[50] The importance of Abraham's intercession for the development of the remnant motif lies in the aspect of the preserving function of the minority of the righteous remnant for the majority of the wicked. For the sake of the righteous remnant Yahweh would in his righteousness forgive the wicked city. This notion is widely expanded in the prophetic utterances of the Ser-

---

[49]It is not so much the "saving grace of the just," so Speiser, Genesis, p. 135, that brings about salvation in this narrative, but as Noth, Überlieferungsgeschichte, p. 259, explains ". . . es wird deutlich, dass die Menschen in dieser Welt nur durch freies Handeln Gottes selbst gerettet werden können, nicht durch irgendeine eigene Gerechtigkeit, mit der sie sich selbst und andere vor dem göttlichen Gericht bewahren könnten." Cf. von Rad, Genesis, p. 290; Warne, op. cit., p. 56; Marie-Louise Henry, Jahwist und Priesterschrift. Zwei Glaubenszeugnisse des Alten Testaments (Arbeiten zur Theologie, 3; Stuttgart, 1960), pp. 15ff.; Kaiser, Einleitung, p. 81.

[50]See von Rad, OTT, I, 394-95.

vant of Yahweh who works salvation "for many."[51]

The account of Gen. 19 relates the "unique event"[52] of the destruction of Sodom and Gomorrah by means of a natural catastrophe.[53] The cities and the plain were totally annihilated. The destruction included even "what grew on the ground" (Gen. 19:25). However, the goal of this narrative is not the destruction of the cities as such, but the salvation of Lot and his immediate family.[54] Lot and his two daughters constitute the sole surviving remnant. The salvation of this remnant is due to the grace of Yahweh and does not demonstrate an early appearance of "the doctrine of merit."[55] It should be noted that the salvation of Lot is neither attributed to his own righteousness nor to that of Abraham.[56]

---

[51]Isa. 53:5, 10; cf. Kurt Galling, Deutsche Theologie (Berlin, 1939), pp. 86ff.; von Rad, Genesis, p. 209; idem, OTT, I, 395; Warne, op. cit., p. 134.

[52]Westermann, Forschung am AT, p. 49.

[53]For a discussion of the physical aspects of the catastrophe, see F. G. Clapp, "Geology and Bitumens of the Dead Sea Area," Bulletin of the American Association of Petroleum Geologists (1936), 881-909; F. M. Abel, Geographie de la Palestine (Paris, 1938), II, 467-68; J. P. Harland, "Sodom and Gomorrah: The Location and Destruction of the Cities of the Plain," BA, V (1942), 17-32; VI (1943), 41-54; idem, "Sodom," IDB, IV, 395-97; "Sodom and Gomorrah," The Biblical World, ed. by Charles F. Pfeiffer (Grand Rapids, Mich., 1966), 543; Sarna, op. cit., p. 142.

[54]Westermann, Forschung am AT, p. 73.

[55]Sarna, op. cit., pp. 149-51, aruges that Lot was saved through the merit of Abraham. "The patriarch had established the principle that the wrathful judgment of God could be averted through the merit of an innocent nucleus; so God delivered Lot from the catastrophe through the merit of Abraham" (p. 150). We have seen above that the "merit" of an innocent nucleus, namely the few righteous in Sodom, was but the occasion for the demonstration of Yahweh's righteous mercy. To construe the statement that "God remembered Abraham" (Gen. 19:29) into a demonstration of "the doctrine of merit" is overinterpreting the implication of this phrase.

[56]Procksch, Genesis, p. 123: "Lot wird nicht kraft seiner Gerecht-

The ancient narrator underlines this fact by relating that this remnant was spared because Yahweh had "mercy on him" (Gen. 19:16). A comparison of the two "unique events" from which a remnant was saved, i.e., the flood and the destruction of Sodom, is necessary to illustrate the similarities and differences with regard to the remnant motif. In both cases the judgment was brought about by a natural catastrophe, here "brimstone and fire" (Gen. 19:24), there water; here as there it is a visitation of God, an intricate unity between judgment and salvation; here as there the salvation of a remnant is not due to merit on the part of the remaining survivors but to the grace of Yahweh. In Gen. 19, however, there is a remarkable emphasis on the motif of preserving life[57] and the motif of fleeing or escaping from destruction.[58] We have already had occasion to observe that the motif of preserving life is an essential part of the future aspect of the remnant motif. It is in this tradition, i.e., the Sodom story, where it has for the first time found explicit expression in the Hebrew Bible.[59]

---

igkeit, sondern durch Jahves Erbarmen gerettet." Von Rad, Genesis, p. 215: "When a man is delivered from judgment, it is a matter for God only."

[57]Gen. 19:17, 19, 20.

[58]Gen. 19:17, 19, 20, 22.

[59]The statement of Lot's daughters "There is not a man to come in to us" (Gen. 19:31) does not indicate an ancient myth about the origin of man (so A. Lods, "La caverne de Lot," Revue de l'histoire des religions, 95 [1927], 204-219) nor is it a fragment of a myth of the destruction of mankind (so S. H. Hooke, "Genesis," in Peake's Commentary on the Bible, ed. by M. Black and H. H. Rowley [London, 1962], p. 191; idem, Middle Eastern Mythology [Baltimore, 1963], p. 141). It rather indicates that Lot and his daughters are the only surviving remnant of the catastrophe and that therefore a connubiality which would assure continuity of life for the family of Lot was no longer possible within the framework of the local group and that, as a result, the future life of the remnant was threatened.

3. The Jacob-Esau Tradition.--The remnant motif appears in connection with the threat to the existence of the clan of Jacob in the Jacob-Esau cycle of Genesis.[60] The background for the occurrence of the remnant motif lies in the rivalry between Esau and Jacob which developed into a family feud. The relationship between the two brothers deteriorated to such an extent that Jacob feared the complete extinction of his seed.[61] In order to preserve at least part of his offspring, Jacob divided his camp into two companies, so that if one company would be destroyed, the other company which is left (hanniš'ār) would be for an escaping (p^elêṭāh).[62] Jacob placed his complete hope for the future of his clan upon the p^elêṭāh In the prayer of Jacob[63] the narrator shows that for Jacob the hope of survival ultimately rested upon God:

> For it was you who said, 'I will be very good to you, and I will make your offspring like the sands of the sea which are too numerous to count.'[64]

D. M. Warne has pointed out that we have here an association of the remnant motif with the election tradition.[65] Implicit in Jacob's reminding

---

[60]See especially W. E. Müller, op. cit., p. 45; Warne, op. cit., pp. 57-58. Modern critical scholarship assigns the pertinent passages under discussion to the Yahwistic stratum of Genesis.

[61]Gen. 32:11(12).

[62]Gen. 32:8(9).

[63]Procksch, Genesis, pp. 184-85, argues convincingly against J. Skinner, Genesis (ICC; 2nd ed.; Edinburgh, 1930), p. 406, Gunkel, Genesis, p. 357, and others who consider it a later expansion of the Yahwistic narrative by pointing out that it is composed in the purest Yahwistic language. Cf. von Rad, Genesis, p. 313; Speiser, Genesis, p. 252.

[64]Gen. 32:12(13). Translation of Speiser, Genesis, p. 253.

[65]Warne, op. cit., p. 58.

Yahweh of the promise to the fathers is that Jacob had no righteousness or merit of his own to offer upon which he could claim the preservation of a remnant,[66] so that the salvation of the remnant depended solely upon the grace and mercy of Yahweh. This prayer, then, is extremely significant not only for connecting for the first time the election tradition,[67] i.e., the promise to the fathers, with the remnant motif, but it reveals once more that the remnant can escape judgment only through God's grace. With regard to the wider theological implications of Heilsgeschichte von Rad states aptly, ". . . God's preservation of Jacob is in a wider sense the same preservation that Israel as a whole experienced."[68] The narrator, thus, shows that the preservation of Jacob and his clan is a prototype of the preservation of Israel as a whole.

4. The Joseph Tradition.--The remnant motif is present at the focal point of the whole Joseph cycle, viz. the scene of recognition. Joseph confronts the fearful brothers by saying, "And God sent me before you to preserve for you a remnant [šᵉʾērîṯ][69] on earth, and to keep alive

---

[66]This is made explicit earlier in Jacob's prayer where he pleaded his unworthiness, vs. 10(11).

[67]H.-J. Zobel, "Ursprung und Verwurzelung des Erwählungsglaubens Israels," ThLZ, 93 (1968), 8, shows that the Exodus experience and the salvation of Israel from her pursuers does not constitute the birth of the election tradition because all aspects of this tradition are at this point already present. Cf. Samuel R. Külling, Zur Datierung der "Genesis-P-Stücke" (Kampen, 1964), p. 283.

[68]Von Rad, Genesis, p. 310.

[69]S. R. Driver, The Book of Genesis (Westminster Commentary; 14th ed.; London, 1943), p. 362, Skinner, op. cit., p. 487, H. E. Ryle, The Book of Genesis (Cambridge, 1914), p. 402, and Procksch, Genesis, p. 404, believe that שְׁאֵרִית here has the meaning of "descendants," since all the members of the family have been preserved. W. E. Müller, op. cit., p. 46, points out, however, that the translation "remnant" is indeed appropriate, since the tribe in narrowly escaping destruction is like a remnant which

for you many survivors [p^{e}lêṭāh]"[70] (Gen. 45:7).

There exists a considerable difference of opinion among critical scholars with regard to the source stratum to which this key text (Gen. 45:7) is supposed to belong. Gunkel,[71] supposes that vs. 7a belongs to J and 7b to E. Procksch and others assign all of vs. 7 to J,[72] while a number of scholars believe that vs. 7 belongs to E.[73] Against Gunkel's splitting up of this verse assigning it to two source strata it has been pointed out that š^{e}ʾērîṯ and p^{e}lêṭāh are combined as a formula elsewhere.[74] Those who assign vs. 7 to E take their main clue from the appearance of Elohim in vs. 7b. Yet it has been pointed out that the

---

is the bearer of hopes for the future existence. That this term has such connotations is shown in the Jacob-Esau narrative in which a participle of שׁאר is used in a substantive-like sense in connection with the survival of the whole clan of Jacob. The use of this noun emphasizes the peril the tribe had escaped. The conjunction of שְׁאֵרִית with פְּלֵיטָה indicates further the notion of escaping from destruction.

[70]We should possibly read with the LXX and Samartinanus פְּלֵיטָה instead of לִפְלֵיטָה, so that the infinitive לְהַחֲיוֹת receives an object, see BHK, p. 69. Herntrich, TDNT, IV, 202 n. 31, believes that this emendation commends itself, because "שְׁאֵרִית and פְּלֵיטָה are combined as a formula elsewhere." Ruppert, Die Josephserzählung der Genesis, p. 123, suggests that the Massoretes have changes פְּלֵיטָה into לִפְלֵיטָה, because the brothers did at that time not yet constitute a "great escaped band." This supposition would probably be correct, if they had operated with our literary-critical and traditio-historical methods.

[71]Gunkel, Genesis, p. 457; similarly Driver, Genesis, p. 362.

[72]Procksch, Genesis, p. 404; W. E. Müller, op. cit., p. 46; recently also von Rad, Genesis, p. 392; and Speiser, Genesis, p. 340.

[73]Skinner, Genesis, p. 486; Ryle, op. cit., p. 402; Herntrich, TDNT, IV, 202; Warne, op. cit., pp. 59-61; Ruppert, op. cit., pp. 115-16.

[74]Herntrich, TDNT, IV, 202 n. 31; cf. Ruppert, op. cit., p. 116.

solution is not that simple, because the change of divine names is an insufficient means for the distinction of source strata.[75] Those who support in one way or another the Documentary Hypothesis maintain that in Genesis the supposed E source strata does not use Yahweh.[76] Rather it is supposedly a direct witness to J.[77] On the other hand the supposed J source stratum is supposedly employing the term Elohim at times in Genesis and Speiser believes that "the present passage is especially well suited to just this kind of usage."[78] On this basis those who subscribe to the Documentary Hypothesis have to assign this verse to J. In addition one can point to the particular use of a form of šʾr as a designation for the salvation of a whole group that is threatened with destruction. This term is so used in the Jacob-Esau cycle[79] in which the whole clan of Jacob escapes destruction. Literary critics assign this particular passage to the Yahwist. It is certain that the whole of Gen. 45:7 belongs to a single early tradition and cannot be assigned to the supposed Elohist or his time.[80]

---

[75]S. P. Metzger, "Noch einmal der Gottesname im Hexateuch," Neue kirchliche Zeitschrift, 34 (1925), 49ff.; M. H. Segal, "El, Elohim and Yahweh in the Bible," JQR, 46 (1955/56), 89-115; idem, The Pentateuch, pp. 3-14; S. Mowinckel, Erwägungen zur Pentateuch Quellenfrage (Trondheim, 1964), p. 61.

[76]Eissfeldt, OTI, p. 183.

[77]Recently the existence of an independent source stratum E has been questioned again. Mowinckel, Erwägungen zur Pentateuch Quellenfrage, p. 115, prefers to interpret much of the E material as later supplements to and redactions of J which he designates as "Jahwista invariatus" and the later developments are the work of the "Jahwista variatus."

[78]Speiser, Genesis, p. 340. [79]Gen. 32:8(9).

[80]The assigning of Gen. 45:7 to E by Herntrich, Warne, and Ruppert forecloses for them the recognition that this passage constitutes the highlight of Joseph's self-revelation and leads to erroneous theological interpretations. Ruppert, op. cit., pp. 229-30, for instance explains

It is noteworthy that the threat to the life and future existence of the clan of Jacob is in this instance connected with lack of food brought about by a famine. Thus we have up to this point four different kinds of threats in connection with which the remnant motif appears: flood, brimstone and fire, family feud, and famine.

Previous investigators of the remnant motif have overlooked the remarkable relationship between the threat to life and existence and the surviving remnant as the bearer of life for the future in the scene of recognition of the Joseph cycle.[81] Joseph attempts to draw attention to a most important idea: the providential guidance of God, which has turned all the dark actions of Joseph's brothers into salvation for all of them. Thus Joseph states, "God sent me before you to preserve life" (Gen. 45:5b).[82] The great theological and programmatic significance of these words receives further emphasis by expressions in vs. 7, "to preserve for you a remnant" and "to keep alive for you many survivors." The ideas of preserving "life," of preserving a "remnant," and of keeping "alive" many "survivors," represent a further demonstration of the basic connection of the remnant motif with the problem of existence.[83] Here

---

that this passage reflects the Assyrian threat to Israel at the time of the composition by E. See Appendix, pp. 466-67.

[81]As an exception appear the succinct remarks of G. H. Davies, "Remnant," A Theological Word Book of the Bible, ed. by Alan Richardson (2nd ed.; New York, 1962), p. 190.

[82]See on this especially Gerhard von Rad, Die Josephsgeschichte (BS, 5; 4th ed.; Neukirchen-Vluyn, 1964), pp. 19-20.

[83]The connection between the idea of life and the remnant is of greater importance than its connection with the idea of righteousness in the ethical sense of this word. When Schilling, op. cit., pp. 146ff., attempts to derive the remnant motif from the sphere of ethics, he has

again, as in the flood story and in the Sodom story, which depicted judgments of mankind or parts thereof from which a remnant survived as bearers of life for the future, we have a remnant in whom life is preserved for the future. Joseph himself is a mihyāh (Gen. 45:5), i.e., a place where life is to be found and a nucleus of life has been preserved.

The Joseph cycle with its remnant motif indicates a further development in the connection between the remnant motif and the election tradition. The first such explicit connection was encountered in the prayer of Jacob (Gen. 32:12[13]) in the Jacob-Esau cycle in which the clan of Jacob was preserved on account of being the heir to the promise to the fathers.[84] The vision of Joseph is turned to the future, because in the preservation of a surviving remnant the nucleus of a "great people"[85] was preserved. God sent Joseph for his brothers to preserve a remnant as a nucleus of the people.[86] This remnant in turn is the depository of the promises to the fathers by God.[87] That the preservation of this remnant, which constitutes the nucleus of the "people," is a pure act of grace on the part of God is obvious from the words of Joseph spoken to his brothers. It is a divine act of salvation. In this sense

---

missed the fundamental connection between the ideas of life and the remnant by placing a too one-sided emphasis on the ethical notion of righteousness. See the critique by G. Fohrer, "Neuere Literatur zur alttestamentlichen Prophetie," ThR, XX (1952), 348-50.

[84]Gen. 50:24.

[85]Gen. 50:20.

[86]Gen. 45:5b, 7-8.

[87]H. Gross, "Rest," Bibeltheologisches Wörterbuch, ed. by J. B. Bauer (2nd ed.; Graz, 1962), II, 1002.

"'remnant' is a word of hope."[88] If the essential kernel of the prophetic remnant motif is given when the election of Israel is referred to, then we have here already an inkling of the remnant motif of the eighth century prophets.[89]

B. The Remnant Motif in the Elijah Cycle

Scholars have pointed to the remnant motif in a number of passages in the Elijah cycle.[90] Werner E. Müller has attempted to find this motif in various parts[91] of the Elijah and Elisha stories aside from the key sections in the scenes on Mt. Carmel[92] and Mt. Horeb.[93] Othmar Schilling, however, has pointed out that the remnant terminology employed in the parts other than the Mt. Carmel and Mt. Horeb scenes is too vague to allow

---

[88]Von Rad, Genesis, p. 394; Ruppert, op. cit., p. 197, states "Thus also for the brothers, the 'remnant' (45:7), the kernel of the people of Israel, the glance into the future can be a hopeful one . . . ."

[89]With Sellin, in Der alttestamentliche Prophetismus, p. 152, Herntrich, TDNT, IV, 202, and Ruppert, op. cit., p. 124, against Schilling, op. cit., p. 162. Cf. J. Paterson, "Remnant," Hasting's Dictionary of the Bible, rev. by F. C. Grant and H. H. Rowley (New York, 1963), p. 841.

[90]Meinhold, Studien zur israelitischen Religionsgeschichte, pp. 2-32; Sellin, Prophetisums, p. 158; A. von Gall, Βασιλεία τοῦ θεοῦ. Eine religionsgeschichtliche Studie zur vorkirchlichen Eschatologie (Heidelberg, 1926), p. 32; Herntrich, TDNT, IV, 202; W. E. Müller, op. cit., pp. 46-49; Schilling, op. cit., pp. 137-40; Warne, op. cit., pp. 61-67; Garofalo, La nozione profetica del "Resto d'Israele," pp. 39-50; idem, "Residuum Israelis," VD, 21 (1941), 239-43.

[91]W. E. Müller, op. cit., p. 46 n. 6: 1 Ki. 18:22, 40; 19:3, 4, 14, 17; 2 Ki. 9:15; 10:11, 14, 17, 19, 21, 24, 25, 28.

[92]1 Ki. 18:22, 40.

[93]1 Ki. 19:3, 4, 14, 18.

an inclusion in a discussion of the remnant motif in the Elijah tradition.[94] The present investigation will therefore pay attention mainly to the remnant motif in the scenes on Mt. Carmel and Mt. Horeb.

The question of the unity of 1 Ki. 18, which contains the remnant motif in the narrative of Mt. Carmel, has often been discussed. Hugo Gressmann argued that two distinct traditions are here united, viz. Elijah's encounter with Obadiah with the rain inducing sequel (18:2b-16 and 18:41-46) and the ordeal of the priests of Baal (18:17-40).[95] He is followed by Albrecht Alt who believes that a false unity was imposed by editorial introductions in 18:1 and 18:41.[96] Georg Fohrer, Ernst Würthwein, and Odil H. Steck take up this lead and consider the scene on Mt. Carmel as an independent narrative.[97] The present writer, however, sees no compelling reasons to dissent from Otto Eissfeldt and other scholars,[98]

---

[94]Schilling, op. cit., p. 198 n. 242.

[95]Hugo Gressmann, Die älteste Geschichtsschreibung und Prophetie Israels (2nd ed.; Göttingen, 1921), p. 269.

[96]Albrecht Alt, "Das Gottesurteil auf dem Karmel," Kleine Schriften zur Geschichte des Volkes Israel (München, 1953), II, 135ff.

[97]Georg Fohrer, Elia (AThANT, 53; 2nd ed.; Zürich, 1968), pp. 37-38; Ernst Würthwein, "Die Erzählung vom Gottesurteil auf dem Karmel," ZThK, LIX (1962), 132; Odil Hannes Steck, Überlieferung und Zeitgeschichte in den Elia-Erzählungen (WMANT, 26; Neukirchen-Vluyn, 1968), pp. 9, 79-83.

[98]O. Eissfeldt, Der Gott Karmel (Berlin, 1953), pp. 32ff.; idem, "Die Komposition von I Reg 16, 29-II Reg 13, 25," Das ferne und nahe Wort. Festschrift für L. Rost, ed. by Fritz Maas (BZAW, 105; Berlin, 1968), 49-58; D. R. Ap-Thomas, "Elijah on Mount Carmel," PEQ, XCII (1960), 147-48; H. H. Rowley, "Elijah on Mount Carmel," BJRL, 43 (1960), 190ff.= Men of God. Studies in Old Testament History and Prophecy (London, 1963), pp. 37ff.; John Gray, I & II Kings. A Commentary (Philadelphia, 1963), pp. 343-44.

especially since we believe, contrary to A. Alt and Martin Noth,[99] that the Baal of Carmel was not an obscure local deity, the destruction of whose shrine by fanatical Yahwists was the historical basis of the tradition of the ordeal on Mt. Carmel, but that this divinity was the Phoenician-Canaanite fertility god Baal-Melkart.[100] Alt has shown that in all likelihood 1 Ki. 18:20-40 rests upon actual historical fact.[101] The drought-Carmel narrative dates according to Steck from the early reign of Jehu (841-814/13).[102]

---

[99]Noth, The History of Israel, p. 242 n. 6.

[100]This identification is accepted by de Vaux, Ancient Israel, p. 280; Bright, A History of Israel, p. 227 n. 53; Rowley, op. cit., p. 64; W. F. Albright, Archaeology and the Religion of Israel (3rd ed.; Baltimore, Md., 1953), pp. 156-57, 229; idem, Yahweh and the Gods of Canaan, p. 243; Harrelson, Interpreting the Old Testament, p. 203; Ringgren, Israelite Religion, p. 261; Heaton, The Hebrew Kingdoms, p. 83; W. H. Schmidt, Alttestamentlicher Glaube und seine Umwelt, pp. 122-23; O. Eissfeldt, "Baʿalšamēn und Jahwe," Kleine Schriften (Tübingen, 1963), II, 171-98.

[101]Alt, Kleine Schriften, II, 139ff., cf. J. J. Stamm, "Elia am Horeb," Studia biblica et semitica. Festschrift Th. C. Vriezen (Wageningen, 1966), p. 328.

[102]Steck, op. cit., p. 133. For the date of Jehu's reign, see Edwin R. Thiele, The Mysterious Numbers of the Hebrew Kings (2nd ed.; Grand Rapids, Mich., 1965), pp. 66-68. The late dating of the Elijah tradition is almost completely abandoned. A date around 800 B.C. or slightly higher or lower is the most common, see R. Kittel, Die Bücher der Könige (Handkommentar zum Alten Testament, I. Abt.; Göttingen, 1900), pp. 159ff.; I. Benzinger, Die Bücher der Könige (Kurzer Hand-Commentar zum AT, IX; Freiburg i. Br., 1899), p. 106; H. Gunkel, Elias, Jahwe und Baal (Tübingen, 1906), pp. 43-44; C. Steuernagel, Lehrbuch der Einleitung in das Alte Testament (Tübingen, 1912), p. 370 (still in the 9th but not later than 8th cent. B.C.); A. Jepsen, Nabi (München, 1934), p. 68 (between 800 and 722 B.C.); W. E. Müller, op. cit., pp. 40-41; R. H. Pfeiffer, Introduction to the Old Testament (New York, 1948), p. 403 (about 800 B.C.); Fohrer, Elia, pp. 42-44; Eissfeldt, Komposition, p. 58; A. Weiser, Introduction to the Old Testament, transl. by D. M. Barton (London, 1961), p. 176; Gray, I & II Kings, p. 336 (before 825 B.C.).

The remnant motif appears here in connection with Israel's political experiences and her greatest religious crisis. Omri (880-874/73) had put Israel on the map of the ancient Near East and Ahab (874/73-853) carried further his father's policies.[103] An alliance with Phoenicia, which brought great economic prosperity to Israel, was sealed by Ahab's marriage to Jezebel, daughter of Ethbaal, king of Tyre (1 Ki. 16:31). This alliance was mutually advantageous for the economic situation of both Tyre and Israel[104] as well as for the political situation as a counterbalance to Damascus. The sudden emergence of Elijah, "the greatest of the early prophets,"[105] during the reign of Ahab discloses the life-and-death struggle which then had arisen between Yahwism and resurgent Canaanite religion and culture.[106] As Solomon's wives worshiped their respective gods in temples built for them,[107] so Jezebel, a worshiper of the Tyrian deities Baal-Melkart and Asherah had a temple to

---

[103]For the political history of the Omride dynasty, see Bright, History of Israel, pp. 220-31; Noth, History of Israel, pp. 241-46.

[104]For the material prosperity of the Omride dynasty the best witness is the archaeological evidence from the new capital Samaria, see P. R. Ackroyd, "Samaria," Archaeology and Old Testament Study, ed. by D. Winton Thomas (Oxford, 1967), pp. 343-54, with bibliography.

[105]J. P. Hyatt, Prophetic Religion (Nashville, 1947), p. 18; cf. J. Lindblom, Prophecy in Ancient Israel (Philadelphia, 1962), p. 74, Elijah is "the outstanding figure among the early prophets."

[106]The study by Leah Bronner, The Stories of Elijah and Elisha (Pretoria Oriental Series, Vol. VI; Leiden, 1968), pp. 35-138, shows that the writer of the Elijah and Elisha narratives wrote these stories as deliberate polemics against Canaanite Baal worship to protest against paganism as represented by the Baal cult.

[107]1 Ki. 11:1-8.

Baal-Melkart built in Samaria.[108] But Jezebel was apparently not satisfied with the permission to worship her god in the temple that Ahab had built for her and her staff, which numbered 450 prophets of Baal and 400 prophets of Asherah. She sought to make the cult of Baal the official religion of the court and the ruling class. The prophets of Baal and Asherah enjoyed official status.[109] The influence of Baalism upon the people was apparently so great that the masses of Israelites were "limping with two different opinions."[110] Loyal Yahwists soon met persecution. As Jezebel's policies encountered resistance, she resorted to even harsher measures: the execution of prophets of Yahweh.[111] Thus there had arisen in the time of Ahab a conflict between two incompatible religions and cultures, Yahwism and Baalism.[112] Elijah's struggle against the latter was "a fight to the finish."[113] Elijah himself had been forced to hide for a long time. When he emerged he stood alone against the ene-

---

[108] 1 Ki. 16:32-33.

[109] 1 Ki. 18:19.

[110] 1 Ki. 18:21. For different interpretations of this verse, see James A. Montgomery, The Books of Kings, ed. by H. S. Gehman (ICC; Edinburgh, 1951), pp. 301, 310.

[111] 1 Ki. 18:4.

[112] Heaton, The Hebrew Kingdoms, p. 249, maintains that "it is improbable that her [Jezebel's] importations introduced to Israel anything that was really new. The paganism of Tyre simply reinforced the Canaanite pressure on Yahwism. . . ." What was new, however, was Jezebel's active propagation with an almost missionary-like zeal for her gods which curtailed for the first time in the history of Israel the right of the prophets of Yahweh to speak freely and unhindered the word of Yahweh without reprisals (Bright, History of Israel, p. 226; Bronner, op. cit., pp. 8-9). Thus Baalism threatened to envelope Yahwism; see J. Mauchline, "I Kings," Peake's Commentary on the Bible, ed. by M. Black and H. H. Rowley (London, 1962), p. 345.

[113] Rowley, Men of God, p. 43.

mies of Yahwism. At the time of the contest on Mt. Carmel, when the "great religious assembly"[114] had gathered, Elijah states that he is the only remnant of the prophets of Yahweh: "I, even I only, am left [ʾănî nôṯartî . . . lᵉbaddî]; a prophet of the Lord."[115] This sentence means more than "to place as its only function emphasis on the superior number [of Baal prophets] over against Elijah."[116] It indicates that Elijah is the only surviving prophet of Yahweh, who publicly stood up for Yahwism at the time when the life of each prophet of Yahweh was threatened. One hundred prophets of Yahweh had gone into hiding when Jezebel cut off the lives of the prophets of Yahweh.[117] It is obvious that the remnant motif appears here in connection with a religio-cultural threat and not with a politico-military one. This observation is of importance in view of Müller's attempt to derive the remnant motif from a politico-military sphere.[118] Up to this point the appearance and development of the remnant motif in the Hebrew Bible is completely separate from the sphere of warfare and politics. In the scene on Mt. Carmel the usage of the remnant motif follows the pattern which the early traditions of Genesis reflect, namely a remnant is left from a past calamity. We will see shortly that a new note is struck with regard to this pattern in the scene on

---

[114] So von Rad, OTT, II, 16.

[115] 1 Ki. 18:22. There is no reason to suppose that this verse is a later addition to the original narrative of the scene on Mt. Carmel, see Steck, op. cit., p. 17 n. 2.

[116] Steck, ibid.

[117] 1 Ki. 18:4; 19:10, 14.

[118] W. E. Müller, op. cit., pp. 22-27.

Mt. Horeb. What is new here is that Elijah represents a remnant of the prophets of Yahweh, i.e. a remnant of one loyal to Yahweh within an apostate Israel. The other appearance of the remnant motif in the Elijah tradition shows further developments.[119]

The remnant motif is present in the narrative of Elijah on Mt. Horeb in 1 Ki. 19:9-18. Fohrer[120] employed in his analysis of the theophany at Mt. Horeb a method too much dependent on literary criticism at the expense of proper traditio-historical considerations. Steck,[121] on the other hand, appears to make a strong case for a threefold redaction in which a later narrator adds vss. 7-8, 9aba, 11, 12-18 to the older layers of vss. 1-3a and 3b-6. The whole process of redaction of the scene on Mt. Horeb appears to have been finished still during the lifetime of Elijah, probably during the reigns of Hazael of Syria[122] and Jehoahaz of

---

[119]For a general discussion of the "new" or "traditional" in Elijah, see C. A. Keller, "Wer war Elia?" ThZ, 16 (1960), 298-301.

[120]The traditio-historical analysis of the theophany at Horeb in 1 Ki. 19 by Fohrer, Elia, pp. 38-39, leaves an original kernel of 1 Ki. 19:3b, 8b, 9-12, 13, 15a-18. But Fohrer is ambiguous because on p. 43 he claims that the oldest stratum of the Horeb narrative closes with vs. 13 and vss. 15-18 are later expansions. Furthermore, Fohrer fails to recognize that vss. 14 and 18 cannot be assigned to different strata of redaction, because these verses correspond to each other. In vs. 14 וָאִוָּתֵר refers most likely to the previously mentioned slaying of the prophets of Yahweh, but now with reference to the "people of Israel" it indicates that Elijah considers himself as the last remnant of the faithful of Yahweh. Vs. 18 refers to this when speaking of the remnant of 7,000. The modification in vs. 18 depends on vs. 14. Von Rad, OTT, II, 21, states, "These words [vs. 18] are at once the climax of the story and the key to its meaning, for they are, of course, the answer to Elijah's complaints that he was the only remaining loyal worshipper of Yahweh."

[121]Steck, op. cit., pp. 27-28.

[122]The study of A. Jepsen, "Israel und Damaskus," AfO, 14 (1941-44), 153-72, has made it likely that Hazael, king of Damascus, came on the

Israel toward the latter part of the ninth century B.C.[123] J. J. Stamm has shown that there is nothing in 1 Ki. 19 which would cause a denial of the narrative's historicity.[124]

On Mt. Carmel Elijah appeared as the only loyal remnant of Yahweh's prophets in a Herculean effort of public contest. On Mt. Horeb Elijah appears in a private theophanic confrontation with Yahweh. The reason for Elijah's long journey to Mt. Horeb is not made particularly clear. It seems to indicate that his triumph at Mt. Carmel was momentary.[125] Some have suggested that his journey to Mt. Horeb indicates a pilgrimage.[126] At any rate it is obvious that he had the desire to pour out his troubles to Yahweh at the place where Yahweh had already shown himself so plainly.[127] His most grievous complaint was his conviction that the

---

throne as a usurper at about the same time as Jehu of Israel, i.e., in 841 B.C. Cf. M. F. Unger, Israel and the Arameans of Damascus (London, 1957), pp. 75-82, 158-63; R. A. Bowman, "Hazael," IDB, II, 538; H. Bardtke, "Hasael," Biblisch-historisches Handwörterbuch, ed. by B. Reicke and L. Rost (Göttingen, 1966), II, col. 650.

[123]Steck, op. cit., pp. 94-95. See Appendix II, p. 471.

[124]Stamm, "Elia am Horeb," pp. 328-30; also M. Buber, The Prophetic Faith, Harper Torchbooks (New York, 1960), p. 105. See Appendix II, p. 471.

[125]Gray, I & II Kings, p. 362.

[126]Von Rad, OTT, II, 20; Schmidt, Glaube, p. 52. However, Noth Überlieferungsgeschichte, p. 152, and Steck, op. cit., p. 110, have raised serious questions concerning this supposition.

[127]The correspondence betwen the scene on Mt. Horeb and the Sinai tradition has been pointed out many times, see Kittel, op. cit., pp. 151f.; Gunkel, Elias, pp. 23, 71 n. 25; A. Šanda, Die Bücher der Könige (Exegetisches Handbuch zum AT; Münster, 1911), I, 447; Gressmann, Geschichtsschreibung, p. 268; Montgomery, op. cit., p. 313; H. Seebass, Mose und Aaron, Sinai und Gottesberg (Abhandlungen zur Evangelischen Theologie, 2; Bonn, 1962), pp. 14ff., 72; Gray, I & II Kings, pp. 363-64; Jörg Jeremias, Theophanie. Die Geschichte einer alttestamentlichen Gattung

cause of Yahwism was utterly lost in Israel and that he is now the only loyal remnant of all of God's people.

> I have been very jealous for the Lord, the God of hosts; for the people of Israel have forsaken thy covenant, thrown down thy altars, and slain thy prophets with the sword; and I, even I only, am left [waʾiwwāṯēr ʾanî lᵉbadî]; and they seek my life to take it away.[128]

This text refers to the reasons for the jealousy of Elijah on Mt. Carmel.[129] In Elijah's view Israel as a whole has forsaken the covenant relationship between her and Yahweh, which was the essence of the faith of which he was the protagonist. Yahweh's altars had been thrown down.[130] The reference to the slaughter of the prophets may refer to the persecution of Jezebel before the scene on Mt. Carmel[131] or it may possibly be a reference to such an unrecorded slaughter between the ordeal on Mt. Carmel

---

(WMANT, 10; Neukirchen-Vluyn, 1965), pp. 107, 109, 112, 162; von Rad, OTT, II, 20; R. B. Y. Scott, The Relevance of the Prophets (2nd ed.; New York, 1968), pp. 74-75; Fohrer, Elia, pp. 55-58; Heaton, The Hebrew Kingdoms, p. 257; Steck, op. cit., pp. 110-25. The last mentioned scholar has investigated the problem of the correspondence in great detail and concludes that the question of the dependence of the Horeb scene on the Sinai tradition can at the present state of research hardly be answered. That there are many affinities is obvious, but the problem of dependence is extremely complex.

[128] 1 Ki. 19:14 also 10. R. M. Frank, "A Note on 3 Kings 10:10, 14," CBQ, 25 (1963), 410-14, attempts to find the original length of 1 Ki. 19:14 by eliminating "thrown down thy altars, and slain thy prophets with the sword" as a gloss which was inserted because of 18:30, 13. But in order to maintain his thesis Frank makes 18:22 dependent on 19:14. Frank's thesis is too arbitrary to be convincing. The most likely solution is that 19:14 is dependent on the earlier Elia tradition, especially 18:13; 18:30; 18:22; 18:18; 19:1; 19:2-3. Cf. Steck, op. cit., pp. 22-23.

[129] Steck, op. cit., pp. 127, 116 n. 10, 120 n. 3.

[130] Cf. 1 Ki. 18:30.

[131] Cf. 1 Ki. 18:4, 13.

and the theophany on Mt. Horeb.[132] Now Elijah considers himself as the only loyal remnant of Israel.[133] Apparently the victory on Mt. Carmel had no lasting outward effect on the people of Israel, so that the entire future of Yahwism and of Israel as Yahweh's covenant people depends on the only loyal remnant Elijah.[134] The life of even the last loyal remnant of Yahweh, the only remaining protagonist of Yahwism on whom the future of Israel's faith and the people as such depended, is threatened.

The theophanic answer which Elijah received from Yahweh was in the highest degree reassuring: "Yet I will leave seven thousand in Israel, all the knees that have not bowed to Baal, and every mouth that has not kissed him."[135] The theophanic speech of Yahweh (1 Ki. 19:15-18), of which this is the final part, has its climax neither in the commission of Elijah[136] nor in the appointment of the avengers[137] whose task is to

---

[132]So Gray, I & II Kings, p. 365.

[133]In the scene on Mt. Carmel, Elijah refers to himself in almost identical terminology as the only loyal remnant, but not of the people of Israel, because they were "limping with two different opinions" (1 Ki. 18:21).

[134]Warne, *op. cit.*, p. 65; cf. J. Pedersen, Israel, Its Life and Culture (Copenhagen, 1926), III-IV, 518.

[135]1 Ki. 19:18. Fohrer, Elia, p. 61, argues that the announcement of the destructive judgment (*Vernichtungsgericht*) and the preservation of a remnant in 1 Ki. 19:17-18 do not go back to Elijah but reflect the situation of doom of later prophecy. But Fohrer misinterprets these vss. through his belief that they depict a destructive judgment. This is not the case. Do not these verses refer to a *Mahngericht* instead, because a remnant will be spared? Furthermore, he misses the essential correspondence between vss. 14 and 18 and of vs. 14 to the events in the career of Elijah. See *supra*, n. 120, and Steck, *op. cit.*, pp. 17 n. 2, 23 n. 1.

[136]1 Ki. 19:15-16.

[137]1 Ki. 19:17.

chastise the nation from without[138] and from within.[139] As von Rad[140] has shown by pointing to the correspondence between vss. 14 and 18, the climax is rather found in vs. 18 where the assurance is given that the judgment has its limit in a remnant of seven thousand loyal worshipers of Yahweh.[141] The answer to Elijah's emphatic complaint that he alone is left has a twofold nature. Firstly, Elijah is not the "only" remnant, because there will be[142] seven thousand more loyal worshipers of Yahweh. Secondly, it makes clear that the destructive judgment despite its terrible nature and despite Israel's apostasy[143] will not lead to complete annihilation of Israel![143a]

There are three new notes struck here in Israel's history which need some further consideration. Firstly, there is the note of Israel's apostasy, a theme well known from the "writing" prophets of the eighth century B.C. Hans Walter Wolff has shown that Hosea had connections with the prophetic movement of the Northern Kingdom and recognized that there

---

[138]Hazael of Syria, 2 Ki. 8:7ff.

[139]Jehu of Israel, 2 Ki. 9:1ff.

[140]Von Rad, OTT, II, 21; cf. Stamm, "Elia am Horeb," p. 334, Steck, op. cit., p. 23 n. 1.

[141]That this is but a round number needs no emphasizing. It is nevertheless a small minority of the whole of Israel as interpreters have indicated, see Kittel, op. cit., p. 154; Šanda, op. cit., I, 452; Steck, op. cit., p. 91 n. 3.

[142]Norman H. Snaith, I Kings (IB; Nashville, 1954), p. 164, points out that "the actual Hebrew refers definitely to the future."

[143]Compare 1 Ki. 19:17 with 19:14.

[143a]See Appendix II, p. 471.

are lines of connection with Israelite prophecy of the ninth century B.C.[144] Hosea refers many times to Israel's apostasy.[145] If the dating of the scene on Mt. Horeb is correct,[146] then one can say that already at this early date as later by Hosea and not first by Amos,[147] Israel is depicted in apostasy from Yahweh. The second new note struck in prophetic proclamation is that Yahweh moves against his people in destructive judgment by means of a foreign nation. Steck believes that vs. 18 contains the motif of the "war of Yahweh."[148] He thinks that this motif aids in answering the question of the origin of Yahweh's judgment of Israel through a foreign nation.[149] There are, however, a number of considerations which decisively weaken Steck's assumption. Vs. 18 does not contain any Holy War terminology. The war which leaves the remnant of vs. 18 is a war against Israel which would mean a complete reversal of the tradition of the "war of Yahweh" at this early date. The wars which will diminish Israel will come from within _and_ without as vs. 17 clearly shows. Furthermore, there is the serious problem whether the "war of Yahweh" tradition played a role at that time, since the classical period of the

---

[144]Hans Walter Wolff, _Hosea_ (BKAT, XIV; 2nd ed.; Neukirchen-Vluyn, 1965), pp. 19, 152, 178, 201-202, 211, 242, 272, 279; idem, "Hoseas geistige Heimat," in _Gesammelte Studien zum Alten Testament_ (TB, 22; München, 1964), pp. 243ff.

[145]Hos. 4:3, 10; 9:12a, 16b; 14:1.

[146]See Steck, _op. cit._, p. 95.

[147]Von Rad, _OTT_, II, 136.

[148]Steck, _op. cit._, p. 105.

[149]_Ibid._, p. 105 n. 2.

"wars of Yahweh" is the time of the Judges.[150] It seems best to be rather cautious in assigning 1 Ki. 19:17-18 to the tradition of the "war of Yahweh."[151] The third new note struck in the scene on Mt. Horeb relates directly to the development of the remnant motif. Here in the scene on Mt. Horeb we have for the first time a remnant spoken of as a future entity.[152] Yahweh "will leave" a remnant of seven thousand in Israel.[153] Up to this point in the history of Israel a remnant was al-

---

[150]For a discussion of these problems, see von Rad, Der Heilige Krieg im alten Israel, pp. 50ff., R. Bach, Die Aufforderungen zu Flucht und Kampf im alttestamentlichen Prophetenspruch (WMANT, 9; Neukirchen-Vluyn, 1962), pp. 101ff.; Rolf Rendtorff, "Reflections on the Early History of Prophecy in Israel," Journal for Theology and Church, IV (1967), 23-25; Schmidt, Glaube, p. 93.

[151]The interrelation in 1 Ki. 19:17 between foreign ruler and Israelite ruler as the means of punishing Israel cannot be equated with the idea of Yahweh punishing Israel by a foreign nation as in "classical" prophecy, cf. Amos 2:14-16; Micah 4:11-13; Isa. 19:1-3; 30:27-33; 31:4; Eze. 38f.; Jer. 6:1-6; 22:7; 51:27; Joel 4:9; Hag. 2:21-22. J. A. Soggin, "Der prophetische Gedanke über den Heiligen Krieg als Gericht gegen Israel," VT, 10 (1960), 79-83.

[152]This does not deny the emphasis in Genesis that the remnant is the bearer of the promises of God. There is in 1 Ki. 19:17-18, however, the distinct note that although there are certainly to be terrible judgments, nevertheless a remnant in Israel will survive to stand before Yahweh, see supra, n. 142; W. E. Müller, op. cit., p. 48; von Rad, OTT, II, 21; Stamm, "Elia am Horeb," p. 334.

[153]1 Ki. 19:18. Steck, op. cit., p. 105 n. 4, is partly right in stressing that the remnant constitutes an entity left after military action, but he misses the point in two respects: (a) The judgment against Israel is according to 1 Ki. 19:17 a military and a non-military one, because one can hardly describe the foretold slaying by the prophet Elisha as an action of war if the slaughter of Elijah on Mt. Carmel serves as a prototype of the slaying by Elisha. No record of a slaughter inspired by Elisha has survived. (b) Steck gives the impression that vss. 17-18 are vaticinia ex eventu. That this is not the case is made likely by the difficulty that the suffering inflicted by Hazael followed rather than preceded the rise of Jehu, which would be in a different sequence in the case of a vaticinium ex eventu. The future aspect of vs. 18 is obvious. A. Jepsen, Nabi, p. 68 n. 2, rejects rightly the notion that 1 Ki. 19:19 is a vaticinium ex eventu based on the catastrophe of 722 B.C. Jepsen

ways an entity left from a past catastrophe. But now a remnant is envisioned in the future as a divine limit to a destructive judgment appointed by God against Israel. While in the Biblical flood story a remnant is left of mankind, correspondingly a remnant will be left here of Israel. As the remnant left of mankind constituted the nucleus for a new mankind, so the remnant that will be left of Israel constitutes the nucleus of a new Israel. The future existence of Israel as Yahweh's covenant people depends on the small remnant of seven thousand.[154] What we have here is the *locus classicus* of the promised remnant[155] in the sense that we meet in this passage for the first time in the history of Israel the promise of a future remnant that constitutes the kernel of a new Israel.[156] Although the remnant that will be saved will consist of those who had remained loyal and faithful to Yahweh, who had been sifted along ethico-religious lines,[157] it will have its existence only because of Yahweh's

---

would like to go to the time of Jeroboam II and understand 1 Ki. 19:17-18 in retrospect to the time of Hazael, Jehu, and Elisha, but this would mean that vs. 18 is a *vaticinium ex eventu*. There is, however, no reason for this in vs. 18. Furthermore, it would be very strange that a text would be formed that would speak of an exclusive remnant of loyal Yahwists at a time when the Aramaean wars left an Israel still saturated with apostasy to the cult of Baal.

[154]W. E. Müller, *op. cit.*, p. 48: "Die siebentausend sind die Garanten dieses Fortbestandes Israels, weil sie sich an Jahve gebunden wissen. . . ." Von Rad, *OTT*, II, 20: "He [Elijah] is, however, permitted to know that even so Jahweh is to continue to bless Israel, from the remnant a new Israel will arise."

[155]So Joachim Jeremias, *Abba* (Göttingen, 1966), p. 121.

[156]Otto Procksch, *Theologie des Alten Testaments* (Gütersloh, 1950), p. 580; Warne, *op. cit.*, p. 67; E. Jacob, *Theology of the Old Testament*, transl. by A. W. Heathcote and P. J. Allcock (London, 1958), p. 323.

[157]This Sellin, *Prophetismus*, p. 158, has correctly emphasized over against Gressmann's notion of the remnant as an exclusive nature-mythological entity before Amos.

gracious action.[158] This is an aspect of the remnant motif which we have encountered already in Genesis. Therefore we encounter a fusion of old and new aspects in the remnant motif of the "greatest of the older prophets."

C. The Remnant Motif in Amos

Amos, the shepherd and dresser of sycamore trees from Tekoa[159] in Judah, is "perhaps the most important prophet in the history of Israelite prophecy and religion."[160] Since Wellhausen[161] the first so-called "writing prophet" has been considered by many scholars as a consistent prophet of doom whose message lacks any ray of hope for the future.[162]

---

[158]Ruppert, op. cit., p. 124, sees in the remark that the survivors did not bow their knee to Baal a "Lohngedanke." But it is incorrect to interpret the remnant who have rejected the worship of Baal and will be saved as expressing any notion of human merit or divine reward for human faithfulness, because explicit emphasis is placed upon the action of Yahweh in the salvation of the remnant. Cf. Harrelson, Interpreting the Old Testament, p. 206: "The survivors will be those who have not submitted to the worship of Baal--yet it is Yahweh who alone can spare them. . . . He preserves this remnant not primarily because of its moral purity--for how could it happen that only the pious survive? Yahweh in his mercy gives a fresh start to his people. . . ." Von Rad, OTT, II, 21: "The remnant doubtless consists of those who had been faithful; but their preservation had been decided even before the start of the coming troubles." Stamm, "Elia am Horeb," p. 334.

[159]Amos 1:1; 7:14, 15.

[160]Harrelson, Interpreting the Old Testament, p. 339.

[161]J. Wellhausen, Prolegomena to the History of Ancient Israel, Meridian Books (Cleveland, 1957), pp. 472ff.; idem, Die Kleinen Propheten (4th ed.; Berlin, 1963), pp. 67ff.

[162]This view is maintained among others by the following scholars: A. Weiser, Die Profetie des Amos (BZAW, 53; Giessen, 1929), pp. 185-89, but see now his more cautious approach in Das Buch der zwölf Kleinen Propheten (ATD, 24; 4th ed.; Göttingen, 1965), pp. 159-63; G. Hölscher, Die Ursprünge der jüdischen Eschatologie (Giessen, 1925), p. 14; Th. C. Vriezen, "Prophecy and Eschatology," SVT, I (1953), 205; R. S. Cripps,

It is certainly correct that Amos proclaimed the coming judgment in more radical terms than any other "writing prophet." The reasons for the necessity of the imminent judgment of Yahweh are outlined as gross social injustice and superficial religious practice. Yahweh will not continue to tolerate corruption in the courts,[163] corruption in the markets,[164] corruption in high society,[165] and the cruel suffering which they cause.[166] Israel's religious practice is a contemptible sideshow.[167] Its religious tradition is merely a cloak for pride and complacency.[168] Israel had no inkling of her true position vis-à-vis Yahweh! Time and time again with one calamity after another, such as famine, drought, failure of harvest, failure in war, judgment through epidemics, and damage by wild animals,[169] Yahweh attempted to shake Israel out of her complacency, but she paid no heed.[170] Thus Israel must now hold herself in readiness to meet

---

A Critical and Exegetical Commentary on the Book of Amos (2nd ed.; London, 1960), pp. 190-91; G. Fohrer, "Remarks on Modern Interpretation of the Prophets," JBL, LXXX (1961), 315; H. W. Wolff, Amos (BKAT, XIV/6; Neukirchen-Vluyn, 1968), pp. 124-25, 128-29.

[163]Amos 5:12; 6:12.

[164]Amos. 8:5, 6.

[165]Amos 3:10, 12, 15; 4:1-3; 6:4-7.

[166]Amos 2:7, 8; 5:11, 12. Cf. H.-J. Kraus, "Die prophetische Botschaft gegen das soziale Unrecht Israels," EvTh, 15 (1955), 295ff.; Arvid S. Kapelrud, Central Ideas in Amos (2nd ed.; Oslo, 1961), pp. 48-50.

[167]Amos 4:4, 5; 5:21-24.

[168]Amos 2:9-11; 3:2; 5:18; 9:7. Cf. von Rad, OTT, II, 136-38.

[169]The means through which judgment comes is not as important as the fact that Yahweh is coming in judgment. For the descriptions and means of judgment, see R. Mayer, "Sünde und Gericht in der Bildersprache der vorexilischen Prophetie," BZ, 8 (1964), 28ff.; H. Graf Reventlow, Das Amt des Propheten bei Amos (FRLANT, 80; Göttingen, 1962), pp. 82ff.

[170]Amos 4:6ff.

her God in judgment. Amos is the prophet of the eleventh hour.[171] The crucial question is whether or not Amos is indeed as consistent a prophet of doom as he is depicted in many quarters of modern scholarship. There are some scholars who regard such passages that mention survivors in connection with the coming judgment as a means on the part of the prophet of heightening the threat of destruction.[172] Other scholars deny such passages (aside from 9:8-15) to Amos, because they view him as a pure preacher of judgment who cannot have entertained any hope whatever for the future.[173] And again a third group of scholars maintains that in order to do justice to the total message of Amos the notion of judgment and doom must neither be underestimated nor overestimated.[174] The latter

---

[171]Samuel Amsler, "Amos, prophète de la onzième heure," ThZ, 21 (1965), 318-28; idem, Amos. (Commentaire de l'Ancien Testament, XIa; Neuchatel, 1965), p. 207; Preuss, Jahweglaube, p. 159.

[172]Mowinckel, Psalmenstudien II, pp. 266-67, 277; Cripps, op. cit., pp. 190-91, 268, 297, 319-20; H. H. Krause, "Der Gerichtsprophet Amos, ein Vorläufer des Deuteronomisten," ZAW, 50 (1932), 238-39; E. W. Heaton, The Old Testament Prophets, Pelikan Book (Baltimore, Md., 1964), p. 144; and others.

[173]For the older literature, see Karl Cramer, Amos. Versuch einer theologischen Interpretation (BWANT, 15; Stuttgart, 1930), pp. 130ff.; Pfeiffer, Introduction to the Old Testament, pp. 582-83; Th. H. Robinson, Die zwölf Kleinen Propheten: Hosea bis Micha (Handbuch zum AT, 14; Tübingen, 1938), p. 105; Weiser, Das Buch der zwölf Kleinen Propheten, p. 161; Cripps, op. cit., pp. 190-91; Hughell E. W. Fosbroke, The Book of Amos. (The Interpreter's Bible, 6; Nashville, 1956), p. 770; "The categorical note of Amos' prediction of doom admits of no qualification." Wolff, Amos, pp. 119, 133, 135, 138; R. Smend, "Das Nein des Amos," EvTh, 23 (1963), 415.

[174]This observation was made already many decades ago by W. Cossmann, Die Entwicklung des Gerichtsgedankens bei den alttestamentlichen Propheten (BZAW, 29; Giessen, 1915), p. 163: "Man darf den Umfang der Gerichtswirkung bei Amos nicht unter- noch überschätzen."

believe that the genuine words of Amos contain not only doom but carry also an aspect of future hope within them. There is a juxtaposition of doom and hope also in the prophecy of Amos.[175] In view of these contradictory positions the present writer must proceed with utmost caution in his investigation of the remnant motif in such passages of Amos which contain the remnant terminology.[175a]

While the previous generation of critical Old Testament scholars

---

[175]Without attempting to be exhaustive the following may be mentioned: Meinhold, op. cit., pp. 33-63; Herbert Dittmann, "Der heilige Rest im Alten Testament," Theologische Studien und Kritiken 87 (1914), 609-610; Cramer, op. cit., pp. 132-33; R. de Vaux, "Le 'reste d'Israël' d'après les Prophètes," RB, 42 (1933), 528; Herntrich TDNT, IV, 202; Schilling, op. cit., pp. 22ff.; Garofalo, Nozione, pp. 50-61; G. A. Danell, Studies in the Name Israel in the Old Testament, (Uppsala, 1946), pp. 120-21, 133 n. 93; Procksch, Theologie, p. 175; E. Würthwein, "Amos-Studien," ZAW, 62 (1950), 10-52; Victor Maag, Text, Wortschatz und Begriffswelt des Buches Amos (Leiden, 1951), pp. 28-29, 247-57; Franz Hesse, "Amos 5, 4-6. 14f.,; ZAW, 68 (1956), 13-16; Warne, op. cit., pp. 69ff.; John D. W. Watts, Vision and Prophecy in Amos (Leiden, 1958), pp. 25, 48; Jacob H. Groenbaek, "Zur Frage der Eschatologie in der Verkündigung der Gerichtspropheten," Svensk Exegetisk Årsbok, XXIV (1959), 11, 14; Buber, The Prophetic Faith, p. 105; T. J. Meek, Hebrew Origins, Harper Torchbooks (New York, 1960), p. 181; Kapelrud, op. cit., pp. 50-51, 56, 79; B. Vawter, The Conscience of Israel: Pre-exilic Prophets and Prophecy (New York, 1961), p. 55; P. Mamie, "Le livre d'Amos: Les châtiments et le 'reste d'Israël'," Nova et Vetera, 37:3 (1962), 217-23; J. P. Hyatt, "Amos." Peake's Commentary on the Bible, ed. by M. Black and H. H. Rowley (London, 1962), p. 617; idem, Prophetic Religion, p. 100; Lindblom, Prophecy in Ancient Israel, pp. 350 n. 124, 374; E. Jenni, "Remnant." IDB, IV, 32; idem, "Eschatology," IDB, II, 128; Reventlow, op. cit., pp. 19ff.; R. Fey, Amos und Jesaja (WMANT, 12; Neukirchen-Vluyn, 1963), p. 53 n. 2; Harrelson, Interpreting the OT, p. 349; K.-D. Schunck, "Strukturlinien in der Entwicklung der Vorstellung vom 'Tag Jahves'," VT, XIV (1964), 324-25; Herrmann, Die prophetischen Heilserwartungen im Alten Testament, pp. 124-25; von Rad, OTT, II, 137; idem, Die Botschaft der Propheten, p. 103; Eissfeldt, OTI, p. 79; J. Scharbert, Die Propheten Israels bis 700 v. Chr. (Köln, 1965), p. 121; C. Westermann, Tausend Jahre und ein Tag, Taschenbuch (Gütersloh, 1965), pp. 205-206; K. W. Neubauer, "Erwägungen zu Amos 5, 4-15," ZAW, 78 (1966), 304-308; Preuss, Jahweglaube, pp. 158-61.

[175a]See Appendix II, pp. 471.

stressed the originality, uniqueness, and individualism of classical prophecy,[176] the present generation of Old Testament scholars has come to recognize more and more that these critics exaggerated these traits of classical prophecy. Von Rad sums up the recent results of scholarship by saying that the prophets "were in greater or lesser degree conditioned by old traditions which they re-interpreted and applied to their own times."[177] Amos also takes up some of these old traditions of Yahwistic faith. He used the old election tradition.[178] Through Amos Yahweh says, "You only have I known of all the families of the earth. . . ."[179] Whether this refers to the exodus tradition[180] or the tradition of the bestowal of the land[181] is not as important as the recognition that it is an election tra-

---

[176]We refer to only a few representative scholars: Wellhausen, Prolegomena, p. 474, speaks of the classical prophets as the "founders of ethical monotheism," as accomplishing the "individualisation of religion." K. Marti, The Religion of the Old Testament, (London, 1907), pp. 147-48, wrote: "The God whom the prophets serve . . . is a spiritual personality of an entirely ethical character. . . . Henceforth the closest union between religion and ethics is of the very essence of prophetic religion. . . . Religion and ethics form a whole, religion being the roots and supplying the dynamic, and ethics the fruit and displaying the effects." B. Duhm, Israels Propheten (2nd ed.; Giessen, 1922), pp. 459-60.

[177]Von Rad, OTT, II, 3; cf. Scott, The Relevance of the Prophets, p. 209.

[178]Edzard Rohland, Die Bedeutung der Erwählungstraditionen Israels für die Eschatologie der alttestamentlichen Propheten (München, 1956), pp. 56-59; von Rad, OTT, II, 133: "We have no understanding of Amos' preaching at all unless we note the way in which he over and over again comes to grips with the election concept, and how it was the nerve of a great part of his message."

[179]Amos 3:2a.

[180]Rohland, op. cit., p. 56f.; cf. Heaton, The Hebrew Kingdoms, p. 270.

[181]Wolff, Amos, pp. 122, 215; idem, Amos' geistige Heimat (WMANT, 18; Neukirchen-Vluyn, 1964), pp. 6, 38.

dition which was taken very seriously by both Amos and Israel. Israel seems to have confronted Amos' message of judgment with the election tradition by emphasizing that since Yahweh has chosen Israel[182] he will also forgive her transgressions. Amos in taking up this very election tradition concludes that Israel has no advantage over other nations:[183] she cannot hide herself behind Yahweh's election. Because of her election Yahweh says, "I will punish you for all your iniquities."[184] Israel's election is in actual fact the very basis of Yahweh's imminent judgment.

As Amos reacted to the popular notion of the election tradition, so he attacked the popular belief that the Day of Yahweh (yôm YHWY)[185] is a day of salvation for Israel as a nation.[186] Instead the Day of

---

[182]Cf. Ex. 34:6-7; Hos. 6:1.

[183]Amos 9:7.

[184]Amos 3:2b; Jacob, op. cit., p. 207.

[185]For the tradition of the Day of Yahweh, see L. Černy, The Day of Yahweh and some Relevant Problems (Prague, 1948); G. von Rad, "The Origin of the Concept of the Day of Yahweh," JSS, 4 (1959), 97-108; Rohland, op. cit., pp. 275ff., 281-82; G. Fohrer, "Zehn Jahre Literatur zur alttestamentlichen Prophetie," ThR, (1962), 333-34; Lindblom, Prophecy in Ancient Israel, pp. 317ff.; C. F. Whitley, The Prophetic Achievement (London, 1963), 199ff.; Schunck, op. cit., pp. 319ff.; Jeremias, Theophanie, pp. 97-100; Herrmann, Heilserwartungen, pp. 121-24; F. M. Cross, "The Divine Warrior in Israel's Early Cult," in Biblical Motifs: Origins and Transformations, ed. by A. Altman (Studies and Texts, III; Cambridge, Mass., 1966), pp. 19ff.; M. Weiss, "The Origin of the 'Day of the Lord'--Reconsidered," HUCA, XXXVII (1966), 29-60; Preuss, Yahweglaube, pp. 170-79; Hans-Peter Müller, Ursprünge und Strukturen alttestamentlicher Eschatologie (BZAW, 109; Berlin, 1969), pp. 69-85.

[186]It is generally conceded that Amos took up the popular catchword Day of Yahweh, meaning the time when God would shower upon Israel the fullness of his favors and really prove to the world that she was Yahweh's chosen people. Weiss, op. cit., p. 48, has challenged the notion of a pre-Amos origin of the tradition of the Day of Yahweh, ". . . 'the Day of the Lord' in whatever form it took in prophetical literature is connected directly or indirectly with the discussed prophecy of Amos." But if Weiss is right in pointing out at the close of his discussion that

Yahweh will be "darkness and not light, and gloom with no brightness in it."[187] It is the aim of Amos to destroy such popular Israelite hopes of salvation which are based on false interpretations of Yahweh's past actions.[188] Along with these popular notions there existed in Israel the idea that if God's people should ever meet with a catastrophe, Israel as a whole would remain as a remnant among the nations to be the bearer of divine election and promise and experience a glorious future.[189] Amos confronts this self-assurance with an emphatic No.

The messenger saying of Amos 3:12 has customarily been thought to contain the remnant motif.

> Thus says the Lord: 'As the shepherd rescues from the mouth of the lion two legs, or a piece of an ear, so shall the people of

---

the Day of Yahweh "has its roots in the ancient motif-complex of the theophany-description" (p. 60), then the question of a pre-Amos origin of the tradition of the Day of Yahweh is raised anew. Whether the variegated and multiple aspects of the prophetic tradition of the Day of Yahweh can all derive from the influence of the single text in Amos 5:18ff. remains highly questionable.

[187]Amos 5:20.

[188]Wolff, Amos, pp. 123-24, has shown anew that the received election tradition (Amos 2:9; 3:2; 9:7) indicates how Yahweh has shown himself in the past for the salvation of Israel, but that because Israel neglected her responsibility which grew out of these saving actions of the past Yahweh will now come for judgment (Amos 1:4, 7, 8; 2:13; 3:2, 14, 15; 5:17, 27; 6:8, 14; 7:8; 8:2; 9:1-4).

[189]The following passages express indirectly the popular remnant idea; 3:2; 3:12; 5:3; 6:9; 9:1, 10. Cf. Cramer, op. cit., p. 130; W. E. Müller, op. cit., p. 50; Schilling, op. cit., pp. 25ff.; Maag, op. cit., p. 247; E. Jenni, "Remnant," IDB, IV, 32: "Amos seems to assume on the part of his opponents a popular remnant idea bearing the stamp of eschatological salvation. . . ." Herrmann, Heilserwartungen, p. 125 n. 25; Warne, op. cit., p. 71; H. Gottlieb, "Amos and Jerusalem," VT, XVIII (1967), 449; Vawter, op. cit., p. 55; J. Nelis, "Rest Israels," Bibel-Lexikon, ed. by H. Haag (2nd ed.; Einsiedeln, 1968), col. 1473.

> Israel who dwell in Samaria be rescued with the corner of a couch and part of a bed.'[190]

The simile which the prophet uses is fairly clear. Amos does not deny that there will be a "rescue" which can be expected from the impending destruction. There will indeed be a remnant. But what kind of remnant will it be? Some have understood this text to describe a "torn and bruised Remnant";[191] others believe that the *tertium comparationis* is "smallness."[192] But these suggestions fall short in that they do not apply the comparison consistently. The former shepherd Amos employed a picture from shepherd life. It was the shepherd's duty when an animal was torn by a wild beast to bring evidence for such loss.[193] The smallest

---

[190]The last part of vs. 12 is problematical. A number of interpreters believe that this saying concludes with the short clause ". . . so shall the people of Israel be rescued" (so Weiser, *Amos*, p. 147; Maag, *op. cit*., pp. 16-17; Amsler, *Amos*, p. 191; H. H. Rowley, *The Biblical Doctrine of Election* [London, 1950], p. 72; etc.). But it seems best for the sake of literary and metrical reasons to consider vs. 12 as a rhetorical unit (so Fosbroke, *op. cit*., VI, 798; Jacob M. Myers, *Hosea-Joel-Amos-Obadiah-Jonah*, [The Laymen's Bible Commentary, 14; Richmond, Va., 1959], p. 117; Cripps, *op. cit*., pp. 161-62; Wolff, *Amos*, p. 235). For attempted textual solutions of the *crux interpretum* in 3:12b, see W. R. Harper, *A Critical and Exegetical Commentary on Amos and Hosea* (New York, 1905), pp. 80-83; J. Reider, "DMSQ in Amos 3," *JBL*, 67 (1948), 245-48; I. Rabinowitz, "The Crux at Amos III 12," *VT*, XI (1961), 228-31; H. Gese, "Kleine Beiträge zum Verständnis des Amosbuches," *VT*, XII (1962), 427-32; H. A. Moeller, "Ambiguity at Amos 3:12," *Bible Translator*, 15 (1964), 31-34. See Appendix II, p. 472.

[191]Rowley, *The Biblical Doctrine of Election*, p. 72; cf. W. Nowack, *Die Kleinen Propheten*, (Göttinger Handkommentar zum Alten Testament; Göttingen, 1922), p. 135: "Nur ein kümmerlicher Rest wird aus dem Gericht übrig sein."

[192]Schilling, *op. cit*., p. 34; cf. Cripps, *op. cit*., p. 161: ". . . the number of the voluptuous rich who will escape will be neglibible." Jacob, *op. cit*., p. 323.

[193]Ex. 22:12(13); Gen. 31:39; cf. "Code of Hammurabi" # 266, *ANET*[3], p. 177.

"rescued" pieces could serve as proof for the total loss. Thus Amos used the verbal catchword "rescued" with bitter irony. Surely there will be a rescued remnant, but it will only indicate the total loss of the nation. Emphasis is placed here on the "meaninglessness of the remnant."[194] Israel like the animal will be torn apart by an irresistible foe and the "rescued" remnant is of no meaning for the future of Israel as a nation. The remnant motif is here employed as an absolute threat against the national existence of Israel.

Amos comes again to speak of a remnant in the saying against the women of Samaria (Amos 4:1-3).

> The Lord Yahweh has sworn by his holiness: 'Behold, the days are coming upon you, when they shall take you away with ropes, even your remnant [*ʾaḥarîṯ*] with fish prongs.'[195]

The term *ʾaḥarîṯ* is of considerable importance for our discussion. It has been translated in a variety of ways. Among the more prominent suggestions are "posterity,"[196] "hind-part,"[197]

---

[194]With Warne, *op. cit*., p. 71, and the widespread support of interpreters. See Appendix II, p. 472.

[195]Amos 4:2. The translation is by the present writer. S. J. Schwantes, "Note on Amos 4:2b," *ZAW*, 79 (1967), 82-83, has shown that צנות in all likelihood should be translated "rope" as in Akkadian, *CAD*, 16, p. 201, and Enūma eliš, I:72=*ANET*³, p. 61. The סירות דוגה is some kind of fishing utensil, not "fishhooks" but a type of harpoon with which the deportees are goaded along like cattle. Cf. Wolff, *Amos*, pp. 244-45; Maag, *op. cit*., p. 138; Amsler, *Amos*, p. 194.

[196]F. Zorell, *Lexicon Hebraicum et Aramaicum Veteris Testamenti*, p. 38; N. H. Snaith, *The Book of Amos* (Nashville, 1946), p. 69; Fosbroke, *op. cit*., VI, 802; Maag, *op. cit*., pp. 19, 122, 138, follows L. Köhler by translating "Brut" in the sense of posterity.

[197]B. Duhm, *Die Zwölf Propheten* (Tübingen, 1910), p. 7; idem, *Anmerkungen zu den Zwölf Propheten* (Giessen, 1911), p. 6; K. Marti, *Das Dodekapropheton* (Kurzer Hand-Commentar zum AT, XIII; Tübingen, 1904), p. 179; Robinson, *op. cit*., p. 84; Nowack, *op. cit*., p. 136; Kraeling,

"last,"[198] and "remnant."[199] ʾaḥarît with the unusual meaning of "hind-part" presupposes the textual emendation of ʾeṯkem into ʾapḵen for which there is no support from the versions. It also contradicts the other uses of this term in the book of Amos.[200] Furthermore, it has been pointed out that it is used as a stylistic form of the "irreale Synchorese."[201] It seems that the translation "posterity" is too interpretative, for it limits the meaning of the term in the original. It would refer only to the progeny of the women of Samaria. It again is in conflict with the other uses in Amos. The translation "last" derives from the idea of "least important,"[202] which implies a value judgment that is difficult to substantiate in this verse. In view of these considerations it seems least objectionable to translate "remnant." This is also clearly the meaning of this term in the passage of Amos 9:1.[203] This translation avoids an undue limitation of the meaning of the term; it does not require textual emendation nor pose grammatical or contextual difficulties.

Commentary on the Prophets, II, 158; KB², p. 35. Cramer, op. cit., p. 35, translates "Ende."

[198]RSV, Jerusalem Bible; Heaton, The Hebrew Kingdoms, pp. 271-72.

[199]GB, p. 27; BDB, p. 31; E. Sellin, Das Zwölfprophetenbuch (KAT; Leipzig, 1929), p. 216; S. R. Driver, The Books of Joel and Amos (Cambridge Bible for Schools and Colleges; 2nd ed.; Cambridge, 1934), p. 168: "residue"; Cripps, op. cit., p. 167: "residue"; Weiser, Das Buch der Zwölf Kleinen Propheten, p. 150: "was von euch übrig ist"; Wolff, Amos, p. 241: "Rest." See Appendix II, p. 472.

[200]Amos 8:10; 9:1.

[201]Gese, op. cit., pp. 436f.; cf. Wolff, Amos, pp. 241-42.

[202]KB, p. 33, and NAB.

[203]This finds support through a linguistic study of this term.

If the translation "remnant" is correct, the question arises as to what is meant by it. Does it refer to the remainder of the women of Samaria or their offspring? The latter suggestion is supported by some.[204] However, the parallelism between vs. 2d and vs. 2c lends strong support to the view that the remnant still refers to the women of Samaria themselves. Taken in this sense it heightens the picture of their fate. The women of Samaria will be deported by their captors with ropes just like cows. Those who are unwilling, the obstinate remnant of them, will be forced along with other strange tools. Thus Amos again speaks of a remnant which is of no importance for the future of the national existence of Israel. It is noteworthy to point out that Amos does not deny that there will be a remnant left when the foe comes, but this remnant has no significance for Israel as a nation.

The remnant motif appears in the very obscure passage of Amos 6:9-10,[205] which is apparently a fragmentary saying. These verses contain one of the most difficult <u>cruces interpretum</u> of the entire book of Amos.[205a] The background is a time of plague which may have attended a siege. The epidemic is so severe that the inhabitants of the house die. "And if ten men remain in one house, they shall die" (6:9). But if there is a survivor in the house of ten (6:10), he is so fearful when the search party comes to bury the dead that he will not mention the name of Yahweh, lest Yahweh will break out in anger against him. The single surviving remnant is thus as if he were dead; no hopes for the future can be placed

---

[204]Maag, <u>op. cit</u>., p. 122; Heaton, <u>The Hebrew Kingdoms</u>, p. 271.

[205]Only a few of the recent scholars doubt the genuineness of this saying; see Lindblom, <u>Prophecy in Ancient Israel</u>, p. 224; Wolff, <u>Amos</u>, p. 119.

[205a]See Appendix, p. 468.

in him. Amos leaves open the possibility of a remnant being left in a house, but he emphasizes the utter ineffectiveness and hopelessness of this remnant. Again Amos attacks with all forcefulness the false hope which Israel had placed in a remnant. ✓

The remnant motif is encountered in the cycle of visions in the book of Amos which contains the "autobiographical style"[206] of the prophet. The fifth vision (9:1-4) was most likely received at the cult center of Bethel[207] or possibly in Jerusalem.[208] The judgment against God's people comes even as they worship him. The cult center is set in motion; the capitals are smitten; moreover, the entire edifice is about to collapse to shatter the heads of all the worshipers. This apostate people is about to be brought to an end:

> And their remnant /ʾaḥarît/ I will slay with the sword: no refugee of them shall flee, no escapee /pālît/ of them shall escape.[209]

The remnant terminology is employed twice in close proximity. The two remnant terms throw light upon each other. The latter term contains a strong indication for the meaning of the former. This stern message of

[206]This is taken as a sure sign of authenticity by Wolff, Amos, p. 130.

[207]This is the most widely accepted supposition, see Wellhausen, Die Kleinen Propheten, p. 94; Marti, Dodekapropheton, p. 221; Driver, Joel and Amos, p. 220; Sellin, Zwölfprophetenbuch, p. 265; Nowack, op. cit., p. 154; Robinson, op. cit., p. 105; Cripps, op. cit., p. 255; Fosbroke, op. cit., p. 845; Hyatt, Amos, p. 625; Amsler, Amos, p. 239; etc.

[208]R. Vuilleumier, La tradition cultuelle d'Israël dans la prophétie d'Amos et d'Osée (Neuchatel, 1960), p. 72; Harrelson, Interpreting the Old Testament, p. 353.

[209]Amos 9:1b. The translation is by the present writer. See Appendix, pp. 468-69.

judgment contains overtones of ḥērem. In ancient Israelite legal tradition the ban was also applied to those who adopted foreign cults.[210] In the Deuteronomic tradition the ban appears also as a threat against Israel should they not separate themselves from everything that is connected with a foreign cult.[211] The terms ḥrb, mlṭ, and plṭ are employed in corresponding usages in passages dealing with the ban.[212] In the middle of the eighth century B. C. there is certainly much in Israel's worship which indicates a syncretism with the cult of Baal.[213] This harsh message of judgment against the worshipers indicates that Yahweh is moving against his people because they have adulterated their traditional faith. The punishment will be so severe that even the remnant that escaped from the earthquake will fall by the sword. No one will be able to get away or escape. Total destruction will come upon them.

This represents what R. Fey has aptly described as a "borderline statement"[214] in the proclamation of Amos. It indicates to what extremes the prophet must resort in order to shake his people out of their false sense

---

[210]Ex. 22:19(20). For the age of this text, see E. Gerstenberger, Wesen und Herkunft des "apodiktischen Rechts" (WMANT, 20; Neukirchen-Vluyn, 1965), p. 28.

[211]Deut. 7:2, 26. Steck, op. cit., p. 107.

[212]Deut. 13:1b; Josh. 6:21; 8:22, 24, 26; 10:28-40; 11:8, 11-12; 1 Sam. 15:3; 30:17.

[213]See notably Hosea 2:13; 3:4; 4:13; 8:5-6, 11; 10:1-2, 5-6; 11:2. J. Mauchline, Hosea (The Interpreter's Bible; Nashville, 1956), pp. 554-55; P. R. Ackroyd, "Hosea," Peake's Commentary on the Bible, ed. by M. Black and H. H. Rowley (London, 1962), p. 604; H. G. May, "The Fertility Cult in Hosea," AJSL, 48 (1931/32), 73-98.

[214]Fey, op. cit., pp. 49, 114. See Appendix, p. 469.

of security. It was apparently not enough to proclaim in bitter irony that the remnant of Israel that would remain after the coming catastrophe would be meaningless as far as Israel's national existence was concerned. Amos had to destroy any hope that had any connection with the popular expectation of Israel.

The threat of complete annihilation is not limited to Israel alone. This threat appears also in connection with the remnant motif in the cycle of sayings against the nations (1:3–2:16). This cycle forms an independent tradition of words of Amos.[215] It is noteworthy that Amos as a messenger of Yahweh speaks against the foreign nations as much as against Israel. In the judgment saying against Philistia (1:6–8)[216] the four Philistine cities of Gaza,[217] Ashdod,[218] Ashkelon,[219] and Ekron[220] are charged with the crime of slave-traffic.[221] The punishment which will fall upon the cities will be so severe that even "the remnant [<u>šeʾērîṯ</u>] of the Philistines shall perish."[222] This must certainly mean more than that "the nation [is] no longer in its strength."[223] Amos predicted the

---

215 Cf. A. Weiser, <u>Die Profetie des Amos</u>, pp. 85–116; Kapelrud, <u>Central Ideas in Amos</u>, pp. 17–33; Reventlow, <u>Das Amt des Propheten bei Amos</u>, pp. 56–75; Fey, <u>op. cit.</u>, pp. 44–48; N. K. Gottwald, <u>All the Kingdoms of the Earth</u> (New York, 1964), pp. 94–114; W. H. Schmidt, "Die deuteronomistische Redaktion des Amosbuches," <u>ZAW</u>, 77 (1965), 174–83; Wolff, <u>Amos</u>, 164–85.

216 Amos 1:6–8.

217 Amos 1:6–7.

218 Amos 1:8a.

219 Amos 1:8b.

220 Amos 1:8c.

221 Wolff, <u>Amos</u>, pp. 191–92; Gottwald, <u>All the Kingdoms of the Earth</u>, pp. 98–99.

222 Amos 1:8d.

223 Cripps, <u>op. cit.</u>, p. 191.

doom of even "the remnant of the Philistines," i.e., all of those that remained after the destruction of the four cities of Philistia. The guilt of Philistia is the same as the guilt of the other nations including Israel, namely the offence against humanity. Yahweh is the "guardian of justice and right"[224] and those who neglect the ancient standards of human rights are met with divine justice.

The recognition that the remnant motif is employed by Amos as a threat of utter destruction in only these two passages (9:1 and 1:8) is of utmost importance. We have already noted that the remnant motif is used in a negative sense with regard to the national existence of Israel where the remnant has no meaning and significance for the future of Israel as a nation (3:12, 4:1-3; 6:9-10). Amos does not appear to be a consistent prophet of doom.[225] Amos only once proclaimed in a borderline statement the total annihilation of all worshiping Israelites while it was his normal custom to proclaim the end of national existence. This is clearly supported by the threat contained in the dirge of Amos 5:1-3.[225a]

> Hear this word which I take up over you in lamentation,
> O House of Israel:
> 'Fallen, no more to rise,
> is the virgin of Israel;
> forsaken on her land,
> with none to raise her up.'
> For thus says the Lord God:

---

[224]Kapelrud, Central Ideas in Amos, p. 48.

[225]Ibid., p. 79; idem, "New Ideas in Amos," SVT, XV (1966), 196; cf. Krause, op. cit., p. 229: "Amos ist kein systematischer Denker." Preuss, Jahweglaube, p. 181.

[225a]See Appendix, p. 469.

'The city that went forth a thousand
shall have a hundred left,
and that which went forth a hundred
shall have ten left
to the house of Israel.'[226]

There seems to be an apparent contradiction between the first saying and the second saying. The former speaks of the fall of Israel and the latter of a remnant of ten percent of the fighting men. For this reason a number of interpreters have either considered the second saying as a gloss[227] or as an independent but misplaced saying.[228] Yet A. Weiser has convincingly argued that the first saying presents a picture for which the second saying gives the reason.[229] Thus there is no real contradiction between the two sayings. Aside from giving the reason the second saying also presents a threat against Israel.[230] Amos describes in a kind of matter-of-fact language the military disaster that was to befall the nation without specifying whether the loss of ninety percent of Israel's fighting men was due to the application of the ban[231] or to death in battle. The loss of ninety percent clearly indicates decimation but not complete destruction: a remnant of ten percent was to be left over from

---

[226]Amos 5:1-3.

[227]So Oort; see Weiser, Die Profetie des Amos (Giessen, 1929),p.178.

[228]So Gressmann, Köhler, Balla; see Weiser, Profetie, p. 179; Robinson, op. cit., p. 88; Fosbroke, op. cit., VI, 810.

[229]Weiser, Profetie, pp. 179-80. Wellhausen, Die Kleinen Propheten, p. 81, had long before Weiser pointed out that vs. 3 is "der Grund der Klage."

[230]Against Weiser with Fohrer, Introduction, p. 434.

[231]One must be careful not to speak too easily of a decimation through the ban as is done by Herrmann, Die prophetischen Heilserwartungen des Alten Testaments, p. 125 n. 25.

the military catastrophe. Thus the importance of the second saying (5:3) is the loss of ninety percent and the remnant of ten percent. The immediate question that arises is, what significance has this remnant for the future existence of the "house of Israel," i.e. the Northern Kingdom? H. Gressmann has correctly pointed out that the emphasis in vs. 3 is not placed on the fact that some will escape the destruction, but rather on how few will be spared.[232] Thus it is Amos' contribution to the further development of the remnant motif in prophetic literature to attach the aspect of smallness to it for the first time. The popular notion that Israel as a whole will remain on the day of battle is transformed by Amos into a threat against the national existence of Israel.[233] The number of the surviving remnant will be so small that Israel as a nation will be unable to recuperate from the disaster. Because the national existence of Israel is threatened the prophet laments, "Fallen . . . is the virgin of Israel."[234] Only a remnant of Israel will remain but not Israel as a remnant. The conclusion reached by A. Weiser that "in the true statements of Amos one cannot speak of the salvation of a 'remnant,' not even in 3:12; 5:1ff.; 6:9f. . . ."[235] cannot be supported in its comprehensiveness. It is obvious that the remnant motif in the passages referred to by A. Weiser cannot be used for the establish-

---

[232]Gressmann, Der Ursprung der israelitisch-jüdischen Eschatologie, p. 229.

[233]For the new element of threat in the message of Amos, see von Rad, OTT, II, 136.

[234]Amos 5:2.

[235]Weiser, Profetie, p. 312.

ment of Israel as a nation. But this does not mean that they do not speak of the preservation of a remnant. The question of the significance of the saved remnant for the national existence of Israel must be clearly distinguished from the question whether or not a remnant is saved at all. The genuine words of Amos have up to now indicated that a remnant will be saved (except 9:1ff.). This Amos has affirmed, but in his attempt to destroy the popular remnant hope he made it unequivocally clear that this remnant is ineffective and meaningless for the future of Israel's national existence. Amos' usage of the remnant motif with its emphasis on the meaninglessness, ineffectiveness, and smallness of the remnant for Israel's national future is a more effective contrast to the popular hopes of Israel than would have been expressions of a complete denial of a remnant.

But Amos intends to do more than to destroy Israel's false hopes. He confronts Israel in such a radical way in order to shake her out of a false sense of security, to bring to her attention her desperate situation before Yahweh, to warn her of the real danger of complete destruction, and to provoke reformation.

Following this threatening dirge and corresponding to it[236] Amos presents words of future hope and life (5:4-6, 14-15).[237]

---

[236]Hans Wildberger, "Jesajas Verständnis der Geschichte," SVT, IX (1963), 111 n. 2; G. Fohrer, "Die Struktur der alttestamentlichen Eschatologie," in Studien zur alttestamentlichen Prophetie (BZAW, 99; Berlin, 1967), p. 49.

[237]Vss. 14-15 are considered secondary by many critics among them Weiser, Profetie, pp. 183-94; Cripps, op. cit., p. 191 n. 1; Snaith, Amos, p. 93; Nowack, op. cit., p. 145, only vs. 15; Robinson, op. cit., p. 91, only vs. 14b; Fosbroke, op. cit., VI, 815; and now also Wolff, Amos, pp. 119, 133-35, 138. There is a growing number of scholars who argue strong-

For thus says the Lord to the house of Israel:
'Seek me and live;
but do not seek Bethel,
and do not enter into Gilgal
or cross over to Beer-sheba;
for Gilgal shall surely go into exile,
and Bethel shall come to nought.
Seek the Lord and live,
lest he break out like fire in the house of Joseph,
and it devours, with none to quench it for Bethel.[238]

This saying opens with the messenger formula and is addressed to the "house of Israel."[239] Two imperatives open this speech of Yahweh which is so divergently interpreted. "Seek" and "live" serve as a Leitmotiv of the entire passage. These terms are related to each other as cause to effect.[240] F. Hesse argues on grammatical grounds that these two imperatives correspond to each other in a final (or telic) rather than in a consecutive sense.[241] This would mean that life is the goal of the seeking of Yahweh. This lends support to the conclusion that the phrase "seek me and live" contains a promise of salvation in the form of an exhortation.[242] Thus the passage of Amos 5:4-6 (and vss. 14-15) has an ex-

---

ly for the authenticity of vss. 14-15, see especially Cramer, op. cit., pp. 40-43; Maag, op. cit., pp. 28-29, 32; Franz Hesse, "Amos 5, 4-6. 14f," ZAW, 68 (1956), 1-17; Danell, Studies in the Name Israel in the Old Testament, pp. 121-22; Hyatt, Amos, p. 622; K. Neubauer, "Erwägungen zu Amos 5, 4-15," ZAW, 78 (1966), 292-316; W. Zimmerli, The Law and the Prophets, transl. by R. E. Clements (New York, 1965), p. 68; H. Gottlieb, "Amos and Jerusalem," VT, XVII (1967), 451-54; Heaton, The Hebrew Kingdoms, p. 274. See Appendix, p. 469.

238Amos 5:4-6.

239There is no reason to eliminate בית ישׂראל as Weiser, Profetie, p. 190, proposed because of the analogy with 5:1, 3.

240Neubauer, op. cit., p. 309.

241Hesse, ZAW, 68 (1956), pp. 4 n. 22.

242Wolff, Amos' geistige Heimat, pp. 30ff., designates Amos 5:4-5 as a Mahnrede which has a number of similarities with the wisdom tra-

traordinary position[243] in the book of Amos in which otherwise the judgment theme predominates. J. P. Hyatt states, "Here are the most hopeful passages in Amos' message."[244]

The imperative "seek" gives a positive invitation to the Israelites. The verb "seek" is often used in the Hebrew Bible in the specific sense of going to a sanctuary in order to seek an oracle[245] or to participate in the cult.[246] A. Weiser supposes that the phrase "seek me" is connected from the start with the cultic seeking of Yahweh.[247] This suggests that the people were to seek Yahweh at the cult center or centers.[248] This supposition is, however, absolutely negated in vs. 5:

---

dition. He concludes, "Aus dieser Welt weisheitlichen Denkens und Redens werden die Mahnworte des Amos in ihrer antithetischen Struktur und mit ihrem Tatfolgeaufweis, der die Einsicht weckt, durchaus verständlich." For a critique of the supposed wisdom influence on Amos, see J. L. Crenshaw, "The Influence of the Wise upon Amos," ZAW, 79 (1967), 42-52.

[243]See especially Gottlieb, op. cit., p. 449.

[244]Hyatt, Amos, p. 621.

[245]Gen. 25:22; 1 Sam. 9:9; cf. 2 Ki. 3:11; 8:8; 22:18.

[246]Ps. 24:6. The meaning of participation in the cult of a sanctuary seems intended in Amos 5:5.

[247]Weiser, Profetie, p. 190. He undergirds his argumentation by pointing to Amos 4:4 "come to Bethel" and explains that "'Gott suchen' ist vielleicht geprägte liturgische Form, die mit der Wallfahrt zum Heiligtum zusammenhängt." Cf. Neubauer, op. cit., pp. 454-63.

[248]This conclusion is reached by Weiser, Profetie, p. 190. Kapelrud, Central Ideas in Amos, pp. 35-37, believes that there is a distinction between the דרש in vss. 4, 6, 14 and vs. 5. The latter verse stresses the idea that Yahweh could not be found at Bethel and Gilgal, but the former passages emphasize that Yahweh is still to be sought at the cult center. Yahweh had rejected Bethel and Gilgal, but "Amos advised the people of the Northern Kingdom to seek Yahweh in Jerusalem" (p. 37). The distinctions of the term are artificially applied by Kapelrud and lead away from the meaning of the text. Amos attacks the cult

"Do not seek Bethel, or do not enter into Gilgal or cross over into Beer-sheba." Yet it is fairly certain that "seek" has cultic overtones.[249] In vs. 4 Amos provokes his hearers by the use of cultic language in the Yahweh-word, while at the same time he opposes the cult of the Northern Kingdom.[250] W. Harrelson says aptly, "Yahweh is not to be found in the pilgrimages to the sacred places, in the offerings there made."[251] The inevitable question is whether the command "seek me and live" is merely a provocation or whether it is not also the task of Yahweh's prophet to explicate the new meaning of these words? J. P. Hyatt[252] affirms that Amos explains at least in part, what he means in 5:14-15.[253] The supposition that 5:14-15 are Amos' own explanation and interpretation of the Yahweh-word in 5:4-6 is supported by the fact that 5:14-15 are neither introduced nor close with the messenger formula. Let us quote the interpretation of Amos in 5:14-15:

> Seek good, and not evil,
> that you may live;
> and so the Lord, the God of hosts, will be with you,
> as you have said.

---

centers of Bethel, Gilgal, and Beer-sheba as examples of worship at any cult center. Cf. Gottlieb, op. cit., p. 453.

[249]For details see Weiser, Profetie, pp. 190ff.; Neubauer, op. cit., p. 311.

[250]Weiser, Profetie, p. 191, with detailed arguments. Cf. Hesse, ZAW, 68 (1956), p. 5; Neubauer, op. cit., p. 311.

[251]Harrelson, Interpreting the Old Testament, p. 348.

[252]Hyatt, Amos, p. 622.

[253]For the opposite view we may cite Weiser, Profetie, p. 192, who states that Amos "betrachtet . . . es nicht als seine Aufgabe, sich in eine nähere Erörterung darüber einzulassen, worin das eigentliche Jahwesuchen bestehe. . . ."

Hate evil, and love good,
   and establish justice in the gate;
it may be that the Lord, the God of hosts,
   will be gracious to the remnant of Joseph.

"Seek good, and not evil" is the condition for the result expressed next, namely life. Thus the purpose and the goal of the "seeking of good" is life. This is clearly indicated by the <u>le</u>^{e}<u>ma</u>^{c}<u>an</u> which introduces the telic (final) clause.[254] Thus vs. 14a has the character of a promise of salvation just as vs. 4a. Furthermore, vs. 14b has no meaning independent of vs. 14a. Therefore it is only natural that vs. 14b must build upon vs. 14a.[255] The fact that the predicate and the subject is separated by <u>kēn</u> does not justify the removal of the verb in order to attach it to vs. 14a.[256] <u>kēn</u> refers in vs. 14b directly to Yahweh and asserts that Yahweh will do this only "so,"[257] i.e., Yahweh acts upon the premise that the house of Israel will fulfill the condition laid down in vs. 14a.

---

[254]See Ronald J. Williams, <u>Hebrew Syntax: An Outline</u> (Toronto, 1967), pp. 64, 87; cf. Hesse, <u>ZAW</u>, 68 (1956), p. 4 n. 22.

[255]So Weiser, <u>Profetie</u>, p. 188, against Köhler who attempts to isolate vs. 14b and then joins it to vs. 14a in a causal relationship. On the other hand Weiser objects to the authenticity of these verses mainly on stylistic grounds. He argues that the opening of vs. 14b וִיהִי־כֵן is clumsy and reveals a later epexegesis. Neubauer, <u>op. cit</u>., pp. 304-305, argues against Weiser by pointing out that vs. 14b is formally an independent main clause which begins with a ו <u>copulativum</u> and a jussive which according to Gesenius-Kautzsch takes the place of regular imperfect. Therefore, it is hardly possible to consider the ו to have the simple coordinative meaning "and" and to take vs. 14b as the continuation of the telic clause of vs. 14ab. In this construction the ו would remain untranslated. Thus the supposed awkwardness of vs. 14b which Weiser criticizes and which leads him to reject the whole verse has been removed by careful grammatical and syntactical analysis.

[256]Maag, <u>op. cit</u>., pp. 157-58, reconstructs the whole word-order of both clauses and is therefore forced to insert another ו. But his reconstruction lacks textual support and seems to be conditioned by his own preconceived notions.

[257]The consideration of Robinson, <u>op. cit</u>., p. 91, to eliminate

If vss. 14a and 14b stand in a cause-effect relationship to each other and if the "live" in vs. 14b contains cultic overtones just as the "live" in vs. 4b--and there is no evidence to the contrary--then Yahweh's command to "seek" him is interpreted by Amos to mean to "seek good, and not evil." Emphasis is then placed upon the correction of erroneous notions of cultic salvation. Salvation or life is gained in a quite different way than is popularly believed. Salvation or life is not automatically received by the cultic pronouncement of salvation in the oracle of salvation at the cult center. Contrary to this notion the people have first to "seek good, and not evil" (vs. 14a). Then, and only then, that may take place what the oracle of salvation to which they refer so lightly promises, namely that "Yahweh . . . will be with you" (vs. 14c). In this connection the full phrase "Yahweh, the God of hosts" fits the context and must not be eliminated as a later interpretation.[258] It is rather certain that Amos recites intentionally cultic formulations.[259] The cultic phrases "seek me" and "seek Yahweh" have identical meanings and are interpreted in a new way by the phrase "seek good" (vs. 14a).[260] These three phrases are identical in meaning to the extent that if these imperatives are followed by the people of Israel, they will issue in life.

---

vs. 14b as a secondary addition because כֵּן can be understood as an absolute expression which needs no continuation is not convincing.

[258]So Neubauer, op. cit., p. 306, against Sellin, Dodekapropheton, p. 231; and Weiser, Profetie, p. 188. Robinson, op. cit., p. 90, Maag, op. cit., p. 32, Amsler, Amos, p. 205 and others have no objection to this phrase.

[259]For the cultic association of the phrase "Yahweh, God of hosts," see von Rad, OTT, I, 18-21; Schmidt, Alttestamentlicher Glaube und seine Umwelt, pp. 107f.

[260]Sellin, op. cit., p. 230, and Gottlieb, op. cit., p. 451.

Thus it is Amos' intention to interpret the two former expressions (vss. 4 and 6) by the latter (vs. 14).

A key question is, what does Amos mean by "good"? In the history of research two main answers have been given, namely "ethical monotheism" and "pre-Deuteronomic propaganda."[261] The former point of view was most prominent around the turn of the century and stressed Yahweh as the "guardian of universal ethics."[262] The latter view mainly emphasizes Amos' attack against the cult of the Northern Kingdom.[263] It seems most appropriate, however, to begin an interpretation of "good"[264] from the immediate context. Amos rejected as acceptable worship the mere seeking of Yahweh at the cult centers (5:5-6) and its services (5:21-23) to the neglect of practicing justice in common life.[265] Amos equates the "seeking of Yahweh" with the "seeking of good." The phrase "seek good, and not

---

[261]A detailed discussion of these views is provided by Gottlieb, op. cit., pp. 451-54.

[262]This phrase is from Robinson, op. cit., p. 77: "Das Grosse und Bleibende in der Verkündigung des Amos ist, dass er Jahwe als Hüter universaler Moral verstehen gelehrt und damit den nationalen Henotheismus seiner Zeitgenossen durch den ethischen Monotheismus abgelöst hat."

[263]This view is maintained by Kapelrud, Central Ideas in Amos, pp. 35-37, who himself seems to be dependent on Engnell.

[264]For the theological background of the "good," see Smend, EvTh, 23 (1963), pp. 405ff.

[265]Against Neubauer, op. cit. p. 306, who believes that Amos proposed a way of salvation completely separate from the cult. But vss. 21-24 can hardly have proposed the abolition of the entire ritual system of the Northern Kingdom. Rather Amos insists that a faith in Yahweh which does not issue in social justice and righteousness in conduct cannot hope in salvation based on mere ritual acts.

evil" (vs. 14a) is further interpreted by the chiasm "hate evil, and love good" (vs. 15a). To this a further admonition is added in vs. 15b: "establish justice in the gate." The demand of Yahweh is "justice" and "righteousness" on the part of the people. The "justice in the gate" is primarily social justice. 5:7 condemns those who neglect justice and righteousness; 5:10 attacks those who hate and detest the ones who yet defend justice and truth; and 5:11 threatens the ones who take advantage of the poor and extort unjust levies. In 5:12 these acts are expressly described as "transgressions" and "sins." Amos criticizes constantly the transgressions of ancient Israelite law.[266] The intention of Amos' usage of such negative expressions is obvious. He attempts to bring Israel to repentance. Thus the passages of 5:7, 10-13 are designed to serve the task of showing his hearers their guilt and the passage of 5:14-15 is aimed at leading them to the only way of salvation. The final aim of the "seeking of Yahweh,"[267] which is the "seeking of good," is to turn them from their

---

[266]It is hardly likely that Amos refers only to certain legal traditions such as the priestly Torah (so J. Begrich, Die priesterliche Tora [BZAW, 66; Berlin, 1936], pp. 63-88) or the Book of Covenant (so Reventlow, Das Amt des Propheten bei Amos, p. 75), because there are also statements which point to disobedience of the more general guidance of God in history. Cf. Smend, EvTh, 23 (1963), pp. 405ff.; Wolff, Amos, pp. 32-36; Neubauer, op. cit., p. 314 n. 105.

[267]Claus Westermann, "Die Begriffe für Fragen und Suchen im Alten Testament," Kerygma und Dogma, VI (1960), 22, suggests that the "seeking" in Amos can take place only through the prophet. As the priest in the cult is the mediator in the "seeking" of Yahweh, so Amos transfers the "seeking" through a new mediator, the prophet. This is an intriguing suggestion but seems to lack any direct support from the book of Amos itself. There is in no place in Amos an intimation that the people must come to Amos to seek Yahweh.

evil ways and to cause them to do "justice" and "righteousness" in their common life.[268]

At this point it is appropriate to emphasize that Amos is not a consistent prophet of unrelieved doom.[269] For Amos the important matter was to point with bitter irony to the false popular notions of salvation and future hope in Israel and to call the people to repentance,[270] to induce them to return to Yahweh. By his call to "seek Yahweh" and to "seek good" and thus to "live," Amos did not proclaim an unconditional promise of a happy future.[271] To have "life" means of course to be spared from judgment.[272] But "life" is conditional; it is dependent upon the "seeking" of Yahweh and of good. Only a revelation from Yahweh

---

[268]Amos does not identify religion with ethics or morality, although it appears that piety is almost fulfilled in the "seeking" of good and in "establishing" righteousness. But Amos qualifies the "seeking" of good at the same time by the "seeking" of Yahweh. Cf. Hans Wildberger, "'Glauben' im Alten Testament," ZThK, 65 (1968), 150.

[269]Hyatt, Prophetic Religion, p. 100; Kapelrud, "New Ideas in Amos," SVT, XI (1966), 196.

[270]It is noteworthy that the direct invitation to repentance recedes in the message of Amos, but one can hardly say that the topic of repentance has in Amos "no meaning" (so E. Würthwein "Busse und Umkehr im Alten Testament," TWNT, IV, 983). In 5:4-6, 14 there is clearly a calling and exhorting aimed at a return to God without the use of the term repentance. Amos speaks directly of repentance in 4:6, 8-9, 10, 11 not so much in the form of an exhortation, but in the form of a denunciation. Amos states that the people did not return to Yahweh. But this repeated note is made just for the reason of calling Israel in the last minute to return to their God. A return to Yahweh has not yet taken place; may this return take place as yet in the last minute! Cf. Y. Kaufmann, The Religion of Israel (Chicago, 1960), p. 367; Danell, op. cit., pp. 120-21.

[271]For the conditional nature of the announcement of doom in Amos see Vuilleumier, op. cit., p. 25; Kapelrud, Central Ideas in Amos, pp. 58-59; Reventlow, Das Amt des Propheten bei Amos, p. 54; Neubauer, op. cit., p. 515.

[272]Marti, Dodekapropheton, p. 188.

gave Amos the assurance that Yahweh was still a merciful God, who once had chosen Israel, and that his gracious purpose still stood and would indeed be realized if the people would return from their self-assurance and act with justice and righteousness.[273] The question with which Amos confronted his people was one of ultimate concern; it was the question of death or life.[274] Life would be theirs only on the condition of their return to Yahweh. When this condition is fulfilled, then, and only then, will Yahweh perhaps be gracious to the "remnant of Joseph" (5:15).

What does Amos mean by the crucial term "remnant of Joseph" (<u>šeʾērîṯ yôsēp̱</u>)[275]? Does this term originate with Amos or did it exist prior to him? Does it designate the Northern Kingdom as a whole or a decimated Israel? Does it refer to a temporal or eschatological entity? These and other questions arise immediately for anyone who is acquainted with the problem of the remnant motif in Amos. The proposed answers to these questions vary widely. If these questions are to be answered in one way or another with any degree of certainty, then solutions must be sought on the basis of the background of the ideas, concepts, and polemics of the prophet Amos himself and the prior development of the remnant motif.

We have noted that Amos had taken up phrases and formulations from

---

[273]Hesse, <u>ZAW</u>, 68 (1956), pp. 1ff.; cf. Lindblom, <u>Prophecy in Ancient Israel</u>, p. 350 n. 14.

[274]H. W. Wolff, "Hauptprobleme alttestamentlicher Prophetie," <u>EvTh</u>, 15 (1955), 149=now also in <u>Gesammelte Studien zum Alten Testament</u> (<u>TB</u>, 22; München, 1964), p. 209.

[275]W. E. Müller, <u>op. cit</u>., p. 52, and Warne, <u>op. cit</u>., p. 72, do not even discuss the question of the identity of the "remnant of Joseph" nor do they investigate its meaning in Amos.

the cultic way of salvation. He has taken up the traditions of the Day of Yahweh and Israel's election. In each case Amos used these concepts and formulations for polemical purposes[276] in order to shake Israel out of her complacency and self-assurance, to confront her with the question of death and life, and to spur her on to return to her God. Amos has shown himself to be a master of great skill in employing these motifs as a re-interpreted polemic to drive home his message for doomed Israel. Israel's consciousness of her election rested upon the fact that Yahweh had "known"[277] her of all the nations and had shown this to the nations of the earth in the exodus experience.[278] S. Herrmann has shown that Amos stands also in "the tradition of the house of Joseph."[279] The term "remnant of Joseph" can hardly have been coined by Amos. It too was taken up from popular belief.[280] It was probably connected with the tradition of the house of Joseph which was rather prominent in the Northern Kingdom.[281] The stereotyped form of the term "remnant of Joseph" supports

---

[276]Neubauer, op. cit., pp. 304-16.

[277]Amos 3:2.

[278]Amos 2:9-10; 3:2; 9:7b; cf. Wolff, Amos, pp. 122-23; Rohland, op. cit., pp. 58-63.

[279]Herrmann, Heilserwartungen, p. 119. He also shows that Amos used the characteristically Northern Israelite election tradition in order to make his point.

[280]So already Sellin, Der alttestamentliche Prophetismus, p. 150. Cf. Schilling, op. cit., p. 26; Preuss, Jahweglaube, pp. 180ff.

[281]We have already seen that in Amos 3:2 the remnant motif is connected with the election tradition.

the idea that it was a known entity, for it would indeed be surprising if no explanation of a newly coined term would have survived had Amos coined it. It can hardly be doubted that such a formulalike term would have needed an explanation had it been newly formed. This term may ultimately have its origin in the climax of the Joseph cycle as related in Gen. 45:7: "And God sent me before you to preserve for you a remnant on earth, and to keep alive for you many survivors." In this passage the remnant is a temporal entity consisting of the entire clan of Jacob. Israel may have applied these notions to herself believing that she as a whole temporal entity will be the "remnant of Joseph" when the Day of Yahweh comes to destroy the surrounding nations. If this suggestion is correct, then Amos can have taken up this term from popular Israelite belief--as he has taken up other ideas, phrases, terms, and traditions--in order to use it polemically against the false popular hopes that were connected with it. In the course of his polemic he fills then this term too with new meaning.

Having discussed the origin of this term we must turn to the question of its meaning. It will be seen that the term "remnant of Joseph" cannot refer to the Northern Kingdom contemporary with Amos.[282] It is

---

[282]This view has found supporters ever since Wellhausen, Die Kleinen Propheten, p. 82. So also Mowinckel, Psalmenstudien II, p. 265. More recently it has been taken up again by Lindblom, Prophecy in Ancient Israel, p. 350 n. 124: The "remnant of Joseph" is "North Israel as a whole"; Mamie, op. cit., p. 222: "Ephraim et Manassé, c'est-à-dire du royaume du Nord"; Gottwald, All the Kingdoms, p. 115: "the present Israelites, who are a mere shadow of their former selves"; Kraeling, Commentary on the Prophets, I, 164: "the Northern Kingdom . . . safely reduced"; Nelis, op. cit., col. 1473.

certainly true that Israel was decimated by calamities (4:6-11).[283] But Israel still believed that it was wealthy and prosperous (6:13).[284] The suggestion that the "remnant of Joseph" refers to Judah is too far-fetched to be credible.[285] From the available evidence the term "remnant of Joseph" cannot have meant a decimated present entity. It must refer to an entity of the future,[286] because the condition for "life" had to be met first.[286a]

Amos was attempting to call Israel to return to Yahweh by exhorting the people to "seek good, and not evil" (5:14). On the basis of the fulfillment of this condition to return, Yahweh would "perhaps . . .

---

[283]See Sellin, Das Zwölfprophetenbuch, I, 231; and especially Weiser, Profetie, p. 186. The subjective remarks of Amos that Israel "is so small" (7:2, 5) are used by Gottwald, All the Kingdoms, p. 115, and Lindblom, Prophecy in Ancient Israel, p. 340 n. 104, in support of their view. These references cannot be used as evidence for the actual condition of Israel, because they are a pathetic diminution on the part of the prophet.

[284]Bright, A History of Israel, pp. 238-42.

[285]This interpretation was advanced over half a century ago by Meinhold, op. cit., p. 47. This farfetched suggestion has not attracted any following. Meinhold himself admits that "Joseph" in Amos refers always to the Northern Kingdom (p. 50). Since Meinhold is not willing to grant that Amos exhibits a tension between doom and salvation for Israel he is forced to this strange suggestion.

[286]The majority of scholars understand the term "remnant of Joseph" as a future entity, see especially J. Boehmer, "Die Eigenart der prophetischen Heilspredigt des Amos," Theologische Studien und Kritiken, 76 (1903), 35; Dittmann, op. cit., p. 610; Sellin, Der alttestamentliche Prophetismus, p. 105; Driver, Joel and Amos, p. 186; Cramer, op. cit., p. 40; Müller, op. cit., pp. 53-53; Schilling, op. cit., pp. 26-29; Procksch, Theologie des Alten Testaments, pp. 175, 580-81; Maag, op. cit., p. 200; Jenni, IDB, II, 128; Schunck, op. cit., p. 323; Herrmann, Heilserwartungen, p. 125; Kapelrud, SVT, XV (1966), p. 205; Ringgren, Israelite Religion, p. 258; Preuss, Jahweglaube, pp. 160-161; etc.

[286a]See Appendix II, pp. 473-74.

be gracious to the remnant of Joseph" (5:15b).[287] The "perhaps" of 5:15b expresses also the grief of Amos which came with the realization that not the entire nation would return to their God by seeking to do justice and righteousness.[288] Only those who would seek Yahweh would "perhaps" live through the coming judgment. They would be the "remnant of Joseph." The tension which Amos' message produced through the juxtaposition of doom and salvation is bridged by the prophet by means of the remnant motif. The mass of Israelites who refused to return to Yahweh would perish in the judgment to come upon the nation, but a remnant, those who returned to Yahweh, would "perhaps" be spared. F. Hesse expresses this in the following way:

> Both sentences keep their validity: Sinners have to be destroyed for the sake of the holiness of Yahweh, and the

---

[287]Grammatically the phrase שְׁאֵרִית יוֹסֵף can be translated either as "the remnant of Joseph" (so the majority) or "a remnant of Joseph" (so Dittmann, op. cit., p. 610; and others, recently also in Wolff, Amos' geistige Heimat, p. 31).

[288]Weiser, Profetie, pp. 186-87, points to the supposed problem of a lack of logic in Amos' message if 5:14-15 is from the prophet himself. He believes that there is an inconsistency in the invitation to repent as directed to the whole house of Israel while only an uncertain salvation of a remnant is promised in vss. 14-15. If the remnant is the body who are saved by their conversion, then it is absurd, argues Weiser, for this salvation to be made uncertain through the modifying "may be." Against this one must object that an inadvertency in logic is not of itself evidence against Amos' authorship of 5:14-15. But when this has been said, the question may be raised whether the logic in these passages is so weak as Weiser thinks. The "may be" of vs. 15b does not contradict the general exhortation to repent. Rather it intensifies the call to return to Yahweh, for if Yahweh would be gracious to all the people then Israel would not be concerned to return to Yahweh. This is to say that even if Israel returns salvation is still dependent on God's free grace. Cf. E. K. Dietrich, Die Umkehr im Alten Testament und im Judentum (Stuttgart, 1936), p. 51; Danell, op. cit., pp. 121-22; Neubauer, op. cit., p. 307 n. 74.

> people of Yahweh must experience salvation for the sake of the given promise.[289]

The ʾûlay (perhaps, may be)[290] indicates that the freedom of God is preserved also in the promise of the salvation of a "remnant of Joseph." The realization of the promise of the remnant is neither automatic nor humanly controllable through the fulfillment of the condition to return to their God. A right to salvation cannot be earned. Everything is dependent upon God's free grace.

In popular belief Israel regarded herself confidently as the remnant of the nations to whom salvation would be granted on the Day of Yahweh when those around them would be destroyed. Amos attacked this view by making salvation conditional. In popular belief the "remnant of Joseph" was taken as a term referring to the salvation of the temporal nation on the Day of Yahweh. Amos insisted that only those who would return to Yahweh could hope for salvation. Amos unequivocally affirmed that Israel as a national entity would not be saved on the Day of Yahweh. Only that part of the nation which would seek Yahweh by seeking good would "perhaps" be saved. The intimate connection of the remnant motif with the tradition of the Day of Yahweh is here evident.[291] Just as the concept of the Day of Yahweh is here an eschatological idea, so the "remnant of Joseph" is an entity of eschatological expectation. The nation will

---

[289]Hesse, ZAW, 68 (1956), p. 16; cf. Jenni, IDB, II, 128.

[290]For the meaning of the "may be" in 5:15b, see Fey, op. cit., pp. 52-53; Neubauer, op. cit., p. 307 n. 74.

[291]See especially Schunck, VT, XIV (1964), 323.

come to an end, but there will be a remnant left by the eschatological catastrophe. The "remnant of Joseph" is the Israel of the Day of Yahweh.[292] This "remnant of Joseph" will consist of those who have returned to Yahweh by having sought good. To identify the "remnant of Joseph" more closely leads to speculation because one would be forced to go beyond the scanty evidence.[293] Yet Amos stands here within an old tradition. Elijah too speaks of a remnant that returned to Yahweh to be spared in judgment.[294] In the Elijah tradition, however, the remnant is an entity that is already present. Amos introduces a new aspect which would never be lost sight of in the future appearance of the remnant motif in prophetic literature. In Amos the remnant is an entity of eschatological expectation.[295] Thus in Amos we encounter for the first time a connection of the remnant motif with eschatology.

---

[292]Schilling, op. cit., p. 28.

[293]Boehmer, op. cit., p. 35, identifies the "remnant of Joseph" as the "pious ones." So also Dittmann, op. cit., p. 610; L. Duerr, Ursprung und Ausbau der israelitisch-jüdischen Heilandserwartung (Berlin, 1925), pp. 40ff.; Maag, op. cit., pp. 199-200. Vawter, op. cit., p. 91, identifies them as the "Israel of faith," while Ringgren, Israelite Religion, p. 258, refers to them as "penitent individuals." It seems that Preuss, Jahweglaube, p. 181, goes too far in identifying the "remnant of Joseph" as a "Gemeinde der Frommen." Schilling, op. cit., p. 41, reads a later idea into Amos when he designates the "remnant of Joseph" as a "heiliger Rest."

[294]1 Ki. 19:18.

[295]With Gressmann, Der Ursprung der israelitisch-jüdischen Eschatologie, p. 235; Sellin, Prophetismus, p. 150; F. Dreyfus, "Reste," Vocabulaire de théologie biblique, ed. by X. Léon-Dufour (Paris, 1962), col. 909; Maag, op. cit., pp. 199-200; Jenni, IDB, II, 128; Schunck, op. cit., p. 323; Herrmann, Heilserwartungen, p. 124; Preuss, Jahweglaube, p. 181, against Lindblom, Prophecy in Ancient Israel, p. 363, who believes that "the authentic revelations of Amos show no traces of a positive eschatology. . . . There is in the revelations of Amos no hint of a remnant that will be saved." Lindblom affirms, of course, that Amos

Amos 5:14-15 demonstrated that the prophet was able by his employment of popular notions of the remnant motif to transfer it on the one hand into a biting polemic against the popular hopes connected with it and on the other hand to imbue it with new meaning of lasting importance for its future development in prophetic literature. In this significant passage in the book of Amos it becomes apparent that the remnant motif contains the dual aspects of judgment and salvation: while only a remnant will remain (judgment), yet there will be a remnant (salvation). In the sense that the remnant has its basis in Yahweh's grace it is the result of God's action for man.[296] At the same time it has its basis in the justice and righteousness of man, in his return to Yahweh, in his doing good. In this sense the human action is immensely intensified in the salvation of the remnant.[297] Yet for Amos human action cannot be a substitute for God's action nor can God's action be a substitute for human action. Each has its proper sphere. There will be no remnant without God's grace just as little as there will be a remnant without man's return to God. Thus Amos is able to bridge the chasm between doom and salvation with the

---

contains a "negative eschatology." He arrives at this conclusion by regarding Amos as a consistent prophet of doom who uses the phrase "remnant of Joseph" as a mere dimunition in his intercession and compassion for Israel. That this is an inadequate interpretation has been shown above.

[296]Herntrich, TDNT, IV, 202, places a too one-sided emphasis on the "action of God" as the basis for the remnant. Note also the criticism by Schilling, op. cit., pp. 4-5; G. Fohrer, "Neuere Literatur zur alttestamentlichen Prophetie," ThR, XX (1952), 348-59; Preuss, Jahweglaube, pp. 180-81.

[297]H. Wildberger, "Jesajas Verständnis der Geschichte," SVT, IX (1963), 103, points out that with the remnant idea human decision receives an "unerhörte Bedeutung."

remnant motif.[298] It is his means of lessening the tension between the proclamation of judgment and the proclamation of salvation. Amos' hope for an eschatological remnant is conditioned by the divine "perhaps" and the human response.

The remnant motif appears once more in another section of the book of Amos, i.e., the epilogue (9:8b-15). Scholars have rightly maintained that the epilogue is made up of three distinct sayings.[299] Of importance for our study is the second saying: a prophecy of promise (9:11-12). The authorship of the epilogue as a whole, including the second saying, is one of the most debated questions of the book of Amos.[300]

---

[298]The remnant motif is not only "niederschmetternd" (so Gressmann, Ursprung, p. 229) and therefore part of the eschatology of doom (Unheilseschatologie). The object of salvation, according to Gressmann, is not the remnant but the new people. But Gressmann overlooks the fact that the new people is directly related to the remnant and grows out of it. The present writer cannot see why Gressmann, p. 237, believes that the remnant motif connects only insufficiently and artificially the proclamation of judgment and salvation. Gressmann is not objective, because he depreciates the proclamation of salvation as something "subprophetic" borrowed from popular belief.

[299]This view has been adopted by many since it was first suggested by Marti, Dodekapropheton, pp. 224-26; A. Winter, "Analyse des Buches Amos," Theologische Studien und Kritiken, 83 (1910), 361-62; L. Köhler, Amos (Giessen, 1917), pp. 154-55; Maag, op. cit., pp. 61-62; Fosbroke, op. cit., VI, 850-53; Weiser, Das Buch der zwölf Kleinen Propheten, I, 204; Hyatt, Amos, p. 625; Reventlow, Das Amt des Propheten bei Amos, pp. 94-95; Harrelson, Interpreting the Old Testament, p. 355; Amsler, Amos, pp. 245-46; and others.

[300]Ever since Wellhausen, Die Kleinen Propheten, p. 96, declared in 1892 that 9:13-15 represents "Rosen und Lavendel statt Blut und Eisen" and that 9:8-15 cannot derive from Amos for the reason that "nachdem er [Amos] grade vorher alle seine früheren Drohungen weit überboten hat, kann er ihnen nicht plötzlich die Spitze abbrechen, nicht aus dem Zorne Jahves zum Schlusse Milch und Honig fliessen lassen," the majority of scholars deny the authorship of the whole epilogue. There have been, however, many attempts to ascribe all or at least part of the epilogue to Amos, see Boehmer, op. cit., pp. 38-39, 44 n. 1; Sellin, Prophetismus, pp. 32-33; W. Eichrodt, Die Hoffnung des ewigen Friedens im Alten Testa-

Before we enter into a detailed discussion of the remnant motif in 9:11-12, we will present our translation of this saying:

'In that day I will raise up the falling[301] booth of David,
and repair its breaches,
and raise up its ruins,
and rebuild it as in the days of old,

---

ment (Gütersloh, 1920), pp. 95-101; Krause, op. cit., pp. 228-29; Driver, Joel and Amos, pp. 122-26; Cramer, op. cit., pp. 47-49, 177ff., gives a valuable survey of the older research; Danell, op. cit., pp. 134-35; J. Hempel, Worte der Propheten (Berlin, 1949), p. 144; idem, "Die Wurzeln des Missionswillens im Glauben des Alten Testaments," ZAW, 66 (1954), 253; W. Zimmerli, "Gericht und Heil im alttestamentlichen Prophetenwort," Der Anfang, 11 (1949), 38; A. Neher, Amos. Contribution à l'étude du prophétisme (Paris, 1950); Maag, op. cit., pp. 6-62, 246-51: vs. 12 is an exilic or post-exilic interpolation; Rohland, op. cit., pp. 59, 230ff., follows Maag; G. J. Botterweck, "Zur Authentizität des Buches Amos," BZ, N.F. 2 (1958), 188-89; E. Hammershaimb, Amos fortolket (2nd ed.; Copenhagen, 1958), pp. 131-39; Watts, op. cit., pp. 25, 48ff., 80f.; Kaufmann, The Religion of Israel, p. 368; I. Engnell, "Amos," SBU, (2nd ed.; Copenhagen, 1962), I, cols. 65f.; Heschel, The Prophets, p. 37; Reventlow, Das Amt des Propheten bei Amos, pp. 90-95; Harrelson, Interpreting the Old Testament, p. 365: only 9:8-10 genuine; Kapelrud, Central Ideas, pp. 53-59: only 9:8-10 genuine; Fey, op. cit., pp. 54ff.: only vs. 12a is a later interpolation; B. Otzen, Studien über Deuterosacharja (Acta Theolgica Danica, VI; Assen, 1964), p. 131; idem, "Rest," Gads Dansk Bibel Leksikon, ed. by E. Nielsen and B. Noack (Copenhagen, 1966), II, cols. 605-7; Scharbert, Propheten Israels, pp. 91f., 130ff.: genuine but overlaid with later material; idem, Heilsmittler im Alten Testament und im Alten Orient (Freiburg, 1964), pp. 159f., Eissfeldt, OTI, p. 400: only 9:8-10 genuine; R. E. Clements, Prophecy and Covenant (SBT, 43; London, 1965), p. 111; von Rad, OTT, II, 138; R. A. Carlson, "Profeten Amos och Davidsriket," RoB, 25 (1966), 74-78; H. P. Müller, Ursprünge und Strukturen alttestamentlicher Eschatologie (BZAW, 109; Berlin, 1969), p. 213: vs. 12 late interpolation.

[301]The articular use of the Qal active participle of נפל clearly refers to the noun סכה with which it agrees in number and gender. W. Gesenius-E. Kautzsch, Hebräische Grammatik (28th ed.; Halle, 1909), # 116d shows that the adjectival participle is here used in the present time as threatening the fall of the "booth of David." This view does not support G. Bergsträsser, Hebräische Grammatik (Hildesheim, 1962), p. 69 n. c, who argues for the predicative use in past time translating "die (ein)-gefallene." But Bergsträsser has to admit that the regular use of the active participle stresses "überwiegend Gleichzeitigkeit" with the main clause and not infrequently "Vorzeitigkeit." The latter certainly applies here whereby syntactically and contextually there is sufficient reason for translating "falling." This is grammatically justifiable. Already

so that they may possess the remnant of Edom.
and all the nations over whom[302] my name is called,'
says Yahweh who does this.

From the outset we should be careful not to dismiss Amos' authorship of this oracle merely because it comes rather unexpectedly and without any direct connection with the preceding passages. That this in itself is no decisive argument against the authenticity of 9:11-12 has been demonstrated by scholars who support[303] and reject[304] its authorship by Amos. The opening phrase "in that day," which is used four more times in generally considered genuine passages of Amos,[305] does not provide sure indications for Amos' authorship of this passage.

What does the phrase "I will raise up the falling [or as others prefer fallen] booth of David" mean? There is here certainly a reference to the David tradition. Some critics have felt that the reference to the dynasty of David is not what would be expected of Amos who worked in the Northern Kingdom.[306] Recently G. von Rad counters this weighty argument

---

B. Duhm, Die Zwölf Propheten (Tübingen, 1910), p. 20, translates the participle in the adjectival sense. See also Cramer, op. cit., p. 48: "die zerfallende Hütte Davids"; Rohland, op. cit., p. 230: "die baufällige Hütte Davids"; the Jerusalem Bible translates "the tottering hut of David." NEB: "David's fallen house"; NAB: "fallen hut of David." See Appendix, p. 470.

[302]Already J. Halévy, "Recherches bibliques-Le livre d'Amos," Revue Semitique, 11 (1903), 298-99, has pointed out that אֲשֶׁר is the subject of יִירְשׁוּ. Cf. Cramer, op. cit., p. 48 n. 8; Maag, op. cit., p. 61. Snaith, Amos, p. 144; Rohland, op. cit., p. 230; Kraeling, Commentary on the Prophets, I, 180; Jerusalem Bible, also the commentaries by Marti, Nowack, Driver, Robinson, Cripps, Weiser, Amsler.

[303]Hammershaimb, Amos, p. 136; Engnell, SBU, I, col. 61; Reventlow, Das Amt des Propheten bei Amos, p. 92.

[304]Kapelrud, Central Ideas, p. 56; Cripps, op. cit., pp. 69-71; and others.

[305]Amos 2:16; 8:3, 9, 13.

[306]See Cripps, op. cit., p. 71.

by pointing out that Amos was a Judean who addressed himself to ancient sacral traditions. He asks whether it would "not surprise us if there had been absolutely no mention of the traditions in which he was most at home [as a Judean]?"[307] E. Rohland has shown that Amos used the David tradition.[308] The historical argument adduced against the authenticity of vs. 11 has to do with the problem that Yahweh promises to raise up the falling or fallen[309] booth of David. It is asserted that this is something that could not have been written in the time of Amos when the booth of David, the dynasty of David, still existed. K. Budde,[310] however, has pointed out many years ago that nopelet does not mean "destroyed." He also argued that the term "booth of David" does not refer to "house" in the sense of dynastic lineage; instead it is a term referring to united Israel. If it is granted that nopelet does not mean "destroyed," then the argument that "this expression could [not] be used in the time of Amos, when both realms were still living side by side"[311] looses its force. H. Graf Reventlow says that "Amos maintains . . . a conception for all Israel.

---

[307]Von Rad, OTT, II, 138; idem, Die Botschaft der Propheten, p. 107.

[308]Rohland, op. cit., pp. 230-33; cf. Fey, op. cit., p. 54; Clements, Prophecy and Covenant, p. 112; von Rad, OTT, II, 138; Gottlieb, op. cit., pp. 455-57, argues that here are also motifs of the New Year Festival; John H. Hayes, "The Usage of Oracles Against Foreign Nations in Ancient Israel," JBL, 87 (1968), 91, shows links between royal theology and nation oracles; Preuss, Jahweglaube, pp. 140-41; H.-P. Müller, op. cit., p. 213.

[309]Grammatically the present sense of the participle is just as correct as the past meaning, see Cripps, op. cit., p. 271 n. 1.

[310]K. Budde, "Zu Text und Auslegung des Buches Amos," JBL, 44 (1925), 115ff.

[311]Kapelrud, Central Ideas, p. 57.

But this does not fit after 586, but exactly in the time of Amos itself."[312] In view of these considerations it would seem sound to interprest vs. 11 as a proclamation which expresses that the "booth of David" has "fallen" with the disintegration of Israel into two kingdoms at the time of the death of Solomon and that since that time it is "falling" through the continual loss of much of its former power and splendor as is indicated by the whole chain of events--political, social, and religious--which followed the division of the united monarchy to the time of Amos.[313] It is possible that Amos,[314] like Isaiah after him,[315] referred to the division of the Davidic kingdom as a great misfortune. Also here Amos addresses himself to the Northern Kingdom. In vs. 11 the prophet proclaims that Yahweh will raise up this diminished booth of David with its breaches and ruins and intends to rebuild it as "in the days of old," in the days of its Davidic greatness. Since the olden days, the time when Yahweh made a covenant with David, there is a promise still outstanding[316] which needs to be fulfilled.

---

[312]Reventlow, Das Amt des Propheten bei Amos, p. 92. Even Gottlieb, op. cit., p. 456, who denies Amos' authorship of 9:11-12, admits that there is really no necessity to see a reference to 586 here.

[313]Cf. Danell, op. cit., pp.134-35; Maag, op. cit., p. 246ff.; Engnell, SBU, I, col. 61; Reventlow, Das Amt des Propheten bei Amos, p. 133; Clements, Prophecy and Covenant, pp. 49 n. 1, 111-12; Preuss, Yahweglaube, pp. 140-41; H.-P. Müller, op. cit., p. 213. See Appendix II, p. 474.

[314]Amos 6:6.

[315]Isa. 7:17; 9:1-6; cf. Gottlieb, op. cit., p. 457.

[316]A related idea is expressed in Micah 5:1-3; see Rohland, op. cit., p. 232; H.-P. Müller, op. cit., pp. 213-14. For the promise connected with the Davidic covenant tradition, see Dennis J. McCarthy, Der Gottesbund im Alten Testament,(SBS, 13; 2nd ed.; Stuttgart, 1967), pp.

For many critical scholars vs. 12 appears even more problematical than vs. 11. The most offensive reference in this verse is the phrase "remnant of Edom."[317] Because of these words vs. 12a is rejected by some who otherwise defend the authenticity of 9:11-12,[318] mainly because it is understood to refer to events connected with the fall of Jerusalem in 586 B.C. There are some who support the authenticity of 9:8b-15, but consider all of vs. 12 as an interpolation for the same reasons.[319] The main reason for extracting all or part of vs. 12--and for some even all of 9:8b-15--is the emphasis on Edom. It is believed that this nation has been singled out because it turned against Judah at that nation's hour of greatest distress in 586 B.C.[320] When vs. 12a is understood in a negative sense, then this argument would indeed have conclusive force,

---

70-77; Martin Rehm, Der königliche Messias im Licht der Immanuel-Weissagung des Buches Jesaja (Eichstätter Studien, 1; Kevelaer, 1968), pp. 7-16; Delbert R. Hillers, Covenant: The History of a Biblical Idea (Baltimore, Md., 1969), pp. 111-19.

[317]The LXX has an interesting variant reading: ὅπως ἐκζητήσωσιν οἱ κατάλοιποι τῶν ἀνθρώπων which reflects a Hebrew Vorlage of לְמַעַן יִדְרְשׁוּ שְׁאֵרִית אָדָם, i.e., "that the remnant of men may seek [the Lord]." The object "the Lord" is found in codex Alexandrinus, see A. Rahlfs, Septuaginta (7th ed.; Stuttgart, 1962), II, 511 apparatus. In Acts 5:17 where these verses are quoted the object is included. However, the LXX reading with its own variants can hardly be used to change the Hebrew text, see Marti, Dodekapropheton, p. 226; Driver, Joel and Amos, pp. 228-29; Cramer, op. cit., p. 48 n. 7; Kraeling, Commentary on the Prophets, I, 180.

[318]On historical grounds with the support of metri causa reasons Hans Schmidt, Der Prophet Amos (Tübingen, 1917), p. 103 n. 1, and recently again Fey, op. cit., p. 55 n. 2.

[319]So Maag, op. cit., p. 61, and recently Preuss, Jahweglaube, p. 140 n. 72 and H. P. Müller, op. cit., p. 213 n. 112, who follow Maag.

[320]Obad. 10-14; cf. Cripps, op. cit., pp. 273, 321-22.

provided that there was enmity between Edom and Israel only at that time. This is, however, not the case. The history of rivalry between the two nations began early and continued for many centuries. It dates back to the time of Israel's journey to Canaan.[321] Later on Saul fought Edom.[322] David was able to conquer it and he dealt harshly with the Edomites.[323] During the time of Jehoshaphat the Edomites raided Judah in the company of others but were overcome.[324] Jehoshaphat attempted to re-open the port of Ezion-geber with no success.[325] About 100 years before Amos Edom gained her independence during the reign of Jehoram (Joram).[326] King Amaziah (796-767 B.C.) was able to capture the Edomite capital Sela and in so doing killed many.[327] In or near the time of Amos Uzziah (767-740/39 B.C.) of Judah restored the port of Elath which was also a way-station on the international trade route with South Arabia.[328] The statement that Uzziah "built Elath and restored it" (2 Ki. 14:22) should not be construed to mean that "Uzziah . . . conquered all of Edom. . . ."[329] If Judah had regained all of Edom it could be expected that it

---

[321]Nu. 20:14-21; 21:4; Jd. 11:17-18.

[322]1 Sam. 14:47.

[323]2 Sam. 8:13, 14; 1 Chr. 18:13; 1 Ki. 11:15, 16.

[324]2 Chr. 20.

[325]1 Ki. 22:48.

[326]2 Ki. 8:20-22; 2 Chr. 21:8-10.

[327]2 Ki. 14:7; 2 Chr. 25:11, 12.

[328]2 Ki. 14:22; 2 Chr. 26:2.

[329]So Yohanan Aharoni, The Land of the Bible: A Historical Geography, transl. by A. F. Rainey (Philadelphia, 1967), pp. 313-14.

would be so stated inasmuch as it was explicitly stated that Edom had gained independence (2 Ki. 8:20-22; 2 Chr. 21:8-10). It is more in accord with the evidence that Edom was partially subjugated by Uzziah. This long history of friction and rivalry between Edom and Israel seems to be one reason why Edom is singled out for special mention in 9:12a. Another reason for the special mention of Edom is the very recent or contemporary, but illfated, attempt to bring all of Edom again under the control of Israel (Judah) as it had been in the days of old under David. This historical context presents the clue for the meaning of the phrase "remnant of Edom." By "remnant of Edom" the prophet refers to that part of Edom which is still independent, which is still to be "possessed" by the booth of David. The "remnant of Edom" as much as the other nations must again be brought under the rule of David so that on the one hand the Davidic empire may again be restored to its splendor, power, and limits[330] "as in the days of old," and on the other hand that Edom too may share in the covenant promise of David.[331] Past interpreters have overlooked the fact that this word about Edom is considerate and positive as compared to the sayings about Edom from exilic or post-exilic times. The positive

---

[330]So also Hammershaimb, Amos, p. 134; Otzen, Studien über Deuterosacharja, p. 131; and Gottlieb, op. cit., pp. 456-57.

[331]This point has been made recently by Ulrich Kellermann, "Der Amosschluss als Stimme deuteronomistischer Heilshoffnung," EvTh, 29 (1969), 181, who is puzzled by the fact that this passage in contrast to the other sayings about Edom from exilic and post-exilic times "stellt ein besonnenes, positives wort für Edom dar, da hier auf jede hasserfüllte Bemerkung verzichtet wird. Edom wird zwar vor den andern Völkern gesondert gennannt, ihnen aber in der Behandlung gleichgesetzt. Die . . . Edomiter werden durch ihre Integration in das Davidreich an dessen Segen teilhaben."

nature of this statement makes an exilic or post-exilic date of vs. 12 virtually impossible. In order that all of Edom--as much as the other nations--may share in the outstanding covenant promise of David also the "remnant of Edom," which is not yet re-united with Israel, must be "possessed" by God's people.

The present chapter has shown that the remnant motif has a rich and varied history in Israelite thought prior to Isaiah. Having examined the origin and development of the remnant motif antecedent to Isaiah, our next task is to investigate the remnant motif of the prophet Isaiah, to delineate the relationships of Isaiah's remnant motif to its prior history, and to study his contribution to the further development of this motif.

PART FOUR

THE REMNANT MOTIF OF ISAIAH OF JERUSALEM

The present chapter endeavors to investigate the usage and development of the remnant motif in the available materials of Isaiah of Jerusalem and to ascertain to what extent it played a role in his proclamation and theology. It will be necessary on methodological grounds to distinguish between the various phases of Isaiah's prophetic activity and to assign as far as possible the Isaianic pericopes to the respective periods of the prophet's work. The materials which contain the remnant motif are divided along the line of sayings that relate to Israel and those that pertain to the nations.

A. The Remnant Motif and Israel

1. The Remnant Motif in Isaiah's Early Career (740-734 B.C.).--The ministry of Isaiah, the son of Amoz,[1] at Jerusalem was, during its earlier part, contemporary with the work of Hosea in North Israel. Isaiah's fellow Judaean Amos preached in the Northern Kingdom, shortly before Hosea. The looming threat of the Assyrian power which is felt but not named by Amos,[2] and to which Hosea refers specifically,[3] becomes for Isaiah a concrete fact which fills the background and provides the oc-

[1]Isa. 1:1.

[2]Amos 5:27.

[3]Hos. 5:13; 8:9, 9:3; 10:6.

casion for the crisis of his life work. The time in which Isaiah was called to his prophetic activity was indeed the beginning of a most critical period for both Israel and Judah. Shortly before he received his call to the prophetic office, Tiglath-Pileser III (745-727)[4] inaugurated a new period in the history of Assyria by conquering both Babylonia and Syria.[5] Isaiah watches how the Northern Kingdom is forced to pay tribute to Assyria in 738 B.C.,[6] how her territory is partitioned and depopulated in 733 B.C. after Ahaz of Judah had called for help against the Syro-Ephraimitic coalition,[7] and how her national existence ended in 722 B.C. with the capture of Samaria by Assyrian military might.[8] Ahaz himself had become an Assyrian vassal and introduced an Assyrian altar into the Jerusalem temple in deference to his new overlord.[9] Judah re-

---

[4]For the dates see J. A. Brinkman, "Mesopotamian Chronology of the Historical Period," in Oppenheim, Ancient Mesopotamia, p. 347.

[5]On that period see W. W. Hallo, "From Qarqar to Carchemish: Assyria and Israel in the Light of New Discoveries," BA, 23 (1960), 33-61, now in The Biblical Archaeologist Reader, 2, ed. by D. N. Freedman and E. F. Campbell, Jr. (Garden City, New York, 1964), pp. 152-88 (the latter is hereafter cited as BAR, 2); Bright, A History of Israel, pp. 252-62; Noth, The History of Israel, pp. 257-69.

[6]For this date see Thiele, Mysterious Numbers, p. 95; A. L. Oppenheim in ANET^3, p. 282; Hallo, BAR, 2, p. 171.

[7]2 Ki. 16:7; 2 Chron. 28:16. See Appendix II, p. 474.

[8]For a discussion of the conflicting historical data by Shalmaneser V and Sargon II, both of whom claim to have captured Samaria, see Hayim Tadmor, "The Campaigns of Sargon II of Asshur: A Chronological Study," JCS, XII (1958), 22-40; Thiele, Mysterious Numbers, pp. 144-48.

[9]2 Ki. 16:10-18. Cf. W. F. Albright, Archaeology and the Religion of Israel (3rd ed.; Baltimore, Md., 1953), pp. 161-2.

mained subservient to Assyria until 705 B.C. when Hezekiah joined an open revolt of subjected peoples following the death of Sargon II in that year. In 701 B.C. Sennacherib stood with his army before the gates of Jerusalem, having already reduced forty-six of Judah's fortified cities to rubble. Their inhabitants are deported,[10] and Hezekiah is shut up in Jerusalem "like a caged bird."[11] The slaughter in Judah must have been fearful,[12] but Jerusalem was not taken. At about 690 B.C. Sennacherib threatened Judah and Jerusalem a second time.[13] But the Israelite capital escaped destruction once more. This brief outline of historical events indicates that during the years of Isaiah's prophetic activity North Israel experienced complete national ruin and Judah found herself in one of her most critical periods.

Isaiah's ministry in Jerusalem introduced into Judah the classical prophetic tradition already apparent in the Northern Kingdom through the work of Amos and Hosea.[14] Isaiah addressed kings, officials, priests, and the common people of the various strata of society. Under the long reign of King Uzziah (792/91 to 740/39),[15] in fame second only to Solomon's, Judah reached the summit of her power. Military strength and

---

[10]ANET[3], pp. 287-8.

[11]DOTT, p. 67; cf. ANET[3], p. 288.

[12]See Isa. 1:4-9. Cf. Bright, History of Israel, p. 269.

[13]The present writer adopts the so-called "two-campaign theory." See infra, n. 438.

[14]See Harrelson, Interpreting the Old Testament, p. 231.

[15]These are the dates of Thiele's chronology of the Hebrew kings, (Mysterious Numbers, pp. 125ff.) which has found widespread acceptance; see Hallo BAR, 2, 154; John Gray, "Chronology of the Old Testament," in

economic wealth had reached a new peak. The increasing prosperity, says W. F. Albright, "was not canalized for the exclusive benefit of the aristocracy and wealthy merchants . . . [but was] in the hands of [all] individuals."[16] Isaiah addressed the "inhabitants of Jerusalem" as well as the "men of Judah."[17] His ministry extended to all classes of people; he lived in their traditions and was well acquainted with their cult.[18] He had close connections with the court and knew about the workings of politics.[19] The multiplicity of his relationships seems to correspond to his complex message and its inherent adaptability. Since his ministry lasted over a period of many decades,[20] it is not at all surprising to

---

Peake's Commentary on the Bible, ed. by M. Black and H. H. Rowley (London, 1962), pp. 70-71; S. J. De Vries, "Chronology of the OT," IDB, I, 580-99; etc. Siegfried H. Horn, "The Chronology of King Hezekiah's Reign," AUSS, II (1964), 40-52, has further refined an area open to criticism in Thiele's chronological scheme, making it an even greater breakthrough in the study of Old Testament chronology. The rival chronological system is by W. F. Albright, "The Chronology of the Divided Monarchy of Israel," BASOR, 100 (1945), 16-22; idem, "New Light from Egypt on the Chronology and History of Israel and Judah," BASOR, 130 (1953), 4-11. Albright's chronological tables are slightly revised in his The Biblical Period from Abraham to Ezra, Harper Torchbook (New York, 1963), pp. 116-7. For a penetrating criticism of Albright's chronology, see E. R. Thiele, "The Synchronisms of the Hebrew Kings--A Re-evaluation," AUSS, I (1963), 131-7, and his Mysterious Numbers, pp. 60-2.

[16]W. F. Albright, "The Biblical Period," in The Jews, ed. by L. Finkelstein (New York, 1949), pp. 39f., quoted by Abraham J. Heschel, The Prophets: An Introduction, Harper Torchbooks (New York, 1969), p. 62.

[17]Isa. 5:3.

[18]Isa. 1:10-17.

[19]Isa. 7:1-9.

[20]Some recent scholars extend Isaiah's ministry beyond the close of the eighth century B.C.; see among others G. Ernest Wright, Isaiah (Layman's Bible Commentaries; London, 1965), p. 14: "The prophetic ministry of Isaiah took place in Jerusalem in the half-century between about 740 and 690 B.C." J. Yeoman Muckle, Isaiah 1-39 (Epworth Preacher's Commentaries; London, 1960), p. 1: "Isaiah's ministry began in the year

find varying aspects and emphases in his message which at times become more apparent and at other times recede into the background depending on the different historical situations and circumstances.

The proclamation of Isaiah, says G. von Rad, "is the most powerful theological phenomenon of the whole Old Testament."[21] The concept of the majestic "holiness" of Yahweh, which is closely connected with the ancient Jerusalemite tradition, holds a central position in the teaching of Isaiah. The titles "Holy One of Israel" (qᵉdôš yiśrāʾēl),[22] "Mighty One of Israel" (ʾᵃbîr yiśrāʾēl),[23] "Yahweh of hosts" (YHWH ṣᵉbāʾôṯ)[24] "Lord" (ʾādôn),[25] and "King" (melek)[26] are all proclamations of his exalted

---

of king Uzziah's death. . ., it is certain that he was still prophesying in 701, and quite possible that he continued some years beyond that date."

[21]Von Rad, Die Botschaft der Propheten, p. 115; idem, OTT, II, 147: "The preaching of Isaiah represents the theological high water mark of the whole Old Testament."

[22]Isa. 1:4; 5:19, 24; 10:20; 30:11, 12, 15; 31:1; much disputed passages are 12:6; 17:7; 29:19; 37:23=2 Ki. 19:22. O. Procksch, "ἅγιος," TDNT, I, 92-94, claims that the epithet קְדוֹשׁ יִשְׂרָאֵל has been coined by Isaiah. This supposition has been challenged by G. W. Ahlström, Psalm 89. Eine Liturgie aus dem Ritual des leidenden Königs (Lund, 1959), who argues convincingly that this epithet in Ps. 89:19 is older than Isaiah. The same has been argued with reference to Ps. 89, which uses this epithet in vs. 19, by O. Eissfeldt, "Das Lied Moses Dt 32:1-32 und das Lehrgedicht Asaphs Ps. 78," Berichte über die Verhandlungen der Sächsischen Akademie der Wissenschaften zu Leipzig, Phil.-hist. Klasse, 104/5 (1958), 33-4. See also the reservations of O. Kaiser, Der Prophet Jesaja, Kap. 1-12 (ATD, 17; 2nd ed.; Göttingen, 1963), p. 7 n. 10; and Hans Wildberger, Jesaja (BKAT, X/1; Neukirchen-Vluyn, 1965), pp. 23-4.

[23]Isa. 1:24.

[24]Isa. 1:9, 24; 6:3, 5. See the excursus on יהוה צְבָאוֹת in Wildberger, Jesaja, pp. 28-9.

[25]Isa. 1:24; 3:1.

[26]Isa. 6:5.

"holiness" and sovereignty. The concept of Yahweh's "holiness" has two corresponding aspects.[27] H. Ringgren[28] has noted that it signifies on the one hand the unapproachability and awesomeness, even the danger of the God who is wholly other primarily when offended. On the other hand it signifies beneficience: the "Holy One of Israel" is the kindly God who has chosen Israel and has mercy upon his people,[29] because he is the "Holy One" of Israel. They are his "sons,"[30] his "vineyard,"[31] and he calls them "my people."[32]

Yahweh's "holiness" expresses itself in judgment. He is angry with "this people" for they do not do justice and righteousness.[33] ṣ^e^dāqāh seems to have been a typically Jerusalemite ideal.[34] But the chief sin on the part of God's people and their leadership is a lack of faith,[35]

---

[27]For the dialectical relationship of the dual nature of Isaiah's concept of "holiness," see now Fey, Amos und Jesaja. Abhängigkeit und Eigenständigkeit des Jesaja, pp. 105-20.

[28]Ringgren, Israelite Religion, p. 74.

[29]Isa. 17:7; 10:20; cf. Helmer Ringgren, The Prophetical Conception of Holiness (Leipzig, 1948), pp. 6, 23f.

[30]Isa. 1:2-4.

[31]Isa. 5:1-7.

[32]Isa. 1:3; 3:12, 15; 10:2; 5:13.

[33]Isa. 5:16, 25-29; 9:7; 10:3-4; 28:22.

[34]Isa. 1:21, 26; 28:16-17; Ps. 72:1, 3, 7; 122; Gen. 14:17ff.; cf. Ahlström, op. cit., pp. 79-80; N. W. Porteous, "Jerusalem-Zion: The Growth of a Symbol," in Verbannung und Heimkehr. Festschrift für Wilhelm Rudolph (Tübingen, 1961), 235-52; Hans Wildberger, "Jesajas Verständnis der Geschichte," SVT, IX (1963), 109ff.; R. A. Rosenberg, "The God Ṣedeq," HUCA, 36 (1965), 161-77; Preuss, Jahweglaube, p. 162.

[35]Isa. 7:9; 28:16; 30:15; cf. Hans Walter Wolff, Frieden ohne Ende. Eine Auslegung von Jesaja 7, 1-7 und 9, 1-6 (BS, 35; Neukirchen-Vluyn, 1962), pp. 22-24; A. H. J. Gunneweg, "Heils- und Unheilsverkündigung in Jes. VII," VT, XV (1965), 33.

i.e., the distrust in Yahweh's guidance in history. Yahweh worked with his people in the past and he does so still, but as a judge. Yet he does not bring judgment upon his people without warning and exhortation. Through the preaching of his prophet Isaiah, he attempts to draw his people to himself.[36] The punishment that is meted out aims for a positive result.[37] To punish is not Yahweh's natural but his alien, paradoxical work.[38] Due to the varying situations Isaiah's proclamation of judgment reflects a corresponding development in the various stages of Isaiah's ministry.[39] Yet Isaiah's message was not wholly one of doom, not even in the earliest period of his activity. Assured as he was of judgment, he did not believe at any time, in contrast to Amos, that the people would be utterly destroyed. All his life Isaiah entertained the hope, repeatedly frustrated,[40] that the judgments would serve as a purge, as a refiner's fire. Though the punishment would bring a break with the old, its purpose is to bring to fruition the promise for the new.[41] One often

---

[36]Isa. 5:1-7.

[37]Isa. 9:7ff.

[38]Isa. 28:21; 22:4; cf. Heaton, The Hebrew Kingdoms, p. 320.

[39]Isa. 2:12-17; 3:1-11; 3:25-4:1; 5:5-6; other expressions appear in 29:7-8; 31:5. The reason for the change is made clear in the following passages, 8:18; 18:7; 31:9. For the various stages of Isaiah's judgment message, see Karl Budde, "Über die Schranken, die Jesajas prophetischer Botschaft zu setzen sind," ZAW, 41 (1923), 154-203; Willy Cossmann, Die Entwicklung des Gerichtsgedankens bei den alttestamentlichen Propheten (BZAW, 29; Giessen, 1915), pp. 49ff.; Bernhard Duhm, Israels Propheten (2nd ed.; Tübingen, 1922), pp. 149ff.; Fey, op. cit., pp. 125-7; Georg Fohrer, Das Buch Jesaja (Zürcher Bibelkommentare; 2nd ed.; Zürich, 1966), I, 5-16.

[40]Isa. 22:1-14.

[41]Isa. 1:21-26; 17:12-14; 24:14-18; 29:6-8.

encounters in Isaiah of Jerusalem dark expressions of doom prior to words of hope.[42] The judgment may on the whole be said to serve a purging purpose.[43] It aimed to bring about a return of the people to their God. A most illuminating passage, which reflects Isaiah's struggle to make salvation possible in face of inevitable judgment, is preserved in Isa. 28:14-22.[44] This pericope speaks of Yahweh's strange work of judging his own people.[45] Judgment and salvation can be pronounced together because both are radically united in the very "holiness" of Yahweh. As the "Holy One" Yahweh judges; as the "Holy One of Israel" he does not turn from his people nor from his city.[46] Thus we find that Isaiah of Jerusalem is not an unrelieved preacher of doom.[47] It is of fundamental importance for a correct understanding of the proclamation of Isaiah of Jerusalem--and for a proper and adequate interpretation of the Isaianic remnant motif--to be cognizant of the fact that a constitutive factor in the original Isaianic proclamation is the dialectical relationship of

---

[42]Isa. 9:1; 11:1.

[43]Isa. 3:8, 14, 25; 5:14-15; 6:11; 7:16-17; 23:20; 32:9-14.

[44]For this passage see Fey, op. cit., pp. 120-5.

[45]For similar passages such as Isa. 1:21-26, see Wildberger, Jesaja, pp. 58-66; and for Isa. 18:20; 28:7-13 and 30:15-17 with their "expansions," see Claus Westermann, Basic Forms of Prophetic Speech, transl. by H. C. White (Philadelphia, 1967), pp. 171ff.

[46]"This people," Isa. 6:10; 8:6, 11, 12; 9:16; 28:11, 14; 29:13, 14, is nevertheless "my people," Isa. 1:3; 3:12, 15; 5:13; 10:2.

[47]Lindblom, Prophecy in Ancient Israel, p. 188: ". . . the antithesis of doom and salvation was constitutive of Isaiah's message from the very beginning."

judgment and salvation.[48] To eliminate all passages of hope is to impose, as J. Philip Hyatt says, "a strait jacket of logical consistency of our own making."[49] The remnant motif is rooted in this dialectic of judg-

---

[48]G. Fohrer, "Zehn Jahre Literatur zur alttestamentlichen Prophetie (1951-1960)," ThR, 28 (1962), 347, claims that Isaiah of Jerusalem has neither a message of salvation nor a remnant idea. The same flat denial of a juxtaposed message of "threats of destruction" and "promises of salvation" in Isaiah has been voiced by him already in his essay "Remarks on Modern Interpretation of the Prophets," JBL, LXXX (1961), 315. Yet Fohrer is not willing to designate Isaiah as an "Unheilsprophet." He concedes that Isaiah is a prophet of "bedingter Verheissung" in "Jesaja 1 als Zusammenfassung der Verkündigung Jesajas," Studien zur alttestamentlichen Prophetie (BZAW, 99; Berlin, 1967), pp. 165-6; idem, Das Buch Jesaja, I, 12-16. Sheldon H. Blank, Prophetic Faith in Isaiah (2nd ed.; Detroit, 1967), pp. 4-8, distinguishes rigidly between the "historical Isaiah" and the "Isaiah of legend." The former is characterized by a message of absolute doom and destruction while the latter's message is of salvation and hope. Heaton, The Hebrew Kingdoms, pp. 320-1, accepts only the "oracles of doom" as authentic Isaianic material. On the other hand, the great majority of scholars reject such neat and simplistic separation of oracles of doom and salvation and argue that inherent in Isaiah's message itself is an interrelated juxtaposition of doom and salvation. A selected list of the latter would include the following, if we limit ourselves to studies that were written after the late 1940's: Hyatt, Prophetic Religion, p. 96; Hempel, Worte der Propheten, pp. 45-6, 117-29; John Bright, The Kingdom of God (Nashville, 1953), p. 83; idem, "Isaiah," Peake's Commentary on the Bible, ed. by M. Black and H. H. Rowley (London, 1962), p. 490; Th. C. Vriezen, "Prophecy and Eschatology," SVT, I (1953), 207; idem, An Outline of Old Testament Theology (Newton, Mass., 1958), p. 61; idem, The Religion of Ancient Israel, transl. by H. Hoskins (Philadelphia, 1967), pp. 221-4; Rohland, Die Bedeutung der Erwählungstraditionen Israels für die Eschatologie der alttestamentlichen Propheten, pp. 145ff.; Buber, The Prophetic Faith, pp. 141ff.; J. J. Stamm, "Die Immanuel-Weissagung und die Eschatologie des Jesaja," ThZ, 16 (1960), 449; C. R. North, "Isaiah," IDB, II, 733-4; Fey, op. cit., pp. 120ff.; Harrelson, Interpreting the Old Testament, pp. 234ff.; Clements, Prophecy and Covenant, pp. 49ff.; Herrmann, Heilserwartungen, pp. 126ff.; von Rad, OTT, II, 155ff.; Childs, Isaiah and the Assyrian Crisis, p. 64; Preuss, Jahweglaube, p. 162-3; Scott, The Relevance of the Prophets, p. 81; Heschel, The Prophets, p. 95; Eissfeldt, OTI, p. 310, etc.

[49]Hyatt, Prophetic Religion, p. 97.

ment and salvation as will be seen in the following investigation.

It has recently been claimed by Ursula Stegemann that Isaiah's inaugural vision is "cited in recent times only rarely as a passage supporting the presence of Isaianic remnant theology."[50] Stegemann supports her claim by referring to two studies in which the call vision of Isaiah is so used: one prepared in 1942[51] and another in 1955.[52] Such a judgment can only arise from a lack of proper research. There are in fact a large number of studies which affirm the presence of the remnant motif in the inaugural vision.[53] Yet we must proceed with great caution in our investigation of the remnant motif in the first

---

[50]Ursula Stegemann, "Der Restgedanke bei Isaias," BZ, 13 (1969), 167. See the critique against her arguments, supra, pp. 38-40.

[51]Ibid., p. 167 n. 23. There she refers to Schilling, "'Rest' in der Prophetie des Alten Testaments", pp. 58-61. Cf., supra, pp. 24-27.

[52]R. Dreyfus, "La doctrine du 'Reste d'Israël' chez les prophète Isaïe," Revue des Sciences Philosophiques et Théologiques, 39 (1955), 361.

[53]The following list does not aim to be exhaustive: Garofalo, La nozione profetica del 'Resto d'Israele', pp. 74-6; L. Dennefeld, Les grands Prophètes (La Sainte Bible, VII; Paris, 1946), p. 42; Danell, op. cit., pp. 162ff.; I. Engnell, The Call of Isaiah (Uppsala, 1949), pp. 13-15; Rowley, The Biblical Doctrine of Election, p. 73; Bright, The Kingdom of God, p. 88; Reiji Hoshizaki, "Isaiah's Concept of the Remnant" (unpublished M.Th. thesis, Southern Baptist Theological Seminary, Louisville, Kentucky, 1955), pp. 72, 78-9; L. G. Rignell, "Das Immanuelszeichen," Studia Theologica, XI (1957), 100-2; Jacob, Theology of the Old Testament, p. 323; Warne, op. cit., pp. 36-7; Lindblom, Prophecy in Ancient Israel, pp. 188-9, 356; J. Mauchline, Isaiah 1-39, Torch Bible Paperbacks (London, 1962), p. 33; Harrelson, Interpreting the Old Testament, pp. 232-3; J. Milgrom, "Did Isaiah Prophesy During the Reign of Uzziah?" VT, XIV (1964), 173 n. 6; Wright, Isaiah, pp. 36-7; Eissfeldt, OTI, p. 310; Scharbert, Propheten Israels, pp. 210-1; I. P. Seierstad, Die Offenbarungserlebnisse der Propheten Amos, Jesaja und Jeremia (2nd ed.; Oslo, 1965), pp. 108-9; Vawter, The Conscience of Israel, p. 204; Preuss, Jahweglaube, p. 182.

period of Isaiah's prophetic activity not only because of the delicate nature of our sources but also because of the danger of a priori argumentation that can arise in connection with the manifold problems of Isaiah research.

Chapter 6 of Isaiah is generally considered to contain Isaiah's own report of his call. There can hardly be any doubt but that Isa. 6 is the prophet's autobiographical account. This can be recognized by the consistent "I-style"[54] which is present throughout this call narrative.[55] The authenticity of the core of Isaiah's call narrative is almost universally acknowledged.[56] In vs. 1 his call is dated "in the year that King

---

[54]This designation is used by Seierstad, op. cit., p. 43. E. Jenni, "Jesajas Berufung in der neueren Forschung," ThZ, 15 (1959), 321ff., speaks of Isaiah's "Selbstbericht." This term has been taken up by R. Knierim, "The Vocation of Isaiah," VT, XVIII (1968), 47, as "self-report."

[55]Vss. 1, 5, 6, 8, 11.

[56]As far as the present writer is aware only C. F. Whitley, "The Call and Mission of Isaiah," JNES, 18 (1959), 38-48, has claimed a post-Isaianic date for Chapter 6. According to Whitley, syntactical, word statistical, and historical (vss. 11-13) comparisons prove that Isa. 6 cannot be written by Isaiah of Jerusalem, but that it must stem from a post-exilic writer. The construction of the two introductory clauses in vs. 1 can very well be correct; cf. Wildberger, Jesaja, pp. 231-2. Even if they were incorrect, an incorrect syntactical construction is no proof for or against someone's authorship; cf. Knierim, op. cit., p. 47 n. 1. The observation that several terms occur only in later traditions is no compelling reason for the assumption that Isa. 6 is written by a later writer. It could very well be possible that some expressions in Isa. 6 may begin with Isaiah of Jerusalem or have existed in oral traditions even at an earlier date. Furthermore, Whitley leaves out of consideration those parts in Chapter 6 which reflect traditions clearly older than Isaiah. Note the negative reactions to Whitley's theory by Jenni, ThZ, 15 (1959), 321 n. 1, and G. Fohrer, "Zehn Jahre Literatur zur alttestamentlichen Prophetie (1951-1960)," ThR, 28 (1962), 63. On the autobiographical nature of Isaiah's account, see especially J. P. Love, "The Call of Isaiah," Interpretation, XI (1957), 282-96; Eissfeldt, OTI, p. 310; Fohrer, Introduction, p. 364; Kaiser, Einleitung, p. 173.

Uzziah died," i.e., the year 740/39 B.C.[57] If we endeavor to know whether or not Isaiah of Jerusalem could have used the remnant motif from the very beginning of his ministry, it is of no little significance to ascertain as far as possible just when Isaiah recorded his call vision. Did he write down his experience immediately after the event or shortly later or at the end of his ministry? Everyone who is acquainted with the problems of Isaiah's call narrative knows that these questions are subject to heated scholarly debate and that they have a definite bearing on the development of Isaiah's theology as well as the formation of the remnant motif. M. M. Kaplan[58] has revived the old hypothesis that Isa. 6 is not Isaiah's inaugural vision.[59] His chief reason for rejecting the common view that Isa. 6 is the prophet's inaugural vision is the saying of the hardening of the heart.[60] Kaplan states, "In my opinion, such unqualified and irredeemable destruction could not have constituted the burden of an inaugural message."[61] Therefore it is assumed that Isaiah

---

[57]The dates proposed for the year of Uzziah's death range from 748 (Engnell, Call of Isaiah, p. 25) or 747 (Eichrodt, Der Heilige in Israel, p. 47) to 735 (A. Jepsen, Die Quellen des Königsbuches /Halle, 1953/, pp. 45-6; followed by Kaiser, Einleitung, p. 173; idem, Der Prophet Jesaja, Kap. 1-12 /ATD, 17; 2nd ed.; Göttingen, 1963/, p. 58). The most common dates are those of Albright's chronological scheme with 742 and 740/39 of the chronology of Thiele, Mysterious Numbers, pp. 125ff. The present writer follows the latter's chronology at this point.

[58]M. M. Kaplan, "Isaiah 6:1-11," JBL, 45 (1926), 251-9.

[59]This was already held by C. P. Caspari, Commentar til de tolv første Capitler af Propheten Jesaja (1867), pp. 240-5 and S. Mowinckel, Profeten Jesaja (Oslo, 1925), pp. 16, 20ff., as cited by Seierstad, op. cit., p. 43 n. 4.

[60]Isa. 6:9-10.

[61]Kaplan, op. cit., p. 253.

must have been an active prophet for a long period of time before he received the temple vision. It is claimed that Isaiah's unsuccessful ministry caused a feeling of hopelessness in the prophet which is the cause for the development of the theory of the hardening of the heart. Though Kaplan did not make many disciples,[62] other scholars have felt that the theme of the hardening of the heart does actually represent a later reflection on the part of the prophet, which must be taken as an indication that the inaugural vision was written down at a later time in the prophet's experience.[63] The scholars who argue for a later recording of the inaugural vision see the problem boldly stated as follows: If the outcome of Isaiah's prophetic work is predetermined, i.e., if there is nothing that the people can do to change God's judgment—whatever that judgment may be—if, indeed, the prophet is to utter his proclamation in

---

[62]Milgrom, op. cit. p. 172-3, agrees with Kaplan, but assigns Isa. 1:10-6:13 to the reign of Uzziah and assumes a continuation and transformation of the message of Isa. 6. F. Horst, "Die Visionsschilderungen der alttestamentlichen Propheten," EvTh, 20 (1960), 198, leans toward Kaplan's view.

[63]This alternative has been adopted by Franz Hesse, Das Verstokkungsproblem im Alten Testament (BZAW, 74; Berlin, 1955), pp. 59-91, who cites the relevant literature on this problem in Isa. 6 up to 1955. Thus we may merely add here the more recent literature of some of those who follow this theory: Love, op. cit., p. 291: Isa. 6 is "the product of much later reflection"; R. B. Y. Scott, "Biblical Research and the Work of the Pastor: Recent Study in Isaiah 1-39," Interpretation, XI (1957), 265: ". . . the prophet looked back over his experience to the call which he was describing at a later time"; Curt Kuhl, The Prophets of Israel, transl. by R. J. Ehrlich and J. P. Smith (Richmond, Va., 1960), p. 79; Scharbert, Propheten Israels, p. 205; Blank, Prophetic Faith, p. 4; Preuss Jahweglaube, p. 184. Eissfeldt, OTI, p. 310, states "that Isaiah has given to his experience [of the call] a deliberate artistic form, though whether immediately after or much later cannot be decided."

such a way that the people will not understand, then why bother with the prophecy in the first place? It is precisely this problem which leads I. Engnell and A. J. Heschel[64] to suggest that the saying of the hardening of the heart has nothing to do with Judah but speaks of North Israel. But there are serious and weighty objections to be raised both against Kaplan's hypothesis as well as against the hypotheses which claim that the opening section of Isaiah's commission by Yahweh (vss. 9-11) is the product of later reflection or refers to the Northern Kingdom and not to Judah. All of the queries mentioned above appear to be raised because of the unwillingness to admit that God would ask something of such a terrible nature of his prophet. It is in this connection that H. Wildberger has raised the question whether we are actually in a position to measure the limits of what God can expect of his prophet.[65] We must not apply an *a priori* standard of our own making as an absolute canon of judgment as to what God can or cannot ask of his servant. The most serious limitation of Kaplan's hypothesis is the date that is given at the opening of Isa. 6. It is precisely this insurmountable objection that caused J. Milgrom[66] to date all of Isa. 1:10-6:13 to the reign of Uzziah. In this way he attempted to leave room for reflection on the part of Isaiah before he committed this material to writing in the year of Uzziah's death. This is, however, a very unlikely suggestion, because there is no evidence that

---

[64]Engnell, *Call of Isaiah*, pp. 51-2; Heschel, *Prophets*, p. 90. This view was held already by Danell, *op. cit.*, p. 166 n. 9.

[65]Wildberger, *Jesaja*, p. 240.

[66]Milgrom, *op. cit.*, pp. 171ff.

a call vision was ever appended at the end of a section of a prophet's work. K. Budde has shown conclusively that Isa. 6 has been placed at the head of the Denkschrift reaching most likely to Isa. 9:6. E. Jenni seems to be right when he says that all attempts that make the message of the hardening of the heart a part of a later reflection of Isaiah render this message innocuous.[67] It appears that we must reckon with the fact that Isaiah actually received this terrible commission in his inaugural vision at the beginning of his prophetic career.[68] The vividness of the whole scene gives support to the view that Isaiah recorded this vision soon after his temple experience. Some scholars have in recent times attempted to blaze new trails for interpreting the difficult saying of the hardening of the heart. It is quite likely that prophetic tradition furnished Isaiah with the motif of the hardening of the heart.[69] A. F. Key has suggested that Isaiah's words were laden with magical power which would bring about the execution of the judgment because the time of repentance was past. "The prophet becomes the divinely appointed execu-

---

[67] Jenni, ThZ, 15 (1959), 338-9.

[68] For scholars supporting this view before 1955, see Hesse, Verstockungsproblem, pp. 84-89, to which we may add the following: Hyatt, Prophetic Religion, p. 34; T. Henshaw, The Latter Prophets (London, 1958), p. 112; Gottwald, A Light to the Nations, pp. 322-3; Jenni, ThZ, 15 (1959), 338-9; Muckle, Isaiah, pp. 26-7; Buber, The Prophetic Faith, p. 131; Eichrodt, Der Heilige in Israel, p. 16; Lindblom, Prophecy in Ancient Israel, pp. 186-7; Harrelson, Interpreting the Old Testament, pp. 231-3; Kaiser, Einleitung, p. 173; Elmer A. Leslie, Isaiah (Nashville, 1963), pp. 24-5; von Rad, OTT, II, 155; Seierstad, op. cit., pp. 46-7; Wright, Isaiah, p. 36; E. J. Young, The Book of Isaiah, Chapters I-XVIII (Grand Rapids, Mich., 1965), p. 232; Fohrer, Jesaja, I, 101-2; Heaton, The Hebrew Kingdoms, p. 331; Wildberger, Jesaja, pp. 239-40; Stegemann, op. cit., p. 168.

[69] Von Rad, OTT, II, 153.

tioner."[70] Even if one would be reticent to follow the suggestion that repentance was ruled out for Judah,[71] one is tempted to affirm that the continued rejection of the message of Isaiah will inevitably lead to a hardening of the heart. It is just at this point where G. von Rad objects. He counters that this interpretation makes the concept of the hardening of the heart dependent on the human reaction to it, while in Isa. 6 it is presented as an act of God executed by his prophet. He warns:

> Any attempt to come to terms with what Isaiah says about hardening of the heart by the way of understanding the words indirectly, that is to say, by taking them as the secondary result of theological reflexion, and therefore as the way out from a theological dilemma

---

[70]Andrew F. Key, "The Magical Background of Isaiah 6:9-13," JBL, 86 (1967), 204.

[71]Isaiah proclaims repentance (6:10; 9:12; 10:20-23; 19:22?; 30:15; 31:6). The question of the relationship of the commission of the hardening of the heart to the possibility of repentance is analogous to the question of the relationship of the commission of the hardening of the heart to the call to faith or the proclamation of salvation. Hesse's (Verstockungsproblem, pp. 83ff.) dictum that the commission of the hardening of the heart is to be understood only in the sense of a prevention of repentance must be considered an a posteriori judgment. Faith stands alongside repentance as an expression of a turning away from false political hopes and a turning to Yahweh (7:9; 28:16; 30:15). Repentance and faith receive the promise of salvation. Those who do not return will receive the announcement of judgment (7:9; 28:16; 30:15; over against 1:15ff.; 6:10; 9:12-13; 14:27). Isa. 7:1-9 is nothing but an empty lie, if the warning to Ahaz has "no longer any real possibility" as Hans-Joachim Kraus, Prophetie und Politik (München, 1952), p. 73, has claimed, because Isaiah is to preach the hardening of the heart. For highly instructive interpretations of Isaiah's message of repentance, see Erich K. Dietrich, Die Umkehr im Alten Testament und im Judentum (Stuttgart, 1936), pp. 57ff.; Hempel, Worte der Propheten, pp. 130-3; Fohrer, "Remarks on Modern Interpretation of the Prophets," JBL, 80 (1961), 314; A. H. J. Gunneweg, "Heils- und Unheilsverkündigung in Jes VII," VT, XV (1965), 27-34; Preuss, Jahweglaube, pp. 183, 192; von Rad, OTT, II, 151-5.

> or an account of a general law of the psychology of religion, is, from the point of view of hermeneutics, a priori to import a standpoint from outside the text itself.[72]

Thus we must not bring a priori consideration to the saying of the hardening of the heart. G. von Rad suggests that we need to understand this saying in a new way. Any understanding of it merely as punishment means to understand it as the end, the final stage of a long process, while in its present context it stands at the beginning of a new work of Yahweh with his people. It stands at the beginning of Isaiah's ministry. This means that it must be read with reference to the history of salvation, as something that points into the future. For Isaiah the hardening of the heart of God's people is a particular work of Yahweh's historical dealings with Israel.[73] Acts of judgment will be effected through Isaiah's prophetic word. What is new in Isaiah is that it effects such judgments not only in the external history of the world but also in the most hidden recesses of the human heart. When Isaiah summed up the net result of his earliest ministry, he said that Yahweh "is hiding his face from the house of Jacob."[74] Yet the amazing fact is that the message of Isaiah was nevertheless accepted by a little group.[75] This interpretation[75a] grows out of the present position of the text. It eliminates all speculative hypotheses and the problems they raise, and it has the advantage

---

[72] Von Rad, OTT, II, 152-3.

[73] See here especially the penetrating treatment of von Rad, OTT, II, 42-43; 89ff., 155; idem, Die Botschaft der Propheten, pp. 119-23; and also Stegemann, op. cit., p. 168.

[74] Isa. 8:17.

[75] Isa. 8:16.

[75a] See Appendix, pp. 470-71.

of accounting for the dual result of Isaiah's message, which represents one of the greatest difficulties of the traditional interpretations of the message of the hardening of the heart. If this new interpretation is adopted, all the serious objections to the view that Isa. 6 faithfully records Isaiah's inaugural vision which came to him at the time of his call have been removed.

The matter of the date of recording the inaugural vision[76] has a direct bearing on the usage of the remnant motif by Isaiah of Jerusalem. Isaiah's reaction to the message of the hardening of the heart is the question, "How long, O Lord?"[77] It seems to reflect more than merely a sign of Isaiah's love for his people.[78] This question of despair has an implicit bearing on the remnant motif. The intent of this question of utter consternation has been variously explained. Some hold that it refers to the duration of Isaiah's commission,[79] while others see the re-

---

[76]Isaiah's autobiographical account of his inaugural vision is usually divided into three main parts: (1) The description of Yahweh's majesty in his temple (vss. 1-4); (2) the cleansing of the prophet in preparation for his commission (vss. 5-7); and (3) the commissioning of the prophet by Yahweh (vss. 8-13). Cf. Eissfeldt, OTI, p. 310. N. Habel, "The Form and Significance of the Call Narratives," ZAW, 77 (1965), 309ff., has studied the Gattung of call narratives in the Old Testament and found certain structural elements that are present in these materials. He divides Isaiah's inaugural vision as follows: (1) The divine confrontation, vss. 1-2; (2) the introductory word, vss. 3-7; (3) the commission, vss. 8-10; (4) the objection, vs. 11a; and (5) the reassurance, vss. 11b-13. The "call structure" is also present in the call narratives of Jeremiah, Ezekiel, and Deutero-Isaiah as well as in other Old Testament call narratives.

[77]Isa. 6:11.

[78]Schilling, op. cit., p. 58; Young, op. cit., pp. 261-2.

[79]So E. König, Das Buch Jesaja (Gütersloh, 1926), p. 96; Ch. Boutflower, The Book of Isaiah (London, 1930), p. 31; J. Skinner, The Book of the Prophet Isaiah, Chapter I-XXXIX (Cambridge Bible for Schools and

sult of his activity emphasized.[80] It seems rather likely that both are contained[81] in it. In addition this pregnant question indicates that the prophet had to assimilate his new experience into his current thought and faith which, as for every Israelite, was conditioned by the expectation that in the end God wants salvation and not destruction. Israel and Isaiah live in this fundamental situation of salvation. Certainly Israel's unfaithfulness to Yahweh's covenant requirement has brought a rift in the people's relationship to their God. Yet this covenant relationship was not abrogated or cancelled. In the final analysis Isaiah expresses the belief, by asking this question, that the hardening of the heart is not the end. He had further expectations for his people. This question is a sign of hope on the part of Isaiah based upon his faith in the election of Israel. The following divine answer is received in 6:11b-13 upon Isaiah's remonstrance against the finality of

---

Colleges; Cambridge, 1930), p. 50; S. H. Blank, "Traces of Prophetic Agony in Isaiah," HUCA, XXVII (1956), 82-3; Volkmar Herntrich, Der Prophet Jesaja, Kapitel 1-12 (ATD, 17; Göttingen, 1957), p. 109; Buber, The Prophetic Faith, p. 132; E. J. Kissane, The Book of Isaiah, I-XXXIX (2nd ed.; Dublin, 1960), I, 74; John Bright, "Isaiah-I," Peake's Commentary on the Bible, ed. by M. Black and H. H. Rowley (London, 1962), p. 494; Mauchline, Isaiah, p. 92.

[80]So Karl Budde, Jesajas Erleben. Eine gemeinverständliche Auslegung der Denkschrift des Propheten (Kap. 6, 1-9, 6) (Gotha, 1928), pp. 20f.; Otto Procksch, Jesaja I (KAT, IX; Leipzig, 1930), p. 58; Engnell, The Call of Isaiah, pp. 44-5; Eichrodt, Der Heilige in Israel, pp. 16-7; Muckle, op. cit., p. 27; Leslie, op. cit., p. 25; Fohrer, Jesaja, I, 102; idem, Introduction, p. 373 n. 74; Seierstad, op. cit., p. 168; Bernhard Duhm, Das Buch Jesaja (5th ed.; Göttingen, 1968), p. 69; Stegemann, op. cit., p. 168.

[81]This has been already supposed by Heinrich Ewald, Jesaja mit den übrigen-älteren Propheten (2nd ed.; Göttingen, 1867), p. 327; Franz Delitzsch, Biblical Commentary on the Prophecies of Isaiah, transl. by J. Martin (Grand Rapids, Mich., 1949), I, 201-2; Kaiser, Jesaja, p. 66; Heaton, The Hebrew Kingdoms, p. 331.

Yahweh's judgment:

11b And he said:
'Until cities lie waste
without inhabitants,
and houses without men,
and the land is left[82] a desert,
12 and Yahweh removes men far away,
and desolation is great in the midst of the land.[83]
13 And though a tenth remain in it,
it will be consumed[84] again,

---

[82]The Niphal תִּשָּׁאֶה is awkward as compared to the Qal of שׁאה. The LXX reads καὶ ἡ γῆ καταλειφθήσεται ἔρημος according to Alfred Rahlfs, Septuaginta (Stuttgart, 1962), II, 574. The LXX reading suggests a Vorlage of תִּשָּׁאֵר which has been suggested also in the apparatus of BHK and BHS. The translation with the reading of MT is not impossible and is supported by 1QIsa, but the root שׁאה I is otherwise not attested in the Niphal. In Isa. 17:12 the Niphal is used of the root שׁאה II, which must not be confused with the root שׁאה I, see KB, p. 935. It seems best to follow the reading of the LXX which is suggested by many commentators as well as BHK, BHS, and KB.

[83]The LXX translates vs. 12 as follows: καὶ μετὰ ταῦτα μακρυνεῖ ὁ θεὸς τοὺς ἀνθρώπους, καὶ οἱ καταλειφθέντες πληθυνθήσονται ἐπὶ τῆς γῆς. "But after this God will remove men, but the ones who are left will be numerous on the earth." The μακρυνεῖ translates the Hebrew רִחַק and καταλειφθέντες stands for עֲזוּבָה. The second part of this verse has in the LXX been reinterpreted to give it a positive meaning. Engnell, The Call of Isaiah, p. 14, has also seen a positive reinterpretation in the first part of this verse where he attaches the meaning of μακροθυμεῖ evidently by mistake to μακρυνεῖ and translates "will become forbearing." Such a meaning is not supported by H. G. Liddell and R. Scott, A Greek-English Lexicon, ed. by H. S. Jones (9th ed.; Oxford, 1940). G. W. Lampe, A Patristic Greek Lexicon (Oxford, 1968), p. 825, lists μακρύνω with usages by the early fathers with the meaning of "to prolong" and "to remove to a distance," but not with a meaning as advanced by Engnell. Cf. I. L. Seeligmann, The Septuagint Version of Isaiah (Leiden, 1948), pp. 63-4; Wildberger, Jesaja, p. 233.

[84]The difficult term here is בער which in the Piel has in Isa. 3:14 and 5:5 the meaning of "to consume, devour." This meaning fits also contextually better here, because no "burning" is mentioned or has been implied in the prior destruction. It seems therefore best to follow here Budde, Jesajas Erleben, pp. 28-9; H. W. Hertzberg, Der Erste Jesaja (Leipzig, 1936), p. 17; Kaiser, Jesaja, pp. 57, 66; Seierstad, op. cit., pp. 107-8; Buber, The Prophetic Faith, p. 133, against KB, p. 140; R. B. Y. Scott, "Isaiah, Chapters 1-39," The Interpreter's Bible, ed. by G. A. Buttrick (Nashville, 1956), V, 213; Eichrodt, Der Heilige in Israel, p. 14; Fohrer, Jesaja, I, 93.

like a terebinth or an oak,[85]
of which, at felling, a stock remains.

---

[85]1QIs[a] reads משלכת for בשלכת to which Symmachus' translation of αποβαλουσα and the translation of the Vulgate "quae expandit ramos suos" (Dennefeld, _op. cit._, p. 42) should be compared. Furthermore, 1QIs[a] reads במה for the MT בם. These variants have led some scholars to important reinterpretations of this difficult passage. F. Hvidberg, "The Maṣṣēba and the Holy Seed," _Interpretationes ad Vetus Testamentum pertinentes_ (Oslo, 1955), pp. 97-9; S. Iwry, "Maṣṣēbāh and Bāmāh in 1QIsaiah[A] 6[13]," _JBL_, 76 (1957), 228; W. F. Albright, "The High Place in Ancient Palestine," _SVT_, IV (1957), 254f.; W. H. Brownlee, "The Text of Isaiah VI, 13 in the Light of DSIa," _VT_, I (1951), 296-8; and G. R. Driver, "Isaiah I-XXXIX: Textual and Linguistic Problems," _JSS_, XIII (1968), 38, take במה to mean "high place." Iwry, however, was forced to make four emendations proposing the following text כאלה וכאלון (ו)אשר(ה) (ה)משלכת (מ)מצבת במה and translated, "Like a terebinth, or an oak, or an Asherah, when flung down from the sacred column of an high place." He argues that the relative particle אֲשֶׁר "when," never occurs in poetry and should therefore be emended to וַאֲשֵׁרָה. This double emendation of one word alone makes his results hardly convincing. Furthermore, it is a mistake to make an invariable rule out of a tendency in Hebrew poetry, because a number of examples can be produced for the use of אֲשֶׁר in Isaianic poetry from the first eleven chapters alone 1:26 (twice); 1:30; 2:20, 22; 5:5; 7:25; 11:16. Albright's treatment is not without difficulties either. He was able to solve the metrical problem by making only two emendations. He accepts the reading משלכת and gives it a feminine plural pointing to overcome the grammatical difficulty of Hvidberg's suggestion, who had read it as a feminine singular where it agreed with "terebinth," but not with the nearer word "oak," which is masculine. But Albright too had to emend the אשר into אשרה. He was also forced to prefix the preposition ב to מצבה. Thus he arrived at the following translation, "Like the terebinth goddess and the oak of the Asherah,/Cast out with the stelae of the high place." Brownlee's reconstruction attempted to solve the metrical problem by separating the phrases "as a terebinth and as an oak" into two separate stichs, where they would appear in poetic parallelism. This involved the transposition of one Hebrew word. There is, however, no textual support for such a transposition, not even from the versions. Driver reads 1QIs[a] אֲשֶׁר מֻשְׁלֶכֶת מִצֶּבֶת בָּמָה and translates this verse "if there be but a tenth part (of its people) in it, it shall turn and be for burning like an oak or a terebinth which is cast away from the site of a high place." He retains the relative particle and avoids any emendation, but he proposes a verbal noun צֶבֶת with the derivative meaning of "site" from "standing, position." However, this noun is used once only in the OT in Ruth 2:16 of a "bundle" of ears of corn. The cognate languages give no support to Driver's proposed meaning for this noun. J. Sawyer, "The Qumran Reading of Isaiah 6, 13," _ASTI_, 3 (1964), 111-3, vocalizes במה as בַּמֶּה taking it as an interrogative pronoun which opens a new clause. He translates, "Wherein is the holy seed? Its stump!" Sawyer has thus recognized the

A holy seed is its stock.[86]

In reply to Isaiah's question, which in the words of G. Fohrer "pre-

---

most serious difficulty which the other reconstructions contain, namely that the last clause of vs. 13 is also present in 1QIs^a. The former attempts fail at this crucial point by leaving out on *a priori* grounds any consideration of the last line. This has been admitted more recently by Brownlee (*The Meaning of the Qumran Scrolls for the Bible* /New York, 1964/ pp. 238-9). Millar Burrows, *More Light on the Dead Sea Scrolls* (New York, 1958), p. 148, points out that the word במה, which is taken to mean "high place" may "still at least equally well mean 'in them,' as the Masoretic text takes it." This is admitted by Iwry, *op. cit.*, p. 229, and Brownlee, *op. cit.*, p. 239. The latter is now convinced that "high place" is not the intended meaning of the scroll, because the scribe left a space before במה, which Brownlee interprets now as a mark of punctuation. However that may be, it seems fairly certain that במה is a longer spelling for בם. N. H. Tur-Sinai, "A Contribution to the Understanding of Isaiah i-xii," in *Scripta Hierosolymitana*, VIII, (1961), 169, takes מצבת as referring to "new planting," which suggests "the new growth to come forth after the trees have been entirely denuded of foilage and fruit." It is noteworthy that the Syriac reads *neṣb^{e}teh*. In Imperial Aramaic and Syriac the substantive of נצב means "plantation, growth, vine," while the verb means "to plant"; cf. *DISO*, p. 184. The last line of vs. 13 makes clear that מצבת was not understood as "pillar" or "sacred column." The only other usage of this term in the Hebrew Bible aside from the two occurrences in vs. 13 is in 2 Sam. 18:18, where its meaning is as usual "grinding stone." In view of these unsolved difficulties it seems best to stay with the MT despite its problems, with Eichrodt, *Der Heilige in Israel*, p. 14; Mauchline, *Isaiah*, p. 93; Kaiser, *Jesaja*, p. 57; Fohrer, *Jesaja*, I, 94; Wildberger, *Jesaja*, pp. 230-3, the RSV, and the Jerusalem Bible against the NEB.

[86]The last three words of the Hebrew text זרע קדש מצבתה are not translated in the LXX. From this many commentators have drawn the conclusion that the LXX *Vorlage* did not contain these words and that therefore they must be declared a secondary addition. Engnell, *Call of Isaiah*, pp. 13-14, however, has pointed out that these words are only missing in Vaticanus and the rest of the Hexplaric recension whereas they are found as σπέρμα ἅγιον τὸ στήλωμα αὐτῆς in Aquila, Theodotion, and in Origen with an asterisk; Symmachus translates σπερμα αγιον η αντιστασις (cf. J. Ziegler, *Isaias. Septuaginta Vetus Testamentum Graecum* /Göttingen, 1939/, XIV, 61, 144). K. Budde, *ZAW*, 41 (1923), 166ff., has clearly shown that the Hebrew words must have existed in the *Vorlage* of the LXX translator, though they were omitted due to homoioteleuton. In addition it should be noted that the Targum contains these three words. Wildberger, *Jesaja*, p. 234, correctly points out that the exegetes who want to eliminate the last clause as a late gloss cannot do so on the basis of the LXX. The fact that 1QIs^a contains these words too makes it virtually impossible to extract these words on the basis of text-critical analysis.

supposes that Yahweh will vex but not destroy,"[87] Yahweh announced a thorough devastation and depopulation, including the deportation of the inhabitants of the land. Vs. 12b heightens the picture of doom of vs. 11b. Even if so much as the tenth of the population should be spared, that one-tenth cannot consider itself as a saved remnant, as vs. 13a indicates. Another wave of destruction will consume it.[88] To speak in the metaphor of the tree: the new shoots will be consumed by the grazing flocks so that only the root stock remains. The destruction will be as thorough as when a tree is felled and the only residue is its root stock.

It is obvious that the remnant motif is present in the expression of the remaining tenth[89] as also in the stock or stump that is left over.

---

[87]Fohrer, Introduction, p. 373 n. 34.

[88]Seierstad, op. cit., p. 108, argues against George B. Gray, The Book of Isaiah, I-XXIX (ICC; Edinburgh, 1912), I, 111, and Procksch, Jesaja, p. 59, that the remaining tenth does not experience a second judgment, but that already in vs. 13a the note of a promise is struck by the grazing of the animals which indicates that there are "für den überlebenden Rest unbegrenzte viehwirtschaftliche Möglichkeiten." It must be pointed out against Seierstad that the MT of vs. 13a cannot be construed to contain a promise but continues the theme of destruction of vss. 11-12.

[89]Karl Marti, Das Buch Jesaja (Kurzer Hand-Commentar zum Alten Testament; Tübingen, 1900), p. 68, points out that the remaining tenth refers to Judah after the "ten tribes" of North Israel were exiled. Marti, of course, considers vss. 12-13 as a post-exilic explanatory addition to vs. 11. Gray, Isaiah, I, 111, counters against Marti's late dating of the last two verses of Isa. 6 that "his [Marti's] arguments are hardly quite conclusive; for it is perhaps hypercritical to claim that men cannot be removed (v. 12) from an already (v. 11) desolate country; and the use of Yahweh in words attributed to Yahweh-particularly at some distance from the beginning of the speech, is hardly sufficient by itself to prove that v. 12 was not the original continuation of v. 11." The same applies to Scott's supposition that vs. 13 must be a supplementary expansion and qualification of vss. 11-12 which "is surely evident from the contradiction between the complete depopulation pictured in the earlier verses and the survival of a tenth. . . ." IB, V, 212. For

The idea of the tenth appeared already in connection with the remnant motif in the Sodom story of the earliest stratum of Genesis (Gen. 18:22b-33). In Isaiah, however, the idea of the tenth contains no positive aspect. It has the character of a threat. A denial of the presence of the remnant motif in the first part of vs. 13 can only derive from a false understanding of the nature of this motif[90] or from a one-sided interpretation of it.[91] The remnant motif is here used in a negative

---

a critical discussion of the so-called "later" additions to Isaiah's inaugural vision, see Fey, op. cit., p. 105 n. 2. With regard to the identification of the one-tenth it would be difficult from a mathematical point of view to designate Judah as a whole as the "tenth" (so also Friedrich Giesebrecht, Beiträge zur Jesajakritik [Göttingen, 1890], p. 79) of "twelve tribes." In the present context it is most natural to interpret the tenth as the decimated remnant of Judah.

[90]Sheldon H. Blank, "Traces of Prophetic Agony in Isaiah," HUCA, XXVII (1956), 81-92, denies the idea of a remnant in Isa. 6:13. However, it must be noted that when Blank speaks of a "remnant" he has invariably the "doctrine of a holy remnant" in mind which excludes any negative aspect from the remnant motif, and sees it only as a motif of promise and hope.

[91]As a typical example of a one-sided use of the remnant motif, we may cite Lindblom, Prophecy in Ancient Israel, pp. 360ff. He treats the remnant motif within the general framework of eschatology where "'the remnant'. . . becomes eschatological as an element in predictions of a new age. When the term is simply applied to the survivors of some devastation it has, of course, no eschatological content" (p. 362). The first of these two aspects is for Lindblom the constitutive one. He links the remnant motif with "positive eschatology." Whenever he speaks of the "Isaianic idea of the remnant" (pp. 362 n. 136; 367 n. 145; 369) he means that it is the positive and not the negative view that comes to expression by it. "To Isaiah the idea of the remnant serves to evoke hope and, at the same time, summon to repentance" (p. 367 n. 145). It is because of this one-sided view of the Isaianic remnant motif that Lindblom is led to reject Isa. 10:22-23, because "here the thought is that only a remnant will be saved, presupposing a pessimistic view of the future of Israel" (ibid.). Our investigation of the remnant motif in the Old Testament prior to Isaiah of Jerusalem has shown that the remnant motif has been used both in "positive" and "pessimistic" ways. Thus one must be most careful not to read one aspect into all uses or to use a certain aspect as a canon for determining the authenticity of Isaianic materials on a priori grounds. It is at this point that Lind-

sense[92] to illustrate the magnitude of the disaster which will come over "this people."[93] The picture is fairly clear: destruction will be experienced by Israel in two stages, so that the remnant of the people will shrink more and more. At first Judah will be hit with calamity as a whole, then the decimated remnant[94] will also experience destruction until only an irreducible remnant is left over, as it were, the stump of a terebinth or an oak that remains at felling.

The thought continues in vs. 13c: "A holy seed is its stock."[95] The problem of the authenticity of this line is one of the hotly debated issues in Isaiah. There is no scholarly consensus in either direction. While scholars of high reputation and deep learning reject the Isaianic authorship of vs. 13c,[96] there are scholars of equal erudition who see no

---

blom has failed, while he has many valuable insights about Isaiah's remnant motif.

[92]See here especially the correct assessment of Meinhold, Studien zur israelitischen Religionsgeschichte, pp. 92-4.

[93]Isa. 6:9, 10.

[94]Duhm, Jesaja, p. 69, points out that it is likely that "der 'zehnte Teil' mag eine Reminiszenz aus Am 5,3; 6,9.10 sein." Fey, op. cit., pp. 60-1, argues that Isaiah employs Amos' idea of decimation of Amos 5:3 in his threat of 6:10.

[95]The textual problems of this line have already been discussed, supra, n. 86.

[96]Among those who see the last three words of the Hebrew text as an addition are the following: Marti, Jesaja, p. 69; Meinhold, op. cit., pp. 94-5; G. W. Wade, The Book of the Prophet Isaiah (Westminster Commentary; London, 1911), p. 43; Gray, Isaiah, I, 111; H. Schmidt, Die grossen Propheten, p. 32; G. H. Box, The Book of Isaiah (London, 1916), p. 45; Duhm, Jesaja, p. 70; Procksch, Jesaja, p. 52; Scott, Isaiah, V, 212-3; Mauchline, Isaiah, p. 63; Fey, op. cit., p. 106 n. 2; Leslie, op. cit., p. 25; Wright, Isaiah, pp. 36-7; Fohrer, Jesaja, I, 103; Heaton, The Hebrew Kingdoms, p. 331. See Appendix, p. 471.

objections to its genuineness.[97] On the whole the latter appear to outweigh in numbers the former; yet it is not so much the quantity of numbers that weighs most in such matters as the quality of the arguments. The fact that the last three words of Isa. 6 are lacking from some of the best manuscripts of the Septuagint has been a major reason for the rejection of these words by many scholars. It appears that this is an inadequate ground for omitting these words, especially in view of the fact that their omission in the Greek manuscripts can be so much more simply explained as a homoioteleuton--as has been shown as early as 1923[98]--than their insertion into the Hebrew[99] and all the other authorities.[99a]

---

[97]The following should be mentioned: Delitzsch, Isaiah, p. 203; C. von Orelli, Der Prophet Jesaja (Kurzgefasster Kommentar; 3rd ed.; München, 1904), p. 34; H. Dittmann, "Der heilige Rest im Alten Testament," Theologische Studien und Kritiken, 87 (1914), 603ff.; Skinner, Isaiah, p. 51; Budde, ZAW 41 (1923), 167-9; F. Feldmann, Das Buch Isaias (Exegetisches Handbuch zum Alten Testament, XIV; Münster, 1925), p. 77; König, Das Buch Jesaja, p. 97; Boutflower, op. cit., pp. 32-3; Hertzberg, op. cit., p. 18; J. Fischer, Das Buch Isaias, Teil 1 (Die heilige Schrift des Alten Testaments; Bonn, 1937), p. 64; Schilling, op. cit., pp. 59-60; Danell, op. cit., p. 167f.; Engnell, Call of Isaiah, pp. 50-1; Hempel, Worte der Propheten, p. 46; Rowley, The Biblical Doctrine of Election, p. 73; Bright, The Kingdom of God, p. 88; Dreyfus, RSPT, 39 (1955), pp. 362-6; H. S. Gehman, "The Ruler of the Universe: The Theology of First Isaiah," Interpretation, XI (1957), 270; Köhler, Old Testament Theology, p. 231, Rignell, StTh, XI (1957), 100; J. Ziegler, Das Buch Isaias (Echter-Bibel; Würzburg, 1958), p. 37; Warne, op. cit., pp. 80-2; Buber, op. cit., p. 133; Kissane, Isaiah, I, 74; Vawter, op. cit., p. 204; Lindblom, Prophecy in Ancient Israel, p. 356; Harrelson, Interpreting the Old Testament, pp. 232-3; Scharbert, Propheten Israels, pp. 210-1; Seierstad, op. cit., p. 109; Eissfeldt, OTI, p. 310.

[98]Budde, ZAW, 41 (1923), 167ff.

[99]Additional support for the inclusion of these words in the Hebrew text comes now from 1QIs[a] which contains these words as in the Masoretic text.

[99a]See Appendix II, p. 475.

In addition, it would, indeed, not be surprising to find some explicit hint of the positive aspect of Isaiah's proclamation already in his inaugural vision. This would certainly be no anomaly since scholars have repeatedly pointed out that Isaiah's inaugural vision contains the essential contents of his entire message.[100]

It has been noted above that there is no contradiction between the message of the hardening of the heart and the proclamation of salvation by Isaiah. F. Hesse has pointed out that if the Holy One of Israel would completely annihilate his own covenant people this would mean "that he questions his own existence."[101] If the entire inaugural vision could be interpreted along the line of total and complete destruction to the exclusion of any aspect of implicit salvation, only then could it appear that vs. 13c introduces a "foreign" aspect into the call narrative of Isa. 6.[102] But even if this position were defensible, one would still have to ask why it could not be possible that the paradoxical nature of Isaiah's proclamation of judgment and salvation could

---

[100] A number of scholars among which are those who reject and accept the last three words of Isa. 6 are agreed that Isaiah's actual message is contained in his call vision. Prochsch, Theologie des Alten Testaments, p. 178: "Jesajas Theologie liegt in seiner Berufungsvision beschlossen." Lindblom, Prophecy in Ancient Israel, pp. 188-9: "The antithesis of doom and salvation was constitutive to Isaiah's message from the very beginning. . . . In the inaugural vision . . . the contents of his prophetic message were defined." Fohrer, Jesaja, I, 14: "Die eigentliche Botschaft Jesajas ist grundlegend durch sein Berufungserlebnis geprägt worden." A. Gelin, "The Latter Prophets," in Introduction to the Old Testament, ed. by A. Robert and A. Feuillet, transl. by P. W. Skehan et al. (New York, 1968), p. 290: "This inaugural vision is like a resume of Isaias' whole career and all his key ideas."

[101] Hesse, Verstockungsproblem, p. 89.

[102] This approach has been adopted among others by Stegemann, op. cit., p. 169.

not also be reflected in the inaugural vision. Yet aspects of salvation are implicitly expressed at various points in the inaugural vision. Doom and salvation are united in the concept of the "holiness" of Yahweh.[103] When Isaiah was confronted in his temple vision by Yahweh's "holiness," he could not but cry, "Woe is me! For I am lost" (6:5). The judgment aspect of divine holiness is apparent in this cry of despair. Who can stand in the presence of the Lord of the universe! Isaiah, however, is not consumed; the heavenly attendants perform an act of purification with holy fire through which the saving aspect of Yahweh's "holiness" becomes an event[104] in the experience of Isaiah. His sinfulness and guilt are removed (6:7); new life is given to him. W. Eichrodt pertinently remarks, "The deadly fire turns into a cleansing agent, the gracious will of God gives new life through its heat."[105] So the prophet himself may be considered the proleptic representative of the future remnant, because he was confronted by Yahweh's "holiness" and emerged as a cleansed and purified individual.

Isaiah's cleansing experience "symbolizes Yahweh's cleansing and forgiveness of Israel," says W. Harrelson.[106] It enables Isaiah to accept his commission and also makes it possible for him to raise the

---

[103]J. Muilenburg, "Holiness," IDB, II, 621; W. H. Schmidt, Glaube, pp. 135-40; Wildberger, Jesaja, p. 24: "Im Begriff der Heiligkeit Jahwes ist eindeutig das Moment der freundlichen Zuneigung eingeschlossen."

[104]For the event-character of Yahweh's holiness, see W. H. Schmidt, Glaube, p. 138.

[105]Eichrodt, Der Heilige in Israel, p. 15.

[106]Harrelson, Interpreting the Old Testament, p. 232.

question, "How long?" That this question expresses implicit hope for the future of Israel has been pointed out above. These aspects of hope and salvation find explicit expression in vs. 13c after the threatening aspect of the remnant motif came to expression in vss. 11b-13b.

The hopeful aspect of the remnant motif has come to expression in the clause "a holy seed is its stock" (vs. 13c).[107] How are we to understand this sentence? On the basis of Job 14:7-9 it may be gathered that it was common knowledge that the root stock which was left in the ground at the felling of a tree was able to sprout again and thus bring forth new life.[108] The felling of the tree certainly meant its destruction, but

---

[107]Stegemann, op. cit., p. 169, speaks of the "Totalität der Katastrophe" which is "gemildert" through vs. 13c. This softening of the completeness of the destruction is taken in conjunction with the lack of the last three words in the LXX as sure signs that indicate that vs. 13c is a gloss. Stegemann's interpretation of Isa. 6 fails to recognize that there are positive aspects implicit in this inaugural vision and that the first part of vs. 13 obviously contains the remnant motif in its threatening aspect and cannot be interpreted to express total and complete destruction, because the stump, as it were, of the oak or terebinth still remains. In a similar vein Fey, op. cit., p. 107 n. 3, denies an Isaianic origin of vs. 13c because "der Verfasser des Zusatzes . . . biegt den Sinn von 13a.ba in doppelter Weise um: er deutet den Wurzelstumpf von Eiche und Terebinthe nicht als Zeichen der Vernichtung, sondern als Zeichen der Hoffnung, und er setzt das restliche, Zehntel des Feldertrages trotz v. 12 gleich 'restlicher Menschengruppe'." Fey seeks to interpret 6:11b-13 with the aid of 5:8-10 and thus takes the desolation of the land in 6:12 to indicate that the population is "restlos" removed from it. Since he believes that the population is completely removed, the "tenth" of vs. 13a must then of necessity refer to the "Zehntel des Feldertrages" and not to the "Zehntel der Bevölkerung." This interpretation, however, is completely unwarranted. There is no indication whatever in vs. 12 that the entire population is exiled. As a result there is no need nor any reason to read in vs. 13a a "Zehntel des Feldertrages." In its context it refers to a tenth of the people. Cf. Gray, Isaiah, I, 111.

[108]G. Dalman, Arbeit und Sitte in Palastine (Gütersloh, 1942), VII, 43-5; H. Grapow, Die bildlichen Ausdrücke im Ägyptischen (Berlin, 1924), p. 101. The Elder Pliny states in his Naturalis historia, XV. 30 with regard to the laurel tree, "vivacissima [est] radix; ita ut si truncus in auruerit, recisa arbor mox laetius fructificat."

not the destruction of the life in the root stock. The root stock is thus the seat of new life.[109] Thus the idea of life which is basic to the remnant motif in general is implicit in the picture of the root stock in the inaugural vision of Isaiah. Taken as a whole the picture which is painted in Isaiah's call vision is fairly clear. The root stock which is left at the felling of the tree is both a symbol for the destruction of the nation and a symbol of resurgent life which will grow out of the reduced remnant.[110] Yahweh punishes to save; he destroys to rebuild. The end in view in God's purpose[111] is not destruction but salvation.[112] This, in the final analysis, is the answer to the human cry of despair, "How long, O Lord?"

---

[109]Gehman, op. cit., p. 270; ". . . the stump, however, is not dead, but it will send forth new shoots from among which in due course a new tree will develop."

[110]The duality of Isaiah's message is reflected in vs. 13. This is no surprise, because it is contained in the notion of the "holiness" of Yahweh, the purification and forgiveness of Isaiah, and the question "how long." Cf. Gottwald, A Light to the Nations, p. 323; Seierstad, op. cit., pp. 107-8; Lindblom, Prophecy in Ancient Israel, p. 188.

[111]For a discussion of the "plan" of Yahweh in Isaiah, see Johannes Fichtner, "Jahves Plan in der Botschaft des Jesajas," ZAW, 63 (1951), 16-33.

[112]Form-critical analysis of the Old Testament call narratives has shown that "words of personal reassurance and comfort are a common feature of all call narratives." So N. Habel, "The Form and Significance of the Call Narratives," ZAW, 77 (1965), 312. That this should not be construed as a conclusive proof for the authenticity of the final line of 6:13 is without question. Nevertheless it does give additional support to the genuineness of vs. 13c, because the vital strands of the prophet's total message are often incorporated into the call narrative. There can be no doubt that the remnant motif is a part of Isaiah's total proclamation. It is also worthwhile to consult the form-critical discussion of prophecies of doom and salvation by Klaus Koch, The Growth of the Biblical Tradition: The Form-Critical Method, transl. by S. M. Cupitt (New York, 1969), pp. 200-20; and Childs, Isaiah and the Assyrian Crisis, pp. 47ff. Childs has clearly shown that there is an interrelation and combination of doom and salvation in Isaiah.

The root stock that remains is a "holy seed."[113] K. Budde has argued convincingly that no objection should be taken to the words "holy seed" by Isaiah.[114] In 1:4a the opposite designation, "seed of evildoers," is used.[115] Just as much as the "Holy One of Israel" is the "father"[116] of the "seed of evildoers" so he is the "father" of the "holy seed." Insofar as Yahweh's "holiness"[117] has such a prominent place in the earlier part of the inaugural vision and brings judgment[118] and salvation[119] to the prophet himself,[120] it is a natural corollary that the twofold aspects of divine

---

[113]Köhler, Old Testament Theology, p. 231, follows the LXX ἀπὸ τῆς θήκης αὐτῆς and reconstructs the reading of the Vorlage as מִמַּצַּבְתָּהּ which he uses for his translation, "out of the stump comes holy after-growth." This certainly improves the text, but the lectio difficilor of the Masoretic text is to be preferred on text-critical grounds.

[114]Budde, Jesajas Erleben, pp. 24-5. Budde could have also referred to הר קדשׁי in 11:9a; cf. Fey, op. cit., p. 107 n. 2.

[115]This phrase is used again in Isa. 14:20.

[116]Cf. Wildberger, Jesaja, p. 22.

[117]Scholars have repeatedly pointed out that the idea of holiness appears to be an ancient Jerusalemite tradition from pre-Israelite times, so more recently E. Jenni, "Jesajas Berufung in der neueren Forschung," ThZ, 15 (1959), 331-4; Werner H. Schmidt, "Jerusalemer El-Traditionen bei Jesaja," ZRGG, XVI (1964), 312; idem, Königtum Gottes im Ugarit und Israel (BZAW, 80; 2nd ed.; Berlin, 1966), pp. 28-9; Wildberger, Jesaja, p. 24.

[118]Isa. 5:16; 30:12ff.; 10:17. The holiness of the Holy One must consume like a fire everything that injures the holiness.

[119]Isa. 10:20; 17:7; 29:19. In the concept of Yahweh's holiness the aspect of friendly aid and help is included.

[120]Fey, op. cit., p. 114: ". . . im Akt der Entsündigung Jesajas ist die Totalität von Unheil und Gericht schon durchbrochen und ein Zeichen der Zuwendung Jahwes aufgerichtet." Cf. Seierstad, op. cit., p. 100.

holiness are also brought to bear on the people. They will experience judgment (vss. 11b-13b), but a "holy seed" will emerge for future existence. Thus the whole question of the continued existence of God's covenant people is raised. The "holy seed" is holy only after the cleansing experience brought about by a confrontation with the divine holiness analogous to the confrontation and cleansing experience of Isaiah.[121] After the annihilation of the nation a holy people will sprout out of the remaining root stock. It will be holy, for it has experienced cleansing judgment. Because of this experience it will stand in the right relationship of faith and trust and obedience to Yahweh.[122] It will then be the carrier of election. In short, these considerations lead to the conclusion that Isaiah uses the remnant motif with its threatening and saving aspect right from the start of his prophetic ministry. The "holy seed" is the outgrowth of the nascent life contained in the root stock;[123] the holy remnant is a reality of the future and as such an element in

---

[121]H. Gross, "Rest," Bibeltheologisches Wörterbuch, ed. by J. B. Bauer (2nd ed.; Graz, 1962), II, 1001, points out that the purification of the prophet is exemplary for the remnant which "steht in Solidarität mit dem Propheten und wird folglich in seiner Wesensart grundlegend bestimmt durch die Teilhabe an der göttlichen Heiligkeit, die . . . auch den Rest umgestaltet und neu prägt Is 6,13: 4,3." Cf. Johannes Hempel, Gott und Mensch im Alten Testament (Stuttgart, 1936), pp. 140ff.; Buber, Prophetic Faith, p. 133.

[122]Schilling, op. cit., pp. 60-1, has overemphasized the "ethical point of view" in connection with the moral obligation on the part of the remnant. He reads strong "ethical" overtones into the inaugural vision of Isaiah and misses the close connection between the Isaianic remnant motif and the Isaianic call to faith.

[123]Schilling, op. cit., pp. 60, 74; E. Osterloh, "Rest," Biblisch-Theologisches Handwörterbuch, ed. by E. Osterloh and H. Engelland (3rd ed.; Göttingen, 1964), p. 494.

Isaiah's eschatology.[124] Isaiah stands here in the tradition of Amos' usage of the remnant motif.

These conclusions do not lend support to the theories centering around a twofold development of Isaiah's remnant motif nor to the theory that Isaiah's remnant motif contained at first only a negative aspect. Following J. Meinhold[125] some scholars like W. E. Müller[126] and others[127] have argued that Isaiah's proclamation lacked the remnant motif at the beginning of his ministry, i.e., that he did not expect any remnant at first. The events connected with the Syro-Ephraimitic war brought about

---

[124]Lindblom, Prophecy in Ancient Israel, pp. 188-9, 367, has placed correct emphasis on the eschatological nature of the remnant motif in vs. 13c. But we must object to the expressions which view the remnant motif as one of Isaiah's "original ideas" (p. 188), "a quite new idea" (p. 367), and the one in which he holds that "Isaiah [is] the first prophet to whom the idea of the remnant motif was revealed" (p. 187). As regards the former notion of the novelty of the remnant motif in Isaiah, Lindblom overlooks the fact that there has been already a long history of the remnant motif in Israel prior to Isaiah, even with regard to the positive aspect of it. The notion of the remnant motif as "revealed" to Isaiah must be restricted to mean that Isaiah was the first to whom it had been "revealed" in his inaugural vision.

[125]Meinhold, Studien zur israelitischen Religionsgeschichte, pp. 92ff., has himself actually adopted suggestions of Giesebrecht, Beiträge zur Jesajakritik, pp. 84ff. Giesebrecht and Meinhold do speak of a threefold "picture of the future" in Isaiah's message. Isaiah believed according to these exegetes at first in an indestructible existence of Israel. But during the Syro-Ephraimitic crisis Isaiah gained the certainty that North Israel would vanish. As a result the prophet believed that Judah would be the "remnant." However, the future development of events brought about the conviction that also Judah will fall under judgment and that only a remnant of Judah will remain.

[126]W. E. Müller, op. cit., pp. 55ff.

[127]W. E. Müller's thesis has been taken up more recently by J. Fichtner, "Jahves Plan in der Botschaft des Jesajas," ZAW, 63 (1951), 28-30, and Herrmann, Heilserwartungen, pp. 128-9.

an emphasis on the remnant motif which to a larger or smaller degree was from then on a part of the proclamation of the prophet. This theory is not supported by the text of Isaiah. Even if one were to leave out of consideration the positive evidence for the remnant motif in Isa. 6:13 for the earliest period of the prophet's ministry, one can have no doubt that Isaiah believed in a remnant before the Syro-Ephraimitic crisis because he named his son *šeʾār yāšûḇ* at a considerable time earlier than his confrontation with King Ahaz[128] on which occasion *šeʾār yāšûḇ* must have been at least old enough to walk. G. Ernest Wright[129] among many others is correct in maintaining that Isaiah's proclamation contained the remnant motif right from his inaugural vision. But he makes it a "sign of judgment" for the early period of Isaiah's activity. It seems that there is no support from Isaiah's early message for such an interpretation. An exclusively negative aspect of the remnant motif during Isaiah's early career can be maintained only by eliminating passages of hope from that period. We have seen that Isaiah's inaugural vision opened up before the prophet the majestic "holiness" of Yahweh with its aspects of terror and destruction as well as forgiveness and salvation. The prophet himself experienced both and became thereby a proleptic representative of the future remnant.[130] Upon his commissioning he asked the anxious but hopeful question, "How long?" The reply of Yahweh contained a twofold answer corresponding to the aspects of his "holiness":

---

[128]Isa. 7:1-9.

[129]Wright, *Isaiah*, p. 36.

[130]*Supra*, pp. 243-44.

the nation will be destroyed but out of its remains a "holy seed," a purified, believing, and trusting remnant, will spring forth to new life. As an entity of eschatological expectation it will be the heir of election and of the promises given to the people through the house of David.

These observations are carried forward by Isaiah in a saying (1:21-26) from his early period of activity.[131] Here the message of a remnant is developed in a most convincing way without the employment of any remnant terminology. The effective picture of a refiner's cleansing is used. The prophetic diatribe (Scheltrede) opens in the form of a lament on Jerusalem (vss. 21-23) which has become the "harlot" (vs. 21). Isaiah adopted Hosea's figure of speech,[132] using it in his own way. The tertium comparationis by Isaiah is not harlotry in the sense of apostasy from Yahweh and idolatry by worshiping Canaanite deities, rather it is the unfaithfulness on the part of Zion. The contrast is between "harlot"

---

[131]It is generally agreed that Isa. 1:21-26 belongs to the prophet's early career before the Syro-Ephraimitic crisis, see especially Schmidt, Die grossen Propheten, pp. 56-7; Eichrodt, Der Heilige in Israel, p. 37; Fohrer, Jesaja, I, 5; Kaiser, Jesaja, p. 15; idem, Einleitung, p. 173 n. 1; Wildberger, Jesaja, p. 58. Only Leslie, op. cit., pp. 115-6, placed this saying recently into Isaiah's last period. However, he does not offer any explanation. Herrmann, Heilserwartungen, p. 128, places it "in die Mitte jesajanischen Denkens" which presumably is a time later than the early period of Isaiah's ministry. He does so because he argues that the remnant motif was absent during the early period. Yet, it is generally conceded that on the whole the materials in the first six chapters of Isaiah derive with few exceptions from Isaiah's early period. In addition the content of this passage shows that Jerusalem had not yet experienced the events of 734/33 B.C. There is also no mention of danger of war. Furthermore the content of vs. 23 is closely related to such sections as 3:12-15; 5:22-24 and 10:1-4 which belong to Isaiah's early period of activity. These considerations strongly point to a date for the saying of 1:21-26 in Isaiah's early period. See Appendix, p. 471.

[132]Hos. 1:2; 2:7; 3:3; 4:12-15; 9:1.

and "faithfulness." Jerusalem's unfaithfulness consists of a lack of "justice" and "righteousness" (vs. 21). In the midst of this indictment, which employs Isaianic key terms, we find pictures that depict with extraordinary vividness and power the disintegration of order and the corruption of justice: "Your silver has become dross, your wine is mixed with water" (vs. 22). The prophet takes up this picture in his threat[133] which begins with vs. 24.

24 Therefore the Lord says,
the Lord of hosts
the Mighty One of Israel:
'Ah, I will vent my wrath on my enemies
and avenge myself on my foes.
25 I will turn my hand against you
and will smelt away your dross as with lye
and remove all your alloy.
26 And I will restore your judges as at the first,
and your counselors as at the beginning.
Afterward you shall be called the city of
righteousness,
the faithful city.'[134]

---

[133]As so often the transition from diatribe to threat is procured by לָכֵן in vs. 24, see Westermann, Basic Forms of Prophetic Speech, pp. 169ff.; Fohrer, Introduction, pp. 351ff.; Kaiser, Einleitung, p. 227; Koch, op. cit., pp. 211f. Westermann suggested that the designations of "diatribe" and "threat" be discarded and replaced by "announcement of judgment" which then would comprise the elements of "indictment" (diatribe) and "sentence" (threat). However, Fohrer has objected by pointing out that there are diatribes or invectives which are found in prophetic materials independent of threats. Therefore, the designation "announcement of judgment" would be inexact. He noted also that the designation "threat" leaves open the matter of whether or not what is threatened actually comes to pass. This fits the situation better because many threats were retracted (Amos 7:1-6 etc.) or were never realized (Isa. 22:14; etc.). Due to these strictures it seems best to retain for the present the designations diatribe and threat.

[134]It is especially noteworthy that the prophetic speech stands in a chiastic relationship to the speech of Yahweh, i.e., vs. 24b corresponds to vs. 23, vs. 25 to vs. 22, vs. 26b to vs. 21a, see Fey, op. cit., p. 64.

The one who speaks[135] this threat is none other than the holy and powerful God, the "Mighty One of Israel."[136] What will he do? He will turn in wrathful judgment[137] against his enemies (vs. 24b). The enemies are here not identified as the enemies of Israel but as the Jerusalemites themselves. Isaiah announces a kind of a Day of Yahweh. Yahweh moves against his own city.[138] But surprisingly the picture neither refers to the destruction of Jerusalem nor to the complete annihilation of Judah. In this opening part of the threat Yahweh's deep involvement comes to expression, i.e., his holy passion cannot tolerate the corruption that is

---

[135]The נְאֻם יהוה is typical for the messenger speech, but it is used here with a long series of titles אדון, יהוה צבאות, אביר ישראל, which apart from its last member appears again in 19:4.

[136]Though this title is used only here in the Hebrew Bible it reflects patriarchal traditions. It should be understood as a variation of אֲבִיר יַעֲקֹב (Gen. 49:24; Isa. 49:26; 60:16; Ps. 132:2, 5). Cf. L. Rost, "Die Gottesverehrung der Patriarchen im Lichte der Pentateuchquellen," SVT, 7 (1960), 346-59; F. M. Cross, "Yahweh and the Gods of the Patriarchs," HThR, 55 (1962), 225-59; J. P. Hyatt, "Was Yahweh Originally a Creator Deity?" JBL, 84 (1967), 369-77.

[137]Both verbs נחם and נקם belong to the terminology of the Day of Yahweh. In the Song of Moses both are used in close proximity in connection with the announcement of the Day of Yahweh (Deut. 32:35-36). The synonymous parallelism of "vindicate" and "have compassion" (Hithpael התנחם) in the latter poem is especially noteworthy. The root נקם appears frequently in connection with the Day of Yahweh (Deut. 32:41, 43; Isa. 34:8; 35:4; Nah. 1:2 etc.). Cf. Wildberger, Jesaja, pp. 64, 65.

[138]It appears that here we already meet motifs which Isaiah elaborated more explicitly later on in his ministry. Yahweh turns against his own city, which is a reversal of tradition of the Day of Yahweh in a sense similar to Amos in 5:18-20. In close connection with this is the tradition of the inviolability of Zion which plays a considerable role in Isaiah (Isa. 8:9-10; 17:12-14) and the battle of the nations motif (Isa. 2:2-4). Cf. Childs, Isaiah and the Assyrian Crisis, pp. 51-2; G. Wanke, Die Zionstheologie der Korachiten (BZAW, 97; Berlin, 1966), pp. 113-7; Lutz, Jahve, Jerusalem und die Völker, pp. 173ff.

carried on in the chosen city. Zion, the faithful city, has succumbed to bribery and is running after gifts. Yet God's affection for this people rings even in the denunciation. "There is sorrow in God's anger. It is an instrument of purification, and its exercise will not last forever."[139] The picture of the smelting practice shows unequivocally that the coming judgment is for the purpose of purging and cleansing[140] but not for annihilation. Isaiah does not proclaim the total destruction and complete annihilation of Israel or Jerusalem; he does say, however, that Yahweh will remove the "alloy" (vs. 25c). The removal of the alloy indicates the preservation of the purest residue. This means that hope remains for the future. "The door to hope is only through the purifying fire."[141] The purifying fire will leave a purified or holy remnant. There is clear evidence in this threat that the remnant motif does not contradict nor stand in the way of Isaiah's message of judgment. "The remnant idea . . . is completely harmonious with Isaiah's announcement of judgment."[142] The purified remnant is the entity by which continuity between the past and the future is established. It is the vital link between judgment and salvation.

In vs. 26 the remnant is the community which emerges from the sifting process of the refiner's fire as purified and holy. It is characterized as making room for "righteousness" and "faithfulness." This

---

[139]Heschel, The Prophets, p. 83.

[140]See here especially E. Balla, Die Botschaft der Propheten (Tübeingen, 1958), pp. 129-30; Bright, The Kingdom of God, pp. 88-9; Wildberger, Jesaja, p. 65; Fohrer, Jesaja, I, 43-4.

[141]Wright, Isaiah, p. 26.

[142]Wildberger, Jesaja, p. 65.

means, of course, that in Zion, God's chosen city, the kind of judges and counselors will be restored "as at first." To the "as at first" in vs. 26a corresponds the parallel expression "as at the beginning" in vs. 26b. Isaiah measures the future era with the measuring stick of the past epoch. Most likely Isaiah refers here to the beginnings of the history of Jerusalem under the rule of David.[143] In another place Isaiah speaks of Jerusalem as "the city where David encamped."[144] He correlates the early history of Israelite Jerusalem with the future Zion. Over against the ʾaḥarê-kēn (afterward) of the ideal time of the past is placed the ideal time of future salvation. This is important for a correct understanding of Isaianic eschatology. H. Wildberger points out that the Isaianic phrases "in the latter days,"[145] "in the latter time,"[146] and "the latter day"[147] correspond to the "afterward" in the present passage.[148] This points to a future age in which a decisive change will take place and a new beginning will be made. In that future age the remnant, cleansed in the purifying judgment, will constitute the nucleus of the new community which is patterned after the ideal age of the past.[148a] It is within this framework only that we must speak of an eschatology

---

[143]*Ibid*.; Fohrer, *Jesaja*, I, 44.

[144]Isa. 29:1.

[145]Isa. 2:2.

[146]Isa. 9:1 (Heb. 8:23).

[147]Isa. 30:8.

[148]Wildberger, *Jesaja*, p. 66.

[148a]See Appendix II, p. 475.

of Isaiah.[149] The remnant motif is an essential aspect of Isaiah's eschatology.[150] According to the present passage the future time of salvation is not envisioned as anything more than a return to the ideal past. The Zion of the purified and holy remnant will again correspond to the civitas dei of the past. Heilszeit and Urzeit correspond to each other. Yet the change from the present to the future does not take place along the line of a regular continuous development within normal historical processes, but as vs. 25a reveals it comes about by the hand of Yahweh.

---

[149]For Isaiah's "eschatology" see Th. C. Vriezen, "Prophecy and Eschatology," SVT, 1 (1953), 199-229; J. Lindblom, "Gibt es eine Eschatologie bei den alttestamentlichen Propheten?" Studia Theologica, VI (1952), 79-114; idem, Prophecy in Ancient Israel, 00. 366-9; Herrmann, Heilserwartungen, pp. 126-44. A categorical denial of any pre-exilic eschatology including an eschatology of Isaiah is maintained by G. Fohrer, "Die Struktur der alttestamentlichen Eschatologie," ThLZ, 85 (1960), 401-20=Studien zur alttestamentlichen Prophetie (BZAW, 99; Berlin, 1967), pp. 32-58; idem, "Zehn Jahre Literatur zur alttestamentlichen Prophetie (1951-1960)." ThR, 28 (1962), 356ff.; Fohrer also denies the presence of the remnant motif in Isaiah, see his "Review of Der Prophet Jesaja, Kap. 1-12 by O. Kaiser," ThLZ, 87 (1962), col. 748.

[150]W. Zimmerli, Der Mensch und seine Hoffnung im Alten Testament (Göttingen, 1968), p. 114: "Ganz gegenständlich ist Heilshoffnung und gegenwärtiges Leid um das Volk Gottes in . . . 1,21-26 verbunden. . . ." Herrmann, Heilserwartungen, pp. 127-8, remarks that in this saying the "Gedankenfluss von der Unheils- zur Heilsbotschaft organisch hinübergleitet." Hempel, Worte der Propheten, p. 138, speaks of the "Rest [als]. . . eine Zukunftsgrösse des Glaubens," G. Beer, "Zur Zukunftserwartung Jesajas," in Studien zur semitischen Philologie und Religionsgeschichte. Festschrift für Julius Wellhausen, ed. by K. Marti (BZAW, 27; Giessen, 1914), p. 27, states that the remnant "ist für Jesaja eine zukünftige Grösse. . . ."; K. Fullerton, "Viewpoints in the Discussion of Isaiah's Hopes for the Future," JBL, 41 (1922), 67: "Again, there are admittedly genuine hopes in Isaiah, 1:21-26, the doctrine of the Remnant. . . ."; von Gall, op. cit., p. 170: "So schliesst der Rest, der bleibt, zweierlei ein, einmal das Gericht, und sodann den Anfang eines Neuen." Gressmann, Eschatologie, p. 231: "Israel soll nicht gänzlich vernichtet, sondern geläutert werden. Die schlechten Elemente werden beseitigt, nur die guten bleiben zurück und bilden den Kern des Neuen Volkes." It is strange that Fohrer, Jesaja, I, 45, is so much at pains to deny what is

Finally it must be pointed out that in a larger sense Isa. 1:21-26 represents an elucidation of the Zion tradition, i.e., one of the Israelite election traditions[151] which plays an important role in the proclamation of Isaiah. Among the motifs that are connected with Zion the motif of righteousness is taken up by Isaiah who connects it with the motif of faithfulness. Both of these motifs are related to the remnant motif. This indicates Isaiah's freedom to use ancient traditions and motifs and to modify them by joining them. In this process new aspects are attached to the various motifs and further connections are established which receive more elaboration in Isaiah's future proclamation. According to the present passage Isaiah knows nothing of a mythically founded election nor does he know anything of an inviolability of Zion which is

---

largely the scholarly consensus on this passage: "Von der Vorstellung eines heiligen Restes bei Jesaja kann auch bei diesem einmalig aufblitzendem Gedanken an ein Teil- oder Läuterungsgericht keine Rede sein. Erst recht handelt es sich nicht um die Ankündigung einer künftigen Heilszeit und also gar um eine eschatologische Botschaft." Fohrer operates with an extremely narrow definition of eschatology in which he nearly equates eschatology with apocalypticism and a one-sided view of the remnant motif derived from post-exilic Judaism. He is forced, however, to admit that the judgment is only partial, but he fails to account for the juxtaposition of judgment and salvation and the remnant which links the past with the future.

[151]See here especially Rohland, op. cit., pp. 145-62; cf. N. W. Porteous, "Jerusalem-Zion: The Growth of a Symbol," Verbannung und Heimkehr. Festschrift für W. Rudolph (Tübingen, 1961), pp. 235-52; J. H. Hayes "The Tradition of Zion's Inviolability," JBL, 82 (1963) 419-26; J. Schreiner, Sion-Jerusalem, Jahwes Königssitz (München, 1963), pp. 243ff.; von Rad, OTT, II, 155-69; Lutz, Jahve, Jerusalem und die Völker, pp. 17ff., Preuss, Jahweglaube, pp. 150-5; H.-P. Müller, Ursprünge und Strukturen alttestamentlicher Eschatologie, pp. 86-101. Different conclusions are reached by Wanke, Die Zionstheologie der Korachiten, pp. 100-17. On Wanke, see the review of the present writer in AUSS, VI (1968), 229-32. For a recent evaluation of the Zion tradition in Isaiah, see James M. Ward, Amos & Isaiah: Prophets of the Word of God, pp. 228-56. See Appendix II, pp. 475-76.

guaranteed through cultic acts. The elction which comes to expression here corresponds to the faithfulness of the elected ones. The present community of Zion will indeed experience judgment. The purging fire will leave a purged remnant which will receive leaders whose deepest concern will be the preservation of justice and righteousness. The "Holy One of Israel" will judge his city to leave a purged, purified, and holy remnant as the carriers of the divine election. This remnant serves as the link between the ideal Urzeit and the future Heilszeit; it is an eschatological entity from which the new community of the future springs forth.

The remnant motif is contained in another saying from the early period of Isaiah's ministry. It will be seen that it has a number of affinities with Isa. 1:21-26, because it is also concerned with the remnant of Jerusalem. We present a translation of the passage in which the remnant is mentioned, i.e., Isa. 4:2-3.

2 In that day
  the branch of Yahweh[152] shall be
    for beauty and glory,
  and the fruit of the land shall be
    for pride and adornment
      for the survivors of Israel.[153]

---

[152]For the MT צמח יהוה the LXX gives ἐπιλάμψει ὁ θεός, "God will shine forth," which seems to have derived from the Hebrew צחח, "to make bright," KB, 800, or the Aramaic צמחא="brightness," see Joseph Ziegler, Untersuchungen zur Septuaginta des Buches Isaias (Münster, 1934), p. 107. Aquila, Symmachus, and Theodotion read ανατολη κυριος, the Vulgate has germen domini, and the Peshitta follows with denḥeh d^{e}mārjâ, i.e. "appearance, glory of the Lord," (see Wildberger, Jesaja, p. 154.). The Targum translates משיחא דיהוה which shows that its Vorlage was צמח The Targum understood this term in a Messianic sense. 1QIs^{a} supports the superior MT.

[153]1QIs^{a} adds ויהודה; see Millar Burrows, The Dead Sea Scrolls

3 And the one who is left in Zion,
  and remains in Jerusalem,
shall be called holy,
every one who is recorded for life[154] in Jerusalem.[155]

The authenticity of 4:2-6 of which the above verses are the first part is much disputed. Many scholars deny[156] an Isaianic authorship while others support it.[157] Some serious objections have been raised against

---

of St. Mark's Monastery. Vol. I: The Isaiah Manuscript and the Habakkuk Commentary (New Haven, Conn., 1950), Pl. IV. This addition is not original.

[154]JB: "noted down for survival"; NAB: "marked down for life."

[155]BHK and BHS print this along with 4:4-6 as prose. Duhm, Jesaja, pp. 51-2; T. K. Cheyne, The Prophecies of Isaiah (5th ed.,; New York, 1890), I, 26-8; Scott, Isaiah, V, 194-5; Leslie, op. cit., p. 204, and RSV consider it also as prose. On the other hand, a rhythmical and poetic structure is recognized by Marti, Jesaja, p. 71; Gray, Isaiah, I, 76; H. Schmidt, Die grossen Propheten, pp. 112-3; Procksch, Jesaja, p. 83; Hertzberg, op. cit., p. 31; Eichrodt, Der Heilige in Israel, p. 63; Kissane, Isaiah, I, 43; Fohrer, Jesaja, I, 70-1. I. W. Slotki, Isaiah (Soncino Books of the Bible; London, 1949), pp. 20-1, and Wildberger, Jesaja, p. 151, regard only vs. 2 as poetry. The present writer follows the majority of exegetes as regards to poetical structure of vss. 2-3.

[156]Since Duhm, Jesaja, pp. 51ff., there has been a growing number of scholars who consider 4:2-6 as secondary: Marti, Jesaja, p. 76; Gray, Isaiah, op. cit., I, 77-8; Aage Bentzen, Introduction to the Old Testament (2nd ed.; Copenhagen, 1952), II, 108; Pfeiffer, Introduction to the Old Testament, p. 439; Eichrodt, Der Heilige in Israel, p. 63; A. Weiser, Introduction to the Old Testament, transl. by D. M. Barton (London, 1961), p. 188; Kaiser, Jesaja, pp. 41-2; Scott, Isaiah, V, 194; Leslie, op. cit., pp. 203-4; Wildberger, Jesaja, p. 153; Fohrer, Jesaja, I, 71; Heaton, The Hebrew Kingdoms, p. 320.

[157]But since Duhm there has been likewise no lack of scholars who support the Isaianic authorship of the whole section or parts thereof: von Orelli, op. cit., p. 23; Steuernagel, Einleitung, p. 479; Feldmann, op. cit., p. 63; Procksch, Jesaja, p. 83, considers vss. 2-3 as authentic; König, op. cit., p. 81; Gressmann, Der Messias, p. 159; Budde, ZAW, 50 (1932) 44ff., follows B. Stade, ZAW, 4 (1884), 149-51, maintaining the authenticity of vss. 2-4 in the order of 4, 3, 2; Fischer, Isaias, p. 42; Schilling, op. cit., pp. 62ff., maintains the authenticity of 4:1-3; Danell, op. cit., p. 163; Herntrich, Der Prophet Jesaja, Kap. 1-12, pp. 62ff.; Rowley, The Biblical Doctrine of Election, p. 75; Buber, Prophetic Faith, p. 29; Kissane, Isaiah, I, 41; Kaufmann, The Religion of

the genuineness of 4:2-3.[158] Yet H. Wildberger has reminded us that a final judgment either way depends upon the exegesis of the passage under

---

Israel, p. 386; Bright, Isaiah-I, p. 493; Lindblom, Prophecy in Ancient Israel, pp. 356 n. 129, says that this passage is substantially authentic; Mauchline, Isaiah, p. 76; Wright, Isaiah, p. 30; Gelin, op. cit., p. 286; Martin Rehm, Der königliche Messias im Licht der Immanuel-Weissagungen des Buches Jesaja (Kevelaer, 1968), pp. 254ff. In view of this list of scholars who support parts or all of 4:2-6 as authentic, it is strange that Ward, op. cit., p. 242, states that 4:2-4 "is universally regarded as a postexilic supplement to the book" and accepts this "consensus concerning 4:2-6, and therefore need not discuss the passage in detail." See Appendix II, p. 476.

[158]Our discussion limits itself to 4:2-3 because these verses contribute directly to the remnant motif. It is widely recognized that they can be understood as an oracle independent of the prior and following sections. The following formal arguments have been advanced against the genuineness of vss. 2-3: (1) The prosaic form of this section testifies to the work of a later editor, so T. K. Cheyne, Introduction to the Book of Isaiah (London, 1895), p. 20. Gray, Isaiah, I, 77, admits that the alleged absence of rhythm and the slight amount of parallelism "may be in large part due to textual corruption, or incorrect analysis of the rhythm and parallelism." An increasingly large number of scholars have made convincing proposals for the poetic structure of vss. 2-3 as well as 4:2-6, supra, n. 155. (2) Collections of prophetic material are apt to conclude with secondary expansions, so Wildberger, Jesaja, p. 153. At first sight this argument seems to carry much weight. The following considerations must be kept in mind before this argument can have conclusive force. In order to have a so-called "secondary expansion" in 4:2ff., one would have to assume that Chapters 2-4 would have been at one point an independent collection of words of Isaiah, so Fohrer, Jesaja, I, 4, and Wildberger, Jesaja, p. 153. But the very criterion for determining an independent collection is the "concluding promise" of 4:2-6. It seems that here is a case of weak logic. If 4:2-6 is a "concluding promise" of a longer collection one must not assume therefore that it must of necessity be a "secondary expansion." This type of argumentation is suspect, because even in admittedly genuine Isaianic material (1:21-26) there is the juxtaposition of words of judgments with words of hope. Furthermore, if one would agree to consider 2-4 as an independent collection, then the collection in Chapter 5 does not contain a "concluding promise." This disturbs the consistency of the main criterion for distinguishing collections of materials. Since the "concluding promise" is an inconsistent means for determining collections, it would seem that Procksch, Jesaja, p. 20; Scott, Isaiah, V, 158, etc., have a stronger case in taking Chapters 2-5 as a collection from Isaiah's early period. (3) The use of certain expressions point to a late date. (4) "The ideas and thought of the passage," says Gray, Isaiah, I, 77, "alone are sufficient to render a late date . . . probable." The last two objections will be dealt with in our discussion of vss. 2-3.

discussion.[159] It is therefore necessary to proceed step by step in the following discussion.

The introductory formula *bayyôm hahûʾ*[160] connects this passage with the preceding oracles. At the same time it is an eschatological formula which points to the future action of Yahweh, as H.-P. Müller has recently shown anew.[161] It is therefore not surprising that this usage makes this formula as well as the entire passage suspect of being an editorial

---

[159]Wildberger, *Jesaja*, p. 153.

[160]The formula בַּיּוֹם הַהוּא does not always mean the eschatological Day of Yahweh. It may refer to a past or contemporaneous time (cf. Ex. 32:28; Jud. 3:30; 4:23; 1 Sam. 14:23) or it is intended simply as a kind of temporal conjunction or adverb (cf. Gen 15:18; 26:32; 30:35; 48:20; Ex. 5:6; Nu. 9:6; Deut. 27:11; etc; Isa. 3:7; 4:1; 20:6; 22:12; 29:18; 30:23; Jer. 39:16b; 48:41; 49:22, 26; 50:30; Eze. 24:26, 27; 29:21; 30:9; 38:14; 45:22; Amos 2:16; Hag. 2:23; Zech. 2:15; 3:10), so P. A. Munch, *The Expression bajjôm hāhū, Is it an Eschatological Terminus Technicus?* (Avhandlinger utgitt av Det Norske Viderskaps-Akadenvi i Oslo, II/2; Oslo, 1936), p. 59. But this is by no means always so as Munch holds. In a number of passages (Isa. 4:2; 5:30; 7:18, 20, 23; 10:20, 27; 11:10, 11; 17:4, 9; 22:20, 25; 23:15; 24:21; 25:9; 26:1; 27:1, 2, 12, 13; 28:5; Jer. 4:9; 30:7, 8; 46:10; Amos 8:9, 13; Ob. 8; Mic. 2:4; 5:9; Zeph. 1:9, 10; 3:11, 16; etc.), says Sigmund Mowinckel, *He That Cometh*, p. 268 n. 5, it is an eschatological formula. Hans Wildberger, "Jesajas Verständnis der Geschichte," *SVT*, IX (1963), 112-3, denies an eschatological meaning in Isa. 2:20; 3:18; 4:2; 11:10, 11; 12:1, 4; 17:7; 19:16; 23:15; 28:5; 29:18; 31:7. Here it is supposedly a formula which connects secondary reinterpretations with Isaianic materials. On the other hand, A. Lefèvre, "L'expression 'en ce jour-là' dans le livre d'Isaïe," *TCJP*, 4 (Mélanges bibliques A. Robert; Paris, 1957), 174-9, investigates all passages in Isaiah which contain this formula concluding--after eliminating as secondary only 2:20, 11:10-16; 17:7; 19:16-25; 23:13-18 and 31:7--that this formula has not yet a fully eschatological meaning, but contains a tendency to acquire it, because it means in Isaiah never "un jour banal" but always a day filled with Yahweh's manifestation. For a general discussion of the formula "in that day," see Preuss, *Jahweglaube*, pp. 174-5.

[161]Hans-Peter Müller, *Ursprünge und Strukturen alttestamentlicher Eschatologie*, pp. 86ff.

expansion.[162] However, one must be cautious. The repeated usage of the introductory formula bayyôm hahû᾿ is attested in a good number of authentic materials from Isaiah of Jerusalem from various periods of his ministry. This formula appears in 7:18-19, which contains a threat against Judah, in 7:20, which speaks of a sweeping destruction, and in 7:23, which refers to the Assyrian invasion. These three oracles are Isaiah's own re-interpretations of the sign of doom against Judah.[163] Contrariwise, the oracle of promise[164] in Isa. 10:24-27 stems from Isaiah. It too contains the formula "in that day."[165] In view of the usages of this formula in passages which contain genuine oracles of doom and of salvation, one cannot maintain with any degree of certainty that the appearance of this formula in 4:2a is a sign for the secondary origin of 4:2ff. The present poem is, of course, an announcement of salvation, which follows an announcement of judgment (2:25-4:1). The alternation of judgment and salvation is not alien to Isaiah of Jerusalem. Isa. 1:21-26 demonstrates that the alternation of judgment and salvation is a definite and constitutive part of Isaiah's message. This is supported from our examination of Isaiah's inaugural vision, which indicated that the juxtaposition of doom and hope is present in Yahweh's holiness

---

[162]So Wildberger, Jesaja, p. 153, and others.

[163]Fohrer, Jesaja, I, 117; cf. Joachim Becker, Isaias-der Prophet und sein Buch (SBS, 30; Stuttgart, 1968), pp. 54, 57ff.

[164]Scott, Isaiah, V, 245; Leslie, op. cit., p. 111.

[165]Isa. 10:27. Compare also the usage of the formula "in that day" in the Isaianic passages of Isa. 22:20, 25.

(6:3). Isaiah's own experience of cleansing demonstrates that judgment and salvation are two sides of Yahweh's action. Isaiah's cry of despair after his commissioning rings with hope for his people (6:11). In 6:13 doom and salvation come to expression through the remnant motif itself. These observations cause us to believe that the shift from threat to promise is no conclusive reason against the Isaianic origin of 4:2f.[166]

The thought of the previous announcements of judgment climaxes in 4:1 with the dreadful picture of seven women begging one man to take them in marriage.

> 4:1 And seven women shall take hold of
> one man in that day,
> saying, 'We will eat our own bread
> and wear our own clothes,
> only let us be called by your name;
> take away our reproach.'

The "one man" is a representative of the survived remnant which will return from the many men who will go forth in battle against the enemy. Isaiah expresses here again the threatening aspect of the remnant motif.[167] The phrase "in that day,"--it is missing in the LXX but present in 1QIs^a--points to Yahweh's day of judgment when few men will be left in Jerusalem. The corresponding formula bayyôm hahûʾ in 4:2 carries on where 4:1 leaves off, i.e., it shows the other side of the work of Yahweh by referring to the future community which God assures the remaining survivors of Zion.

Immediately following the formula "in that day" appears the term

---

[166] Against Wildberger, Jesaja, p. 153.

[167] Cf. Isa. 6:13a.

ṣemaḥ YHWH. This expression is of great importance for a correct understanding of the present poem. The word ṣemaḥ appears also in Jer. 23:5: ṣemaḥ ṣaddîq; 33:15: ṣemaḥ ṣedāqāh; Zech. 3:8: ṣemaḥ ʿabdî; and 6:12: ʾîš ṣemaḥ šemô. In both of these books these expressions are designations of the Messianic king of the future age. They are usually understood as indications that in the time of Jeremiah and Zechariah the term ṣemaḥ become a terminus technicus for the Messiah.[168] In both texts in Jer. leḏāwiḏ is expressly added; in Zech. emphasis is placed upon Zerubbabel as the promised scion of David. But in Isa. 4:2 we find a different emphasis. Here it is a "branch of Yahweh" and not a "branch" for David. This indicates at once that here we have a usage of ṣemaḥ that differs from the later Messianic passages in Jer. and Zech. A decisive argument against the Messianic interpretation of ṣemaḥ YHWH is the parallelism of perî-hāʾāreṣ in 4:2b. Since the latter phrase cannot be taken to refer to the Messiah, it follows that the former should be understood in a sense that correspondes to the latter, namely in the sense of "growth, vegetation of Yahweh."[169] The obviously non-Messianic and literal meaning of

---

[168]See especially the extended discussion in Rehm, op. cit., pp. 254-6. Wildberger, Jesaja, p. 154, argues that in Jeremiah this term is not yet a Messianic title but means merely "Nachkomme." J. G. Baldwin, "Ṣemaḥ as a Technical Term in the Prophets," VT, XIV (1964), 93, still maintains that the usage of this term in 4:2 has sacrificial overtones and that 4:2-6 as a whole is Messianic.

[169]So among recent interpreters Duhm, Jesaja, p. 51; Gray, Isaiah, I, 78; H. Schmidt, Die grossen Propheten, p. 113; Procksch, Jesaja, pp. 83-4; Scott, Isaiah, V, 194; Kissane, Isaiah, I, 47-8; Bright, Isaiah-I, p. 493; Kaiser, Jesaja, p. 42; Fohrer, Jesaja, I, 71; Rehm, op. cit., p. 255; Wildberger, Jesaja, pp. 154-5.

ṣemaḥ in 4:2 is a clear indication of the early date of the present passage.[170] J. Mauchline seeks in the expression ṣemaḥ YHWH a reference to the remnant which will survive the judgment.[171] But this identification fails on account of the parallelism where the parallel expression "the fruit of the land" is referred to for the survivors of Israel. It is therefore more natural to interpret the two parallel expressions as designations for the growing and fruitful vegetation of the land after the dreadful devastation.[172]

The promise of the natural fertility of the land is given to the pᵉlêṭaṯ-yiśrāʾēl. This expression occurs only here in Isaiah, but the noun pᵉlêṭāh appears four more times in the book of Isaiah.[173] In the Hebrew Bible it is most common in contexts of warfare[174] where it designates the escaped remnant.[175] It is neither a late expression in Hebrew thought[176] nor does it contain an aspect that would be foreign to Isaiah

---

[170] So especially Kissane, Isaiah, I, 47, and Bright, Isaiah-I, p. 493.

[171] Mauchline, Isaiah, p. 76.

[172] In analogy to פְּרִי הָאָרֶץ we find such phrases as פְּרִי הָאֲדָמָה (Gen. 4:3; Deut. 26:2, 10; 28:4, 11, 18, 42, 51; 30:9; Jer. 7:20; Mal. 3:11; Ps. 105:35) and צֶמַח הָאֲדָמָה (Gen. 19:25; cf. Isa. 61:11; Ps. 65;11). Inasmuch as Yahweh lets the trees grow (Gen. 2:9 וַיַּצְמַח) מִן־הָאֲדָמָה, it does not appear strange that one can speak of צֶמַח יהוה, even if this expression does not appear in any other place in the Hebrew Bible.

[173] Isa. 10:20; 15:9; 37:31, 32.

[174] Jd. 21:12; 2 Sa. 15:14; etc.

[175] Contrariwise in the case of the פְּלֵיטָה of foreign nations, the survivors that escaped will be destroyed (Isa. 15:9; 1 Chron. 4:43).

[176] It is used in the Jacob cycle in Gen. 32:8(9), in the Joseph cycle in Gen. 45:7, and in the tribal feud with reference to the פְּלֵיטָה לְבִנְיָמִן in Jd. 21:17.

of Jerusalem.[177] In 4:2 it is not explicitly stated that Yahweh will leave "survivors" from Israel; this is nevertheless the whole tenor of this passage.[178] An extra-Biblical parallel from the time of Isaiah contains this idea. The Panamumwa Inscription, which dates from between 733/32 and 727 B.C., uses a verbal form of plṭ with reference to the gods who "saved" (plṭwʾ) King Yaudi from ruin.[179] In Isa. 4:2 we find that Yahweh will leave "survivors of Israel," i.e., in Zion/Jerusalem as is explicated in vs. 3.

In 4:3 the pᵉlêṭaṯ-yiśrāʾēl are identified with the hannišʾār bᵉṣîyôn wᵉhannôṯār bîrûšālaim. It is well known that pᵉlêṭāh and deritives of pᵉlêṭāh are closely related. Pᵉlêṭāh appears five times parallel with šᵉʾērîṯ,[180] four times parallel with the substantival use of the Niphal participle of pᵉlêṭāh,[181] and once parallel with the noun šᵉʾār.[182] These parallel appearances in materials from early to late periods point at once to the antiquity of the terminology, its long history, and its closeness of meaning. The parallelism of the Niphal forms of plṭ and ytr in 4:3 indicates a synonymous meaning of these terms.[183] Thus we find in 4:2-3

177Danell, op. cit., pp. 162-3.

178Cf. Isa. 2:12; 3:1, 13-14; 17.

179KAI, II, 223 Nr. 215:2.

180Gen. 45:7; Isa. 15:9; 37:32=2 Ki. 19:31; 1 Chr. 4:43; Ezr. 9:14.

181Gen. 32:9; Ex. 10:5; Isa. 4:2, 3; Neh. 1:2, 3.

182Isa. 10:20.

183Compare also Ex. 10:5, 15; Josh. 11:11, 14; 1 Sam. 25:22, 34; Jer. 34:7.

the remnant terminology for the first time in close proximity in Isaiah.

The "survivors of Israel" are identified with the remnant in Zion/Jerusalem (4:3). They are not those who are left behind after the ruin of the city, but those who remain after the purifying judgment (1: 21-26).[184] They are not left over because they did not bend their knees before Baal and did not kiss him (1 Ki. 19:18), but because Yahweh's faithfulness has let him not to make a complete end.[185] The faithfulness on the part of Yahweh is rooted in his holiness which saves as much as it judges.[186] The aim of the divine work is the uncovering of his holiness in order that it might fill the whole earth (6:3). The goal of Yahweh's election of Israel at Sinai was to make it a gôy qaḏôš [187] and a ᶜām qaḏôš.[188] This aim had been frustrated by Israel's unfaithfulness. Yet the divine purpose remains the same. Isaiah is to proclaim the destruction of Israel, so that the goal of Yahweh's purpose can be reached in the remnant that remains and inherits the election promises. Isaiah's use of the names, Israel, Zion, and Jerusalem in connection with the remnant indicates that the election traditions associated with these names will be transferred to the remnant.[189] In addition the remnant in Zion/

---

[184] Kissane, Isaiah, I, 48.

[185] See here the remarks of Herntrich, Jesaja, pp. 66-8.

[186] Supra, pp.243, 244.

[187] Ex. 19:6.

[188] Deut. 7:6; 14:2, 21; 26:19; 28:9; cf. Hans Wildberger, Jahwes Eigentumsvolk (Zürich, 1960), pp. 95ff.

[189] Wildberger, Jesaja, p. 157.

Jerusalem "shall be called holy" (4:3). Just as Isaiah himself experienced the cleansing judgment of God through the act of purification with burning coals, which caused him to emerge as the proleptic representative of the remnant, so the remnant in Zion/Jerusalem will have gone through the cleansing judgment of Yahweh[190] in the day of visitation. It will then be called holy. O. Kaiser remarks, "[The remnant] cannot take credit . . . for this holiness on account of its own works for it is created through God's electing judgment."[191] Though Isaiah can speak of the "holy mountain" (11:9), the holiness in the present passage is a characteristic of the remnant and not of Zion/Jerusalem. We cannot, therefore, agree with H. Wildberger who claims that in 4:3 "Zion/Jerusalem is called holy."[192] Vs. 3 does not speak of the holiness of Zion/Jerusalem nor of the holiness of Israel/Judah nor of the holiness of the inhabitants of Zion/Jerusalem, but of the holiness of the remnant in Zion/Jerusalem.[193] The lô explicitly refers the holiness to the remnant.[194] Inasmuch as it is typical of Isaiah to speak of the q^{e}dôš yiśrā'ēl[195] and the har q^{o}dšî,[196] it is not surprising to find that the mem-

---

[190]Cf. Isa. 1:21-26.

[191]Kaiser, Jesaja, p. 43.

[192]Wildberger, Jesaja, p. 157.

[193]Against Herntrich, Jesaja, pp. 68-9, who attempts to distinguish between "being holy" and "being called holy." In the present writer's opinion such a distinction is artificial.

[194]Procksch, Jesaja, p. 85.

[195]Isa. 1:9; 5:19, 24; 30:11, 12, 15; 31:1; disputed passages are 10:20; 12:6; 17:7; 29:19; 37:23=2 Ki. 19-22.

[196]Isa. 11:9.

bers of the future remnant will be called qadôš. In 6:13c Isaiah had already struck this theme with the zeraᶜ qodeš.[197] The first intimation of the holy remnant of the inaugural vision is further explicated here in 4:3.

Another aspect of the holy remnant comes to expression in the phrase "every one who is recorded for life" (4:3d). Though the origin and exact interpretation of this concept is still not settled,[198] it is fairly clear that the holy remnant will be spared in judgment, because their names have been written down in the book of life. This places emphasis on the fact that the holy remnant will not be spared because of their qualifications, but because of God's determination to work out his purpose in history. It indicates also that God has determined them for life in advance of the destructive judgment.[199] In either case it is God's action that leaves a holy remnant. The idea that God had already determined the remnant and that it constitutes a limit to the destructive judgment was first encountered in the Elijah cycle, "Yet I will leave seven thousand in Israel" (1 Ki. 19:18).[200] It can be easily recognized that Isaiah follows here an old tradition, but he adapts it in his own way by connecting it with the idea of the preservation of life. This idea

---

[197]Supra, pp. 344-8.

[198]For detailed discussions, see Kaiser, Jesaja, p. 43; Fohrer, Jesaja, I, 71-2; Wildberger, Jesaja, pp. 157-9.

[199]So more recently Herntrich, Jesaja, p. 69; Kaiser, Jesaja, p. 43; Fohrer, Jesaja, I, 72; Wildberger, Jesaja, p. 157.

[200]Supra, pp. 168-9.

is a constitutive part of the remnant motif from its earliest appearance in extra-Biblical and Biblical thought.[201] In prophetic materials the connection between the remnant motif and life was explicitly encountered in Amos 5:14, 15: "Seek good, and not evil, that you may live, . . . it may be that the Lord, the God of hosts, will be gracious to the remnant of Joseph."[202] In the present poem Isaiah does not make the possibility of life a result of human action; he emphasizes the exclusive action of Yahweh.[203] The same emphasis was expressed by Isaiah in 1:21-26.[204] This militates against O. Schilling's excessive emphasis on the ethical action of man which makes possible his belonging to the remnant.[205] Furthermore, Isaiah's use of life does not refer to an "eschatological-supratemporal type of existence"[206] nor to eternal life as such. What he expresses is that the holy remnant, which will emerge from the eschatological day of judgment, will witness the abundant growth of the vegetation of the land (4:2), which ensures continued life in contrast to normal circumstances when life is most precarious after a major national catastrophe.

In short, Isaiah proclaims in this announcement of salvation (4:2-3) that from the nation of Israel, which will experience destruction

---

[201] *Supra*, Chapters II and III.

[202] *Supra*, pp. 198-9.

[203] See Rohland, *op. cit.*, pp. 115-6, 158-62.

[204] *Supra*, pp. 250ff.

[205] Schilling, *op. cit.*, pp. 22ff.

[206] *Ibid.*, p. 63.

in the eschatological day of Yahweh, "survivors of Israel" will emerge and remain in Zion/Jerusalem. This eschatological community will emerge, because for them the judgment did not serve as a destructive but as a cleansing agent. It will owe its existence and life to Yahweh's holiness and to his faithfulness to the election promises which are connected with the names Israel and Zion/Jerusalem. It will be a holy remnant, because Yahweh has purged and purified it. This saying refers neither to a supra-historical future aeon in discontinuity with the present age nor to a heavenly Jerusalem nor to a remnant with eternal life. According to Isaiah the holy remnant will be a product of the inbreaking of God in the present aeon; the holy remnant is an eschatological entity through which continuity between the past and the future is preserved.

Thus we have investigated the pertinent materials from Isaiah's early career and have gained an important picture of Isaiah's remnant motif during the beginnings of his ministry.

2. The Remnant Motif in Isaiah's Career During the Syro-Ephraimitic War (734-733 B.C.).--The pericope of Isa. 7:1-17 has a central position in the *Denkschrift* (testimony book)[207] of Isaiah which, according to the modern view of the composition of prophetic books,[208] extends from

---

[207]This term was coined by Budde, *ZAW*, 41 (1923), 165; idem, *Jesajas Erleben*, pp. 1-5. It has been adopted by many scholars, see Kaiser, *Jesaja*, p. 68; Wildberger, *Jesaja*, p. 234; Harrelson, *Interpreting the Old Testament*, p. 235; R. Kilian, *Die Verheissung Immannuels, Jes. 7, 14* (SBS, 35; Stuttgart, 1968), p. 14, etc.

[208]A most instructive discussion of the development of the present book of Isaiah has recently come from Lindblom, *Prophecy in Ancient Israel*, pp. 245ff.

6:1-9:6. The dramatic incidents related in Isa. 7 are written in the style of a third person report.[209] O. Eissfeldt sums up the scholarly opinion regarding the historicity of 7:1-9 in the following words: ". . . there can hardly be any doubt that the narrative is in all essentials completely trustworthy."[210] The occasion for these incidents are events in the political life of Judah when the Syro-Ephraimitic War of 734-733 B.C.[211] threatened the existence of the Davidic dynasty and the Judaean

---

[209]Scholars have repeatedly pointed out that underlying Chapter 7 seems to be Isaiah's autobiographical account, because Chapters 6 and 8 are certainly autobiographical reports in the first person; see Gray, Isaiah, I, 112; Kaiser, Jesaja, p. 68; Fohrer, Jesaja, I, 105; Donner, Israel unter den Völkern, pp. 9-10. Eissfeldt, OTI, p. 311, points out correctly against Gray that we have hardly the right to assimilate Chapter 7 to Chapters 6 and 8 by changing the third person into the first. Cf. Scott, Isaiah, V, 213; Kilian, op. cit., p. 14.

[210]Eissfeldt, OTI, p. 311. Sheldon H. Blank, "Immanuel and Which Isaiah," JNES, XIII (1954), 83ff.; idem, "Traces of Prophetic Agony in Isaiah," HUCA, XXVII (1956), 87; idem, Prophetic Faith in Isaiah, pp. 30-32, considers Isa. 7:1-12, 14-16 as a prophetic legend from an "Isaiah of legend." Similarly, C. F. Whitley, "The Call and Mission of Isaiah," JNES, XVIII (1959), 43, considers 7:3 as an editorial insertion. But these suppositions have found no support. Georg Fohrer, Die symbolischen Handlungen der Propheten (AThANT, 54; 2nd ed.; Zürich, 1968), p. 78: "Die Behauptung, dass Jes. 7, 3 und 8,1-4 ungeschichtlich und legendarisch seien, kann schwerlich ernst genommen werden."

[211]The exact date of the Syro-Ephraimitic War is difficult to determine. Joachim Begrich, "Der syrisch-ephraimitische Krieg und seine weltpolitischen Zusammenhänge," ZDMG, 83 (1929), 213-37, has proposed a date for the Syro-Ephraimitic War from June/July 734 to the fall of Damascus in 732 B.C. But Albrecht Alt, "Tiglatpilesers III. erster Feldzug nach Palästina," in Kleine Schriften des Volkes Israel (München, 1953), II, 150-62, was able to re-evaluate the complicated history of this period with the aid of newly discovered evidence from Nimrud referring to Tiglath-Pileser III's campaign to Palestine between 734-32 B.C. Donner, op. cit., pp. 59-63, has recently reassessed the problem of the Syro-Ephraimitic War dating it from the spring/summer 734 to the spring/summer 733 B.C. On the other hand, Gottwald, All the Kingdoms of the Earth, pp. 149-53, 202, dates the Syro-Ephraimitic crisis from 735-32 B.C. Gottwald believes in a supposed pro-Assyrian party in Judah under the leadership of Ahaz. According to the Eponym Chronicle, Tiglath-Pileser III was engaged in an expedition to Palestine in 734 which was

state. Under King Uzziah (Azariah) Judah had a prominent part in the anti-Assyrian coalition which had been formed among the western nations to protect themselves against Assyrian expansionism. Tiglath-Pileser III (745-727 B.C.) was at that time the outstanding conqueror on the throne in Nimrud. He applied the age-old method of large-scale deportations of vanquished peoples[212] and extended his influence into Syria and Palestine in repeated campaigns.[213] His first encounter with a league of Syrian and Palestinian states, which was headed by Uzziah (Azariah), evidently took place in 742.[214] The rulers who subsequently paid tribute to Assyria include the kings of Byblos, Tyre, Damascus (Rezin), Samaria

---

directed against Philistia. It seems altogether probable that this campaign must have had some connection with an anti-Assyrian coalition by the states of the west. It appears that after this campaign which did not touch heavily upon Israel--Tiglath-Pileser III crossed Israelite territory only in the Sharon--Pekah, King of Israel, and Rezin, King of Damascus, pressed heavily against Ahaz of Judah, which lead the latter to call on Assyria for help (2 Ki. 16:7, 8). Tiglath-Pileser's action in his campaign of 733 against Israel--his conquest of Galilee, Gilead, and the coastal region, which were reorganized into Assyrian provinces,--may have been in response to Ahaz' call for aid. According to this reconstruction the Syro-Ephraimitic War may be dated from 734-733 B.C. For the historical evidence and slightly differing reconstructions see Thiele, Mysterious Numbers, pp. 130-1; Aharoni, The Land of the Bible: A Historical Geography, pp. 327-33; V. Pavlovsky und E. Vogt, "Die Jahre der Könige von Juda und Israel," Biblica, 45 (1964), 341: "In den ersten Monaten des Jahres 733 griffen sie Ahaz mit Heeresmacht an." See Appendix II, p. 476.

[212]ANET^3, p. 282.

[213]See Pavlovsky-Vogt, op. cit., pp. 348-54; Aharoni, The Land of the Bible, pp. 327-30.

[214]ANET^3, pp. 282f.; with Thiele, Mysterious Numbers, pp. 125ff., against H. Tadmor, "Azriyau of Yaudi," Scripta Hierosolymitana, 8 (1961), 232-71, who suggests the date of 738 B.C. for this campaign. To arrive at this date Tadmor is forced to interpret the sequence of entries on the "Display Inscription" geographically rather than chronologically. This is completely unwarranted.

(Menahem), and even the queen of Arabia.[215] Soon afterwards the political order in Palestine changed completely. Uzziah (Azariah) died in 740/39.[216] In the same year Pekah, son of Remaliah, murdered Pekahiah, son of Menahem, King of Israel. Pekah apparently rose to power on the wave of bitterness caused by the complete submission to Assyria,[217] and with his rise a new coalition against Assyria was formed, headed by Pekah and by Rezin of Damascus (Aram). In 735 Ahaz deposed Jotham thereby becoming sole ruler of Jerusalem (Judah). Ahaz refused to join the new anti-Assyrian coalition. As a result Pekah and Rezin declared war on Judah and ascended against Jerusalem.[218] The purpose of the Syro-Ephraimitic advance against Jerusalem was to replace Ahaz with "the son of Tabe-el" (7:6)[219] in order to bring the Judean state to join the anti-

---

[215]ANET[3], p. 282.

[216]Supra, n. 15.

[217]Aharoni, The Land of the Bible, p. 327.

[218]Leslie, op. cit., p. 47, states that vs. 1 is Isaiah's own brief summary of the Syro-Ephraimitic attack upon Judah and its outcome. Kilian, op. cit., p. 15, see here the hand of a redactor at work.

[219]Albrecht Alt, "Menschen ohne Namen," Kleine Schriften (München, 1959), III, 213, suggests that this individual was "ein Mann von nichtköniglicher Herkunft, aber in gehobener Stellung, sei es in einem der Nachbarreiche oder wahrscheinlicher am Hofe von Jerusalem selbst." Kaiser, op. cit., pp. 73-4, follows Alt. A different identification has been suggested by W. F. Albright, "The Son of Tabeel," BASOR, 140 (1955), 34-5, connecting the name Tabe-el with an almost contemporary Assyrian cuneiform text which mentions an Aramaean land called Bêt Tâb'ēl (cf. E. Vogt, "'Filius Tāb'ēl' (Is. vii, 6)," Biblica, 37 [1956], 263f.; F. L. Moriarty, "The Immanuel Prophecies," CBQ, 19 [1957], 228; H. Junker, "Ursprung und Grundzüge des Messiasbildes bei Isajas," SVT, 4 [1957], 182 n.2). However, M. Noth has pointed out that the reading of ṭāb-'el in the Akkadian text is not quite assured, see Wolff, Frieden ohne Ende. Eine Auslegung von Jes. 7,1-7 und 9,1-6, p. 15. The supposition that Ben Tabeel may have been a son of Uzziah or Jotham by an Aramaean prin-

Assyrian league. This threat to the existence of the Davidic dynasty and Judah was the reason that Ahaz's "heart and the heart of his people shook as the trees of the forest shake before the wind" (7:2). As Jerusalem is under siege[220] Yahweh instructed Isaiah,

> Go forth to meet Ahaz,
> you and Shear-jashub your son,
> at the end of the conduit
> of the upper pool
> on the highway to the Fuller's Field.[221]

This word of Yahweh commands Isaiah to go and confront King Ahaz in Jerusalem at an appointed place. Isaiah is told to take his son šᵉʾār yāšûb with him to this historic meeting. The symbolic name of Isaiah's oldest son is most appropriately translated "A-Remnant-Shall-Return."[222] The intended meaning of this name at the time of the birth of this boy, which must have been at least two years prior to the present events, is unknown, because one can only speculate about the circumstances in which the name Shear-jashub was given. It indicates, however, that Isaiah's

---

cess (so Albright, Moriarty, Bright, A History of Israel, p. 256 n. 11) is pure conjecture and has found little acceptance. (see Donner, op. cit., p. 12 n. 2; Gottwald, All the Kingdoms of the Earth, p. 122 n. 41; Scharbert, op. cit., p. 228; Eichrodt, Der Heilige in Israel, p. 81; Rehm, op. cit., p. 34). Fohrer, Jesaja, I, 108 is undecided between three different suggestions, i.e., Alt's, Albright's, and the view that Tabeel is an official in the court of Damascus.

[220]Isa. 7:1, 2. Cf. Heschel, The Prophets, p. 64. There is no reason to suppose as Gottwald, All the Kingdoms of the Earth, p. 155, does that Isaiah's meeting with Ahaz preceded the siege.

[221]Isa. 7:3b. The present writer follows the translation of the RSV, but adopts the strophic arrangement of Fohrer, Jesaja, I, 104.

[222]For the large number of suggestions for translating this name and the validity of their linguistic and syntactical argumentations, see Gerhard F. Hasel, "Linguistic Considerations Regarding the Translation of Isaiah's 'Shear-jashub'," AUSS, IX (1971), 36-46.

proclamation contained the remnant motif already some years prior to the present events.

The crucial question, however, at the time of this historic meeting is, what has the name of the boy to say to Ahaz in this particular situation? Isaiah's mission at this very moment was to quell the fear of Ahaz and his people and to make him and Judah rely on Yahweh and Yahweh alone (7:4-9).[223] Below it will be seen that Isaiah most creatively

---

[223]There is still no agreement among scholars with regard to the Gattung of 7:1-9. In a study published first in 1951 von Rad, Der Heilige Krieg im alten Israel, pp. 56ff., maintained that Isaiah actualized and adapted an old "Kriegsansprache" from the setting in the Holy War. It has two parts, an "exhortation" in vss. 4-6 and a "promise" in vss. 7-9. This suggestion has been adopted by E. Würthwein, "Jesaja 7, 1-9. Ein Beitrag zum Thema 'Prophetie und Politik'," Theologie als Glaubenswagnis. Festschrift für K. Heim, ed. by H. Faber (Hamburg, 1954), pp. 51-2; M. Saebø, "Formgeschichtliche Erwägungen zu Jes. 7,3-9," Studia Theologica, XIV (1960), 57-8; Wolff, Frieden, p. 18; and Kilian, op. cit., p. 18. Ward, Amos & Isaiah: Prophets of the Word of God, p. 190, states that 7:1-9 is a "battle oracle," but denies that Isaiah revived with it the old tradition of the Holy War. L. G. Rignell, "Das Immanuelszeichen. Einige Gesichtspunkte zu Jes. 7," StTh, XI (1957), 104 designated vss. 7-9 as a "Gerichtsorakel." He is followed by J. H. Hayes, "The Usage of Oracles Against Foreign Nations in Ancient Israel," JBL, 87 (1968), 83, who uses the term "judgment speech" for the section in 7:5-7. J. J. Stamm, "Die Immanuel-Weissagung und die Eschatologie des Jesaja," ThZ, 16 (1960), 439, considers 7:2-9 as a prophetic "Mahnrede." A similar position is taken by Fohrer, Jesaja, I, 105, who takes it to be a "begründete Mahnrede." H. Wildberger, "'Glauben' im Alten Testament," ZThK, 65 (1968), 133, proposed that 7:3-9 is a "Heilsorakel" and not direcetly a "Kriegsorakel." Isaiah decisively modifies the ancient oracle of salvation by adding the conditional aspect of vs. 9b: "If you will not believe, surely you shall not be established." He states, "Damit ist die alte Form des Heilsorakels in der Tat entscheidend variiert: Die Heilsprophetie ist gezügelt, aber die Gültigkeit der göttlichen Zusage an sich ist nicht in Frage gestellt; die Unheilsprophetie ist in Schranken gewiesen, ohne dass die Berechtigung ihres Anliegens überfahren wäre. Heil und Glaube gehören zuhauf [zusammen]" (p. 133). Koch, The Growth of the Biblical Tradition: The Form-Critical Method, p. 213, supports Wildberger by citing evidence which shows that 7:3ff. follows the structure of the prophecy of salvation. Note also Wildberger's exposition in Jesaja, pp. 268-72.

links the remnant motif with faith. But before this relationship can be delineated we must analyze very carefully the significance of the presence of Isaiah's son with the symbolic name šeʾār yāšûb. The question is not so much whether this name is the "key term"[224] in Isa. 7 or whether it "contains the programme of the entire Isaianic proclamation,"[225] but rather what has come to expression by this name at this particular time in the life and history of Ahaz and Judah? Does the name šeʾār yāšûb expresses only a threat[226] or only hope?[227] Does it express both threat and hope,[228] or is it to serve in contrast only as a

---

[224]So Rignell, StTh, XI (1957), 100.

[225]So Kaiser, Jesaja, p. 71.

[226]So von Orelli, op. cit., p. 35; Robert H. Kennett, The Composition of the Book of Isaiah in the Light of History and Archaeology (London, 1910), pp. 10-1; Bentzen, Jesaja I, p. 56; Sheldon H. Blank, "The Current Misinterpretation of Isaiah's Sheʾar Yashub," JBL, 67 (1948), 211-5; idem, Prophetic Faith, p. 32; E. W. Heaton, "The Root שאר and the Doctrine of the Remnant," JTS, III (1952), 36; idem, The Old Testament Prophets, Penguin Books (Baltimore, 1961), p. 144; idem, The Hebrew Kingdoms, p. 332; Wright, Isaiah, p. 37; Becker, Isaias, p. 46 n. 22; Kilian, op. cit., pp. 16-7; J. Nelis, "Rest Israels," Bibel-Lexikon, ed. by H. Haag (2nd ed.; Einsiedeln, 1968), col. 1473. A slightly different view is propounded by Ward, op. cit., p. 269, who sees in this name only a "prediction of conquest."

[227]König, Jesaja, p. 101; H. Lindsjo, "A Study of the Hebrew Root שוב and Its Religious Concepts" (unpublished Ph.D. disseration, University of Chicago, 1939), p. 44; Young, op. cit., p. 271; F. Rienecker, "Rest," Lexikon zur Bibel (5th ed.; Wuppertal, 1964), col. 1139: "personifizierte Verheissung." Meinhold, Religionsgeschichte, pp. 108ff., argues that with the name of Isaiah's oldest son the remnant motif in Isaiah began to take shape. See Appendix II, p. 476.

[228]So Gray, Isaiah, I, 116; Duhm, Jesaja, p. 71; Mowinckel, Psalmenstudien II, pp. 279-80; H. Schmidt, Die grossen Propheten, p. 81; G. Hölscher, Die Ursprünge der jüdischen Eschatologie (Giessen, 1925), p. 4; Skinner, Isaiah, p. 54; Procksch, Jesaja, p. 113; Hertzberg, op. cit., p. 38; W. E. Müller, op. cit., p. 56; J. A. Bewer, The Book of Isaiah, Ch. 1-39 (New York, 1950), p. 28; Herntrich, Jesaja, p. 117;

warning[229] or as an exhortation[230] for king and people? This multiplicity of possibilities indicates the difficulty of arriving at a fairly certain interpretation of the name. Yet the present writer believes that an adequate and proper interpretation of this name can be achieved by an analysis of the two elements which make up the short sentence of the name, its relation to the Isaianic remnant motif, and its particular *Sitz im Leben*. A linguistic analysis shows that it is a verbal sentence name[231] with the subject *šeʾār* in an emphatic position.[232] Our investigation above has shown that forms of the root *šʾr* are used in connection with threats from the natural, social, political, and religious spheres

---

J. Fichtner, "Jahves Plan in der Botschaft des Jesajas," *ZAW*, 63 (1951), 32; Rignell, *StTh*, XI (1957), 113; Warne, *op. cit*., p. 85; Th. C. Vriezen, *An Outline of Old Testament Theology* (Newton, Mass., 1958), p. 360; N. W. Porteous, "Jesajabuch," *Die Religion in Geschichte und Gegenwart*, ed. by K. Galling (3rd ed.; Tübingen, 1959), III, 602-3; Buber, *op. cit*., p. 134; Eichrodt, *Der Heilige in Israel*, p. 83; Vawter, *The Conscience of Israel*, p. 206; Wolff, *Frieden*, p. 17; Fey, *op. cit*., pp. 115 n. 1, 140; Donner, *op. cit*., p. 11; Harrelson, *Interpreting the Old Testament*, p. 236; Herrmann, *Heilserwartungen*, p. 129; R. E. Clements, *The Conscience of the Nation: A Study of Early Israelite Prophecy* (London, 1967), p. 68; Stegemann, *op. cit*., pp. 173ff.

[229]There are some exegetes who interpret this name as a solemn warning to Ahaz, see Kissane, *Isaiah*, I, 77; Leslie, *op. cit*., p. 48; Kraeling, *Commentary on the Prophets*, II, 64; Rehm, *op. cit*., p. 36.

[230]Among interpreters who argue for this emphasis only Fohrer, *Jesaja*, I, 106-7, denies any aspect of promise and/or threat in addition to exhortation. The following scholars opt for exhortation as additional aspects, Schilling, *op. cit*., p. 64; Rignell, *StTh*, XI (1957), 100; Scott, *Isaiah*, V, 215; J. Lindblom, *A Study of the Immanuel Section in Isaiah*, p. 10 n. 3; Preuss, *Jahweglaube*, p. 191 n. 172.

[231]See the detailed discussion in Hasel, *AUSS*, IX (1971), 36-46.

[232]This is not at all an anomaly in Hebrew verbal sentences, see C. Brockelmann, *Grundriss der vergleichenden Grammatik der semitischen Sprachen* (Hildesheim, 1961), II, 170ff.; K. Schlesinger, "Zur Wortfolge im hebräischen Verbalsatz," *VT*, 3 (1953), 381-90.

that endanger the existence of historical entities.[233] This means that forms of the root _š'r_ cannot be uniquely linked to a single threat. It has also become apparent that the noun _š^e'ār_--as well as other verbal and nominal forms of _š'r_--is used to express negative _and_ positive aspects of the remnant motif.[234] This noun carries within itself a dual polarity. This in turn indicates that whenever _š^e'ār_ is used it is likely that this polarity will come to expression.[235] As a result the emphatic position of _š^e'ār_ in this name cannot be taken as an absolute indicator that it must be a threat[236] or conversely that it must be a promise.[237] In an attempt to gain a correct understanding of the symbolic name of Isaiah's son one must heed the warning of J. Lindblom who says that "the term 'remnant' [in this name] must not be taken in isolation, but should be seen in connection with the totality of Isaiah's message."[238] It is,

---

233 It was shown that the evidence from the ancient Near Eastern sources and from the Hebrew Bible does not support the notion propounded by W. E. Müller, _op. cit._, pp. 5-21, which has been accepted without attempts at confirmation by von Rad, _OTT_, II, 21-2; Wildberger, _Jesaja_, pp. 155-6; Wolff, _Frieden_, p. 17; Ruppert, _Die Josephserzählung der Genesis_, p. 122; Stegemann, _op. cit._, p. 163. Müller has argued that the remnant idea has its origin in Assyrian military practice. For a presentation of the evidence from ancient Near Eastern materials, see Chapter II; for the evidence of Hebrew remnant terminology, see pp. 386-388, and for the chronological investigation of the Hebrew remnant motif up to Isaiah, see Chapter III. Yoshiaki Hattori, "The Prophet Ezekiel and His Idea of the Remnant" (unpublished Th.D. dissertation, Westminster Theological Seminary, 1968) has presented a penetrating study of the remnant motif in Ezekiel. Hattori, however, has not dealt with the ancient Near Eastern background nor with the Hebrew remnant motif prior to this post-exilic prophet.

234 _Supra_, pp. 386-7.

235 So also Stegemann, _op. cit._, pp. 174-5.

236 _Supra_, n. 226.

237 _Supra_, n. 227.

238 Lindblom, _Immanuel_, p. 9.

therefore, natural to relate the term šeʾār to the remnant motif of Isaiah as it has come to expression prior to the events of 734–733. The dual aspects of judgment and salvation are constitutive components of Isaiah's remnant motif[239] as expressed in his inaugural vision (6:13),[240] in the saying with the picture of the refiner's fire (1:21-26), and the poem of the holy remnant in Zion (4:1-3). The same juxtaposition of doom and hope is explicitly expressed in pericopes from later periods (10:20ff.; 17:10-16; 28:5-6; etc.). This cumulative evidence leads to the inevitable conclusion that the element šeʾār[241] in the name of Isaiah's son contains the two aspects of doom and hope, i.e., that it is both a threat and a promise at one and the same time. Now the question still remains, what does this term mean for Ahaz and Judah at this critical juncture? Who will be the part that will experience destruction? Who will be the residual part that will be saved? It is virtually impossible

---

[239]Against Lindblom, Immanuel, p. 8, who believes that "in Isaiah the idea of the remnant is a promise, not a threat."

[240]Ward, Amos & Isaiah: Prophets of the Word of God, pp. 158ff., has argued very convincingly on the basis of stylistics that there is a correlation between the first and the second half of Isa. 6 and that the positive aspect of the remnant motif in 6:13c is not alien to the whole tenor of the inaugural vision. The key to the relation between Isaiah's own lostness and salvation and the people's destruction and a renewal in holiness is the motif of purging. Stylistically vss. 9-10 reaches its climax in "and be healed." The second part of Isaiah's commissioning, vss. 11-13, reaches its climax in "a holy seed is its stump." Ward states, "Stylistically the two parts, each of which is in the form of a speech of God, are identical. Each is set in poetic parallelism except for the final clause of each, which stands out as the stressed line" (p. 160).

[241]Aside from its appearance in the name in 7:3 שְׁאָר appears twelve times (Isa. 10:19, 20, 21, 22; 11:11, 16; 14:22; 16:14; 17:3; 21:17; 28:5) in the book of Isaiah. It occurs another fourteen times in other parts of the Hebrew Bible.

to consider the whole of Israel, i.e., North Israel and South Israel, as the remnant, because this stands in direct contradiction to Isaiah's message of the remnant.[242] It is also incongruous with the motif of the remnant as used by other pre-exilic prophets, who envision the remnant invariably as a part of the whole. There can be no doubt but that the term *šeʾār* stands here too for a remnant as a part of the whole. Thus it will be only a remnant--but still a remnant. This dual emphasis is underlined by the emphatic position of *šeʾār*, which can perhaps be best related in translation by underlining the subject "A-*Remnant*-Shall-Return." G. Fohrer[243] has recently supported the old suggestion[244] that the symbolic name proclaims the possibility that Judah will be the remnant of the whole Israel. But the interpretation of *šeʾār* as a political entity runs aground. W. E. Müller, the foremost representative of the political interpretation of the remnant motif, forcefully rejected this suggestion.

> This understanding would come close to the questionable popular understanding of the remnant and were inexplicable in view of the indicated seriousness of the Isaianic proclamation of judgment.[245]

It is incongruous to hold that Isaiah proclaims that Judah will enter into judgment[246] and at the same time that Judah is the remnant.

At this point we must bring the second element of the name *šeʾār*

---

[242]The present writer is not aware that this view has any serious supporter.

[243]G. Fohrer, *Die symbolischen Handlungen der Propheten* (2nd ed.; Zürich, 1968), pp. 29-30.

[244]Meinhold, *Religionsgeschichte*, p. 110.

[245]W. E. Müller, *op. cit.*, p. 56.

[246]Isa. 6:9-10, 12-13; 1:21-26; 17:5-6; 5:29; 8:5-8; 10:16-19; 3:25-4:1; etc.

yāšûb into the discussion not only because, as the predicate, it qualifies the subject but also because it explicates its meaning. But also with regard to the predicate *yāšûb* scholarly opinion is divided. Some scholars argue that *yāšûb* has a secular meaning referring to those who return home from battle.[247] The majority of scholars, however, support the "religious signification"[248] of *yāšûb*,[249] i.e., a return to God. Symbolic names of children of eighth century prophets are used with religious meanings. This is the case with the names of the children of Hosea.[250] A religious return is the invariable meaning of extra-Biblical

---

[247]So Blank, *JBL*, 67 (1948), 215. More recently Wolff, *Frieden*, pp. 17-18, takes a mediating position by suggesting that the second element in this name means both "return from battle" and "return to Yahweh." Kilian, *op. cit.*, pp. 16, 51ff., takes up Wolff's suggestion that the second element means return from battle. He argues that it does not mean also return to Yahweh, because he thinks that such a positive notion is alien to Isaiah's remnant motif. Rowley, *The Biblical Doctrine of Election*, p. 74, thinks that it means possibly "a return to their homes by survivors who had scattered in terror to hide." There is, however, no evidence in support of these positions.

[248]The term is Lindblom's, *Immanuel*, p. 10.

[249]For the literature of the Jewish and Christian tradition up to the critical period of scholarship and the literature of critical scholarship up to 1940, see Garofalo, *La nozione profetica del 'Resto d'Israele'*, p. 80 n. 103. In addition the following may be mentioned: H. Schmidt, *Die grossen Propheten*, pp. 57, 81; de Vaux, *RB*, 42 (1933), 30f.; E. K. Dietrich, *Die Umkehr im Alten Testament und im Judentum* (Stuttgart, 1936), pp. 71-2; Hertzberg, *op. cit.*, p. 38; W. E. Müller, *op. cit.*, pp. 56ff.; Schilling, *op. cit.*, p. 65; Hyatt, *Prophetic Religions*, p. 103; Slotki, *op. cit.*, p. 83; Bewer, *Isaiah*, p. 28; Herntrich, *Jesaja*, p. 117; Fichtner, *op. cit.*, 29; Procksch, *Theologie des Alten Testaments*, p. 659; H. W. Wolff, "Das Thema 'Umkehr' in der alttestamentlichen Prophetie," *ZThK*, 48 (1951), 145-6; Balla, *Die Botschaft der Propheten*, p. 130; Warne, *op. cit.*, pp. 84ff.; Eichrodt, *Der Heilige in Israel*, p. 83; Kissane, *Isaiah*, I, 77; Jenni, "Remnant," *IDB*, IV, 33; Herrmann, *Heilserwartungen*, p. 129; Stegemann, *op. cit.*, p. 175; etc.

[250]Hos. 1:2-9; cf. Fohrer, *Die symbolischen Handlungen der Propheten*, pp. 25-7.

personal names from Mari and Ugarit which have as one of their elements a form of the root twb.[251] Isaiah speaks clearly of a religious signification when he refers to himself and his children: "I and the children whom the Lord has given me are signs and portents in Israel from the Lord of hosts who dwells on Mount Zion" (8:18). In this connection U. Stegemann points out,

> A 'sign' however means a guarantee for the presence of Yahweh; it is an expression of His might and greatness, interpretation and strengthening of His word, and support of His threats as well as promises.[252]

Furthermore, we must not forget that the whole import of the encounter between Isaiah and Ahaz is a confrontation between religion and politics. In 7:2-9 the political sphere appears to become transposed into the religious sphere. Isaiah's message in this critical situation was to release Ahaz and Judah from the fear of the enemies who threaten the existence of the Davidic dynasty. Isaiah admonishes with the word of Yahweh ʾal-tîrah: those who threaten your existence and life are only "smoldering stumps of firebrands" (7:4). The prophet makes clear that one of the possible courses of action which Ahaz could follow, namely to yield to the military pressure and join the Aramaean-Israelite alliance against Assyria, is a futile option. Another course of action was still open for the king. He could yield to his political counselors and seek the protection of Assyria by joining into a covenant relationship with that mighty power. But Isaiah called upon Ahaz to abandon any trust in such a political alliance. Ahaz is called upon to follow a third course of

---

[251] Cf. Hasel, AUSS, IX (1971), 36-46. See Appendix, p. 472.

[252] Stegemann, op. cit., p. 175.

action, namely to rely exclusively and absolutely upon Yahweh.[253] "If you will not believe, surely you shall not be established" (7:9b). This demand of faith in Yahweh is not utopian;[254] it is putting covenant relation over against covenant relation. Ahaz is called upon to choose the covenant relation which is based upon the religious principle of faith, "that is steadiness, through confidence in God's presence and power,"[255] instead of a covenant relation[256] which is based upon the political principle of military might. Faith in this context is not faith in the prophetic word nor even in the first instance faith in God, but an attitude of trust, confidence, and steadiness based upon one's knowledge of God and his promises.[257] The attitude of faith creates the con-

---

[253] Buber, Prophetic Faith, p. 135, coined the term "theopolitics" in connection with Isaiah's call to use faith in God in place of human covenants.

[254] Rolf Rendtorff, Men of the Old Testament (Philadelphia, 1968), p. 91: "Isaiah called on the king to remember those fundamentals on which Israel had in past times built up its life. His political counsels have been described as utopian. But that kind of argument ignores that fact that in ancient time the direct historical puissance of the gods was thought to be a reality not inferior, but actually superior, to that of weapons. Isaiah, therefore, was not telling the king to choose between political realism and religious enthusiasm; on the contrary, he was asking him which reality he thought had the more weight--the power of Israel's God, or the troops of his . . . allies."

[255] Leslie, op. cit., p. 48.

[256] Würthwein, "Jesaja 7," pp. 56ff., argues that for Isaiah the issue is Yahweh's covenant or the pact with Assyria which involved the recognition of foreign gods. Cf. Donner, op. cit., pp. 13ff.; William McKane, Prophets and Wise Men (SBT, 44; London, 1965), pp. 133-5.

[257] H. Wildberger, "'Glauben', Erwägungen zu האמין," Hebräische Wortforschung. Festschrift zum 80. Geburtstag von W. Baumgartner (SVT, XVI; Leiden, 1967), pp. 377-8; idem, "'Glauben' im Alten Testament," ZThK, 65 (1968), 133.

dition on which alone Yahweh can intervene as a helping power in the distress of king and people.[258] The <u>ta'amînû</u> in vs. 9b corresponds to the word of salvation in vs. 4 <u>'al-tîrāh</u> which is already defined by <u>hiššāmēr</u>, <u>hašqeṭ</u>, and <u>lebābkā 'al-yērak</u>.[259] Isaiah does not promise unconditional salvation. King and people must take their stand on Yahweh or their existence will not be guaranteed. The name <u>še'ār yāšûb</u> is in this connection an exhortation to king and people for an unconditional return to Yahweh in faith. There are overtones of the Nathan oracle present here,[260] but the promise of the continuity of the election of the Davidic dynasty as well as of Judah is made conditional on faith. The salvation of the remnant will depend on the decision to return to Yahweh in faith.[261] In other words faith is the <u>criterium distinctionis</u> between the surviving

---

[258]Lindblom, <u>Prophecy in Ancient Israel</u>, p. 342; Procksch, <u>Theologie des Alten Testaments</u>, p. 181: "Faith is no jump into nothingness, but into God's bosom."

[259]See on this especially H. P. Müller, "Imperative und Verheissung im Alten Testament: Drei Beispiele," <u>EvTh</u>, 28 (1968), 564-7.

[260]There are scholars who forcefully argue that Yahweh's promise of the continuance of the Davidic dynasty is particularly in view here, see Würthwein, "Jesaja 7," pp. 58ff.; Wilhelm Visher, <u>Die Immanuelbotschaft im Rahmen des königlichen Zionsfestes</u> (Theologische Studien, 45; Zollikon-Zürich, 1955), pp. 16ff.; H. Junker, "Ursprung und Grundzüge des Messiasbildes bei Isaias," <u>SVT</u>, IV (1957), 181ff.; O. Loretz, "Der Glaube des Propheten Isaias an das Gottesreich," <u>Zeitschrift für katholische Theologie</u> 82 (1960), 40-73, 159-81; Wildberger, <u>ZThK</u>, 65 (1968), 133ff.; John J. Scullion, "An Approach to the Understanding of Isaiah 7:10-17," <u>JBL</u>, 87 (1968), 288ff.

[261]Eichrodt, <u>Theology of the Old Testament</u>, II, 434, says that "the reality of the remnant depends entirely on faith. . . ." O. Michel, "Glaube: πίστις," <u>Theologisches Begriffslexikon zum Neuen Testament</u>, ed. by L. Coenen <u>et al</u>. (Wuppertal, 1967), 567, states the following: "The continuation of the people rests solely in the certain trust in the Eternal One."

remnant and the perishing masses. Isaiah realized that only a remnant would muster faith in Yahweh[262] and thus secure salvation. Yet by taking his son "A-Remnant-Shall-Return" with him to the fateful encounter with king and people he exemplified his belief that a "remnant" of Judah would return to Yahweh in faith.[263] He exhorted and encouraged his lis-

---

[262]The passage in Isa. 28:16 corresponds to 7:9b: "He who believes [הַמַּאֲמִין] will not be in haste." Another parallel is in Isa. 30:15: "In quietness and trust shall be your strength." R. Smend, "Zur Geschichte von האמין," Hebräische Wortforschung. Festschrift zum 80. Geburtstag von W. Baumgartner (SVT, XVI; Leiden, 1967), 284, concludes that in 7:9 and 28:16 the meaning is "faith in God."

[263]Von Rad, Der Heilige Krieg im alten Israel, pp. 7ff., maintains that the old tradition of the Holy War (or better war of Yahweh) was renewed by Isaiah during the Syro-Ephraimitic crisis. Indeed, Isaiah envisioned the universal work of Yahweh in history along the lines of the tradition of the Holy War. In the words of von Rad, "Isaiah actualized in the difficulty of the Syro-Ephraimite war . . . the old ways of holy war" (p. 57). But von Rad himself qualifies that "Isaiah did not really renew the idea of olden times, because it did not know yet . . . the contrast between divine and human actions" (p. 58) which is present in Isaiah. Von Rad maintains that the exhortation "do not fear" and the concept of faith derive both from the Holy War tradition. G. Fohrer, "Zehn Jahre Literatur zur alttestamentlichen Prophetie (1951-1960)," ThR, 28 (1962) 333, has raised the searching question whether one can really speak of an actualization in view of such basic differences. "Is not something present in Isaiah which has nothing to do any longer with the idea of holy war?" One may add that there is no evidence in the Old Testament which points in the direction that a Holy War was fought against part of Yahweh's own people as is the case here, namely the Northern Kingdom. H. M. Dion, "The Patriarchal Traditions and the Literary Form of the 'Oracle of Salvation'," CBQ, 29 (1967), 198-206, arrives at the conclusion that the formula אַל־תִּירָא "does not really pertain to the most ancient traditions of the holy war" (203) but is a later accretion. For a criticism of von Rad's failure to deal with the origins of Holy War in Israel--and in turn with its mythological elements in earliest Israel--and as practiced by pre-Yahwistic or non-Israelite peoples, see F. M. Cross, Jr. "The Divine Warrior in Israel's Early Cult," Biblical Motifs: Origins and Transformations, ed. by A. Altmann (Studies and Texts, III; Cambridge, Mass., 1966), pp. 17ff., and Patrick D. Miller, Jr., "Holy War and Cosmic War in Early Israel" (unpublished Ph.D. dissertation, Harvard University, 1963). As regards the faith motif in Isa. 7, von Rad, OTT, II, 159, argues "that the demand for faith too has its home in the old cycles" of the Holy War tra-

teners not to fear for their existence and life but to decide in confident faith and trust for Yahweh, who through their attitude of faith would be their real strength and power and assure their continued existence and life. The reality of the existence of the remnant depends wholly on faith.[264]

---

dition. The thesis that faith is a constituent part of the Holy War tradition rests solely on conjecture. Von Rad is not able to cite a single example for his assertion that there can be no doubt "that in the old holy wars a word . . . of faith in Yahweh had an important function" (Der Heilige Krieg, p. 10). In the account of the Red Sea crossing (Ex. 14:31) and in Gideon's struggle with the Midianites (Jd. 7) faith in Yahweh was the result of God's action, which made faith possible but not part of the exhortation given before the action. In Isaiah we have something completely different: Isaiah demanded faith now in order to make existence rest on a future action of God. In view of these differences one must be most cautious with regard to Isaiah's "actualization" of Holy War traditions. Weiser, TWNT, VI, 189 n. 122, points out that von Rad's attempt to look for the Sitz im Leben of the faith motif in the Holy War tradition fails because it does not adequately account for the breadth of the Old Testament concept of faith. Similarly Fohrer, Jesaja, I, 107 n. 50, points out that the expressions "fear not" and "be quiet" as well as the faith motif, which is encountered first in Gen. 15:6, appear in such a great variety of contexts that they cannot be derived from the ideas of the Holy War. Preuss, Jahweglaube, pp. 115-6, states, "Nicht als unmöglich erscheint die Vermutung, dass Gen. 15 auch insoweit noch eine alte Tradition bewahrt hat, als der Vollzug des 'Glaubens' . . . seinen Urgrund ebenfalls in der nomadischen Existenz hat und nicht im Heiligen Krieg oder im sakralen Jahwebund. . . ." Wildberger, "'Glauben' im Alten Testament," ZThK, 65 (1968), 133f., argues that faith belongs to the "Formensprache" of the oracle of salvation but admits that in Deut. 20:4; Josh. 8:1; Deut. 1:20-1, 1:29-32; 3:22, 7:17-24; 31:6; Josh. 1:9; cf. Num. 14:9, there is no explicit reference to faith. In Gen. 15:1b-6, which Wildberger classifies as an oracle of salvation, faith is the result of God's saving word. In view of the radical distinctions and basic changes which are present in Isaiah's development of the faith motif in Chapter 7 it would seem best to refrain from linking it to and deriving it from the tradition of the Holy War. In the present writer's view the faith motif is much too complex and variegated to trace its origin to the tradition of the wars of Yahweh.

[264]According to Weiser, TWNT, VI, 189, "ist Glaube und Sein für Jesaja identisch; denn auch in dem bekannten Wort Js. 7, 9 . . . ist das 'Bestand haben' im Sinne der menschlichen Gesamtexistenz . . . nicht etwa als Lohn für den Glauben gedacht, so dass der Glaube die Vor-

We are now in a position to summarize briefly to what extent and in which way the remnant motif came to expression in the first pericope from the time of the Syro-Ephraimitic war. Our discussion has shown that the symbolic name *šeʾār yāšûb* contains the dual polarity of doom and salvation, i.e., it is both threat and promise. As such the presence of the son is an exhortation to Ahaz and Judah in their crisis hour to return to Yahweh. The continual existence of the Davidic dynasty and of Judah has been made dependent on faith. Of course, Isaiah realizes that only a remnant will decide for faith rather than political expediency, but still a remnant will turn to its God in an attitude of trust, confidence, and steadiness, creating the condition for Yahweh to intervene. Faith alone will be the *criterium distinctionis* between the surviving remnant and the perishing masses. What is new here is that Isaiah imbues the term *šeʾār* with a radically religious content. The remnant that returns to Yahweh will be a religious entity characterized by true faith in God. The child's name contains the whole content of the massage of 7:2-9. The imminence of the disaster is by no means subdued, but the aspect of promise and hope is also emphasized. The hope of the future is bound up with faith. Without faith there will be no existence and life; with faith there will be existence and life. The remnant will have its existence through the attitude of faith in Yahweh.

---

aussetzung der Existenz wäre, sondern--da das כִּי demonstrativ-explikativ zu verstehen ist--ist damit die Identität von Glauben und Bestand (=Existenz) ausgesprochen; positiv gewendet wurde der Sinn des Wortes also lauten: im Glauben selber liegt die besondere Seinsweise und der Bestand des Gottesvolkes."

The remnant motif has also been seen in the "endlessly discussed"[265] passage of the Immanuel sign.[266] A number of scholars maintain that there is, to say the least, a close relationship between the remnant motif and the Immanuel sign.[267] Though it is not possible within the scope of the present study to engage in a detailed investigation of the Immanuel prophecy of 7:10-17, we must nevertheless discuss various aspects of this pericope. This is mandatory because of the variety of positions that have been taken with regard to the supposed reference of the remnant motif in the Immanuel prophecy. The present writer follows the general communis opinio which holds that 7:10ff. is closely connected with 7:1-9[268] and that the sign of 7:10ff. is the guarantee of the truth

---

[265]So Lindblom, Immanuel, p. 15.

[266]Extensive literature on the Immanuel prophecy is cited by J. J. Stamm, "Neuere Arbeiten zum Immanuel Problem," ZAW, 68 (1956), 46-53; Kilian, Die Verheissung Immanuels, Jes 7,14; and Rehm, op. cit., pp. 30-121, 355-75. The study by Rehm contains the most comprehensive bibliography on the Immanuel problem, while Kilian's little book contains highly instructive critiques of major interpretations of the Immanuel sign.

[267]Such a relationship is pointed out with greater or lesser emphasis and variation by the following: A. E. Skemp, "'Immanuel' and the 'Suffering Servant of Yahweh', a Suggestion," Expository Times, 44 (1932), 94; F. Dreyfus, "La doctrine du reste d'Israël chez le prophète Isaïe," Revue des Sciences Philosophiques et Théologiques, 39 (1955), 371-3; H. Junker, "Ursprung und Grundzüge des Messiasbildes bei Isajas," SVT, IV (1957), 187-9; L. Rignell, "Das Immanuelszeichen. Einige Gesichtspunkte zu Jes. 7," StTh, XI (1957), 113; Warne, op. cit., p. 88; Buber, Prophetic Faith, pp. 140-1; Vawter, The Conscience of Israel, p. 205; Wolff, Frieden, pp. 43ff.; A. H. J. Gunneweg, "Heils- und Unheilsverkündigung in Jes. VII," VT, XV (1965), 32; H. Kruse, "Alma Redemptoris Mater. Eine Auslegung der Immanuel-Weissagung Is 7,14," Trierer Theologische Zeitschrift, 74 (1965), 15ff.; von Rad, OTT, II, 165; Preuss, Jahweglaube, p. 183; Rehm, op. cit., p. 121; Stegemann, op. cit., pp. 184-5.

[268]Procksch, Jesaja I, p. 119, thinks that this second unit has a new situation, namely the scenery has shifted to "the house of David," i.e., the royal palace. This view is adopted by Lindblom, Immanuel, p. 15, but rejected by Wolff, Frieden, p. 26, who points out that the

of the former unit.[269] It is quite likely that each saying in 7:1–8:16 follows "in strict chronological order."[270]

Our investigation has shown that the boy "A-Remnant-Shall-Return" was to hold up before Ahaz the exhortation to make the decision of faith. This name implicitly expressed the result of a decision against faith. On the whole the presence of the boy Shear-jashub was to aid the king to reach the right decision,[271] i.e., to abandon his plans to call upon Tiglath-Pileser for aid and thereby to join into a pact with Assyria. If one keeps in view the weight of the decision which Ahaz was called to make as the leader of his people and if one tries to do justice to the political dilemma in which the king found himself in this perilous hour, one may indeed understand why he hesitated. At the same time it becomesplausible why a "sign"[272] is offered to Ahaz. The purpose of the sign in 7:10 was to authenticate the previous word of Yahweh (7:4-9) not in the sense that a miracle would be wrought by Yahweh but to encourage Ahaz to make the decision of faith. Ahaz is not asked to believe merely on the basis of the prophetic word. Yahweh is actually offering a confirmation of his counsel and proof for the truth of Isaiah's word. But Ahaz does not yield. His pious refusal to ask for a sign (7:12) indicates

---

address of the court (7:13) is anticipated by 7:2 and expressed in the plural of 7:9b. Cf. Kilian, op. cit., p. 32; Rehm, op. cit., p. 36; Kaiser, Jesaja, p. 76 n. 3.

[269]Cf. Kissane, Isaiah, I, 80-1.

[270]Fohrer, Introduction, p. 367.

[271]Kilian, op. cit., p. 98.

[272]For recent discussions on the word אות, see K. H. Rengstorf, "σημεῖον," TWNT, VII, 211; Lindblom, Immanuel, pp. 16ff.; Rehm, op. cit., pp. 115-20.

that he has made his decision not to bind himself to Yahweh in faith when he was confronted with the second word of Yahweh. It also shows that he had come to recognize that the former word of Yahweh is reliable.[273] A new word of Yahweh on the lips of Isaiah reproaches Ahaz for his obstinacy which not only wearies men but also God (7:13). In this connection the subtle shift of personal pronouns is significant. In 7:11 Isaiah demanded that Ahaz ask for a sign of "your God," but now the prophet says that Ahaz wearies "my God!" This remarkable distinction indicates that the God of Isaiah is no longer the God of Ahaz or, in other words, that Ahaz had made his decision to call upon Assyria for aid rather than to trust confidently in Yahweh.[274] Therefore (lāḵēn)[275] Yahweh himself will give a sign (7:14). This is the so-called Immanuel

---

[273]With Kilian, op. cit., p. 98, against Kaiser, Jesaja, p. 78.

[274]Wolff, Frieden, p. 30: "Eine Entscheidung ist gefallen. Der Gott Jesajas ist nicht mehr der Gott des Achas." Kaiser, Jesaja, p. 79: "Der Prophet weiss, dass die Entscheidung bereits gefallen ist. Der König und seine Begleiter haben sich . . . im Überhören des konkreten Anrufs von Jahwe getrennt."

[275]There can be hardly any doubt about the import of the introductory term, which brings the new sign in relationship to the previously reproached refusal of Ahaz. J. J. Stamm, "Die Immannuel-Weissagung. Ein Gespräch mit E. Hammershaimb," VT, IV (1954), 31, has pointed out that in Isaiah לָכֵן introduces only diatribes and threats. Wolff, Frieden, p. 32, considers 7:14 according to form-critical analysis as a threat. Kilian, op. cit., p. 99, argues, "Geht man von der Gesamtsituation aus, in der das göttliche Zeichen von V. 14 angekündigt wird, und erkennt man, dass V. 9b auf Grund der Absage des Ahas in V. 12 zum Drohwort geworden ist, und nimmt man ferner die Droheinleitung von V. 14 ernst, dann dürfte zweifelsohne feststehen, dass Jesaja selbst das Zeichen von V. 14 als Drohwort versteht." However, both Wolff and Kilian believe that the formal threat of 7:14 can still contain a message of promise. Cf. Eichrodt, Der Heilige in Israel, pp. 86-93; Junker, SVT, IV (1957), 187; G. Fohrer, "Zu Jesaja 7,14 im Zusammenhang von Jesaja 7, 10-22," in Studien zur alttestamentlichen Prophetie (BZAW, 99; Berlin, 1967), pp. 168-9; Stegemann, op. cit., p. 184.

sign. It is the conception and birth of a boy who shall be called Immanu-El "God-With-Us." Since Ahaz and his counselors have turned from Yahweh in disbelief the Immanuel sign is a threat, an announcement of doom, for them and all who follow their course. The sign is not a "God-With-You" but a "God-With-Us." Despite the promises of vss. 15-16 the catastrophe of vs. 17 will break in upon Ahaz, his people, and his father's house. It will be of such a terrible nature that nothing comparable has been experienced since the division of the monarchy.[276]

But the name "God-With-Us" contains at the same time a promise of salvation, which comes to expression in the name's first element ᶜimmānû Various attempts have been made to identify the traditio-historical origin of this element. H. W. Wolff has argued that this element and therefore the whole name is rooted in the war of Yahweh tradition.[277] W. Vischer, on the other hand, has attempted to show that ᶜim is "An essential, if not the main concept of the Davidic covenant . . . ."[278] Thus the name Immanuel does not belong to the war of Yahweh tradition but

---

[276]With Eichrodt, Der Heilige in Israel, pp. 88-90; Kaiser, Jesaja, pp. 82-4; Fohrer, Jesaja, I, 114-6; Scott, Isaiah, V, 220; Kilian, op. cit., pp. 99ff., against Lindblom, Immanuel, pp. 21ff., who interprets the entire unit of 7:10-17 as a second "warranting sign" to induce Ahaz to decide for faith.

[277]Wolff, Frieden, pp. 42-3, with references to Jd. 6:12, 13, 16; Deut. 20:4; Nu. 14:43; Josh. 1:9; 7:12, 2 Sam. 5:10; Ps. 46:8, 11.

[278]Vischer, op. cit., p. 22, with references to Ps. 89:21, 22, 25; 2 Sam. 23:5. Similar to Vischer's view is that of Lindblom, Immanuel, p. 22, who sees in this name a "cultic cry of joy" much like Ps. 46:7, 11 and Amos 5:14.

to the David tradition. In a recent study H. D. Preuss[279] has shown that the motif of the "mit-Sein Gottes" ("being-with" of God) is an unattached motif[280] which cannot be limited to the war of Yahweh tradition nor to the David tradition. Originally the "being-with" of God motif was a promise of divine presence in wanderings. During the united and divided monarchy it has turned into a general formula of God's present help as a typical expression of Israelite faith and trust.[281] These considerations lead to the conclusion that the "being-with" of God motif cannot be aligned with a particular tradition. At the same time they demonstrate that the name "God-With-Us" has a strongly positive character. Thus M. Noth's old dictum that Immanuel is a name of trust has been confirmed.[282] As a result additional weight is placed upon the twofold aspect of the Immanuel sign, the name contains a hopeful aspect,[283] so that here too the dual polarity of doom and hope or judgment and salvation is present.[284]

---

[279]H. D. Preuss, ". . . ich will mit dir sein!" ZAW, 80 (1968), 154: "Der Gott, welcher sein geleitendes Mitsein verheisst, geht selber mit seinem Segen, seinem Bestand und seiner (militärischen) Hilfe. Er geleitet die Seinen, und er streitet (dabei) für sie, streitet für die zu ihm gehörende Sippe oder Gruppe . . . so dass der Zusammenhang von Jahwekrieg und nomadischer Existenz . . . nicht unwahrscheinlich ist."

[280]For the distinction between "unattached motifs" and "attached motifs," see Koch, op. cit., pp. 56-7.

[281]Preuss, ZAW, 80 (1968), 159.

[282]M. Noth, Die israelitischen Personennamen im Rahmen der gemeinsemitischen Namengebung (BWANT, 10; 2nd ed.; Hildesheim, 1966), p. 160, describes Immanuel as a "Vertrauensnamen." Cf. Rehm, op. cit., p. 64.

[283]Wolff, Frieden, p. 42, states, "Zuversichtliches Bekenntnis spricht der Name aus."

[284]Warne, op. cit., p. 88.

The identity of Immanuel is a matter of much scholarly debate. The enigmatic Immanuel has been identified with the Messiah,[285] a son of Ahaz[286] a royal son,[287] and a son of Isaiah.[288] Others adopt a collective interpretation in which Immanuel describes children of many mothers.[289] Another type of collective interpretation which is often joined with allegorical emphases, identifies Immanuel with the new Israel.[290] Of immediate interest for the study of Isaiah's remnant motif is the identification of Immanuel with the remnant. A. E. Skemp suggested that "Immanuel . . . was a personification of the righteous 'rem-

---

[285]This line of interpretation is followed by many scholars. A very detailed defense of this position has recently been provided by Rehm, op. cit., pp. 30-120. A recent critique is provided by Kilian, op. cit., pp. 59-66.

[286]Among those who identify Immanuel with Hezekiah, son of Ahaz, are Buber, Prophetic Faith, pp. 139-45; J. Steinmann, Le prophète Isaïe, sa vie, son oeuvre et son temps (Paris, 1950), p. 89f.; Lindblom, Immanuel, pp. 18-9, 24; Scharbert, Propheten Israels, pp. 234-6; E. Vogt, "Sennacherib und die letzte Tätigkeit Jesajas," Biblica, 47 (1966), 427; Mowinckel, He That Cometh, pp. 110-9; E. Hammershaimb, Some Aspects of Old Testament Prophecy from Isaiah to Malachi (København, 1966), pp. 20f. For criticisms of this view, see Wolff, Frieden, pp. 35f.; Kilian, op. cit., pp. 67-71.

[287]So among others Vischer, op. cit., pp. 47-52; Scott, Isaiah, V, 218-9. For a critique, see Rehm, op. cit., pp. 100-3.

[288]So recently N. K. Gottwald, "Immanuel as the Prophet's Son," VT, VIII (1958), 36-47; Donner, op. cit., p. 18; Rohland, op. cit., p. 170 n. 2; Becker, op. cit., p. 31. For critiques, see Kilian, op. cit., pp. 78-83; Preuss, Jahweglaube, pp. 144ff.; Rehm, op. cit., pp. 86-8.

[289]More recently this interpretation has found supporters in L. Köhler, "Zum Verständnis von Jesaja 7,14," ZAW, 67 (1955), 48-50; Kaiser, Jesaja, pp. 81ff.; Fohrer, Jesaja, I, 113ff.; W. McKane, "The Interpretation of Isaiah VII 14-15," VT, XVII (1967), 213-4; Stegemann, op. cit., p. 184. For critiques see Kilian, op. cit., pp. 84-7; Rehm, op. cit., pp. 88-9.

[290]So recently Rignell, StTh, XI (1957), 112ff., and Kruse, op. cit., pp. 23ff.

nant'. . . ."[291] H. Kruse also identifies Immanuel with the holy remnant.[292] He interprets the ^{c}almāh symbolically as representing Zion[293] and allegorizes as follows:

> The allegory was fit as nothing else to be used by the prophet in the present situation. . . . One could describe the entire answer to the king in the following way: 'the country is in the position of a pregnant one, and the coming birth pangs will be greater than they needed to be. But in spite of all of this something comforting will come from it: a small remnant bound to God; only you, O king, will have no part in it'.[294]

Kruse explicates further that the "remnant bound to God" contains germinatively also the Messiah.[295] In the present writer's opinion Kruse's allegorical interpretation is abortive. In the first place the identification of ^{c}almāh with a child-bearing Zion would represent in Isaiah's time such a strange idea[296] that one could expect at least a more explicit explanation on the part of the prophet if he had actually intended such an unusual identification.[297] Secondly, the plural "us" in the name Immanuel should not be taken as proof that a collective meaning is intended and that therefore the "us" points to a remnant, i.e., the new

---

[291]Skemp, op. cit., p. 94.

[292]Kruse, op. cit., p. 31.

[293]Ibid., p. 23.

[294]Ibid., p. 31.

[295]Ibid., p. 35.

[296]There is quite a difference between the designation "mother" for Israel in Hos. 2:4, 7; 4:5 and the term "young woman" in Isa. 7:14. The term "mother" cannot be used to prove that ^{c}almāh must be an allegorical designation for Zion/Jerusalem, see Kilian, op. cit., p. 92.

[297]Wolff, Frieden, p. 34.

Israel. This line of reasoning is contradicted by vss. 14 and 16 which remain consistently in the singular. Furthermore, the hermeneutics involved in Kruse's argumentation is highly questionable. It is one thing to interpret allegorically but it is quite different to make Isaiah use allegory in this instance. Unconvincing is also L. Rignell's interpretation of ᶜalmāh which sees it as a symbol for Israel. Israel will give birth to Immanuel, who is a symbol of the remnant, i.e., the "new Israel."[298] M. Rehm points out against Rignell that Isa. 8:8 speaks of Immanuel as a king, i.e., as a royal person and not as a collective new Israel.[299] The identification of 8:8 militates against both the allegorical and the symbolic interpretation.

The element "with us" in the name Immanuel seems to elaborate the idea of "my God" in vs. 13 in contrast to the notion of "your God" in vs. 11. The distinction between "your God" and "my God" certainly corresponds to the twofold aspect of the Immanuel sign, namely judgment for Ahaz and those who follow his decision of disbelief and salvation for those who turn to Yahweh in faith. R. Kilian expresses the polarity succintly: "judgment for Ahaz, salvation for the others."[300] Who are the others for whom the Immanuel sign is a guarantee of salvation and hope? The inevitable answer from the context of the Immanuel sign is that the others are those who return to Yahweh in faith.[301] In short, the Immanuel sign

---

[298]Rignell, StTh, XI (1957), 112-5.

[299]Rehm, op. cit., p. 110.

[300]Kilian, op. cit., p. 100.

[301]Kilian, op. cit., p. 104, who as at pains to argue that there is no positive remnant motif in Isaiah, must nevertheless admit that the Immanuel sign contains salvation for the remnant: "Nur wenn in der

is a sign of doom for those who disbelieve and a sign of salvation for those who believe.

According to H. W. Wolff the Immanuel sign answers the question of the identity of the faithful remnant in a different way.[302]

> The answer in the new [Immanuel] sign is as follows: The remnant, that is 'us,' the Immanuel clan, which names the child, which confesses in confidence what Ahaz did not want to say despite an ultimate exhortation.[303]

Wolff's identification of the remnant with the Immanuel clan[304] is ambiguous. It is not clear just what he means by the designation "Immanuel-Sippe." It may be merely a descriptive term of the faithful remnant. If this is the case, then the remnant is mystified, because it seems to derive from an ancestor by the name Immanuel. But this is obviously not what Wolff means, for the so-called Immanuel clan names the child to be born with the name Immanuel. One receives the impression that Wolff himself interprets the term <u>ᶜalmāh</u> collectively as the Immanuel clan. He assigns the task of the "young woman" to the Immanuel clan, i.e., in 7:14,

---

Verkündigung des Jesaja eine positive Restvorstellung aufweisbar wäre, könnte der Gerichtscharakter der Verse 14-17 zwar aufrechterhalten bleiben, doch könnte dann zugleich in Immanuel--wenn auch reichlich verborgen und geheimnisvoll--für den gläubigen Rest Heil verkündet sein."

[302]Wolff, <u>Frieden</u>, p. 43. We must be reminded, however, that Wolff envisages a dual meaning in the second element of the name of Isaiah's oldest son: it means a return to Yahweh and a return from battle. The idea of a return from battle is suggested by Wolff, because of the war of Yahweh tradition, which is supposedly actualized in 7:1-9. For the problems of the war of Yahweh tradition in 7:1ff., see <u>supra</u>, n. 263.

[303]Wolff, <u>Frieden</u>, p. 43.

[304]Preuss, <u>Jahweglaube</u>, p. 183, takes up Wolff's idea of an Immanuel clan: "Die öfter genannten 'Wir' und 'Uns' (7,14; 8,10; 9,5) scheinen als Glaubende (7,10ff.), als Jünger Jesajas, als 'Immanuel-Sippe' eine Rolle zu spielen."

the "young woman" will name the child, but according to Wolff the Immanuel clan will do that. If he does indeed interpret collectively by equating ᶜalmāh with the Immanuel clan and the Immanuel clan with the remnant, then the devastating criticism which he advances against such a collective interpretation[305] applies likewise to himself. The present writer is unable to accept Wolff's identification of the remnant with the dubious Immanuel clan. On the other hand, Wolff and other scholars rightly emphasize the dual meaning of the Immanuel sign.[306] It is a threat for Ahaz and those who follow him, but a sign of promising hope and salvation for those who decided to return in faith to Yahweh. For the former it will mean "God-Against-Them" but for the latter it will indeed mean "God-With-Us." They will emerge as the future remnant.

It has been suggested that Immanuel will rule over the faithful remnant of the future.[307] Though the idea of the rulership of Immanuel

---

[305]Ibid., pp. 34-5.

[306]Wolff, Frieden, p. 48: "Unter einem umfassenden Gericht verborgen, bezeugt das Zeichen einem Rest das Heil." Junker, SVT, IV (1957), 189: "Ahaz und das gegenwärtige Volk von Juda hat nur das Gericht zu erwarten, und Heilszeichen ist Immanuel nur für den 'Rest', der aus diesem Gericht gerettet wird. . . ." Gunneweg, VT, XV (1965), 32: ". . . eine mögliche Identifizierung des Immanuel . . . ist zu suchen im Jesajakreis, innerhalb des Restes." Warne, op. cit., p. 88: "It /the sign/ bears a threat to the king and the rest of the sinful nation but a promise to the Remnant." Von Rad, Die Botschaft der Propheten, p. 132, very cautiously interprets the Immanuel sign also as a reference to the remnant: "Ohne Frage hat Jesaja einem tiefgreifenden Sichtungsvorgang entgegengesehen, und es ist nichts dagegen einzuwenden, wenn man in dieser Hinsicht terminologisch vereinfachend von einer Restvorstellung spricht. Man mag dann im Immanuelzeichen einen Hinweis auf den Rest sehen. . . ." Idem, OTT, II, 165.

[307]Buber, Prophetic Faith, p. 140, states, "Immanuel is the king of the remnant, from which the people will renew itself." More cautious expressions are given by others; Vawter, op. cit., p. 205, believes that Immanuel will restore and confirm the reign of right and righteousness

is absent in the pericope of 7:10-17 it is present in the much disputed hymn of 9:1-6,[308] which is often interpreted in relation to the Immanuel sign. If the suggestion that Immanuel will rule the future remnant is correct, as seems probable, then it would logically follow that Immanuel himself will be a member of the eschatological remnant.

Time and again Isaiah's gathering together of a circle of disciples has been described as his "practical step of creating the remnant in which he believed."[309] This inference is drawn from Isa. 8:16-18, a passage which stems from the Syro-Ephraimitic war.[310]

---

among the restored remnant of which he himself is a part. Eissfeldt, OTI, p. 318, states in connection with 9:1-6 that the remnant will be ruled by a member of the Davidic line. This view, Eissfeldt believes, is perfectly reconcilable with the Immanuel prophecy. Rehm, op. cit., p. 143, explicates in connection with 9:1-6 that the child is a part of the saved remnant and that it will be the ruler over the remnant.

[308]Eissfeldt, OTI, pp. 317-8, concludes that it is probably Isaianic. So also Eichrodt, op. cit., pp. 87ff.; Kaiser, Jesaja, p. 99ff.; Wolff, Frieden, p. 63; Lindblom, Immanuel, pp. 40f.; Rehm, op. cit., pp. 131-5; Becker, op. cit., pp. 22-7. Recently Fohrer, Jesaja, I, 138f., follows those critics who deny the genuineness of this passage. For a discussion of the arguments advanced against the genuineness, see Rehm, op. cit., pp. 132ff.

[309]Gray, Isaiah, I, 155; cf. Skinner, Isaiah, p. lxiv; Hyatt, Prophetic Religion, p. 103. F. Maass, "Wandlungen der Gemeindeauffassung in Israel und Juda," Theologica Viatorum. Jahrbuch der kirchlichen Hochschule Berlin (Berlin, 1950), II, 23; G. Hölscher, "Jesaja," ThLZ, 77 (1952), col. 689; Dreyfus, RSPT, 34 (1955), 382-3; Jacob, Theology of the Old Testament, p. 246; Warne, op. cit., p. 88; T. W. Manson, The Teachings of Jesus (2nd ed.; Cambridge, 1959), p. 176; G. A. F. Knight, A Christian Theology of the Old Testament (2nd ed.; London, 1964), p. 204; H. Gottlieb, "Amos und Jerusalem," VT, XVII (1967), 447; Preuss, Jahweglaube, p. 183.

[310]A number of interpreters take this passage to indicate Isaiah's withdrawal from public ministry during the Syro-Ephraimitic war, so recently Fohrer, Jesaja, I, 132; Heaton, The Hebrew Kingdoms, pp. 335-6; Kaiser, Jesaja, pp. 94-5. Eichrodt, Der Heilige in Israel, p. 93, places 8:16-17 after 8:1-2 and 8:18 after 8:4 and points out that it belongs to the same time as the Immanuel prophecy.

16 Bind up the testimony,
seal the teaching among my disciples.
17 I will wait for the Lord,
who is hiding his face from the house of Jacob,
and I will hope in him.
18 Behold, I and the children whom the Lord has given me
are signs and portents in Israel
from the Lord of hosts,
who dwells on Mount Zion.

This passage does not identify the disciples of the prophet as "the nucleus of the remnant"[311] nor is there any reference about "consolidating the remnant."[312] The inference that Isaiah set about to "create"[313] a faithful remnant in his disciples is unwarranted. The prophet, his children,[314] and his disciples cannot be equated simply with the remnant. Surely Isaiah himself experienced a cleansing purge at his call (Isa. 6: 5-7). He alone is purified and forgiven "in the midst" of an unclean people. As such Isaiah is a proleptic representative of the future

---

[311]So Knight, op. cit., p. 204.

[312]So Skinner, Isaiah, p. lxiv; Manson, op. cit., p. 176.

[313]So Gray, Isaiah, I, 155; Hyatt, Prophetic Religion, p. 103; Maass, Theologica Viatorum, II, 23; Preuss, Jahweglaube, p. 183.

[314]According to Jacob, op. cit., p. 324, Shear-jashub will constitute the nucleus of the remnant. Gunneweg, VT, XV (1965), 28, points out that in the ancient Near East and in Israel there is no distinction between the name and the one who carries it. Therefore Gunneweg deduces that the child Shear-jashub, as the carrier of the name, is himself a part of the remnant which returns. The difficulty with Gunneweg's line of reasoning is the idea of returning to Yahweh. The future remnant, which Yahweh will save in the terrible catastrophe, will consist of those who have returned in faith to God. Whether such an act can be ascribed to a child of a few years of age is highly questionable. On the other hand, one can argue that this boy had not yet turned from Yahweh and therefore does not need to return to him in faith; he is still one with God and thus belongs to the remnant. But this could apply equally to all children of Shear-jashub's age who would then too have to belong to the remnant and be saved in the catastrophe. In the present writer's view it seems best not to identify Shear-jashub with the remnant. Shear-jashub is a proleptic representative of the remnant, a guarantee that a remnant will remain.

remnant.[315] According to this passage Isaiah and his followers--his children and disciples--are not the remnant or part thereof; they are "signs and portents in Israel" (8:18) pointing forward to the eschatological remnant which will emerge from the future catastrophe.[316] Nowhere does Isaiah identify with clarity who will belong to the future remnant. Isaiah, his children, and his disciples are proleptic representatives of the eschatological remnant. They are a guarantee and pledge that everything the prophet has spoken will come to pass. They are a guarantee and pledge that Aram and Ephraim will experience destruction (8:1-4) and that Judah itself will not remain as a remnant after it had refused to return and believe in Yahweh (7:1-9).[317] They are at the same time a guarantee and pledge that a remnant will emerge from the coming judgment. This eschatological remnant of the future will be composed of

---

[315]Procksch, Theologie des Alten Testaments, p. 659, states, "Das Haupt dieses Restes ist der Prophet selber, der in seinen Söhnen und Jüngern . . . eine Glaubensgemeinde schafft, die sich von der massa perditionis abscheidet (8,16-18)." That Isaiah himself is the head of the remnant is pure conjecture. In not one instance does Isaiah picture himself as the head of the remnant.

[316]H. Schmidt, Die grossen Propheten, p. 81, remarks correctly that the small band of disciples is to be seen as "das Unterpfand . . ., dass ein solcher 'Rest' da sein wird." Duhm, Jesaja, p. 85, speaks of a "verkörperte Antizipation der Zukunft." Procksch, Jesaja, p. 138: "Jesaja mit seinen Söhnen . . . weiss sich ins Volk gestellt als Vorzeichen des Künftigen (v. 18)." Herntrich, Jesaja, p. 154, interprets the "signs and portents" as follows: "Sie weisen hin auf das Kommende, sie sind 'Typen', die etwas vorwegbilden, was sich ereignen wird. . . ." E. Jenni, "Eschatology," IDB, II, 129: "The prophet himself . . . together with his children and disciples, constitutes for the coming community the pledge of salvation (8:16-18; 14:32)." Lindblom, Prophecy in Ancient Israel, p. 368.

[317]So especially Fohrer, Jesaja, I, 133.

those who have returned to Yahweh in faith, from whom Yahweh has not hidden his face (8:17),[318] but it will become an actual reality only during the purifying judgment of Yahweh which will sweep away all those who decided against faith and God.[319] The remnant motif bridges two opposing aspects in Isaiah's proclamation, namely the conviction that Israel will be met with judgment and the expectation that after the judgment there will be salvation.[320]

3. The Remnant Motif in Isaiah's Later Career (716/15-ca. 701 B.C.).--In the midst of a threat and diatribe directed against Samaria, "the proud crown of the drunkards of Ephraim" (28:1), and a diatribe and threat against the drunken priests and befuddled prophets (28:7-13), there appears an oracle of salvation which contains the remnant motif (28:5-6). The alternation from doom to hope between 28:1-4 and 28:7-13 along with arguments based on terminology and ideas have prompted scholars to regard these two verses as an insertion by a later hand.[321] Other scholars consider this brief oracle to derive from Isaiah of Jerusalem.[322] It is, therefore, necessary to turn briefly to the question

---

[318]Von Rad, OTT, II, 187.

[319]Cf. Isa. 6:13; 1:21-26; 4:2-3; 7:2-9.

[320]B. Otzen, "Rest," Gads danske Bibel Leksikon, ed. by E. Nielsen and B. Noack (København, 1966), II, col. 606.

[321]For a discussion up to 1922, see K. Fullerton, "Viewpoints in the Discussion of Isaiah's Hopes for the Future," JBL, 41 (1922), 29ff. Among more recent exegetes we may mention Scott, Isaiah, V, 313-4; Leslie, op. cit., p. 204; Wright, Isaiah, p. 69; Fohrer, Jesaja, II, 48-9.

[322]Giesebrecht, Jesajakritik, p. 63; Meinhold, Religionsgeschichte, p. 154; Skinner, Isaiah, p. 221; König, op. cit., p. 250; Procksch, Jesaja, pp. 351-2; Schilling, op. cit., pp. 69-70; Danell, op. cit., p.

of authenticity. C. Steuernagel[323] has dealt with the argument used by H. Hackmann, M. Brückner, T. K. Cheyne, K. Marti, and others, namely that threats and promises are diametrically opposed in Isa. 28–32 and that the promises must therefore be considered as secondary additions. C. Steuernagel insists rightly that threat and promise are not mutually exclusive as can be clearly demonstrated from 28:23–29 where in parabolic description God's destroying and healing action in history is presented in combined forms. It may be added that the ambivalence of doom and hope is present also in 1:21–26 from Isaiah's early period of activity.[324] It is a part of Isaiah's whole proclamation. R. Fey has pointed out that this feature of Isaiah's proclamation appears to be rooted in the dialectic of the Isaianic motif of the holiness of Yahweh which consists of a correlation of judgment and salvation.[325] It seems that from the viewpoint of the ambivalence of doom and hope this short promise in 28:5–6 is not incongruent with Isaianic movement of thought and theology. The question of terminology and ideas is most appropriately considered within the interpretation of 28:5–6.

184; Dennefeld, op. cit., pp. 106–7; Warne, op. cit., pp. 94–5; Kissane, Isaiah, I, 299; Muckle, op. cit., p. 96; Bright, Isaiah–I, p. 508; Mauchline, Isaiah, p. 199; Lindblom, Prophecy in Ancient Israel, p. 467; W. Eichrodt, Die Hoffnung des ewigen Friedens im alten Israel (Beiträge zur Förderung christlicher Theologie, 25; Gütersloh, 1920), p. 45; idem, Der Herr der Geschichte, Jesaja 13–23/28–39 (Die Botschaft des Alten Testaments, 17/II; Stuttgart, 1967), p. 121; A. Gelin, "The Latter Prophets," in Introduction to the Old Testament, ed. by A. Robert–A. Feuillet, transl. by P. W. Skehan et al. (New York, 1968), p. 290. See Appendix II, p. 476.

[323]Steuernagel, Einleitung, p. 500.

[324]Supra, pp. 251ff.

[325]Fey, Amos und Jesaja, pp. 105–43.

5 In that day the Lord of hosts will be
a crown of glory
and a diadem of beauty,
to the remnant of his people;
6 and a spirit of justice
to him who sits in judgment,
and a strength to those
who turn back the battle at the gate.

The introductory formula *bayyôm hahûʾ*[326] is a constituent part of the opening section of this oracle; it belongs to the meter of the first verse.[327] It refers to a future which has been changed through divine action. Insofar as Yahweh's action in history can be designated as eschatological and clearly distinguished from apocalyptic, one can say that *bayyôm hahûʾ* refers to the eschatological time of judgment out of which salvation will come.[328] If this interpretation is correct, then it becomes even more obvious that this oracle does not fit into the present context.[329] G. A. Danell makes a special effort to keep vss. 5-6 in their present context but with little success.[330] He is forced to identify "the remnant of his people" with Judah, which is abortive as will be seen shortly. W. Eichrodt has repeatedly suggested that 28:5-6 belongs

---

[326]See the discussion of this formula earlier in this chapter, *supra*, pp. 260ff.

[327]See Procksch, *Jesaja I*, p. 351; Kissane, *Isaiah*, I, 300; Fohrer, *Jesaja*, II, 47.

[328]With Procksch, *Jesaja*, pp. 351-2; Fohrer, *Jesaja*, II, 48; Bright, *Isaiah-I*, p. 508; Lindblom, *Prophecy in Ancient Israel*, p. 467; Schilling, *op. cit.*, p. 69; Kissane, *Isaiah*, I, 304.

[329]The attempts of König, *Jesaja*, pp. 250-1, and Kissane, *Isaiah*, I, 304, to harmonize the ideas of 28:5-6 with the previous and following materials are not convincing.

[330]Danell, *op. cit.*, p. 184.

to Isaiah's early period of ministry.[331] This supposition has some merit. But it seems more likely that the passage belongs to the period of disturbance following the death of Sargon II in 705 B.C.[332] when Hezekiah of Judah became a leader of a coalition in revolt against Assyria. The present position of this oracle within Chapters 28-32 whose materials date almost exclusively from Isaiah's later period supports this suggestion. As such it may have served as a warning and exhortation to Hezekiah and Judah to trust in Yahweh of hosts for their strength rather than in their own strength and those of their allies. This oracle was probably placed after the oracle against Ephraim because of the terminological correspondence between the language of 28:5 and 28:1, 3.[333]

The remnant motif has come to expression in the designation <u>šeʾār ʿammô</u>. The term <u>šeʾār</u> is typically Isaianic (7:3). The designation <u>šeʾār ʿammô</u> occurs also in Isa. 11:11, 16. These are the only usages of the combination <u>šeʾār ʿammô</u> in the Hebrew Bible. This combination is used with a completely different sense in these passages in Isaiah as compared to the only closely corresponding designation <u>šeʾār ʿam</u> in Neh. 10:28(29); 11:1. There is merely a correspondence in language between Isa. 28:5 (11:11, 16) and Neh. 10:28(29); 11:1; the ideas expressed by these designations in the two books lack any correspondence whatever.

---

[331]Eichrodt, <u>Die Hoffnung des ewigen Friedens im alten Israel</u>, p. 45; idem, <u>Herr der Geschichte</u>, p. 120-1.

[332]So Procksch, <u>Jesaja</u>, p. 251: "Das Fehlen des Messias spricht eher für die Spätzeit, wenn auch nicht mit völliger Beweiskraft." Cf. Gelin, <u>op. cit</u>., p. 290.

[333]Eichrodt, <u>Herr der Geschichte</u>, p. 121: "Dass die Ehrenprädikate von der zierenden Krone und vom herrlichen Kranz an ähnliche Ausdrücke in V. 1 und 3 anklingen, ist zwar richtig und mag den Anlass zur Einschiebung an dieser Stelle gegeben haben."

Interpreters have identified *p^e^lêṭaṯ* time and again with Judah.[334] This identification is usually made on the basis of the present context of 28:5-6. Insofar as 28:1-4 speaks of the doom of Ephraim it is argued that 28:5-6 speaks of the salvation of Judah. However, the traditio-historical picture is more complicated. In the first place it is clear that the oracle of 28:1-4 must have been originally spoken before 722 B.C. and is here repeated as a parabolic warning to Judah. Secondly, the short oracle of salvation of 28:5-6 was very likely placed after 28:1-4 because of the corresponding language. Thirdly, it was probably placed before the threat of 28:7-13 to serve as an exhortation and warning to Hezekiah and Judah not to rely upon political alliances but to trust for strength in Yahweh of hosts lest judgment should fall upon them and there will be only a "remnant of his people" left. These general considerations make it improbable to identify "the remnant of his people" with Judah. Our investigation of the remnant motif in Isaiah has so far shown that Isaiah of Jerusalem has invariably spoken of a remnant *from* Judah. O. Schilling has pointed out that if one supposes that *p^e^lêṭaṯ* means Judah after Ephraim has disappeared, it would be most incongruous that the community whose leaders practice justice and right (28:5-6) would immediately thereafter be described as a community whose leaders reel and stagger with wine and stumble in giving judgment (28:7).[335]

---

[334]Giesebrecht, *Jesajakritik*, p. 63; T. K. Cheyne, *Introduction to the Book of Isaiah* (London, 1895), p. 181; Duhm, *Jesaja*, p. 196; Danell, *op. cit.*, p. 184; etc.

[335]Schilling, *op. cit.*, p. 70.

This difference in description points to different communities.

The identity of šeʾār ʿammô depends in the last analysis on the interpretation of the oracle in which this reference occurs. "The remnant of his people" is pictured as that entity which will have Yahweh of hosts as their "crown of glory" (ʿaṭereṯ ṣeḇî) and "diadem of beauty" (ṣep̂îraṯ tip̄ʾārāh). Both of these phrases are used only here in the Hebrew Bible. The term ṣeḇî appears also in 28:1 in connection with the "glorious beauty" of the fading flower of Ephraim and in 4:2 in connection with the "branch of Yahweh" which shall be glorious. T. K. Cheyne has argued that "it is natural to say that the fertility of the soil is a glory to Israel, natural too to speak of Samaria as the glory of Ephraim,"[336] but it is "not natural" to describe Yahweh as a "crown of glory." Therefore, one must postulate that the hand of a "late supplementer"[337] was here at work. In the present writer's opinion it is rather precarious to claim to know just what is "natural" or "not natural" for a writer. But let us pursue the matter of linguistic correspondence of 28:5 with 28:1ff. and 4:2 a little further. The term ʿaṭereṯ appears again in 28:1, 3 but in connection with the drunkards of Ephraim, so that there is no real correspondence of figures. ṣep̂îrāh is not used elsewhere in Isaiah.[338] The term tip̄ʾārāh appears in 28:1, 4 and in 4:2 and a number of other pas-

---

[336]Cheyne, Introduction, p. 181.

[337]Ibid.

[338]The only other two appearances in the Old Testament are in Eze. 7:7, 10.

sages in the book of Isaiah.[339] This term is used in connection with a wide variety of ideas,[340] which does not allow us to decide what is "natural" or "not natural" for Isaiah. The outcome is that while some of the terms of 28:5 are used in 4:2 and 28:1, 2 they do not occur in the same *status constructus* combination and do not express the same idea. If these terms would appear in identical phrases or combinations with a different idea, it would seem more credible that different writers were at work. But as it stands the mere usage of certain terminology cannot be used for or against Isaiah's authorship. Different subject matter requires different figures. Furthermore, T. K. Cheyne assumes that 28:5-6 was inspired by expressions of 28:1-4. But this is hardly likely, because of the great differences of the figures of speech.[341]

The description of *šeʾār ʿammô* as an entity to whom Yahweh of hosts will be a glorious crown and a beautiful diadem is a stark contrast to the rejection of Yahweh on the part of the Judean king and people by relying upon an alliance with a foreign nation. The designation "Yahweh of hosts" in connection with the remnant motif is not accidental. It is a typically Isaianic combination (1:9; 1:21-26; 6:5). Isaiah uses this designation consciously putting theological weight upon it.[342] In the present passage it implies that Yahweh will be the security, power, and pride of *šeʾār ʿammô*. This is emphasized explicitly by the fact that Yahweh

---

[339] Isa. 3:18; 10:12; 13:19; 20:5.

[340] Cf. *KB*, pp. 1036-7.

[341] So Eichrodt, *Herr der Geschichte*, p. 121.

[342] Wildberger, *Jesaja*, p. 28.

of hosts will be the glorious crown and beautiful diadem of <u>šᵉʾār</u> <u>ᶜammô</u> In other words <u>šᵉʾār</u> <u>ᶜammô</u> is an entity whose trust will not be in the power and strength of political alliances but in Yahweh of hosts. This indicates that <u>šᵉʾār</u> <u>ᶜammô</u> will have followed Isaiah's counsel to return to Yahweh and become a community of faith,[343] which will have fulfilled the condition to make it possible for Yahweh to have them emerge from the future judgment. "The remnant of his people" must therefore be identified with the eschatological remnant.[344] The judges of this future remnant will be endowed with "a spirit of justice" (<u>lᵉrûaḥ</u> <u>mišpāṭ</u>)[345] which will enable them to judge justly (28:6). The motif of justice and just judgment is prominent in connection with the future remnant in Isaiah.[346] Those who thus judge will not "acquit the guilty for a bribe, and deprive the innocent of his right" (5:23) nor "stumble in giving judgment" (28:7).[347] Yahweh of hosts will be a "strength" to those who de-

---

[343]J. Meinhold, "Einige Bemerkungen zu Jes. 28," <u>Theologische Studien und Kritiken</u>, 66 (1893), 22-3, has pointed out long ago that "the remnant of his people" consists of those who will be saved from the future judgment by Yahweh and must not be identified with Judah or Ephraim or both. H. Dittmann, "Der heilige Rest im Alten Testament," <u>Theologische Studien und Kritiken</u>, 87 (1914), 611, points out that in Isaiah the remnant is an eschatological entity which will be made up out of the believers of the people. Skinner, <u>Isaiah</u>, p. 221, states that "the remnant of his people" means "a converted remnant." Procksch, <u>Jesaja</u>, p. 352: "Der שְׁאָר עַמּוֹ . . . ist die bekehrte Glaubensgemeinde, die das Gericht überstanden hat." Fohrer, <u>Jesaja</u>, II, 48: "Der Ausdruck Rest . . . ist hier längst zu einem neuen Begriff geworden, der die glaubende Gemeinde der Heilszeit meint." Cf. Lindblom, <u>Prophecy in Ancient Israel</u>, pp. 467-8.

[344]Cf. Isa. 1:21-26; 4:2-3; 6:13.

[345]This idea is different from the one in Isa. 4:4 where the רוּחַ מִשְׁפָּט is a "spirit of judgment," i.e., an agent of cleansing.

[346]See Isa. 1:21-26, <u>supra</u>, pp. 320ff. and Wildberger, <u>Jesaja</u>, pp. 86-7, 89. See Appendix II, p. 477.

[347]For a discussion of the importance of the term מִשְׁפָּט as regards

fend the city, because they trust in him and not in their own strength nor in that of their allies. Isaiah had repeatedly threatened those who trust in their own strength and in that of their allies.[348] One is hardly able to dispute that the content and main ideas of this brief oracle are in harmony with the future hopes of Isaiah[349] and the Isaianic remnant motif.

From the same collection of sayings of Isaiah in Chapters 28-32,[350] i.e., the so-called Assyrian cycle, which contains mostly materials from the period of 705-701 B.C., comes another saying which contains the remnant motif. The diatribe[351] and threat of 30:15-17 probably derives from the period of Hezekiah's plan to seek the help of Egypt (30:1-2) at about 705(3)-701 B.C.[352]

---

moral demands and religious obligations and the right attitude to Yahweh, see Lindblom, Prophecy in Ancient Israel, pp. 346-60.

348Isa. 3:2; 30:16-17; 31:3.

349Bright, Isaiah-I, p. 508, states that "the theology is certainly Isaianic." Hertzberg, op. cit., p. 94, who believes that 28:5-6 are not genuine, admits that "die Worte . . . sind aber in seinem [Jesajas] Geiste gesagt. . . ."

350Fohrer, Introduction, p. 365, speaks of seven minor collections which together with other materials gradually came to constitute the entire prophetical writing. A less differentiated picture of composition is drawn up by Kaiser, Einleitung, pp. 174-6. But Kaiser agrees with Fohrer that Chapters 28-32 derive from Isaiah's last period of ministry. Cf. Harrelson, Interpreting the Old Testament, pp. 244-5.

351Childs, Assyrian Crisis, p. 37, prefers the term "invective" to "diatribe."

352Eissfeldt, OTI, p. 316, dates it between 705-701 B.C. Kaiser, Einleitung, p. 174, believes too that it comes from the period of the Syro-Palestinian revolt in 705(3)-701 B.C. So also Leslie, op. cit., pp. 74, 77-8; Scott, Isaiah, V, 330-1; Duhm, Jesaja, p. 16; Procksch, Jesaja, pp. 347-8; Wright, Isaiah, p. 68; Mauchline, Isaiah, p. 207; Bright, Isaiah-I, p. 510; Kissane, Isaiah, I, 324; Donner, op. cit., pp. 161-2;

15 For thus says the Lord God,
the Holy One of Israel,
'In returning and rest[353] you shall be saved;
in quietness and trust shall be your strength.'
And you would not.
16 But you said, 'No! We will speed upon[354] horses,'
therefore you shall speed away;
and 'We will ride upon swift[355] steeds,'
therefore your pursuers shall be swift.
17 A thousand shall flee[356] at the threat of one,
at the threat of five you shall flee,
till what is left of you shall be like a flagpole
on the top of a mountain,
like a signal on a hill.[357]

Interpreters are agreed that 30:15 contains the essence of Isaiah's

---

and others. H. Schmidt, *Die grossen Propheten*, p. 93, and recently Fohrer, *Jesaja*, II, 96, consider this passage to derive from the period of Hezekiahs earlier reign and date it between 711-705 B.C. Herrmann, *Heilserwartungen*, believes that vs. 17 reflects the situation of Sennacherib's campaign in 701 B.C.

[353]Fohrer, *Jesaja*, II, 101 n. 117, connects נחת with the verb נוח in 7:2 and translates "Vertragstreue." Therefore he takes the hapax legomenon שׁוּבָה not in the sense of "returning, conversion, coming back" but interprets it with the aid of Mic. 2:8 to mean "abgewandt vom Kriege" (turned away from war). However, the postulated meaning of נוח in Isa. 7:2 is not firmly secured and would be unique. Furthermore in 30:15 נַחַת is used parallel to הַשְׁקֵט just as in Isa. 7:14 the verb נוח is used as a synonym of שׁקט. This is a definite pointer in the direction that the meanings of both are closely related. Thus there is no real support for the translation of "Vertragstreue" for נַחַת. Isaiah's concern is primarily to call for trust *in* Yahweh rather than to counsel to be faithful to the covenant with Assyria. שׁוּבָה certainly derives from שׁוּב and not from ישׁב as Fohrer thinks. The phrase שׁוּבֵי מִלְחָמָה in Mic. 2:8 is textually not well supported. It must be noted too that מִלְחָמָה is not present in Isa. 30:15 and that the singular is used and not the plural. Thus there is really no binding reason to depart from the traditional translation.

[354]1QIs[a] reads אל for על.

[355]1QIs[a] reads ואל for ועל.

[356]The Hebrew text lacks "will flee." The LXX reads διὰ φωνὴν ἑνὸς φεύξονται χίλιοι.

[357]The translation is by the present writer.

proclamation in summary form. The purpose of Yahweh for his people is laid out in powerful language. The fourfold call to Judah to return to God and rest in calm surrender to the divine will, and to practice quietness of mind and trust confidently in Yahweh circumscribes and interprets the call for faith.[358] Isaiah's earlier message to Ahaz, which was given under somewhat similar circumstances, makes it plain that Judah's security and future existence does not lie in military action and political alliances but in confident faith in Yahweh.[359] But the nation was at cross-purposes with her God. Isaiah repeatedly warned Hezekiah and Judah not to enter into a new alliance and pointed away from trust in human strength to faith in divine power.[360] Judah as a nation still refuses God's offer. As is indicated by the phrase "and you would not" (30:15b).[361] Judah's total rejection of Yahweh's purpose for them is expressed in the words of 30:16. Through Judah's emphatic No the only avenue to salvation is closed, and Judah calls down upon itself national disaster. The promise of deliverance is turned into judgment.[362] Judah's efforts in battle will come to nought "till what is left of you [*nôṯartem*] shall be like a flagpole on the top of the mountain, like a

---

[358]See especially Fey, *op. cit.*, p. 130; Eichrodt, *Herr der Geschichte*, pp. 176-7.

[359]Cf. Isa. 7:4, 9; 7:10-17; 28:16.

[360]Isa. 28:7-13; 28:14-22; 29:9-12; 29:13-14.

[361]In Isa. 28:12b the phrase "yet they would not hear" is analogous to the one in 30:15b.

[362]Fey, *op. cit.*, p. 131: "Das Nein Israels löst . . . ein Umschlagen des Heilsangebots Jahwes in Unheilsankündigung aus. In ungeahnter Weise nimmt Jahwe das Volk beim Wort."

signal on a hill" (30:17b). Surely a remnant will be left.[363] But the picture of the lonely flagpole and signal indicates Judah's abandoned state and the loss of her military might. The import of this simile is pointedly summed up by W. Eichrodt:

> The picture of the flag pole and the signal on the mountain designates impressively the complete solitude and loneliness of those who have fled from being alone with God into the presence of men.[364]

Isaiah's oracle is to hold up before Judah the futility of her efforts to seek security in her own machinations.

This oracle contains Isaiah's typical threefold sequence: offer of salvation by Yahweh--rejection by Israel--rejection of Israel by Yahweh. This sequence is manifested also in Isaiah's early and middle periods of ministry.[365] It is important to recognize that certain basic ideas remained constant--despite other changes in Isaiah's message--during the decades of his ministry. Among them are the radical either-or of self-sufficiency or faith in Yahweh; the judgment as a result of the rejection of the call for faith; and the idea that salvation can be gained[365a] only through a return to God. Furthermore, it is significant that Isaiah does not here soften the message of judgment for Judah by a theory of a remnant which promises a blessed future existence to Judah. Here as elsewhere Isaiah's threat to Judah's national existence is radical, because of her rejection of Yahweh's offer. This oracle is therefore an exhortation to each listener to return to Yahweh in faith in order to be-

---

[363]Duhm, Jesaja, p. 221; Kissane, Isaiah, I, 333.

[364]Eichrodt, Herr der Geschichte, p. 178.

[365]Isa. 5:1-7; 8:5-8; 17:10-11; 28:7-13 (from late period).

[365a]See Appendix II, p. 477.

long to those who can experience salvation in the future judgment, as much as it is a dire threat to those who reject the divine offer.

The diatribe[366] of Isa. 1:4-9, which opens with a typical woe (zārîm) exclamation[367] and changes then into an implicit exhortation,[368] contains the remnant motif. It dates from the time shortly after the Assyrian assault against Judah. The historical events are vividly portrayed in 1:7f. when strangers (zārîm) ravaged Judah's countryside and her towns. Jerusalem alone is left as an isolated capital. These bitter experiences were met in Israel in 701 B.C.[369] when the Assyrian conqueror Sennacherib shut up Hezekiah in his capital "like a bird in a

---

[366]The German "Scheltwort," is translated with "diatribe" (so Koch, The Growth of the Biblical Tradition: The Form-Critical Method, pp. 191f.) or "invective" (so Childs, op. cit., p. 21.).

[367]E. Gerstenberger, "The Woe-Oracles of the Prophets," JBL, 81 (1962), 249-63, has offered new insights into the usage of woe-oracles providing at the same time a reply to Westermann, Basic Forms of Prophetic Speech, pp. 189ff.

[368]With Wildberger, Jesaja, p. 20, against Childs, Assyrian Crisis, p. 22, who takes the concluding part of this oracle as a lament. The latter follows Kaiser, Jesaja, pp. 5-6 who considers 1:2-9 as a unit and believes that Isaiah very likely has announced this accusation of Yahweh when the people assembled in the Jerusalem temple on a day of lamentation. "Der Sitz im Leben wäre demnach eine Klagefeier. Während die Gemeinde von dem Propheten ein Heilsorakel erhoffte, antwortete er mit diesem Ruf zur Besinnung auf die eigene Schuld." Wildberger, Jesaja, p. 21, points out against Kaiser that nowhere in this pericope is the impression given that Isaiah speaks to men who observe a day of lamentation. He advances the guess that these words were spoken during a Zion festival. One can probably never be sure on which occasion these words were spoken.

[369]Most commentators are agreed regarding the date of 701 B.C. for this oracle. The attempt of E. Robertson, "Isaiah Chapter I," ZAW, 52 (1934), 231ff., to date 1:2-7 into the time between the fall of Damascus in 732 B.C. and the destruction of Samaria in 722 B.C. is unsuccessful. Equally unconvincing is the attempt of Danell, op. cit., pp. 156-9, who seeks to date 1:4-9 shortly after 722 B.C. For other suggestions, see König, Jesaja, p. 43, who himself dates this in the time of Jotham.

cage"[370] and took forty-six of Judah's strong cities and drove out 200,150 of her inhabitants as booty. The remnant motif is encountered in the last two verses of this pericope.

8 And the daughter of Zion is left
like a booth in a vineyard,
like a shed in a cucumberfield,
like a besieged city.[371]
9 If Yahweh of hosts
had not left us a few[372] survivors,[373]

---

[370] ANET[3], p. 288; DOTT, p. 67; cf. 2 Ki. 18:13-16.

[371] Wildberger, Jesaja, p. 19, emends נְצוּרָה into בַּצִּירָה and repoints כְּעִיר into כַּעֲיִר to read "wie ein Eselsfüllen im Pferch." This is a notable endeavor to make better sense out of difficult Hebrew. However, the "foal of a donkey" does not correspond as well to "shed" and "booth" as does עִיר. The MT reads "like a guarded city." But the versions differ: The LXX reads ὡς πόλις πολιορκουμένη; the Targum reads כקרתא דצירין עלה; the Peshitta reads m'dînâ ḥebîštâ; the Vulgate reads "sicut civitas quae vastatur." The versions do then support נְצוֹרָה, i.e., the Niphal participle of צוּר, which the RSV and Jerusalem Bible have adopted. Gray, Isaiah, I, 14, suggests a different translation, "like a tower for the watch," which is related to Duhm's translation, "wie eine Burg der Wacht" (Jesaja, p. 27). But עיר does not mean "tower" or "Burg" and נצורה does not mean "watch (Wacht)." This invalidates also Kaiser's translation "Wachtkastell" (Jesaja, p. 5). It seems that the versions provide the best suggestion. The consonants of the MT remain the same. Through changes in pointing the reading first suggested by H. Ewald, Jesaja mit den übrigen älteren Propheten (2nd ed.; Göttingen, 1867), pp. 374-5, and adopted by Delitzsch, Dillmann, Procksch, Donner, Fohrer, BHK, BHS, and others, is accepted.

[372] The adverb מְעַט serves to underline the smallness of a number, see Isa. 10:25; 16:14; 26:20. Just because it is absent in the LXX, Peshitta, and Vulgate one should not eliminate it, especially since it is present in 1QIs[a]. כִּמְעַט has also the meaning of "almost" (KB, p. 546). The Athnah has, therefore, been placed by some exegetes under the previous word, which would allow כִּמְעַט to be moved to the next line. Wildberger, Jesaja, p. 19, rejects this transposition on logical grounds. Without the mercy of Yahweh Zion would be completely and not "almost" like Sodom and Gomorrah.

[373] The LXX has in place of שָׂרִיד the word σπέρμα, the Vulgate translates "semen." J. Fischer, In welcher Schrift lag das Buch Isaias der LXX vor? (BZAW, 56; Giessen, 1930), p. 18, believes that this is merely a free translation on the part of the LXX translators. Ziegler, Untersuchungen zur Septuaginta des Buches Isaias, p. 106, suggests that

we would have been like Sodom,
we would have resembled Gomorrah.[374]

There is no doubt that a Jerusalemite speaks here. Isaiah's authorship is undisputed. Isaiah does not speak here of the remnant of Israel. The "daughter of Zion is left [notrāh]" (1:8a). The phrase "daughter of Zion" is a designation for the inhabitants of Jerusalem (5:3; 8:14; 10:24, 32). The picture which Isaiah paints is clear. Judah has been overrun by the enemy and is left desolated. Only Jerusalem is left in the midst of the disaster of which Isaiah had warned king and people. H. Wildberger[375] reminds us that the name "Zion" here calls to remembrance the promises connected with the city of God, while "Jerusalem" expresses more the political and secular aspect. Through the expression "daughter of Zion" shines the Zion tradition. "The 'daughter of Zion' is the carrier of the promises connected with the mountain of God, but she needs to note, that these do not provide any security which can be separated from one's faithfulness to the covenant."[376] Isaiah's demand for faith in Yahweh's covenant faithfulness relativized the promises connected with Mount Zion.[377] The

---

the translator was influenced by the Greek phrase καταλιπεῖν . . . σπέρμα from Deut. 3:3 which contains in the Hebrew also שָׂרִיד. A similar Greek phrase is found in the apocryphal Widom of Solomon 14:6 ἀπέλιπεν . . . σπέρμα.

374The translation is by the present writer.

375Wildberger, Jesaja, p. 29.

376Ibid.

377Isa. 7:2-9; 7:10-17; 8:6-8; 1:21-26; 29:1-8; 17:12-14; 2:2-4. Cf. Rohland, op. cit., pp. 145-78; John H. Hayes, "The Tradition of Zion's Inviolability." JBL, 82 (1963), 449-26. Herrmann, Heilserwartungen, pp. 141-4; von Rad, OTT, II, 155-69; Wildberger, Jesaja, pp. 78-90; Childs, Assyrian Crisis, pp. 50-9.

promises connected with Zion preserve their hopeful meaning only on the condition that Israel will return to Yahweh in faith. Much of Zion's glory has vanished, as the deft illustrations of the "booth in a vineyard" and the "shed in a cucumberfield" and the "besieged city" (1:8b) clearly portray.

A proper understanding of Isaiah's usage of the remnant motif seeks an answer to the question whether or not the prophet had the future remnant in mind when he spoke of the "daughter of Zion" which alone is left of Judah. Is this the purified remnant, i.e., the "holy seed" (6:13c) or "holy" remnant (4:3), of which he spoke decades earlier? The answer to this question is an emphatic No.[378] The context shows that these "survivors" are not the community of faith which would emerge from God's purging judgment as the eschatological remnant. In 1:9 Isaiah declares that only because of Yahweh's grace and mercy "a few survivors [sārîd]"[379] were left. Had it not been for the strength of "Yahweh of hosts," and especially for his grace,[380] the whole nation would have been wiped off

---

[378]Childs, Assyrian Crisis, p. 22: "The people who have been spared are not 'a holy remnant', . . ." Hermann, Heilserwartungen, p. 128 n. 9: "Doch handelt es sich hier um keine Zukunftserwartung." Bright, Isaiah-I, p. 490: "Isaiah did not regard the survivors of 701 as the purified remnant of Israel."

[379]Scott, Isaiah, V, 170, points out that the term שָׂרִיד may have been deliberately chosen here by Isaiah, because שְׁאָר "had acquired special associations in Isaiah's early period, . . ." Yet it is noteworthy that in Isa. 37:4 the שָׂרִיד of the events of 701 are designated as שְׁאֵרִית. Only in Isa. 1:9 does the prophet use the term שָׂרִיד and it is possible that he stressed by its use the notion of fleeing, which is implicit in this term. Cf. supra, pp. 196ff.

[380]Herntrich, Jesaja, p. 9: ". . . nur durch seine [Gottes] Gnade ist dieser Rest bewahrt." Mauchline, Isaiah, p. 52: "Had it not been for God's mercy, the destruction would have been utter (v. 9), like that of Sodom, without survivor." Mowinckel, He That Cometh, p. 135:

the face of the earth as Sodom and Gomorrah had been in the time of Abraham (Gen. 18-19).[381] In this instance Isaiah makes use of the historical meaning of the remnant motif. He looks back upon a past event and reflects on the historical situation. In this connection the comparison of Jerusalem with Sodom and Gomorrah is not surprising, because the Genesis narrative too looks back upon a past event.[382] The *tertium comparationis* is not the means of destruction but its totality. Surely Israel is not yet totally destroyed; but in what way will she react to this punishment? Isaiah's reflection on the past catastrophic event that left only a small historical remnant leads him implicitly to look towards the future. In referring to the rebelliousness of the people and the punishment for their breach of a most solemn covenant,[383] which is Yahweh's "alien work,"[384] Isaiah raises the question, Will Israel understand that the time given her is but a time of probation? Yahweh extended his

---

". . . Yahweh has, of His undeserved grace, 'left us a remnant' (Isa. i, 9)." Eichrodt , *Der Heilige in Israel*, pp. 28-9: "Auch der klägliche Rest selbständiger Existenz ist der Hauptstadt ja nur durch Gottes unverdiente Nachsicht geblieben (V. 9), . . ."

[381]For the usage and meaning of the remnant motif in the narrative of the cities of the Plain, see *supra*, pp. 147-52.

[382]Against Wildberger, *Jesaja*, p. 30: "Der Vergleich mit Sodom und Gomorrha überrascht, diese Städte sind ja nicht durch Kriege zerstört worden." Wildberger is determined to connect the Isaianic remnant motif with the war of Yahweh tradition. The very connection between the destruction of Judah by war in the time of Sennacherib and the destruction of Sodom and Gomorrah by a natural catastrophe in Isaiah indicates that the lines of connection and the traditio-historical relationship of the pre-Isaianic and Isaianic remnant motif cannot be singularly linked to the war of Yahweh tradition.

[383]Isa. 1:4.

[384]Isa. 28:21.

grace in order to give the "few survivors" another chance to return to him in faith.[385] Because these "survivors" are not the future remnant, but have the potentiality of belonging to it,[386] Isaiah speaks of this future entity in other sayings that derive from this period of his prophetic activity.

The pericope of Isa. 10:20-23 contains the dual polarity of Isaiah's remnant motif.

20 In that day the remnant of Israel
and the survivors of the house of Jacob
will no more lean upon him that smote them,
but[387] will lean upon Yahweh,
the Holy One of Israel, in truth.
21 A remnant will return,
the remnant of Jacob,
to the mighty God.
22 For though your people, O Israel
were like the sand of the sea,
a remnant would return from them.
Destruction is decreed,[388]
overflowing with righteousness.

---

[385]Wildberger, Jesaja, p. 27: "Die heisse Hoffnung Jesajas, dass die Entronnenen zu einem 'Rest, der umkehrt' (שְׁאָר־יָשׁוּב), werden möchten (7:3), ist offensichtlich der eigentliche Grund, warum Jesaja dieses Wort gesprochen hat." Eichrodt, Der Heilige in Israel, p. 29: ". . . wer die Bedeutung des Restes aus der Verkündigung Jesajas kennt, hört die unausgesprochene Frage, die darin liegt: wird man des letzte Angebot verstehen, das der Herr der Heerscharen den mit knapper Not dem Tode Entronnenen macht?"

[386]Cf. 1 Ki. 19:18.

[387]The ו is here used adversatively. Cf. Williams, Hebrew Syntax, p. 72 # 432.

[388]Tur-Sinai, Scripta Hierosolymitana, 8 (1961), 184-5, suggests that כִּלָּיוֹן חָרוּץ be taken as the conclusion of vs. 23, which he likes to place after vs. 25. There is, however, no textual support for this twofold transposition. The close terminological and sequential relationship with Isa. 1:27 militates against Tur-Sinai's proposal. Cf. Th. C. Vriezen, "Prophecy and Eschatology," SVT, I, (1953), 208 n. 3. G. R. Driver, "Isaiah I-XXXIX: Textual and Linguistic Problems," JSS, XIII

23 For an annihilation, even a decisive one,[389]
the Lord,[390] Yahweh of hosts, is making
in the midst of the land.[391]

Many scholars attribute this oracle to Isaiah of Jerusalem.[392]

(1968), 42, connects the Hebrew חָרוּץ with the Arabic ḥaraḍa "wasted by disease" and deletes יהוה צְבָאוֹת with the Syro-hexaplaric recension for metrical reasons. On the basis of these propositions Driver translates: "a remnant shall return, in which is sickly wasting,/ (Yet it is) overflowing with righteousness;/ for the Lord is working something final and determined within the whole land; . . ." It seems that the lectio difficilor of the MT is original.

[389]The ו seems to be explicative introducting a qualifying clause (Williams, Hebrew Syntax, p. 72 #434). Leslie, ibid., translated, "For an end, and that decisive, . . ." It is of course grammatically also possible to take the Niphal participle נֶחֱרָצָה as a substantive (cf. Isa. 28:22; Procksch, Jesaja, p. 172). Others again see here an example of hendiadys, see König, Jesaja, p. 150 n. 5; Kaiser, Jesaja, p. 117; Young, op. cit., I, 370 n. 54.

[390]Fohrer, Jesaja, I, 160, and Leslie, op. cit., p. 52, extrapolate אדני, but without reason.

[391]The translation is by the present writer.

[392]Giesebrecht, Jesajakritik, pp. 71-6; S. R. Driver, An Introduction to the Literature of the Old Testament, Meridian Books (Cleveland and New York, 1956), p. 210; von Orelli, Jesaja, p. 57; Owen C. Whitehouse, Isaiah I-XXXIX (The New-Century Bible; New York, 1905), pp. 166-7; H. Schmidt, Die grossen Propheten, pp. 111-2; Skinner, Isaiah, p. 98; George Adam Smith, The Book of Isaiah (2nd ed.; New York, 1927), I, 150-1; Boutflower, op. cit., pp. 238-9; de Vaux, RB, 42 (1933), 529 n. 5=Bible et Orient (Paris, 1967), p. 29 n. 1; Schilling, op. cit., pp. 66f.; Danell, op. cit., pp. 175-6; Dennefeld, op. cit., p. 57; Bewer, Isaiah, p. 36; Rowley, The Biblical Doctrine of Election, p. 74; Vriezen, SVT, I (1953), 208 n. 3; Kissane, Isaiah, I, 127; C. Kuhl, The Prophets of Israel, transl. by R. J. Ehrlich and J. P. Smith (Richmond, Va., 1960), p. 77; Steinmann, op. cit., p. 53; Muckle, Isaiah, pp. 44-5; Bright, Isaiah-I, p. 458; Gross, op. cit., II, 1001; Heschel, The Prophets, p. 94; Mauchline, Isaiah, p. 125; Leslie, op. cit., pp. 51-2, 108; Schunck, op. cit., p. 323; Eissfeldt, OTI, p. 312; Scharbert, Die Propheten, p. 255; Young, The Book of Isaiah, I, 368-71; Ringgren, Israelite Religion, pp. 258, 274; E. H. Maly, Prophets of Salvation (New York, 1967), pp. 91-2; Rehm, op. cit., p. 189; Scott, The Relevance of the Prophets, p. 81; Ward, op. cit., pp. 269-70.

Some have thought that vss. 20-21 are Isaianic, but vss. 22-23 are not;[393] others claim that the whole passage is from a late usually post-exilic editor.[394] T. K. Cheyne has argued on the ground of style that 10:20-23 is non-Isaianic.[395] D. M. Warne, on the other hand, arrives at the conclusion that "the words and phrases . . . reflect Isaiah's style."[396] The former himself concedes that "the whole passage is to a great extent a mosaic of Isaianic expressions and images; . . ."[397] It appears that

---

[393]So Procksch, Jesaja, p. 171, and more recently also Lindblom, Prophecy in Ancient Israel, p. 367 n. 145. Lindblom denies the authenticity of vss. 22-23, because of their negative emphasis and his theory that the Isaianic remnant motif contains only a positive aspect. Isa. 6:13; and 1:21-26 alone prove that Lindblom's emphasis is too one-sided. This applies also to Mowinckel, Psalmenstudien II, p. 279.

[394]Cheyne, Introduction, pp. 51-4, with detailed arguments on stylistic and historical grounds. Meinhold, Religionsgeschichte, p. 138, argues that vss. 20-23 must be secondary, because the ideas cannot be brought into harmony with Isaiah's message. Steuernagel, Einleitung, p. 481, argues against Isaiah's authorship on the basis of the position of 10:20-23 within an oracle against Assyria. G. Beer, "Zur Zukunftserwartung des Jesaja," in Studien zur semitischen Philologie und Religionsgeschichte. Festschrift für Julius Wellhausen (BZAW, 27; Giessen, 1914), 27, denies the genuineness of 10:20-27 on the basis of his peculiar view that Isaiah proclaimed throughout his entire ministry that Jerusalem will be taken by the Assyrians. Every saying which is contrary to this must have been interpolated into Isaiah's message. Gray, Isaiah, I, 203-4, argues that the prose of 10:20-23 within a section of poetry 10:5-34 shows it to be secondary. The following writers consider 10:20-23 also secondary but add no new arguments: Duhm, Jesaja, pp. 101-2; Hertzberg, op. cit., p. 55; Wolff, ZThK, 48 (1951), 141 n. 29; Bentzen, Introduction to the Old Testament, II, 108; Eichrodt, Der Heilige in Israel, pp. 130-1; Kaiser, Jesaja, p. 116; Fohrer, Jesaja, I, 160; Kraeling, Commentary on the Prophets, I, 79; Becker, op. cit., p. 60. See Appendix II, p. 477.

[395]Cheyne, Introduction, p. 52.

[396]Warne, op. cit., p. 97; cf. Kissane, Isaiah, I, 126: ". . . the thoughts and the languages are characteristic of Isaiah."

[397]Cheyne, Introduction, p. 52.

arguments based on stylistic considerations are indecisive as to determining genuineness. At this point it is well to remind ourselves of the words of R. Fey that "terminological connections and picture connections are not rare in the (indesputable) sayings of Isaiah."[398] With regard to the process of separating the genuine from the non-genuine the candid confession of B. Duhm in his introductory remarks to Isa. 10:5-34 is highly instructive: "In separating what is genuine from the added interpolations a certain subjective process is, of course, inevitable."[399] Nevertheless, truly scientific investigation of the Scriptures must aim to be as objective as possible by taking all phenomena into consideration and yet being aware of one's subjective limitations.

G. B. Gray's argument that 10:20-27 must be late, because Isaiah "would not allow fine poems to dribble out in prose conclusions"[400] is hardly convincing. In the first place 10:20-23 must be separated from the following. Secondly, some scholars have indeed considered 10:20-23 as poetry.[401] Whether poetry or not one can hardly deny Isaianic authorship on account of its supposed prose. G. B. Gray himself admits that "Isaiah wrote prose as well as poetry, . . ."[402] It is probable that

---

[398]Fey, op. cit., p. 126 n. 1.

[399]Duhm as quoted by Whitehouse, Isaiah, p. 167. This statement is omitted in the later editions of Duhm's commentary.

[400]Gray, Isaiah, I, 203.

[401]See Kaiser, Jesaja, p. 117; Fohrer, Jesaja, I, 159-60; the Jerusalem Bible takes vss. 20-21 as poetry. Kissane, Isaiah, I, 125, considers it as poetry placing vss. 20-23 before 11:1.

[402]Gray, Isaiah, I, 203.

10:20-23 is an independent saying placed here for reasons to be discussed below. The present position of this oracle hardly provides a well-founded basis upon which definite conclusions concerning the authorship of this pericope can be reached.[403]

Time and again the argument has been advanced that 10:20-23 reflects historical inaccuracy.[404] We may cite as a case in point B. Duhm's much quoted epigram: "Ahaz trusted in Assyria (2 Ki 16), but was not beaten; Hezekiah was beaten but did not trust in Assyria."[405] This statement is certainly true but it juxtaposes historical events to which this oracle does not seem to refer. The statement upon which B. Duhm reflects is a phrase in 10:20, namely to "lean upon him that smote them." If this phrase is interpreted to refer to Tiglath-Pileser's campaign which broke up the Syro-Ephraimitic coalition, then there would be some serious historical difficulty.[406] But a good

---

[403]Against Steuernagel, Einleitung, p. 481; cf. supra, n. 394.

[404]Cheyne, Introduction, p. 52: "The passage is also in no vital relation to the facts of Isaiah's time . . . it is deficient in historical accuracy." Gray, Isaiah, I, 203: "The writer is oblivious of the chronology of Isaiah's age." S. H. Blank, "Traces of Prophetic Agony in Isaiah," HUCA, XXVII (1956), 88: "10:20-23 /is/ out of context in the writings of the eighth century Isaiah . . . /and is/ perfectly at home in a different historical context." Kaiser, Jesaja, pp. 117-8, argues that it is difficult to ascribe 10:20-23 to Isaiah, because there are no words preserved from him which go beyond the year 701. Kaiser's argument is rather weak because 1:4-9 are admittedly "from the year 701 or shortly thereafter" (p. 5). Cf. Wright, Isaiah, p. 14, who places the close of Isaiah's ministry down in 690 B.C.

[405]Duhm, Jesaja, p. 101.

[406]Kaiser, Jesaja, p. 117, points out against Steinmann's attempt to place this saying in the year 738 B.C. when Menahem paid tribute to Tiglath-Pileser that at that time the Assyrians did not smite Israel, because no battle took place.

number of scholars point out that this is not the historical situation which this phrase describes. Judah had been a dependency of Assyria since 734/33 B.C. when Ahaz called upon Tiglath-Pileser for aid against the threat of the Syro-Ephraimitic league. But Judah itself had not felt the blow of the Assyrian military force before 701 B.C. In that year Judah suffered tremendous losses of land and people so that Hezekiah surrendered to Sennacherib and acceded to his demands.[407] The national policy of Judah was again oriented to "him that smote them" (vs. 20).[408] There can be hardly any doubt but that the events of 701 B.C. provide the context for the historical allusions of this saying. If this is granted it appears that the oracle of 10:20-23 dates from the time of Isaiah, i.e., shortly after the events of 701 B.C.[409] There are then

---

[407]See 2 Ki. 18:13-27; Isa. 36:1-22.

[408]A number of interpreters understand the phrase "will no more lean upon him that smote them" to refer to the Syro-Ephraimitic war when Assyria smote Ephraim and subsequently date 10:20-23 to that period (cf. von Orelli, Jesaja, p. 56; Danell, op. cit., p. 175; Kissane, Isaiah, I, 127; Kuhl, op. cit., p. 77; Rehm, op. cit., p. 189). But here Duhm, Jesaja, p. 101, is correct in pointing out that Ahaz leaned for support on Assyria but was not smitten. That this does not refer to Ahaz and his time is obvious from the expression that they "will lean upon Yahweh" (10:20c). Ahaz did certainly not lean upon Yahweh.

[409]So H. Schmidt, Die grossen Propheten, p. 111-2; de Vaux, RB, 42 (1933), 529 n. 5; Bewer, Isaiah, p. 36; Bright, Isaiah-I, p. 498; Maly, op. cit., pp. 91-2. Giesebrecht, op. cit., p. 71-6, believes that vss. 22-23 are from an earlier period in Isaiah's career and are a later insertion due to Isaiah himself. In the midst of consolation they introduce a discordant note of threatening. Similar suggestions have been put forth more recently. Scott, Isaiah, V, 244, thinks that vss. 22-23 come from the prophet's earliest period and correspond to the ominous tone of the message given him in his original commission. Mauchline, Isaiah, p. 125, believes that these verses come from an earlier stage in the prophet's ministry before the "doctrine of the remnant became prominent." But our study has indicated that the remnant motif was a constituent part right from the beginning of Isaiah's ministry. Leslie, op. cit., pp. 51-2, dates these two verses to the Syro-Ephraimitic war. Giesebrecht, Scott, Mauchline, and Leslie date vss. 20-21 to 701 B.C. In-

thus far no reasons which speak decisively against the Isaianic origin of this oracle. If we are not deceived, it appears that 10:20-23 is a genuine oracle of Isaiah of Jerusalem which he delivered shortly after the events of 701 B.C.

The present position of this independent oracle within an oracle apparently directed against Assyria is probably best explained by the principle of catchword combinations. The term *šeʾār* in 10:19 seems to have been the clue for the placing of 10:20-23 after 10:19, because *šeʾār* appears four times in 10:20ff.[410]

The phrase *šeʾār ʿeṣ* in 10:19 uses a picture which compares Assyria[411] to the trees of a forest which will be left so few in number

---

sofar as the juxtaposition of judgment and salvation appears frequent (cf. 6:13; 1:21-26; 7:2-9, 10-17) there is no need to separate 10:20-23.

[410]On the linking together of oracles by key words, see Scott, *Isaiah*, V, 125; Kaiser, *Jesaja*, p. 118; Rehm, *op. cit*., pp. 188-9; Warne, *op. cit*., p. 96; Whitehouse, *op. cit*., p. 167.

[411]Duhm, *Jesaja*, p. 97, and Kaiser, *Jesaja*, p. 116, suppose that 10:16-19 originated during the time of the Seleucids in the second century B.C. For cogent criticisms of this dating, see Gray, *Isaiah*, I, 203-4, and especially Meinhold, *Studien zur israelitischen Religionsgeschichte*, pp. 139-43. The latter exposes the fallacy of the underlying linguistic reasoning which derived Συρία (=Seleucids) from Ἀσσυρία. Fohrer, *Jesaja*, I, 158, speaks merely of a late date without going into specifics. Budde, *ZAW*, 41 (1923), 194-7, argues against the late date proposed by Fullerton, *op. cit*., 1ff., and proposes that this saying is not directed against Assyria but describes the destruction of Judah from the early period of Isaiah's prophetic activity. This view has been adopted by Procksch, *Jesaja*, p. 169; Eissfeldt, *OTI*, p. 308, 313; Scott, *Isaiah*, V, 243; Becker, *op. cit*., p. 60. On the other hand, there are many scholars who support the view that this is an Isaianic oracle against Assyria: H. Schmidt, *Die grossen Propheten*, pp. 103-5; Boutflower, *op. cit*., pp. 237-8; König, *Jesaja*, pp. 149ff.; Dennefeld, *op. cit*., p. 56; Steinmann, *op. cit*., p. 251-2; Herntrich, *Jesaja*, pp. 197-8; Eichrodt, *Der Heilige in Israel*, pp. 127-8; Bright, *Isaiah-I*, p. 498; Leslie, *op. cit*., p. 107; Wright, *Isaiah*, pp. 46-8; Mauchline, *Isaiah*, p. 124; Muckle, *op. cit*., pp. 43-4; Young, *op. cit*., pp. 364ff.; Kissane, *Isaiah*, I, 125ff.; Ward, *op. cit*., pp. 250ff.; Rehm, *op. cit*., p. 188.

that even a child can write them down.[412] It seems that the threatening and the hopeful aspects of the remnant motif come to expression in 10:19. Assyria will not be completely destroyed, for there will be a "remnant of trees" left. Some trees will indeed remain. These, however, will be so few in number that even a child can write them down. The destruction of the large majority and the survival of at least a few are here intricately connected.

Let us then turn to a discussion of the content of the oracle of 10:20-23. The introductory phrase of the oracle has much the same meaning as the "in that day" in 4:2 and 28:5.[413] In the present passage it seems to refer to a period of time that is still future. At that time Yahweh will be the center of hope for the remnant. If one keeps this future time in which truthful allegiance will be given to Yahweh separated from apocalyptic notions,[414] one is able to interpret this formula eschatologically.[415]

Who are the *šeʾār yiśrāʾēl* which are identified with the parallel

---

[412]The LXX translates καὶ οἱ καταλειφθέντες ἀπ' αὐτῶν which shows that the translator leaves the picture of the forest which is present also in vs. 18, and interprets these words with reference to people. Cf. Ziegler, *Untersuchungen zur Septuaginta*, p. 82.

[413]See the discussions of this introductory formula, *supra*, pp. 260-62.

[414]Johann Michael Schmidt, *Die jüdische Apokalyptik* (Neukirchen-Vluyn, 1969); idem, "Forschung zur jüdischen Apokalyptik," *Verkündigung und Forschung*, 14 (1969), 44-69, has presented most valuable studies regarding the history of research of Jewish apocalyptic which aid an appreciation of apocalyptic as distinguished from eschatology.

[415]With Mowinckel, *He That Cometh*, p. 268 n. 5, and Schunck, *op. cit.*, p. 323, against Wildberger, *SVT*, IX (1963), 112-3.

designation "survivors of the house of Jacob"? G. A. Danell[416] has revived an old interpretation which identifies the "remnant" with Judah.[417] The supporters of this interpretation argue that when the Assyrians destroyed North Israel it was a blow to the existence of the whole of Israel, that is to say to South Israel too. Aside from the historical difficulty which this interpretation places on the phrase which states that they "will no more lean upon him that smote them," there are other insurmountable difficulties. Judah did not stop leaning upon Assyria after the events of 722 B.C. which obliterated the Northern Kingdom. She continued to lean upon Assyria until Sargon II died in 705 B.C. Hezekiah then freed himself from Assyria but did not lean upon Yahweh. He sought an alliance with Egypt. Isaiah repeatedly spoke out against this leaning of Judah upon political pacts and alliances and Judah's refusal to lean upon Yahweh.[418] These difficulties militate against the simple identification of the remnant with Judah, so that this interpretation is virtually impossible. The context shows clearly that on that future day "the remnant of Israel and the survivors of the house of Jacob" will lean upon their God in truth. This qualification points inevitably toward a period that is yet in the future. It is therefore necessary to regard the "remnant" as a future remnant, i.e. a remnant <u>from</u> Israel. We may

---

[416]Danell, <u>op. cit</u>., p. 175.

[417]Giesebrecht, <u>Jesajakritik</u>, pp. 71ff. It is because of this identification that Meinhold, <u>Religionsgeschichte</u>, p. 138, is unable to place this saying into any period of Isaiah's ministry.

[418]Isa. 7:2-9; 7:10-17; 28:14-16; etc.

paraphrase vs. 20 as follows: In the eschatological time after renewed destruction has fallen upon the nation there will be a remnant from Israel left which will reject political alliances and rely in faith upon Yahweh, the Holy One of Israel.

It is obvious that this remnant will be a community of faith. There is an unquestionable correlation between the leaning on Yahweh in "truth" and the demand for "faith" in 7:2-9.[419]

The synonymous use of šeʾār and šeʾērîṯ is paralleled by the identification of "Israel" with the "house of Jacob" (vs. 20). The latter term is typical of eighth century prophecy. It is used by Isaiah[420] and it appears relatively often in the various parts of the book of Isaiah.[421] It is also used by Amos[422] and Micah.[423] It is probably not accidental that the designation "house of Jacob" appears in the Pentateuch aside from Gen. 46:27 only once more in the Sinai pericope (Ex. 19:3). Israel encountered Yahweh's might and his divine help in the Exodus experience. It appears then that the prophet used the designation "house of Jacob" deliberately to call to remembrance that those who

---

[419]Wildberger, ZThK, 65 (1968), 152 n. 110, points out that the אֱמֶת in 10:20, which is usually translated with "truth," may because of its connection with 7:9 be rendered as "faith." See Appendix II, p. 477.

[420]Isa. 2:5; 8:17.

[421]The infrequent designation "house of Jacob" is used remarkably often in the book of Isaiah: 2:5, 6; 8:17; 10:20; 14:1; 29:22; 46:3; 48:1; 58:1, i.e., it appears nine times of the twenty-one times it occurs in the Hebrew Bible in the book of Isaiah.

[422]Amos 3:13; 9:8.

[423]Mic. 2:7; 3:9; cf. 4:2.

lean upon God truthfully and trustingly can count upon the saving action of Yahweh and will also be the inheritors of the election promises connected with the patriarch Jacob.

Vs. 21 explicates vs. 20. The name of Isaiah's oldest son Shear-jashub, is introduced in the form of a sentence which provides a commentary on it. The hopeful aspect of the name comes to expression in the sentence, "A remnant will return." The prophet is certain that there will be a remnant from Israel. The idea of the remnant in this verse serves to provoke hope and, at the same time, is a summons to repentance.[424] The remnant which will return is more closely defined with the "remnant of Jacob." The designation "Jacob" parallels "Israel" in vs. 20. Yet "Jacob" is used again to emphasize the idea that this faithful remnant will be the carrier of the election promises made to this founding father of Israel. However, in typically Isaianic fashion the absolute election promises are made conditional. The election promises are placed in direct correlation with the faithfulness of the elected ones.

The attitude characteristic of the future remnant, namely their leaning upon Yahweh in truth (vs. 20), is now defined as a return to the mighty God. Tersely expressed one can say negatively: no repentance, no remnant. Israel is summoned once more to return to Yahweh, the mighty God. The question with which the prophet here confronts the survivors in Judah after Sennacherib's invasion is this, Will you at least now return in faith, and trust in your God whose covenant guarantees the salvation you desire? The prophet emphatically states that the remnant will

---

[424]Lindblom, Prophecy in Ancient Israel, p. 367 n. 145.

return to ʾel gibôr (cf. 9:5).[425] This term is here used with reference to Yahweh, not to make him a national deity, but to indicate that the Holy One of Israel, who in bringing the promise also brings judgment, is actually a "mighty God." He is the kind of God who evokes trust and faith.

There is no contradiction between 10:20-21 and 10:22-23 as some have supposed on the basis of the opposite meanings of the remnant motif which are developed in the two parts of this oracle.[426] God's judgment is an integral part of his salvation as is evident from Isaiah's inaugural vision (6:5-7). The sequence of thought in 10:20-23 is the same as in 1:27-28. D. M. Warne[427] points out that the juxtaposition of salvation and judgment was used to prevent any misunderstanding of God's promise, whereby the remnant could claim to be a privileged group.

---

[425]For the problem of the meaning of this term in Isa. 9:5, see the detailed discussion of Rehm, op. cit., pp. 153-6, who cites most of the relevant secondary literature. Cf. Becker, op. cit., pp. 22-7, 58-9. Walter Harrelson, "Nonroyal Motifs in Royal Eschatology," Israel's Prophetic Heritage. Essays in honor of James Muilenburg, ed. by B. W. Anderson and W. Harrelson (New York, 1962), p. 153, shows that the prophet has taken the motifs and images with which the coming ruler is described from the early history of Israel, especially the Gideon narrative. The name אל גבור is taken to correspond to Gideon's designation גבור החיל in Jd. 6:12.

[426]Mowinckel, Psalmenstudien II, p. 279, states that 10:22f. is a redaction of exegetical reflection. Lindblom, Prophecy in Ancient Israel, p. 367 n. 145, expresses the opinion that vss. 22f. "are obviously secondary, forming a sort of commentary on the preceding statement. Here the thought is that only a remnant will be saved, presupposing a pessimistic view of the future of Israel. To Isaiah the idea of the remnant serves to evoke hope. . . ." Procksch, Jesaja, p. 171: "Dort herrscht Optimismus, hier Pessimismus." These three scholars work with the theory that all true remnant passages in Isaiah are positive in tone. They fail to recognize that Isaiah's remnant motif contains both positive and negative aspects.

[427]Warne, op. cit., p. 98.

The ominous tone of vs. 20 is obvious. The prophet seems to speak in direct address to Israel, i.e., the dead patriarch, thereby declaring to the living Israelites that what God had formerly promised, namely to make them as the sand of the sea,[428] will not prevent him from bringing about a decisive end to Israel's national existence. This is the second time Isaiah refers to the Abraham cycle in connection with the negative aspect of the remnant motif.[429] This too is typically Isaianic. The original motif of promise has been made conditional. No matter how many there will be in number not more than a mere remnant of them will be left, because the multitude is unwilling to return to Yahweh. The principle herein stated is for the purpose of confuting a false reliance upon the election promise given first to Abraham (Gen. 22:17) and repeated to Jacob (Gen. 32:13). It will not do to have physical, patriarchal ancestry in order to be spared in the future judgment.[430]

Destruction is decreed for the multitude of the people (vs. 22b). The issue is whether Israel would take the occasion for a renewal of faithful obedience. The decisive annihilation announced in vs. 23 points to the end of national existence, the end of an era, but not the end of life and existence for all Israelites. With this oracle of doom the prophet exhorted his listeners to choose now for God and thus for their own future. In his judgment Yahweh of hosts would save those who return

---

[428]Cf. Gen. 22:17; 32:13.

[429]In Isa. 1:9 Sodom and Gomorrah is mentioned.

[430]Young, op. cit., p. 370. Young is not right in the view that when Israel will have become as the sand of the sea that only then a remnant will return. If our dating of the present oracle is correct, then Israel was no longer like the sand of the sea, but a very diminished nation.

to him, but bring utter annihilation for those who refused.

The juxtaposition of salvation and judgment in 10:20-23 appears to be in complete harmony with Isaiah's proclamation and theology. The terminology and movement of thought are Isaianic too. The twofold aspect of the remnant motif accords with Isaiah's usage of the remnant motif. The historical situation befits the time of 701 B.C. There seems to be no decisive reason which would lead us to believe that 10:20-23 is not from Isaiah of Jerusalem. In this oracle Isaiah made explicit certain aspects which were implicit from the early part of his ministry. The motif of faith which was always so intricately connected with the remnant motif has now an explicit object. It is faith in Yahweh. This was certainly implied in 7:1ff. and 28:14-16. The motif of returning became explicitly a return to Yahweh, the mighty God.

Another oracle from the prophet's late period of ministry points to a new future. The promise of 37:30-32 reads as follows:

30 And this shall be the sign for you:
This year will be eaten the aftergrowth,[431]
and in the second year the wild growth;[432]

---

[431]The word סָפִיחַ occurs elsewhere only in Lev. 25:5, 11, where it refers to the grain that grows of itself on the sabbatical year when no regular sowing took place.

[432]KB, p. 654, connects the hapax legomenon שָׁחִיס with סָחִישׁ of the parallel account in 2 Ki. 19:29 to mean "grain that shoots up of itself in the second year." John Gray, I & II Kings (Philadelphia, 1963), p. 628 n. a, takes the term of 2 Ki. 19:29 from the one in Isa., pointing out that שָׁחִיס may be a cognate with Arabic šahasa, the second form of which means "to miss the target." Hence the Hebrew term may mean grain from seed which has fallen in waste places. Gray, therefore, translates "random growth." Both Fohrer, Jesaja, II, 178, and Eichrodt, Herr der Geschichte, p. 234, translate "Wildwuchs." This is also the suggested meaning of Scott, Isaiah, V, 370: "what grows wild." The Jerusalem Bible reads "what sprouts in the fallow."

but in the third year sow and reap,
plant vineyards and eat[433] their fruit.
31 And the survivors of the house of Judah, those who were left,[434]
shall again take root below, and bear fruit above;
32 For from Jerusalem shall go forth a remnant,
and survivors from Mount Zion.[435]
The zeal of Yahweh of hosts shall accomplish this.[436]

This prose oracle is generally regarded as Isaianic.[437] A number

---

[433]BHK and BHS suggest the reading וְאָכְלוּ with 2 Ki. 19:29 instead of וְאָכוֹל. The Qere, ואכלו, supports this suggestion. 1QIs^a has ואכולו which seems to support again 2 Ki. 19:29 and the Qere.

[434]It is surprising that BHS omitted the significant substitution of the Masoretic feminine adjectival modifier הנשארה with והנמצה in 1QIs^a. This substantive is coordinated by a connective ו with the previous subject of the sentence to form a compound subject. The variant ואספה in 1QIs^a as compared to the Masoretic ויספה may be nothing more than a different spelling. There is also the omission of the prepositional ל before מעלה. All in all, the reading of 1QIs^a 37:31 differs from the traditional text in wording, structure, and content. S. Iwry, "והנמצא- A Striking Variant Reading in 1QIs^a," Textus, V (1966), 34-43, argues that the substitution of the substantive for the adjectival modifier looks more like an intelligent gloss than a mere alteration brought about by remote analogy. Iwry investigated the root מצא and suggested on the basis of usages in Chronicles, 2 Kings, and Ezra that the noun נמצא means "'one that is left over,' 'a survivor,' 'one in captivity,' 'a refugee'"(p. 42). The usage of this substantive in 1QIs^a implies that deliverance and regeneration will come not only to the remnant of Judah (in Jerusalem) but to any exiled survivor of Israel. Thus he rightly proposes that this textual variant is a secondary gloss and that the Masoretic text is superior.

[435]1QIs^a has "Jerusalem" and "Mount Zion" in reverse order!

[436]The translation is by the present writer.

[437]So virtually all commentaries. In the last decade of the past century Cheyne, Introduction, pp. 223-4, argued that it is post-Isaianic, because "the ideas and phraseology are not Isaianic." The phrase "house of Judah" supposedly takes the place of Isaiah's "house of Jacob." But Cheyne argues on insufficient grounds. Out of the six appearances of "house of Jacob" Cheyne assigns 2:5, 6; 10:20; 14:1; 29:22 to a late date and only 8:17 to the time of Isaiah. If Isaiah used only once, according to Cheyne, "house of Jacob," he could likewise use once "house of Judah." A single usage of a certain designation does not make it more Isaianic than another designation of similar meaning. Instead the sequence of "Judah . . . Jerusalem" is typically Isaianic, cf. 3:8; 22:21; 36:7. J. Gray, I & II Kings, p. 628, points to "the fact that in

of scholars suggest that it derives from Sennacherib's second invasion of Judah, which cannot have taken place before 690/89 B.C.[438]

---

two other oracles of Isaiah where relief is promised, Isa. 7:14-16 and Isa. 20, a three-year interval is figuratively suggested as here" which indicates the Isaianic origin of 37:30-32. Cheyne, Introduction, p. 224, suggests that "the high honor given to the 'remnant' and to Jerusalem is in accordance with the later eschatology; . . ." J. Gray, I & II Kings, p. 629, on the other hand, points out that "the conception of the remnant is characteristic of Isaiah of Jerusalem, . . ." Our investigation up to this point has shown this to be correct. Hardly anyone would doubt that Isaiah had much to say about Jerusalem. Fohrer, Jesaja, II, 185, is according to the present writer's knowledge, the only recent commentator who believes that 37:30-32 is non-Isaianic. He believes much like Cheyne that the eschatology reflected in this passage is late. Fohrer, of course, argues that Isaiah has no eschatology and no hopeful remnant motif. Duhm, Jesaja, p. 273, believes that 37:30 is genuine but vss. 31-32 are non-Isaianic, because the remnant terminology is eschatological as in 4:2. We have shown above that 4:2-3 does not contain any ideas and concepts which would make an Isaianic authorship impossible. As the eschatological ideas of 37:30-32 are best treated along with our discussion of this oracle. A selective list of the large number of supporters of Isaiah's authorship may include the following: Skinner, Isaiah, p. 291; Mowinckel, Psalmenstudien II, p. 278; König, Jesaja, p. 310; Procksch, Jesaja, p. 458; Hertzberg, op. cit., p. 126; Schilling, op. cit., p. 74; Danell, op. cit., pp. 185-6; Bewer, Isaiah, p. 94; Scott, Isaiah, V, 369; idem, The Relevance of the Prophets, p. 81; Heschel, The Prophets, p. 83; Lindblom, Prophecy in Ancient Israel, p. 467; J. Gray, I & II Kings, pp. 628-9; Leslie, op. cit., p. 95; Harrelson, Interpreting the Old Testament, p. 244; Eissfeldt, OTI, p. 329; Wright, Isaiah, pp. 81-2; Eichrodt, Herr der Geschichte, p. 247.

[438]Among the supporters of a two-invasion theory are Bright, A History of Israel, pp. 282-7; idem, Isaiah-I, pp. 514-5; Wright, Isaiah, pp. 18-9, 80-1; J. Gray, I & II Kings, p. 623; Harrelson, Interpreting the Old Testament, p. 244f.; etc. For a full bibliography of treatments on the subject up to 1926, see Leo L. Honor, Sennacherib's Invasion of Palestine (New York, 1926), pp. 117-22. For more recent discussions, see H. H. Rowley, "Hezekiah's Reform and Rebellion," BJRL, XLIV (1962), 404-6, and footnotes there, also Siegfried H. Horn, "Did Sennacherib Campaign Once or Twice Against Hezekiah," AUSS, IV (1966), 1-28. Child's, Isaiah and the Assyrian Crisis, pp. 11-18, 69-103, 120, is a very ardent supporter of a one-invasion theory. In the present writer's opinion he has not been able to show conclusively that only a one-invasion theory is possible or absolutely called for. His form-critical study did not contribute significantly towards the solution of the historical problem. Furthermore, he has not been able to meet all the problems involved in the one-invasion theory nor has he been able to answer many of the objections raised against it. We are grateful to him for having

This suggestion is probably correct.[439]

The "sign" (ʾôṯ) here is not, as often in the Hebrew Bible, a miracle.[440] It is employed in typically Isaianic fashion (cf. 7:10ff.; 8:1).[441] It serves as guarantee for the predicted departure of Sennacherib in order to encourage, support, and assure Hezekiah that the time of hardship will come to an end. By the third year the threat to the existence and life of "the survivors of the house of Judah" (pᵉlêṭāṯ bêṯ-yehûḏāh) will be removed and sustenance will again come forth in its normal way.

It is significant that Isaiah uses the name Judah to identify the survivors more closely. He does not use the name Israel. This may probably be taken as an indication that the prophet does not here refer to the purified remnant of the future[442] and that he considered Judah to have passed, at least partially, through the process of decimation which he was shown in his call vision (6:11-13b). Much of what had been re-

---

reminded us again of the complex nature of the historical problems and for his attempt to get at the problem from a different angle.

[439]No problems are posed with regard to the present location of this prose oracle. Scott, Isaiah, V, 369, suggests that vss. 30-32 should come between vs. 35 and vs. 36 of this chapter. This had already been proposed by von Orelli, Jesaja, p. 130, who cites Köhler and Klostermann. Leslie, op. cit., p. 95, follows Scott. Eichrodt, Herr der Geschichte, p. 247, places vss. 30-32 after vs. 34. He considers vs. 35 as a later insertion.

[440]The following passages may serve as examples: Ex. 7:3; 10:1-2; Nu. 14:11; Deut. 6:22; 7:19; 11:3; Pss. 65:9; 105:27.

[441]Cf. Rehm, op. cit., pp. 117f.

[442]With Kissane, Isaiah, I, 401, against Bright, The Kingdom of God, pp. 90-1, who believes that Isaiah had hoped that these "survivors of the house of Judah" would turn out to be the purified remnant which Yahweh would bless.

vealed to Isaiah in this inaugural vision had come to pass: The enemy was in the land, the nation experienced decimation, yet survivors, "those who remained" (hannᵉš'ārāh) of the house of Judah, had been left over. The nation had not yet come to a full end. Though the escaped survivors take root and bear fruit, they are not the "holy seed" (6:13c). Isaiah did not simply identify the future remnant with this decimated nation.

About a decade earlier when the first siege of Jerusalem was lifted after the Judean countryside had gone through a most terrible devastation not a thought was given to the God whose judgment it was and whose purpose had brought it to pass (22:1-14).[443] On that glad day when the Assyrian army lifted the choking siege the people celebrated on the rooftops with wild joy, banqueting and carousing, but with never a thought to the God who had saved them or for the repentance to which he had been trying to drive them. Isaiah observed the people's reaction and cried

---

[443]While most commentators assign 22:1-14 to the period of Sennacherib's first invasion, the exact circumstances are much debated. Recently Scott, Isaiah, V, 289, followed by Leslie, op. cit., p. 69, supposes a date of 711 B.C. and interprets 22:1-14 as a revelry on the brink of disaster. While this interpretation is not entirely impossible, the present writer agrees with those who see here the rejoicing over deliverance, see Skinner, Isaiah, p. 175; Gray, Isaiah, I, 364; Steuernagel, Einleitung, p. 492; König, op. cit., p. 219; Bright, Isaiah-I, p. 504; Mauchline, Isaiah, pp. 171-2; Wright, Isaiah, p. 62; Eichrodt, Herr der Geschichte, p. 93; Fohrer, Jesaja, I, 249; Heaton, The Hebrew Kingdoms, pp. 342-3; Ward, op. cit., p. 230. Childs, Assyrian Crisis, p. 26, is very cautious with regard to the dating of 22:1-14, which he considers on form-critical grounds as a unity consistent with the Isaianic invective-threat pattern. He feels that 22:1-14 simply does not provide the necessary information which would allow it to be related directly to a known historical event. Yet he believes that the lifting of the siege of Jerusalem produced wild rejoicing (p. 27). It should, of course, not be ruled out entirely that 22:1-14 could even date from the period after the second invasion.

out with bitterness, "Surely this iniquity will not be forgiven you till you die" (22:14). This word of Yahweh was not repealed.

The nation experienced another onslaught of Assyrian military might. Still some survivors of the house of Judah escaped. They are a historical remnant. A number of times Isaiah speaks of such a historical remnant (6:13ab; 1:8-9; 30:17). The historical usage of the remnant motif must not be confused with the eschatological remnant of the future. These are related but not identical aspects of the remnant motif as used by Isaiah of Jerusalem. The future remnant will emerge or go forth from the historical remnant of the decimated nation which will again undergo judgment. This appears to be the thought of vs. 32. The very reason why the historical remnant, the escaped survivors of the house of Judah, must take root and bear fruit is to make it possible that from them a *š^{e}ʾērîṯ* i.e., the future remnant, shall go forth (*tēṣēh*). The prophet used here the feminine noun *š^{e}ʾērîṯ* instead of the masculine *š^{e}ʾār* because of the chiastic parallel *p^{e}lêṭāh* which is also feminine.[444]

The future remnant will come forth from Zion/Jerusalem. Some have seen here a reference to the spreading out of the Judeans to the countryside.[445] However, it is entirely consistent with Isaiah's proclamation

---

[444]So Procksch, *Jesaja*, p. 458. Whenever a noun of the root is used in the Hebrew Bible with the noun פְּלֵיטָה it is invariably the feminine noun שְׁאֵרִית and not שְׁאָר (cf. Gen. 45:7; Isa. 30:32=2 Ki. 19:31, Isa. 15:9; 1 Chr. 4:43; Ezr. 9:14). The only exception is Isa. 10:20 where the formula שְׁאָר יִשְׂרָאֵל appears parallel to פְּלֵיטַת בֵּית־יַעֲקֹב. The use of שְׁאָר in 10:20 instead of שְׁאֵרִית is due to the stereotyped formula שְׁאָר יִשְׂרָאֵל. The usage of שְׁאֵרִית with פְּלֵיטָה in 37:30 is therefore entirely normal and consistent with the practice of other Old Testament writers and cannot be used as an argument against the genuineness of this oracle as Cheyne, *Introduction*, p. 224, proposes.

[445]Procksch, *Jesaja*, p. 458; Kissane, *Isaiah*, I, 401; Leslie, *op. cit.*, p. 95.

and theology to interpret vs. 32 differently. The escaped survivors of the house of Judah which reside in Jerusalem are the vital nucleus out of which the future remnant will go forth. Isaiah encouraged and assured Hezekiah by the "sign" that through God's grace sustenance will be forthcoming for the escaped survivors, i.e., the historical remnant. The implied purpose is to give them another opportunity to turn to Yahweh in faith in order to make it possible for Yahweh to spare them in the purging process of the future judgment par excellence. The invasion of Sennacherib serves as another warning judgment of Yahweh. Isaiah knows that not all will even now turn to Yahweh in faith. But the hope of the future lies with the few faithful ones who will heed God's promptings. They will emerge from the escaped survivors of the house of Judah as the future remnant[446] that will go forth from Zion/Jerusalem.

Though Zion/Jerusalem is the center of renewal for the people who hold on to the covenant faith when the storm has passed, the prophet does not appear to speak in this prose oracle of the military or political inviolability of Zion/Jerusalem.[447] He did prophesy that the future remnant will go forth[448] from Zion/Jerusalem, i.e, from the residence of the

---

[446]Bright, The Kingdom of God, p. 91, is therefore not right when he states, "The Remnant hope, then,could have nothing to do with the actual nation, . . ." Isaiah's remnant motif is intricately connected with the actual nation insofar as the future remnant will emerge out of the nation. This does not mean, of course, that Isaiah did not predict national ruin.

[447]On the various aspects of the Zion tradition especially as reflected in the Psalmic materials, see Sidney L. Kelly, Jr., "The Zion-Victory Songs: Psalms 46, 48, and 76" (unpublished Ph.D. dissertation, Vanderbilt University, 1968).

[448]The "going forth" of 37:32 is not identical with the "going forth" of 2:3b. In the latter verse תּוֹרָה and דְּבַר־יהוה will go

escaped survivors of the house of Judah. God's support for the continued existence of the community formed by faith in Yahweh and characterized by their righteous and just deeds is expressed in the last line of this oracle: "The zeal of Yahweh of hosts shall accomplish this" (37:32b).[449] It is not merely human skill and power that will bring this about; it is divine initiative, the quality of the zeal of Yahweh, his ardent interest in his people, by which Isaiah explains the emergence of the future remnant. According to 1:21-26 the inhabitants of Zion/Jerusalem will meet with judgment. The purging fire will leave a purged remnant, which will be the carriers of the election traditions connected with the Zion motif.[450] In the same early period of his prophetic ministry Isaiah proclaimed that the remnant in Zion/Jerusalem "shall be called holy" (4:3). The purged remnant of 1:21-26 and the holy remnant residing in Zion/Jerusalem of 4:2-3[451] are identical. They are, however, not the same as the escaped survivors of the house of Judah of 37:31. The former are identical with the future remnant of 37:32 that will go forth from the escaped survivors of the house of Judah in Zion/Jerusalem. It is not at all contradictory for Isaiah to prophesy the ruin of Judah and at the same time to speak of the future remnant which will go forth from Zion/Jerusalem. The prophet appears to stress that the utter punishment of

---

forth, while here the שְׁאֵרִית and פְּלֵיטָה will go forth. It is obviously impossible to equate both.

[449] Scott, Isaiah, V, 370, states that "this last line is appropriate in the present context . . . but is not so in 9:7, where an editor has copied it from this passage." Cheyne, Introduction, p. 244, says that vs. 32b is a "verbal quotation" from 9:6. Scott is correct in stressing that vs. 32b is appropriate in the present context.

[450] Supra, pp. 251ff.

[451] Supra, pp. 257ff.

the nation for its sins does not remove from Yahweh's hands the power to transform Zion/Jerusalem into the center of the faithful remnant of the future. This glorious hope expressed by Isaiah is an affirmation of trust in Yahweh's power and his determination to fulfill his promise to Israel and to work out his purpose for his people. It is also a summons to his hearers to join into this trusting relationship with Yahweh. Yahweh will not be defeated in Israel's ruin; he will make his future remnant go forth from Zion/Jerusalem, i.e., from those few escaped survivors of the house of Judah that are left in the old Davidic city.

The last passage in which the remnant motif occurs in connection with Israel is the oracle of salvation of 11:10-16, which, by reason of its style, terminology, and ideas, is generally regarded as post-Isaianic.[452] On the other hand, there have been scholars who have seen no decisive reason to deny the authenticity of this oracle.[453] Since the remnant terminology is present only in vs. 11 and vs. 16 it is possible to limit our discussion to the interpretation of these two verses

---

[452]Since B. Stade rejected in the year 1883 the Isaianic authorship of the end of the so-called book of Immanuel, namely 11:10-12:6, many scholars have followed him in considering 11:10-16 as deriving from a later period, in the case of some indeed from a much later period. Cf. Giesebrecht, Jesajakritik, pp. 25-52; Cheyne, Introduction, pp. 59-67; Eissfeldt, OTI, p. 317; etc.

[453]August Dillmann, Der Prophet Jesaja (Leipzig, 1890), p. 121; Driver, An Introduction to the Literature of the Old Testament, pp. 210-1; von Orelli, Jesaja, pp. 54-5; König, Jesaja, p. 169; Schilling, op. cit., p. 68; Danell, op. cit., pp. 176-9; Slotki, op. cit., pp. 57ff.; Buber, Prophetic Faith, p. 148; Kaufmann, The Religion of Israel, pp. 390-1; Kissane, Isaiah, I, 138-9, considers vss. 11-12, 15-16 as non-genuine; Mauchline, Isaiah, pp. 130-2; Scharbert, Propheten Israels, p. 340, considers vss. 11, 15-16 as genuine; Young, op. cit., pp. 394ff.; Wright, Isaiah, leaves the question of authenticity open. See Appendix II, pp. 477-78.

which are most closely related to each other in thought.

11 In that day the Lord will raise his hand a second time[454]
to redeem the remnant of his people[455]
which is left from[456] Assyria, and from Egypt,
and from Pathros, and from Cush,[457] and from Elam,
and from Shinar, and from Hamath, and from the
coastlands of the sea.[458]

16 And there will be a highway for the remnant of his people,
which is left from Assyria,
as there was for Israel
in the day when they came up from the
land of Egypt.[459]

---

[454]The LXX reads τοῦ δεῖξαι. Von Orelli, Jesaja, p. 54, adds לִשְׁלֹחַ. BHK emends שֵׁנִית to שְׂאֵת in order to supply the somewhat weak יוֹסִיף with a verb. BHS suggests that שֵׁנוֹת should be read for שֵׁנִית. The LXX reading does not point directly to שְׂאֵת, but its reading could be introduced to fill the brachylogy. It is hardly likely that a scribal error can produce the difficult שֵׁנִית from the simple שְׂאֵת as BHK implies. In any case the lectio difficilor would more likely be the original. The emendation of שֵׁנוֹת is a tempting suggestion, because the confusion of ו and י is not infrequent. However, this expression is not otherwise attested in the Old Testament. 1QIs[a] seems to support the MT, but the vertical stroke of the י is unusually long so as to leave open the possibility of a ו (cf. M. Burrows, ed. The Dead Sea Scrolls of St. Mark's Monastery, Vol. I, Plate X). It appears that the most natural explanation is that in the expression שָׁלַח יָדוֹ the verb can possibly be omitted as understood (cf. König, Jesaja, p. 165; Duhm, Jesaja, p. 109). Young, op. cit., p. 395 n. 23, points to a somewhat similar usage in the Hittite Annals of Muršiliš II, col. III, 58: da-a-an KAŠ-ŠI nam-ma pa-a-un = "for the second time again I went."

[455]The RSV translates "the remnant which is left of his people." It seems better, however, not to tear apart the phrase "the remnant of his people."

[456]The Jerusalem Bible translates "from the exile of" for which there is no textual basis.

[457]The RSV translates Ethiopia. Kaiser, Jesaja, p. 130, suggests Nubia.

[458]Many commentators delete וּמֵאִיֵּי הַיָּם, because it is missing in the LXX (cf. Procksch, Jesaja, p. 156; Leslie, op. cit., p. 247; etc.). Its presence in 1QIs[a] supports the MT.

[459]The translation is by the present writer. A difficult question is whether or not these verses are poetic or prose. The decisive

The introductory formula "in that day" is used here in the same way as in the remnant passage of 10:20 (cf. 4:2; 28:5). The reference to the future action of Yahweh is not an alien element in the message of Isaiah of Jerusalem. It seems to be significant that there is a correlation between the day of God's future action and the day of God's past action for Israel in vs. 16. This thematic correspondence between Heilszeit and Urzeit is an Isaianic notion which is also very prominent in the pericope of 1:21-26[460] in which the remnant motif is also prominent. In 1:21ff. Isaiah points out that the time of the future remnant will correspond to the ideal time of the past; in 11:11ff. God will act in the future for "the remnant of his people" in the same mighty manner in which he had acted in the past for the salvation of Israel of old. Though the occasions of God's action may not be the same, the ideological schema is identical.

One of the crucial questions revolves around the meaning of God's

---

argument against the genuineness of 11:10-16 is according to Cheyne, Introduction, p. 62, the sudden disappearance of "the beautiful metre of vss. 1-8." It is the prose of these verses which decides for Cheyne that 11:10-16 is post-Isaianic, while all other arguments are undecisive. Similarly Kissane, Isaiah, I, 138-9, rejects vss. 11-12, 15-16, because they are written in prose. Gray, Isaiah, I, 222, discusses the question of prose versus poetry of this section pointing out the disagreement among scholars. He decides that 11:9-11, 16 are prose. The RSV seems to follow Marti in taking 11:12-16 as poetry. Kissane, Isaiah, I, 135ff., considers only vss. 10, 13-14, as poetry. The Jerusalem Bible treats the whole section as poetry as does Fohrer, Jesaja, I, 170-1; Kaiser, Jesaja, pp. 130-1; Leslie, op. cit., pp. 247-8; Eichrodt, Der Heilige in Israel, p. 144. This difference of opinion as to whether there is here actually prose makes it impossible to build an argument for or against Isaianic authorship. There is, of course, no doubt about the observation that Isaiah wrote prose as well as poetry.

[460] Supra, pp. 253ff.

recovering "the remnant of his people" a second time (vs. 11a). Many interpreters think that the prophet refers to a second ingathering of exiles after the first return had taken place in the days of Zerubbabel and Ezra.[461] This interpretation is possible only if 11:11 (or 11:11-16) is placed very late in the post-exilic period.[462] But since there are weighty arguments--to be mentioned in the following paragraphs--against such a late post-exilic date, a more probable explanation will be proposed. J. Bright, who himself suggests a post-exilic date, points out that "there is no necessary implication that a return from exile has already taken place; . . ."[463] This is correct. The assumption that "second time" refers to a second ingathering of exiles is not supported by the text. The context makes clear the fact that the first time in which Yahweh recovered his people was the exodus deliverance to which vs. 16 refers.[464] The "second time" then refers to a new action of God which corresponds to the exodus deliverance.

---

[461]Duhm, Jesaja, p. 109; Eichrodt, Der Heilige in Israel, p. 145; Leslie, op. cit., p. 248; Kaiser, Jesaja, p. 131; Fohrer, Jesaja, I, 171; etc.

[462]Duhm, Jesaja, p. 110, proposes the date of 170-160 B.C. for 11:11-16. Kaiser, Jesaja, pp. 131-2, thinks of the time of the Seleucids. M. Treves, "Little Prince Pele-Joez," VT, XVII (1967), 464-77, assigns all of 11:1-12:6 to the years 170-163 B.C. Such late dates are virtually impossible because of the date of 1QIs[a].

[463]Bright, Isaiah-I, p. 499.

[464]Direct or indirect references to the Exodus tradition are relatively rare in the book of Isaiah. Direct references of the exodus from Egypt appear in 10:24-26 and 11:15-16; indirect references appear in 4:3-6 and in Chapter 35. All of these passages are of disputed authorship. Yet it is not impossible for Isaiah of Jerusalem to have referred to this great Israelite election tradition. Cf. Rohland, op. cit., pp. 112-8.

There can be no doubt but that the exile of the Northern Kingdom is postulated by the references to Assyria (vss. 11, 16). But the other important nation which is repeatedly mentioned is Egypt and not Babylon as one would expect if the exile also of Judah were postulated. Judah's exile in Babylon is not even so certainly intimated as some scholars seem to think. Admittedly "the remnant of his people" are not only gathered from Assyria and Egypt, the two main places of deportation and refuge (vs. 16), but also from other areas. An identification of these areas is important. Pathros is a designation for Upper Egypt.[465] Cush refers to the southern part of Egypt which is more or less equivalent with modern Ethiopia. Elam seems to designate the territory east of Babylonia.[466] Shinar appears to refer to Babylonia known anciently as Sumer and Akkad.[467] It should, however, be pointed out that as far as the present writer is aware there is no cuneiform record in which Shinar appears as a designation for Babylonia.[468] Hamath is a city located on the Orontes River in North Syria. The expression "coastlands of the sea" refers to the indented coast and islands of the Mediterranean. G. B. Gray said that the latter phrase is "never used by Isaiah of Jerusalem, [but] is a favorite with Deutero-Isaiah, . . ."[469] As a matter of fact, the expression

---

[465] T. O. Lambdin, "Pathros," IDB, III, 676.

[466] Bright, Isaiah-I, p. 499.

[467] T. Jasobson, "Shinar," IDB, IV, 332.

[468] Speiser, Genesis, pp. 67, 106, points out that in Gen. 10:10; 11:2; 14:2, 9 the Hebrew term is equivalent to the cuneiform šumer(u), "Sumer."

[469] Gray, Isaiah, I, 226.

"coastlands of the sea" occurs only in 11:11 and 24:15 and never in the latter portions of the book of Isaiah.[470]

Some hold that this long enumeration of places from Pathros to the end of vs. 11 is an editorial expansion due to the desire to list names of the later diaspora in Seleucid Syria and Ptolemaic Egypt.[471] This seems hardly likely in view of Y. Kaufmann's emphasis that in Hebrew there is no basis for understanding Assyria and Egypt as Seleucid Syria and Ptolemaic Egypt respectively.[472] He argues that in late Biblical literature the land that is east of the Euphrates may be called Assyria and Babylonia,[473] but that no writer designates the land west of the Euphrates as Assyria or Babylonia. Since the Seleucid capital of Antiochia was in the west, the Seleucid kingdom is never styled Assyria.

The enumeration of territories in vs. 11b seems to be related to the two main places of Assyria and Egypt. One may wonder whether or not some of these territories are actual provinces of Assyria and Egypt mentioned in reversed order. Pathros and Cush seem to refer to Egypt.[474] Elam, Shinar, and Hamath were tributaries of Assyria.[475] The fact that

---

[470]The plural "isles" alone is found fifteen times in the various parts of the so-called First, Second, and Third Isaiah.

[471]Duhm, Jesaja, p. 109: "V. 11b zählt die Länder der Diaspora auf, . . . die einzelnen Provinzen des seleucidischen und des ptolemäischen Reiches. . . ." König, Jesaja, p. 169; Fohrer, Jesaja, I, 171 n. 98; Kraeling, Commentary on the Prophets, II, 82.

[472]Kaufmann, The Religion of Israel, p. 350 n. 2.

[473]Ezr. 5:13; 6:22; Neh. 13:6.

[474]So Danell, op. cit., p. 176.

[475]So Mauchline, Isaiah, p. 130.

Babylon is neither specifically mentioned nor clearly intimated is the most serious obstacle to a post-exilic date for the passage under discussion.[476] Those considerations make a pre-exilic date more probable than a date when the name Babylon could not have been omitted. If there is then no other way to interpret this passage but to go back to pre-exilic times, the time of Isaiah is no more impossible than the time of Jeremiah. The emphasis on deportees from Israel and Judah makes a date in the latest period of Isaiah's work more likely than one in his earlier ministry.

It is impossible to disprove that in Isaiah's time scattered Israelites were to be found in all the territories mentioned in vs. 11. The well-known Assyrian practice of deporting tribes and peoples does not make it impossible that Tiglath-Pileser III, Sargon II, and Sennacherib may have settled their Israelite and Judean captives in Assyria and territories tributary to Assyria. It was an Assyrian practice to resettle conquered territories with deportees. Though there is no mention in the Hebrew Bible of Israelites having gone into captivity in Egypt, this possibility should not be ruled out entirely. An Egyptian expedition against Judah and Israel is reported from as early as the time of Rehoboam.[477] From the days of David and Solomon Egypt had provided asylum for hard-pressed men of Judah and for political adversaries.[478] During

---

[476]Danell, op. cit., pp. 176-7; Mauchline, Isaiah, p. 132.

[477]1 Ki. 14:25-28. According to Egyptian sources, Shishak (=Sheshonk) I, also invaded Israel, see ARE, IV, #709-22; ANET[3], pp. 263-4; Martin Noth, Könige I (BKAT, IX/1; Neukirchen-Vluyn, 1968), pp. 330-2; B. Mazar, "The Campaign of the Pharaoh Sheshonk to Palestine," SVT, IV (1957), 57-66.

[478]1 Ki. 11:14-25, 26-40. Cf. Noth, Könige I, pp. 251ff.

Isaiah's time there was a pro-Egyptian faction in Judah.[479] Political dissenters of the pro-Assyrian policies of Ahaz may have sought refuge in Egypt, the other great political power of Isaiah's day. It is, therefore, entirely conceivable that an Egyptian diaspora may have existed in the south. It could have been made up of voluntary and/or forced emigration of Israelites.[480] Fugitives from the outlying districts of Judah may have taken refuge in Egypt, the Judean ally, when Sennacherib attacked to quench the rebellion of western nations in the last years of Isaiah's ministry. It is not improbable that in Isaiah's last days there were Israelites in Egypt.[481]

This oracle pronounces that "the remnant of his people" (*šeʾār ʿammô*) will be gathered from these territories (vss. 11, 16). The remnant terminology in vs. 11 and vs. 16 is Isaianic.[482] Those who support and deny Isaianic authorship point out alike that the oracle of 11:10(11)-16 contains on the whole Isaianic expressions.[483] What is new is that it is a return from Assyria and Egypt (vss. 11, 16), i.e., it is a bringing back of the scattered remnant of God's people who are left by the enemy. The remnant here does not refer to the escaped survivors in

---

[479] Isa. 30:1-7; 31:1-3.

[480] Such a diaspora of emigrants may be indicated for the Aramaean Damascus in 1 Ki. 20:34.

[481] Even such a critic as Cheyne, *Introduction*, p. 60, admits that "in support of his [Isaiah's] authorship one might urge the references to Assyria and Egypt and other countries within his ken."

[482] The same designation is used in 28:5, *supra*, pp. 304ff.

[483] Mauchline, *Isaiah*, p. 131: "Yet the language used in vss. 10-16 is on the whole, characteristic of Isaiah." Cheyne, *Introduction*, p. 60: "In support of his authorship one might urge . . . the presence of Isaianic expressions. . . ."

Jerusalem but to those who were left over in foreign nations.[484] This gathering in of "the remnant of his people" is envisioned without any reference to Isaiah's general emphasis on repentance and faith as a condition for salvation. The usage of the remnant is here unique insofar as it is not employed in connection with judgment or with the purged remnant of Zion. It seems that essentially two solutions to this problem can be proposed: one is to argue that this is evidence for a non-Isaianic origin of this oracle; the other is to propose that the prophet's remnant motif was not so rigid and fixed as to exclude any latitude for varying ranges of emphases. In the present writer's opinion the latter position is the more defensible in view of Isaiah's total message and usage of the remnant motif. If the passage of Amos 9:11-12 is genuine,[485] it would then, against this background, not seem unreasonable to grant a related idea also in Isaiah.[486] Our investigation of the Isaianic remnant motif has shown that the prophet has not cast this motif into a stereotyped mold but employs it with a varying range of applicability. This corresponds to the undogmatic flexibility of Isaiah's proclamation[487] which was conditioned by the length of his ministry

---

[484]Procksch, Jesaja, pp. 157-9, and Schilling, op. cit., p. 68, are right in pointing out that there is here a different use of the remnant motif from what it is elsewhere in Isaiah.

[485]Supra, pp. 208ff.

[486]This would seem to be supported even from the point of view of Isaiah's dependence on Amos, see Fey, op. cit., pp. 57ff. On the other hand, Isaiah's independence would be maintained by his own development of his thinking and his own emphasis.

[487]Herrmann, Heilserwartungen, p. 126, emphasized the flexibility of Isaiah's message in the following words: "Die Vielzahl seiner Beziehungen entspricht die Vielschichtigkeit seiner Botschaft, ihre innere

and by the varying historical circumstances.

Finally we must be aware of the relationship of the remnant motif to the total emphasis of the oracle. In the oracle of 11:11-16 the prophet is not speaking primarily of the return of the remnant of Israel, i.e., those who are left in foreign countries after the destruction, though it may be that the thought of such a return lies at the foundation of what he says. Rather, he is thinking of a deliverance of such a magnitude that it can only be performed by Yahweh. It will take nothing less than divine initiative to overcome the obstacle for an assembling of his people. Emphasis is placed upon the idea that Yahweh's purpose to prepare a people for himself can not be thwarted, not even by a dispersion of the remnant of his people. As once before when Yahweh had brought up his people out of the land of Egypt, so once again he will bring up his people over a highway to the promised land. The emphasis throughout this oracle is on Yahweh's mighty action: Yahweh destroys, indeed he "removes men far away" (6:12), but he also recovers and saves them.[488]

B. The Remnant Motif and the Nations

After our investigation of Isaiah's remnant motif as related to Israel, one looks eagerly forward to an examination of the remnant motif

---

Wendigkeit, die durchaus kein glattes klares Programm darbietet, sonder wandlungs- und anpassungsfähig sich durch die spannungsreiche judäische Geschichte von den dreissiger Jahren bis zum Ende des 8. Jahrhunderts bewegt. . . . Das bedeutet im Einzelfalle nicht Exklusivität und Einseitigkeit, . . ." Cf. Schilling, op. cit., p. 68; Stegemann, op. cit., p. 182f.

[488]This is again characteristic Isaianic theology as in Isa. 6:5-11.

in the utterances concerning foreign nations. Almost all oracles concerning foreign nations in which the remnant motif is present belong to the collection of utterances in Isa. 13:1-23:18.[489] Similar collections are to be found in other prophetic books (Amos 1-2; Jer. 46-51; Eze. 25-32). The present writer will again follow the same methodology of studying the remnant motif in chronological sequence in the respective oracles concerning foreign nations.

1. Syria.--The oracle concerning Damascus in the section of 17:1-6 is a threat against the Aramean kingdom. It must therefore have been uttered before the fall of Damascus in 732 B.C. The content presupposes the Syro-Ephraimitic coalition against Judah and it may therefore be assigned to the prophet's early period of activity, namely to 735/34 B.C.[490] when such an oracle would have served to reassure Judah.

The first part of this doom oracle closes with an ironic comparison in which the remnant motif plays a key role.

3 The fortified city will disappear from Ephraim,
  and the kingdom from Damascus,
and the remnant of Aram will be[491]

---

[489]There is general agreement among scholars that Isa. 13:1-23:18 represents an independent collection of oracles which is a part of the threefold eschatological structure of Isa. 1-39, namely prophecies concerning Israel, Isa. 1-12; prophecies concerning foreign nations, Isa. 13-23; eschatological prophecies and promises of salvation, Isa. 24-35. Cf. Eissfeldt, OTI, pp. 306ff.; Fohrer, Introduction, pp. 365ff.; Kaiser, Einleitung, pp. 174f.

[490]Bright, Isaiah-I, p. 502; Leslie, op. cit., p. 45; Donner, Israel unter den Volkern, pp. 41-3; Harrelson, Interpreting the Old Testament, p. 241; Eissfeldt, OTI, p. 313; Wright, Isaiah, p. 57; Fohrer, Jesaja, I, 212; Eichrodt, Der Herr der Geschichte, p. 50. See Appendix II, p. 478.

[491]1QIs^a has יהוה instead of יהיו, which seems to be a scribal mistake.

like the glory[492] of the sons of Israel,
says Yahweh of hosts.[493]

At the present moment Damascus formed a fortress between Ephraim, i.e., North Israel, and Assyria.[494] Isaiah predicts the fall of the Syrian kingdom. The disappearance of the "kingdom" from Damascus, the capital of Syria or Aram, means the loss of political independence.[495] The second part of vs. 3 speaks then of "the remnant of Aram" (*šᵉʾār ʾarām*), i.e., those who have been left over when destruction had come. Does the subtle comparison of the Aramean remnant with the glory of the Israelites express a glorious future for the former? At first sight this may seem to be so. But as a matter of fact this comparison is bitter irony on the part of Isaiah. What the glory of the Israelites means is explicated in the second part of the oracle. In 17:4-6 Isaiah uses a series of pictures to describe the ruin of the glory of Jacob, i.e., Ephraim. The third figure of speech compares the glory of the Israelites with the few olives that are left (*nišʾar*) after the olive tree has been shaken with a stick (vs. 6). The remnant of Aram will be as negligible a remainder as the survivors of North Israel who are compared to the few olives left

---

[492] BHS suggests that one should perhaps read with the Targum שְׁאָר אֲרָם וּכְבוֹדוֹ="the remnant of Aram and its glory." 1QIs[a] supports the MT which seems to be the superior reading.

[493] The translation is by the present writer.

[494] With Duhm, *Jesaja*, p. 132; Skinner, *Isaiah*, p. 142; Gray, *Isaiah*, I, 298; Leslie, *op. cit.*, p. 45; Kissane, *Isaiah*, I, 190; Eichrodt, *Herr der Geschichte*, p. 51, against Whitehouse, *op. cit.*, p. 216; von Orelli, *Jesaja*, p. 72; Fohrer, *Jesaja*, I, 214, who see in the "fortified city" a reference to Samaria. This would be premature in this stanza which is concerned with Syria.

[495] So Fohrer, *Jesaja*, I, 214; Scott, *Isaiah*, V, 272.

after a harvest. Those who are left in Syria (Aram) will be no better off than those who remain of the people of Ephraim.[496] The remnant motif is here employed to emphasize that almost nothing will remain of Syria (Aram) or of Ephraim (North Israel). The Syro-Ephraimitic league will come to nought. Isaiah depicts here the near events of Aram and Israel and does not speak of an eschatological future. It must also be noted that because a remnant remains, no matter how negligible it is, the remnant is a nucleus of existence and life of the respective nations. This aspect, however, is not specifically developed by Isaiah in this oracle.

2. Philistia.--The oracle of 14:28-32, which contains a prophetic warning against the premature rejoicing of Philistia, is definitely dated according to its present superscription[497] in the year of the death of Ahaz of Judah, i.e., 716/15 B.C.[498] Perhaps as early as 715 B.C. Ashdod

---

[496]This negative aspect is vastly underestimated by Schilling, op. cit., p. 76, who interprets the remnant motif in 17:3, 5-6, only in positive terms.

[497]Joachim Begrich, "Jesaja 14, 28-32. Ein Beitrag zur Chronologie der israelitisch-jüdischen Königszeit," Zeitschrift der Deutschen Morgenländischen Gesellschaft, 86 (1933), 69-73, has in the present writer's opinion confirmed the originality of the setting given in the superscription. See now also S. Erlandsson, The Burden of Babylon (Lund, 1970), pp. 68-9.

[498]A discussion of the various dates that have been proposed prior to 1964 is provided by Donner, op. cit., pp. 111-2. He points out that the difficulty of fixing exactly the year of the death of Ahaz has led many scholars to seek dates ranging from 727, 722, 719, 716/15, to 705 B.C. Donner himself believes that the years 722-720 are the only possibility for this oracle, because he thinks that the "rod" which has been broken refers to Shalmaneser V, who probably died in 722 B.C. Gottwald, All the Kingdoms of the Earth, p. 164, suggests the same date as Donner for the same reasons, but takes the originality of the superscription more seriously than Donner does. He, therefore, suggests that this oracle was used again in 715 B.C. and then supplied with a superscription referring to the death of Ahaz. Most recent commentators favor the date of 715 B.C. on account of the superscription and historical events revolving around the Philistine city of Ashdod; see Bright, Isaiah-I, p.

began to scheme a rebellion against Assyria.[499] Sargon II reports that king Azuri of the city of Ashdod "schemed not to deliver tribute any more and sent messages (full) of hostilities against Assyria, to the kings living in its neighborhood."[500] Presumably envoys had also come to the Judean king. They are referred to as "the messengers of the nation" (14:32). The present oracle is spoken to warn and exhort in this concrete historical situation.

28 This oracle came in the year King Ahaz[501] died:
29 'Do not rejoice, O Philistia, all of you
  that the rod which smote you has been broken,
for from the serpent's root will come forth an adder,
  and its fruit will be a flying serpent.
30 And the poor will feed in my pastures,[502]

55; Fohrer, *Isaiah*, I, 201. Recent investigations of the complicated history of the reign of Hezekiah have conclusively shown that Ahaz' reign and life ended in 716/15 B.C.; see Thiele, *Mysterious Numbers*, pp. 134-40; idem, "Synchronisms of the Hebrew Kings," *AUSS*, I, (1963), 121-38; II (1964), 120-36; Horn, *AUSS*, II, (1964), 40-52.

[499]H. Tadmor, "The Campaigns of Sargon II of Assur," *JCS*, 12 (1958), 79-80, discussed the complex question of the dating of the Ashdod revolts in the light of the newest but still inconclusive events. Cf. Gottwald, *All the Kingdoms of the Earth*, pp. 164-5; Fohrer, *Jesaja*, I, 201-2; Wright, *Isaiah*, pp. 144-5.

[500]*ANET*[3], p. 286.

[501]J. A. Bewer, "The Date in Isa. xiv, 28," *AJSL*, 54 (1937), 62; idem, *Isaiah*, p. 44, emended אָחָז, Ahaz, to וָאֶחֱזֶה, "then I saw," which has now been taken over by *BHS* as a reading which should perhaps be adopted. This removal of the name Ahaz is dictated by the problem of the date of the oracle. If we keep the preserved text which is supported by the versions, we may hardly understand the superscription to indicate the occasion for rejoicing for Philistia; we must regard the reference as a matter of dating. Cf. Eissfeldt, *OTI*, p. 313.

[502]*BHK* and *BHS* point out that a few MSS read בכורי which can be pointed to suggest בְּכָרַי, "in my pastures." The Masoretic reading can be taken to contain possibly a *plene* reading. This emendation first suggested by J. B. Koppe in the late 18th century has been adopted by many including Duhm, *Jesaja*, p. 124; Procksch, *Jesaja*, p. 202; König, *Jesaja*, p. 187; Bright, *Isaiah-I*, p. 501; Eichrodt, *Herr der Geschichte*,

and the needy will lie down in safety;
but I will kill[503] your root[504] with famine,
and your remnant I will slay.[505]
31 Howl, O gate; cry, O city;
melt away, O Philistia, all of you!
For smoke is coming from the north,
and no one is numbering[506] its ranks,'[507]
32 And what shall one answer the messengers
of the nations?[508]

---

p. 32; Fohrer, Jesaja, I, 201; Jerusalem Bible. Cheyne and Marti emend the MT into בְּהָרַי, "on my mountains," which is the translation also of Kissane, Isaiah, I, 171, while he follows Koppe's emendation! The reading "on my mountains" is hardly likely, because it would normally be written עַל־הָרַי, 28:25. Cf. Gray, Isaiah, I, 270.

[503]With BHS which cites in support of the emendation וְהֵמִית the LXX ἀνελεῖ and the Targum of codex Reuchlinianus and the critical apparatus in it. Cf. Donner, op. cit., pp. 110-1.

[504]The LXX reads σπέρμα σου = זַרְעֲךָ; the Targum contains בנך. There is, however, no reason to follow Duhm, Jesaja, p. 125, and the Jerusalem Bible translating "your posterity." 1QIs[a] supports the superior MT.

[505]1QIs[a] and the Vulgate support אֲהַרֹג instead of the MT יַהֲרֹג. This is one of the thirteen readings the RSV adopted from 1QIs[a], see M. Burrows, The Dead Sea Scrolls (New York, 1955), pp. 305ff. Among recent commentators the following accept the reading of 1QIs[a] and Vulgate: Eichrodt, Herr der Geschichte, p. 32; Leslie, op. cit., p. 58; Fohrer, Jesaja, I, 201. The Jerusalem Bible avoids partially the problem by translating "killing."

[506]1QIs[a] reads מודד = מוֹדֵד of "to number, measure" for the MT בּוֹדֵד, which the RSV and Leslie, op. cit., p. 58, translates as "straggler" and the Jerusalem Bible as "deserter." The substitution of the two letters is a common scribal error. The reading of 1QIs[a] is also accepted by Bright, Isaiah-I, p. 501, and Childs, Assyrian Crisis, p. 60.

[507]Following Marti's proposed עַמּוּדָיו, "its pillars," for the MT מוֹעָדָיו. It lacks, however, any textual support. BHS suggests "its strength" (KB, p. 683), במו עֻדָיו.

[508]The LXX, Syriac, and Targum read "nations." 1QIs[a] supports the MT.

'Yahweh has founded Zion,[509]
and in her the afflicted of his people will find refuge.'[510]

This is a difficult oracle. For our present purpose many of the problems can be omitted.[511] This word contains a warning directed to Philistia, because of that nation's premature rejoicing evoked by the death of some great Assyrian king.[512]

The historical situation is in some ways similar to that of the Syro-Ephraimitic crisis. When Hezekiah had become ruler over Judah he was steering a course away from Assyrian vassalage. The Philistine city of Ashdod sent emissaries to Hezekiah to urge Judah to join into an anti-Assyrian coalition.[513] The choice of Hezekiah was much the same as that of Ahaz about two decades earlier. Is he going to call the Assyrians or is he going to join the coalition? Or will he listen to Isaiah?

---

[509]The כִּי at the beginning is recitative, introducing direct speech and should therefore not be translated. Cf. Williams, Hebrew Syntax, p. 75 #452.

[510]The translation is by the present writer.

[511]K. Fullerton, "Isaiah 14:28-32," AJSL, 42 (1925), 1ff., has questioned the genuineness of 14:30a, 32b, mainly by the way in which the "poor," "needy," and "afflicted" are introduced. He concludes that these terms must be taken in a religious sense to designate the pious much as used in the Psalms of the late period. Recently Childs, Assyrian Crisis, pp. 60-1, has shown that these terms are constituent parts of the ancient Zion tradition. He concludes, "It is evident that the prophet is not attempting a new political or religious formulation, but drawing material from the ancient traditions to remind Israel of her relation to Yahweh." Cf. Kapelrud, SVT, XV (1966), 193ff.

[512]The exact Assyrian king in question is still a matter of scholarly debate, see the discussions by Gray, Isaiah, I, 266-7; Scott, Isaiah, V, 266; Donner, op. cit., pp. 112ff.

[513]The textual problem of 14:32 makes an interpretation of the role of the messengers or king(s) and nation or nations difficult. The general meaning, however, seems fairly clear, namely to read this oracle together with Isa. 18 and 20 as concerned with the Philistine revolt

Isaiah addressed Philistia and her emissaries and in so doing instructed Judah on how to react with faith to the offer of rebellion. Philistia has no cause to glory, because it will be destroyed. The judgment over Philistia will result in complete annihilation. Even the "root" of Philistia, from which the nation derives its life, will be killed (vs. 30c). In the same way the "remnant" (<u>šeʾērîṯ</u>) of Philistia, i.e., those who have been left over after the first strike, will also suffer destruction. As there will be a "remnant of Aram" so will there be a "remnant" of Philistia, but the latter will experience utter annihilation. The remnant motif is here employed in its negative aspect.

On the other hand, Isaiah instructs Israel of the proper answer to those who seek an alliance. A stark contrast is drawn between disaster for Philistia and safety in Zion. J. M. Ward has rightly pointed out that "this oracle does not set Philistia's vulnerability over against the invulnerability of Yahweh's nation of Judah, . . ."[514] Yet just what use did Isaiah make here of the Zion tradition? If one takes vs. 32 to refer to the inviolability of Zion for all of Judah, one faces not only a contradiction with other clear statements of the prophet in which destruction is implied,[515] but one misinterprests vs. 32. According to Isaiah's message in vs. 32 only the "afflicted of his people" will find refuge (<u>yeḥsû</u>) in Zion, only the "poor" and "needy" will lie there in

---

against the Assyrians under Sargon II. Cf. Gottwald, <u>All the Kingdoms of the Earth</u>, pp. 164-6.

[514] Ward, <u>op. cit</u>., p. 254.

[515] Isa. 8:14f. 32:9-14; cf. Childs, <u>Assyrian Crisis</u>, p. 60.

safety (labetah).[516] Salvation in Zion cannot be taken for granted by all. The reason why only the "afflicted" and "poor" and "needy" will find security in Zion is not because it is Zion, but because Yahweh is its founder (28:16). In 30:15 Isaiah declared that salvation lies in returning and rest, and early in his ministry he announced that only those will be established who believe in Yahweh (7:9). It appears that the "afflicted" and "poor" and "needy" are identical with the community of faith in Judah from which the future remnant will emerge.[517] They will find true deliverance in Yahweh alone. Thus we find that within the form of an oracle to the nations the Zion tradition is employed both as a testimony to the absolute sovereignty of Yahweh over the nations, and as an exhortation to Israel to seek for safety only in her God and to remind her that true existence and life cannot be found outside the proper relationship of confidence and trust in Yahweh.

3. Arabia.--The difficult oracle concerning Arabian tribes in 21:13-17 is directed to localities in northwest and central Arabia: Dedan (vs. 13), Tema (vs. 14), and Kedar (vs. 16). There is reason to believe that the historical context of these brief prophecies[518] is most

---

[516] H. Wildberger, "'Glauben' im Alten Testament," ZThK, 65 (1968), 151: "Es gibt also bei aller Fragwürdigkeit blosser Heilsprophetie ein legitimes Wissen um Geborgenheit in Gott und auf seinem heiligen Berg, das theologisch durchaus gerechtfertigt ist und dem Wesen des Jahweglaubens entspricht."

[517] Many directly identify the "afflicted" and "poor" and "needy" with the remnant, see H. Gross, "Rest," Bibeltheologisches Wörterbuch, ed. by J. B. Bauer (2nd ed.; Graz, 1962), II, 1001-2; Jenni, "Remnant," IDB, IV, 33; Procksch, Theologie des Alten Testaments, p. 193. It appears, however, more appropriate to designate them as the proleptic representatives of the future remnant.

[518] Scholars generally divide 21:13-17 into two parts on the basis

probably the Assyrian attempt to gain control of Arabian tribes, which according to the report of Sargon II had never been tributaries to any overlord.[519] Such information as we have indicates that Sargon II led an expedition against the Arabs at about 715 B.C.[520] This was followed by campaigns against the Arabs under Sennacherib (705-681 B.C.)[521] and by his son and successor Esarhaddon (681-669 B.C.).[522] It is quite possible, therefore, that 21:13-17 may have come from Isaiah himself in the time of Sargon II or Sennacherib, i.e., in 715 or later.[523]

---

of its style: (1) 21:13-15 is a poetic oracle; and (2) 21:16-17 is a prose oracle. Cf. Gray, Isaiah, I, 359-60; Duhm, Jesaja, p. 157; Scott, Isaiah, V, 288; Leslie, op. cit., p. 130; RSV and Jerusalem Bible. On the other hand there are some scholars who take also vss. 16-17 as poetry, see Kissane, Isaiah, I, 229; Eichrodt, Herr der Geschichte, p. 88.

[519]ANET[3], p. 286. On the other hand, Tiglath-Pileser III tells us that in the course of his campaigns in the west he penetrated into Arab territories, so that two Arab queens sent tribute to him, see ANET[3], pp. 283-4. S. Cohen, "Tema," IDB, IV, 533, makes 21:14 refer to Tiglath-Pileser's campaign in 738 B.C. This date, however, is not certain, because of the difficulty of dating his expeditions.

[520]Reference is made to "the tribes of Tamud, Ibadidi, Marsimanu, and Haiapa, the Arabs who live, far away, in the desert (and) who know neither overseers nor official(s) and who had not (yet) brought their tribute to any king." ANET[3], p. 286; cf. ARAB, II, #17f.

[521]ATAT[2], p. 121.

[522]ANET[3], pp. 291-2.

[523]A date in the time of Isaiah and Isaianic authorship is accorded to 21:13-17 by the following scholars: König, Jesaja, p. 215; Boutflower, op. cit., p. 179; Procksch, Jesaja, p. 273, only 12:13-15; Kissane, Isaiah, I, 228-9; Mauchline, Jesaja, p. 168; Scharbert, Propheten Israels, p. 262; Wright, Isaiah, p. 62; etc. Some scholars are undecided with regard to the genuineness of 21:13-17: Whitehouse, op. cit., p. 247; Hertzberg, op. cit., p. 80; Scott, Isaiah, V, 288; Eichrodt, Herr der Geschichte, pp. 89-90. Other scholars definitely suggest dates later than Isaiah of Jerusalem. Bright, Isaiah-I, p. 504, dates it to about 650 B.C., thinking of Arab incursions and Ashurbanipal's reaction against them; Cheyne, Introduction, p. 131, thinks of 589 B.C. for 21:13-15 when Nebuchadnezzar moved into Palestine; Bewer, Isaiah, p. 57; Leslie,

In the first part of 21:13-17 the inhabitants of Tema, an important caravansary lying on the junction point of two great trade routes through the Arabian desert, are called upon to provide food and drink for their fugitive brethren of the tribe of Dedan. It is clearly stated that these refugees (vs. 14) had "fled from the sword . . . and from the press of battle" (vs. 15). The Temaites are counselled to aid this escaped remnant which is in danger of perishing in the steppe (vs. 13). The prophet's counsel contains the recognition stated in Amos 1-2 that the basic laws of God are not limited to national or tribal boundaries but have universal validity.

In 21:16-17 Kedar is addressed:

16 For thus the Lord[524] said to me:
'Yet a year[525] like the years of a hireling,
and all the glory of Kedar shall end;
17 and the remnant[526] of the number of archers of the

---

op. cit., p. 119; and Fohrer, Jesaja, I, 245, point to a date of about 540 B.C. when Nabonidus moved against the Arabs. With the evidence of Assyrian moves against the Arabs in Isaiah's time it may appear that there is ample historical context to place 21:13-17 into that period.

[524]1QIs[a] has יהוה.

[525]1QIs[a] reads שלוש שנים. It is entirely possible that a number has dropped out, for the tertium comparationis seems to require a plural instead of the singular. In Isa. 16:14, which contains the same comparison, "three years" is the tertium comparationis.

[526]Zorell, Lexicon Hebraicum et Aramaicum Veteris Testamenti, p. 813, and BHS a repointing of the Masoretic וּשְׁאָר into וְשָׁאַר, which would simplify the long construct chain. The Jerusalem Bible translates "hardly any will be left." The difficulty with this suggestion is that the Qal is used only in 1 Sam. 16:11 where there is itself a textual problem. In Isa. 28:1 there is an analogous status constructus chain. It may therefore be best to keep the Masoretic pointing.

mighty of the sons of Kedar will be few,
for Yahweh, the God of Israel, has spoken.'[527]

The remnant motif appears here in connection with the warriors of the tribe of Kedar, which will be few. The implication of vs. 17 is that the fighting power of this famous Arab tribe will be broken.[528] The remnant terminology is employed in the threat against the Kedarites. The fact that only a small remnant of the warriors of Kedar will remain indicates, on the one hand, destruction of the glory of Kedar; but, on the other hand, it also indicates that Kedar will not suffer complete destruction. While the present force of Kedar will be diminished, the seeds of future existence and life for this Arabian tribe are preserved in the remnant.

4. Babylon.--The oracle against Babylon, 14:22-23, is considered by many interpreters to be part of the framework[529] of 14:4b-21 due to its position after this ode. While W. Eichrodt[530] and especially H. L.

---

[527]The translation is by the present writer.

[528]It is noteworthy that in the Assyrian campaign records of the seventh century B.C. the Kedarites (Assyrian Qidri, Qadri) are referred to in such a way as to indicate that by this time the name of this tribe was practically synonymous with Arabs. The fact that in 21:13-17 distinct Arabian tribes are mentioned-without Kedar having a collective meaning of Arabs-may indicate an earlier date than the seventh century B.C.

[529]Most modern scholars consider 14:1-4a and 14:22-23 as the framework of the ode of 14:4b-21, see Duhm, Jesaja, pp. 116, 122; Steuernagel, Einleitung, pp. 487-8; Procksch, Jesaja, p. 193; Gottfried Quell, "Jesaja 14, 1-23," Festschrift F. Baumgärtel zum 70. Geburtstag 14. Januar 1958, ed. by J. Herrmann and L. Rost (Erlangen, 1959), 131ff.; Scott, Isaiah, V, 258-9; Mauchline, Isaiah, p. 143; Bright, Isaiah-I, p. 500. On the other hand, Kissane, Isaiah, I, 159; defends the unity of 14:3-23, arguing that vss. 20d-23 form a strophe of normal length. He believes that Babylon should be exchanged for Assyria.

[530]Eichrodt, Herr der Geschichte, pp. 29-30

Ginsberg[531] have presented a persuasive defense of the Isaianic authorship of 14:4b-21 by relating it to Assyria, the "concluding oracle" mentioning Babylon is believed to be out of place and therefore is generally regarded to be editorial. Is 14:22-23 really the prose conclusion[532] of 14:4b-21 added by a later hand to superimpose artifically the name of Babylon upon an oracle about Assyria? Or is 14:22-23 an independent fragmentary oracle[533] against Babylon which was placed here because it dates from about the same period and belongs, according to Isaiah's pattern of grouping foreign oracles along the lines of a geographical scheme, to those referring to the east? The present writer believes that the latter option is the more probable one. The typical middle and end formula n^{eʾ}um Yahweh appears twice in the middle and once at the end of 14:22-23 marking it as an oracle. This usage of the formula is typical

---

[531] H. L. Ginsberg, "Reflexes of Sargon in Isaiah After 715 B.C.E.," JAOS, 88 (1968), 47-53. He argues that this is an "ode on the death of Sargon," which fits admirably with the circumstances surrounding the death of Sargon II in 705 B.C., and he demonstrates that the ideology and diction of 14:4b-21 are not only compatible with Isaianic authorship, but are positive arguments in its favor. Ginsberg, of course, is not the first to argue that this ode applies to Sargon II. The first to do so on the basis of the cuneiform text which says about Sargon II that "he was not buried in his house" was P. Dhorme, "Le pays bibliques et l'Assyrie," RB, 7 (1910), 389. A. Parrot, Nineveh and the Old Testament (London, 1955), pp. 49-51, also favors the identification of Sargon II as the fallen monarch, as does Gottwald, All the Kingdoms of the Earth, p. 176. Boutflower, op. cit., pp. 71ff., suggests that Tiglath-Pileser alone corresponds with the picture in 14:4-23, while Eichrodt believes that Sennacherib is the most likely historical figure alluded to in this section. Even if the identity of the Assyrian ruler is still debated, there is an increasing consensus that 14:4b-21 refers to Assyria, Herr der Geschichte, pp. 29, 30.

[532] Bright, Isaiah-I, p. 500; Scott, Isaiah, V, 258.

[533] So Mauchline, Isaiah, p. 143; and now also Erlandsson, op. cit., pp. 123-5.

of eighth century prophecy, i.e., Amos and Hosea.[534] Isaiah himself employs this formula in other places in connection with oracles concerning foreign nations.[535] Since this formula is not used within the materials of 13:1-14:21, it points to an independent oracle.

The historical context for 14:22-23 seems to be connected with the circumstances which surround the events during the reign of Hezekiah when the Babylonian embassy of the indefatigable rebel king Merodach-Baladan II appeared in Jerusalem.[536] This was more than an official visit of courtesy.[537] The king of Babylon sought to incite to rebellion the Assyrian vassals in the far west. Thus Merodach-Baladan was actually engaged in organizing a coalition against Assyria. If the events of the Babylonian emissaries are correctly connected with the illness of Hezekiah, then it is probable that the date should be taken as coming very soon after 705 B.C., before Sennacherib had consolidated his position on the throne of Assyria.[538] The narrative of Isa. 39:1-8=2 Ki. 20:12-19 was probably

---

[534]It is used twenty-one times in Amos and four times in Hosea. In Amos it appears thirteen times at the end, twice in the middle, and in the remaining cases it is at the opening. Wolff, Amos (BKAT, XIV/6; Neukirchen-Vluyn, 1967), p. 174. Cf. Westermann, Basic Forms of Prophetic Speech, pp. 189-9; Koch, The Growth of the Biblical Tradition, pp. 214ff.

[535]Isa. 17:3, 6=Syria; 19:4=Egypt. In Amos 2:11, 16 this formula is also used in connection with oracles to nations.

[536]2 Ki. 20:12-19; Isa. 39:1-8.

[537]André Parrot, Babylon and the Old Testament (London, 1958), p. 75; Gray, I & II Kings, p. 638.

[538]The dating of the arrival of the Babylonian emissaries in this period is supported by a number of scholars, see Scott, Isaiah, V, 379; Leslie, op. cit., p. 81; Bewer, Isaiah, p. 97; Wright, Isaiah, p. 84; Fohrer, Jesaja, II, 201; Oppenheim, Ancient Mesopotamia, p. 162. There are some recent commentators that prefer a date about a decade earlier

preserved because of the role of the prophet Isaiah at the coming of the Babylonian embassy. It may be recalled that this was also the very time when Hezekiah made overtures to join an alliance with Egypt. The prophet's opposition to Hezekiah's policies regarding Egypt are clearly indicated in Isa. 28-31. As Isaiah denounced the plan to join with Egypt in an anti-Assyrian plot,[539] so the prophet appears to have attached Babylon's invitation to join an anti-Assyrian coalition with an oracle against that nation, part of which is preserved in 14:22-23.

22 'And I will rise up against them,'
  says Yahweh of hosts.
'And I will cut off from Babylon
  name and remnant,[540]
  offspring and posterity,'[541] says Yahweh.
23 'And I will make it a possession of the hedgehog,
  and pools of water;
and I will sweep it with the broom of destruction,'
  says Yahweh of hosts.[542]

---

when Babylon also revolted against Assyria and Marduk-apal-iddina was finally subdued by Sargon II; see Gray, I & II Kings, pp. 606, 637; Mauchline, Isaiah, p. 236; Muckle, op. cit., p. 129; Eichrodt, Herr der Geschichte, p. 268. It seems that the later date fits better the historical circumstances of Assyria, Babylonia, and Judah.

[539]Isa. 18:1-7; 20:1-6.

[540]BHK suggests that one point שְׁאָר with the Syriac as שְׁאֵר, "flesh" (KB, 938). Leslie, op. cit., p. 126, translates accordingly "flesh." Scott, Isaiah, V, 264, accepts the same repointing but would translate "blood relative." The Syriac, however, is by itself a very poor source for textual emendations; see Leona G. Running, "An Investigation of the Syriac Version of Isaiah: III," AUSS, IV (1966), 146-8; idem, "Syriac Variants in Isaiah 26," AUSS, V (1967), 57-8. BHS omits the Syriac variant. It is noteworthy that 1QIs^{a} reads שארית, which could be so written in analogy to 2 Sam. 14:7. There is no doubt about the fact that the term means in this formula "remnant." Cf. supra, pp. 166ff.

[541]For the hendiadys, see Williams, Hebrew Syntax, p. 17 #72.

[542]The translation is by the present writer.

This fragmentary oracle predicts the utter destruction and complete desolation of Babylon. The use of the two co-ordinated phrases of "name and remnant" and "offspring and posterity" shows that full extermination is only achieved when all possibilities for new life are eliminated. Each pair of nouns, and both pairs combined, express in the fullest manner the idea of progeny; they indicate that where one of these remains the possibility of existence and renewal is given. But Babylon is to be utterly cut off. Any potential of life and renewal will be annihilated. The destruction of Babylon is as complete as that announced over Philistia (14:28-32), in which also the remnant motif was used in the negative sense.

This oracle concerning Babylon seems to have been placed here because it comes from about the same time period as 14:4b-21 and because it fits into Isaiah's geographical pattern of foreign oracles, which follows generally the order of east, west, north, south, center,[543] Assyria and Babylon being the areas in the east.

Isaiah reacted against the Babylonian urgings to join an anti-Assyrian plot just as vigorously as he did against Hezekiah's policy to join an alliance with Egypt.[544] The reason for this is that Judah is to rely upon Yahweh of hosts. He is the sovereign not only of Judah but of all nations. Hezekiah and his people must find their security in Yahweh,

---

[543]See especially Fohrer, Introduction, pp. 367-8.

[544]If our connecting 14:22-23 with the Babylonian invitation to join an anti-Assyrian coalition is correct, then it is not only possible but likely that Isaiah was the author of this fragmentary oracle. Cf. Scott, Isaiah, V, 259: ". . . it is possible . . . that Isaiah was the author."

the Holy One of Israel, and not in pacts with foreign nations.[545]

5. Moab.--The remnant motif appears once more in connection with a foreign nation. The origin, context, literary unity, date, and authorship of the oracle concerning Moab, Isa. 15-16, have occasioned considerable scholarly discussion. O. Procksch characterized these chapters as "the child of pain of exegesis."[546] Yet these chapters are of unusual beauty and reflect great depth of feeling. In our discussion of these chapters we must limit ourselves to aspects that have an indirect or direct bearing on the purpose of our investigation.

It is widely recognized that most of the long oracle goes back to an independent source.[547] It is not quite clear whether this source is

---

[545] Gottwald, All the Kingdoms of the Earth, p. 185: ". . . the thought of Isaiah displays a curiously thoroughgoing dialectic, for he discerns the judgment of God as a racing fire striking hither and yon among the nations, in one and the same cluster of events consuming both sides, . . . Those who strive to hold that judgment at arm's length, . . . who fail to read in the punishment of another their own call to repentance--all such will stumble and fall to their own destruction."

[546] Procksch, Jesaja, p. 208.

[547] This is the conclusion reached by most critics since it was first suggested by Wilhelm Gesenius in 1820. The following may be cited: Steuernagel, Einleitung, p. 489; E. Sellin, Einleitung in das Alte Testament (2nd ed.; Leipzig, 1914), p. 82; Gray, Isaiah, I, 271; Skinner, Isaiah, p. 131; Feldmann, op. cit., p. 208; König, Jesaja, pp. 193-4; Wade, op. cit., p. 107; Procksch, Jesaja, p. 223; W. F. Albright, "Review of Introduction to the Old Testament by Robert H. Pfeiffer," JBL, 61 (1942), 119; Pfeiffer, Introduction to the Old Testament, pp. 444-5; M. Diman (=Haran), "An Archaic Survival in Prophetic Literature," Yedi'oth, 13 (1947), 7-15 (Hebrew); Scott, Isaiah, V, 268; Kaufmann, op. cit., p. 383; Kissane, Isaiah, I, 177; A. H. Van Zyl, The Moabites (Pretoria Oriental Series, III; Leiden, 1960), p. 20; Mauchline, Isaiah, p. 149; Wilheml Rudolph, "Jesaja XV-XVI," Hebrew and Semitic Studies presented to G. R. Driver, ed. by D. Winton Thomas and W. D. McHardy (Oxford, 1963), pp. 130, 142; Gottwald, All the Kingdoms of the Earth, p. 173; Eichrodt, Herr der Geschichte, p. 42.

of non-Hebrew[548] or Hebrew origin.[549] The case of those who argue for a Hebrew origin seems to rest upon a better foundation than the one of those who believe in a non-Hebrew origin.

Though the present writer does not agree in every detail with W. Rudolph in his analysis of these chapters,[550] he does concur in ascribing 15:9; 16:2, 12, 13-14 to a later prophet who used the earlier poem for his own purposes. Insofar as two of these later additions, i.e., 15:9 and 16:13-14, contain the remnant motif, it is of considerable interest to determine, if possible, the author of these additions. Be-

---

[548]The advocates of a non-Hebrew origin of this source fall into three groups: (1) Pfeiffer, Introduction to the Old Testament, pp. 444f., followed by Bewer, Isaiah, p. 45; Mauchline, Isaiah, pp. 149f.; and Leslie, op. cit., p. 251, suggests a Moabite origin. If this were the case then the sympathy expressed in some sections would be genuine, but the triumphant tone would be completely incompatible. (2) Diman (=Haran), op. cit., pp. 7ff., believes that this poem is of a pre-Israelite origin and celebrates an Amorite defeat of Moab. This theory has been adopted by Gottwald, All the Kingdoms of the Earth, p. 173. (3) Van Zyl, op. cit., p. 21, believes on linguistic grounds that a Moabite origin is ruled out and suggests that it originated as a mocking song among Bedouins.

[549]The advocates of the Hebrew origin of this source are in the majority and point to the antiquity of the place names, the beautiful Hebrew with characteristic Hebrew linguistic and stylistic peculiarities, and to historical circumstances in ancient Israel, see Albright, JBL, 61 (1942), 119; Steuernagel, Einleitung, p. 489; Feldmann, op. cit., p. 208; Ferdinand Hitzig, Des Propheten Jonas Orakel über Moab (BZAW, 41; Giessen, 1925), pp. 34f.; Scott, Isaiah, V, 268; Rudolph, op. cit., p. 142; Eissfeldt, OTI, pp. 320-1; Wright, Isaiah, p. 57; Eichrodt, Herr der Geschichte, pp. 42-3.

[550]Rudolph's study of the oracle concerning Moab published in 1963, op. cit., pp. 131ff., has contributed decisively to a better understanding of the difficult chapters of Isa. 15-16. His success in bringing new insights to bear on all problems may be measured by the way in which such an independent scholar as Eichrodt has adopted most of the former's suggestions in his commentary of 1967.

fore this can be achieved it is necessary to consider briefly the probable date of the underlying poem which has been re-used by the author of the additions.

An ever increasing number of scholars concur that the poem which underlies the oracle concerning Moab is of pre-Isaianic origin.[551] The archaic flavor of the poem points to a time earlier than Isaiah, making a late pre-exilic or post-exilic date virtually impossible. A number of scholars[552] have recently again argued very forcefully for the old suggestion that it is best to assign the underlying prototype to either the ninth or early eighth century B.C.[553] It could either come from the time

---

[551]The post-exilic dates suggested by Duhm, Jesaja, p. 126, i.e., the time of Alexander Jannaeus (104-78 B.C.) for the final edition and of John Hyrcanus (135-105 B.C.) for the origin of the source must be ruled out on the basis of 1QIs[a]. The dates of Gray, Isaiah, I, 270, fifth century B.C., Pfeiffer, Introduction to the Old Testament, p. 445, i.e., 550-450 B.C., Leslie, op. cit., p. 250, fifth century B.C., and Fohrer, Jesaja, I, 204, post-exilic (?) are unacceptable because "the kingdom of Moab had disintegrated already in that period" (Van Zyl, The Moabites, pp. 21 n. 7, 36-37). Bentzen, Introduction to the Old Testament, II, 107, places Isa. 15-16 before the exile. In 1942 W. F. Albright, JBL, 61 (1942), 119, had advanced the suggestions that both this poem and its re-use in Jer. 48 refer to an irruption of Arab tribes into Transjordan at about 650 B.C., which ended Moab's existence as a strong autonomous state. He then argued that the events described in the poem refer to the fate of Moab at that time. This hypothesis was adopted by two of Albright's students and is incorporated in their commentaries on Isaiah, viz. Bright, Isaiah-I, p. 501, and Wright, Isaiah, p. 57. However, Albright changed his mind recently and argued that the poem underlying Isa. 15-16 and Jer. 48 stems from a single ninth century prototype; see Yahweh and the Gods of Canaan, p. 23 n. 57.

[552]Rudolph, op. cit., pp. 142-3; cf. Eichrodt, Herr der Geschichte, p. 42. Albright, Yahweh and the Gods of Canaan, p. 23 n. 47; cf. König, Jesaja, p. 193; Steuernagel, Einleitung, p. 489; Feldmann, op. cit., p. 208; Hitzig, op. cit., pp. 34-35; Sellin, Einleitung in das AT, p. 82.

[553]The claim of W. W. Graf Baudissin, Einleitung in die Bücher des Alten Testaments (Leipzig, 1901), p. 358, that in this case Ephraim or Judah would have to be named as the destroyer of Moab is without support. There is likewise no evidence for the attractive suggestion made

of Joash of Judah (835-796 B.C.) or from the time of Jeroboam II of Israel (793/92-753 B.C.),[554] or even from the time of Jehoram of Israel (852-841 B.C.). During the times of each of these kings Moab experienced attacks from outside enemies which seems to have inspired a writer to produce the poem on Moab.

This old Hebrew poem probably would not have been preserved had not a later prophet re-used it (16:13). The most natural suggestion is that this prophet was Isaiah of Jerusalem.[555] The a priori argument that Isaiah would not have used older material is without force.[556] Just as the great prophet Jeremiah used this old material for his pericope about Moab (Jer. 48) so Isaiah employed it in his time. It this supposition is correct, Isaiah would then appear to be the author of the prophetic words which are preserved in 15:9; 16:2, 12, 13-14, thereby adapting and sup-

---

by many that Jonah, the son of Amittai, is the author of the poem, see Steuernagel, Einleitung, p. 489; Sellin, Einleitung in das AT, p. 82; Hitzig, op. cit., pp. 34-35, etc. It is clear that the original composition celebrated the defeat of Moab. But in the present writer's opinion it remains problematical whether or not this poem constitutes the "älteste Schriftprophetie des Alten Testaments," so Rudolph, op. cit., p. 142, and similarly Eichrodt, Herr der Geschichte, p. 42, because it is not quite clear whether it is an elegy, so Wade, op. cit., p. 107; Gray, Isaiah, I, 271; Procksch, Jesaja, p. 223, Mauchline, Isaiah, p. 146, or a mocking or taunt song, so Van Zyl, op. cit., pp. 20-1.

[554]König, Jesaja, p. 193, believes that the time of Joash is the only possibility due to 16:1, 3-5 which is directed to Judah. Rudolph, op. cit., pp. 130, 142, favors the time of Jeroboam II.

[555]So Rudolph, op. cit., p. 142; Van Zyl, op. cit., p. 22; Eichrodt, Herr der Geschichte, pp. 47-8; Procksch, Jesaja, p. 226; Kissane, Isaiah, I, 175; etc. Both Cheyne, Introduction, pp. 83-85, and Gray, Isaiah, I, 277, who argue for a post-exilic date of the poem, the interpolations, and epilogue, admit that there is nothing in the style or language of 15:9; 16:2, 12, 13-14, which would prove these passages to be post-Isaianic. Cf. Erlandsson, op. cit., pp. 69-70.

[556]Against Procksch, Jesaja, p. 223.

plementing the original poem and making it apply to concrete situations contemporaneous with his ministry. As a result this <u>māśśā'</u> was incorporated in the collection of oracles concerning foreign nations in the book of Isaiah.

By the re-use and adaptation of this old material the prophet was able to emphasize effectively that Judah should not rely upon Moab for help. In using this material he had a powerful argument to illustrate to his contemporaries that the Moabites had not been able to withstand the pressures from outside in earlier times, from enemies much less formidable than the powerful Assyrians that confronted Judah and Moab at this time. He reminded them also that Moab was unable to rebuff Tiglath-Pileser III at about 732 B.C.[557] and that during the recent attack of the Gidiriya[558] the population of at least one Moabite city was killed. Isaiah may have used this old poem at the time of 713-711 B.C. when Judah and Moab were on close terms and when Moab joined an anti-Assyrian coalition.[559] At this time the prophet seems to have adapted it by the supplementations of 15:9; 16:2, 12. Thus it had become the instrument of a powerful message in the concrete historical situation of 713-711 B.C. The remnant motif appears in 15:9.

9 For the waters of Dimon[560] are full of blood;
yet I will bring upon Dimon even more;

---

[557] <u>ARAB</u>, I, 282-9; Van Zyl, <u>op. cit</u>., pp. 36-7.

[558] For the varying identification of Gidiriya with Kedar tribes, Gederoth in Judah, or Gader in Transjordan, see Gottwald, <u>All the Kingdoms of the Earth</u>, p. 174.

[559] Van Zyl, <u>op. cit</u>., p. 150.

[560] On the basis of $1QIs^a$ and the Vulgate some scholars and RSV and

for the survivors of Moah a lion,[561]
and for the remnant of the land.[562]

This insertion together with 16:2, 12, gives the whole poem a new emphasis. These verses taken together constitute a poignant threat given in the direct speech of Yahweh, which sets them apart from the rest of the poem. It constitutes an announcement of judgment upon Moab which will go beyond the prior destruction. Though the battle at the waters of Dimon colored the water red with blood still there was a surviving remnant left over. But even these survivors (*p^e^lêṭaṯ*) of Moab, this remnant (*š^e^ʾērîṯ*), will have no safety. Despite their flight to the fords of Arnon (16:2) and the prayers to their gods,[563] there will be no security for the survivors of Moab. When Yahweh strikes in judgment all en-

---

the Jerusalem Bible adopted Dibon. However, H. M. Orlinsky, "Studies in St. Mark's Scroll-V," *Israel Exploration Journal*, 4 (1954), 5-8; idem, "Qumran and the Present State of Old Testament Text Studies: The Septuagint Text," *JBL*, 78 (1959), 28, has convincingly argued that Dimon is the original meaning.

[561] *BHS* lists the emendation of Hoffmann, *ZAW*, 3, 104, cited in Procksch, *op. cit*., p. 214, אֶרְאֶה, "I have a vision." *BHS* also suggests יִרְאָה, "fear." The latter has been used by Rudolph, *op. cit*., p. 135. Kissane, *Isaiah*, I, 180, suggests אֲנִיָּה, "sorrow." But it seems that it is not necessary to deviate from the MT, which is supported by 1QIs[a] and the versions.

[562] *BHS* points אדמה as אֲדַמֶּה, "I speak a parable about the remnant." Scholarly emendations such as אֶדְמְעָה, "let me shed tears," or אֵימָה, "terror," or אֱדֹם, "Edom," or אַדְמָה, "Admah," can be multiplied. It seems to be easier to multiply guesses than to justify them. The translation follows the RSV with the exception of Dimon.

[563] The Moabite king Mesha sacrificed the crown prince to the national god, to whose anger the king attributed the subjection of his people in the time of Omri and Ahab, cf. 2 Ki. 3:27. In this connection it is significant that according to the Moabite Stone the disasters of Moab are attributed to the displeasure of the gods. Cf. *DOTT*, p. 196.

deavors of men are useless and their gods are as nothing.

Thus a new tone is introduced into the old poem about Moab's suffering. The pro-Moabite sentiments and aspects of sympathy as well as the illfated attempts of the human survivors have been turned into a mere prelude to even more severe punishment. The complete helplessness and utter impotence of foreign gods are laid bare. The ones who have been punished and the ones who seek a pact, i.e., Moab and Israel, are confronted with the God who destroys all human pride. This is a different way of saying that the only real safety is in faithful reliance upon Yahweh, the Holy One of Israel.

At a later time a further word of Yahweh was appended to this announcement of judgment whose fulfillment was still oustanding. The time of the addition of 16:13-14 was probably the period of revolt that followed the death of Sargon II in 705 B.C. Moab was also implicated in this revolt.[564] It was the time in which Isaiah also spoke out against Babylon[565] and Egypt.[566] Thus it would be entirely compatible if Isaiah would on this occasion again address himself to Moab. If this suggestion is correct, the concluding verses, i.e., 16:13-14, of the oracle concerning Moab would then have been added to the oracle concerning Moab at about 705 B.C. or shortly thereafter.

13 This is the word which Yahweh spoke concerning
Moab in the past.

---

[564]Van Zyl, op. cit., p. 151; Bright, A History of Israel, p. 268.

[565]Isa. 14:22-23; supra, pp. 360ff.

[566]Isa. 30:1-7; 31:1-3.

14 But now Yahweh has spoken, saying,
'In three years like the years of a hireling,
the glory of Moab will be brought into
contempt, despite[567] all his great multitude,
and the remnant[568] will be small, a trifle,
insignificant.'[569]

The expression "in the past" (<u>meʾaz</u>) in vs. 13 points to an older saying of Yahweh. Many commentators believe that it refers to the poem which Isaiah re-used. Those who support a Hebrew origin of the poem generally suggest that it comes from an "earlier prophet."[570] If this is accepted, then one does not need to assume that Isaiah refers only to the word of Yahweh in 15:9 and 16:2, 12, which are in a narrow sense the only word of Yahweh in Isa. 15-16. In a larger sense every word of a prophet is a word which Yahweh has spoken.

---

[567]The preposition ב has been variously interpreted. König, <u>Jesaja</u>, p. 192; Procksch, <u>Jesaja</u>, p. 223; Fohrer, <u>Jesaja</u>, I, 212, take it in the sense of "including." The adversative use of this preposition in the present passage is the common view. However, it is possible to take it in the instrumental sense and translate, "the glory of Moab will be brought into contempt by all the great multitude" (cf. Williams, <u>Hebrew Syntax</u>, p. 47 #243). In this case the great multitude would be the agent that brings the contempt upon Moab. Cf. Leslie, <u>op. cit</u>., p. 255.

[568]In place of the Masoretic וּשְׁאָר the LXX reads καὶ καταλειφθήσεται = וְנִשְׁאַר, "and it (there) will be left." <u>BHS</u> suggests to point it וְשָׁאַר, "and he will leave." This is possible. But in view of the fact that the Qal is used only once in the Hebrew Bible it is not probable. Procksch, <u>Jesaja</u>, p. 224, proposed the emendation וּשְׁאָרוֹ, "and his (her) remnant," cf. <u>BHS</u>. These are all attempts to remove the <u>lectio difficilor</u>. 1QIs[a] supports the superior MT.

[569]The translation is by the present writer.

[570]Scott, <u>Isaiah</u>, V, 268. Cf. Rudolph, <u>op. cit</u>., p. 142: the poem is "die ältests Schriftprophetie"; Eichrodt, <u>Herr der Geschichte</u>, p. 42: the poem is "die älteste schriftlich vorliegende prophetische Kundgebung," and many others.

[571]Against G. B. Gray, <u>Isaiah</u>, I, 295, with König, <u>Jesaja</u>, p. 193; Rudolph, <u>op. cit</u>., p. 141.

A new word of Yahweh is spoken in vs. 14. Within the period of three years Moab's regained independence and prosperity will again meet disaster. Just as the earlier prayers of Moab for deliverance were not to be answered, so now in her new time of recovery Moab's glory will again be laid low. Since only a remnant (<u>šeʾār</u>) will survive, the great multitude will disappear in battle or through deportation. The threefold emphasis on the smallness and powerlessness of the remnant stresses the folly of Judah if it were to rely upon such an impotent ally.

The remnant motif is here used in its dual aspect: The threatening aspect is the more prominent one and comes to expression by the prediction that the great multitude of Moab will be reduced so that only a small and weak remnant will survive. The hopeful aspect is expressed by the idea that a remnant will remain. Even the new visitation that will come upon Moab will not bring about the complete end and full extermination of the Moabite nation. The remnant which will be left constitutes the nucleus of life necessary for the future existence of Moab. The assumption that this remnant will be a regenerated faithful community is without foundation. The remnant motif is here employed with reference to immediate historical events which are to take place, and has no eschatological meaning. The same use of the remnant motif has been observed in the other oracles concerning foreign nations.

PART FIVE

SUMMARY AND CONCLUSIONS

The first section of our investigation provided the necessary background by way of a review of research as regards the remnant motif in modern Biblical scholarship. It became immediately apparent that many disparate positions and contradictory theories concerning the origin, development, and meaning of the remnant motif in the Hebrew Bible have been held by various scholars. It was also noted that there is a bewildering disparity of opinion among Old Testament scholars with regard to the interpretation of the appearance, usage, and importance of the remnant motif in the proclamation and theology of Isaiah of Jerusalem. Our survey of research has made it imperative to examine the remnant motif in a number of interrelated areas in order to be able to cope with the problems of the origin and early history of the remnant motif in ancient Israel as adequately as possible.

The second part of our study is devoted to one of these areas, i.e., it examines the remnant motif in ancient Near Eastern literary texts. The results of the investigation of the Sumerian, Akkadian, Hittite, Ugaritic, and Egyptian literary records are of considerable importance not only for an understanding of the extra-Biblical remnant motif but also for the appreciation and interpretation of the remnant motif in the Biblical traditions. Werner E. Müller argued on the basis of an almost exclusive utilization of Egyptian, Hittite, and Assyrian annals that the remnant motif originated from the socio-political sphere as a breakdown of a supposed principle of "complete physical destruction" as practiced in Assyrian warfare.[1] Aside from W. E. Müller's dubious interpretation of the Assyrian materials to abstract this supposed "principle,"[2] the evidence of the ancient Near Eastern literary remains proves that his theory concerning the origin of the remnant motif is untenable. Equally untenable is the derivation of the remnant motif from Babylonian myth[3] or from Babylonian cult.[4]

Let us briefly summarize the findings of our examination of the various ancient Near Eastern literary texts. The remnant motif is securely anchored in the extant literary remains of the Sumerians. It is present in the Sumerian flood account, the Sumerian King List, a lamentation over the destruction of Ur, and a hymn. It is especially prominent in the Sumerian flood tradition as available in the flood story and the various forms of the King List. This flood tradition is of considerable importance for the origin and development of the remnant motif in extra-Biblical materials because all later Mesopotamian traditions of the great flood including the Ugaritic and Hebrew flood stories are related to the Sumerian prototype. Despite the fact that the theme of the great flood which destroyed mankind with the exception of a handful of the hu-

---

[1]W. E. Müller, Die Vorstellung vom Rest im AT, pp. 8-18. The origin of the remnant motif as propounded by Müller has been accepted by von Rad, Wildberger, Wolff, Ruppert, Steck, and Stegemann, supra, p. 22 n. 105.

[2]W. E. Müller, Die Vorstellung vom Rest im AT, pp. 17-18; supra, pp. 97-100.

[3]So Hugo Gressmann, Der Ursprung der israelitisch-jüdischen Eschatologie, pp. 229-38.

[4]So Mowinckel, Psalmenstudien II, pp. 276-82.

man race became popular around the twenty-first century B.C., it is fairly certain that the memory contained in this tradition is much older. The Sumerian flood tradition places much emphasis upon the motif of the destruction of mankind and correspondingly upon the motif of the survival of a remnant. Although the surviving remnant in the Sumerian flood account was exceedingly small it preserved the "seed of mankind" and thus bridged the abyss of total destruction by linking the existence of mankind in the antediluvian era with man's existence in the postdiluvian era. One of the key elements in the Sumerian flood account is the idea that the surviving remnant did preserve the life and existence of mankind. On the whole we may conclude that the extant Sumerian literary materials use the remnant motif as the vehicle of thought to express a twofold idea: (1) Through the survival of a remnant of human entities the continuity of existence and the preservation of life of these entities is guaranteed; and (2) the life and existence of human entities ceases when no remnant survives. This dual polarity of the remnant motif is present from its earliest rise in the first great civilization of Mesopotamia.

The remnant motif is present in a large variety of genres of Akkadian literature. In epic texts it plays a role in Enūma eliš, the Atraḫasis Epic, the Gilgamesh Epic, and the Erra Epic. The Babylonian epic of creation, Enūma eliš, exhibits the remnant motif in connection with the theme of a rebellion among gods. It appears that this is the only Mesopotamian example of the use of the remnant motif with divine entities. A rebellion among the gods ends after some have been slain and the remainder of the rebellious gods "saved and preserved their lives"

(Tablet IV:109) by giving up their struggle and pledging allegiance to valiant Marduk. It has been suggested that the developments of these events derive from and apply to historical conditions: The rebellious gods correspond to a rebellious vassal whose leaders will be eliminated; this will cause the remainder to save themselves by accepting renewed vassalage.

The Old Babylonian story of the flood as available in the Atraḫasis Epic is of great importance for an understanding and interpretation of the Akkadian or more specifically Babylonian usage of the remnant motif. According to the consensus of scholarly opinion the flood story preserved in the Atraḫasis Epic has as its prototype the Sumerian flood account. The announced aim of the flood was the "total destruction" (Tablet III:iii:37; iv:44) of mankind as in its prototype. What is new is that the flood comes as the climax of a series of attempts on the part of the gods to control mankind's rebellion against the established order.[5] The aim of the prior plague, famine, and drought was to "diminish" the human race, but the aim of the flood is man's "total destruction."[6] This motif is correlated with the motif of the survival of a remnant of mankind. Much emphasis is again placed upon the notion of saving life. Despite the fact that the surviving remnant was for the moment very meager and woefully small, it preserved life and possessed the ingredients

---

[5]G. Pettinato, "Die Bestrafung des Menschengeschlechts durch die Sintflut. Die erste Tafel des Atramḫasīs-Epos eröffnet eine neue Einsicht in die Motivation dieser Strafe," Orientalia, N. S. 37 (1968), 165-200.

[6]This motif is used only in connection with the flood in the Atraḫasis Epic, see supra, p. 71 n. 89.

of renewal and regeneration. The remnant motif of the Gilgamesh Epic is very similar to that of the Atraḫasis Epic. The deluge sent by the gods swept away all but the last vestige of human life on earth. The future of the human race and civilization hinged on the fate of the remnant of mankind contained in the precarious craft. With the safe landing of the boat and the appeasement of Enlil the existence of mankind was assured for the future. In these two epics the remnant motif is the means of expressing the idea that in the face of a most devastating threat to all human existence a remnant survived through which man's continued existence was assured and civilization was saved.

The Erra Epic, which dates from the Middle Babylonian period, demonstrates a new aspect in the usage of the remnant motif in Akkadian epic literature. The remnant motif appears in this epic in connection with the destruction of Babylonian cities. The small remnant left after the destruction of Babylon and the other cities of Akkad has the inherent potential to sprout like a "seed" and thus replenish that which was lost. It also assures the future pre-eminence of Akkad in which the city of Babylon will have special prominence. In the Erra Epic we have an instance of a threat by a foreign enemy against a national entity. The Akkadians, i.e., Babylon with the other Akkadian cities, are threatened with extinction. But the gods of the Akkadians intervene to save a remnant. This is the first instance in Akkadian literature where the remnant motif is used to refer to a national entity. In this sense we have here a parallel to a usage of the remnant motif in the prophetic materials of the Hebrew Bible. The idea of "the remnant of the people" of Akkad is encountered once more in an Akkadian "prophetic" text which is, however, too fragmentary to permit definite conclusions.

The remnant motif has a prominent place in the Assyrian royal inscriptions and war annals as had already been noted by W. E. Müller. The present writer has extended his research to the whole range of this literature from the time of Shalmaneser I (1274-1245 B.C.) to the overthrow of the Assyrian empire. In these records the remnant motif is used exclusively in connection with the enemies of Assyria. This means that another aspect of the remnant motif in Akkadian literary texts comes to light. When the remnant motif appears in these records it is always in connection with an enemy of Assyria. At times remnant terminology is employed to express the total annihilation of a hostile military force, or the population of an enemy city or territory, or an enemy tribe, or other kinds of hostile social and political entities. More frequent, however, is the use of the remnant motif to express the idea that a "remnant" of a hostile entity was able to "escape" and thereby saved its "life." It is reported that sometimes such an escaped remnant was caught and completely destroyed or pardoned and left in their own territories or lands or it was deported. There is no doubt that in these Assyrian records the remnant motif is closely connected with the Assyrian practice of warfare and Assyrian political policy. The aim of Assyrian political policy and thus military practice was the complete subjugation of other nations, city-states, or tribes. The main object was to break the political independence and national sovereignty of these political and social entities in order to make them useful for Assyria. This Assyrian aim certainly involved instances of total annihilation when an insubmissive and obstinate enemy was encountered. On the other hand, there is no evidence that the Assyrians acted according to a so-called "principle of complete physical destruction" as W. E. Müller has argued.[7] This consideration alone renders impossible his contention that the remnant motif has its origin in the breakdown of such a supposed principle. The fact that the earliest appearances of the remnant motif in Akkadian literature antedate by many centuries the appearance of the remnant motif in the Assyrian royal inscriptions and annals is a clear proof that the remnant motif did not originate from the sphere of Assyrian political and military practice.

In Assyrian annalistic literature we have another terminological and conceptual witness which indicates that the remnant motif is grounded in circumstances in which the existence of various social structures and human entities is threatened with full extinction and complete annihilation. Here again the dual aspect of the remnant motif comes to expression. When no remnant of the hostile entity was left it meant the cessation of the existence of that entity; conversely when a remnant was able to escape or was left by the Assyrians the existence and life of that entity was preserved with all the innate potentialities of renewal and restoration.

The remnant motif is present in religious and historical texts of the Hittite literary remains. "The Song of Ullikummi" of the mythological Kumarbi cycle refers to a remnant of mankind. The "Plague Prayers of Mursili II" speak of a remnant of the Hittite nation which is threatened with complete destruction by the continued ravages of the plague.

---

[7] Supra, pp. 97-100.

The preserved parts of the annals of the various Hittite kings, which antedate the Assyrian annals by many centuries, contain the remnant motif in essentially the same way as the Assyrian annals. While the remnant motif in the extant Hittite literary records is not as prominent as in the much more abundant Akkadian materials, it too is used with references to the survival of a remnant of mankind, a remnant of the national entity, and a remnant of entities hostile to the Hittites.

The remnant motif has also turned up in various literary remains from Ugarit. The recently discovered flood story is too fragmentary to allow definite conclusions about the remnant motif. The so-called "Legend of King Krt" contains the remnant motif in connection with the death of the royal house of Krt. The physical and political disasters that befell the house of Krt left the old ruler Krt as the sole remnant. But Krt preserved by his survival the future of his dynasty. He married again and new offspring issued from this second marriage. The remnant motif appears here at the center of the life-and-death theme which is the main motif of the Krt cycle. In the mythological Baal and Anath cycle the remnant motif appears again in juxtaposition to the life-and-death problem. "Men" on earth are faced with extinction due to a calamitous drought. But the "remnant" of men are saved through life-giving rain. As a result human life is preserved and mankind continues to exist. These clear instances of the remnant motif in Ugaritic literary texts emphasize again the inextricable interrelationship between the threat to human life and the survival of the remnant which preserves life and existence.

The remnant motif is much more prominent in Egyptian texts than has previously been recognized.[8] It appears in mythological, "prophetic," religious, and historical literary records.[9] The myth of "The Book of the Divine Cow," which is believed to transpose actual historical events into the world of the gods, may reflect events of a time considerably earlier than the fifteenth century B.C. to which the oldest extant version is assigned. According to this myth the destruction of mankind was caused by man's rebellion against their creator god. The complete annihilation of the human race is averted by the intervention of the god Re. The "small remainder" of the decimated human race is promised to replenish the world with inhabitants. Man's rebellion, his punishment, and the preservation of human existence by means of a remnant are three key motifs which this myth has in common with the Mesopotamian flood tradition. Within recognized limits this Egyptian myth may be said to take the place of the flood tradition which seems to be lacking in Egyptian literary records.

The remaining Egyptian literary texts that exhibit the remnant motif refer to various threats such as physical illness, civil disorder, and war. In some cases there appears to be a combination of threats such as political disorder and natural catastrophe. In texts other than those classified as historical ones, in which the remnant motif is used only with reference to Egypt's enemies, the remnant invariably survives.

---

[8]W. E. Müller, Die Vorstellung vom Rest im AT, pp. 6-8, limited his discussion of the remnant motif in Egyptian literary texts to two references in the so-called "prophetic" texts. Warne, op. cit., pp. 19-22, cites in addition to Müller only one instance of the remnant motif from Seti I.

[9]Supra, pp. 116ff.

Two texts of the "prophetic" or controversial literature refer to a remnant of Egypt which survives and thereby guarantees continued existence for the nation. In historical texts terms such as "remnant" and "survivors" are used as a rule only when the remnant of an enemy has been or is going to be destroyed. The deportees and prisoners of war, which are as a matter of fact a remnant, are in these texts never so designated. On the whole the remnant motif, and in this case also the remnant terminology, appears in connection with such entities as an individual, a group of people, Egypt as a nation, and the human race. It may or may not be surprising that the remnant motif in the extant Egyptian literary texts exhibits the same polarity of positive and negative aspects which we have encountered in the Sumerian, Akkadian, Hittite, and Ugaritic literary materials. It is used in the same intricate relationship to the life-and-death tension and stresses the loss or preservation of life and human existence.

One of the important results of our investigation of the extra-Biblical remnant motif in the relevant ancient Near Eastern texts is a recognition that the appearance of the remnant motif in these texts antedates the appearance of the remnant motif in the Hebrew Bible. This conclusion raises the question of the origin of the remnant motif as well as the matter of borrowing and influence of one upon the other. An answer to the question of the origin of the remnant motif must take into consideration the large variety and multiple applicability of the remnant motif. It would be rather precarious to argue that the remnant motif arose in connection with the threat of war, for instance, to the exclusion of consideration of other threats. The large variety of threats in the natural, social, and political spheres--flood, famine, drought, plague, pestilence, rebellion, war, and natural death--indicates the diffusion of the remnant motif during its long history. The remnant motif is not limited to a single _Gattung_ of literature. It appears with such genres as myth, epic, legend, prophecy, prayer, hymn, letter, and annal. The manifold connections and multiple relations of the remnant motif are also recognizable through its usage with such human entities as an individual, a family, clan, tribe, army, city, nation, and mankind. The remnant motif is used both with memories of long past catastrophes and with virtually contemporary cataclysmic events. The reason for the complexity of the remnant motif, its widespread distribution, its long range of usage, its variegated applicability, lies within the nature of this motif itself. The origin of the remnant motif may be discovered by considering the common denominator which is present, explicitly or implicitly, in all its usages. This common denominator may be designated as the life-and-death problem, i.e., man's existential concern. The constant emphasis on the loss or preservation of life and existence when the remnant motif appears indicates that it is not only intrinsically coupled with man's existential concern to live and to preserve life when his existence is threatened, but that it has its actual origin in the tension or problem of human existence. The remnant motif arose out of the fundamental question of man's continued existence. When the very life of mankind or a human entity is threatened, the immediate existential question arises whether or not this threat will wipe out life and existence or whether a remnant will survive to preserve life and human existence. As such the remnant motif serves as a vehicle of thought whereby positive and negative answers are given to the question of existence out of which it arises. Depending on whether or not a remnant survived it can express the negative notion of total destruction and complete cessation of life and thus the end of the existence of an entity, or conversely, it can express the positive notion that in and through the surviving remnant the life and existence of the threatened entity was secured for the future despite the loss of part of it. No remnant means no life, a remnant means life and existence. The remnant possesses the immense innate potentialities of renewal, regeneration, and restoration.

The much discussed question of the age of the remnant motif must now be answered by way of stating that the exact date of its origin cannot be expected. It appears to be as old as threats to human existence and man's concern to survive. As far as the extant sources allow us to judge it found first expression in connection with the threat to mankind's existence in the Mesopotamian flood tradition which appears to go back to the third millennium B.C. The implications arising out of the connection between the first appearance of the remnant motif in the Mesopotamian flood tradition and the origin of the remnant motif may not be unimportant.

One of the basic motifs of the ancient Near Eastern flood narratives is the decision of the god or gods to destroy mankind. The presupposition of this decision is that the god or gods who decided to create man can also decide to destroy him. In this sense the flood is primeval event. This points to the area where flood story and creation story belong together: The creation of man leaves open the possibility of the destruction. This possibility was realized in the flood. The complementary character of creation and flood accounts, which are combined aside from the primeval history in Genesis already in the Old Babylonian Atraḫasis Epic, is hereby clearly indicated. The correlation of creation and flood in these two epic narratives and also the same distribution of creation and flood accounts in the ancient Near East means that man's knowledge of his creation and the creation of his world belongs to and is a part of his knowledge of the possibility of his end or destruction. It must be noted that such a destruction transcends the death of an individual as well as a locally limited catastrophe. The whole existence of mankind is involved in the flood just as the whole existence of mankind is involved in creation. To conceive the possibility of total destruction opens up for man a completely new understanding of human existence, namely the continuity of mankind's existence on the basis of the salvation of a remnant of the human race. Through the surviving remnant of mankind man's existence is preserved and will go on. The observation that the earliest appearance of the remnant motif is found in the ancient Near Eastern flood tradition thus receives unusual importance. Man's existential concern drove him back to his beginnings for an answer to the problem of life and existence. Conceiving that his creation left open the possibility of destruction, a new answer to his fundamental problem came to him by the recognition of the survival of a remnant in a catastrophe that threatened the very existence of mankind. If these considerations are correct, we may conclude that the remnant motif has its origin in the problem of human existence in connection with man's struggle for an answer to the problem of the possibility of the destruction of mankind. The answer was conceived in the recognition that mankind's continuous existence is assured and preserved on the basis of the divine salvation of a remnant.

An investigation of the Hebrew remnant motif should commence with an examination of the remnant terminology in the Hebrew Bible. Space did not permit the inclusion of this study in the present form of this monograph. It will have to suffice to give a brief summary of the results. The Hebrew remnant motif comes to expression through the usage of verbal and nominal derivatives of five separate Hebrew roots. A study of these roots in their manifold connections in their particular contexts, with careful considerations of the semantic usages in their sentence- and word-combinations, and their Semitic cognates led to new results.

It has become apparent that the derivatives of šʾr represent the focal point of the terminological expression of the Hebrew remnant motif. Derivatives of plṭ/mlṭ, ytr, śrd, and ʾhr cluster to a larger or smaller degree around this focal point. The Semitic cognates of the Hebrew root šʾr emphasize in the majority of cases the remaining part without any reference to or implication of the loss of the larger whole or balance.[10] The Hebrew derivatives of šʾr designate that part which is left over after the removal of a small part, the balance, or the larger whole. In a few instances some forms also designate the whole without the loss of any part. The variety of threats in connection with which derivatives of šʾr occur in the Hebrew Bible precludes the view that forms of šʾr are

---

[10] Against Eric W. Heaton, "The Root שאר and the Doctrine of the Remnant," JTS, N.S. III (1952), 28, who had claimed that the Semitic languages confirm the fundamental sense of שאר which implies that the residual part is less important than the larger number or quantity which has been in some way disposed of.

uniquely connected with the language of the wars of Yahweh.[11] Derivatives of *plṭ* appear predominantly with human entities. The nominal form *p^{e}lêṭāh* describes the "*escaped* remnant" from general war, war of Yahweh, and eschatological judgment. Other forms of *plṭ* describe in most cases an escaping. Forms of *ytr* are used very frequently in connection with a large variety of material things and human entities. Various shades of meaning come to expression by these derivatives such as "excess, surplus, rest, remnant, and residue." It is wrong to read a single shade of meaning into every usage of a form of *ytr* or to consider a certain shade of meaning basic and determinative for all other shades of meaning.[12] The nominal form of *śrd* is used almost exclusively with human entities which are "surviving" or are not "surviving." In some instances the noun *ʾaḥarîṯ* is used in the sense of "remnant."

The derivatives of all five roots are employed either to express the negative notion of total annihilation or the positive notion of the survival of a remnant. The positive notion is the more frequent one in the 223 usages of derivatives of *šʾr*, the dominant one in the eighty usages of derivatives of *plṭ* and the 248 usages of derivatives of *ytr*, and the less frequent one in the twenty-eight nominal forms of *śrd*. When used in the positive sense in connection with human entities neither

---

[11]Against Hans Wildberger, *Jesaja* (BKAT, X/2; Neukirchen-Vluyn, 1966), p. 155.

[12]Against Roland de Vaux, "Le 'reste d'Israël' d'après les Prophètes," *RB*, 42 (1933), 528 n. 1.

the fragmentary nature of the residual part nor the painful loss of the other part is of greatest importance. Rather the surviving or escaping remnant is itself a new whole which possesses all potentialities of renewal and regeneration. The bi-polarity of the negative and positive notions in the Hebrew remnant terminology must never be lost sight of. The fact that at times forms of a certain root are used in connection with the negative notion of total loss and at other times the same forms or other forms of the same root are employed with the emphasis on the positive notion prevents a reading of a certain semantic value such as "backward-looking"[13] or "forward-looking"[14] or "excess"[15] into virtually each appearance of a form of a particular root of the Hebrew remnant terminology. It must be emphatically maintained that each individual context, stylistic usage, sentence- and word-combination puts a certain semantic value upon the form of a Hebrew root in its particular usage. The semantic value established on the basis of these considerations is absolute and must not be blurred by superimposing another semantic value from a different context.

The third chapter of the present study is devoted to an examination of the history of the Hebrew remnant motif from its earliest appearance in the Hebrew Bible to Isaiah of Jerusalem. The main outline of the Hebrew remnant motif has taken shape in the very early stages of

---

[13]Heaton, JTS, N.S. III (1952), 29.

[14]So Donald M. Warne, "The Origin, Development and Significance of the Concept of the Remnant in the Old Testament" (unpublished Ph.D. dissertation, Faculty of Divinity, University of Edinburgh, 1958), pp. 9ff.

[15]De Vaux, RB, 42 (1933), 528 n. 1.

ancient Israel and found its earliest written expression in the earliest materials in Genesis. W. E. Müller[16] had correctly recognized that the first references to the remnant motif antedate its usage in prophetic materials. The first explicit usage of the remnant motif is found in the Hebrew flood story. There is hardly any doubt about the notion that the Hebrew flood story is related to the Mesopotamian flood tradition which also contains the remnant motif. Both traditions go back to a common tradition in which the remnant idea must have played a dominant role in connection with the existential question of life and death, destruction and survival. The ancient Israelite narrator in Genesis surrounds the flood story with his own theological insights. This means that the earliest explicit reference to the Hebrew remnant motif appears in a particular religious context and ideology, namely it is from the start securely anchored in salvation history. It plays a role in the judgment and salvation theme. The final aim of God, however, is salvation and not doom. This is apparent from the emphasis on the survival of a remnant. This remnant which survived the great flood constitutes the nucleus of mankind in which mankind's future existence was secured.

In the Abraham-Lot story the remnant motif is used in connection with revolutionary reflections about God's righteousness: for the sake of divine righteousness the minority of a righteous remnant has a preserving function for the wicked majority. Thus a city which on the whole is wicked is saved. Stress is placed on the saving of life. The Jacob-

---

[16]W. E. Müller, Die Vorstellung vom Rest im AT, pp. 41-9.

Esau cycle and the Joseph cycle connect the remnant motif with the election tradition. On the whole the remnant motif is used in Genesis in connection with mankind, a city, a clan, and the nucleus of God's people. The salvatio-historical emphasis is evident in the overarching correlation between the salvation of a remnant of the human race and the nucleus of the people of God. It is further solidified through the connection of the remnant motif with the promise to the fathers and the sure accomplishment of the plan of salvation in defiance of all obstacles and fears. V. Herntrich takes an extreme position by arguing that the remnant motif originated out of the "action of God" in which "God creates the remnant."[17] Thus the question of a temporal origin of the remnant motif has lost its significance, because it is subsumed by the "question of the witness to the reality of God."[18] V. Herntrich correctly emphasizes the gracious action of God, but overstates his case. In the theocentric conception of history in the oldest layer of Genesis God is considered to be the one who shapes all history. But this fact does not cause the human side in the events to be curtailed or neglected.[19]

The Hebrew remnant motif undergoes considerable development in the scenes on Mt. Carmel and Mt. Horeb in the Elijah cycle. Baalism threatened to envelope Israelite Yahwism. Thus the remnant motif comes here to view in connection with a religio-cultural threat that cuts to the very

---

[17]Herntrich, TDNT, IV, 200-201.

[18]Herntrich, TDNT, IV, 201; F. Rienecker, "Rest," Lexikon zur Bibel (5th ed.; Wuppertal, 1964), cols. 1138-40, is the only scholar to the present writer's knowledge who follows Herntrich at this point.

[19]See especially Artur Weiser, Introduction to the Old Testament, p. 100.

existence of Israel. In the scene on Mt. Carmel Elijah considers himself as the only surviving prophet of Yahweh who publicly defended Yahwism against Baalism. Just as in the early traditions of Genesis, the remnant is here a remnant left after a past calamity, namely the persecution of the Yahweh prophets by queen Jezebel. In the scene on Mt. Horeb, new significant developments of the remnant motif become apparent. Elijah considers himself now as the only loyal and faithful remnant of Yahweh in an apostate Israel which has forsaken the Lord's covenant. The existence of even this last faithful remnant of a loyal Israel was threatened. The theophanic reply of Yahweh to Elijah's complaint that he "alone is left" climaxes in the assurance that Yahweh will leave a remnant of 7,000 in a <u>future</u> judgment. Israel's apostasy will be punished by the sword (war) from within and without, but this judgment will not lead to complete annihilation. A remnant of 7,000, sifted along ethico-religious lines, will be preserved to constitute the nucleus of a new Israel faithful to Yahweh. As in the Genesis materials the faithful remnant will owe its existence primarily to the gracious mercy of Yahweh and not to their own merit. This means that traditional aspects of the remnant motif in Genesis are taken up in relevant passages of the Elijah cycle where the remnant motif undergoes considerable development: The threat is due to Israel's apostasy; the judgment of Israel will come in the near future in the form of war; the sifting takes place along ethico-religious lines; the remnant will constitute the kernel of a new Israel faithful to Yahweh and his covenant requirements; it will be saved primarily as an act of the grace of God. Brief though the encounter with the remnant motif in the Elijah cycle may be, yet new features have been delineated that play an increasingly important part in the "writing" prophets of the eighth century B.C.

Amos is the first "writing" prophet who makes extensive use of the remnant motif. He attacks, it seems, the popular notion that Israel as a whole will remain as a remnant among the nations when the Day of Yahweh brings divine judgment. Amos exposes the fallacy of the popular appropriation of the remnant motif by using it to a large extent to express doom and destruction for Israel. The most drastic statement of Amos is found in 9:1-4, where he speaks of the complete destruction of even the remnant of Israel. This is a borderline expression which is qualified by other sayings. Amos speaks of a remnant in a number of instances. There was to be a remnant of the women of Samaria (4:1-3), one survivor of ten men in a house (6:9-10), and the decimation of Israel's fighting men (5:3). However, in each of these cases the remnant motif was used to indicate the meaninglessness and ineffectiveness of the remaining survivors for the future existence of Israel as a national entity. Israel could not hope to continue to exist on the basis of this remnant. Thus Amos employs the remnant motif from popular belief as a dire threat against the national existence of Israel. Just as he used cultic language to attack the false popular notions of salvation gained through the cult, so he bitterly attacks and treats with irony the popular remnant idea bearing the stamp of self-confident salvation. Israel cannot simply equate itself with the remnant. There was to be a remnant from Israel, but it would be utterly meaningless for the future of the nation (3:12). Thus Amos attempted to destroy the popular notion that Israel would remain as a remnant in the coming disaster and that it would automatically continue to be the bearer of divine election which would have the assurance of a glorious future.

Amos so bitterly attacked the popular misappropriation of the remnant motif in order to shake Israel out of her complacency, to bring to her attention her desperate situation before Yahweh, and to provoke a return to Yahweh. Amos challenged Israel to "seek Yahweh" in order that she might "live" (5:4-6). This was a promise of salvation conditioned by Israel's response. This indicates that there is actually a possibility for a remnant to remain. It will be a remnant <u>from</u> Israel, a remnant faithful to Yahweh. The "remnant of Joseph" (5:15) will survive the eschatological Day of Yahweh for it had been sifted along ethico-religious lines. It is a remnant that sought Yahweh. As a result it will live. The divine "perhaps" indicates grief on the part of Amos. It shows also that the promise of the future remnant of the eschatological Day of Yahweh is neither automatic nor humanly controllable. In Amos the remnant motif is used for the first time in an eschatological sense. At the same time it must be noted that Amos' remnant motif is closely connected with the notion of life. This is an emphasis that is paralleled with aspects of the remnant motif in Genesis and the Elijah cycle. If Amos 9:11-12 comes from the prophet himself, as seems probable, another aspect of the remnant motif comes to the fore. The "remnant of Edom" will participate with the other nations in the outstanding promise of the David tradition. This emphasizes further that the eschatological remnant is largely an entity of religious instead of national destination.

In short, the encounter of the remnant motif in Amos reveals a threefold usage. Firstly, Amos employed the remnant motif to refute the popular remnant expectation which claimed all of Israel as the remnant. He made it a motif of doom for the nation. Secondly, he used the remnant motif to show that there will indeed be a remnant from Israel. The sifting will take place along ethico-religious lines. Here the remnant motif contains the notion of doom for those who do not return to Yahweh and the notion of eschatological salvation for those who choose to return to Yahweh. Amos is the first Hebrew writer to connect the remnant motif with eschatology. There is here again a very close link between the remnant motif and life as in the earliest stratum of Genesis and in the Elijah cycle. Finally, Amos enlarged the remnant motif to include also the "remnant of Edom" among and with the neighboring nations as a recipient of the outstanding promise of the David tradition. This indicates that Amos sees the remnant not so much as an entity of national dimensions but as an entity of religious importance and destination.

The Hebrew remnant motif has thus a rich and varied history prior to the prophetic ministry of Isaiah of Jerusalem. It is, therefore, evident that the remnant motif was not one of Isaiah's "original ideas."[20] At the same time it is obvious that the remnant motif has a much more prominent place in the Isaianic pericopes than in the earlier parts of the Hebrew Bible. The aim of the chronological examination of the Isaianic remnant motif was to obtain as accurate a knowledge as possible of the beginnings of Isaiah's usage of the remnant and to trace its development and application to Israel and the nations during the many years

---

[20] So Lindblom, Prophecy in Ancient Israel, p. 188.

of the prophet's activity. The results of our investigation do not support the suggestions that the remnant motif was absent in the first phase of Isaiah's ministry.[21] It is likewise not correct to maintain that the remnant motif had at first only a negative emphasis and acquired only later in Isaiah's ministry a positive aspect.[22] The inaugural vision (6:1-13) clearly indicates that Isaiah used the remnant motif in its negative and positive aspect and in its non-eschatological and eschatological sense right from the outset of his ministry. It demonstrates that the remnant motif in Isaiah's thought and theology is related to Yahweh's holiness. Isaiah himself experienced a confrontation with judgment and salvation issuing from Yahweh's holiness which made him a proleptic representative of the remnant of the future. The remnant motif is thus a leading element in Isaiah's proclamation of judgment and salvation right from the start of his prophetic activity. Isaiah speaks of a "holy seed" (6:13c) which will emerge after Yahweh's cleansing judgment has fallen upon the nation. He is thus the first to speak of a "holy" remnant. This idea, however, is embryonically present already in the notions of a faithful remnant as first encountered in the Elijah cycle and in Amos. Isaiah's notions of a "holy" remnant is a main element of his eschatology.

In Isa. 1:24-26 the Holy One of Israel will judge Zion. A purified and holy remnant will emerge from the divine fire of purification which will fall upon Israel. This purged remnant will constitute the nu-

---

[21]Against Giesebrecht, Meinhold, W. E. Müller, Fichtner, Herrmann.

[22]Against Wright.

cleus of a new community of the future age which will live in Zion and be the heir of the election traditions. The eschatological *Heilszeit* of the purified and holy remnant corresponds to the ideal *Urzeit* of the past. The basis of salvation is shifted to a future action of God in which the hand of Yahweh brings about the inauguration of the new age with the remnant. Isa. 4:2-3 declares that Yahweh will leave survivors *in* Zion/Jerusalem, i.e., after the purging judgment has fallen upon Israel. The surviving remnant owes its existence to Yahweh's faithfulness and not to human merit. It will be called "holy" not because of any qualification of its own but because of God's mercy. This "holy" remnant is "recorded for life" (4:3) because of God's determination to work out his purpose in history. It should be emphasized that this eschatological remnant will be neither a supra-historical entity nor a remnant with eternal life nor a remnant in a heavenly Jerusalem. It will be an eschatological entity on the basis of its emergence through the inbreaking of God into history.

Isaiah impregnated the remnant motif with new aspects during the Syro-Ephraimitic crisis. The confrontation of Isaiah and his son Shear-jashub, "A-*Remnant*-Shall-Return," with king Ahaz was intended to exhort king and people to return to Yahweh in faith. The context of the whole message of 7:2-9 is crystallized in the name "A-*Remnant*-Shall-Return." This name expresses the dual polarity of doom and salvation. It is a threat to those who decide for political expediency as much as it is a promise for those who decide for faith in Yahweh. Faith, as a matter of fact, is the *criterium distinctionis* between the masses that will perish and the remnant that will survive. The attitude of faith, confidence, and trust in Yahweh on the part of some Israelites will create the condition for Yahweh to intervene in their behalf and for a remnant to emerge from the eschatological catastrophe. From henceforth the notions of remnant and faith are inseparable for Isaiah.

The so-called Immanuel sign (7:10-17) contains both threat and promise. It is threat for those who refuse to decide for faith and promise for those who decide for faith. Immanuel himself is a part of the remnant if not its actual ruler. The idea that Isaiah set about to "create"[23] a faithful remnant or "consolidated"[24] it in his disciples and children goes far beyond the implications of Isa. 8:16-18. The prophet, his children, and his disciples are "signs and portents" pointing forward to the future remnant. Though they are indeed propleptic representatives of this future remnant, they are not to be identified with it.

The remnant motif also plays a prominent role in Isaiah's message and theology during the later part of his prophetic work. It appears in Isa. 28:5-6, a saying probably spoken at the time of Hezekiah's plan to join an alliance with Egypt. Here the prophet exhorts the king to decide for God rather than Egypt by stressing that "the remnant of his people" will have its power, security, and glory in Yahweh and not in political alliances. Isa. 30:15-17 stems from the same historical situation. Isaiah's typical threefold sequence is here present: offer of salvation by Yahweh--rejection by Israel--rejection of Israel by Yahweh. The offer of deliverance is turned upon the rejection by Israel into an

---

[23]So G. B. Gray, Hyatt, Maass, Preuss.

[24]So Skinner and T. W. Manson.

announcement of judgment. The remnant motif appears thus in its negative aspect. Here as elsewhere Isaiah's threat to national existence is radical.

The events of Assyria's invasion of 701 B.C. left Judah as a decimated state. The pericope of Isa. 1:4-9 dates from shortly after these events. In it Isaiah speaks of a remnant of the daughter of Zion. Although the survivors of the events of 701 B.C. are designated as a remnant, they are not the purified remnant which will emerge from Yahweh's judgment. Isaiah uses here the remnant motif in a way familiar from earlier usages in the Hebrew Bible. The prophet designates the survivors of a past catastrophe as a remnant. For the sake of convenience we may call this remnant left of a past historical event the historical remnant as distinguished from the eschatological remnant. The adjectives "historical" and "eschatological" are not intended to make the latter suprahistorical and the former historical; they are merely used to distinguish between a remnant that is present from a past event and one that will emerge from a future action of God and have the qualifications of the eschatological remnant. Thus the distinction between the two lies not only in the sphere of past and future but also in the nature of the remnant itself. Isaiah's urgent hope is that the survivors of 701 B.C. will return to Yahweh and become the community from which the eschatological remnant will emerge.

The "remnant of Israel" in 10:20-21 refers to a remnant left from Israel after the eschatological judgment will have fallen upon Israel. Isaiah's unwavering certainty that a remnant of Israel will return to Yahweh provokes hope and summons his hearers to repentance. The following two verses, 10:22-23, use the negative aspect of the remnant motif: those who reject Yahweh will be rejected by him. The juxtaposition of salvation and judgment in 10:20-23 is typical of Isaiah's thought and theology.

In Isa. 37:30-32 we encounter a combination of the historical and eschatological usage of the remnant motif. The survivors of Israel that are left in Zion/Jerusalem are the historical remnant from which the eschatological remnant will emerge. The emergence of the future remnant is due to divine initiative.

Two verses, Isa. 11:11, 16, speak of a remnant of Israel that is scattered among various peoples, especially the nations of Assyria and Egypt. This remnant will be brought back to their homeland by divine action. This is another aspect of the historical usage of the remnant motif.

Isaiah of Jerusalem employed the remnant motif also in connection with foreign nations. Amos was the first Hebrew writing prophet to use the remnant motif in oracles concerning foreign nations. In Isaiah this usage is much more frequently encountered than in Amos. The "remnant of Aram" is mentioned in Isa. 17:3 in an oracle concerning Syria which was spoken before the fall of Damascus in 732 B.C. The remnant motif is here used as a threat to Aram=Syria predicting that it will become impotent as a military power. This oracle is an exhortation to Israel not to rely upon Syria for help. In Isa. 14:28-32 the remnant motif is used with reference to Philistia. The historical occasion for this oracle was likely the anti-Assyrian revolt of ca. 715 B.C. Isaiah predicts the destruction of even the remnant of Philistia. It was also to instruct

Judah on how to react to the revolt which was brewing at that time. In Isa. 21:17 Isaiah announces that the archers of the tribe of Kedar will be few. The fighting power of this famous Arab tribe will come to nought. The fragmentary oracle of 14:22-23, which seems to date from shortly after the events of 705 B.C. announces the complete annihilation of Babylon. It comes in connection with the Babylonian urgings to join an anti-Assyrian plot. The remnant motif also occurs in connection with Moab in the Isaianic additions of 15:9 and 16:13-14 to an old poem about Moab. The survivors will experience renewed decimation. It is noteworthy that the main emphasis as regards the use of the remnant motif in these oracles concerning foreign nations is throughout negative. The remnant motif is employed to express the utter destruction of Philistia and Babylon; it is used with reference to Syria, Kedar, and Moab to express the notion that their might will be broken and that a powerless remnant may remain.

It is evident that Isaiah of Jerusalem employed the remnant motif from the beginning of his prophetic career. It continued to play an important part in his message and theology throughout the many decades of his activity. Isaiah did not create the idea of a remnant. The remnant motif was already part of the tradition in which he stood. The Isaianic remnant motif has various aspects and divers connections but these are present in all essentials right from the start of his ministry. Isaiah's remnant motif is a part of his proclamation of judgment and salvation and thus is a key element of his theology. Depending on the historical situation and his particular emphasis Isaiah uses the remnant motif in a negative sense as a threat of dire judgment or employs it in a positive sense to exhort, to summon to repentance, and to instill hope. The bi-polarity comes to expression when one group is threatened and another group is encouraged to trust in God. This bi-polarity is present from the outset of his prophetic work and is preserved throughout his long ministry. This is to say that there is no time in his work where the remnant motif was used only in a positive or only in a negative sense.

Isaiah speaks of a "holy" or "purified" remnant which is to emerge in the future as a result of the inbreaking of God into history. As such the remnant is an eschatological entity. At the same time Isaiah speaks of a remnant of Israel or a nation in a non-eschatological sense. While he does this his main concern is to call Israel back to God and to make her create the condition by which some are able to become members of the eschatological remnant, the purified and holy remnant of the future. It is, therefore, no mistake to consider the remnant motif as a key element of Isaiah's theology. It is evident that Isaiah has not cast his usage of the remnant motif into a stereotyped mold. At the same time it must be maintained that the remnant motif is for Isaiah from the first to the last intensely theological. He does not know the distinction of a "secular-profane" and a "theological" remnant motif.[25] What has been designated in this study as the historical remnant is just as theological a usage of the remnant motif as the eschatological aspect of the remnant motif.

The remnant motif is as clearly associated with Isaiah's call for faith as it is connected with his call for repentance. Isaiah relates the remnant motif to the various election traditions, especially the Zion

---

[25]So Stegemann, W. E. Müller, and others.

tradition and the David tradition. At the same time it has become evident that the remnant motif is not a constituent element or definite part of a particular tradition. The remnant motif is an unattached motif from the point of view of form-criticism, for it is not a part of a particular Gattung. At the same time it is an independent motif from the point of view of transmission history, for it is not uniquely joined to a single tradition.

The early history of the remnant motif in the Hebrew Bible shows that it was originally not eschatological, and that it did not arise in the cult. Its usage in extra-Biblical and Biblical materials indicates that it arose out of man's existential concern to secure his life and existence. In the Hebrew Bible it was from the start incorporated into salvation history and became gradually employed to express future expectations of Yahwistic faith. In Amos it received for the first time a distinctly eschatological emphasis. Isaiah of Jerusalem solidified the eschatological usage. The eschatological or holy remnant, purified by a divine purging, was for Isaiah an object of faith and a future reality. This element of the Isaianic remnant motif proved to be of great importance for later prophecy and the further development of Israelite eschatology.

It is an established fact that the remnant motif appears at crucial turning points in history when man's life and existence are threatened with extermination. The lasting contribution of the prophetic movement in ancient Israel, which herself faced ruinous disaster, is to have provided a basis for the survival of a remnant in its urgent call to return to God. Without the fulfillment of this condition there would be no future remnant. The urgent prophetic call to turn to God in faith, confidence, and trust is ultimately also the only basis for the survival of modern man whose existence is threatened with global ruin at the present crucial turning point in history.

Modern man's precarious situation, being characterized by the possibility of nuclear annihilation, by large scale destruction of human life caused by the ecological crisis, by the menacing problems of mass starvation and overpopulation as well as uncertain political, social, and economic conditions and widespread racial and national unrest, has led to an unprecedented insecurity and anxiety and intense quest to secure life and preserve existence on the part of people of all strata of society. Modern men are confronted in the Biblical message of the remnant with a life-and-death question, the question of ultimate reality. Ultimate survival, the deepest securing of one's existence, and the most satisfying inner experience comes on one basis alone and that is a whole-hearted and complete return to God in letting him be the Lord of all one's longings, desires, and hopes. If the remnant kerygma brings about such a positive response, then that which no agency other than the divine can give will be received, namely true security, real peace, genuine love, and lasting hope with the assurance that one is a member of the remnant.

LIST OF ABBREVIATIONS

AE	Erman, Adolf. *The Ancient Egyptians: A Sourcebook of their Writings*. New York, 1966.
AFO	*Archiv für Orientforschung*
AHw	Soden, Wolfram von. *Akkadisches Handwörterbuch*. Wiesbaden, 1965ff.
AJSL	*American Journal of Semitic Languages and Literature*
ANET^3	Pritchard, James B., ed. *Ancient Near Eastern Texts Relating to the Old Testament*. 3rd ed. Princeton, N. J., 1969.
AnOr	Analecta Orientalia
ARAB	Luckenbill, Daniel D. *Ancient Records of Assyria and Babylonia*. 2 vols. Chicago, 1926, 1927.
ARE	Breasted, J. H., ed. *Ancient Records of Egypt: Historical Documents from the Earliest Times to the Persian Conquest*. 5 vols. Chicago, 1906-07.
ArOr	*Archiv Orientalni*
AS	Luckenbill, Daniel D. *The Annals of Sennacherib*. Chicago, 1924.
ATAT^2	Gressmann, Hugo, ed. *Altorientalische Texte und Bilder zum Alten Testament*. 2 vols. 2nd ed. Berlin, 1926, 1927.
ATD	Das Alte Testament Deutsch
AThANT	Abhandlungen zur Theologie des Alten und Neuen Testaments
AUSS	*Andrews University Seminary Studies*
BA	*The Biblical Archaeologist*
BAR	*The Biblical Archaeologist Reader*
BASOR	*Bulletin of the American Schools of Oriental Research*
BDB	Brown, F.; Driver, S. R.; Briggs, C. A. *A Hebrew and English Lexicon of the Old Testament*. Oxford, 1959.
BHK	Kittel, R. *Biblia Hebraica*. 7th ed. Stuttgart, 1951.
BHS	Elliger, K. et Rudolph, W. *Biblia Hebraica Stuttgartensia*. Stuttgart, 1968ff.
BiOr	*Bibliotheca Orientalis*
BJRL	*Bulletin of the John Rylands Library*
BKAT	Biblischer Kommentar Altes Testament
BS	Biblische Studien
BWANT	Beiträge zur Wissenschaft vom Alten und Neuen Testament
BZ	*Biblische Zeitschrift*
BZAW	Beihefte zur Zeitschrift für die alttestamentliche Wissenschaft
CAD	Oppenheim, A. Leo, *et al*., eds. *The Assyrian Dictionary*. Chicago, 1956ff.
CBQ	*Catholic Biblical Quarterly*
CT	*Cuneiform Texts from Babylonian Tablets in the British Museum*
DISO	Jean, Charles F., and Hoftijzer, Jacob. *Dictionaire des inscriptions sémitiques de l'ouest*. Leiden: E. J. Brill, 1965.
DOTT	Thomas, D. Winton, ed. *Documents from Old Testament Times*. New York, 1961.
ET	*The Expository Times*

EvTh	*Evangelische Theologie*
FRLANT	Forschungen zur Religion und Literatur des Alten und Neuen Testaments
GB	Gesenius, W., and Buhl, F. *Hebräisches und Aramäisches Handwörterbuch über das Alte Testament*. 17th ed. Berlin, 1949.
GE	Gilgamesh Epic
HAT	Handbuch zum Alten Testament
HK	Handkommentar zum Alten Testament
HThR	*Harvard Theological Review*
HUCA	*Hebrew Union College Annual*
IB	The Interpreter's Bible
ICC	International Critical Commentary
IDB	*The Interpreter's Dictionary of the Bible*. Edited by G. A. Butterick. 4 vols. Nashville, 1962.
JAOS	*Journal of the American Oriental Society*
JB	Jerusalem Bible
JBL	*Journal of Biblical Literature*
JCS	*Journal of Cuneiform Studies*
JEA	*Journal of Egyptian Archaeology*
JEOL	*Jaarbericht van het Vooraziatisch—Egyptisch Gezelschap 'Ex Oriente Lux'*
JNES	*Journal of Near Eastern Studies*
JQR	*Jewish Quarterly Review*
JSS	*Journal of Semitic Studies*
JTS	*Journal of Theological Studies*
KAI	Donner, H., and Röllig, W. *Kanaanäische und aramäische Inschriften*. 3 vols. Wiesbaden, 1962-1964.
KAT	Kommentar zum Alten Testament
KB	Koehler, L., and Baumgartner, W. *Lexicon in Veteris Testamenti Libros*. Leiden, 1958.
KB^2	Koehler, Ludwig, und Baumgartner, Walter. *Hebräisches und Aramäisches Lexikon zum Alten Testament*, unter Mitarbeit von B. Hartmann und E. Y. Kutscher. Lieferung I. Leiden, 1967.
LXX	Septuagint
MAOG	Mitteilungen der Altorientalischen Gesellschaft
MT	Masoretic Text
MVAG	Mitteilungen der Vorderasiatisch (-Ägyptisch)- en Gesellschaft
NAB	New American Bible
NEB	New English Bible
OTI	Eissfeldt, Otto. *The Old Testament: An Introduction*. New York, 1965.
OTT	Rad, Gerhard von. *Old Testament Theology*. 2 vols. Edinburgh, 1962, 1965.
PBS	Publications of the Babylonian Section
PEQ	*Palestine Exploration Quarterly*
RB	*Revue biblique*
SANT	Studien zum Alten und Neuen Testament
SBS	Stuttgarter Bibel-Studien
SBT	Studies in Biblical Theology
SBU	Svensk Biblisk Uppslagsverk
RoB	*Religion och Bibel*
RSV	Revised Standard Version
StTh	*Studia Theologica*

SVT	Supplements to Vetus Testamentum
TB	Theologische Bücherei
TDNT	Theological Dictionary of the New Testament. Edited by G. Kittel. Grand Rapids, Mich., 1964ff.
ThR	Theologische Rundschau
TWNT	Theologisches Wörterbuch zum Neuen Testament. Edited by G. Kittel and G. Friedrich. Stuttgart, 1932ff.
ThLZ	Theologische Literaturzeitung
ThZ	Theologische Zeitschrift
UT	Gordon, Cyrus H. Ugaritic Textbook. (AnOr, 38). Rome, 1965.
VD	Verbum Domini
VT	Vetus Testamentum
WMANT	Wissenschaftliche Monographien zum Alten und Neuen Testament
ZA	Zeitschrift für Assyriologie
ZAW	Zeitschrift für die alttestamentliche Wissenschaft
ZDMG	Zeitschrift der Deutschen Morgenländischen Gesellschaft
ZDPV	Zeitschrift des Deutschen Palästina-Vereins
ZThK	Zeitschrift für Theologie und Kirche

The RSV is used throughout unless otherwise noted.

BIBLIOGRAPHY

Abel, F.-M. Géographie de la Palestine. 2 vols. Paris, 1933, 1938.
Achtemeier, E. R. "Righteousness in the OT." IDB, (1962), IV, 80-85.
Ackroyd, P. R. "Hosea," Peake's Commentary on the Bible. Edited by M. Black and H. H. Rowley. London, 1962.
________. "Samaria." Archaeology and Old Testament Study. Edited by D. Winton Thomas. (Oxford, 1967). Pp. 343-54.
Aharoni, Y. The Land of the Bible: A Historical Geography. Translated by A. F. Rainey. Philadelphia, 1967.
Ahlström, G. W. Psalm 89. Eine Liturgie aus dem Ritual des leidenden Königs. Lund, 1959.
Aistleitner, J. Die mythologischen und kultischen Texte aus Ras Schamra. 2nd ed. Budapest, 1964.
________. Wörterbuch der ugaritischen Sprache. Edited by Otto Eissfeldt. 2nd ed. Berlin, 1963.
Albright, W. F. Archaeology and the Religion of Israel. 3rd ed. Baltimore, Md., 1953.
________. The Biblical Period from Abraham to Ezra. Harper Torchbook. New York, 1963.
________. Yahweh and the Gods of Canaan. Garden City, N. Y., 1968.
________. "Abram the Hebrew: A New Archaeological Interpretation." BASOR, 163 (1961), 36-54.
________. "The Chronology of the Divided Monarchy of Israel." BASOR, 100 (1945), 16-22.
________. "The High Places in Ancient Palestine." SVT, IV (1957), 242-58.
________. "New Light from Egypt on the Chronology and History of Israel and Judah." BASOR, 130 (1953), 4-11.
________. "The Son of Tabeel." BASOR, 140 (1955), 34-35.
________. Review of Introduction to the Old Testament by Robert H. Pfeiffer. JBL, 61 (1942), 111-26.
Alt, A. "Das Gottesurteil auf dem Karmel." Kleine Schriften zur Geschichte des Volkes Israels. (München, 1953), II, 135-49.
________. "Menschen ohne Namen." Kleine Schriften zur Geschichte des Volkes Israels. (München, 1959), III, 17-68.
________. "Tiglatpilesers III. erster Feldzug nach Palästina." Kleine Schriften zur Geschichte des Volkes Israels. (München, 1953), II, 150-62.
Altmann, A., ed. Biblical Motifs: Origins and Transformations. Studies and Texts, III. Cambridge, Mass., 1966.
Amsler, S. Amos. Neuchâtel, 1965.
________. "Amos, prophète de la onzième heure." ThZ, 21 (1965), 318-38.
Anderson, G. W., and Harrelson, W., eds. Israel's Prophetic Heritage. Essays in Honor of James Muilenburg. New York, 1962.
Anderson, G. W. "Isaiah XXIV-XXVII Reconsidered." SVT, IX (1963), 118-26.

Anthes, R. "Mythologies in Ancient Egypt." *Mythologies of the Ancient World*. Edited by S. N. Kramer. (Garden City, N. Y., 1961). Pp. 15-92.

Ap-Thomas, D. R. "Elijah on Mount Carmel." *PEQ*, XCII (1960), 146-55.

Bach, R. *Die Aufforderungen zur Flucht und zum Kampf im alttestamentlichen Prophetenspruch*. WMANT, 9. Neukirchen-Vluyn, 1962.

Baldwin, J. G. "Ṣemaḥ as a Technical Term in the Prophets." *VT*, XIV (1964), 93-97.

Balla, E. *Die Botschaft der Propheten*. Edited by Georg Fohrer. Tübingen, 1958.

Bardtke, H. "Hasael." *Biblisch-historisches Handwörterbuch*. (Göttingen, 1966), II, 650.

Baudissin, W. W. Graf. *Einleitung in die Bücher des Alten Testaments*. Leipzig, 1901.

Baumgärtel, F. *Die Eigenart der alttestamentlichen Frömmigkeit*. Schwerin, 1932.

Becker, J. *Isaias-der Prophet und sein Buch*. SBS, 30. Stuttgart, 1968.

Beer, G. "Zur Zukunftserwartung Jesajas." *Studien zur semitischen Philologie und Religionsgeschichte. Festschrift für Julius Wellhausen*. Edited by Karl Marti. (Giessen, 1914). Pp. 13-35.

Begrich, J. *Die priesterliche Tora*. *BZAW*, 66. Berlin, 1936.

________. "Jesaja 14, 38-32. Ein Beitrag zur Chronologie der israelitisch-jüdischen Königszeit." *ZDMG*, 86 (1933), 66-79. Reprinted in *Gesammelte Studien zum Alten Testament*. Edited by W. Zimmerli. (TB, 21; München, 1964). Pp. 121-31.

________. "Das priesterliche Heilsorakel." *ZAW*, 52 (1934), 81-92.

________. "Der Syrisch-Ephraimitsche Krieg und seine weltpolitischen Zusammenhänge." *ZDMG*, 83 (1929), 213-37.

Bentzen, A. *Introduction to the Old Testament*. 2 vols. 2nd ed. Kopenhagen, 1952.

________. *Jesaja I*. Kopenhagen, 1944.

Benzinger, I. *Die Bücher der Könige*. Kurzer Hand-Commentar zum Alten Testament, IX. Freiburg i. Br., 1899.

Bergsträsser, G. *Hebräische Grammatik*. Reprographic reprint from 1918 edition. Hildesheim, 1962.

Bewer, J. A. *The Book of Isaiah, Ch. 1-39*. New York, 1950.

________. "The Date in Isa. xiv, 28." *AJSL*, 54 (1937), 62.

Biggs, R. D. "More Babylonian 'Prophecies'." *Iraq*, XXIX (1967), 117-32.

Black, M. and Rowley, H. H., eds. *Peake's Commentary on the Bible*. London, 1962.

Blank, S. H. *Prophetic Faith in Isaiah*. 2nd ed. Detroit, 1967.

________. "The Current Misinterpretation of Isaiah's Sheʾar Yashub." *JBL*, 57 (1948), 211-15.

________. "Immanuel and Which Isaiah?" *JNES*, XIII (1954), 83-86.

________. "Traces of Prophetic Agony in Isaiah." *HUCA*, XXXVII (1956), 81-92.

Boehmer, J. "Die Eigenart der prophetischen Heilspredigt des Amos." *Theologische Studien und Kritiken*, 76 (1903), 35-47.

Böhl, F. M. Th. de Liagre. "Gilgameš." *Reallexikon der Assyriologie und der vorderasiatischen Archäologie*. (Berlin, 1968), III, 357-72.

________. "Religieuze Teksten uit Assur (VI-IX)." *JEOL*, 7 (1940), 403-17.

Bonnet, H. "Kuh." Reallexikon der ägyptischen Religionsgeschichte. (Berlin, 1952). Pp. 402-405.

________. "Mythus." Reallexikon der ägyptischen Religionsgeschichte. (Berlin, 1952). Pp. 496-501.

________. "Prophezeihung." Reallexikon der ägyptischen Religionsgeschichte. (Berlin, 1952). Pp 608-609.

________. "Sonnenauge." Reallexikon der ägyptischen Religionsgeschichte. (Berlin, 1952). Pp. 733-35.

Borger, R. Einleitung in die assyrischen Königsinschriften. Handbuch der Orientalistik, Ergänzungsband, V. Edited by B. Spuler. Leiden, 1961.

________. Handbuch der Keilschriftliteratur. Band I: Repertorium der sumerischen und akkadischen Texte. Berlin, 1967.

________. "Zu den Asarhaddon-Verträgen aus Nimrud. Nachtrag." ZA, 22 (1964), 261

Botterweck, G. J. "Zur Authentizität des Buches Amos." BZ, 2 (1958), 176-89.

Boutflower, C. The Book of Isaiah (Chapters I-XXIX) in the Light of the Assyrian Monuments. London, 1930.

Box, G. H. The Book of Isaiah. London, 1916.

Brandon, S. G. F. Creation Legends of the Ancient Near East. London, 1963.

Bowman, R. A. "Hazael." IDB, (1962), II, 538.

Breasted, J. H., ed. Ancient Records of Egypt: Historical Documents from the Earliest Times to the Persian Conquest. 5 vols. Chicago, 1906-1907.

________. The Dawn of Conscience. Chicago, 1933.

Brinkman, J. A. "Mesopotamian Chronology of the Historical Period." Ancient Mesopotamia (2nd ed.; Chicago, 1968). Pp. 335-52.

Bright, J. A History of Israel. Philadelphia, 1959.

________. The Kingdom of God. Nashville, 1953.

________. "Isaiah-I." Peake's Commentary on the Bible. Edited by M. Black and H. H. Rowley. London, 1962.

Brockelmann, C. Grundriss der vergleichenden Grammatik der semitischen Sprachen. 2 vols. Hildesheim, 1961.

Bronner, L. The Stories of Elijah and Elisha. Pretoria Oriental Series, VI. Leiden, 1968.

Brown, F., Driver, A. R., and Briggs, C. A. A Hebrew and English Lexicon of the Old Testament. Oxford, 1959.

Brownlee, W. H. The Meaning of the Qumran Scrolls for the Bible. New York, 1964

________. "The Text of Isaiah VI, 13 in the Light of DISa." VT, i (1951), 296-98.

Brunner-Traut, E. Altägyptische Märchen. Düsseldorf-Köln, 1963.

Buber, M. The Prophetic Faith. Harper Torchbooks. New York, 1960.

Budde, K. Jesajas Erleben. Eine gemeinverständliche Auslegung der Denkschrift des Propheten Jesaja (Kap. 6, 1-9, 6). Gotha, 1928.

________. "Über die Schranken, die Jesajas prophetischer Botschaft zu setzen sind." ZAW, 41 (1923), 154-203.

________. "Zu Text und Auslegung des Buches Amos." JBL, 43 (1924), 46-131; 44 (1925), 63-122.

Burrows, M. The Dead Sea Scrolls. New York, 1955.
_______. More Light on the Dead Sea Scrolls. New York, 1958.
_______. An Outline of Biblical Theology. Philadelphia, 1946.
_______, ed. The Dead Sea Scrolls of St. Mark's Monastery: Vol. I: The Isaiah Manuscript and the Habakkuk Commentary. New Haven, 1950.
Campbell, J. C. "God's People and the Remnant." Scottish Journal of Theology, 3 (1950), 78-85.
Carlson, R. A. "Profeten Amos och Davidsriket." Religion och Bibel, 25 (1966), 57-78.
Cassuto, U. A Commentary on the Book of Genesis. Translated by I. Abrahams. 2 vols. Jerusalem, 1961, 1964.
Černy, L. The Day of Yahweh and Some Relevant Problems. Prague, 1948.
Cheyne, T. K. Introduction to the Book of Isaiah. London, 1895.
_______. The Prophecies of Isaiah. 5th ed. New York, 1890.
Childs, B. S. Isaiah and the Assyrian Crisis. SBT, II/3. London,1967.
Civil, M. "The Sumerian Flood Story." Atra-ḫasīs: The Babylonian Story of the Flood. (Oxford, 1969). Pp. 138-45.
_______. "Texts and Fragments (36)." JCS, XV (1961), 79-80.
Clapp, F. G. "Geology and Bitumens of the Dead Sea Area." Bulletin of the American Association of the Petroleum Geologists, (1936), 881-909.
Clay, A. T. A Hebrew Deluge Story in Cuneiform and Other Epic Fragments in the Pierpont Morgan Library. Yale Oriental Series, V/3. New Haven, 1922.
Clements, R. E. Prophecy and Covenant. SBT, 43. Naperville, Ill., 1965.
_______. The Conscience of the Nation. A Study of Early Israelite Prophecy. London, 1967.
Cohen, S. "Tema." IDB, (1962), IV, 533.
Cornill, C. H. Der israelitische Prophetismus. 20th ed. Strassburg, 1920.
Cossmann, W. Die Entwicklung des Gerichtsgedankens bei den alttestamentlichen Propheten. BZAW, 29. Giessen, 1915.
Cramer, K. Amos. Versuch einer theologischen Interpretation. BWANT, 3. Folge Heft 15. Stuttgart, 1930.
Crenshaw, J. L. "The Influence of the Wise upon Amos." ZAW, 79 (1967), 42-52.
Cripps, R. S. A Critical and Exegetical Commentary on the Book of Amos. 2nd ed. London, 1960.
Cross, F. M. "The Divine Warrior in Israel's Early Cult." Biblical Motifs: Origins and Transformations. Edited by A. Altmann. (Studies and Texts, III; Cambridge, Mass., 1966). Pp. 3ff.
_______. "Yahweh and the Gods of the Patriarchs." HThR, 55 (1962), 225-59.
Dalman, G. Arbeit und Sitte in Palästina. 7 vols. Gütersloh, 1928-42.
Danell, G. A. Studies in the Name Israel in the Old Testament. Uppsala, 1946.
Davies, G. H. "Remnant." A Theological Word Book of the Bible. Edited by Alan Richardson. (2nd ed. New York, 1962). Pp. 188-91.
de Buck, A. The Egyptian Coffin Texts. Oriental Institute Publications, 34. 2 vols. Chicago, 1935, 1938.

Deimel, A. "Diluvium in traditione babylonica." VD, VII (1927), 186-91.
Delitzsch, Franz. A New Commentary on Genesis. Translated by S. Taylor. 2 vols. New York, 1899.
Delitzsch, Friedrich. Assyrisches Handwörterbuch. Leipzig, 1896.
________. Assyrische Lesestücke. 3rd ed. Leipzig, 1885.
Dennefeld, L. Les grands prophètes. La Sainte Bible, VII. Paris, 1946.
de Vaux, R. Ancient Israel: Its Life and Institutions. Translated by J. McHugh. London, 1961.
________. Studies in Old Testament Sacrifice. Cardiff, 1964.
________. "Jerusalem and the Prophets." Interpreting the Prophetic Tradition. Edited by Harry M. Orlinsky. (New York, 1969). Pp. 275-300.
________. "Le 'reste d'Israël' d'après les Prophètes." RB, 42 (1933), 526-39. Reprinted in R. de Vaux, Bible et Orient. (Paris, 1967). Pp. 25-39.
De Vries, S. J. "Chronology of the OT." IDB, (1962), I, 580-99.
Dexinger, F. Sturz der Göttersöhne oder Engel vor der Sintflut? Wiener Beiträge zur Theologie, XIII. Wien, 1966.
Dhorme, P. "Le pays bibliques et l'Assyrie." RB, 7 (1910), 368-90.
Dietrich, E. K. Die Umkehr im Alten Testament und im Judentum. Stuttgart, 1936.
Dillmann, A. Der Prophet Jesaja. Leipzig, 1890.
________. Genesis. Translated by W. B. Stevenson. 2 vols. Edinburgh, 1897.
Diman (=Haran), M. "An Archaic Survival in Prophetic Literature." Yedi'oth, 13 (1947), 7-15.
Dion, H. M. "The Patriarchal Traditions and the Literary Form of the 'Oracle of Salvation'." CBQ, 29 (1967), 198-206.
Dittmann, Herbert. "Der heilige Rest im Alten Testament." Theologische Studien und Kritiken, 87 (1914), 603-18.
Donner, H. Israel unter den Völkern. Die Stellung der klassischen Propheten des 8. Jahrhunderts v. Chr. zur Aussenpolitik der Könige von Israel und Juda. SVT, XI. Leiden, 1964.
________, und Röllig, W. Kanaanäische und aramäische Inschriften. 3 vols. Wiesbaden, 1962-1964.
Dossin, G., ed. Lettres. Archives royales de Mari, 4. Paris, 1951.
Dreyfus, F. "La doctrine du 'Reste d'Israël' chez le prophète Isaïe." Revue des Sciences Philosophiques et Théologiques, 39 (1955), 361-86.
________. "Reste." Vocabulaire de théologie biblique. Edited by X. Leon-Dufour. (Paris, 1962). Pp. 908-11.
Driver, G. R. Canaanite Myths and Legends. Edinburgh, 1956.
________. "Isaiah I-XXXIX: Textual and Linguistic Problems." JSS, XIII (1968), 36-57.
Driver, S. R. The Book of Genesis. Westminster Commentary. 14th ed. London, 1943.
________. The Books of Joel and Amos. Cambridge Bible for Schools and Colleges. 2nd ed. Cambridge, 1934.
________. An Introduction to the Literature of the Old Testament. Meridian Books. Cleveland and New York, 1956.
Dürr, L. Ursprung und Ausbau der israelitisch-jüdischen Heilandserwartung. Berlin, 1925.

Duhm, B. Anmerkungen zu den Zwölf Propheten. Giessen, 1911.
_______. Das Buch Jesaja. 5th ed. Göttingen, 1968.
_______. Israels Propheten. 2 nd ed. Tübingen, 1922.
_______. Die Zwölf Propheten. Tübingen, 1910.
Ebeling, E. Der akkadische Mythos vom Pestgotte Era. Berliner Beiträge zur Keilschriftforschung, II/1. Berlin, 1925.
_______. Bruchstücke eines politischen Propagandagedichtes aus einer assyrischen Kanzlei. MAOG, 12/II. Leipzig, 1938.
_______. Keilschrifttexte aus Assur religiösen Inhalts. Wissenschaftliche Veröffentlichung der Deutschen Orientgesellschaft, 34. Band II. Leipzig, 1923.
Edzard, D. O. Die "zweite Zwischenzeit" Babyloniens. Wiesbaden, 1957.
Eichrodt, W. Der Heilige in Israel: Jesaja 1-12. Die Botschaft des Alten Testaments, 17/I. Stuttgart, 1960.
_______. Der Herr der Geschichte, Jesaja 13-23/28-39. Die Botschaft des Alten Testaments, 17/II. Stuttgart, 1967.
_______. Die Hoffnung des ewigen Friedens im alten Israel. Beiträge zur Förderung christlicher Theologie, 25. Gütersloh, 1920.
_______. Israel in der Weissagung des Alten Testaments. Zürich, 1951.
_______. Theology of the Old Testament. Translated by J. A. Baker. 2 vols. Philadelphia, 1961,1967.
Eissfeldt, O. Der Gott Carmel. Berlin, 1963.
_______. The Old Testament. An Introduction. Translated by P. R. Ackroyd. New York, 1965.
_______. "Baʿalšamēn und Jahwe." Kleine Schriften. (Tübingen, 1963), II, 171-98.
_______. "Die Komposition von I Reg 16, 29-11 Reg 13,25." Das ferne und nahe Wort. Festschrift L. Rost. Edited by Fritz Maass. (Berlin, 1968). Pp. 49-58.
_______. "Das Lied Moses Dt 32:1-43 und das Lehrgedicht Asaphs Ps 78." Berichte über die Verhandlungen der Sächsischen Akademie der Wissenschaften zu Leipzig, Phil.-hist. Klasse, 104/5 (1958), 26-43.
Elliger, K. Leviticus. HAT, I/4. Göttingen, 1966.
Engnell, I. Amos. 2nd ed. Copenhagen, 1962.
_______. The Call of Isaiah. An Exegetical and Comparative Study. Uppsala, 1949.
_______. Studies in Divine Kingship in the Ancient Near East. 2nd ed. Oxford, 1967.
Erlandsson, S. The Burden of Babylon. A Study of Isaiah 13:2-14:23. Lund, 1970.
Erman, A. The Ancient Egyptians: A Sourcebook of their Writings. Harper Torchbooks. Translated by A. M. Blackman. New York, 1966.
_______. The Literature of the Ancient Egyptians. Translated by Aylward M. Blackman. London, 1927.
Ewald, H. Jesaja mit den übrigen älteren Propheten. 2nd ed. Gottingen, 1867.
Faber, H. ed. Theologie als Glaubenswagnis. Festschrift für Karl Heim zum 80. Geburtstag. Furche-Studien 23. Bd. Hamburg, 1954.
Falkenstein, A. Sumerische Götterlieder. 2 vols. Heidelberg, 1959, 1960.
_______. "Sumerische Beschwörungen aus Bogazköy." ZA, 45 (1939), 8ff.

Falkenstein, A. und Soden, W. von. Sumerische und akkadische Hymnen und Gebete. Zürich, 1953.
Feldmann, F. Das Buch Isaias. Exegetisches Handbuch zum Alten Testament, XIV. Münster, 1925.
Feuillet, A. "La communauté messianique dans la prédication d'Isaïe." Bible et Vie Chrétienne, 20 (1957/58), 38-52.
Fey, R. Amos und Jesaja. Abhängigkeit und Eigenständigkeit des Jesaja. WMANT, 12. Neukirchen-Vluyn, 1963.
Fichtner, J. "Jahwes Plan in der Botschaft des Jesajas." ZAW, 63 (1951), 16-33.
Finegan, J. Light from the Ancient East. 2nd ed. Princeton, 1959.
Finkelstein, J. J. "The Antediluvian Kings: A University of California Tablet." JCS, XVII (1963), 38-51.
________. "Bible and Babel." Commentary, 26 (1958), 431-44.
Fischer, J. Das Buch Isaias, Teil 1. Die Heilige Schrift des Alten Testaments. Bonn, 1937.
________. In welcher Schrift lag das Buch Isaias der LXX vor? BZAW, 56. Giessen, 1930.
Fohrer, G. Das Buch Jesaja. 3 vols. 2nd ed. Zürich, 1967-68.
________. Die symbolischen Handlungen der Propheten. 2nd ed. Zurich, 1968.
________. Elia. AThANT, 53. 2nd ed. Zürich, 1968.
________. Introduction to the Old Testament. Translated by D. C. Green. Nashville, 1968.
________. "Jesaja 1 als Zusammenfassung der Verkündigung Jesajas." Studien zur alttestamentlichen Prophetie. (Berlin, 1967). Pp. 148-66.
________. "Neuere Literatur zur alttestamentlichen Prophetie." ThR, XIX (1951), 277-346; XX (1952), 193-271, 295-361.
________. "Remarks on Modern Interpretation of the Prophets." JBL, 80 (1961), 309-19.
________. Review of Der Prophet Jesaja, Kap. 1-12 by Otto Kaiser. ThLZ, 87 (1962), cols. 746-49.
________. "Die Stuktur der alttestamentlichen Eschatologie." ThLZ, 85 (1960), cols. 401-20.
________. "Zehn Jahre Literatur zur alttestamentlichen Prophetie (1951-1960)." ThR, 28 (1962), 1-75, 235-97, 301-74.
________. "Zu Jesaja 7, 14 im Zusammenhang von Jesaja 7, 10-22." Studien zur alttestamentlichen Prophetie. (Berlin, 1967).
Fosbroke, H. E. W. The Book of Amos. IB, 6. Nashville, 1956.
Frank, R. M. "A Note on 2 Kings 19:10,14." CBQ, 25 (1963), 410-14.
Fullerton, K. "Isaiah 14:28-32." AJSL, 42 (1952), 1ff.
________. "Viewpoints in the Discussion of Isaiah's Hopes for the Future." JBL, 41 (1922), 1-101.
Gadd, C. J. "The Cities of Babylonia." The Cambridge Ancient History. Revised ed. (Cambridge, 1964).
Gaehr, T. J. "Shear-jashub; or the Remnant Sections in Isaiah." Bibliotheca Sacra, 79 (1922), 363-71.
Gall, A. von. Βασιλεία τοῦ θεοῦ. Eine religionsgeschichtliche Studie zur vorkirchlichen Eschatologie. Religionswissenschaftliche Bibliothek, 7. Heidelberg, 1926.
Galling, K. Deutsche Theologie. Berlin, 1939.

Gardiner, A. H. "The Defeat of the Hyksos by Kamose." JEA, II (1916), 95-110.

________. "New Literary Works from Ancient Egypt." JEA, I (1914), 100-106.

Garelli, P., ed. Gilgameš et sa légende; études recueillies par Paul Garelli. . . . Paris, 1960.

Garofalo, S. La nozione profetica del 'Resto d'Israele.' Contributo alla teologia del Vecchio Testamento. Lateranum, N.S. AN. VIII N. 1-4. Romae, 1942.

________. "Residuum Israelis." VD, 21 (1941), 239-43.

Gaster, T. H. Myth, Legend, and Custom in the Old Testament. New York, 1969.

Gehman, H. S. "The Ruler of the Universe: The Theology of First Isaiah." Interpretation, XI (1957), 269-81.

Gelin, A. "The Latter Prophets." Introduction to the Old Testament. Edited by A. Robert and A. Feuillet. Translated by P. W. Skehan, et al. New York, 1968.

Gerstenberger, E. Wesen und Herkunft des "apodiktischen Rechts." WMANT, 20. Neukirchen-Vluyn, 1965.

________. "The Woe-Oracles of the Prophets." JBL, 81 (1962), 249-63.

Gese, H. "Kleine Beiträge zum Verständnis des Amosbuches." VT, XII (1962), 417-38.

Gesenius, W. und Buhl, F. Hebräisches und Aramäisches Handwörterbuch über das Alte Testament. 17th ed. Berlin, 1949.

________, und Kautzsch, E. Hebräische Grammatik. 28th ed. Halle, 1909.

Giesebrecht, F. Beiträge zur Jesajakritik. Göttingen, 1890.

Ginsberg, H. L. The Legend of King Keret, A Canaanite Epic of the Bronze Age. BASOR, Supplementary Studies, 2-3. New Haven, 1946.

________. "Reflexes of Sargon in Isaiah After 715 B.C.E." JAOS, 88 (1968), 47-53.

Gössmann, F. Das Era-Epos. Würzburg, 1956.

Goetze, A. Die Annalen des Muršiliš. MVAG, 38. Leipzig, 1933.

________. Kulturgeschichte des Alten Orients: Kleinasien. Handbuch der Altertumswissenschaft, III. 2nd ed. München, 1957.

________. Madduwattaš. MVAG, 32. Leipzig, 1928.

________. "Die Pestgebete des Muršiliš." Kleinasiatische Forschungen. Edited by F. Sommer and H. Ehelolf. (Weimar, 1930), I, 161-251.

________. "Warfare in Asia Minor." Iraq, XXV (1963), 124-30.

Gordon, C. H. Ugaritic Handbook. Roma, 1947.

________. Ugaritic Literature. Roma, 1949.

________. Ugaritic Textbook. AnOr, 38. Rome, 1965.

Gordon, E. I. Sumerian Proverbs: Glimpses of Everyday Life in Ancient Mesopotamia. Philadelphia, 1959.

Gottlieb, H. "Amos und Jerusalem." VT, XVII (1967), 430-63.

Gottwald, N. K. A Light to the Nations. An Introduction to the Old Testament. New York, 1959.

________. All the Kingdoms of the Earth. New York, 1964.

________. "Immanuel as the Prophet's Son." VT, VII (1958), 36-47.

Grapow, H. Die bildlichen Ausdrücke im Ägyptischen. Berlin, 1924.

________. Studien zu den Annalen Thutmosis des Dritten und zu ihnen verwandten historischen Berichten des neuen Reiches. Berlin, 1949.

Gray, G. B. The Book of Isaiah, Chapters I-XXXIX. ICC. Edinburgh, 1912.
Gray, J. I & II Kings. A Commentary. The Old Testament Library. Philadelphia, 1963.
________. The KRT Text in the Literature of Ras Shamra: A Social Myth of Ancient Canaan. 2nd ed. Leiden, 1964.
________. "Chronology of the Old Testament." Peake's Commentary on the Bible. Edited by M. Black and H. H. Rowley. London, 1962.
________. "Texts from Ras Shamra." Documents from Old Testament Times. Edited by D. Winton Thomas. (New York, 1961). Pp. 118-33.
Grayson, A. K., and Lambert, W. G. "Akkadian Prophecies." JCS, XVIII (1964), 7-30.
Gressmann, H. Die älteste Geschichtsschreibung und Prophetie Israels. 2nd ed. Göttingen, 1921.
________. Der Messias. FRLANT, 43. Göttingen, 1929.
________. The Tower of Babel. Edited by Julian Obermann. New York, 1928.
________. Der Ursprung der israelitisch-jüdischen Eschatologie. FRLANT, 6. Göttingen, 1905.
________, ed. Altorientalische Texte und Bilder zum Alten Testament. 2 vols. Berlin, 1926, 1927.
________. "Foreign Influences in Hebrew Prophecy." JTS, XXVII (1926), 241ff.
Grönbaek, J. H. "Zur Frage der Eschatologie in der Verkündigung der Gerichtspropheten." Svensk Exegetisk Årsbok, XXIV (1959), 5-21.
Gröndahl, F. Die Personennamen der Texte aus Ugarit. Studia Pohl, 1. Rome, 1967.
Gross, H. "Rest." Bibeltheologisches Wörterbuch. Edited by Johannes B. Bauer. (2nd ed.; Graz, 1962), II, 1000-1003.
Gunkel, H. Elias, Jahve und Baal. Tübingen, 1907.
Gunn, B. "The Religion of the Poor in Ancient Egypt." JEA, III (1916), 81-94.
Gunneweg, A. H. J. "Heils- und Unheilsverkündigung in Jes. VII." VT, XV (1965), 27-34.
Gurney, O. R. The Hittites. 2nd ed. Baltimore, Md., 1966.
________, and Finkelstein, J. J. The Sultantepe Tablets I. London, 1957.
________. "Hittite Prayers of Mursili II." Annals of Archaeology and Anthropology. XXVII (1940), 1-163.
Güterbock, H. G. The Song of Ullikummi. New Haven, 1952.
________. "The Deeds of Suppiluliuma as Told by His Son, Mursili II." JCS, X (1956), 41-69; 75-98; 107-30.
________. "Hittite Mythology." Mythologies of the Ancient World. Edited by S. N. Kramer. (Garden City, N. Y., 1961). Pp. 139-79.
________. "The Song of Ullikummi. Revised Text of the Hittite Version of a Hurrian Myth." JCS, V (1951), 135-61; VI (1952), 8-42.
Habel, N. "The Form and Significance of the Call Narratives." ZAW, 77 (1965), 297-323.
Haldar, A. Associations of Cult Prophets Among the Ancient Semites. Uppsala, 1945.
Halevy, J. "Recherches bibliques-Le livre d'Amos." Revue Sémitique, 11 (1903), 1-31,97-121, 193-209, 289-30; 12 (1904), 1-18.
Hallo, W. W. "Beginning and End of the Sumerian King List in the Nippur Recension." JCS, XVII (1963), 52-57.

Hallo, W. W. "From Qarqar to Carchemish: Assyria and Israel in the Light of New Discoveries." BA, 23 (1960), 33-61. Reprinted in BAR, 2. Edited by D. N. Freedman and E. F. Campbell, Jr. (Garden City, N. Y.., 1964). Pp. 152-88.

________. "On the Antiquity of Sumerian Literature." JAOS, 83 (1963), 167-76.

Hämmerly-Dupuy, D. "Some Observations on the Assyro-Babylonian and Sumerian Flood Stories." AUSS, VI (1968), 1-18.

Hammershaimb, E. Amos fortolket. 2nd ed. Copenhagen, 1958.

________. Some Aspects of Old Testament Prophecy from Isaiah to Malachi. Kobenhaven, 1966.

Hamp, V. "Rest, heiliger R. I. Altes Testament." Lexikon für Theologie und Kirche. (Freiburg, 1963), VIII, 1252-3.

Harper, W. R. A Critical and Exegetical Commentary on Amos and Hosea. New York, 1905.

Harland, J. P. "Sodom." IDB. 1962. Vol. IV.

________. "Sodom and Gomorrah: The Location and Destruction of the Cities of the Plain." BA, V (1942), 17-32; VI (1943), 41-54.

Harper, E. T. "Die Babylonischen Legenden von Etana, Zu, Adapa und Dibbarra." Beiträge zur Assyiologie und semitischen Sprachwissenschaft, (1894), 390-521.

Harrelson, W. From Fertility Cult to Worship. Garden City, N. Y., 1969.

________. Interpreting the Old Testament. New York, 1964.

________. "Nonroyal Motifs in Royal Eschatology." Israel's Prophetic Heritage. Essays in Honor of James Muilenburg. Edited by B. W. Anderson and W. Harrelson. New York, 1962.

Hasel, G. F. "Linguistic Considerations Regarding the Translation of Isaiah's 'Shear-jashub'." AUSS, IX (1971), 36-46.

________. "Remnant." IDBSuppl. (1976), pp. 735-36.

________. "'Remnant' as a Meaning of ᵓaḥarît," in The Archaeology of Jordan and Other Studies. Edited by L. T. Geraty. Berrien Springs, Mi., 1980.

Hattori, Y. "The Prophet Ezekiel and His Idea of the Remnant." Unpublished Th.D. dissertation, Westminster Theological Seminary, 1968.

Hayes, J. H. "The Tradition of Zion's Inviolability." JBL, 82 (1963), 419-26.

________. "The Usage of Oracles Against Foreign Nations in Ancient Israel." JBL, 87 (1968), 81-92.

Heaton, E. W. The Hebrew Kingdoms. The New Clarendon Bible: Old Testament, Vol. IV. London, 1968.

________. The Old Testament Prophets. Pelikan Book. Baltimore, Md., 1964.

________. "The Root שׁאר and the Doctrine of the Remnant." JTS, N.S., III (1952), 27-39.

Heidel, A. The Gilgamesh Epic and Old Testament Parallels. 2nd ed. Chicago, 1949.

Helck, W., and Otto, E. Kleines Wörterbuch der Ägyptologie. Berlin, 1956.

Hempel, J. Gott und Mensch im Alten Testament. BWANT, Dritte Folge, Heft 2. 2nd ed. Stuttgart, 1936.

________. Worte der Propheten. Berlin, 1949.

Hempel, J. "Die Wurzeln des Missionswillens im Glauben des Alten Testaments." ZAW, 66 (1954), 244-72.

Henry, M.-L. Glaubenskrise und Glaubensbewährung in den Dichtungen der Jesajaapokalypse. BWANT, 86. Stuttgart, 1967.

Henshaw, T. The Latter Prophets. London, 1958.

Herntrich, V. Der Prophet Jesaja, Kapitel 1-12. ATD, 17. Göttingen, 1957.

________. "λεῖμμα κτλ." TWNT. Edited by Gerhard Kittel. Stuttgart, 1942; IV, 198-215; TDNT. 1967. Vol. IV, 196-209.

Herrmann, S. Die prophetischen Heilserwartungen im Alten Testament. BWANT, 87. Stuttgart, 1965.

________. Untersuchungen zur Überlieferungsgestalt mittelägyptischer Literaturwerke. Deutsche Akademie der Wissenschaften zu Berlin, Institut für Orientforschung, Veröffentlichung N. 33. Berlin, 1957.

________. "Prophetie in Israel and Ägypten." SVT, IX (1963), 47-65.

Hertzberg, H. W. Der Erste Jesaja. Leipzig, 1936.

Heschel, A. J. The Prophets. New York, 1962.

________. The Prophets: An Introduction. Harper Torchbooks. New York, 1969.

Hesse, F. Das Verstockungsproblem im Alten Testament. BZAW, 74. Berlin, 1955.

________. "Amos 5, 4-6. 14f." ZAW, 68 (1956), 1-17.

Hillers, D. R. Covenant: The History of a Biblical Idea. Baltimore, Md., 1969.

Hilprecht, H. V. The Babylonian Expedition of the University of Pennsylvania. Series D, Vol. V. Philadelphia, 1910.

Hitzig, F. Des Propheten Jonas Orakel über Moab. BZAW, 41. Giessen, 1925.

Hölscher, G. Die Ursprünge der jüdischen Eschatologie. Giessen, 1925.

________. "Jesaja." ThLZ, 77 (1952), 683-94.

Holt, J. M. The Patriarchs of Israel. Nashville, 1964.

Honor, L. L. Sennacherib's Invasion of Palestine. Contributions to Oriental History and Philology, No. 12. New York, 1926.

Hooke, S. H. "Genesis," Peake's Commentary on the Bible. Edited by M. Black and H. H. Rowley. London, 1962.

________. In the Beginning. The Claredon Bible, VI. Oxford, 1947.

________. Middle Eastern Mythology. Baltimore, Md., 1963.

Horn, S. H. "Did Sennacherib Campaign Once or Twice Against Hezekiah?" AUSS, IV (1966), 1-28.

________. "The Chronology of King Hezekiah's Reign." AUSS, II (1964), 40-52.

Horst, F. "Die Visionsschilderungen der alttestamentlichen Propheten." EvTh, 20 (1960), 193-205.

Hoshizaki, R. "Isaiah's Concept of the Remnant." Unpublished M.Th. thesis, Southern Baptist Theological Seminary, Louisville, Kentucky, 1955.

Houwinck Ten Cate, P. H. J. "Mursilis' Northwestern Campaigns--Additional Fragments of His Comprehensive Annals." JNES, XXV (1966), 162-91.

Hvidberg, F. "The Maṣṣeba and the Holy Seed." Nederlands theologisch Tijdschrift, 56 (1955), 97-99.

Hyatt, J. P. Prophetic Religion. Nashville, 1947.

________. "Amos," Peake's Commentary on the Bible. Edited by M. Black and H. H. Rowley. London, 1962.

________, ed. The Bible in Modern Scholarship. Nashville, 1965.

________. "Was Yahweh Originally a Creator Deity?" JBL, 84 (1967), 369-77.

Iwry, S. "Maṣṣēbāh and Bāmāh in 1Q Isaiah^{A} 6 13." JBL, 76 (1957), 225-32.

________. "והנמצא--A Striking Variant Reading in 1AIs^{a}." Textus, V (1966), 34-43.

Jacob, E. Theology of the Old Testament. Translated by A. W. Heathcote and P. J. Allcock. London, 1958.

Jacobsen, T. The Sumerian King List. Assyriological Studies, 11. Chicago, 1939.

________. "Ancient Mesopotamian Religion: The Central Concerns." Proceedings of the American Philosophical Society, 107 (1963), 473-84.

________. "Formative Tendencies in Sumerian Religion." The Bible and the Ancient Near East. Essays in Honor of William Foxwell Albright. Edited by G. Ernest Wright. (Garden City, N. Y., 1965). Pp. 353-68.

________. "Book Review of Lamentation over the Destruction of Ur by S. N. Kramer." AJSL, LVIII (1941), 219-24.

Jastrow, Morris. Aspects of Religious Belief and Practice in Babylonia and Assyria. New York and London, 1911.

________. Hebrew and Babylonian Traditions. London, 1914.

________. Die Religion Babyloniens und Assyriens. 2 Bände. Giessen, 1905-12.

Jean, C.-F., and Hoftijzer, J. Dictionnaire des inscriptions sémitiques de l'ouest. Leiden, 1965.

Jenni, E. "Eschatology." IDB, (1962), II, 126-32.

________. "Jesajas Berufung in der neueren Forschung." ThZ, 15 (1959), 321-39.

________. "Remnant." IDB, (1962), IV, 32-33.

Jepsen, A. Die Quellen des Königsbuches. Halle, 1953.

________. Nabi. München, 1934.

________. "Israel und Damaskus." AfO, 14 (1941-44), 153-72.

Jeremias, A. Babylonisches im Neuen Testament. Leipzig, 1905.

Jeremias, Joachim. "Der Gedanke des 'Heiligen Restes' im Spätjudentum und in der Verkündigung Jesu." Zeitschrift für die neutestamentlichen Wissenschaft, 42 (1949), 184-94. Reprinted in J. Jeremias, Abba. (Göttingen, 1966). Pp. 121-32.

Jeremias, Jörg. Theophanie. Die Geschichte einer alttestamentlichen Gattung. WMANT, 10. Neukirchen-Vluyn, 1965.

Jirku, A. Der Mythus der Kanaanäer. Bonn, 1966.

________. Kanaanäische Mythen und Epen aus Ras Schamra-Ugarit. Gütersloh, 1962.

Junker, H. "Ursprung und Grundzüge des Messiasbildes bei Isaias." SVT, IV (1957), 181-96.
Kaiser, O. Einleitung in das Alte Testament. Gütersloh, 1969.
________. Der Prophet Jesaja, Kapitel 1-12. ATD, 17. 2nd ed. Göttingen, 1963.
________. "Rest." Biblisch-historisches Handwörterbuch. (Göttingen, 1966), III, 1592-93.
Kammenhuber, A. "Die hethitische Geschichtsschreibung." Saeculum, 9 (1958), 136-55.
Kapelrud, A. S. Central Ideas in Amos. 2nd ed. Oslo, 1961.
________. "New Ideas in Amos." SVT, XV (1966), 193-206.
Kaplan, M. M. "Isaiah 6:1-11." JBL, 45 (1926), 251-59.
Kaufmann, Y. The Religion of Israel. Translated and edited by Moshe Greenberg. Chicago, 1960.
Keller, C. A. "Wer war Elia?" ThZ, 16 (1960), 298-313.
Kellermann, U. "Der Amosschluss als Stimme deuteronomistischer Heilshoffnung." EvTh, 29 (1969), 169-83.
Kelly, S. L., Jr. "The Zion-Victory Songs: Psalms 46, 48, and 76. A Critical Study of Modern Methods of Psalmic Interpretation." Unpublished Ph.D. dissertation, Vanderbilt University, 1968.
Kennett, R. H. The Composition of the Book of Isaiah in the Light of History and Archaeology. London, 1910.
Key, A. F. "The Magical Background of Isaiah 6:9-13." JBL, 86 (1967), 198-204.
Kidner, D. Genesis. Tyndale Old Testament Commentary. Chicago, 1967.
Kienast, B. "Review of Das Era-Epos by Felix Gössmann." ZA, 54 (1961), 244-49.
King, W. L. Legends of Babylon and Egypt in Relation to Hebrew Tradition. London,, 1918.
Kilian, R. Die Verheissung Immanuels, Jes. 7, 14. SBS, 35. Stuttgart, 1968.
Kissane, Edward J. The Book of Isaiah, I-XXXIX. 2nd ed. Dublin, 1960.
Kitchen, K. A. Ancient Orient and Old Testament. Chicago, 1968.
Kittel, R. Die Bücher der Könige. HK, I. Abteilung. Göttingen, 1900.
Knierim, R. "The Vocation of Isaiah." VT, XVIII (1968), 47-68.
Knight, G. A. F. A Christian Theology of the Old Testament. Revised edition. London, 1964.
Koch, K. The Growth of the Biblical Tradition. Translated by S. M. Cupitt. New York, 1969.
Köberle, J. Sünde und Gnade. München, 1905.
Koehler, L. Amos. Giessen, 1917.
________. Old Testament Theology. Translated by A. S. Todd. Philadelphia, 1957.
________. "Zum Verständnis von Jesaja 7, 14." ZAW, 67 (1955), 48-50.
________, und Baumgartner, W. Hebräisches und Aramäisches Lexikon zum Alten Testament, unter Mitarbeit von B. Hartmann und E. Y. Kutscher. Lieferung I. Leiden, 1967.
________, und Baumgartner, W. Lexicon in Veteris Testamenti Libros. Leiden, 1958.
König, E. Das Buch Jesaja. Gütersloh, 1926.
Korošec, V. "The Warfare of the Hittites--From the Legal Point of View." Iraq, XXV (1963), 159-66.

Kraeling, E. G. Commentary on the Prophets. 2 vols. Camden, N. Y., 1966.
Kramer, S. N. From the Tablets of Sumer. Twenty-five Firsts in Man's Recorded History. Indian Hills, 1956.
________. History Begins at Sumer. Garden City, N. Y., 1959.
________. Lamentation Over the Destruction of Ur. Assyriological Study, No. 12. Chicago, 1940.
________. Sumerian Mythology: A Study of Spiritual and Literary Achievement in the Third Millenium B. C. Philadelphia, 1944.
________. The Sumerians. Their History, Culture, and Character. Chicago, 1963.
________, ed. Mythologies of the Ancient World. Garden City, N. Y., 1961.
________. "Cuneiform Studies and the History of Literature." Proceedings of the American Philosophical Society, 107 (1963), 485-527.
________. "Gilgamesh: Some New Sumerian Data." Gilgameš et sa légende. Études recueillies par Paul Garelli. (Paris, 1960). Pp. 59-68.
________. "Sumerian Literature, A General Survey." The Bible and the Ancient Near East. Essays in Honor of William Foxwell Albright. (Garden City, N. Y., 1965). Pp. 327-52.
Kraus, F. R. "Altmesopotamisches Lebensgefühl." JNES, XIX (1960), 117-32.
Kraus, H.-J. Prophetie und Politik. München, 1952.
________. Worship in Israel. Translated by G. Buswell. Richmond Va., 1966.
________. "Die prophetische Botschaft gegen das soziale Unrecht Israels." EvTh, 15 (1955), 295-307.
Krause, H. H. "Der Gerichtsprophet Amos, ein Vorläufer des Deuteronomisten." ZAW, 50 (1932), 221-39.
Kruse, H. "Alma Redemptoris Mater. Eine Auslegung der Immanuel-Weissagung Is 7, 14." Trierer Theologische Zeitschrift, 74 (1965), 15-36.
Kuhl, C. The Prophets of Israel. Translated by R. J. Ehrlich and J. P. Smith. Richmond, Va., 1960.
Külling, S. R. Zur Datierung der "Genesis-P-Stücke." Kampen, 1964.
Laessøe, J. People of Ancient Assyria, their Inscriptions and Correspondence. London, 1963.
________. "The Atrahasīs Epic: A Babylonian History of Mankind." BiOr, XIII (1956), 90-102.
Lambdin, T. O. "Pathros." IDB, (1962), III, 676.
Lambert, W. G. Babylonian Wisdom Literature. Oxford, 1960.
________, and Millard, A. R. Atra-ḫasīs. The Babylonian Story of the Flood. Oxford, 1969.
________. Babylonian Literary Texts. CT, 46. London, 1965.
________. "Enmeduranki and Related Matters." JCS, XXI (1967), 1ff.
________. "The Fifth Tablet of the Era Epic." Iraq, XXIV (1962), 119-125.
________. "Myth and Ritual as Conceived by the Babylonians." JSS, XIII (1968), 104-12.
________. "A New Look at the Babylonian Background of Genesis." JTS, N.S. 16 (1965), 287-300.

Lambert, W. G. "Review of Das Era-Epos by Felix Gössmann." AFO, 18 (1958), 395-401.
Landsberger, B. "Einleitung in das Gilgameš-Epos." Gilgameš et sa légende. Études recueillies par Paul Garelli. (Paris, 1960). Pp. 31-36.
Laroche, E. "Catalogue des textes hittites." Revue hittite et asianique, XIV (1956), 33-38, 69-116; XV (1957), 30-89; XVI (1958), 18-64.
Lefèvre, A. "L'expression 'en ce jour-la' dans le livre d'Isaïe." Mélanges bibliques A. Robert. (Paris, 1957). Pp. 174-79.
Leslie, E. A. Isaiah. Nashville, 1963.
Lewis, J. P. A Study of the Interpretation of Noah and the Flood in Jewish and Christian Literature. Leiden, 1968.
Liddell, H. G., and Scott, R. A Greek-English Lexicon. Edited by H. S. Jones. 2 vols. 9th ed. Oxford, 1940.
Lindblom, J. Prophecy in Ancient Israel. Philadelphia, 1962.
________. A Study on the Immanuel Section in Isaiah. Isa. vii, 1-ix, 6. Lund, 1958.
________. "Gibt es eine Eschatologie bei den alttestamentlichen Propheten?" StTh, VI (1952), 79-114.
Lindsjo, H. "A Study of the Hebrew Root שוב and Its Religious Concepts." Unpublished Ph.D. dissertation, University of Chicago, 1939.
Lods, A. Israel. New York, 1932.
________. "La caverne de Lot." Revue de l'histoire des religions, 95 (1927), 204-219.
Lohfink, N. Das Siegeslied am Schilfmeer. 2nd ed. Frankfurt/Main, 1965.
Loretz, O. "Der Glaube des Propheten Isaias an das Gottesreich." Zeitschrift für kath. Theologie, 82 (1960), 40-73, 159-81.
Love, J. P. "The Call of Isaiah. An Exposition of Isaiah 6." Interpretation, XI (1957), 282-96.
Luckenbill, D. D. Ancient Records of Assyria and Babylonia. 2 vols. Chicago, 1926, 1927.
________. The Annals of Sennacherib. Oriental Institute Publications, Vol. II. Chicago, 1924.
Lutz, H.-M. Jahve, Jerusalem und die Völker. WMANT, 27. Neukirchen-Vluyn, 1968.
Maag, V. Text, Wortschatz und Begriffswelt des Buches Amos. Leiden, 1951.
Maass, F. "Wandlungen der Gemeindeauffassung in Israel und Juda." Theologica Viatorum. Jahrbuch der kirchlichen Hochschule Berlin. (Berlin, 1950). Pp. 16-32.
Mallowan, M. E. L. "Noah's Flood Reconsidered." Iraq, XXVI (1964), 62-83.
Maly, E. H. Prophets of Salvation. New York, 1967.
Mamie, P. "Le livre d'Amos. Les châtiments et le 'reste d'Israël.'" Nova et Vetera, 37 (1962), 217-23.
Manson, T. W. The Teachings of Jesus. 2nd ed. Cambridge, 1959.
Marti, K. Das Buch Jesaja. Kurzer Hand-Commentar zum Alten Testament. Tübingen, 1900.
________. Das Dodekapropheton. Kurzer Hand-Commentar zum Alten Testament, XIII. Tübingen, 1904.
________. The Religion of the Old Testament. London, 1907.

Marti, K. "Der jesajanische Kern in Jes. 6, 1-9." BZAW, 34 (1920), 113-21.
Matouš, L. "Zur neueren epischen Literatur im alten Mesopotamien." ArOr, 35 (1967), 1-25.
Mauchline, J. Hosea. IB. Vol. VI. Nashville, 1956.
________. Isaiah 1-39. Torch Bible Commentary. London, 1962.
________. "I Kings," Peake's Commentary on the Bible. Edited by M. Black and H. H. Rowley. London, 1962.
May, H. G. "The Fertility Cult in Hosea." AJSL, 48 (1931/32), 79-98.
Mayer, R. "Sünde und Gericht in der Bildersprache der vorexilischen Prophetie." BZ, 8 (1964), 22-44.
Mazar, B. "The Campaign of the Pharaoh Sheshonk to Palestine." SVT, IV (1957), 57-66.
McCarthy, D. J. Der Gottesbund im Alten Testament. SBS, 13. 2nd ed. Stuttgart, 1967.
McCown, G. C. "Hebrew and Egyptian Apocalyptic Literature." HThR, XVIII (1925), 257-411.
McKane, W. Prophets and Wise Men. SBT, 44. London, 1965.
________. "The Interpretation of Isaiah VII 14-15." VT, XVII (1967), 208-19.
Meek, T. J. Hebrew Origins. Harper Torchbooks. 3rd ed. New York, 1960.
Meinhold, J. Studien zur israelitischen Religionsgeschichte. Band I: Der heilige Rest. Teil I: Elias Amos Hosea Jesaja. Bonn, 1903.
________. "Einige Bemerkungen zu Jes. 28." Theologische Studien und Kritiken, 66 (1893), 1ff.
Metzger, S. P. "Noch einmal der Gottesname im Hexateuch." Neue kirchliche Zeitschrift, 34 (1925), 38ff.
Meyer, B. F. "Jesus and the Remnant of Israel." JBL, 84 (1965), 123-30.
Meyer, E. Die Israeliten und ihre Nachbarstämme. Halle, 1906.
Michel, O. "Glaube: πίστις." Theologisches Begriffslexikon zum Neuen Testament. Edited by L. Coenen, et al. (5. Lieferung. Wuppertal, 1967). Pp. 565-75.
Milgrom, J. "Did Isaiah Prophesy During the Reign of Uzziah?" VT, XIV (1964), 164-82.
Millard, A. R. "Fragments of Historical Texts from Nineveh: Ashurbanipal." Iraq, XXX (1968), 98-111.
________. "A New Babylonian 'Genesis' Story." Tyndale Bulletin, 18 (1967), 3-18.
Miller, P. D. "Holy War and Cosmic War in Early Israel." Unpublished Ph.D. dissertation, Harvard University, 1963.
Moeller, H. "Ambiguity at Amos 3;12." The Bible Translator, 15 (1964), 31-34.
Montgomery, J. A. The Books of Kings. Edited by H. S. Gehman. ICC. Edinburgh, 1951.
Morenz, S. "Die ägyptische Literatur und die Umwelt." Ägyptologie: Literatur. Handbuch der Orientalistik. Edited by B. Spuler. (Leiden, 1952), I, 194-206.
Morgenstern, J. "The Rest of the Nations." JSS, 2 (1957), 225-31.
Moriarty, F. L. "The Immanuel Prophecies." CBQ, 19 (1957), 226-33.
Mowinckel, S. Erwägungen zur Pentateuch Quellenfrage. Trondheim, 1964.

Mowinckel, S. He That Cometh. Translated by G. W. Anderson. New York-Nashville, 1956.
________. Profeten Jesaja. Oslo, 1925.
________. Prophecy and Tradition. Oslo, 1946.
________. The Psalms in Israel's Worship. Translated by D. R. Ap-Thomas. 2 vols. Nashville, 1962.
________. Psalmenstudien II. Das Thronbesteigungsfest Jahwäs und der Ursprung der Eschatologie. 2nd ed. Amsterdam, 1961.
________. "Die Komposition des Jesajabuches. Kap. 1-39." Acta Orientalia, XI (1933), 267-92.
Muckle, J. Y. Isaiah 1-39. Epworth Preacher's Commentary. London, 1960.
Muilenburg, J. "Form-Criticism and Beyond." JBL, 88 (1969), 1-18.
________. "Holiness." IDB, (1962), II, 616-25.
Müller, H.-P. Ursprünge und Strukturen alttestamentlicher Eschatologie. BZAW, 109. Berlin, 1969.
________. "Imperativ und Verheissung im Alten Testament: Drei Beispiele." EvTh, 28 (1968), 557-71.
________. "Zur Frage nach dem Ursprung der biblischen Eschatologie." VT, XIV (1964), 276-93.
Müller, W. E. Die Vorstellung vom Rest im Alten Testament. Inaugural-Dissertation; Theologische Fakultat, Universität Leipzig. Borsdorf-Leipzig, 1939.
Munch, P. A. The Expression bajjom hāhū, Is it an Eschatological Terminus Technicus? Avhandlinger utgitt av Det Norske Videnskaps-Akademi i Oslo, II/2. Oslo, 1936.
Myers, J. M. Hosea-Joel-Amos-Obadiah-Jonah. The Laymen's Bible Commentary, 14. Richmond, Va., 1959.
Neher, A. Amos. Paris, 1950.
Nelis, J. "Rest Israels." Bibel-Lexikon. Edited by H. Haag. (2nd ed. Einsiedeln, 1968). Cols. 1473-75.
Neubauer, K. W. "Erwägungen zu Amos 5, 4-15." ZAW, 78 (1966), 292-316.
Neugebauer, O. Mathematische Keilschrifttexte. 3 vols. Berlin, 1935-1937.
North, C. R. "Isaiah." IDB, (1962), II, 731-44.
________. "Shear-jashub." IDB, (1962), IV, 311.
Noth, M. The History of Israel. 2nd ed. New York, 1960.
________. Die israelitischen Personennamen im Rahmen der gemeinsemitischen Namengebung. BWANT, 10. 2nd ed. Hildesheim, 1966.
________. Könige I. BKAT, IX/1. Neukirchen-Vluyn, 1968.
________. Überlieferungsgeschichte des Pentateuch. Stuttgart, 1948.
Nougayrol, J. Ugaritica, V. Paris, 1968.
Nowack, W. Die Kleinen Propheten. Göttinger Handkommentar zum Alten Testament, 4. Göttingen, 1922.
Oppenheim, A. L. Ancient Mesopotamia. Portrait of a Dead Civilization. 2nd ed. Chicago, 1968.
________. Letters from Mesopotamia. Chicago, 1967.
________, et al., eds. The Assyrian Dictionary. Chicago, 1956ff.
Orelli, C. von. Der Prophet Jesaja. Kurzgefasster Kommentar. 3rd ed. München, 1904.
Orlinsky, H. M. "Qumran and the Present State of Old Testament Studies: The Septuagint Text." JBL, 78 (1959), 26-33.
________. "Studies in St. Mark's Scroll-V." Israel Exploration Journal, 4 (1959), 5-8.

Osterloh, E. "Rest." Biblisch-theologisches Wörterbuch. Edited by E. Osterloh und H. Engelland. (3rd ed.; Göttingen, 1964). P. 494.

Otten, H. Mythen vom Gotte Kumarbi. Berlin, 1952.

________. "Neue Fragmente zu den Annalen des Muršili." Mitteilungen des Instituts für Orientforschung, 3 (1955), 153-79.

________. "Keilschrifttexte." Mitteilungen der Deutschen Orient-Gesellschaft, 91 (1958), 73-84.

Otto, E. "Annalistik und Königsnovelle." Ägyptologie: Literatur. Handbuch der Orientalistik. Edited by B. Spuler. (Leiden, 1952), I, 140-48.

________. "Die Religion der Ägypter." Religionsgeschichte des Alten Orients. Handbuch der Orientalistik. Edited by B. Spuler. (Leiden, 1964), VIII, 1-75.

________. "Weltanschauliche und politische Tendenzschriften." Ägyptologie: Literatur. Handbuch der Orientalistik. Edited by B. Spuler. (Leiden, 1952), I, 111-19.

Otzen, B. Studien über Deuterosacharja. Acta Theologica Danica, VI. Assen, 1964.

________. "Rest." Gads Danske Bibel Leksikon. Edited by E. Nielsen and B. Noack. (København, 1966), II, 605-607.

Pallis, S. A. The Babylonian Akîtu Festival. Copenhagen, 1926.

Parrot, A. Babylon and the Old Testament. London, 1958.

________. Nineveh and the Old Testament. London, 1955.

________. "Mari." Archaeology and Old Testament Study. Edited by D. Winton Thomas. (London, 1967). Pp. 136-44.

Paterson, J. "Remnant." Hasting's Dictionary of the Bible. Revised by F. C. Grant and H. H. Rowley (New York, 1963). Pp. 841-42.

Pavlovsky, V., und Vogt, E. "Die Jahre der Könige von Juda und Israel." Biblica, 45 (1964), 321-47.

Pedersen, J. Israel, Its Life and Culture. 2 vols. Copenhagen, 1926.

________. "Die KRT Legende." Berytus, 6 (1941), 63-105.

Pettinato, G. "Die Bestrafung des Menschengeschlechts durch die Sintflut. Die erste Tafel des Atramhasīs-Epos eröffnet eine neue Einsicht in die Motivation dieser Strafe." Orientalia, N.S. 37 (1968), 165-200.

Pfeiffer, C. F., ed. The Biblical World. Grand Rapids, MIch., 1966.

Pfeiffer, R. H. Introduction to the Old Testament. New York, 1953.

Piankoff, A. The Shrines of Tut-Ankh-Amon. Edited by N. Rambova. New York, 1955.

Poebel, A. Historical and Grammatical Texts. PBS, V. Philadelphia, 1914.

________. Historical Texts. PBS, IV/1. Philadelphia, 1914.

Porteous, N. W. "Jerusalem-Zion: The Growth of a Symbol." Verbannung und Heimkehr. Festscrift für Wilhelm Rudolph. Tübingen, 1961.

________. "Jesajabuch." Die Religion in Geschichte und Gegenwart. (3rd ed.; Tübingen, 1959), III, 601-606.

Posener, G. Littérature et politique dans l'Égypte de la XIIe dynastie. Paris, 1956.

Preuss, H. D. Jahweglaube und Zukunftserwartung. BWANT, 87. Stuttgart, 1968.

________. "... ich will mit der sein!" ZAW, 80 (1968), 139-73.

Pritchard, J. B., ed. Ancient Near Eastern Texts Relating to the Old Testament. 3rd ed. Princeton, 1969.

Procksch, O. Die Genesis. HK. Leipzig, 1913.

_______. Jesaja I. KAT, IX. Leipzig, 1930.

_______. Theologie des Alten Testaments. Gütersloh, 1950.

_______. "ἅγιος." TDNT. (Grand Rapids, Mich., 1964), I, 88-97.

Quell, G. "Jesaja 14, 1-23." Festschrift für F. Baumgärtel zum 70. Geburtstag 14. Januar 1958. Edited by J. Herrmann und L. Rost. (Erlangen, 1959). Pp. 131-57.

Rabinowitz, I. "The Crux at Amos III 12." VT, XI (1961), 228-31.

Rad, G. von. Die Botschaft der Propheten. München, 1967.

_______. Genesis: A Commentary. Translated by J. H. Marks. Philadelphia, 1961.

_______. Der Heilige Krieg im Alten Testament. 4th ed. Göttingen, 1965.

_______. Die Josephsgeschichte. BS, 5. 4th ed. Neukirchen-Vluyn, 1964.

_______. Old Testament Theology. Translated by D. M. G. Stalker. 2 vols. Edinburgh, 1962, 1965.

_______. "The Origin of the Concept of the Day of Yahweh." JSS, IV (1959), 97-108.

_______. "Josephsgeschichte und ältere Chokma." SVT, I (1953), 120-27.

Rahlfs, A., ed. Septuaginta. 2 vols. 7th ed. Stuttgart, 1962.

Rambova, N., ed. The Shrines of Tut-Ankh-Amon. Bollingen Series, 40/2. New York, 1955.

Rehm, M. Der königliche Messias im Licht der Immanuel-Weissagung des Buches Jesaja. Eichstätter-Studien, 1. Kevelaer, 1968.

Reicke, B., und Rost, L., eds. Biblisch-historisches Handwörterbuch. 3 vols. Göttingen, 1962-66.

Reider, J. "DMSQ in Amos 3." JBL, 67 (1948), 254-58.

Reiner, E. "Plague Amulets and House Blessings." JNES, XIX (1960), 148-55.

Rendtorff, R. Men of the Old Testament. Translated by Frank Clarke. Philadelphia, 1968.

_______. "Reflections on the Early History of Prophecy in Israel." Journal for Theology and Church, IV (1967), 14-34.

Reventlow, H. G. Das Amt des Propheten bei Amos. FRLANT, 80. Göttingen, 1962.

_______. Das Heiligkeitsgesetz formgeschichtlich untersucht. WMANT, 6. Neukirchen-Vluyn, 1961.

Rienecker, F. "Rest." Lexikon zur Bibel. (5th ed.; Wuppertal, 1964). Cols. 1138-40.

Rignell, L. G. "Das Immanuelszeichen. Einige Gesichtspunkte zu Jes. 7." StTh, XI (1957), 99-119.

_______. "Isaiah Chapter I." StTh, XII (1958), 140-58.

Ringgren, H. Israelite Religion. Translated by D. E. Green. Philadelphia, 1966.

_______. The Prophetical Conception of Holiness. Leipzig, 1948.

Robert, A., and Feuillet, A., eds. Introduction to the Old Testament. Translated by P. W. Skehen, et al. New York, 1968.

Robertson, E. "Isaiah Chapter I." ZAW, 52 (1934), 231-36.

Robinson, T. H. Die zwölf Kleinen Propheten: Hosea bis Micha. HAT, 14. Tübingen, 1938.

Roeder, Günther. Die Ägyptische Religion in Texten und Bildern. Die Bibliothek der Alten Welt. 4 vols. Zürich-Stuttgart, 1959-61.

________. Urkunden zur Religion des alten Ägypten. Jena, 1915.

Rohland, E. Die Bedeutung der Erwählungstraditionen Israels für die Eschatologie der alttestamentlichen Propheten. Inaugural-Dissertation, Universität Heidelberg. München, 1956.

Rosenberg, A. "The God Ṣedeq." HUCA, XXXVI (1965), 161-77.

Rost, L. "Die Gottesverehrung der Patriarchen im Lichte der Pentateuch-Quellen." SVT, VII (1960), 346-59.

Rowley, H. H. The Biblical Doctrine of Election. London, 1950.

________. Men of God. Studies in Old Testament History and Prophecy. London, 1963.

________. Worship in Ancient Israel. London, 1967.

________. "Elijah on Mount Carmel." BJRL, 43 (1960), 190-219.

________. "Hezekiah's Reform and Rebellion." BJRL, 44 (1961), 395-461.

Rudolph, W. "Jesaja XV-XVI." Hebrew and Semitic Studies, presented to G. R. Driver in celebration of his 70th birthday. Edited by D. W. Thomas and W. D. McHardy. (Oxford, 1963). Pp. 130-43.

Running, L. G. "An Investigation of the Syriac Version of Isaiah." AUSS, IV (1966), 37-64, 135-48.

________. "Syriac Variants in Isaiah 26." AUSS, V (1967), 46-58.

Ruppert, L. Die Josephserzählung der Genesis. Ein Beitrag zur Theologie der Pentateuchquellen. SANT, XI. München, 1965.

Ryle, H. E. The Book of Genesis. Cambridge Bible for Schools and Colleges. Cambridge, 1914.

Saebø, M. "Formgeschichtliche Erwägungen zu Jes. 7,3-9." StTh, XIV (1960), 54-69.

Saggs, H. W. F. "Assyrian Warfare in the Sargonid Period." Iraq, XXV (1963), 145-54.

Salonen, A. Die Wasserfahrzeuge in Babylonien. Helsinki, 1939.

Šanda, A. Die Bücher der Könige. Exegetisches Handbuch zum Alten Testament, 9. 2 vols. Münster, 1911.

Sandars, N. K. The Epic of Gilgamesh. 2nd ed. Baltimore, Md., 1964.

Sarna, Nahum M. Understanding Genesis. Melton Research Series, I. New York, 1966.

Sawyer, J. "The Qumran Reading of Isaiah 6, 13." Annual of the Swedish Theological Institute, 3 (1964), 111-13.

Scharbert, J. Heilsmittler im Alten Testament und im Alten Orient. Freiburg, 1964.

________. Die Propheten Israels bis 700 v. Chr. Köln, 1965.

Schilling, O. "'Rest' in der Prophetie des Alten Testaments." Unpublished Th.D. Inauguraldissertation, Universität Münster, 1942.

Schmidt, H. Die grossen Propheten. Die Schriften des Alten Testaments, II/2. Göttingen, 1915.

Schmidt, J. M. Die jüdische Apokalyptik. Die Geschichte ihrer Erforschung von den Anfägen bis zu den Textfunden von Qumran. Neukirchen-Vluyn, 1969.

________. "Forschung zur jüdischen Apokalyptik." Verkündigung und Forschung, 14 (1969), 44-69.

Schmidt, N. "The Origin of Jewish Eschatology." JBL, 41 (1922), 102-14.

Schmidt, W. H. "Die deuteronomistische Redaktion des Amosbuches." ZAW, 77 (1965), 168-93.

________. "Jerusalemer El-Traditionen bei Jesaja: Ein religionsgeschichtlicher Vergleich zum Vorstellungsbereich des göttlichen Königtums." Zeitschrift für Religions- und Geistesgeschichte, XVI (1964), 302-13.

Schmökel, H. Das Gilgamesch Epos. Stuttgart, 1966.

________. Das Land Sumer. 3rd ed. Stuttgart, 1962.

Schott, A., und Soden, W. von. Das Gilgamesch-Epos. Stuttgart, 1958.

Schott, S. "Die älteren Göttermythen." Ägyptologie: Literatur. Handbuch der Orientalistik. Edited by B. Spuler. (Leiden, 1952), Vol. I.

Schrader, E. Die Keilinschriften und das Alte Testament. Revised by H. Zimmern and H. Winckler. 3rd ed. Berlin, 1903.

Schreiner, J. Sion-Jerusalem, Jahwes Königssitz. München, 1963.

Schunck, K.-D. "Strukturlinien in der Entwicklung der Vorstellung vom 'Tag Jahwes'." VT, XIV (1964), 319-40.

Schwantes, S. J. "Note on Amos 4:2b." ZAW, 79 (1967), 82-83.

Scott, R. B. Y. Isaiah, Chapters 1-39. IB, Vol. V. Nashville, 1956.

________. The Relevance of the Prophets. 2nd ed. New York, 1968.

________. "Biblical Research and the Work of the Pastor: Recent Study in Isaiah 1-39." Interpretation, XI (1957), 257-68.

Scullion, J. J. "An Approach to the Understanding of Isaiah 7, 10-17." JBL, 87 (1968), 288-300.

Seebass, H. Der Erzvater Israel und die Einführung der Jahweverehrung in Kanaan. BZAW, 98. Berlin, 1966.

________. Mose und Aaron, Sinai und Gottesberg. AThANT, 2. Bonn, 1962.

Seeligmann, I. L. The Septuagint Version of Isaiah. A Discussion of its Problems. Leiden, 1948.

Segal, M. H. The Pentateuch. Jerusalem, 1967.

________. "El, Elohim and Yahweh in the Bible." JQR, 46 (1955/56), 89-115.

Seierstad, I. P. Die Offenbarungserlebnisse der Propheten Amos, Jesaja und Jeremia. 2nd ed. Oslo, 1965.

Sellin, E. Der alttestamentliche Prophetismus. Leipzig, 1912.

________. Einleitung in das Alte Testament. 2nd ed. Leipzig, 1914.

________. Das Zwölfprophetenbuch übersetzt und erklärt. KAT, XII. 2nd ed. Leipzig, 1929.

Simpson, W. K. "The Study of Egyptian Literature, 1925-1965." A. Erman, The Ancient Egyptians. Harper Torchbook. (New York, 1966). Pp. xi-xxxiii.

Skemp, A. E. "'Immanuel' and the 'Suffering Servant of Yahweh,' a Suggestion." ET, 44 (1932), 44-45.

Skinner, J. The Book of the Prophet Isaiah, Chapters I-XXXIX. Cambridge Bible for Schools and Colleges. 2nd ed. Cambridge, 1930.

________. Genesis. ICC. 2nd ed. Edinburgh, 1930.

Smend, R. "Zur Geschichte von האמין." Hebräische Wortforschung. Festschrift zum 80. Geburtstag von Walter Baumgartner. (SVT, XVI; Leiden, 1967). Pp. 285-90.

________. "Das Nein des Amos." EvTh, 23 (1963), 404-23.

Smith, G. A. The Book of Isaiah. 2nd ed. 2 vols. New York, 1927.
Snaith, N. H. The Book of Amos. Nashville, 1946.
_______. The Distinctive Ideas of the Old Testament. Schocken Paperback. New York, 1964.
_______. I Kings. IB, Vol. III. Nashville, 1954.
Soden, W. von. Der Aufstieg des Assyrerreiches als geschichtliches Problem. Der Alte Orient, 37/I-II. Leipzig, 1938.
_______. "Der Assyrer und der Krieg," Iraq, XXV (1963), 131-44.
Soggin, J. A. "Der prophetische Gedanke über den Heiligen Krieg als Gericht gegen Israel." VT, X (1960), 79-83.
Sollberger, E. The Babylonian Legend of the Flood. London, 1962.
Sommer, F., und Falkenstein, A. Die hethitisch-akkadische Bilingue des Hattusili II. (Labarna II.). Abhandlungen der Bayerischen Akademie der Wissenschaften, N. F., 16. München, 1938.
Speiser, E. A. Genesis. The Anchor Bible. Garden City, N. Y., 1964.
_______. "Ancient Mesopotamia." The Idea of History in the Ancient World. Edited by R. C. Dentan. (New Haven, 1955). Pp. 35-76.
Spiegel, J. "Göttergeschichten, Erzählungen, Märchen, Fabeln." Ägyptologie: Literatur. Handbuch der Orientalistik. Edited by B. Spuler. Leiden, 1952. Vol. I.
Spuler, B., ed. Ägyptologie: Literatur. Handbuch der Orientalistik, I/2. Leiden, 1952.
Stamm, J. J. Die akkadische Namengebung. MVAG, 44. Leipzig, 1939.
_______. "Elia am Horeb." Studia biblica et semitica. Festschrift Th. C. Vriezen. (Wageningen, 1966). Pp. 327-34.
_______. "Die Immanuel-Weissagung und die Eschatologie des Jesaja." ThZ, 16 (1960), 439-55.
Staples, W. E. "Epic Motifs in Amos." JNES, XXV (1966), 106-12.
Steck, O. H. Überlieferung und Zeitgeschichte in den Elia-Erzählungen. WMANT, 26. Neukirchen-Vluyn, 1968.
Stegemann, U. "Der Restgedanke bei Isaias." BZ, 13 (1969), 161-86.
Steinmann, J. Le prophete Isaïe, sa vie, son oeuvre et son temps. Lectio Divina, 5. Paris, 1950.
Steuernagel, C. Lehrbuch der Einleitung in das Alte Testament. Tübingen, 1912.
Streck, M. Assurbanipal und die letzten assyrischen Könige bis zum Untergang Niniveh's. Vorderasiatische Bibliothek, VII. 2 vols. Leipzig, 1916.
Struwe, W. "Zum Töpferorakel." Aegyptus: Roccolta di scritti in onore di Giacomo Lumbrosa. (Milano, 1925). Pp. 127-35.
Tadmor, H. "Azriyau of Yaudi." Scripta Hierosolymitana, 8 (1961), 232-71.
_______. "The Campaigns of Sargon II of Assur." JCS, 12 (1958), 22-40, 77-100.
Terrien, S. "Amos and Wisdom." Israel's Prophetic Heritage. Essays in Honor of James Muilenburg. Edited by B. W. Anderson and W. Harrelson. (New York, 1962). Pp. 108-15.
Thiele, E. R. The Mysterious Numbers of the Hebrew Kings. 2nd ed. Grand Rapids, Mich., 1965.
_______. "The Synchronisms of the Hebrew Kings--A Re-evaluation." AUSS, I (1963), 121-38; II (1964), 120-36.

Thomas, D. W., ed. Archaeology and Old Testament Study. Oxford, 1967.
________. Documents from Old Testament Times. Harper Torchbooks. New York, 1961.
Thompson, R. C. The Epic of Gilgamesh. Oxford, 1930.
Thureau-Dangin, F. Rituels accadiens. Paris, 1921.
Treves, M. "Little Prince Pele-Joez." VT, XVII (1967), 464-77.
Tur-Sinai, N. H. "A Contribution to the Understanding of Isaiah i-xii." Scripta Hierosolymitana, 8 (1961), 154-88.
Unger, M. F. Israel and the Arameans of Damascus. London, 1957.
Vanderburgh, F. A. "A Hymn to Bel." JAOS, 29 (1908), 184-91.
Vawter, B. The Conscience of Israel: Pre-exilic Prophets and Prophecy. New York, 1961.
Virolleaud, C. La légende de Kéret, roi des Sidoniens . . . . Paris, 1936.
Vischer, W. Die Immanuel-Botschaft im Rahmen des königlichen Zionsfestes. Theologische Studien, 45. Zollikon-Zürich, 1955.
Vogt, E. "'Filius Ṭāb'ēl' (Is. vii, 6)." Biblica, 37 (1956), 263-64.
________. "Sennacherib und die letzte Tätigkeit Jesajas." Biblica, 47 (1966), 427-37.
Vriezen, T. C. An Outline of Old Testament Theology. Newton, Mass., 1958.
________. The Religion of Ancient Israel. Philadelphia, 1967.
________. "Essentials of the Theology of Isaiah." Israel's Prophetic Heritage. Essays in Honor of James Muilenburg. Edited by B. W. Anderson and W. Harrelson. (New York, 1962). Pp. 128-46.
________. "Prophecy and Eschatology." SVT, I (1953), 199-229.
Vuilleumier, R. La tradition culturelle d'Israël dans la prophétie d'Amos et d'Osée. Neuchâtel, 1960.
Wade, G. W. The Book of the Prophet Isaiah. Westminster Commentary. London, 1911.
Walser, G., ed. Neuere Hethiterforschung. Historia: Einzelschriften, Heft 7. Wiesbaden, 1964.
Wanke, G. Die Zionstheologie der Korachiten. BZAW, 97. Berlin, 1966.
Ward, J. M. Amos & Isaiah: Prophets of the Word of God. Nashville, 1969.
Warne, D. M. "The Origin, Development and Significance of the Concept of the Remnant in the Old Testament." Unpublished Ph.D. dissertation, Faculty of Divinity, University of Edinburgh, 1958.
Watts, J. D. W. Vision and Prophecy in Amos. Leiden, 1958.
Weber, O. Die Literatur der Babylonier und Assyrer, ein Überblick. Der Alte Orient, Ergänzungsband 2. Leipzig, 1907.
Weidner, E. F. Politische Dokumente aus Kleinasien. Boghazköi-Studien, 8-9. Leipzig, 1923.
________. "Der Staatsvertrag Aššurniraris VI. von Assyrien mit Mati'ilu von Bît-Agusi." AFO, 8 (1932), 17ff.
________. "Texte-Wörter-Sachen." AFO, 13 (1939/40), 230-37.
Weippert, M. Die Landnahme der israelitischen Stämme in der neueren wissenschaftlichen Diskussion. FRLANT, 92. Göttingen, 1967.
Weir, M. A Lexicon of Accadian Prayers in the Rituals of Expiation. London, 1934.
Weiser, A. Das Buch der zwölf Kleinen Propheten. ATD, 24. 4th ed. Göttingen, 1963.

Weiser, A. Einleitung in das Alte Testament. Stuttgart, 1939.

________. Introduction to the Old Testament. Translated by D. M. Barton. London, 1961.

________. Die Profetie des Amos. BZAW, 53. Giessen, 1929.

________. "πιστεύω, B. Der at.liche Begriff." TWNT, (1959), VI, 182-97.

Weiss, M. "The Origin of the 'Day of the Lord'-Reconsidered." HUCA, 37 (1966), 29-60.

Wellhausen, J. Prolegomena to the History of Ancient Israel. Meridian Books. Cleveland, 1957.

________. Die Kleinen Propheten. 4th ed. Berlin, 1963.

Westermann, C. Basic Forms of Prophetic Speech. Translated by H. C. White. Philadelphia, 1967.

________. Genesis. BKAT, I/1-3. Neukirchen-Vluyn, 1966-69.

________. Tausend Jahre und ein Tag. Gütersloh, 1965.

________. "Arten der Erzählung in der Genesis." Forschung am Alten Testament. (TB, 24; München, 1964). Pp. 9-91.

________. "Sinn und Grenze religionsgeschichtlicher Parallelen." ThLZ, 90 (1965), cols 489-96.

Whitehouse, O. C. Isaiah I-XXXIX. The New-Century Bible. New York, 1905.

Whitley, C. F. The Prophetic Achievement. Leiden, 1963.

________. "The Call and Mission of Isaiah." JNES, XVIII (1959), 38-48.

Wilcken, U. "Zur ägyptisch-hellenistischen Litteratur." Aegyptica. Festschrift für Georg Ebers zum 1. März 1897. (Leipzig, 1897). Pp. 142-52.

________. "Zur ägyptischen Prophetie." Hermes, 40 (1905), 544-60.

Wildberger, H. Jahwes Eigentumsvolk. Zürich, 1960.

________. Jesaja. BKAT, X/1-4. Neukirchen-Vluyn, 1965-69.

________. "'Glauben,' Erwägungen zu האמין." Hebräische Wortforschung. Festschrift zum 80. Geburstag von Walter Baumgartner. (SVT, XVI: Leiden, 1967). Pp. 372-86.

________. "'Glauben' im Alten Testament." ZThK, 65 (1968), 129-59.

________. "Jesajas Verständnis der Geschichte." SVT, IX (1963), 83-117.

Williams, R. J. Hebrew Syntax: An Outline. Toronto, 1967.

Winckler, H. Keilinschriftliches Textbuch zum Alten Testament. 3rd ed. Leipzig, 1909.

Winter, A. "Analyse des Buches Amos." Theologische Studien und Kritiken, 83 (1910), 323-74.

Wiseman, D. J. Chronicles of Chaldean Kings (626-556 B.C.) in the British Museum. London, 1956.

________. "A New Stela of Aššur-naṣir-pal II." Iraq, XIV (1952), 24ff.

Witzel, M. "Die Klage über Ur." Orientalia, N. S. XIV (1954), 185-234; XV (1946), 46-63.

Wolff, H. W. Amos BKAT, XIV/6-9. Neukirchen-Vluyn, 1968-69.

________. Amos' gestige Heimat. WMANT, 18. Neukirchen-Vluyn, 1964.

________. Frieden ohne Ende. Eine Auslegung von Jes. 7, 1-7 und 9, 1-6. BS, 35. Neukirchen, 1962.

________. Hosea. BKAT, XIV. 2nd ed. Neukirchen-Vluyn, 1965.

________. Immanuel-Das Zeichen dem widersprochen wird. BS, 23. Neukirchen-Vluyn, 1959.

________. "Hoseas geistige Heimat." Gesammelte Studien zum Alten Testament. (TB, 22; München, 1964). Pp. 232-50.

Wolff, H. W. "Probleme alttestamentlicher Prophetie." EvTh, 15 (1955), 116-68.
________. "Das Thema 'Umkehr' in der alttestamentlichen Prophetie." ZThK, 48 (1951), 129-48.
Wright, G. E. Biblical Archaeology. 2nd ed. Philadelphia, 1962.
________. Isaiah. Laymen's Bible Commentaries. London, 1965.
________, ed. The Bible and the Ancient Near East. Essays in Honor of William Foxwell Albright. Garden City, New York, 1965.
________. "Discoveries at Megiddo, 1935-1939." BAR, 2. Edited by D. N. Freedman and E. F. Campbell, Jr. (Garden City, N. Y., 1964). Pp. 225-40.
________. "The Faith of Israel." IB, (1953), I, 349-89.
Woolley, C. Leonard. The Sumerians. New York, 1965.
Wundt, W. Völkerpsychologie. Mythus und Religion, III. 3rd ed. Stuttgart, 1923.
Würthwein, E. "Amos-Studien." ZAW, 62 (1950), 10-52.
________. "Busse und Umkehr im Alten Testament." TWNT, (1942), IV, 976-82.
________. "Die Erzählung vom Gottesurteil auf dem Karmel." ZThK, 50 (1962), 131-44.
________. "Jesaja 7, 1-9. Ein Beitrag zum Thema 'Prophetie und Politik'." Theologie als Glaubenswagnis. Festschrift für Karl Heim. Edited by H. Faber. (Furche-Studien, 23; Hamburg, 1954). Pp. 47-63.
Young, E. J. The Book of Isaiah, Chapters I-XVIII. The New International Commentary on the Old Testament. Grand Rapids, Mich., 1965.
Ziegler, J. Das Buch Isaias. Echter-Bibel. Würzburg, 1958.
________. Isaias. Septuaginta Vetus Testamentum Graecum. Vol. XIV. Göttingen, 1939.
________. Untersuchungen zur Septuaginta des Buches Isaias. Alttestamentliche Abhandlungen, XII. Band, 3. Heft. Münster, 1934.
Zimmerli, W. Ezekiel. BKAT, XIII/1-17. Neukirchen-Vluyn, 1969.
________. The Law and the Prophets. Translated by R. E. Clements. Harper Torchbooks. New York, 1965.
________. Der Mensch und seine Hoffnung im Alten Testament. Göttingen, 1968.
________. "Gericht und Heil im alttestamentlichen Prophetenwort." Der Anfang, 11 (1949), 21-46.
Zimmern, H. Sumerische Kultlieder aus altbabylonischer Zeit. Zweite Reihe. Vorderasiastische Schriftdenkmäler der Königlichen Museen zu Berlin, X. Leipzig, 1913.
Zobel, H.-J. "Ursprung und Verwurzelung des Erwählungsglaubens Israels." ThLZ, 93 (1968), cols. 2-12.
Zorell, F. Lexicon Hebraicum et Aramaicum Veteris Testamenti. Roma, 1954.
Zyl, A. H. Van. The Moabites. Pretoria Orienta Series, III. Leiden, 1960.

INDEXES

INDEX OF SUBJECTS

INDEX OF MODERN AUTHORS

INDEX OF BIBLICAL PASSAGES

INDEX OF HEBREW WORDS

APPENDIX

DISCUSSION OF RECENT LITERATURE

P. 14 n. 69 De Vaux's essay is now translated under the title "'The Remnant of Israel' According to the Prophets," in The Bible and the Ancient Near East, transl. D. McHugh (Garden City, N.Y.: Doubleday, 1971), pp. 15-30.

P. 40 A concise recent study by Rudolf Kilian, "Prolegomena zur Auslegung der Immanuelverheissung," in Wort, Lied und Gottesspruch. Festschrift für Joseph Ziegler, ed. Josef Schreiner (Würzburg: Echter Verlag, 1972), II, 207-215, deals with the remnant idea in Isaiah. He follows primarily Stegemann and feels that Isa 1:21-26 can hardly be used to support a positive remnant idea in Isaiah's early period (against S. Herrmann and J. J. Stamm). That this denial cannot be sustained has already been elaborated (supra, pp. 250-257). Kilian is correct in his emphasis that the name Shear-jašub in 7:3 expresses both hope and doom but that the idea of a return to Yahweh is not intended hardly follows (supra, pp. 280-287). Kilian does not break new ground.

An extremely one-sided position with regard to the remnant idea in Isaiah is maintained by H.-J. Hermisson, "Zukunftserwartung und Gegenwartskritik in der Verkündigung Jesajas," EvTh, 33 (1973), 54-77, who argues that on the basis of Isa 30:17 Isaiah's idea of the remnant is "a meaningless remnant, certainly not receiving salvation, and moreover no positively qualified 'holy' remnant" (p. 55). Hermisson misses even the meaning of the name "A-Remnant-Shall-Return" completely in turning it into a "unique sign of doom." The doom aspect is present in the name but also an undeniable aspect of hope (supra, pp. 280-287).

W. E. Müller's study (supra, pp. 18-22) on the idea of the remnant has been republished in the late fall of 1973 (Neukirchener Verlag, Neukirchen-Vluyn) with its text unchanged but slight expansions in few footnotes. The editor of this republication, H. D. Preuss, provided an "Addition" (pp. 96-126) and a "Bibliography" (pp. 127-134). The primary aim of the 30-page addition is to trace the influence which Müller's study left on later OT scholarship. It is not surprising that his investigation left a virtually indelible mark on especially German OT scholarship. His views on the "secular-political" origin and its later "religious" development have been adopted very uncritically to the present. Preuss has come to recognize that in view of the present study, which he did not receive until "immediately before the finishing of the manuscript" (p. 113) of his "Addition," the origin and development of the remnant idea as portrayed by Müller can no longer be maintained (pp. 16f. n. 15a, 113-116, 126). Preuss does not add anything new in his survey of literature from 1939 to 1972 and closes his review with this study which is now presented in its second edition. With regard to the present study he states, "The remnant idea appears in Israel's surroundings earlier than in the Old Testament. It is not limited to a single genre and is connected with the questions of life and death, security of existence and hope, and is thus filled with religious and not political content. Here one can agree generally with Hasel. This agreement can be maintained also with regard to the investigation of the remnant idea in the Old Testament prior to the time of Isaiah, but hardly for all interpretations of texts from the book of Isaiah" (p. 116). I am fully aware of the present situation with regard to the dating of materials in the book of Isaiah but see no reasons to depart from that which has been said in my study. Additions below will further strengthen the positions taken earlier.

I have been able to publish an article on the "Semantic Values of Derivatives of the Hebrew Root ŠʾR," AUSS, II (1973), 152-169, which may be considered to serve as a supplement to the brief indications on terminology (supra, pp. 386-388) in this study. We have shown that on the basis of cognates in Ugaritic, Aramaic, Palmyrene, Nabatean, Arabic and Syriac that the Hebrew root šʾr is of common West Semitic origin. Our investigation into the semantics of šʾr has revealed that it designates the residual part which is left over or remains after the removal of the balance of a small part, half, or the larger whole. In some cases the remnant also designates the whole without the loss of any part. The semantics of derivatives of šʾr demonstrates its frequent usage (195 out of 223) with human entities, such as mankind as a whole, a people or nation, tribe or clan, group or family, and even a single individual. The great variety of threats in the natural, social, political, and religious spheres precludes a derivation or special connection of the root šʾr and its derivatives with any single threat whether the politico-military practice of total warfare (so W. E. Müller) or the Yahweh Wars (so H. Wildberger, H. P. Müller). The variegated threats and manifold relations of derivatives of šʾr demonstrate that the remnant motif has its origin neither in eschatology (H. Gressmann), myth and cult (S. Mowinckel), election (O. Schilling), etc., but in the life-and-death problem, i.e., the fundamental question of human existence and its continuity.

Basic to the Hebrew root šʾr is a bi-polarity of negative and positive aspects: Negatively derivatives of šʾr can express total loss or painful decimation with emphasis on complete meaninglessness and utter insignificance; positively they can express the immense future potentiality inherent in the remnant, no matter its size. To have a "remnant" (a "name" or "root") means to possess continued existence, guaranteeing life through perpetuation by progeny. This bi-polarity must not be understood or construed as mutually exclusive modes of thought. It interacts constantly by forming different emphases according to the particular semantic value of each individual context, sentence-combination and word-combination. In no case must any semantic value be blurred or obliterated by superimposing another semantic value from a different context.

It is hoped that in the near future I may publish my investigations on the remainder of the OT remnant terminology and other aspects of the biblical remnant idea.

P. 58 Here we can now add a newly published historical Sumerian text which contains the theme of the flood which destroys mankind but leaves a remnant, i.e., the "Lagaš King List." The prologue opens with a description of the world after the flood:

1 After the Flood had swept over
2 and had brought about the destruction of the land--
3 As mankind had been made to endure,
4 as the seed of mankind had been left,
5 as the black-headed people had risen in their clay--
6 When An (and) Enlil
7 the name of mankind having been called,

The translation is by E. Sollberger, "The Rulers of Lagaš, "*JCS*, 21 (1967 [1969]), 282.

The expression "the seed of mankind" (*numun nam-lú-[l]u*$_8$) is identical to the one in the Sumerian Flood Account (supra, p. 55). The preservation of "the seed of mankind" in the flood runs counter to the intention of the gods who had decreed that this very "seed of mankind" is to be annihilated (see the Sumerian Flood Story, lines 157 (supra, p. 53) and 25a (supra, p. 54). In view of this traditio-historical background, it may be suggested that the phrase "the name of mankind having been called" (line 7) does not refer to the creation of man after the flood, even though the creation of man is similarly expressed by the imposition of the name in the cosmogonic prologue to "Gilgameš, Enkidu, and the Nether World" (Kramer, *Sumerian Mythology*, p. 37). The calling of "the name of mankind" seems to refer to man's subordination to the gods who reestablish their authority over them after the flood by calling over man his name so that he again serves the gods.

Pp. 67f. n. 74 On the debate of the translation of the first line, see W. von Soden, "Als die Götter (auch noch) Menschen Waren. Einige Grundgedanken des altbabylonischen Atramḫasīs-Mythus," *Or*, 38 (1969), 415-432, to which W. G. Lambert, "New Evidence for the First Line of Atraḫasīs," *Or*, 38 (1969), 533-538, responded. Von Soden, "Grundsätzliches zur Interpretation des babylonischen Atramḫasīs-Mythus," *Or*, 39 (1970), 311-314, countered again and Lambert answered in "Critical Notes on Recent Publications," *Or*, 40 (1971), 90-98, with von Soden, "Zu W. G. Lamberts 'Further Comments on the Interpretation of Atraḫasīs'," *Or*, 40 (1971), 99-101.

P. 70 n. 82 See now also W. L. Moran, "Atraḫasis: The Babylonian Story of the Flood," *Bib*, 52 (1971), 51-61.

P. 72 n. 95 On *rigmu(m)*, "call, cry, voice," see *AHw* (1972), II, 892f., and on *ḫubūru(m)* II, "noise," *AHw*, I, 352b.

P. 73 n. 97 Von Soden, *Or*, 38 (1969), 425-429, has shown that the interpretation of Pettinato, namely that the "noise" indicates rebellion against the divine rulership, can hardly be maintained.

P. 75 W. W. Hallo, "Antediluvian Cities," *JCS*, 23 (1970[1972]), 62 n. 74, suggests that the older Babylonian traditions of the flood "neither explicitly claim the total destruction of mankind at the Flood nor, in consequence, that all of humanity therefore descended from the lone survivor." The "annihilation" or "total destruction" is referred to by the term gamertu (cf. AHw, I, 278b; CAD, G, 33) which he interprets as "may be nothing more than hyperbole." Nevertheless this term does have its emphasis on "totality" and is never employed in a hyperbolic sense. Furthermore, the Sumerian flood story already refers to "destruction" (nig-gi₁₆-ma) and calls Ziusudra, "The Preserver of the Seed of Mankind," (supra, p. 55) which clearly indicates total destruction of mankind. Though the Atraḫasīs Epic does not explicitly tell us that the world was repopulated through its surviving flood hero, implicitly the ancient Near Eastern flood tradition points in this direction. The newly published "King List of Lagaš" (E. Sollberger, "The Rulers of Lagaš," JCS, 21 (1967[1969]), 279-286) is prefaced by a description of the state of the world after the Flood and speaks of "the seed of mankind [which] had been left" (p. 280 line 4) after the Flood. This is another link showing that only a "seed of mankind" was left in the Flood. By implication mankind descended from this "seed of mankind" (p. 282 n. 72 for Sollberger's evaluation of the various readings which the text allows).

P. 76 It may be noted that the name of the Babylonian flood hero of the Gilgamesh Epic Utnapishtim means "I have found my Life" (so D. O. Edzard, "Die Mythologie der Sumerer und Akkader," Wörterbuch der Mythologie, ed. by H. W. Haussig [Stuttgart: E. Klett, 1965], I, 133). This shows the preoccupation with life of the entire epic in which the flood story figures large. The emphasis on life is already contained in the name of the Sumerian flood hero Ziusudra, which may be rendered "Life of Distant Days" ("Leben-ferner-Tage") according to R. Borger, "Xisusthros," Paulys Realencyclopädie 2.Reihe, 18. Halbband (Stuttgart: A. Druckenmüller, 1967), cols. 2135-2138, esp. 2136.

P. 79 n. 117 The representative new edition of the Erra Epic is by L. Cagni, L'epopea di Erra (Roma: Instituto di Studi del Vicino Oriente, 1969).

Pp. 79f. n. 118 Cagni, Erra, pp. 37-48, disscusses at length the problem of the date. His conclusion follows the suggestion of Lambert who proposed a date in the first half of the ninth century B.C. W. W. Hallo, "Antediluvian Cities," JCS, 23 (1970), 62, n. 63, suggests that the original date "is presumably about the end of the second millennium."

Note also the discussion of the date of the Erra Epic by Wolfram von Soden, "Etemenanki vor Asarhaddon nach der Erzählung vom Turmbau zu Babel und dem Erra-Mythos," Ugarit-Forschungen, ed. by K. Bergerhof, M. Dietrich, O. Loretz, and J. C. de Moor (Neukirchen-Vluyn: Neukirchener Verlag, 1971), III, 253-263, esp. 253f.

P. 82 n. 124 On the question of the flood, see now also Cagni, Erra, pp. 189f.

Pp. 83 n. 127 Cagni, Erra, p. 73 translates as follows:

145 Gli uomini che scamparono al diluvio e videro l'opera eseguita per me
146 (Sebbene?) io alzi le mie armi e distrugga-sopravvivono (ancora).

P. 83 n. 128 On the term *riḫtu*, "remnant," see now *AHw* (1972), II, 968f.: *rēḫtu(m)*, "Rest," and for the adjective *rē/īḫu(m)*, "übrige; übriges," (p. 969a).

P. 84 n. 129 On the Akkadian verb *sâtu*, see now *AHw* (1972), II, 1033a, and on the noun *sittūtu*, "die Übriggebliebenen (the ones left [remaining] over)," *AHw*, II, 1052.

P. 85 n. 134 Cagni, *Erra*, p. 126, has adopted the new reading of *ri-ḫa-ni-iš* and Cagni's translation follows independently the one I proposed: "Išum invece, suo consigliere, lo placò e lasciò indietro un resto!" (p. 127). *AHw*, II, 9686, transliterates in Erra, V, 41: *re-ḫa-ni-iš* and translates "als Übrigbleibende," i.e., "as a remnant." The form *rē/īḫaniš* is, of course, not the common term for "remnant." Cf. K. Deller, "Zur Terminologie neuassyrischer Urkunden," *Wiener Zeitschrift für die Kunde des Morgenlandes*, 57 (1961), 41f.

P. 86 n. 136 See also *ezēbu(m)* in *AHw*, I, 267f. with the meaning "left behind."

P. 91 n. 157 R. Borger (see p. 90 n. 151) has made a convenient collection of the phrase, "The rest of their troops that fled," in the famous Prism of Tiglath-Pileser I, where it appears in this or similar form in I 85-86a, II 1b-3a, III, 12b-14a, IV 27a, V 54-56a and Tablet A, 19 (*Einleitung in die assyrischen Königsinschriften*, p. 126).

P. 93 n. 164 For Tukulti-Ninurta II (890-884), see Wolfgang Schramm, "Die Annalen des assyrischen Königs Tukulti-Ninurta II (890-884 v. Chr.)," *BiOr*, XXVII (1970), 156.

P. 95 n. 176 See now also the new transcription and translation of the annals of Tukulti-Ninurta II by Wolfgang Schramm, "Die Annalen des assyrischen Königs Tukulti-Ninurta II (890-884 v. Chr.)," *BiOr*, XXVII (1970), 147-160, esp. 149, 156:

36 . . . áš-ru-up si-ta-te-šú-un i[g-d]u-ru šadû (KUR-ú) m[ar-ṣu]
"Their remnant fled and they occupied a steep mountain"
40 . . . re-ḫu-te-šú-nu a-<na> šu-zu-ub napišti (ZI.MEŠ)-šú-nu ^{ÍD}Za-ba šap-le-e [. . .]
"Their remnant [crossed] the lower Zab, in order to save their lives" (translations mine).

P. 120 n. 267 On the general subject of "prophecy" in ancient Egypt, the reader should consult G. Lanczkowski, *Altägyptischer Prophetismus* (Wiesbaden: O. Harrassowitz, 1960), and L. M. Ramlot, "Prophétisme et politique en Orient," *Supplément au Dictionnaire de la Bible* (Paris, 1970), VIII, 812-908.

P. 121 n. 269 See now especially the fullfledged study by W. Helck, *Die Prophezeiung des Nfr. tj* (Wiesbaden: O. Harrassowitz, 1970) and Ramlot, *Supplément au Dictionnaire de la Bible*, VIII, 812ff.

P. 136 n. 3 On the relationship between the Gilgamesh epic and the Genesis flood account, see E. Fisher, "Gilgamesh and Genesis: The Flood Story in Context," *CBQ*, 32 (1970), 392-402, who does not distinguish clearly between literary borrowing and an ultimate connection of traditions.

P. 142 On account of philological considerations, it remains very doubtful that the "uproar" of man in the Atraḫasis Epic means or implies "evil conduct" (so again W. M. Clark, "Flood and the Structure of Pre-patriarchal History," *ZAW*, 83 [1971], 185f.) as has been shown by W. von Soden, "Als die Götter (auch noch) Menschen waren. Einige Grundgedanken des altbabylonischen Atramḫasīs-Mythus," *Or*, 38 (1969), 425-429. Caution must be exercised in imposing an ethical motivation onto the Babylonian flood tradition to which in turn the ethical motivation of the Genesis flood narrative is linked. There is no linguistic or conceptual relationship between the "noise" or "uproar" (*rigmum*) in the Babylonian tradition and the "violence" (*ḥāmās*) in Gen 6 (against Clark, *ZAW*, 83 [1971], 186f.).

Pp. 145 n. 31 The discussion on the "righteousness" of Noah (Gen 7:1) has received new impetus in a number of recent studies. It has been shown that the concepts of "righteous" and "life" are closely woven together in the biblical flood story (H. H. Schmid, *Gerechtigkeit als Weltordnung* [Tübingen: Mohr, 1968], p. 106). Since Noah is the first one designated as "righteous (*ṣādîk*)" in the Bible (Gen 6:9; 7:1; cf. H. Graf Reventlow, *Rechtfertigung im Horizont des Alten Testaments* [München: Kaiser, 1971], p. 42 n. 20) special attention is given to this predicate. "God gives life to the *ṣādîk*" (A. Jepsen, "צדיק und צדקה im Alten Testament," *Gottes Wort und Gottes Land. Festschrift H.-W. Hertzberg*, ed. H. Graf Reventlow [Göttingen: Vandenhoeck & Ruprecht, 1965], p. 82). In contrast to the advancement of sin and evil after the fall God lavished out His divine blessings. God (Yahweh) created man and without His divine condescension no one would have been saved in the flood. The saving of Noah in the flood which Noah's "righteousness" has not earned through obedience and the new beginning of God with man after the flood is totally a divine gift of grace (Schmid, *Gerechtigkeit*, p. 106). J. Scharbert, *Prolegomena eines Alttestamentlers zur Erbsündenlehre* [1968], pp. 72f., notes "that therefore it is by no means said that Noah had not earned judgment because he did not stand under the power of sin . . . . Being declared righteous is pure grace which Yahweh did not owe him." See also A. N. Barnard, "Was Noah a Righteous Man?" *Theology*, 74 (1971), 311-314; W. M. Clark, "The Righteousness of Noah," *VT*, 21 (1971), 261-280.

Pp. 156f. n. 80 Hannelis Schulte, *Die Entstehung der Geschichtsschreibung im Alten Israel* (BZAW, 128; Berlin: W. de Gruyter, 1972), p. 30 n. 56, brings forth salient arguments against those scholars who assign Gen 45:7 to the E source stratum. She shows that the various motifs of this passage belong rather to the supposed J stratum. Her emphasis on the theme of "life and death" are important and the connection between

Gen 45:7f. and 50:20 is unmistakable. The intricate relationship between "remnant" (*š^{e}ʾār, p^{e}lêṭāh*) and the theme of "life and death" which is the red thread of the Joseph narrative is crucial for the appreciation of the remnant idea in this section of Genesis. Joseph is presented as "life-bringer" (W. Brueggemann, "Life and Death in Tenth Century Israel," *JAAR*, 40 [1972], 96-109).

P. 166 n. 123 The time of origin of the scene on Mt. Horeb is discussed by H.-C. Schmitt, *Elisa. Traditionsgeschichtliche Untersuchungen zur vorklassischen nordisraelitischen Prophetie* (Gütersloh: G. Mohn, 1972), pp. 124-126, who disagrees with Steck but does not provide cogent arguments for a later date.

P. 166 n. 124. R. A. Carlson, "Elie à l'Horeb," *VT*, 19 (1969), 416-439, has devoted a detailed study to the Horeb scene in the Elijah cycle which should receive careful attention.

The historicity is now questioned by Schmitt, *Elisa*, p. 125, who states that the information of a persecution of Yahweh prophets (1 Ki 18:13; 19:2) as well as the slaughter of the Baal prophets (1 Ki 18: 40; 19:1) "contradict everything that we know of the time of Ahab and is with certainty non-historical." Such skepticism at historical facticity is highly dubious. For a different evaluation of the sources, see J. Bright, *A History of Israel* (2nd ed.; Philadelphia, 1972), pp. 242f.

P. 169 An interesting interpretation of 1 Ki 19:18 is advanced by K. Seybold, "Elia am Gottesberg. Vorstellungen des prophetischen Wirkens nach 1. Könige 19," *EvTh*, 33 (1973), 3-32. He takes the remnant of 7,000 "as a *real* number of about one tenth of the population of Northern Israel which is able to fight, participate in legal action and the cult, so that the judgment meant a decimation of the nation . . ." (p. 16). Such a small group could hardly exist as a nation. The judgment was to effect the loss of national independence. These views are new, but do not commend themselves. The text of 1 Ki 19:18 does not state anywhere or even imply that the 7,000 are to be considered as the lone survivors of a war. This text does not speak of decimation by war but of a remnant of 7,000 which are loyal to Yahweh because they refuse to worship Baal. The struggle from which the remnant would come forth would not consist of a war with a foreign nation but of an internal struggle of the survival of Yahwism. On the other hand, Seybold has rightly recognized that we have here a "promise of a remnant" (p. 17). The concept of the "promised remnant" is at the heart of the remnant idea of the Elijah cycle!

P. 176 n. 175a W. Zimmerli, "Die Bedeutung der grossen Schriftprophetie für das alttestamentliche Reden von Gott," *STV*, 23 (1972), 55, says that "the proclamation of Amos does not seem to go beyond the 'perhaps' of a possible grace for the 'remnant of Joseph'" (cf. Zimmerli, *Grundriss der alttestamentlichen Theologie* [Stuttgart: W. Kohlhammer, 1972], pp. 160-162). On the other hand, W. Rudolph, *Joel-Amos-Obadja-Jona* (KAT, XIII/2; Gütersloh: G. Mohn, 1971), p. 292, rightly points out that Amos speaks twice of the possibility that the coming destruction may not be total: "The coming judgment has a sifting function."

(Cf. J. L. Mays, Amos. A Commentary [Philadelphia: Westminster Press, 1969], p. 102).

P. 180 n. 190 To the suggestions at bringing a solution to the crux interpretum in 3:12 should now be added W. Rudolph, "Schwierige Amosstellen," in Wort und Geschichte. Festschrift für K. Elliger, ed. H. Gese and H. P. Rüger (Neukirchen-Vluyn: Neukirchener Verlag, 1973), pp. 157f., who emends to read w^{e}rôb^{e}dîm šen ^{c}ereṣ "and those who decorated the bed with ivory." See also his Joel-Amos-Obadja-Jona, pp. 159f. Note also I. Willi-Plein, Vorformen der Schriftexegese innerhalb des Alten Testaments (BZAW, 123; Berlin: W. de Gruyler, 1971), pp. 23f.

P. 181 n. 194 Mays (Amos, p. 67) has missed the point by saying that "the saying does not promise the survival of a remnant, however small and wounded, after the coming judgment, but rather shatters any hope of rescue." The picture certainly indicates that a remnant remains (so correctly also Rudolph, Joel-Amos-Obadja-Jona, p. 164), but it is no positive hope of a remnant (against van Hoonacker and Neher). What is rescued as a remnant is not to be conceived of as things but people. Thus Amos does not speak of the impossibility of salvation but of the fact that the "rescued" remnant is meaningless for Israel's national existence. The fact that Samaria is mentioned does not seem to mean that this saying applies only to the wealthy inhabitants of Samaria (against Rudolph, p. 165) but seems to indicate that even these classes of people will not constitute a remnant through which Israel will survive as a nation. The fate of the wealthy urbanites in the fortified capital will be the same as that of the poor of the land in the rural areas.

P. 182 n. 199 E. Jenni, "אחר ʾḥr danach," Theologisches Handwörterbuch zum Alten Testament (München: Kaiser, 1971), I, 115, has suggested that the meaning of "remnant" for ʾaḥarît (אַחֲרִית) is to be eliminated in favor of the meaning "posterity" or "what comes after" in Amos 4:2; 9:1; Jer 31:17; Ezk 23:25; Pss 37:37, 38; 109:13; Dan 11:4. With regard to Amos 4:2 Rudolph, Joel-Amos-Obadja-Jona, p. 161, points out again that "posterity" is nowhere supported in the OT and that this is true of "hindpart" for which the term אָחוֹר (ʾāḥôr) is used so that "remnant" must remain in the text. Plein, Vorformen der Schriftexegese, p. 26, also shows that "what is left over from them," i.e., the "remainder," is the correct meaning in Amos 4:2 and 9:1.

P. 183 Rudolph's emendation (similar to Budde's, JBL, 43 [1924], 127) with the insertion of w^{e}nišʾār nišʾār at the beginning of Amos 6:10 which provides the following translation of 6:9, 10a: "And even if ten people are left over in a single house, they have to die. But if one should be left over, ..." (in Wort und Geschichte. Festschrift K. Elliger [1973], pp. 161f.) has provided better sense. It remains after all questionable on account of its conjectural insertion of two words. The meaning of the text is certainly as Rudolph suggested, but this does hardly give warrant for an emendation.

P. 184 n. 209 Now Rudolph (Wort und Glaube. Festschrift K. Elliger [1973], p. 162) follows Gese (VT, 12 [1962], 436f.) in the translation "and what possibly remains over, I will slay with the sword." (Cf. Rudolph, Joel-Amos-Obadja-Jona, pp. 241f.).

P. 185 n. 214 Wolff, Amos (BKAT, XIV/9; Neukirchener Verlag, 1969), p. 391, states concerning 9:1: "Every remnant idea is thus outrightly rejected." Wolff is not quite correct because a remnant is left after the earthquake but even this remnant will experience destruction by the sword. Wolff apparently does not distinguish here between a positive and negative notion of the remnant.

P. 187 n. 225a On Amos 5:1-3 and the negative aspect of the remnant idea see now also Wolff, Amos, 278, who argues against Preuss that there is here no thought of a "saved remnant." It must be kept in mind that there may be indeed a saved remnant but not one of importance for national existence. Rudolph, Joel-Amos-Obadja-Jona, p. 188, speaks of the "bleeding out of the national body" (similarly Weiser), so that Amos can lament in a funeral dirge.

Pp. 190f. n. 237 The authenticity of Amos 5:14, 15 is also maintained now by Mays, Amos, pp. 99-102, and Rudolph, Joel-Amos-Obadja-Jona, p. 193, who points out that Wolff's (Amos, pp. 294f.) notion of wisdom influence is to be ruled out and that the "small linguistic differences" are negligible.

P. 202 n. 286a Mays, Amos, p. 102, is correct in emphasizing that "the 'remnant of Joseph' refers to those who will be left after the destroying decimation of Yahweh's judgment (1.8; 5.3)." His restriction of the remnant as "not so much a theme of hope for the future" in 5:14 needs to be balanced. More discerning is Rudolph, Joel-Amos-Obadja-Jona, pp. 193, 292, who emphasizes that Amos does here actually speak of a future remnant which will escape total destruction, and that this remnant indicates that the nation qua nation did not choose to return to Yahweh by seeking good.

Pp. 207f. n. 300 Rudolph, Joel-Amos-Obadja-Jona, pp. 278-287, strongly defends the genuineness of Amos 9:11-15, especially against U. Kellermann (EvTh, 29 [1969], 169-183) and the commentary by H. W. Wolff. He concludes after a careful exegesis that "nothing has appeared which would speak against Amos, that to the contrary 'the remnant of Edom' (vs. 12) speaks uniquely in favor of Amos, and that a unity of the entire passage has appeared so that one can with good reasons defend the authenticity just because of vs. 12" (p. 285). Independently of Rudolph the question of the authenticity of Amos 9:11-12 was studied by Klaus Seybold, Das davidische Königtum im Zeugnis der Propheten (FRLANT, 107; Göttingen: Vandenhoeck & Ruprecht, 1972), pp. 17-19, who concludes that these verses belong to Amos in the eighth century B.C. The authenticity is supported also with strong arguments by S. Wagner, "Überlegungungen zur Frage nach den Beziehungen des Propheten Amos zum Südreich," ThLZ, 96 (1971), 661-663. It is striking that scholars such as W. Rudolph, G. von Rad, W. Eichrodt, G. J. Botterweck, I. Engnell, A. Alt ("Vorlesung 'Kleine Propheten' im Wintersemester 1950/51 in Leipzig (Nachschrift)" referred to in Wagner, ThLZ, 96 [1971], 669 n. 18) among others who certainly are under no suspicion of maintaining conservative views have expressed themselves in maintaining genuineness of Amos 9:11, 12.

Pp. 208f. n. 301 On the possibility of "falling" or "fallen" booth of David, see now also S. Wagner, ThLZ, 96 (1971), 661.

P. 211 n. 313 I. Engnell, A Rigid Scrutiny (Nashville: Vanderbilt University Press, 1969), p. 283, suggests that the "booth of David" refers to the kingdom of David. Virtually the same point is made by J. L. Mays, Amos (Philadelphia: Westminster Press, 1969), p. 164. E. Hammershaimb, The Book of Amos: A Commentary (Oxford: Blackwell, 1970), p. 140, suggests that it "is here meant to symbolize the dynasty or kingdom of David." Rudolph, Joel-Amos-Obadja-Jona, p. 280, states that "the former proud house [dynasty] of David is compared to a 'fallen booth,' it thus no longer earns the name house." A highly original suggestion has been put forth by H. Neil Richardson, "Skt (Amos 9:11): 'Booth' or 'Succoth'?" JBL, 92 (1973), 375-381, who rejects a symbolic interpretation of "booth" and argues "that there is here a reference to a city, and . . . that city is not Jerusalem but in fact Succoth, reading sukkōth for sukkath" (p. 376). Against this reading might be suggested that Succoth is regularly written in the OT plene, i.e. sukkôth. The major problem with this hypothesis relates to the problem of the importance of the Transjordanian city of Succoth to be singled out by Amos (Tell Deir ᶜAlla is not the site of Succoth according to its excavator H. J. Franken, Excavations at Tell Deir ᶜAlla [Leiden: Brill, 1969], 4-8; "The Other Side of Jordan," The Hashemite Kingdom of Jordan Annual of the Department of Antiquities, 15 [1970], 5-10). The meaning of "booth (cf. Wagner, ThLZ, 96 [1971], 661f.) as a symbol of the unity of the Israelite kingdom of old remains still the best interpretation.

P. 217 n. 7 A stimulating study which has a direct bearing on the understanding of the interrelationship of the religio-political conditions of Isaiah's career is now provided by John McKay, Religion in Judah under the Assyrians (SBT, II/26; London: SCM Press, 1973), pp. 5-28.

P. 232 n. 75a A number of recent studies have addressed themselves again to the question whether or not Isa 6:1-13 reports the events as they occurred at the call of Isaiah or reflects later events. J. M. Schmidt, "Gedanken zum Verstockungsauftrag Jesajas (Is VI)," VT, 21 (1971), 68-90, follows those who argue that the hardening of the heart passage (vss. 6-9) presupposes some activity on the part of Isaiah. O. D. Steck, "Bemerkungen zu Jesaja 6," BZ, 16 (1972), 188-206, believes to prove that Isa 6 is not an entity to be separated from its present context (p. 203) and reflects the hardening of the heart of the people in the Syro-Ephraimitic War. Steck's idea that Isaiah's "deep insight" that it is Yahweh's own work that the people reject divine help causes him to place Isa 6 before the "memorial book" is interesting. But the concept of "deep insight" does not do justice to the context and does not aid in the solution of the problem. K. Gouders, "Die Berufung des Propheten Jesaja (Jes 6, 1-13)," Bibel und Leben, 13 (1972), 89-106, 172-184, concludes that Isa 6 is a genre sui generis which serves the purpose of the prophet's legitimation before the people. These studies do not add much that is new to the question.

P. 240 n. 96 The decisive argument against the authenticity of Isa 6:13c with the idea of the "holy seed" is for some scholars (O. H. Steck, "Bemerkungen zu Jesaja 6," BZ, 16 [1972], 190f. n. 10; H. -J. Hermisson, "Zukunftserwartung und Gegenwartskritik in der Verkündigung Jesajas," EvTh, 33 [1973], 55 n. 5; cf. J. Vollmer, Geschichtliche Rückblicke und Motive in der Prophetie des Amos, Hosea, und Jesaja [BZAW, 119; Berlin: W. de Gruyter, 1971], pp. 129f. n. 9) the conviction that Isaiah speaks "exclusively of Yahweh's holiness" (Hermisson, p. 55 n. 5). This is hardly correct unless one denies to Isaiah also other passages which speak of holiness in connection with entities other than deity. Isa 11:9 refers to the "holy mountain." Isa 14:10-15 "preserves ancient Canaanite lore of a holy mountain" (so R. J. Clifford, The Cosmic Mountain in Canaan and the Old Testament [Cambridge, Mass.: Harvard University Press, 1972], p. 161) without containing the terminology (on the genuineness of Isa 14, see S. Erlandsson, The Burden of Babylon [Lund: Gleerup, 1970]). Isa 11:9 is genuine (see Rehm, Der königliche Messias, pp. 209-218; and H. Wildberger, Jesaja [BKAT, x/6; 1972], pp. 442-444, 458). If Isaiah can attribute holiness to one entity other than deity, he can certainly attribute this to another entity, i.e., if he can speak of a "holy mountain," he can also speak of a "holy seed." The idea of a "holy seed" coming forth from a cut down root stock (6:13) fits into the thought patterns of Isaiah as the picture of a new ruler arising from the root stock of a cut down tree indicates in Isa 11:1. The idea of a "holy" entity appears again in 4:2f. which has also all signs of being genuine. In short, the conception of holiness is not restricted by Isaiah uniquely to God. On this score Isa 6:13c is to be considered genuine which is another argument in the long list of arguments in support of its genuineness.

P. 241 n. 99a The genuineness of Isa 6:13c and the thought of the holy remnant in Isaiah's early period is defended by P. Auvray, Isaïe 1-39 (Paris: J. Gabalta, 1972), pp. 32, 92f.

P. 250 n. 131 On Isa 1:21-26 and the Isaianic concept of salvation through and after judgment, see now O. H. Steck, Friedensvorstellungen im Alten Testament (Zürich: Theologischer Verlag, 1972), pp. 59ff.

P. 254 n. 148a The concepts of purifying judgment and the correlation between past and future in Isa 1:21-26 is now especially emphasized by J. Vollmer, Geschichtliche Rückblicke und Motive in der Prophetie des Amos, Hosea und Jesaja, pp. 155-160, whose late origin of the Zion tradition (with G. Wanke) must be rejected as the study of Roberts in the following note indicates. The pattern of Urzeit-Endzeit and fusion of the themes of judgment and salvation "into an organic unity" with "the restoration . . . standing at the end of the process of a purifying judgment" is stressed by J. W. Whedbee, Isaiah and Wisdom (Nashville: Abingdon Press, 1971), pp. 139f.

P. 256 n. 151 The reader is directed to a highly stimulating study on the

Zion tradition the title of which summarizes the conclusions reached, J. J. M. Roberts, "The Davidic Origin of the Zion Tradition," JBL, 92 (1973), 329-344. The point of Roberts is to show that "one cannot derive the Zion tradition from the pre-Israelite cult of Jerusalem" and that its "original Sitz im Leben [is] in the era of the Davidic-Solomonic empire" (p. 339). "It [Zion tradition] is best understood as a product of Zion's most glorious days, the golden age of David and Solomon" (p. 344).

Pp. 258f. n. 157 The hotly disputed passage of Isa 4:2-3 is now also defended as Isaianic by Auvray, Isaïe 1-39, pp. 70f., and rightly dated to the early period before 735 B.C. (p. 24).

P. 271 n. 211 Contrary to the customary interpretation that the Syro-Ephraimitic War with Judah came about due to the Assyrian threat which was to be countered by a strong defensive alliance of which Judah was to be a part (so among the virtual common opinion also McKay, Religion in Judah under the Assyrians, p. 5) it has been argued that the Syro-Ephraimitic War must be understood in terms of Damascene expansionism (so B. Oded, "The Historical Background of the Syro-Ephraimitic War Reconsidered," CBQ, 34 [1972], 153-165).

Pp. 276f. n. 227 The aspect of threat is too strongly emphasized for the symbolic name of Isaiah's son "A Remnant Shall Return" by W. Zimmerli, Grundriss der alttestamentlichen Theologie (Stuttgart: W. Kohlhammer, 1972), p. 170. At the same time this name contains the encouragement to be the "remnant" which returns to Yahweh. Wildberger, Jesaja, p. 348, emphasizes that while this name had a warning meaning (for Ahaz) it contains an ambivalence because it also contains expecting salvation.

P. 282 n. 251 One of the staunchest recent propounders of the idea that the second element of the name Shear-jashub, i.e. yašûḇ, means in the first instance a return from battle is G. Sauer, "Die Umkehrforderung in der Verkündigung Jesajas," in Wort-Gebot-Glaube. W. Eichrodt zum 80. Geburtstag, ed. J. J. Stamm, E. Jenni, H. J. Stoebe (Zürich: Zwingli Verlag, 1970), pp. 285f. Sauer goes wrong because he (1) follows W. E. Müller in the derivation of the remnant idea from the political-military sphere and (2) accepts L. Köhler's suggestion that the name is a "naked" relative clause which is now shown to be wrong (see G. F. Hasel, "Linguistic Considerations Regarding the Translation of Isaiah's 'Shear-jashub'," AUSS, 9 [1971], 36-46). Wildberger, Jesaja, p. 278, also sees the dual aspect of judgment and hope with the emphasis on a return of a remnant to Yahweh expressed in this name (cf. H. Gottlieb, VT, 17 [1967], 441f.; H. Gunneweg, VT, 15 [1965], 27-34). Completely unconvincing is E. Lipinski, "Le שאר ישוב d'Isaïe VII 3," VT, 23 (1973), 245f.

Pp. 301f. n. 322 Isa 28:1-6 is assigned by Auvray, Isaïe 1-39, p. 26, to the period of the Syro-Ephraimitic crisis. F. L. Morairty, S. J., "Isaiah 1-39," The Jerome Bible Commentary (Englewood Cliffs, N.J.: Prentice-Hall, 1968), p. 278, takes this section also as genuine.

P. 308 n. 346 Recently Auvray, Isaïe 1-39, p. 247, suggests that the "remnant of his people" in Isa 28:5-6 designates the survivors of both the Northern and the Southern Kingdoms. But this is hardly likely. His emphasis on the conversion of the remnant is nevertheless correct.

P. 312 n. 365a A radical attempt to remove the motif of repentance from Isaiah is made by G. Sauer, "Die Umkehrforderung in der Verkündigung Jesajas," in Wort-Gebot-Glaube. W. Eichrodt zum 80. Geburtstag, ed. J. J. Stamm, E. Jenni, and H. J. Stoebe (Zürich: Zwingli Verlag, 1970), pp. 277-295. He argues strenuously that Isaiah's motif of the remnant is not connected with any concept of repentance. With regard to Isa 30:15 he is right that Fohrer's attempt (who followed Duhm, E. König, and O. Procksch) to interpret šûḇāh does not satisfy but neither does the one he follows, namely to derive it from yšb (first suggested by Gesenius [1853] and supported by M. Dahood). The Isaianic idea of repentance shines through 1:27; 5:25; 6:10, 13; 7:3; 9:11f.; 10:4, 21f.; 12:1; 19:22; 21:12; 23:17; 29:17; 30:15; 31:6; 35:10; 37:7f., 34, 37; 38:8. To reinterpret 6:10, 13; 7:3; 30:15 and to deny that any of the others came from Isaiah of Jerusalem is to force the prophet into a mold of one's own making.

P. 320 n. 394 H. Wildberger, Jesaja (1972), pp. 413f., who questions the authenticity of Isa 10:20-23 points out correctly that this passage is filled with Isaianic terms: šeʾār, yāšûḇ reflects 7:3; "the Holy One of Israel" comes also from Isaiah (cf. 31:15); "the mighty God" is identical to 9:4; "like the sand of the sea" is found in Gen 22:17; 32:13; Hos 2:1; "destruction is decreed" is reminiscent of 28:22; "overflowing with righteousness" reminds of 28:15ff. Does not this Isaianic terminology indeed indicate Isaianic authorship? Auvray, Isaïa 1-39, pp. 135f.; Moriarty, Jerome Bible Commentary, p. 272, added to those listed on p. 319 n. 392, think so. Even Wildberger who holds out for a later period is led to admit even with regard to content that the remnant idea in 10:20-23 "moves remarkably close along the Isaianic line . . ." (p. 415).

P. 327 n. 419 The emphasis on faith in connection with the remnant idea of Isaiah is to be clearly recognized. Sauer, Wort-Gebot-Glaube, p. 286, is correct: "The remnant will alone through its faith--also in and especially through judgment--have existence." Of course, the aspect of repentance must not be denied!

P. 339 n. 453 The important question of the authenticity of Isa 11:10-16 has been the subject of an article by Seth Erlandsson, "Jesaja 11, 10-16 och des historiska bakgrund," Svensk exegetisk Årsbok, 36 (1971), 24-44. He shows on the basis of Assyrian texts that all places mentioned in this section appear in Assyrian records and have a relation to the political interests of Assyria toward the end of the eighth century B.C. Furthermore, the localities can be considered as the places where Israelites from the Northern Kingdom resided. Thus these verses are genuine as is indicated also by the purely Isaianic Zion traditions and David traditions. We can only agree with Erlandsson and have reached the same conclusion of genuineness independently of his investigation. There is no reason whatever to deny 11:10-16 to Isaiah.

P. 349 n. 490 E. Vogt, "Jesaja und die drohende Eroberung Palästinas durch Tiglatpileser," in Wort, Lied und Gottespruch. Festschrift für J. Ziegler, ed. J. Schreiner (Würzburg: Echter Verlag, 1972), pp. 249-255, devoted a study to Isa 17:1-6. He rightly emphasizes that "the remnant of Aram" stands in emphatic position in vs. 3 and that the remnant idea is expressed through (1) the expression "remnant of Aram" (vs. 3), (2) the gleaning of the grain (vs. 5) and the gleaning of the berries (vs. 6). The threatening aspect of the remnant idea is stressed while at the same time an actual remnant remains. He supports our emphasis that this saying "does not express total destruction" (p. 253).

2 5450